Going Places

Recent Titles in the Libraries Unlimited
Real Stories Series
Sarah Statz Cords, Series Editor

The Inside Scoop: A Guide to Nonfiction Investigative Writing and Exposés
Sarah Statz Cords

Real Lives Revealed: A Guide to Reading Interests in Biography
Rick Roche

Women's Nonfiction: A Guide to Reading Interests
Jessica Zellers

Life Stories: A Guide to Reading Interests in Memoirs, Autobiographies, and Diaries
Maureen O'Connor

Going Places

A Reader's Guide to Travel Narratives

Robert Burgin

Real Stories

Sarah Statz Cords, Series Editor

AN IMPRINT OF ABC-CLIO, LLC
Santa Barbara, California • Denver, Colorado • Oxford, England

Library of Congress Cataloging-in-Publication Data

Burgin, Robert.
Going places : a reader's guide to travel narratives / Robert Burgin.
p. cm. — (Real stories series)
Includes index.
ISBN 978-1-59884-972-1 (hardcopy : alk. paper) — ISBN 978-1-61069-385-1 (ebook)
1. Travel writing. I. Title.
G151.B865 2013
910.4—dc23 2012035744

ISBN: 978-1-59884-972-1
EISBN: 978-1-61069-385-1

17 16 15 14 13 1 2 3 4 5

This book is also available on the World Wide Web as an eBook.
Visit www.abc-clio.com for details.

Libraries Unlimited
An Imprint of ABC-CLIO, LLC

ABC-CLIO, LLC
130 Cremona Drive, P.O. Box 1911
Santa Barbara, California 93116-1911

This book is printed on acid-free paper ∞
Manufactured in the United States of America

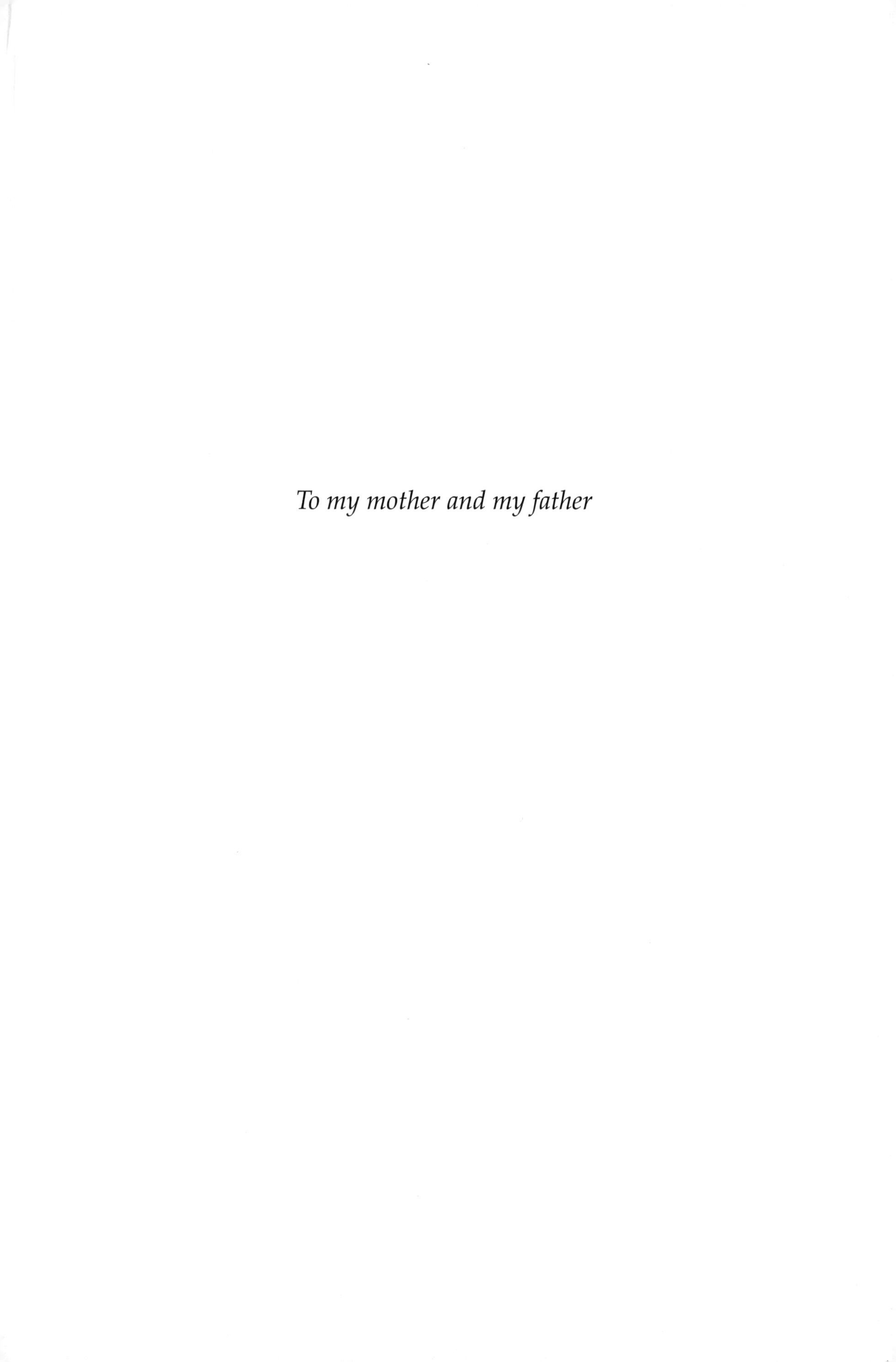

To my mother and my father

Contents

Series Foreword

For years I have been involved in a serious love affair—with nonfiction books.

What a pleasure it continues to be, therefore, to keep meeting other readers who prefer history, biographies, memoirs, travel narratives, current affairs books, or true crime titles (to name but a few nonfiction genres) to the latest novels. I still read fiction—many nonfiction readers do—but more often than not when I am looking for "a good book" what I am really looking for is a "good nonfiction book."

The continuing mission of the reading guides in the *Real Stories* series is to help library staff and all those who work with readers (not to mention readers themselves) learn more about various nonfiction genres and types, as well as to identify specific titles and authors which may be of interest to them. For too many years the tools available to readers' advisors focused exclusively on fiction, but in the recent past the explosion of literary blogs, other online literary commentary, and the inclusion of nonfiction titles in book recommendation databases has helped to augment such classic guides to fiction as Diana Tixier Herald's *Genreflecting* titles and Joyce Saricks's *Readers' Advisory Guide to Genre Fiction*. It is our hope that the specific titles in the *Real Stories* series, which now includes guides to Biographies, Food Writing, Investigative Writing, Life Stories, Travel Narratives, and Women's Nonfiction, will be of particular use to those still looking for cohesive nonfiction genre and subgenre groupings, booklists, and other nonfiction resources.

When I wrote the first book in the series, *The Real Story*, Robert Burgin was my series editor and was kind enough to write that I had provided a "map to the rich and varied world of nonfiction." Robert went on to edit four more books in the series before passing the series editorship on to me, and it seems particularly right that this guide to travel reading, the first book that I have had the pleasure to help shape for publication, is by none other than Robert himself. And what a book it is. Although I included a chapter on Travel narratives in *The Real Story*, Robert has taken my rudimentary start and expanded the Travel genre "map" to include seven distinct Travel subgenres, all with their own classic titles, clearly explained appeal characteristics, and numerous suggestions for further and related reading. In addition to grouping titles together in helpful stylistic groupings and subgenre categories, Robert has also provided numerous access points (Nancy Pearl might call them "doorways") for readers' advisors and readers in the form of subject headings and geographical place names (vitally important information here, as the appeal of travel literature often relies heavily upon its location and setting).

Most importantly, he has written not only a *useful* guide but an *enticing* guide. It was somewhat to my dismay that I found, after reading this book and making a note of many of the titles Robert made me want to read, that my TBR list had grown extensively (I say "dismay," as my TBR list is always too long as it is). I invite you to not only use this guide (and others in the *Real Stories* series) when helping patrons or when performing readers' advisory, but also when you personally need a "good nonfiction book."

Sarah Statz Cords

Acknowledgments

Writing this book has not been a solo journey. I have had many helpful companions on this trip.

A number of individuals have discussed the book with me and, in several cases, have made specific recommendations regarding travel books in particular or readers' advisory in general. These include Dale Cousins, Mahmoud El-Tobgy, Nina El-Tobgy, Ellen Foreman, Elizabeth Skinner, and Duncan Smith, among others. The late Ken Shearer deserves a great deal of credit for encouraging me to pursue the ways in which readers' advisory can be extended to nonfiction in general. Librarians at the Braswell Memorial Library in Rocky Mount (NC), the Wake County Libraries in Raleigh (NC), the Joyner Library at East Carolina University in Greenville (NC), and the Davis Library at the University of North Carolina at Chapel Hill have also assisted me in many ways.

Sarah Statz Cords and Barbara Ittner have been wonderful editors. Both have suggested titles for the book and have recommended ways to strengthen the book and make it far better than it could have been without their efforts. Both have also been extremely encouraging of me and patient with me during the process of writing the book, a process that took much longer than I ever expected.

I would also like to thank my two favorite travel companions, my wife Linda and my daughter Monica, both for supporting me in various ways during the writing of this book and for accompanying me on trips to such wonderful places as Austria, China, France, Germany, London, Paris, and Switzerland. Memories of those trips will always be with me.

This book is dedicated to my late parents, William Jennings Burgin and Mavis Nix Burgin, both of whom passed away while I was conceiving of and writing the book. My parents did two things to instill in me a love of travel and travel narratives. First, when I was a boy, our family rarely traveled. We took just one trip during my youth that would qualify as a family vacation—a weeklong visit to Washington, DC, when I was 14. Ironically, the lack of travel in my youth has made me yearn to travel or read about travel as an adult. I am apparently making up now for something that I did not get as a child.

Second and perhaps more importantly, though, my parents told me about their own travels. My father had joined the Navy in 1945, entering just as World War II had ended and taking part in cleanup operations in the Pacific. He would regale us with tales of Guam or Japan or China, and I could tell from the gleam in his eye that travel had been a special part of his life, even if he no longer went farther than an hour or two beyond our home town. My mother, on the other hand, did not travel until she had retired, and then she would periodically take bus tours to sites within the United States, sites such as Branson, Missouri, or Niagara Falls, or the Pennsylvania Amish

Country. Listening to her talk about these trips and watching her face light up as she remembered the things that she had seen was nothing short of magical.

My parents gave me these two priceless gifts: the love of travel and the love of hearing or reading about the travels of other people. My hope is that this book will, in turn, share those gifts with countless librarians and their readers.

Introduction

There is no Frigate like a Book / To take us Lands away.
—Emily Dickinson, "There is no Frigate like a Book"

We are a species that travels. According to some religious traditions, we have been cast out of Eden and made to wander the earth. According to science, we have migrated out of Africa to populate the world. According to literature, we go on pilgrimages and odysseys. According to popular music, we're leaving on a jet plane or taking to the highway or hitting the road, Jack.

We are also a species that records its travels. Our earliest narratives (*The Legend of Etana, The Epic of Gilgamesh, The Iliad, The Odyssey*) all involve travel, and we have continued this trend by writing a vast number of travel narratives and personal reflections on trips to foreign destinations. Over 1.5 million titles match the subject heading "travel" in WorldCat, including over 800,000 books. Amazon.com shows over 380,000 titles when one searches "travel" in its section on books, and over 280,000 of these are classified into Amazon's travel category.

Of course, only some of these books are travel narratives, as opposed to travel guides or books about travel photography or fiction titles with travel-related themes. Nevertheless, a large number of books can be classified as travel narratives, and consequently, just as we need guidebooks to help us sort through the world's 190-plus countries, as readers and readers' advisors, we need a guidebook to help us make sense of the world of travel narratives and the readers who are drawn to them.

So the purpose of this book is twofold. First, it is intended to assist readers' advisors and readers in navigating a world of books that help them make sense of the world in which they live, a world in which people travel to appreciate the beauty of other places or to wonder at the exotic peoples or plants or animals of another country, to recover from personal tragedy or to discover themselves, to celebrate travel by rail or by foot or by car, or to celebrate living abroad, a world of humorous encounters, or a world of adventurous travel. This book attempts to map this vast world of travel narratives by "chunking" travel narratives into more manageable subgenres and categories that, I hope, reflect the reasons that readers actually read these books.

Second, and more importantly, the book is intended to help librarians better understand their readers by better understanding what motivates them to read books of a certain genre, a certain subgenre, or a certain category within that subgenre. The book is meant to help librarians create better relationships with their users by helping them appreciate why one reader will find Francis Mayes's account of buying and restoring a farm house in Tuscany (*Under the Tuscan Sun*) vivid and sensuous while another calls it "verbose, cliché-ridden, superficial, and materialistic" or why one reader will see Bill Bryson's humor as self-effacing while another considers his humor nasty and irritating. Helping create these relationships is particularly important to recreational nonfiction, which has fewer professional tools, literary blogs, and resources dedicated to its study.

This desire to create stronger relationships with our users is, for me, the key motivation for providing readers' advisory services, which are about much more than simply handing the right book to the right reader. As Liz Burns said on Twitter (quoting Sophie Brookover), readers' advisory is about "building relationships, trust with readers over time."[1] We build those relationships and strengthen that trust by showing our readers that we understand and validate their reading tastes, by creating a space in which they can talk about the books that they read and enjoy, and by helping them better understand their own reading tastes and how to find titles that will be meaningful to them. My hope is that this book will assist librarians in all these ways.

What Is a Travel Narrative?

Determining what titles to include in a book on travel narratives may seem at first to be a relatively straightforward matter, but it is not. Even the judges of the prestigious Dolman Best Travel Book Award have trouble with what looks like the simple definition of a travel narrative:

> After much stimulating discussion over lunch at Blacks, the judging panel of the Authors' Club Dolman travel award have drawn up a long-list of ten books. With such extraordinarily varied submissions, debate inevitably focused around what actually constitutes a travel book: how 'present' does the author have to be, must the narrative be a linear travelogue, and how intrepid does the journey need to be?[2]

I have defined *travel narrative* here to mean a book in which one or more travelers take a voluntary trip to one or more places and share their personal thoughts, perceptions, reactions, and experiences. These narratives are intended to be read and enjoyed in a linear manner, from start to finish, and not referred to simply on an as-needed basis.

To take just one example, Bill Bryson's *A Walk in the Woods: Rediscovering America on the Appalachian Trail* is about the author's hike along the 2,100-mile Appalachian Trail in the United States. There is, in this case, a primary traveler who is the author of the narrative and who shares with us his very personal observations of the Appalachian Trail, of the trip, of himself, of his hiking partner (Steven Katz), and of the people that they meet along the way. It is meant to be read from start to finish and enjoyed as a story. It is by no means intended as a guide for other individuals who plan to hike the Appalachian Trail or as a reference work for people with questions about the Trail.

In the case of *A Walk in the Woods*, we have the simplest situation—a single author, a single trip, and a single destination. However, my definition of *travel narrative* is broad enough to include titles by multiple authors (Nicholas and Micah Sparks, *Three Weeks With My Brother*), titles that involve multiple trips (Cathy N. Davison, *36 Views of Mount Fuji: On Finding Myself in Japan*), and travels that involve multiple destinations (Frances Mayes, *A Year in the World: Journeys of a Passionate Traveller*). There may even be multiple narratives in a single book, as in collections of travel essays by a single author (Tim Cahill, *A Wolverine Is Eating My Leg*) or by multiple authors (*Sand In My Bra And Other Misadventures: Funny Women Write From The Road*).

It is also important to consider what the above definition excludes, that is, what has **not** been included in this book. Understanding what has not been included may help the reader better understand what I mean by the term *travel narrative*.

First and foremost, I have not included travel *guides*, those books that provide information about a specific travel destination and include useful information on what to see, where to stay, where to eat, and where to shop. Canadian library educator Guy Robertson does a good job of explaining the distinction between travel guides and travel narratives by noting that library travel collections typically include "two main divisions: guidebooks and travel literature." Guidebooks, he notes, "include volumes dedicated to specific places all over the world," and their readers have specific needs: "Guidebook users recognize that every trip costs money and requires planning and organization."[3] By contrast, he argues that "travel literature is more personal. The foundation of any work of travel literature is its author's perception of his or her surroundings, and the ways in which that author experienced—or muddled through—various situations."[4]

Sarah Statz Cords makes a similar distinction when she contrasts cookbooks and books about food, noting that the former "are not so much books you read as books you refer to."[5] Travel narratives are mean to be read and enjoyed. Guidebooks are mean to be referred to and used.

Second, I have excluded books that consist primarily of photographs with some added narrative (for example, *Andes* by Mario Vargas Llosa and Pablo Corral Vega or *Australian Colors: Images of the Outback* by Bill Bachman) as well as books that are graphical in nature, i.e., primarily cartoons (Mo Willems, *You Can Never Find a Rickshaw When It Monsoons*). The focus here is on travel narratives, on writing that tells a story.

Third, the books that are recommended here are about travel that is something apart from work, and they are about travel that is voluntary. Consequently, books that do not involve travel *per se* but are instead about the place in which one happens to work, no matter how exotic, are not included. (This includes titles such as Edward Abbey, *Desert Solitaire: A Season in the Wilderness* or Peter Allison, *Don't Look Behind You!: A Safari Guide's Encounters with Ravenous Lions, Stampeding Elephants and Lovesick Rhinos*.) Likewise, books that tell about travel that is involuntary by nature are not included (books by exiles, like Ariel Dorfman's *Heading South, Looking North: A Bilingual Journey*).

These distinctions, by the way, are not always easy to make. It may be a fairly simple matter to exclude guidebooks such as those offered by Frommer, Fodor, Let's

Go, Lonely Planet, Rick Steves, and others, but some titles that I have excluded, like Ina Caro's *Paris to the Past*, are much closer to being narratives, while others that I have included, like Chuck Palahniuk's *Fugitives and Refugees: A Walk in Portland, Oregon*, come very close to being guidebooks.

Why People Read Travel Narratives

People read travel narratives, as they read fiction and other nonfiction genres, for a number of reasons. To borrow from Catherine Ross's excellent work on why readers read nonfiction,[6] we have at least the following:

- People read travel narratives for pleasure. The fact that travel narratives such as Elizabeth Gilbert's *Eat, Pray, Love: One Woman's Search for Everything Across Italy, India and Indonesia* or Peter Mayle's *A Year in Provence* have been best sellers and have spawned movies and television mini-series suggests that many readers find them enjoyable to read and connect with the stories that these narratives tell.
- People read travel narratives because they are interested in a destination or in some other subject that the narrative treats. Readers who love Paris will likely enjoy Adam Gopnik's essays on his expatriate life there (*Paris to the Moon*) or Kathleen Flinn's descriptions of daily life there (*The Sharper Your Knife, the Less You Cry: Love, Laughter, and Tears in Paris at the World's Most Famous Cooking School*). Readers who are interested in the concept of happiness will find Eric Weiner's *The Geography of Bliss: One Grump's Search for the Happiest Places in the World* to be very informative. Readers with an interest in the life of Napoleon will learn much from Julia Blackburn's *The Emperor's Last Island: A Journey to St. Helena*.
- People read travel narratives to gain knowledge about a destination or about some other subject that is the focus of the narrative. This particular reason has become more evident as the world itself has become a smaller, "flatter" place. One gains a better understanding of the protestors gathering in Tahrir Square in Cairo from the insights in Max Rodenbeck's *Cairo: The City Victorious*, for example. Pico Iyer's *Falling Off the Map: Some Lonely Places of the World* helps one comprehend the situation in North Korea and the impact of the recent death of Kim Jong-Il. Numerous travel titles (Ana M. Briongos's *Black on Black: Iran Revisited*, Azadeh Moaveni's *Lipstick Jihad: A Memoir of Growing Up Iranian in America and American in Iran* and *Honeymoon in Tehran: Two Years of Love and Danger in Iran*) help one gain a better sense of what life is like in Iran, just as Jason Elliot's *An Unexpected Light: Travels in Afghanistan* helps one better understand Afghanistan.
- People read travel narratives for the beauty of the text. Several of the writers whose works are recommended here are highly regarded, such as Nobel

Prize winners Octavio Paz (*In Light of India*) and Jose Saramago (*Journey to Portugal: In Pursuit of Portugal's History and Culture*) as well as writers who were mentioned in their lifetimes as potential Nobel Prize winners, like Ryszard Kapuscinski (*Travels with Herodotus*) and W.G. Sebald (*The Rings of Saturn*).

Travel narratives also feature, perhaps more than other genres, a sense of discovery. Interestingly, that sense of discovery may hinge on both differences and similarities. The reader may find that the destination or the people or even the experience featured in the travel narrative is very different from those with which she is familiar, just as Eddy L. Harris (*Native Stranger: A Black American's Journey into the Heart of Africa*) travels to Africa as an African American man hoping to better understand his roots, only to find that he is treated as a stranger there, with more in common with the few white people whom he encounters than with the native Africans.

Conversely, the reader may find that there are similarities and connections between the places, people, and experiences with which she is familiar and those that are the subject of the travel narrative. We feel a common humanity, even with a people as different as the Inuit that Greta Ehrlich describes in *This Cold Heaven: Seven Seasons in Greenland* or the Arabs of the "Empty Quarter," many of whom had never seen a European, in Wilfred Thesiger's *Arabian Sands*. Paul Kriwaczek (*In Search of Zarathustra: The First Prophet and the Ideas that Changed the World*) finds common ideas in seemingly different and often warring religious traditions as he travels through Asia. Alan Tennant (*On the Wing: To the Edge of the Earth with the Peregrine Falcon*) even reflects on the common uncertain future faced by humans and falcons as he follows those birds on their migratory paths.

A travel narrative may also be read as part of the travel that the reader will undertake, is undertaking, or has undertaken. A travel narrative may inspire readers to travel to certain destinations, as Peter Mayle's Provence books or Frances Mayes's Tuscany books certainly did, or it may help prepare a reader intending to travel to a specific place, as Peter Hessler's *Oracle Bones: A Journey between China's Past and Present* did for me prior to the 2009 trip that my wife and I took to China. A travel narrative may serve as a companion on a trip that the reader is currently taking, thus allowing the reader to compare notes with another traveler. A travel narrative may serve as a reminder of a trip taken in the past.

The potential link between travel narratives and the travels that readers may have taken or may take or may wish to take, of course, provides readers' advisors with another way to connect with their readers. In addition to the traditional book-oriented approach to the readers' advisory interaction ("Tell me about a book that you've read and enjoyed"), readers' advisors can ask readers of travel narratives to describe their favorite trips or to talk about trips that they would like to take. The ways in which a reader talks about a favorite trip—the destination, the chance to meet other people, the purpose of the trip, the fact that the reader took a train, and so forth—can be as revealing as the ways in which a reader talks about a favorite book.

Travel narratives may even appeal to readers who can't travel or who don't travel. As an example of the former case, few of us will actually travel to Antarctica, but we can still enjoy the stark beauty of that frozen continent through the writings of Peter Matthiessen (*End of the Earth: Voyaging to Antarctica*), Sara Wheeler (*Terra Incognita: Travels in Antarctica*), Fen Montaigne (*Fraser's Penguins: A Journey to the Future in Antarctica*), Lucy Jane Bledsoe (*The Ice Cave: A Woman's Adventures from the Mojave to the Antarctic*), and others. As an example of the latter case, consider Rita, a reader who was interviewed by one of Catherine Ross's students:

> Somebody did introduce me to Paul Theroux's travel stuff. It was somebody who had been a train buff and they said [to read] *The Great Railway Bazaar* and then of course *Riding the Red Rooster*. . . I did go out and get his *The Old Patagonia Express*. And, my God, that was a wonderful book! And then I got his others, and it was really like being on a train journey. Now, for me, I'm not crazy about train journeys. Getting there has never been half the fun, as far as I'm concerned. So I enjoyed reading it because I didn't have to do any of this dreadful stuff like sitting in this train for ninety-nine hours. But it was still wonderful to read.[7]

The traditional appeal factors that readers' advisors generally rely on (pacing; characterization; story line; frame and setting; tone and mood; and language and style)[8] are also important in understanding why people read travel narratives and why they read the travel narratives that they do. These factors will be explored in more detail in the introductions to the individual chapters of this book, which focus on the specific subgenres of the travel narrative genre.

History of the Travel Narrative

The history of the travel narrative reflects several themes. First, for the majority of the genre's existence, titles that focus on the destination of the travel have been prevalent. Second, in spite of the fact that other subgenres did not become popular until later in the history of the travel narrative, there are early examples of many of them. Third, a number of external factors allowed these other subgenres to increase in popularity during the past two or three centuries.

The earliest works that can be considered travel narratives (and for many years, the majority of the titles in this genre) fit into the subgenre that this book calls "A Sense of Place" (chapter 1), that is, titles where the destination is of primary importance. These include the fragmentary writings by Hecataeus of Miletus, a Greek historian who traveled at length in Europe, Africa, and Asia during the 6th century BC and described both the lands that he visited and the people in those countries; *The Histories* of Herodotus, written in the 5th century BC and including a number of observations of other countries and people made by the author during his travels and presented within the context of the world history that he was constructing;[9] and the ten-volume *Description of Greece*, written in the 2nd century AD by Pausanias and focusing on the various parts of Greece and its cultures.

The prevalence of early travel narratives that focused on the destination of the author was due to a simple fact: prior to the spread of railroads in the 19th century, travel (particularly travel by land) was difficult for most people. Travel from antiquity through early modern times was strenuous, slow, expensive, and dangerous. This response on WikiAnswers by Dr. Judith Patton sums up the situation in the Middle Ages:

> Travel was hard, it was dangerous, and the roads were bad. It took a long time to go anywhere. A man who wanted to go 30 miles by horse could only travel about 10 miles a day. Which means that to cover the 30 miles it took 3 days to get there and another 3 days to get back. So, that means you left your fields, animals, home for 6 days or more to go 30 miles. This was a lot in this time. The people of the middle ages also didn't view night the way we do since there were no lights anywhere at night. Night time was considered a whole different world and the night air dangerous. It was better to stay home unless you had to travel.[10]

Consequently, most people knew other countries or even distant parts of their own countries only through the written or spoken narratives of those few who did travel. Even as late as the 1840s, Richard Dana's travel narrative, *Two Years Before the Mast,* became popular among those going to California during the Gold Rush of the 19th century because it was one of the few sources of information on that region.

Travel narratives of this era of difficult travel easily fit into four of the categories outlined in chapter 1. Readers would have wanted to know about the beauty of the lands that they would never see themselves ("The Beauty of the Place"), the exotic people who lived in those places and their cultures ("Landscapes and People"), the plants and animals of those distant lands ("Appreciating Nature"), and the faraway cities ("Urban Landscapes"). So the writer Herodotus describes for his readers some of the wonders of the ancient world, such as the great pyramid at Giza and the walls of Babylon; discusses the religious beliefs and customs of the Egyptians, Lydians, Babylonians, Scythians, and Thracians; describes the hippopotami, crocodiles, phoenixes, and winged serpents of Egypt; and depicts cities from Babylon to Athens and Sparta.

The advent of faster, less expensive, and safer travel did not, of course, remove any of these motivations for reading travel narratives. Though travel may have become less expensive, it was still too expensive for many, perhaps most, people. (The "Grand Tour," for example, was generally restricted to upper-class Europeans.) Even today, travel is too expensive or too much trouble for many people, and so travel through books that describe destinations may be the only way that many readers will know a place. Likewise, political situations may prevent travel to certain areas of the world, and books like Daniel Metcalfe's *Out of Steppe: The Lost Peoples of Central Asia* or Alfredo José Estrada's *Havana: Autobiography of a City* may be the only way that readers will be able to visit some countries or cities.

Even for those who were able to travel, narratives that focused on destinations have remained popular and useful. These titles can inform readers about places to which they intend to travel and can provide useful information to make their trips easier or more enjoyable. In some cases, the travel narratives take on a more subjective point of view and even provide an "insider's" guide to parts of the destination that the average traveler would not normally see.

In spite of the prevalence of titles in the "A Sense of Place" subgenre, there are many examples of early titles from the other subgenres examined in this book. For instance, it is not surprising that several of the earliest travel narratives can be seen as "Quests," a subgenre examined in chapter 2 and defined as travel narratives that focus on the purpose of the narrative. For example, Pausanias, who lived in the second century AD and wrote the ten-book *Description of Greece,* traveled in search of history and legend (two of the categories in this chapter) and discussed the historical underpinnings of the various Greek states of the time. He wrote about seeing the shields of the soldiers who had died in the battle of Leuctra, for instance, as well as seeing the ruins of the house of the Greek poet Pindar and the statues of Hesiod and Orpheus.

The travels of Faxian, a Chinese Buddhist monk who traveled to India and Sri Lanka between 399 and 412, also featured a strong sense of purpose: to procure Buddhist scriptures, particularly those related to monastic rules, and to highlight Buddhist practices in these countries. His journey is described in his narrative, *A Record of Buddhist Kingdoms, Being an Account by the Chinese Monk Fa-Xian of his Travels in India and Ceylon in Search of the Buddhist Books of Discipline*. A similar purpose inspired the Chinese monk Xuanzang to travel to India and report on his travels in *Great Tang Records on the Western Regions,* published in 646.

Other early travel narratives featured travel in the footsteps of others, a category within the broader subgenre of "The Quest." Japanese poet Matsu Basho's late 17th-century work, *The Narrow Road to the Deep North and Other Travel Sketches,* for example, had as its purpose following in the footsteps of the 12th-century Japanese poet Saigyo Hoshi and visiting all of the sites mentioned in his verses.

Likewise, there are early works that match the definition set out here for "The Journey" (chapter 3), narratives where the most important element is not the destination or the purpose of the travel but the traveler or travelers. Not surprisingly, many of these were religious, because in earlier times, the primary reason for discovering or better understanding one's self was to do so with respect to one's relationship with one's God. Consequently, Nasir Khusraw's 11th-century work, *Safarnama,* is in many ways a journey of self-discovery, motivated by a dream in which a heavenly voice told Khusraw to give up the luxuries of this world and search for wisdom. *Safarnama* describes Khusraw's journeys to holy shrines like Mecca and Medina and his attempts to resolve his spiritual crisis. The 15th-century travels of the Russian merchant Afanasy Nikitin (*The Journey Beyond Three Seas*) are also about self-discovery, in particular his conversion from Christianity to Islam, a conversion that was not particularly smooth and that troubled Nikitin quite a bit.

There are even very early travel narratives that fit into chapter 3's category of "Reflective Journeys," that is, those in which the traveler shares her thoughts and reflections on issues that transcend the journey. We have, for example, *De Reditu Suo,* a poem written in 417 by Rutilius Claudius Namatianus, a wealthy Gallo-Roman who traveled from Rome to his estates in Gaul and used the trip to speculate on the future of Rome following its sacking by the Visigoths. Unlike many other writers of this period, Namatianus did not believe that the world was falling apart as a result of these events but instead was optimistic that things were looking up.

Expatriate narratives, which are the focus of chapter 4, are also represented in the early travel literature. Because he spent nine years in China, the ninth century Japanese Buddhist monk Enin's four-volume diary, *The Record of a Pilgrimage to China in Search of the Law*, may be considered an early expatriate narrative. One of eight Japanese monks who studied in China during that time, his narrative was the first written work by an outsider to document life in China. It is worth noting that he faced many challenges as an expatriate in China, including many that resulted from the Tang dynasty's persecution of Buddhism toward the end of this stay.

Interestingly, the earliest instances of "Travel Humor" (the focus of chapter 6) were works of fiction. A good example is the *True History* of Lucian of Samosata (c. 125–after c. 180), which recounts a fanciful voyage that Lucian and a group of fellow travelers take. The voyage includes a trip to the moon on a giant waterspout, being trapped inside a giant whale, and such fantastic sights as a sea of milk and an island of cheese. The story is mean to parody the travels recounted by other authors, such as Homer and Herodotus. (Lucian encounters Herodotus on an island, where he is being punished for eternity for the many "lies" that he published in his *Histories*.) Lucian himself goes on to state that the story recounted in *True History* is about "things which I have neither seen nor had to do with nor learned from others—which, in fact, do not exist at all and, in the nature of things, cannot exist. Therefore my readers should on no account believe in them."

In a similar manner, the earliest "Travel Adventure" narratives (chapter 7) were epic poems, like Homer's *Iliad* and *Odyssey*, at least parts of which appear to have been based on true events. There were also survival stories like Xenophon's *Anabasis*, which describes the journey of 10,000 Greek soldiers who were stranded deep in enemy territory in Persia around 400 BC and who crossed scorching deserts and snow-covered mountains to reach the Black Sea and the safety of its Greek shoreline cities.

While these early examples of the other subgenres of the travel narrative did exist, however, the popularity of these subgenres and even certain categories within the subgenre of "A Sense of Place" required the presence of various external factors.

One of these factors was "the rise of Romanticism's emphasis on the individual,"[11] which made it possible for the focus of the travel narrative to be on the individual traveler as opposed to the destination. An early example of the change in focus of the travel narrative can be seen in the Scottish explorer Mungo Park (*Travels in the Interior of Africa*):

> Though he certainly could have done so, Mungo Park did not write up a narrative of geographical discovery, observation, or collection, but one of personal experience and adventure. He wrote, and wrote himself, not as a man of science, but as a sentimental hero. He made himself the protagonist and central figure of his own account, which takes the form of an epic series of trials, challenges, and encounters with the unpredictable.[12]

Ironically, both the rise of Romanticism, with its focus on nature and its reaction against the scientific "rationalization" of nature, and the rise of the biological sciences made travel narratives that focused on an appreciation of nature (see chapter 1) even more important. William Bartram's *Travels* and John James Audubon's *Birds of America* were two early titles that reported on the incredible animals and birds of the American continent, and Theodore Roosevelt's *Through the Brazilian Wilderness* focused on the exotic plants and animals encountered by the former U.S. President during his 1913 journey to the jungles of Brazil.

Two of the categories discussed in chapter 1 ("Endangered Places" and "Appreciating Nature") have become more important with the increasing interest in environmental concerns since the 1960s. The popularity of the titles in the "Endangered Places" section (from Tom Bissell's visit to the disappearing Aral Sea in *Chasing the Sea: Lost Among the Ghosts of Empire in Central Asia* to Sara Wheeler's warnings about the melting ice caps in *The Magnetic North: Notes from the Arctic Circle*) derives from the heightened awareness of the planet's fragile ecology and ongoing concerns about global warming. Likewise, many of the titles in the latter category attempt to inform readers about the uncertain future of the animals and plants that are the focus of their authors' travels: kangaroos in Tim Flannery's *Chasing Kangaroos: A Continent, a Scientist, and a Search for the World's Most Extraordinary Creature;* jaguars and other large cats in Richard Mahler's *The Jaguar's Shadow: Searching for a Mythic Cat*; penguins, whales, and seals in Peter Matthiessen's *End of the Earth: Voyaging to Antarctica*; and the plants of the Amazon basin in Mark Plotkin's *Tales of a Shaman's Apprentice: An Ethnobotanist Searches for New Medicines in the Amazon Rain Forest*.

Travel in search of food (chapter 2) also appears to be a relatively recent phenomenon. Though the food customs of other cultures may have been part of early travel narratives, food was not the focus of the narrative or the purpose of the travel. Such books would come much later, after Jean Anthelme Brillat-Savarin's *The Physiology of Taste* (1825) had established the genre of food writing and perhaps after the postwar prosperity of the developed world made it possible for large numbers of people to both travel well and eat well.

Another factor, especially important in the focus of the travel narrative on healing or self-discovery (those of "The Journey" in chapter 3) was the rise of the psychoanalysis of Freud, Jung, and others in the 20th century, which gave credence to the importance of one's inner thoughts and emotions and the need to discover one's self or heal one's self, a motivation that lies at the heart of many travel narratives.

Obviously, the invention and spread of specific modes of transportation influenced the popularity of travel narratives that focus on those modes of transportation (chapter 4, "Getting There Is Half the Fun"). The invention of the first practical automobiles and motorcycles and the development of the safety bicycle in the late 19th century made travel by those modes of transportation and writing about that travel possible. Walking had, of course, been the primary mode of human transportation for most of mankind's existence but was only considered special enough to write about when alternative forms of transportation were available.

This brief historical sketch should serve to remind readers' advisors that although destination may be an important factor in the appeal of travel narratives, it is by no means the only feature that will attract a reader to a book in this genre. Modern travel narratives have expanded well beyond the notion of destination as the major motivation of travel or writing about travel. Readers have many reasons to like a travel narrative, and readers' advisors should keep these in mind as they work with their readers.

Selection Process

The titles that appear in this book have been gleaned from several sources.

- Previously published guides, including Sarah Statz Cords's *The Real Story: A Guide to Nonfiction Reading Interests*, Neal Wyatt's *The Readers' Advisory Guide to Nonfiction*, Nancy Pearl's *Book Lust to Go: Recommended Reading for Travelers, Vagabonds, and Dreamers*, Sarah Anderson's *Travel Companion*, and Maggy Simony's *The Traveler's Reading Guide: Ready-Made Reading Lists for the Armchair Traveler*.
- Lists of award winning travel books (see Appendix A).
- Online databases, including Libraries Unlimited's Readers' Advisor Online (http://www.readersadvisoronline.com/), Any New Books (http://anynewbooks.com/), and Novelist (http://www.ebscohost.com/novelist/).
- Online catalog tools, including LibraryThing and WorldCat.
- Websites such as *National Geographic Traveler* (http://traveler.nationalgeographic.com/), *Condé Nast Traveler* (http://www.concierge.com/cntraveler), *The Guardian*'s travel section (http://www.guardian.co.uk/travel/), *The Telegraph*'s travel section (http://www.telegraph.co.uk/travel/).
- Readers' lists on Amazon.com and Goodreads, including titles recommended by readers on the Amazon.com "Travel Community" discussion forum.
- Other readers' advisory Web resources, gathered and linked at http://rburgin.com/sites/ranf.html. Many of these resources are book lists that have been generated by public libraries. They represent an extremely valuable resource, and librarians should be encouraged to create more of these and put them on the Web. Such an effort would be crowdsourcing at its best.

After compiling a large database of titles from these sources, I used WorldCat to determine the number of libraries holding each title. In general, I have included the titles that were held by the largest number of libraries. I have also included as many award-winning titles as possible, regardless of how widely these are held.

How to Use This Book

The 500-plus travel narratives annotated in this book have been divided into seven chapters, each representing a subgenre of the travel narrative genre, a way in which these titles might appeal to readers. Five of these are based on the rather loose definition of travel as an activity that involves a traveler or travelers who go to a destination by some means, for some purpose, for some length of time. The first five chapters parallel the elements of that definition.

Chapter 1, "A Sense of Place," focuses on titles where the destination is of primary importance. For many readers, the most important focus of a travel narrative will be on a specific place or destination (the crumbling Venice of John Berendt's *The City of Falling Angels* or the barely surviving Montana towns of Jonathan Raban's *Bad Land: An American Romance* or the stark, icy Greenland of Gretel Ehrlich's *This Cold Heaven: Seven Seasons in Greenland*), so the ability of the author to evoke that destination will be an important part of the narrative's appeal.

But while place is important to travel narratives, it is not the only thing that draws readers to books of this genre. As David Carr points out, "Works of travel are also about sampling the tastes of other times and places, of course, and yet they are also about looking for something else. The best of them appear to extend well beyond the constraints of travel, a term that seems almost incidental to the writer's intention."[13]

Consequently, we have six other subgenres, beginning with Chapter 2, "Quests," a chapter that includes titles that concentrate on the purpose of the travel. The traveler may go in search of food, for example, or history or legends or even a concept or idea, like happiness, as in Eric Weiner's *The Geography of Bliss: One Grump's Search for the Happiest Places in the World*. The traveler's purpose may even be to repeat the journey of an earlier traveler, as in Tim Butcher's attempt to retrace the path that 19th-century explorer H.M. Stanley took along the Congo River in *Blood River: A Journey to Africa's Broken Heart*. For some readers, the purpose of the trip will be a key factor in its appeal.

Chapter 3, "The Journey," focuses on travel narratives where the most important element is the traveler or travelers or the process of traveling and what it does to the traveler. These are the titles for readers who believe, like Rilke, that "The only journey is the one within." These are character-driven narratives in which travel plays a healing role or a role in the traveler's discovery of self. These are narratives that may involve the traveler returning to her past or to a place that she has visited before. These are books that tell of Colin Thubron traveling by foot to a sacred Tibetan mountain following his mother's death (*To a Mountain in Tibet*) or Peter Carey taking his manga-obsessed 12-year-old son to Japan to better understand him (*Wrong About Japan: A Father's Journey with His Son*) or Andrew X. Pham returning to the Vietnam of his childhood (*Catfish and Mandala: A Two-Wheeled Voyage through the Landscape and Memory of Vietnam*).

The means of travel is important to the readers who will be drawn to the narratives of Chapter 4, "Getting There Is Half the Fun." For some readers, there is something special about travel by foot or travel by train or a road trip, whether in a car or on a bicycle or a motorcycle. Some readers will enjoy walking the Appalachian Trail with Bill Bryson (*A Walk in the Woods: Rediscovering America on the Appalachian Trail*) or riding the train across the United States with Jenny Diski (*Stranger on a Train: Daydreaming and Smoking around America with Interruptions*) or riding the back roads with William Least-Heat Moon (*Blue Highways: A Journey into America*).

The length of time devoted to the trip defines the titles of Chapter 5, "The Expatriate Life." These narratives represent longer stays, either the one or two years of someone like Pico Iyer (*The Lady and the Monk: Four Seasons in Kyoto*) or the longer stay of Kuki Gallman (*I Dreamed of Africa*), and also include narratives in which the traveler lives with another group of people for a longer time, as Isabel Fonseca does in *Bury Me Standing: The Gypsies and Their Journey* or Bill Buford does in *Among the Thugs*.

The last two chapters of the book highlight two special subgenres, "Travel Humor" and "Travel Adventure." The former represents a subgenre of the travel narrative where the purpose of the narrative is to make the reader laugh. There are a large number of travel narratives that fit this genre, and some of travel's better-known writers (Mark Twain, Bill Bryson, Eric Newby) are practitioners. These are books that will appeal to readers who need a good laugh, whether they are laughing at the unpreparedness of Eric Newby's "short walk" up a previously unclimbed glacial peak (*A Short Walk in the Hindu Kush*) or at the outrageousness of Jennifer Cox's decision to date her way around the planet (*Around the World in 80 Dates*).

Finally, "Travel Adventure" represents a subgenre that borders on another major nonfiction genre, "Adventure." As the introduction to that chapter notes, just as there are disputed territories in the real world of nations, so are there areas of nonfiction where boundaries blur, and some readers will be attracted to the sense of adventure that these travelers experience, to the tension and excitement that Steven Callahan must have felt as he tried to keep himself alive on a five-and-a-half foot inflatable raft for two-and-a-half months (*Adrift: Seventy-six Days Lost at Sea*) or that Colin Angus must have felt as he rafted down the previously untamed Yenisei River in Mongolia and Russia (*Lost in Mongolia: Rafting the World's Last Unchallenged River*).

Just as it is often difficult to state definitively that a given title is a travel narrative, it is also difficult to place a given title into a specific subgenre of the travel narrative genre.

For example, where shall we put Pete McCarthy's hilarious ramblings through Ireland, *McCarthy's Bar*? On the one hand, because McCarthy had visited Ireland as a child, perhaps the title belongs in "The Past Is a Foreign Country," a category in the subgenre "The Journey." On the other hand, his love of the land and the people of Ireland might place the book in "Landscapes and People" in the subgenre "A Sense of Place." A case might also be made that *McCarthy's Bar*, with its search for a sense of belonging, belongs in the category "In Search of an Idea" in the subgenre "Quests." McCarthy, of course, travels by car, and both the rental car of the first half of the book and the dilapidated Volvo of the second half play major roles in the story, which might lead us to categorize the book in "On the Road" in the subgenre "Getting There Is Half the Fun." In spite of all these options, though, the fact that every page of the book is laugh-out-loud funny meant to me that the strongest case was to be made for putting this title in the subgenre "Travel Humor."

But even this decision leaves us with a dilemma: which category within the subgenre "Travel Humor" is the most appropriate? McCarthy provides us with a good bit of background and information about the places that he visits, and so a case might be made for "Wit and Wisdom." Nevertheless, because much of his wandering through

Ireland is tied to his many outrageous rules of travel (most notably "Never Pass a Bar That Has Your Name On It"), I have decided to categorize the book under "Crazy Ideas" with other journeys based on amusing propositions.

On the one hand, the fact that so many of the titles in the book are difficult to categorize makes life difficult for the author of a guide like this and makes life equally or even more difficult for readers' advisors who are trying to match books and readers. On the other hand, it is perhaps a good problem to have and merely reflects the richness of the titles that make up the travel narrative genre. It is a reminder that, just as the blind men found many ways to experience the elephant, there are many ways to experience a book. It is a reminder of the richness of the experience that our readers bring to us.

Organization of the Chapters

Each chapter begins with a definition of the subgenre represented by that chapter. Following the definition is an explanation of the appeal of the subgenre, typically using the six traditional elements of appeal. Each chapter's organization is then explained by listing the categories that make up the subgenre focus of the chapter. The recommended titles are then presented within the categories of the subgenre. For each category, a longer definition is provided.

The first category of each chapter is "Classics," a category including titles that meet the following criteria, established by Tina Frolund in her guide to the classics:[14]

- Age. The term "classic" typically connotes an item of a certain age, and classics are generally those books that have been around long enough to have made an impact. For the purposes of this book, classics are titles that were first published prior to 1990, the watershed year that marks the fall of the Soviet empire and the opening of much of the world to outside travelers. While this date may seem to some readers to be fairly recent, it should be remembered that the travel world did change radically with the opening of the former Soviet Union and its allies and that the Cold War assumptions of pre-1990 travel writing were very different than those of the post-Soviet era.
- Universality. Frolund notes that "Classics explicate our shared human experience," and as pointed out earlier, the classic travel narratives show the reader similarities and connections between the places, people, and experiences with which she is familiar and those that are the subject of the travel narrative. We feel a common humanity with the individuals encountered in these travels, for example, even with a people as different as the Arabs of the "Empty Quarter," many of whom had never seen a European, in Wilfred Thesiger's *Arabian Sands*.
- Multiple levels of meaning. I discussed earlier the difficulties in placing travel narratives into subgenres and categories within those subgenres, and this is particularly true of the classic travel narratives, many of which feature a rich

variety of meanings. For example, is Robert M Pirsig's *Zen and the Art of Motorcycle Maintenance* a journey of self-discovery, a trip through the writer's past, a father–son journey, a motorcycle road trip, or all of the above?

- A great story. Few stories have resonated so well with readers as that of the 17-year-old Marco Polo setting off for Asia in 1271 with his father and uncle and returning to Venice 24 years later, filled with stories of Kublai Khan, camels, and China. Few stories are as compelling as that of the Muslim explorer Ibn Battuta leaving home in 1325 at the age of 21 on a pilgrimage to Mecca and not returning to Morocco for 24 years. The classic travel narratives take advantage of the archetypal nature of the quest and the journey.

- Memorable characters. Many of the classic travel titles feature wonderful, sometimes quirky characters: Peter Mayle's grumpy, fox-hunting neighbor Massot, the perpetual pessimist Faustin, and the clarinet-playing plumber Menicucci, all portrayed in *A Year in Provence*; Karen Blixen's lover, the big-game hunter Denys Finch-Hatton, in *Out of Africa*; the hoboes encountered by Ted Conover in *Rolling Nowhere*; Gertrude Stein and F. Scott Fitzgerald in Ernest Hemingway's *A Moveable Feast*; and the tragic explorer Robert Scott in Apsley Cherry-Garrard's *The Worst Journey in the World*.

- Emotional or thought-provoking experiences. Many of the classic travel narratives reflect strong emotions, as when Peter Jenkins, recently divorced and disillusioned by the war in Vietnam, decides to walk across the United States in order to better understand the country in *A Walk Across America* or when Che Guevara's encounters with the exploitation and mistreatment of mine workers awaken his political consciousness in *The Motorcycle Diaries*. Others are based on fascinating theories (like Bruce Chatwin's thoughts about mankind's nomadic drive in *The Songlines* or Thor Heyerdahl's theory that people from South America could have settled Polynesia, which the author tests in *Kon-Tiki*) that invite the reader to reflect on the author's ideas and experiences.

- Great writing and language at its best. The writers of these classic travel titles represent Nobel Prize winners (V. S. Naipaul, John Steinbeck), highly regarded novelists (Isak Dinesen, Lawrence Durrell, Ernest Hemingway, Washington Irving, Jamaica Kincaid, Michael Ondaatje, George Orwell, James Michener, and Mark Twain), renowned nonfiction writers (Truman Capote and John McPhee), and celebrated poets (Ellen Meloy and Richard Shelton). Their writing and the writing of the other classic travel titles is generally first rate, and language or style is a strong appeal factor for these titles.

Each main entry for the recommended titles in the book includes the basic bibliographic information for the recommended book: author; title; publication information; number of pages; and ISBN. Books that are especially appropriate for book discussions or young adults are also marked by symbols following the ISBN. That information is followed by a brief annotation, typically 100 to 150 words, that attempts to summarize the book and to highlight its potential appeal to readers.

Brief lists of subject headings and categories pertinent to the title follow, as well as a list of places or geographical locations that are covered by the book. These are indexed in the back of the book so that librarians and readers will be able to use subjects and places to access titles. With regard to the places, a few points are in order. First, note that when a foreign city is listed as a geographical location, its country is also listed; for example, Paris and France. However, when a city in the United States or Canada is listed, its state or territory and country are not listed unless that state or territory was a major part of the travel narrative. Second, I have used the current names of countries. For example, in Patrick Leigh Fermor's book on his walk through Europe in the 1930s (*A Time of Gifts: On Foot to Constantinople from the Hook of Holland to the Middle Danube*), he passes through what was then Czechoslovakia. This area is now the Czech Republic and the Slovak Republic, and so I have used the latter names as the title's places or geographical locations. Third, occasionally, when there were simply too many destination countries or states to list, I have designated the destination as "Africa (Various)" or "United States (Various)."

A list of any major awards won by the recommended book is also included. (Those awards are described in Appendix A.) If the recommended book is part of a series, that series is also listed.

For each of the recommended travel narratives, a "Now Try" section is also included. The books in the "Now Try" section represent several titles that individuals who enjoyed the recommended title may also like. These "Now Try" titles may include those written by the author who wrote the recommended title as well as other travel narratives that have similar themes or destinations. "Now Try" titles may include fiction as well as nonfiction titles and may even include a film or a television series.

Every chapter includes a "Consider Starting With . . ." list. These are the six to eight titles that best represent the subgenre under consideration and its categories. For readers who think that they may be interested in a particular subgenre, these are the best titles with which to start. Likewise, each chapter has a list of "Fiction Read-Alikes," which include authors whose works display some of the same characteristics as the nonfiction travel narratives recommended in the chapter.

* * *

A Note on Icons

The Book Group icon indicates that the title is appropriate for book groups or book clubs. Typically, these titles will be those that lend themselves to discussions. Many of these titles will also be best sellers, so that libraries will be likely to have multiple copies.

The Young Adult YA icon indicates that the title is appropriate for young adult or teen readers. Typically, these titles do not contain "adult" themes (such as violence or sexuality) or themes (such as marriage) that might be boring to younger readers. These titles also tend to be faster paced and on an easier reading level.

Notes

1. LizBurns, (@LizB). Post on Twitter.com, November 22, 2011.

2. "Dolman Prize Long-List Announced," May 11, 2011. http://dolmanprize.wordpress.com/about/.

3. Guy Robertson, "Travel Collections: Off the Shelf, On the Road," *Feliciter* 55 (2009): 104.

4. Robertson, "Travel Collections," 105.

5. Sarah Statz Cords, "100 Best-ish Nonfiction Titles: Food and Health," *Citizen Reader* (blog), October 25, 2011, http://www.citizenreader.com/citizen/2011/10/100-best-ish-nonfiction-titles-food-and-health.html.

6. Catherine Ross, "Reading Nonfiction for Pleasure: What Motivates Readers?" in *Nonfiction Readers' Advisory*, edited by Robert Burgin (Westport, CT: Libraries Unlimited, 2004), pp. 105–20.

7. Ross, "Reading Nonfiction for Pleasure," p. 115.

8. Joyce Saricks, *The Readers' Advisory Guide to Genre Fiction* (Chicago: American Library Association, 2009), p. 7.

9. As Canadian library educator Guy Robertson points out, "The first producer of travel literature in Western civilization was Herodotus . . . who included in his *Histories* descriptions of the peoples he encountered during his travels in regions around the Mediterranean and the Black Sea." See Robertson, "Travel Collections," 105.

10. Dr. Judith Patton, post on WikiAnswers. http://wiki.answers.com/Q/Why_didn't_rich_people_travel_in_middle_ages#ixzz1GU3ogTqE (Accessed March 13, 2011). Used with permission.

11. Shannon Butler, *Travel Narratives in Dialogue: Contesting Representations of Nineteenth-Century Peru* (New York: Peter Lang, 2008), p. 1.

12. Mary Louise Pratt, *Imperial Eyes: Travel Writing and Transculturation* (Florence, KY: Routledge, 2007), p. 73.

13. David Carr, "Many Kinds of Crafted Truths: An Introduction to Nonfiction," in *Nonfiction Readers' Advisory*, edited by Robert Burgin (Westport, CT: Libraries Unlimited, 2004), p. 59.

14. Tina Frolund, *Genrefied Classics: A Guide to Reading Interests in Classic Literature* (Westport, CT: Libraries Unlimited, 2007), pp. xiii–xv. Copyright © 2007 by Libraries Unlimited. Reproduced with permission of ABC-CLIO, LLC.

References

Anderson, Sarah. *Sarah Anderson's Travel Companion*. London: Potobello, 2004.

Burns, Liz (@LizB). Post on Twitter.com, November 22, 2011.

Butler, Shannon. *Travel Narratives in Dialogue: Contesting Representations of Nineteenth-Century Peru*. New York: Peter Lang, 2008.

Carr, David. "Many Kinds of Crafted Truths: An Introduction to Nonfiction." In *Nonfiction Readers' Advisory*, edited by Robert Burgin, 47–65. Westport, CT: Libraries Unlimited, 2004.

Cords, Sarah Statz. *The Real Story: A Guide to Nonfiction Reading Interests*. Westport, CT: Libraries Unlimited, 2006.

Frolund, Tina. *Genrefied Classics: A Guide to Reading Interests in Classic Literature.* Westport, CT: Libraries Unlimited, 2007.

Patton, Judith Patton. Post on WikiAnswers. http://wiki.answers.com/Q/Why_didn't_rich_people_travel_in_middle_ages#ixzz1GU3ogTqE (Accessed March 13, 2011.)

Pearl, Nancy. *Book Lust to Go: Recommended Reading for Travelers, Vagabonds, and Dreamers.* Seattle, WA: Sasquatch Books, 2010.

Pratt, Mary Louise. *Imperial Eyes: Travel Writing and Transculturation.* Florence, KY: Routledge, 2007.

Robertson, Guy. "Travel Collections: Off the Shelf, On the Road." *Feliciter* 55 (2009): 104–6.

Ross, Catherine. "Reading Nonfiction for Pleasure: What Motivates Readers?" In *Nonfiction Readers' Advisory,* edited by Robert Burgin, 105–20. Westport, CT: Libraries Unlimited, 2004.

Saricks, Joyce. *The Readers' Advisory Guide to Genre Fiction.* Chicago: American Library Association, 2009.

Simony, Maggy. *The Traveler's Reading Guide: Ready-Made Reading Lists for the Armchair Traveler.* New York: Facts on File, 1993.

Wyatt, Neal. *The Readers' Advisory Guide to Nonfiction.* Chicago: American Library Association, 2007.

Chapter 1

A Sense of Place

My friend sang strange songs when he ran his hand over the boulders by the river, and the beauty of the land was a cold, hard pain in his chest.
—Ellen Meloy, *The Anthropology of Turquoise: Meditations on Landscape, Art, and Spirit*

Definition of "A Sense of Place"

By definition, travel involves a place, a destination to which one journeys. Not surprisingly, then, this book on travel narratives opens with a subgenre devoted to place, a subgenre whose focus is on the destination of the traveler and what she or he finds there.

What the traveler finds may be the unforgettable beauty of the place or a combination of the appeal of the place and its people. The writer may find beauty in a wilderness (a desert or one of the polar regions) or in the crowd and bustle of a major city. The writer may celebrate the fauna and flora of the destination or lament the destructive changes that threaten the beauty of a place. Regardless, the focus is on the destination.

The importance of destination to many travel narratives and to many readers of travel narratives is reflected in the fact that most libraries will classify travel books by the destination (914.1 for Great Britain, 914.3 for Germany, 914.4 for France) and that many of the existing guides to travel narratives are organized by destinations (Nancy Pearl's *Book Lust to Go: Recommended Reading for Travelers, Vagabonds, and Dreamers*, Sarah Anderson's *Travel Companion*, and Maggy Simony's *The Traveler's Reading Guide: Ready-Made Reading Lists for the Armchair Traveler*).

The importance of place is also reflected in the fact that the entry for each of the suggested titles in this book includes a list of places or geographical locations covered by that title. An index of these places is also included so that the reader looking for books on Paris or China or Djibouti can find them easily. Finally, the importance of destination can be seen in the "Now Try" titles at the end of each annotation. Many of these will be based on destination. A quest for food in Spain may generate Read-Alikes that are also set in Spain.

Although one of the major arguments of this book is that destination is not the only factor about a travel narrative that will appeal to a reader, it is also clear that destination is, for many readers, a very important reason for reading and enjoying a particular title.

Appeal of "A Sense of Place"

The most obvious of the six traditional elements of appeal[1] for the titles in this chapter are frame and setting. The focus of these titles is typically on a specific place or destination, and the ability of the author to evoke these places, no matter how foreign or exotic they may be, is of key importance to the reader.

Readers of travel narratives may read about a place they never expect to see in person (the Antarctica of Peter Matthiessen's *End of the Earth: Voyaging to Antarctica*, for example), or about a place they intend to visit (Peter Hessler's *Oracle Bones: A Journey between China's Past and Present*, which I read in preparation for the 2009 trip that my wife and I took to China,) or about a place they have already visited (Roy Blount's *Feet on the Street: Rambles Around New Orleans* should appeal to anyone who has traveled to and fallen in love with New Orleans). In each case, the reading experience is heightened by a focus on the place itself.

Many readers will be drawn to titles simply because they are "about" a specific country or city or part of the world.[2] As noted previously, many guides to travel narratives are arranged, for the most part, by country. But characterization may also be important, particularly for those titles in the "Landscapes and People" section. Typically, an author will not limit her or his descriptions of a place to its geographic features, no matter how beautiful. The individuals that the author encounters are invariably an important part of the scenery.

Other appeal factors, such as writing style, story line, and pacing, will be less important but often present. As with many of the chapters in this book, "A Sense of Place" features several authors who are well known as writers of fiction, poetry, or other nonfiction genres. Readers who enjoy an author's writing style may find their titles in this chapter to be of interest. Examples include Bruce Chatwin (*In Patagonia*) and Peter Matthiessen (*The Tree Where Man Was Born* and *The Birds of Heaven: Travels with Cranes*), both of whom have written a number of novels; Washington Irving (*Tales of the Alhambra*), known for his short stories; John McPhee (*Coming into the Country*), who writes in a number of nonfiction genres; the novelist James Michener (*Iberia: Spanish Travels and Reflections*); and the poets Ellen Meloy (*The Anthropology of Turquoise: Meditations on Landscape, Art, and Spirit*) and Richard Shelton (*Going Back to Bisbee*).

As readers' advisors work with readers who are drawn to books with a heavy focus on the destination or the place, they should remember that titles in other genres may have appeal for these readers: history (especially the history of a specific country or city), anthropology, natural history, environmental or nature writing, or fiction with a strong sense of place. For example, a title such as Farley Mowat's *Never Cry Wolf* may appeal to readers who enjoyed Barry Lopez's *Arctic Dreams: Imagination and Desire in a Northern Landscape*, and a title like Dayton Hyde's *Sandy: The Sandhill Crane Who Joined Our Family* may be of interest to fans of Peter Matthiessen's *The Birds of Heaven: Travels with Cranes*.

Organization of the Chapter

This chapter begins, as will all of the chapters, with "Classics." As noted in the Introduction these are titles that were published prior to 1990 and that display universality, multiple levels of meaning, great stories, memorable characters, emotional or though-provoking experiences, and great writing. These titles are likely to be more familiar to both readers and librarians and will help them better understand the nuances of the subgenre and its further categories. Changes may have affected the places that the travelers visit in these titles, but many of the insights of the authors are still important.

Following the classic works of the subgenre is "The Beauty of the Place," which provides titles that primarily praise the physical beauty of the destination. "Landscapes and People," the third section, represents titles in which the author evokes not only a sense of the beauty of the destination but also an appreciation for the people who live there. The people who are encountered in these books are inextricably part of the destination for these writers.

The destinations of the titles in the fourth section, "Urban Landscapes," are cities, and the appeal of these cities represents something vastly different from the natural beauty of the destinations of the previous sections. By contrast, "Appreciating Nature" represents titles in which the author expresses an appreciation for the fauna and flora of the destination. These living things define the author's destination in each title in this section.

Finally, titles in the "Endangered Places" section focus on the lost beauty of the destination, on the devastating changes that have taken place or will soon take place to the destination and its ecology. The changes may impact environmental features and or they may impact people, but regardless, there is a sense of lost beauty of place in these titles.

Classics

Classics are those travel narratives that were published before 1990, the watershed year that marks the fall of the Soviet empire and the opening of much of the world to outside travelers, and that also display universality, multiple levels of meaning, great stories, memorable characters, emotional or though-provoking experiences, and great writing. These titles are more familiar to readers and librarians and will thereby serve as good entry points into the subgenre of "A Sense of Place" and its various categories. Though the places that the travelers visit in these titles (the Spain of James Michener's

Iberia: Spanish Travels and Reflections or the Hong Kong of Jan Morris's *Hong Kong: Epilogue to an Empire*) may have undergone great changes, many of the insights of the authors are still important, particularly when the writer's focus is on the people of a place, their history and spirit, or on timeless themes, such as the many threats to endangered species and fragile environments.

Bartram, William

Travels and Other Writings. New York: Literary Classics of the United States, 1996 [1791]. 701 pp. ISBN: 9781883011116

In 1773, naturalist Bartram began a four-year journey through the American southern colonies. His *Travels* provide vivid, beautiful depictions of the flora and fauna of this wild area, much of which had never been encountered before, and include Bartram's own masterful drawings as well as reports of his encounters with Native Americans. Written with a deep respect for the magnificence of nature, the book is an excellent portrayal of the wildlife and people of these lands in the early part of the country's history.

Subjects: 18th Century; American History; American Indians; American South; Animals; Plants

Categories: Appreciating Nature; The Beauty of the Place

Places: Alabama; Florida; Georgia; North Carolina; South Carolina

Now Try: In *Guide to William Bartram's Travels*, Brian Sanders has written a companion for readers interested in visiting some of the sites explored by Bartram. Likewise, James Kautz follows in Bartram's footsteps in *Footprints Across the South: Bartram's Trail Revisited*, although Kautz also discusses the many ways in which the area has changed since Bartram visited in the 1770s. The drawings of John James Audubon are, of course, the most famous depictions of the birds of 19th-century America, and *Birds of America* is his best known work. However, the Library of America edition of his *Writings and Drawings* includes his journals, memoirs, and letters as well.

Ibn Battutah, Abu Abdullah Muhammad

The Travels of Ibn Battuta. London: Picador, 2002. 325 pp. ISBN: 9780330491136

Generally regarded as the greatest traveler of the premodern world, the Muslim explorer Ibn Battuta left home in 1325 at the age of 21 to set off on a pilgrimage to Mecca; he would not return to Morocco for 24 years. He visited most of the known Islamic world, traveling more than 75,000 miles, a figure unsurpassed for 450 years. His observations on the world of the relatively peaceful 14th century are fascinating, especially his interactions with other members of the Muslim communities in the countries through which he traveled. Ibn Battuta dictated his account to Ibn Juzayy, a scholar, between 1354 and 1355; the earliest Western edition appears to have been a French translation in the 1850s. This edition of Ibn Battuta's *Travels* is an abridged version of a translation published in four volumes between 1958 and 1994; it is edited by Tim Mackintosh-Smith and includes 25 pages of clarifying footnotes. (In 2011, the *Guardian* listed *The Adventures of Ibn Battuta* as one of the 100 greatest nonfiction titles of all time.)

Subjects: 14th Century; Exploration; Islam; Solo Travelers

Categories: The Beauty of the Place; Landscapes and People

Places: Afghanistan; Africa; Algeria; Bahrain; Bulgaria; China; Egypt; India; Indonesia; Israel; Kenya; Libya; Malaysia; Mali; Mauritania; Morocco; Myanmar; Niger; Oman; Pakistan; Philippines; Russia; Saudi Arabia; Somalia; Spain; Sri Lanka; Syria; Tajikistan; Tanzania; Tunisia; Turkey; Uzbekistan; Yemen

Now Try: Another approach to Ibn Battuta's life and travels is Ross Dunn's *The Adventures of Ibn Battuta: A Muslim Traveler of the Fourteenth Century*, which includes quotations from Ibn Battuta's original writings along with very accessible notes about the places that he visited. Mackintosh-Smith himself has traveled through Islamic countries in the footsteps of Ibn Battutah and has written about these journeys in three books: *Travels with a Tangerine: A Journey in the Footnotes of Ibn Battutah* (which follows Ibn Battutah's path from Morocco to Turkey), *The Hall of a Thousand Columns* (which replicates Ibn Battutah's travels to India), and *Landfalls: On the Edge of Islam from Zanzibar to the Alhambra* (which follows the great Muslim traveler back from India to the Alhambra in Spain). In these three books, Mackintosh-Smith provides a compelling comparison of modern-day and 14th-century Islam. The 2009 IMAX film, *Journey to Mecca: In the Footsteps of Ibn Battuta*, follows the first of Ibn Battuta's journeys, to Mecca. Another early Muslim traveler was Ibn Jubayr, whose pilgrimage to Mecca from 1183 to 1185 is described in *Travels of Ibn Jubayr*. For readers interested in the history of Islam itself, Tom Holland's book, *In the Shadow of the Sword: The Birth of Islam and the Rise of the Global Arab Empire*, can be recommended, and for readers interested in the life of the prophet Muhammad, Karen Armstrong's *Muhammad: A Prophet for Our Time* is excellent. The best known of the early travelers was, of course, Marco Polo, and *The Travels of Marco Polo* is annotated in this chapter.

Byron, Robert

The Road to Oxiana. New York: Oxford University Press, 1982 [1937]. 292 pp. ISBN: 9780195030679

Widely regarded as one of the greatest travel narratives of the 20th century (Paul Fussell called it "the *Ulysses* of travel writing"), *The Road to Oxiana* describes Byron's journey in 1933 and 1934 through the Middle East to Oxiana, a region on the border between Afghanistan and what was then the Soviet Union. Much of the focus of the book is on the Muslim art and architecture that Byron believed were underappreciated in the West, but there are also humorous passages, particularly when Byron is dealing with difficult government officials or trying to coax his automobiles through unfriendly terrain. Byron also sprinkles his manuscript with bits of history, descriptions of landscapes, and stories of the people that he meets along the way.

Subjects: 1930s; Architecture; Art and Artists; Automobiles; Humor; Islam

Categories: The Beauty of the Place; Landscapes and People

Places: Afghanistan; Iran; Iraq; Israel; Lebanon; Russia; Syria

Now Try: While Byron's book is considered by many to be the first great modern travel narrative, it was less well received in its time than titles by Peter Fleming and Evelyn Waugh. Fleming's *Brazilian Adventure* follows an expedition to locate a missing explorer in 1920s Brazil and is that writer's best known work. Waugh wrote several travel narratives, including *Remote People,* about his travels through the British East African colonies, and *When the Going Was Good,* a collection of his shorter prewar pieces. The *New York Times* critic who reviewed the 1982 edition of *The Road to Oxiana* listed a handful of classic travel narratives that he felt were "more charming," including Peter Mayne's *A Year in Marrakesh,* a 1954 work about the author's years in Morocco; Alexander William Kinglake's *Eothen: Traces of Travel Brought Home from the East,* about a journey in Syria, Palestine, and Egypt in the 1830s; and J. R. Ackerley's *Hindoo Holiday: An Indian Journal,* a humorous memoir of the author's five months in India as secretary to a maharaja.

Chatwin, Bruce

In Patagonia. New York: Summit Books, 1977. 205 pp. ISBN: 9780671400453

Chatwin established his reputation as a travel writer with this book, based on a six-month trip to Patagonia, the southernmost portion of South America and an area that Chatwin describes as "the uttermost part of the earth." *In Patagonia* is a book of snippets (97 short sections in all), with the author wandering from vivid descriptions of the landscape to interviews with colorful inhabitants to notes on the region's eccentric history. Subjects range from Darwin to Butch Cassidy and the Sundance Kid. There have been claims that many of the conversations and characters were invented by Chatwin, but the book remains an enthralling evocation of a remote, wild part of the world.

Subjects: Essays; Quick Reads

Categories: The Beauty of the Place; Landscapes and People

Places: Argentina; Chile

Awards: Hawthornden Prize, 1977

Now Try: Chatwin's novel *On the Black Hill* is also about odd characters living in isolation, in this case, identical twin brothers living in a farmhouse on the border of England and Wales. Another Chatwin novel, *The Viceroy of Ouidah,* tells of a Brazilian adventurer who becomes the master of the slave trade in a West African nation. Nicholas Shakespeare's book, *Bruce Chatwin,* is a highly regarded, detailed biography of the enigmatic writer. Readers who are fascinated by the Patagonian region of South American may enjoy Anne Whitehead's *Bluestocking in Patagonia: Mary Gilmore's Quest for Love and Utopia at the World's End,* the true story of an aspiring writer who travels with her husband to found a Socialist utopia in Paraguay.

Frazier, Ian

Great Plains. New York: Farrar Straus Giroux, 1989. 290 pp. ISBN: 9780374217235

In the early 1980s, *New Yorker* writer Frazier moved to Montana and began his travels through and research on the states that make up the American Great Plains. The result is part travel narrative and part history, with superb stories of the people he meets, the colorful history of the region, and the conditions of the area at the time. Frazier visited a number of sites (including the spot where Sitting Bull's cabin once stood, the home town of Western Swing pioneer Bob Wills, a house whose occupants once rescued Bonnie and Clyde, and the house where the *In Cold Blood* murders took place) and reports on all of them with an almost childlike sense of wonder. *Great Plains* is a thoughtful appreciation of what are often dismissed as the "flyover" states.

Subjects: American History; American Indians; Geography; Great Plains

Categories: The Beauty of the Place; Landscapes and People

Places: Colorado; Kansas; Montana; Nebraska; New Mexico; North Dakota; Oklahoma; South Dakota; Texas; Wyoming

Now Try: Frazier's *On the Rez* is a more recent, in-depth look at one of the peoples who lived on the Great Plains, the Oglala Sioux, and their current conditions on the Pine Ridge reservation in South Dakota. Poet Kathleen Norris moved from New York to South Dakota and, after 20 years, wrote her reflections of life in the High Plains in *Dakota: A Spiritual Geography*; her book is far more spiritual and meditative than is Frazier's. Stephen Jones travels through another Great Plains state in his celebration of the Sandhills region of Nebraska, *The Last Prairie: A Sandhills Journal*. Jonathan Raban's *Bad Land: An American Romance* provides both a history and a travel narrative about eastern Montana and is annotated in the "Endangered Places" section of this chapter. Frazier visited the Holcomb, Kansas, house where the murders recounted by Truman Capote's *In Cold Blood* took place; readers will find a strong sense of the American Midwest in that work of true crime. Frazier also visited the Pritchard farmhouse in Lutie, Texas, the site of a famous incident in the career of Bonnie and Clyde; readers interested in that duo, who robbed their way through Midwestern America during the Great Depression, may learn more through books such as Jeff Guinn's *Go Down Together: The True, Untold Story of Bonnie and Clyde* or John Neal Phillips's *Running With Bonnie and Clyde: The Ten Fast Years of Ralph Fults.*

Irving, Washington

Tales of the Alhambra [With Bracebridge Hall, Tales of a Traveler]. New York: Library of America, 1991 [1832]. 1104 pp. ISBN: 9780940450592

Following the **success** of ***The** Sketch Book,* Washington Irving spent the 1820s in Europe in search of new material. In 1828, he moved to Granada,

Spain, and the following year, he took up residence in the historic Alhambra palace, which was built for the last Moorish rulers in Spain. The book contains Irving's dreamlike, romantic descriptions of the area, its music, its history, and its folklore. His observations are told as short sketches and provide insight into the lives of the Spanish people in the early 19th century and into the spirit of Spain.

Subjects: 19th Century; Architecture; Folklore; Islam; Music and Musicians

Categories: The Beauty of the Place; Landscapes and People

Places: Spain

Now Try: James Michener's *Iberia: Spanish Travels and Reflections* (annotated in this section) and Giles Tremlett's *Ghosts of Spain: Travels Through Spain and Its Silent Past* are more recent travel narratives about Spain. For readers who want to learn more about the Alhambra itself, Michael Jacobs's *Alhambra* and Robert Irwin's *The Alhambra* can be recommended. Tahir Shah's *The Caliph's House: A Year in Casablanca* and *In Arabian Nights: A Caravan of Moroccan Dreams* are set in Morocco and not Spain, but Shah's evocation of the former palace in which he and his family live as well as the traditional Arabian stories that they hear is as dreamlike and romantic as Irving's descriptions of the Alhambra and the folklore of Granada. Irving is, of course, best known as the author of the short story, "The Legend of Sleepy Hollow," which he published about 10 years before *Tales of the Alhambra*. Victoria Hislop's novel *The Return* is set in 20th-century Granada, where a young British tourist learns of the fate of a local family during the Spanish Civil War

Lopez, Barry

Arctic Dreams: Imagination and Desire in a Northern Landscape. New York: Scribner, 1986. 464 pp. ISBN: 9780684185781

Arctic Dreams, arguably the most celebrated narrative about the Arctic region of our planet, is an ecstatic appreciation of the area's majesty. Lopez draws thoughtful and powerful lessons on the land and its inhabitants (from narwhals to polar bears to native Eskimos) from more than a dozen trips to the far north over a period of five years. Lopez's writing is wide-ranging and passionate, and he is clearly attuned to the mysterious power of the Arctic, a power that Lopez says derives from "the tension between its beauty and its capacity to take life." In spite of this power, however, the encroachment of civilization and the concomitant threat of destruction to this severe environment loom throughout the book.

Subjects: Animals; Endangered Species; Environment; Exploration; Geography

Categories: Appreciating Nature; The Beauty of the Place; Landscapes and People

Places: Alaska; Arctic Region; Canada

Awards: National Book Award for Nonfiction, 1986

Now Try: Readers who enjoy Lopez's appreciation of Arctic wildlife may also be attracted to his highly regarded earlier book, *Of Wolves and Men*, which focuses on one species of North American mammal. Farley Mowat's classic, *Never Cry Wolf*, is also about wolves as well as being set in the Arctic region of Canada. Other titles about Arctic animals, particularly those that are endangered, include *On Thin Ice: The Changing*

World of the Polar Bear by Richard Ellis and *After the Ice: Life, Death, and Geopolitics in the New Arctic* by Alun Anderson. Arctic narratives in general (like Gretel Ehrlich's beautiful book about the frozen beauty of Greenland, *This Cold Heaven: Seven Seasons in Greenland*, which is annotated in this chapter, under "The Beauty of the Place", or Bill Streever's natural history of the Arctic, *Cold: Adventures in the World's Frozen Places*) should also appeal to readers who enjoyed *Arctic Dreams*.

Marnham, Patrick

So Far From God: A Journey to Central America. New York: Viking, 1985. 253 pp. ISBN: 9780670804498

Marnham takes his title from an old saying by an early Mexican president: "Poor Mexico! So far from God, so close to the United States." The book provides a vivid and sometimes humorous account of his leisurely trip from the United States to Mexico City and on into the northernmost Central American countries. Marnham's colorful account is full of the grime and sweat of the people that he met on his train and bus rides, and he highlights their daily lives and the seemingly endless political conflicts with which they live. His portrait of the civil war in El Salvador is particularly striking.

Subjects: Humor; Rail Travel; Rural Life

Categories: Landscapes and People

Places: Central America; El Salvador; Guatemala; Mexico; Nicaragua

Awards: Thomas Cook Travel Book Award, 1985

Now Try: Readers interested in a good history of Mexico in general should consider Earl Shorris's hefty (800 pages) *The Life and Times of Mexico*. Larry Habegger and Natanya Pearlman edited *Traveler's Tales Central America*, a collection of travel essays on Central America that includes pieces by well-known writers Paul Theroux and Tim Cahill. Like Marnham, Peter Ford travels into a Central American war zone, in his case a border dispute between Nicaragua and Honduras; he writes about his three-month exploration of Central America's east coast in *Around the Edge*. Joan Didion's *Salvador*, in which she portrays terror as a standard tool of politics in 1980s El Salvador, may be of interest as well. Mary Morris also traveled through Mexico and Central America in her narrative of self-discovery, *Nothing to Declare: Memoirs of a Woman Traveling Alone* (annotated in "The Journey" chapter of this book).

Matthiessen, Peter

The Snow Leopard. New York: Viking Press, 1978. 338 pp. ISBN: 9780670653744

Matthiessen's book about his 1973 quest for the elusive, almost mythical snow leopard in the Himalayas operates on two levels. It is both the story of his travels in search of the rare creature and the story of a pilgrimage of understanding into the writer's own soul. Matthiessen, a practicing Buddhist, reflects on the history of Buddhism, on his own Zen-oriented practice, and on the personal pain of his late wife's death from cancer. He intersperses these reflections with more typical travel narrative fare: beautiful descriptions of the exotic birds and animals, the people, and the landscapes that he encounters. Still, it is the quest (whether for the mysterious snow leopard or for inner peace) that is the focus of the book.

Subjects: Animals; Buddhism; Community Life; Conservation; Death and Dying; Grief; Landscape; Memoirs; Spirituality

Categories: Appreciating Nature

Places: Nepal

Awards: National Book Award for Nonfiction, 1979

Now Try: Matthiessen is a prolific writer, and many of his works mix observations about nature and more philosophical, spiritual reflections. *The Cloud Forest*, about his expeditions in the South American wilderness, and *Sand Rivers*, about his safari into Tanzania, are two examples. Readers who were moved by Matthiessen's spiritual thoughts may want to try his *Nine-Headed Dragon River: Zen Journals 1969–1982*, which explores his Zen practice in more detail. Matthiessen won a second National Book Award in 2008 for *Shadow Country*, a work of fiction that tells the story of a sugar cane planter and outlaw who is killed by his neighbors. Like Matthiessen's nonfiction, the novel evokes a strong sense of place, in this case, the undeveloped Everglades of the late 19th century. Other books on rare animals may also appeal: Marq De Villiers and Sheila Hirtle's *Sable Island: The Strange Origins and Curious History of a Dune Adrift in the Atlantic* (about wild horses living on a sand dune in the middle of the Atlantic, 100 miles east of Nova Scotia); Bernd Heinrich's *Mind of the Raven: Investigations and Adventures with Wolf-Birds* (a biologist's examination of these surprisingly intelligent birds); David Quammen's *Monster of God: The Man-Eating Predator in the Jungles of History and the Mind* (annotated in this chapter, under "Appreciating Nature"); and Margaret Mittelbach and Michael Crewdson's *Carnivorous Nights: On the Trail of the Tasmanian Tiger* (about the mysterious marsupial predator that may or may not have been hunted to extinction).

Matthiessen, Peter

The Tree Where Man Was Born. New York: Dutton, 1972. 247 pp. ISBN: 9780525222651

Matthiessen, a writer and an environmental activist, writes about his several trips to East Africa over a dozen-year period. While much of his focus is on the people that he met (the herdsmen and other native Africans as well as the anthropologists studying man's origins and the biologists studying the animals of the area), the most evocative and lyrical language is reserved for his descriptions of nature and the beauty of the African savannah. Some of the science is dated, and some of Matthiessen's attitudes toward the native Africans may strike some readers as racist, but his vivid descriptions of the land and the people are stirring.

Subjects: Animals; Anthropology; Endangered Species; Environment

Categories: Appreciating Nature

Places: Africa; Kenya; Sudan; Tanzania; Uganda

Now Try: Two of Matthiessen's later books, *African Silences* and *Sand Rivers,* are published with *The Tree Where Man Was Born* as *African Trilogy* and should interest readers who care about the people and wildlife of that continent. Matthiessen also writes fiction, and his 1965 novel, *At Play in the Fields of the Lord,* deals with the conflict in a South American jungle between a naive missionary who is trying to convert the local Indians and a mercenary who is hired to kill them. That novel was made into a film with the same name in 1991 and stars Tom Berenger, John Lithgow, and Darryl Hannah.

McPhee, John

Coming into the Country. New York: Farrar, Straus and Giroux, 1976. 438 pp. ISBN: 9780374522872

McPhee writes about Alaska at a very special time in its life as a young state, hovering between old traditions and new regulations, with controversies surrounding the establishment of national park areas and the Alaskan pipeline. McPhee's portrait of the state emerges from a series of stories about his travels and discussions with bush pilots, prospectors, trappers, homesteaders, politicians, and businesspeople, all of whom see Alaska in different ways. McPhee is able to capture the complexity of the state and to do so in an eloquent and nonjudgmental manner. While much has changed about Alaska in the years since the book's original publication, it still provides a fascinating look at the mindset of the inhabitants of the largest of the U.S. states.

Subjects: Community Life; Conservation; Environment; Geography

Categories: Appreciating Nature; The Beauty of the Place; Landscapes and People

Places: Alaska

Now Try: McPhee's writings are as eclectic as they are excellent, and fans of travel narrative may be interested in other McPhee titles, including *The Pine Barrens,* which explores the pinelands that cover nearly half the state of New Jersey, and *La Place de la Concorde Suisse,* about Switzerland and the role of the Swiss Army in its society. Another writer who captures the complexities of Alaska is Margaret Murie, whose memoir, *Two in the Far North,* may be recommended to those interested in the state. McPhee spends a good part of *Coming into the Country* interviewing and discussing the trappers and homesteaders of the upper Yukon; their fate is described in Dan O'Neill's *A Land Gone Lonesome: An Inland Voyage along the Yukon River* (annotated in this chapter). James Michener's long but absorbing novel, *Alaska,* is an excellent fiction read-alike to *Coming into the Country* and follows the development of Alaska from prehistoric times to the present. Edna Ferber's 1958 novel, *Ice Palace,* about Alaska's long journey to statehood, may also be recommended.

Michener, James

Iberia: Spanish Travels and Reflections. New York: Fawcett Crest, 1982 [1968]. 960 pp. ISBN: 9780449207338

Novelist Michener's tribute to his second home is almost one thousand pages long and describes his travels in that country over four decades in a vivid combination of memoir and travelogue. The size of the book reflects the richness of the detail and the breadth of knowledge that Michener provides as he focuses not only on his own experiences and the people he met but also on Spain's food, culture, history, and spirituality. *Iberia* is a very intimate appreciation of the country, what one reviewer described as "a massive, thousand-page love affair with Spain." Michener's obsession with the country corroborates his own claim that Spain haunts the people who go there, and while obviously dated, several reviewers noted that *Iberia* was still helpful to them both before and during recent trips to Spain.

Subjects: Art and Artists; Food; Memoirs; Religion

Categories: The Beauty of the Place; Landscapes and People

Places: Spain

Now Try: A more recent travel narrative about Spain is Giles Tremlett's *Ghosts of Spain: Travels Through Spain and Its Silent Past,* which focuses on the social and political changes that have affected Spain since its Civil War. *The Buried Mirror: Reflections on Spain and the New World,* by Mexican novelist Carlos Fuentes, is more history than travel and focuses on the relationship between Spain and Latin America. Many of Michener's novels are set in specific countries and have the feel of travel narratives; these include *Mexico, Caravans: A Novel of Afghanistan, The Drifters,* and *Poland.* Like *Iberia,* Earl Shorris's *The Life and Times of Mexico* is an enormous (800 pages) history of a Spanish-speaking country; like Michener, Shorris is also a skilled writer, and as one reviewer noted, he "expertly uses the lives of everyday Mexicans to tell the story and draw in the reader."

Moorhouse, Geoffrey

To The Frontier: A Journey to the Khyber Pass. New York: Holt, Rinehart, and Winston, 1985. 285 pp. ISBN: 9780030004544

In the early 1980s, Moorhouse spent three months traveling through the extremely rugged terrain of northwestern Pakistan to its border with Afghanistan, visiting Lahore, meeting members of the Afghan mujahideen, investigating drug smuggling, and climbing the famous Hindu Kush mountains along the way. Moorhouse evokes the stormy beauty and contrasts of this remote part of the world and, in one memorable scene, recalls being awakened one night by what turned out to be the noise of the Russians withdrawing from Afghanistan. The book was originally deemed anti-Islamic and suppressed in Pakistan by that country's government.

Subjects: Mountains; War

Categories: The Beauty of the Place

Places: Pakistan

Awards: Thomas Cook Travel Book Award, 1984

Now Try: Moorhouse had a particular love for India and wrote several travel narratives about the subcontinent, including *Calcutta: The City Revealed* and *Om: An Indian Pilgrimage.* His best-known work, *The Fearful Void* (annotated in this book's chapter "The Journey"), describes his attempt to become the first person to cross the Sahara Desert from west to east by foot and by camel. The best travel narrative about the Hindu Kush, in my humble opinion, is the classic by Eric Newby, *A Short Walk in the Hindu Kush* (annotated in "Travel Humor"). Mohsin Hamid's first novel, *Moth Smoke,* depicts life in a modern Pakistan of gun running and drug trafficking, where a banker in Lahore loses his job, falls in love with the wife of his best friend, and becomes a heroin addict; the book became a cult hit in Pakistan and India and was a finalist for the PEN/Hemingway Award for the best first novel in the United States.

Morris, Jan

Hong Kong: Epilogue to an Empire. New York: Random House, 1988. 359 pp. ISBN: 9780394550978

Welsh travel writer Morris portrays "the last of the great British colonies as it is in its last years" and does so by mixing lessons of the past with portraits of the present, alternating chapters on the city's history with chapters on its culture, geography, politics, and society. The writing is elegant, and Morris captures the vibrant flow of the "Pearl of the Orient." The book was written before 1997, when Hong Kong was returned to China, but Morris does speculate on what this reunification might mean.

Subjects: Asian History; Colonialism; Islands; Society; Women Travelers

Categories: Urban Landscapes

Places: China; Hong Kong

Series: *Vintage Departures*

Now Try: Morris is well known for her portraits of world cities. These include *The World of Venice, The Great Port: A Passage Through New York,* and *Trieste and the Meaning of Nowhere* (annotated in this chapter's section on "Urban Landscapes"). Morris has also published collections of her travel essays, and these include several essays on cities such as Las Vegas and Stockholm (in *Journeys*) or Atlanta, Jerusalem, and Baghdad (in *The World: Travels 1950–2000*). Readers interested in Hong Kong may find two novels worth pursuing: Timothy Mo's *The Monkey King,* about a man who marries into a dysfunctional family in 1950s Hong Kong, and travel writer Paul Theroux's *Kowloon Tong,* about the lives of individuals caught up in the 1997 handover of Hong Kong to China.

Naipaul, V. S.

A Turn in the South. New York: Knopf, 1989. 307 pp. ISBN: 9780394564777

Nobel Prize winner V. S. Naipaul reports on his travels through the American South in the 1980s, in pursuit of a better understanding of that part of the nation. Naipaul's perspective is particularly interesting: he is both an outsider and someone who grew up in a world similar to that of the antebellum South, "the vanished world of sugar-cane fields and huts and barefoot children." Naipaul visits the new cities of the South, tobacco farms, Elvis's birthplace, and former plantations. He meets and listens to a wide range of individuals (rednecks in rusty pickup trucks, poets, Bible-thumping politicians, country music songwriters, and the daughters of sharecroppers) and is sympathetic and understanding of their strong sense of the past.

Subjects: American History; American South

Categories: Landscapes and People

Places: Alabama; Florida; Georgia; Mississippi; New York; North Carolina; South Carolina; Tennessee

Now Try: *A Turn in the South* focuses on the sense of identity among American Southerners, and several of Naipaul's novels also focus on the sense of identity among other groups: *Guerillas* (which takes place on an unnamed Caribbean island) and *A Bend in the River* (which takes place in an unnamed African country after its independence). Readers wanting to know more about Naipaul himself should turn to Patrick French's *The World Is What It Is: The Authorized Biography of V. S. Naipaul.* Wanda Rushing uses the Southern city of Memphis, Tennessee, to explore the importance of place in the current age of globalization in her *Memphis and the Paradox of Place: Globalization in the American South.* John Howard Griffin's classic *Black Like Me* is a travel narrative of sorts, in which a white man darkens his skin and pretends to be a black man as he travels through the American South.

Polo, Marco

The Travels of Marco Polo. New York: Facts on File, 1984 [c. 1300]. 218 pp. ISBN: 9780871968906

The most famous travel narrative of the Middle Ages, Marco Polo's *Travels* recount his journey along the Silk Road through Persia, Tibet, India, and China and the time that he spent in the court of the great Kublai Khan. While modern scholars debate the accuracy of his account and even question whether Polo actually traveled to China, the lively stories tell of the splendor of a world that was as foreign to his European readers as it is to us today.

Subjects: 13th Century; Exploration; Geography; Quick Reads; Silk Road

Categories: The Beauty of the Place; Landscapes and People

Places: China; India; Iran; Italy; Tibet

Now Try: In 1985, Harry Rutstein became the first person to follow Marco Polo's route across Europe and Asia. His adventures are told in *The Marco Polo Odyssey:*

In the Footsteps of a Merchant Who Changed the World, which is annotated in the "Quests" chapter of this book. Denis Belliveau and Francis O'Donnell spent two years retracing Polo's journey and tell about their experience in the lively book, *In the Footsteps of Marco Polo: A Companion to the Public Television Film.* In Italo Calvino's intricate novel, *Invisible Cities,* Marco Polo describes the cities that he has visited on his travels for the aging emperor Kublai Khan. A later, 17th-century Ottoman Turk who traveled widely was Evliya Celebi, and his 10-volume travel writings have been recently abridged into a single volume by Sooyong Kim and Robert Dankoff, *An Ottoman Traveller: Selections from the Book of Travels of Evliya Celebi.*

Raban, Jonathan

Arabia Through the Looking Glass. New York: Simon and Schuster, 1979. 344 pp. ISBN: 9780671250584

This is Raban's first travel book and describes his travels in the Middle East and especially the people he encountered. Raban, who learned Arabic in preparation for the trip, has a knack for meeting people and letting them tell their stories. He explores the worlds of rich Arabs and poor, from the "squeaky clean" Abu Dhabi to the "seedy" Bahrain, and does so with a dry wit.

Subjects: Islam

Categories: Landscapes and People

Places: Abu Dhabi; Africa; Bahrain; Dubai; Egypt; Jordan; Lebanon; Qatar; United Arab Emirates; Yemen

Now Try: Raban discusses his motivations for writing in a collection of travel writing and literary criticism, *For Love and Money.* Anne Caulfield travels through Jordan and falls in love with her tour guide in *Kingdom of the Film Stars: Journey into Jordan,* a book that also provides an insightful look at the country's history and culture. Caulfield's book was inspired by Gertrude Bell's account of her 1905 trip to the same area, *The Desert and the Sown: The Syrian Adventures of the Female Lawrence of Arabia,* even though Bell undertook her journey because she had lost her love.

Raban, Jonathan

Old Glory: A Voyage Down the Mississippi. New York: Simon and Schuster, 1981. 409 pp. ISBN: 9780671250614

Raban travels down the Mississippi River in a 16-foot aluminum boat with an outboard motor, from Minneapolis (where the river first becomes navigable) to the Louisiana bayou (where the river merges with the ocean). Along the way, Raban observes the great river and the diverse lives of the people who live along it. His own lack of experience with a boat on a river and the unpredictable nature of the Mississippi contribute to a dangerously eventful voyage: he is nearly capsized by a towboat, nearly caught in a whirlpool, and becomes romantically involved with the neurotic Sally. Still, Raban's prose is as magnificent as the river, and whether he is discussing what happened to the factories that made pearl buttons out of clam shells or race relations in Memphis, he is an expert observer of America's nostalgic heartland.

Subjects: American South; Midwest; Rivers; Solo Travelers

Categories: Landscapes and People

Places: Louisiana; Minnesota; Mississippi River; Tennessee

Awards: Thomas Cook Travel Book Award, 1981

Series: *Vintage Departures*

Now Try: Raban's observations are interesting for a number of reasons, including the fact that he is an Englishman; Eddy Harris, an African American, provides a different perspective in his narrative about canoeing down the Mississippi in *Mississippi Solo: A River Quest*. His exuberant prose and the stories of the people he meets are reminiscent of Raban's. Mary Morris's *The River Queen* follows her journey down the Mississippi in a houseboat following the death of her father. As a seven-year-old living in Norfolk, England, Raban was inspired by Mark Twain's classic, *The Adventures of Huckleberry Finn*, and anyone wishing to know more about life along the great river would do well to refer to that classic work as well as Twain's *Life on the Mississippi*, which is annotated in this chapter.

Steinbeck, John

The Log from the "Sea of Cortez." New York: Penguin Classics, 1995 [1951]. 288 pp. ISBN: 9780140187441

In addition to being a writer, Steinbeck was also something of an amateur marine biologist, having studied the subject at Stanford. In 1940, he and Ed Ricketts, the head of Pacific Biological Laboratories, sailed along the Gulf of California in search of specimens. The book recounts their trip, including the people they met, the problems they encountered, and the specimens they collected. Steinbeck also discusses the ecological ties among the various marine animals. The book is also important because of its portrayal of Ricketts, whose thinking greatly influenced Steinbeck's writing and who was the basis of several of Steinbeck's characters.

Subjects: Authors; Biology; Oceans; Quick Reads; Scientists; Seas

Categories: Appreciating Nature

Places: California; Mexico

Now Try: Ricketts was the model for "Doc," one of the characters in Steinbeck's novels, *Cannery Row* and *Sweet Thursday*, its sequel; both novels take place in Monterey, California, and have a strong sense of place. Steinbeck and Ricketts sailed around Baja California, but the great naturalist Joseph Wood Krutch writes about the peninsula itself and its desert plants and marine animals in *The Forgotten Peninsula: A Naturalist in Baja California*. Graham Mackintosh spent 500 days backpacking in Baja California, living on rattlesnake, distilled seawater, and the kindness of those he met; the self-proclaimed "most unadventurous person in the world" tells his story in *Into a Desert Place: A 3000 Mile Walk around the Coast of Baja California*.

Teale, Edwin Way

Wandering Through Winter: A Naturalist's Record of a 20,000-Mile Journey Through the North American Winter. New York: St. Martins Press, 1990 [1965]. 370 pp. ISBN: 9780312044589

Teale and his wife Nellie spent four winter months in the late 1950s traveling 20,000 miles by car from California to northeastern Maine, and in this book, he reports on the people, plants, animals, and birds that they encountered. Teale is a naturalist and has an in-depth knowledge of the flora and fauna, which include whooping cranes, California condors, gray whales, giant beavers, and snowy owls. Teale's concern for the preservation of species and environments is understated and never polemical, but an emphasis on the interconnected nature of life underlies his writing. Interestingly, while the focus of the book is clearly on nature, it also provides a record of the people and places in the rapidly changing America of the late 1950s.

Subjects: 1950s; Automobiles; Seasons; Spouses

Categories: Appreciating Nature

Places: Arizona; California; Kentucky; Maine; New Mexico; Texas

Awards: Pulitzer Prize for General Nonfiction, 1966

Now Try: *Wandering Through Winter* is the last of four volumes in which Teale and his wife travel the United States through the four seasons. The other books in the cycle are similar in tone and style and include *North with the Spring* (1951), *Autumn Across America* (1956), and *Journey into Summer* (1960). Teale wrote quite a few other works on natural history, including the charming *A Walk Through the Year*, which consists of an essay for every day of the year. Readers interested in nature as it manifests itself in the different seasons should also try *A Year in the Maine Woods, Summer World: A Season of Bounty*, and *Winter World: The Ingenuity of Animal Survival*, all by biology professor Bernd Heinrich. Other travel narratives that involve longer travels through America, like John Steinbeck's *Travels with Charley: In Search of America* (annotated in the "Getting There Is Half the Fun" chapter) and Peter Jenkins's *A Walk Across America* (annotated in the "Journeys" chapter), may also appeal to readers who enjoyed Teale's books, as may other narratives that involve travel by husbands and wives, such as Edward D. Webster's endearing narrative of travels in Europe, *A Year of Sundays: Taking the Plunge and (Our Cat) to Explore Europe*.

Thesiger, Wilfred

Arabian Sands. New York: Penguin, 1991 [1959]. 347 pp. ISBN: 9780140095142

Arabian Sands describes Thesiger's travels through the southern desert of the Arabian Peninsula, an area so desolate that the Arabs themselves refer to it as the "Empty Quarter." Many of the people he met had never seen a European, and Thesiger's fascination with and love of the Bedouins is a central theme of the book. He shows great respect for their ability to eke out lives in the harshest of conditions and portrays them as cheerful and generous in spite of their hardships. Although this part of the world has changed substantially since the publication of *Arabian Sands*, it remains an important book for understanding the spirit of the Bedouin people.

Subjects: Bedouins; Deserts; Minorities; Islam

Categories: Landscapes and People

Places: Arabian Peninsula

Now Try: Thesiger's interest in the indigenous people of the Middle East may also be seen in *The Marsh Arabs*, in which he travels among the Madan people of the marshlands of southern Iraq; these journeys are also the subject of a book by his traveling companion, Gavin Maxwell, in *A Reed Shaken by the Wind: A Journey Through the Unexplored Marshlands of Iraq*. Thesiger was born in Ethiopia, and his book, *The Danakil Diary: Journeys through Abyssinia, 1930–4*, recounts his travels through what was then the Ethiopian empire of Abyssinia. Alexander Maitland's biography, *Wilfred Thesiger: The Life of the Great Explorer*, was authorized by Thesiger before his death in 2003, and that support gave Maitland access to Thesiger archives.

Thubron, Colin

Behind the Wall: A Journey through China. New York: Atlantic Monthly Press, 1988 [1987]. 306 pp. ISBN: 9780871132420

Armed with a knowledge of Mandarin, Thubron roamed through China in the 1980s, at a time when few Westerners traveled there, and his writing vividly captures the land, the Chinese people, and their customs. His ability to speak the language allowed him to talk with a wide range of individuals, including farmers, businessmen, city dwellers, homemakers, and university students. Thubron writes beautifully and also displays an intimate knowledge of the history of the country, with a particular focus on the devastating impact of the Cultural Revolution and how it robbed an entire generation of a large part of their lives.

Subjects: Asian History

Categories: The Beauty of the Place; Landscapes and People

Places: China

Awards: Hawthornden Prize, 1988; Thomas Cook Travel Book Award, 1988

Now Try: One reviewer suggested that Thubron's book was reminiscent of Mark Salzman's *Iron and Silk*, about that writer's two years of teaching English and studying martial arts in China (annotated in "The Expatriate Life" chapter of this book). Thubron's later book, *Shadow of the Silk Road* (annotated in the "Quests" chapter of this book), begins with his return to China after 20 years, and provides an interesting contrast to *Behind the Wall*. Bill Porter's *Road to Heaven* (also annotated in "Quests") recounts that writer's visit to China to find another group that was deeply affected by the Cultural Revolution of the 1960s and 1970s, the Taoist and Buddhist monks and nuns whose temples were destroyed during that movement.

The Beauty of the Place

Travel narratives in "The Beauty of the Place" category evoke the physical beauty of the author's destination. Readers who are drawn to strong descriptions of beautiful settings (which may be the frozen beauty of Greenland that Gretel Ehrlich describes in *This Cold Heaven: Seven Seasons in Greenland* or the untamed marshes, mountains, and forests that Robert Macfarlane seeks out in *The Wild Places*) will find these titles of interest. The writing is often filled with striking images as the author attempts to capture the ineffable attraction of these destinations.

Readers who are drawn to travel narratives that focus on the physical beauty of the destination may also enjoy fiction with a strong sense of place (the novels of David Guterson, with their evocation of the Pacific Northwest, Cormac McCarthy's Border Trilogy, or James Michener's many country-based novels, like *Mexico*, *Caravans: A Novel of Afghanistan*, or *Poland*). Likewise, histories of specific countries (James Billington's *The Icon and the Axe: An Interpretive History of Russian Culture* or Earl Shorris's *The Life and Times of Mexico*) or other nonfiction genres with a strong focus on place (Adam Hochschild's *King Leopold's Ghost: A Story of Greed, Terror, and Heroism in Colonial Africa* or Farley Mowat's *Never Cry Wolf*) may be of interest.

Albinia, Alice

Empires of the Indus: The Story of a River. London: John Murray, 2008. 366 pp. ISBN: 9780719560040

Albinia follows the Indus River both geographically (upstream from its mouth in Karachi to its source in Tibet) and historically, travelling backward in history to recount the history of Pakistan. Her attention to scholarly detail is impressive, and she also expresses her sorrow and frustration over the ongoing political conflicts that made the trip nearly impossible, as well as over the ecological devastation of the great river, which has led to its frequent flooding. *Empires of the Indus* is well researched and informative and skillfully combines elements of travel narrative, history, and environmental writing.

Subjects: Asian History; Environment; Rivers; Scholarly Writing; Women Travelers

Places: Afghanistan; India; Pakistan; Tibet

Awards: Dolman Best Travel Book Award, 2009

Now Try: A recent exploration of the poorly understood country of Pakistan and its complexities is Anatol Lieven's compelling *Pakistan: A Hard Country*. An earlier account of life in Pakistan by American journalist Ethan Casey, *Alive and Well in Pakistan: A Human Journey in a Dangerous Time*, is also perceptive and is based on both the author's observations and his interviews with a wide range of individuals living in Pakistan. Albinia discusses her frustration over the many conflicts in the region through which the Indus River flows; Amitava Kumar's *Husband of a Fanatic: A Personal Journey Through India, Pakistan, Love, and Hate* tells the story of a Hindu Indian writer living in the United States who married a Pakistani Muslim and explores these conflicts on a more personal level.

Ehrlich, Gretel

This Cold Heaven: Seven Seasons in Greenland. New York: Pantheon Books, 2001. 377 pp. ISBN: 9780679442004

Ehrlich first traveled to Greenland in 1993 and was immediately captivated by both the stunning land and the Inuit who live there; the book describes her repeated journeys there and her attempts to understand the people and how the land has shaped their lives. Ehrlich alternates between chapters describing her own visits and chapters describing the expeditions and research of Danish-Inuit ethnographer Knud Rasmussen and her attempts to follow in his footsteps. Ehrlich's writing is highly metaphorical ("The Arctic's continuously shifting planes of light and dark were like knives thrown in a drawer") and captures the contrasts between the stark, icy beauty of the Inuit's world and the alcoholism, poverty, and depression in which many of them live. The book is also very personal, and Ehrlich is anything but a detached observer; her sense of loss at leaving Greenland and those to whom she became attached is particularly poignant.

Subjects: Exploration; Explorers; Indigenous Peoples; Women Travelers

Categories: Landscapes and People

Places: Arctic Region; Greenland

Awards: *New York Times* Notable Book, 2001

Now Try: Ehrlich claims that her preference for the far north came after she was struck by lightning, an experience that she recounts in *A Match to the Heart: One Woman's Story of Being Struck By Lightning*. Her other book about the Arctic region is *In the Empire of Ice: Encounters in a Changing Landscape,* in which she describes the people who live on the Arctic Ocean. Tete-Michel Kpomassie was living in his native Togo when he happened upon a picture book about Greenland; his tale of traveling to Greenland to live with the Inuit is the subject of a fascinating book, *An African in Greenland*. In *Last Places: A Journey in the North,* Lawrence Millman retraces the route of the Vikings from Norway to Greenland and, like Ehrlich, describes the beauty of these remote places and their people. Ehrlich writes of the clash between tradition and modernity among the Inuit of Greenland; an earlier clash between Christianity and pagan cultures underlies Judith Lindbergh's epic novel of three women in ninth-century Greenland, *The Thrall's Tale*. Although it is set in Alaska, Colleen Mondor's book about working as a charter airline's dispatcher, *The Map of My Dead Pilots: The Dangerous Game of Flying in Alaska,* with its mix of admiration and detachment, may appeal to readers of *This Cold Heaven*.

Fredston, Jill A.

Rowing to Latitude: Journeys Along the Arctic's Edge. New York: North Point Press, 2001. 289 pp. ISBN: 9780374281809

Fredston describes the 20,000 miles that she and her husband logged in skulls and kayaks as they spent their summer months exploring some of the most isolated parts of the Arctic North, rowing icy waters and remote rivers, tracing barren coastlines, surviving storms and polar bears, and being serenaded by humpback whales. The couple encountered many indigenous people and Fredston occasionally takes a brief side trip into the history of the areas they explore, but the book's focus is mostly on the trip and the natural beauty they witnessed, which made it worth facing the many adversities that they confronted.

Subjects: Adventure; Animals; Arctic Region; Environment; Geography; Kayaking; Rivers; Rowing

Places: Alaska; Canada; Greenland; Norway; Sweden

Now Try: The rest of the year, Fredston and her husband (Doug Fesler) live near Anchorage, where they direct the Alaska Mountain Safety Center and teach people how to recognize and deal with avalanches; their book, *Snow Sense: A Guide to Evaluating Snow Avalanche Hazard*, covers that topic in print. Jonathan Waterman details his experiences crossing the Arctic Circle via kayak, skis, and dogsled in *Arctic Crossing: One Man's 2,000-Mile Odyssey Among the Inuit*; much more of his book involves interactions with the Inuit and his observations of their current status. Kim Heacox evokes the beauty of Alaska and his 25 years of living on and kayaking in Glacier Bay in *The Only Kayak: A Journey into the Heart of Alaska*.

Heat-Moon, William Least

River-Horse: The Logbook of a Boat Across America. Boston: Houghton Mifflin, 1999. 506 pp. ISBN: 9780395636268

Because he "wanted to see those secret parts [of the nation] hidden from road travelers," Heat-Moon took a four-month, 5,000-mile journey across the United States, not by car but by water, mainly on a dual-outboard boat named *Nikawa* (Osage for "river horse"). Even though Heat-Moon shares the journey with several companions, it is a very introspective and sometimes lonely trip, less chatty than the author's earlier *Blue Highways*, filled with appreciative descriptions of the beauty of the country as seen from the water and also filled with loosely connected, almost random, observations and historical asides. From his start in New York Bay and up the Hudson River, through various rivers, lakes, and canals (including the Ohio, the Mississippi, and the Missouri) to the Pacific Ocean, Heat-Moon provides an optimistic vision of the American spirit and the future of the country.

Subjects: American History; Environment; Rivers

Category: Reflective Journeys

Places: Allegheny River; Columbia River; Mississippi River; Missouri River; Ohio River; Salmon River; Snake River; United States (Various)

Awards: *New York Times* Notable Book, 1999

Now Try: Ron and Eva Stob sailed a 40-foor trawler over 6,000 miles through the Great Loop, which circumnavigates eastern North America by way of the Mississippi River, the Great Lakes, and the Intracoastal Waterway; their story of overcoming a lack of nautical knowledge is told in *Honey, Let's Get a Boat . . . A Cruising Adventure of America's Great Loop*. Nathaniel Stone followed the Great Loop more or less as he traced the path of a 19th-century Massachusetts fisherman, recounting the experience in the delightful book, *On the Water: Discovering America in a Row Boat*. NPR host Noah Adams traveled the New River from its source in the North Carolina mountains through much of Appalachia; his journey by canoe, car, and bicycle to learn more about this part of the country is told in *Far Appalachia: Following the New River North*. Another very personal river trip is described by ecologist Janisse Ray in *Drifting into Darien: A Personal and Natural History of the Altamaha River*; Ray traveled down the 137-mile river to Darien, Georgia, where it meets the sea, and shares the stories of the people who live along the river.

Macfarlane, Robert

The Wild Places. New York: Penguin Books, 2008 [2007]. 340 pp. ISBN: 9780143113935

Macfarlane went in search of the last wild places in England, Ireland, and Scotland and sees his book as "a prose map that would seek to make some of the remaining wild places of the archipelago visible again, or that would record them before they vanished for good." Macfarlane shares his thoughts on what he means by "wild," provides detailed descriptions of the natural beauty that he encounters, and adds a little local history. The result of his walking, climbing, swimming, and musing is an eloquent and passionate appreciation of untamed places like salt marshes, mountains, forests, beaches, and moors.

Subjects: Authors; Geography; Hiking; Landscape; Mountains

Categories: Appreciating Nature

Places: England; Ireland; Scotland

Awards: Dolman Best Travel Book Award, Shortlist, 2008; *New York Times* Notable Book, 2008

Now Try: Macfarlane's earlier book, *Mountains of the Mind: Adventures in Reaching the Summit*, uses stories of legendary mountain climbers and the author's own climbs to explore the fascination that people have with mountains. Annie Dillard's classic, *Pilgrim at Tinker Creek*, shares Macfarlane's wonderful prose as well as his appreciation of wild places. Macfarlane was inspired by the Scottish mountain climber W. H. Murray, and readers may be interested in Murray's autobiography, *The Evidence of Things Not Seen: A Mountaineer's Tale*, which was completed by Murray's wife after his death in 1996.

Mahoney, Rosemary

Down the Nile: Alone in a Fisherman's Skiff. New York: Little, Brown, and Co., 2007. 273 pp. ISBN: 9780316107457

Mahoney's rich text and eye for detail evoke the beauty of the Nile in this story of her solo rowing trip in 1998 down part of the world's longest river. Along with that glorious scenery, she also offers up historical and cultural insights, particularly those related to the cultural differences that complicated her original, simple idea, "to buy a small Egyptian rowboat and row myself along the 120-mile stretch of river between the cities of Aswan and Qena," starting with the fact that no one in Egypt would sell a woman a rowboat. Mahoney's portrayals of the individuals who live alongside the Nile, especially Amr, a Muslim sailor, whose quiet friendship and generosity enabled her to begin her journey on his own seven-foot skiff.

Subjects: Adventure; Feminism; Islam; Quick Reads; Rivers; Rowing; Solo Travelers; Women Authors; Women Travelers

Places: Africa; Egypt; Nile River

Awards: *New York Times* Notable Book, 2007

Now Try: Mahoney's other books have been well received, including *The Early Arrival of Dreams; A Year in China*, which was a *New York Times* Notable Book in 1990, and *Whoredom in Kimmage: The World of Irish Women*, which was both a *New York Times* Notable Book and a National Book Critics Circle Award finalist in 1994. Mahoney's *The Singular Pilgrim: Travels on Sacred Ground* recounts her travels to some of the world's great pilgrimage sites: Croagh Patrick in Ireland, Lourdes, Santiago de Compostela, Canterbury, and the Ganges River. Another classic tale of travel down the Nile is John Goddard's fascinating *Kayaks Down the Nile*, which describes a 1950 trip that he and two friends made down the 4,125-mile river. Alan Moorehead's classic travel narratives, *The Blue Nile* and *The White Nile*, are annotated in the "Travel Adventure" chapter of this book.

Matthiessen, Peter

End of the Earth: Voyaging to Antarctica. Washington, DC: National Geographic, 2003. 242 pp. ISBN: 9780792250593

Matthiessen describes two voyages that he took to Antarctica and includes particularly beautiful descriptions of the magnificent icebergs and the wildlife he encountered. He ponders a range of topics, from geology and ecology to whaling and seal hunting, and he decries the increasing number of tourists who are damaging the fragile beauty of the area. Matthiessen's prose is sparkling and tight, especially when he describes the landscapes that he sees or the birds that he comes upon, and the book is a sympathetic and admiring look at a harsh but striking part of the world.

Subjects: Animals; Birds; Endangered Species; Environment; Penguins

Categories: Appreciating Nature

Places: Antarctica

Now Try: *The Crystal Desert: Summers in Antarctica* by David G. Campbell is another appreciation of the icy continent, one that mixes natural history with accounts of our attempts to explore it. Pauline and Tim Carr are the only permanent inhabitants of the Antarctic island that they write about in *Antarctic Oasis: Under the Spell of South Georgia,* which contains beautiful photographs as well as an account of their lives among the wildlife there. Jenny Diski uses a trip to Antarctica to reflect on her own life with dysfunctional parents and depression in *Skating to Antarctica,* and though books about various expeditions to Antarctica (like Albert Lansing's *Endurance: Shackleton's Incredible Voyage,* annotated in the "Travel Adventure" chapter, or Caroline Alexander's *The Endurance: Shackleton's Legendary Antarctic Expedition*) are primarily adventure and survival stories, they do provide a strong sense of place and environment.

Meloy, Ellen

The Anthropology of Turquoise: Meditations on Landscape, Art, and Spirit. New York: Pantheon Books, 2002. 324 pp. ISBN: 9780375408854

Meloy is an artist and a naturalist, and in this book, she uses turquoise (the color and the gem) to explore several beautiful places (the Mojave Desert, the Sierra Mountains, the Yucatan Peninsula, the Bahamas, and her own home in southern Utah) and to meditate on our ties to such landscapes and particularly their colors. Meloy's language is sumptuous and poetic (she describes the night as having "the purity of eye-blind dark" and the colors of the mesas as bearing "the temperament of iron"), and her love of nature is palpable. The book is a series of essays and mixes memoir, travel narrative, and natural history to urge the reader to open her or his eyes and take in the details around us.

Subjects: Art and Artists; Deserts; Essays; Geography; Memoirs; Mountains; Women Travelers

Categories: Appreciating Nature

Places: Arizona; Bahamas; California; Colorado; Mexico; Nevada; New Mexico; Utah

Now Try: Meloy, whose book was nominated for a Pulitzer Prize in 2003, died in 2004 at the age of 58. Readers who appreciate the beauty of nature may be interested in her other books, including *Raven's Exile: A Season on the Green River,* about the Colorado River's longest tributary, and *The Last Cheater's Waltz: Beauty and Violence in the Desert Southwest,* in which she uses a visit to Los Alamos to meditate on the human condition. The 1903 classic, *Land of Little Rain* by Mary Austin, paints a lovely portrait of the American Southwest and covers some of the areas that Meloy visits in her books. Naturalist Craig Childs also considers the austere beauty of these landscapes in his lyrical book, *Soul of Nowhere.* Another Utah author whose writing evokes the arid beauty of that region is the American conservationist Terry Tempest Williams. Her powerful mixture of memoir and natural history, *Refuge: An Unnatural History of Family and Place,* juxtaposes the loss of her mother to ovarian cancer with the flooding of the Great Salt Lake and its disastrous consequences for the herons, owls, and egrets that live there. Her meditative *Finding Beauty in a Broken World* takes a similar approach, discussing the brutal attempts to kill off the prairie dogs of the plains and high desert in conjunction with the genocidal war between Tutsis and Hutus in Rwanda, which she visited.

Palin, Michael

Himalaya. New York: St. Martin's Press, 2004. 288 pp. ISBN: 9780312341626

Palin and his BBC television crew spent six months traveling 3,000 miles to film a series on the world's tallest mountain range, and the book ("these diaries," as Palin calls them) captures his thoughts on the trip. The book's chapters are organized by country, and Palin provides witty, entertaining insights about the places he encountered (from the Khyber Pass to the Brahmaputra delta in Bangladesh), the people he met (including the Dalai Lama), and the activities in which he took part (milking a yak, massaging an elephant, and watching bull racing, among others). Palin's descriptions of the breathtaking scenery are complemented by beautiful photographs by Basil Pao.

Subjects: Adventure; Geography; Humor; Mountains; Photography

Categories: Landscapes and People

Places: Bangladesh; Bhutan; China; India; Nepal; Pakistan; Tibet

Now Try: A 3-disc DVD of Palin's *Himalaya* series is also available. Palin has written several travel books related to his work with BBC television, including *Around the World in Eighty Days,* in which he recreates the journey of Jules Verne's hero, Phileas Fogg, and *Sahara,* in which he travels around and through the great desert. In *The Traveler: An American Odyssey in the Himalayas,* Eric Hansen provides a memorial to Himalayan trekker Hugh Swift and includes over 50 color photographs from Swift's own collection. James Hilton's *Lost Horizon* is the classic novel about the utopia known as Shangri-La, which is set in the Himalayas.

Shelton, Richard

Going Back to Bisbee. Tucson, AZ: University of Arizona Press, 1992. 329pp. ISBN: 9780816513024

Shelton is a well-known poet, and he uses his talents to praise the Sonoran desert of southeastern Arizona, an area the author first encountered as an Army draftee and then lived in during the late 1950s and early 1960s. The book tells of a day trip to Bisbee and contains the author's reflections on the natural and human history of the area, on his own life, and on the beauty of the area. Shelton provides a loving portrait of the desert, complete with tarantulas, occasional monsoons, and former copper mines, in a lyrical work that some reviewers have compared to Thoreau's *Walden*.

Subjects: Deserts; Geography; Memoirs

Categories: Appreciating Nature

Places: Arizona; Sonoran Desert

Awards: ALA Notable Book, 1993

Now Try: Shelton has been called "a poet of the Southwest" by *The Saturday Review*, which added that "his language is as dry and bony as his desert landscape." His books of poetry may interest readers who love the deserts of the American southwest; *The Tattooed Desert* won the International Poetry Forum's United States Award in 1970, and *The Bus to Veracruz* was nominated for both the Pulitzer Prize and the National Book Award. Edward Abbey's classic, *Desert Solitaire*, tells of the author's years as a park ranger in Utah and, like *Going Back to Bisbee*, includes reflections on nature of the desert and the need to live in cooperation with the natural world. Gary Paul Nabhan's *The Desert Smells Like Rain: A Naturalist in Papago Indian Country* relates a series of trips taken by an ethnobiologist into the desert that stretches from Arizona to the state of Sonora in Mexico.

Stevenson, Andrew

Kiwi Tracks: A New Zealand Journey. Melbourne, Australia; Oakland, CA: Lonely Planet Publications, 1999. 222 pp. ISBN: 9780864427878

Stevenson spent four months in New Zealand (two on each of the islands that make up the island nation) and focuses on the beauty and the spirit of its places: the national parks, the Fiordland, the Ninety Mile Beach, the Gondwannic forests, and the snow-capped mountains. He mixes personal reflections (some of them quite painful) with discussions with fellow hikers to produce a growing understanding of both the values and culture of the New Zealand people and his own personal values, and he does so with a subtle humor and a clean style.

Subjects: Hiking; Humor; Landscape; Mountains; Quick Reads; Self-Discovery

Category: Discovering One's Self; Landscapes and People

Places: New Zealand

Series: *Lonely Planet Journeys*

Now Try: Alexander Elder's travelogue, *Straying from the Flock: Travels in New Zealand*, is another personal account of a visit to New Zealand and captures the beauty of the country's landscape. Joe Bennett lived ten years in New Zealand before he decided to get to know the country better by hitchhiking around it, an experience that he recounts in *A Land of Two Halves: An Accidental Tour of New Zealand*. Gillian Orrell left her corporate life in London to walk New Zealand and writes about her experience in *New Boots in New Zealand: Nine Great Walks, Three Islands and One Tramping Virgin*. For fiction about New Zealand, two novels stand out: the Booker Prize winner, Keri Hulme's powerful *The Bone People*, about the difficult relationships between three people; and Alan Duff's controversial *Once Were Warriors*, about contemporary Maori life in New Zealand, which was condemned by a number of Maori commentators for its negative and allegedly racist portrayal of the Maori people.

Unsworth, Barry

Crete. Washington, DC: National Geographic, 2004. 170 pp. ISBN: 9780792266433

Unsworth, who won the Booker Prize for his novel, *Sacred Hunger*, travels to Crete with his wife and writes a delightful account of the trip and his impressions of the island, which he calls "among the most beautiful places our earth has to show." Unsworth displays a deep appreciation of the people of Crete and their blend of generosity and stubborn independence, and he dislikes the other tourists who invade the island. This brief work includes a mix of historical fact, myth, and the author's observations on destinations as various as the reputed birthplace of Zeus and the palace of Knossos, which supposedly held the labyrinth of the Minotaur.

Subjects: Islands; Mythologies; Quick Reads; Spouses

Places: Crete; Greece

Series: *National Geographic Directions*

Now Try: Unsworth is a well-regarded novelist, and the first of his novels to be shortlisted for the Booker Prize, *Pascali's Island*, takes place on an unnamed Greek island during the last years of the Ottoman Empire. *Crete on the Half Shell: A Story about an Island, Good Friends and Food* by Canadian chef Byron Ayanoglu is a comical combination of travel narrative and food writing and focuses on the author's efforts to open a curry restaurant in a Crete seaside town. Another Canadian writer, Simone Poirier-Bures, tells the story of her time on Crete as a young girl in a sparkling memoir, *That Shining Place*. Lawrence Durrell's *Prospero's Cell: A Guide To The Landscape And Manners of The Island Of Corfu* (annotated in "The Expatriate Life" chapter of this book) is also set on the island of Crete as is his brother Gerald Durrell's Corfu Trilogy: *My Family and Other Animals; Birds, Beasts, and Relatives*; and *The Garden of the Gods*. Gerald's version of events does not always agree with that of his older brother, however, and many critics believe that at least part of *Prospero's Cell* is fictitious.

Wheeler, Sara

Terra Incognita: Travels in Antarctica. New York: Random House, 1998 [1996]. 351 pp. ISBN: 9780679440789

Wheeler's first book tells about her seven-month stay in Antarctica as a writer-in-residence with the U.S. National Science Foundation. She mixes her experiences with those of early Antarctic explorers like Robert Scott, Ernest Shackleton, and Roald Amundsen to produce an intriguing story of our century-long effort to figure out this coldest and driest of continents. Wheeler describes her own thoughts and feelings and explores how each experience on Antarctica changes her. These inner travels combine with vivid descriptions of the starkly beautiful environment to produce a book that many readers will find transporting.

Subjects: Environment; Explorers; Polar Regions; Scientists; Women Travelers

Places: Antarctica

Now Try: Wheeler later traveled to the Arctic Circle and wrote about her experiences there in *The Magnetic North: Notes from the Arctic Circle*, annotated in this chapter's section on "Endangered Places." Journalist Michael Parfit spent a full season in Antarctica on assignment for *Smithsonian* magazine and reports on the beauty of the frozen continent and the passion of the scientists who work there in *South Light: A Journey to the Last Continent*; he writes with what one reviewer called "a curious blend of poetry and science." Gretchen Legler, another observer sponsored by the National Science Foundation, began *On the Ice: An Intimate Portrait of Life at McMurdo Station, Antarctica* as a journalistic look at the scientists who live and work on Antarctica, but fell in love with a scientist there and expanded the book to include a meditation on lesbian love. Geraldine McCaughrean's *White Darkness* is a thriller set in the Antarctic; it looks at the continent's wild, threatening nature and how that nature brought out the worst in some of its characters.

Landscapes and People

Titles in "Landscapes and People" describe not only the attractiveness of the destination but also the intense beauty of the people who live there. These are the titles that Guy Robertson referred to when he said that travel literature "frequently includes observations on the people that the author meets: their customs and culture and outstanding characteristics."[3]

Readers who like narratives with a strong character focus as well as an evocation of setting can be pointed toward these books. Often, larger issues, such as religious and ethnic conflicts, can be better understood at the level of the single individual. Typically, a wide range of individuals from all levels of the society will be encountered: Jason Elliot talks with wealthy aristocrats and poor tribal horsemen in *Mirrors of the Unseen, Journeys in Iran*; Brian Hall interviews members of all sides of the Baltic conflict in *The Impossible Country: A Journey through the Last Days of Yugoslavia*; and Eric Hansen portrays strippers as well as those working at Mother Teresa's hospice in Calcutta in *The Bird Man and the Lap Dancer: Close Encounters with Strangers*.

Readers who enjoy the focus on the colorful and exotic people encountered in these travel narratives may also find novels that center on individuals from other cultures (Keri Hulme's Booker Prize winner, *The Bone People*, and Alan Duff's *Once Were Warriors*, for example) to be appealing. Biographies or memoirs of these individuals (Theodora Kroeber's *Ishi in Two Worlds* or Rachel Holmes's *African Queen: The Real Life of the Hottentot Venus*) as well as titles in anthropology (Margaret Mead's *Coming of Age in Samoa* or A. A. Chagnon's *Yanomamo: The Fierce People*) may also be of interest.

Bird, Christiane

A Thousand Sighs, A Thousand Revolts: Journeys in Kurdistan. New York: Ballantine Books, 2004. 405 pp. ISBN: 9780345469397

The Kurds are the largest ethnic group in the world without their own country, and travel writer Bird combines travel narrative and history to tell their story. The Kurdistan of her book's title does not exist *per se*, but the 30 million Kurds who represent it live in an arc stretching from Iraq to the former Soviet Union. Bird tells compassionate, detailed stories about the people she met, from an exiled *agha* to Kurdish artists to students whose villages had been destroyed in Saddam Hussein's genocidal Anfal campaign of the 1980s. Their stories create a portrait of the determination of these people to eventually control their own destiny.

Subjects: Asian History; Minorities; Women Travelers

Places: Iran; Iraq; Syria; Turkey

Now Try: Bird became interested in the Kurds during a trip to Iran, which resulted in the riveting book, *Neither East Nor West: One Woman's Journey through the Islamic Republic of Iran*. Archibald Milne Hamilton spent four years between 1928 and 1932 building a road through what was then called Iraq Kurdistan; he tells his story in *Road through Kurdistan: Travels in Northern Iraq*. Hiner Saleem's memoir, *My Father's Rifle: A Childhood in Kurdistan*, is a simply told story of a Kurdish family in the 1960s and 1970s. The 2005 Kurdish film *Turtles Can Fly* depicts life in a Kurdish village on the Iraqi-Turkish border from the point of view of the children there.

Dalrymple, William

Nine Lives: In Search of the Sacred in Modern India. New York: Alfred A. Knopf, 2010 [2009]. 275 pp. ISBN: 9780307272829

Dalrymple moved to India in 1989 and has watched the impact of India's rapid economic changes on the spiritual practices there. *Nine Lives* features stories about nine individuals and how their extreme religious paths are being affected by modernity, including a young Jain nun who plans to starve herself to death, a female mystic who lives in a cremation ground and drinks from skulls, and a well digger who becomes the incarnation of the god Vishnu for three months each year. Dalrymple attempts to let the individuals tell their stories without intruding, and to a large extent, he succeeds. The result is a fascinating and inspiring look at those who keep the old traditions of India alive in the face of great change.

Subjects: Buddhism; Hinduism; Religion; Spirituality

Places: India

Now Try: Dalrymple is well known as the author of several books about Indian history, including *The Last Mughal: The Fall of a Dynasty, Delhi, 1857*, about the uprising that first challenged British rule in India, and *White Mughals: Love and Betrayal in Eighteenth-Century India*, which uses the story of a British officer's marriage to an Indian woman to depict day-to-day life in the Indian colony at the end of the 18th century. Anand Giridharadas, born in the United States of Indian parents, returned to their native country in *India Calling: An Intimate Portrait of a Nation's Remaking*, which focuses on the impact of change on tradition by looking at individuals living in India and their families; the title is annotated in "The Journey" chapter of this book. Amitava Kumar's *Husband of a Fanatic: A Personal Journey Through India, Pakistan, Love, and Hate* tells the story of a Hindu Indian writer living in the United States who married a Pakistani Muslim and began to explore the hatreds between Indians and Pakistanis,

Hindus and Muslims, and fundamentalists and non-fanatics. Aravind Adiga's Booker Prize-winning novel, *The White Tiger*, captures the "new India" through the eyes of a taxi driver. George Saunders's collection of essays, *The Braindead Megaphone*, focuses on a number of unique individuals, including the "Buddha Boy" of Nepal.

Elliot, Jason

Mirrors of the Unseen, Journeys in Iran. New York: St. Martin's Press, 2006. 415 pp. ISBN: 9780312301910

Elliot's account of his four years of travel in Iran avoids the debates of contemporary politics and focuses instead on the people and culture (particularly the art and architecture) of this ancient, misunderstood nation. He met wealthy aristocrats and tribal horsemen; he traveled to secret cocktail parties, ancient ruins, horse breeding farms, and remote mountain villages; and he depicts a people who are proud of their past and contemptuous of the current regime. Elliot mixes historical detail with conversations with ordinary people to produce a beautiful and thought provoking book that provides a refreshing look at the perspective of these citizens on their country.

Subjects: Architecture; Art and Artists; Investigative Stories; Islam

Places: Iran

Now Try: Elliot carried a copy of Robert Byron's classic, *The Road to Oxiana*, with him to Iran, and one reviewer refers to that book as "certainly the wittiest book, and perhaps the wisest, to have been written in English about Iran." (It is annotated in the "Classics" section of this chapter.) Hooma Majd, the Western-educated grandson of an ayatollah, examines Iranian politics and culture in his witty and timely book, *The Ayatollah Begs to Differ: The Paradox of Modern Iran*. Alison Wearing traveled through Iran with a male companion, disguised as a honeymooning couple, and challenges Western notions of Iran in *Honeymoon in Purdah: An Iranian Journey*. Anyone wishing to understand contemporary Iran should also be encouraged to read Azar Nafisi's wonderful story about a secret book club in revolutionary Iran, *Reading Lolita in Tehran: A Memoir in Books*.

Frater, Alexander

Chasing the Monsoon: A Modern Pilgrimage through India. New York: Knopf, 1991. 273 pp. ISBN: 9780394583105

Frater spent two months following the annual monsoon through India, from Cape Comorin on the southernmost tip to the village of Cherrapunji, sometimes referred to as "the wettest place on Earth." The book is more than a reflection on the weather, however; it is a moving, compassionate portrait of the Indian people and the impact of the monsoon on their lives. Some areas welcome the monsoon as relief for their drought; others are devastated by its resulting floods, which destroy homes, possessions, and sometimes lives. Through the variety of responses to the monsoon, Frater is able to portray the complexity of India and her people.

Subjects: Environment; Poverty; Weather

Places: India

Now Try: Frater's *Tales from the Torrid Zone: Travels in the Deep Tropics* is memoir as well as travel narrative and begins with the author's childhood on the tropical island of Vanuatu; he also travels from Fiji to Laos, Senegal to Uganda, and Taiwan to Indonesia. Like *Chasing the Monsoon*, the essays in Mark Tully's *No Full Stops in India* show an appreciation for the country of India and its people as well as a recognition of the terrible poverty and other challenges there. In the novel *Bombay Ice*, author Leslie Forbes uses the monsoon as a metaphor for the chaos of India and the lives of the characters, including a BBC filmmaker who has returned to India out of concern for her sister's marriage. Readers interested in the meteorological aspect of Frater's book (his focus on the monsoon) may also enjoy titles on climate-related issues, such as Tim Flannery's *The Weather Makers: How Man Is Changing the Climate and What It Means for Life on Earth* and James Hansen's *Storms of My Grandchildren: The Truth About the Coming Climate Catastrophe and Our Last Chance to Save Humanity.*

Frazier, Ian

Travels in Siberia. New York: Farrar, Straus and Giroux, 2010. 529 pp. ISBN: 9780374278724

Ian Frazier has made five trips to Siberia (which he describes as "the greatest horrible country in the world") over the past twenty years, and he recounts these in this amusing but sometimes grim book. Frazier's focus on the people of the area comes through both in his overview of Russian history (Mongol chieftains, czars, revolutionaries, Pushkin, Tolstoy, and Stalin) as well as his own observations about the contemporary inhabitants: young border guards, crazy Russian drivers, beautiful Russian women, and village poets. Frazier has a sense of wonder and an eye for detail, and both serve him well in this rather long book (which one reviewer referred to as a "valentine") about an area that comprises one-twelfth of the world's land mass and stretches across eight time zones.

Subjects: Asian History; European History; Geography

Categories: The Beauty of the Place

Places: Russia

Awards: ALA Notable Book, 2011; *New York Times* Notable Book, 2010

Now Try: Frazier's interest in vast, empty spaces can be seen in two of his other works, *Great Plains* (annotated in this chapter) and *On the Rez*, about the American Indian, with a particular focus on the Oglala Sioux of South Dakota's Pine Ridge Reservation and Frazier's own long-time friendship with one of them. There are a number of travel narratives on Siberia, including two by classic travel writer Dervla Murphy: *Through Siberia by Accident*, in which Murphy intended to bicycle through Siberia but was injured and instead went by train, boat, and bus, and the later *Silverland: A Winter Journey Beyond the Urals*, in which she traveled by slow train from start to finish. Colin Thubron's

In Siberia is as grim in its assessment of Siberia as is Frazier's book; it is annotated in this section. The classic fictional account of life in a Siberian labor camp is Alexander Solzhenitsyn's *One Day in the Life of Ivan Denisovich*. Another fiction title set in Siberia is Clair Huffaker's historical novel, *The Cowboy and the Cossack*, about fifteen American cowboys who sail to Vladivostock in 1880 with a herd of 500 cattle for delivery to a famine-stricken town deep in Siberia.

French, Patrick

Tibet, Tibet: A Personal History of a Lost Land. New York: Knopf, 2003. 325 pp. ISBN: 9781400041008

French, the former director of the Free Tibet movement in England, has been fascinated with Tibet ever since the Dalai Lama visited his school in northern England when French was a teenager. *Tibet, Tibet* describes French's visit to Tibet in 1999 and his discussions with local Tibetans about life in that country; he spoke with Buddhist nuns, Tibetan nomads, and exiled monks to portray a nation whose distinctive, centuries-old culture has fallen to Chinese invaders. He combines history and travel narrative to tear down myths about Tibet, including several that center on the Dalai Lama himself, and captures the complexities of the current situation there.

Subjects: Asian History; Buddhism; Culture Clash; Mountains; Nomads; Nuns; Religion; Spirituality

Places: Tibet

Series: *Vintage Departures*

Now Try: Melvyn C. Goldstein explores the intricate history of Tibet and China in his excellent survey, *The Snow Lion and the Dragon: China, Tibet, and the Dalai Lama*. Claire Scobie examines the changes that Chinese occupation has brought to Tibet on a more personal level in her story of her friendship with a Buddhist nun, *Last Seen in Lhasa: The Story of an Extraordinary Friendship in Modern Tibet*, which is annotated in this chapter. Xinran Xinran's novel, *Sky Burial: An Epic Love Story of Tibet*, is based on the true story of a Chinese doctor who embarked on a 30-year journey into Chinese-occupied Tibet to discover the fate of her husband. Another novel set in Tibet is Alai's *Red Poppies*, about the rise and fall of a Tibetan noble family during the rise of Chinese Communism in the first half of the 20th century.

Gargan, Edward

The River's Tale: A Year on the Mekong. New York: Alfred A. Knopf, 2002. 332 pp. ISBN: 9780375405846

In 1998, Gargan began a year-long journey down the 3,000-mile Mekong, from its source in China to its destination, the South China Sea. His slow trip down the river is filled with encounters with individuals, ranging from Tibetan monks to local potters, and highlights the vast cultural differences and political squabbles among the nations through which the Mekong flows as well as the lingering effects of French and American colonialism. Gargan, a former *New York Times* correspondent in Asia, focuses on the contrasts between modernity and traditional life, as in the Internet cafes in towns without electricity or paved streets, or the signs of Pol Pot's genocidal regime surrounding the glory of the Angkor Wat.

Subjects: Asian History; Culture Clash; Rivers

Places: Cambodia; China; Laos; Mekong River; Tibet; Vietnam

Awards: *New York Times* Notable Book, 2002

Series: *Vintage Departures*

Now Try: Milton Osborne's *The Mekong: Turbulent Past, Uncertain Future* focuses more on the history of the river, from the 5th-century Khmer empire that built the Angkor Wat through the post-Vietnam-War era; his book also looks at the ecology of the river and threats such as China's hydroelectric dam projects. In *River of Time: A Memoir of Vietnam and Cambodia*, John Swain (best known for his efforts to free Cambodian colleague Dith Pran from the Khmer Rouge, as portrayed in *The Killing Fields*) portrays the effect of the collapse of Cambodia and South Vietnam on the people who lived there. Norman Lewis's 1951 classic, *A Dragon Apparent: Travels in Cambodia, Laos, and Vietnam*, portrays the charm and grandeur of the countries before the tragedy of Vietnam.

Hall, Brian

The Impossible Country: A Journey through the Last Days of Yugoslavia. Boston: D.R. Godine, 1994. 335 pp. ISBN: 9781567920000

In 1991, Hall was one of the last journalists allowed into Yugoslavia before it collapsed, and his interviews with and portraits of the various religious and ethnic "tribes" in the areas of conflict (Serbs, Croats, and Bosnian Muslims) provide an unbiased account of the convoluted situation there. His depiction of the people of this patchwork country is especially compassionate and puts a human face on the country's dissolution. His visits to Zagreb, Belgrade, and Kosovo and his interspersed sketches of the country's history are recounted in a perceptive and even entertaining manner and reveal a country where, as Hall says, "the truth was more complex, more fundamentally unknowable" than any other.

Subjects: European History; Islam; Minorities; War

Places: Bosnia and Herzegovina; Croatia; Kosovo; Serbia

Now Try: The classic travel narrative on Yugoslavia is Rebecca West's *Black Lamb and Grey Falcon*, which discusses the history and culture of the Balkans and was written just before the Nazi invasion of 1941. Slavenka Drakulic's *The Balkan Express: Fragments from the Other Side of War* is a collection of 18 extremely personal essays that convey the horror of the Balkan wars of the early 1990s. Laura Silber's *Yugoslavia: Death of a Nation* and Misha Glenny's *The Fall of Yugoslavia: The Third Balkan War* are two histories of the conflict that led to the break-up of Yugoslavia. Fiction titles that allow readers to see the war from the point of view of those living through it include Steven Galloway's *The Cellist of Sarajevo,* about four people trying to survive the war, including the cellist who vows to play for 22 days at the site of a mortar attack that killed 22 people waiting in line to buy bread; Scott Simon's *Pretty Birds,* about a half-Muslim woman serving as a sniper during the siege of Sarajevo; and Slavenka Drakulic's *S,* about a half Serb, half Muslim teacher caught up in the Bosnian war. David Remnick's Pulitzer Prize-winning *Lenin's Tomb: The Last Days of the Soviet Empire* is a firsthand account of the dissolution of another communist country (the Soviet Union) and shows the same appreciation of the complexities of that fall as does *The Impossible Country.*

Hansen, Eric

The Bird Man and the Lap Dancer: Close Encounters with Strangers. New York: Pantheon Books, 2004. 228 pp. ISBN: 9780375421266

This collection of nine essays by travel writer Hansen focuses on interesting people and places that the writer encountered in his 20s, 30s, and 40s. He learned about friendship from an elderly Russian dancer and a homeless woman in southern France; he listened to the rich stories of an old Russian woman who cooked for Stravinsky and Balanchine in New York; he interviewed a California biologist who befriended a group of strippers; he worked at Mother Teresa's hospice in Calcutta. Hansen is often funny but never cynical or sentimental in these vignettes. Some reviewers have called Hansen's essays "anthropological," and they do provide a deep appreciation of the breadth and depth of the human experience.

Subjects: Essays; Humor; Quick Reads

Places: Australia; Borneo; California; France; India; Maldives; New York; Vanuatu

Series: *Vintage Departures*

Now Try: Hansen is a well-known travel writer, and three of his other titles, *Stranger in the Forest: On Foot Across Borneo*; *Orchid Fever: A Horticultural Tale of Love, Lust, and Lunacy*; and *Motoring with Mohammed: Journeys to Yemen and the Red Sea,* are annotated in this book. Another collection of travel essays that focus on the individuals encountered is Chuck Thompson's witty *To Hellholes and Back: Bribes, Lies, and the Art of Extreme Tourism,* in which the author reports on meeting eight year old boxers, naked gurus, and a host of others. Taras Grescoe also provides a mix of travel narrative and anthropological observation in his eclectic collection, *The End of Elsewhere: Travels Among the Tourists.* Another collection of essays that look at offbeat locations, events, and characters is Hank Stuever's *Off Ramp: Adventures and Heartache in the American Elsewhere,* which includes stories about a wedding in New Mexico and two friends in Texas who share a passion for decorating. The fascinating and unforgettable people in Lara Vapnyar's short story collection, *Broccoli and Other Tales of Food and Love,* may also remind readers of the characters in *The Bird Man and the Lap Dancer.*

Heat-Moon, William Least

PrairyErth (A Deep Map): An Epic History of the Tallgrass Prairie Country. Boston: Houghton Mifflin, 1991. 624 pp. ISBN: 9780395486023

"PrairyErth" is an old geologic term for the prairie soils, and Heat-Moon digs deep into the figurative soil of a single county in south central Kansas in this densely detailed book. Traveling mostly on foot through the grasslands and prairies, Heat-Moon observes, reports on, and celebrates every aspect of this land: its culture, its history, its physical environment, and most of all, its people: a cowboy named Slim, a failed business owner, a feminist rancher, a former railroad worker, a World War II veteran who claimed to have saved de Gaulle's life, and coyote hunters. Just as Chase County, Kansas, is at the geographic center of the United States, Heat-Moon's thoughts and observations are about the spirit, soul, and potential that lie at the heart of the country.

Subjects: American History; American Indians; Environment; Geography; Great Plains

Categories: Appreciating Nature; The Beauty of the Place

Places: Kansas

Now Try: Heat-Moon has written a number of travel narratives, and several of these (*Blue Highways: A Journey into America, River-Horse: The Logbook of a Boat Across America,* and *Roads to Quoz: An American Mosey*) are annotated in this book. A number of historical novels have been set in Kansas; two of the best are Marilynne Robinson's Pulitzer Prize winner, *Gilead,* which includes the story of the protagonist's grandfather, who had a vision to go to Kansas and fight for the abolition of slavery, and Gordon Parks's *The Learning Tree,* about an African American boy growing up in Kansas in the 1920s.

Hessler, Peter

Oracle Bones: A Journey between China's Past and Present. New York: HarperCollins, 2006. 491 pp. ISBN: 9780060826581

After living in China for a decade, Hessler focuses on everyday people to reveal a modern China that is still linked to its past. He tells about his students' struggles as they left school and entered the work place; about his friend from one of China's ethnic minorities, who migrated to the United States with fake documents; and about the oracle bones scholar who committed suicide during the Cultural Revolution. Hessler also tells his own story, which includes a visit to the underground city in Anyang, going undercover at the Falun Gong demonstrations in Tiananmen Square, and observing anti-American protests in Nanjing. Much as ancient diviners used the oracle bones of the book's title to predict the future, Hessler uses these stories to speculate on the future of the world's most populous country.

Subjects: Archaeology; Asian History; Society

Places: China

Awards: ALA Notable Book, 2007, *New York Times* Notable Book, 2006

Now Try: Two of Hessler's other books on China (*River Town: Two Years on the Yangtze* and *Country Driving: A Journey Through China from Farm to Factory*) are annotated elsewhere in this book. Leslie T. Chang's fascinating *Factory Girls: From Village to City in a Changing China* uses the stories of two teenage girls to symbolize the migration of 130 million Chinese workers from the villages to the cities to work in factories. *New Yorker* writer Jianying Zha's *Tide Players: The Movers and Shakers of a Rising China* describes what she sees as China's move from the political idealism of Tiananmen Square to a pragmatism that allows certain individuals to prosper while pushing to the edge of what the state allows. Justin Hill's novel, *The Drink and Dream Teahouse,* tells how three generations in a rural Chinese town are affected by the Tiananmen Square protests.

Housden, Roger

Saved by Beauty: Adventures of an American Romantic in Iran. New York: Broadway Books, 2011. 290 pp. ISBN: 9780307587732

British poet Roger Housden had long been fascinated with Iran and its culture, poetry, and music, and in the winter of 2008–2009, when Housden was in his 60s, he was able to finally visit the country. His deep appreciation of the artists, writers, filmmakers, and religious scholars he met is clear from his rich descriptions, whether he is visiting one of the country's mosques or the place where writing was invented. He admires the young, creative artists and thinkers who are trying to preserve the best of Iran's centuries-old history while at the same time advocating for a new, more secular culture that values freedom of speech, freedom of religion, and women's rights.

Subjects: Architecture; Art and Artists; Islam; Poets

Places: Iran

Now Try: Housden is best known for his *Ten Poems* series, in which he collects 10 poems by various poets and explains in accompanying essays what each poem has meant to him. Books in the series include *Ten Poems to Change Your Life, Ten Poems to Change Your Life Again and Again,* and *Ten Poems to Set You Free.* Housden has also written *Sacred Journeys in a Modern World,* a travel narrative about his personal spiritual quests, from the Monastery of St. Catherine's in the Sinai Desert to the tomb of the mystic poet Rumi in Turkey. Jamie Maslin's book about his experiences among the youth culture in Iran, *Iranian Rappers and Persian Porn: A Hitchhiker's Adventures in the New Iran,* may also appeal to readers who enjoyed *Saved by Beauty* and want other narratives that provide a different view of the Iranian people than one typically gets.

Langewiesche, William

Cutting for Sign. New York; Pantheon, 1993. 247 pp. ISBN: 9780679411130

Atlantic Monthly correspondent Langewiesche traveled the 1,950-mile border between the United States and Mexico (from San Diego, California, to Brownsville, Texas) and talked with the people who live there to put faces on the tensions and controversies represented by the region. He met ranchers, workers, migrants, border patrol agents, labor organizers, and store owners; he spoke with Anglos, Mexicans, and Native Americans. Langewiesche also provides some historical context as well, and the book is a well-written introduction to the places and the people along the troubled border between the two countries.

Subjects: Foreign Relations; Globalization; Immigrants; Immigration; Investigative Stories; Politics; Quick Reads; Trade

Places: California; Mexico; Texas

Series: *Vintage Departures*

Now Try: Langewiesche has written eight books on a wide range of issues and is highly regarded for his strong, evocative prose. His *Sahara Unveiled: A Journey Across The Desert* remains the classic travel narrative about the Sahara Desert and is annotated below. Another of his books, *The Outlaw Sea: A World of Freedom, Chaos, and Crime,* describes the lawlessness and anarchy of the oceans and recounts piracy, legal disputes, and the conflict between the need for shipping companies to make a profit and the need to preserve the environment. Luis Urrea's *Across the Wire: Life and Hard Times on the Mexican Border* is a more intimate look at the lives of individuals in the U.S.-Mexico border town of Tijuana, and his novel, *Into the Beautiful North,* evokes life in a small Mexican village with its story about four women friends who head north to the United States to find men to bring back and repopulate their village. Ted Conover goes undercover to pose as a Mexican trying to cross that border in his suspenseful book, *Coyotes: A Journey Across Borders With America's Illegal Migrants.* Ruben Martinez follows a single Mexican family as its members journey through illegal crossings and work in the United States in the gritty and poignant *Crossing Over: A Mexican Family on the Migrant Trail.*

Langewiesche, William

Sahara Unveiled: A Journey Across the Desert. New York: Pantheon Books, 1996. 301 pp. ISBN: 9780679429821

Langewiesche crossed 1,200 miles of desert from Algiers to Timbuktu and beyond and reflects on the people who survive on the edge of the great desert: a woman whose husband was disabled in an automobile accident, leaving her with no money and four children; an old drunk who twice survived being lost in the desert; a conceited gun runner who left the author stranded in the desert; a date farmer who believed that one can survive on just milk and dates; and many others. Langewiesche also mixes in the history of the region and, in particular, its tribes: the original nomads, the Tuareg; the descendants of their slaves, the Haratins; and plenty of Islamic fundamentalists. The book is a fascinating blend of history, anecdote, and natural history and an appreciation of a desert and its people.

Subjects: Adventure; African History; Deserts; Nomads

Places: Africa; Algeria; Burkina Faso; Mali; Niger; Senegal; Sahara Desert

Series: *Vintage Departures*

Now Try: Langewiesche visits the famous city of Timbuktu in *Sahara Unveiled,* and Marq de Villiers's combination of history and travel narrative, *Timbuktu:*

The Sahara's Fabled City of Gold, may interest readers who are fascinated with the former trading center. Frank Kryza's *The Race for Timbuktu: In Search of Africa's City of Gold* tells the story of 19th-century British explorers competing to find the legendary city. Geraldine Kennedy's *Harmattan: A Journey Across the Sahara* describes the journey across the Sahara that five Peace Corps volunteers made in the mid-1960s, largely because they thought it would be fun, and the challenges they faced. Fiction readers interested in the Sahara may want to try Paul Bowles's first novel, *The Sheltering Sky,* which follows three Americans who drift through North Africa just after World War II.

Marsden, Philip

The Spirit Wrestlers. London: HarperCollins, 1998. 249 pp. ISBN: 9780002558525

Marsden journeyed through the Caucasus region of post-Soviet Russia to search out "the dissenters and misfits of the Russian fringes," in particular the radical sectarians known as Spirit-Wrestlers and Milk-Drinkers. He visited villages that had not been seen by outsiders since before the revolution and met larger-than-life individuals, such as an exiled Georgian prince, a painter of religious icons, Gulag survivors, and proud Cossack horsemen. With well-chosen details, Marsden paints a unique and vivid portrait of the human spirit that has endured in Russia in spite of the terror of the Soviet era.

Subjects: Asian History; European History; Rural Life; Spirituality

Places: Russia

Awards: Thomas Cook Travel Book Award, 1999

Now Try: Marsden is the author of several travel books, including his first book, *A Far Country: Travels in Ethiopia,* which describes his travels in Ethiopia and evokes the "hallucinogenic" beauty of the country's lakes and mountains, and *The Chains of Heaven: An Ethiopian Romance,* which describes his return trip to that country 20 years later. Marsden visited 17 countries in Europe and the Middle East in writing *The Crossing Place: A Journey Among the Armenians,* which focuses on the Armenian people who scattered after the 1915 genocide at the hands of Turkey. The book won the Somerset Maugham Award in England for the best book by a writer under the age of 35. Fiction readers interested in novels set in Russia have several choices, including Edward Rutherfurd's *Russka: The Novel of Russia,* which portrays the history of Russia through the lives of individual families, and Yuri Rytkheu's *A Dream in Polar Fog,* which follows a Canadian sailor who lives among the Chukchi people of northeastern Siberia.

Maslin, Jamie

Iranian Rappers and Persian Porn: A Hitchhiker's Adventures in the New Iran. New York: Skyhorse Pub., 2009. 265 pp. ISBN: 9781602397910

British author Maslin planned to backpack the length of the Silk Road, beginning in Iran. Unfortunately, he didn't plan the trip very well and ended up stranded in a country that had been demonized by the British and U.S. press. What he found instead were plenty of kind and generous people who were willing to help him in numerous ways: paying for his meals and insisting that he stay at their houses. He also found a vibrant underground youth culture, complete with heavy drinking, illegal parties where the women weren't wearing the *hejab,* and even hardcore pornographic films. In fact, Maslin's first-hand accounts of various aspects of the youth culture in Iran resulted in his being banned from re-entering the country.

Subjects: Islam; Politics; Pop Culture

Places: Iran

Now Try: Maslin's second book, *Socialist Dreams and Beauty Queens: A Couchsurfer's Memoir of Venezuela,* recounts Maslin's experiences "couchsurfing" around Venezuela (i.e., staying in the homes of people he found on the Internet site, couchsurfing.org). The book also explores the policies of Venezuelan president Hugo Chavez. Hooman Majd's *The Ayatollah Begs to Differ: The Paradox of Modern Iran,* much like *Iranian Rappers and Persian Porn,* features a good bit of social commentary in its exploration of the complexities and apparent contradictions of modern Iran. Nicholas Jubber used an epic poem about Persia's ancient rulers as the lens through which he viewed modern Iran and Afghanistan in *Drinking Arak Off an Ayatollah's Beard: A Journey Through the Inside-Out Worlds of Iran and Afghanistan*; he also writes about the Iranians and Afghanis he befriended. Two fictional portraits of the intersection between pop and Islamic cultures are Tahar Ben Jelloun's *Leaving Tangier,* about a Moroccan brother and sister who move to Spain to make new lives, and Michael Muhammad Knight's *The Taqwacores,* about Muslim punks in Buffalo, New York. (One reviewer called Knight's book "*Catcher in the Rye* for young Muslims.")

McConahay, Mary Jo

Maya Roads: One Woman's Journey Among the People of the Rainforest. Chicago: Chicago Review Press, 2011. 260 pp. ISBN: 9781569765487

McConahay is a journalist who became fascinated with Mayan culture in the early 1970s and who has covered Central America for a number of publications. In *Maya Roads,* she focuses on the indigenous Lacandón people, descendants of the ancient Maya, as well as on the politics, archaeology, flora, and fauna of their home, the Central American rain forest. McConahay sees the rain forest as a place of intense beauty but one that has greatly changed in recent years due to civil wars, the destruction of the forests, tourism, and a $40 billion drug trade. The book includes a number of stories of ancient Mayan life and clearly conveys her admiration for the strength and adaptability of these indigenous people.

Subjects: Environment; Indigenous Peoples; Jungles; Mayas; Modernization

Categories: Endangered Places

Places: Guatemala

Now Try: George Lovell's *A Beauty that Hurts: Life and Death in Guatemala* is an examination of the Guatemala military's atrocities against the Maya people. Scott Wallace's *The Unconquered: In Search of the Amazon's Last Uncontacted*

Tribes is the account of a different jungle tribe, one known for their skill at the use of curare-poisoned arrows. Readers who are interested in further exploring environmental issues and indigenous people should consider Eugene Linden's *The Ragged Edge of the World: Encounters at the Frontier Where Modernity, Wildlands, and Indigenous Peoples Meet*, which examines social and environmental changes in a wide range of places, including Vietnam, New Guinea, Borneo, Machu Picchu, Cuba, and Midway Island.

Scobie, Claire

Last Seen in Lhasa: The Story of an Extraordinary Friendship in Modern Tibet. London: Rider, 2006. 242 pp. ISBN: 9781846040054

Scobie, a young journalist, accompanied a group of British botanists on several treks into southern Tibet in search of rare red lilies. On one of the treks, she met Ani, a middle-aged Buddhist nun and yogini, through whom Scobie begins to understand both the beauty of Tibet and the persecution of the land's people at the hands of the Chinese, who are intent on destroying their Buddhist faith. Scobie's affection for Ani shines through her elegant, absorbing prose.

Subjects: Buddhism; Friendships; Investigative Stories; Nuns; Religion; Women Travelers

Places: Lhasa; Tibet

Awards: Dolman Best Travel Book Award, 2007

Now Try: Sun Shuyun's *A Year in Tibet* tells about a year spent in Tibet while making a documentary film; in spite of the fact that Shuyun is Chinese, the local people became close to her and she grew to love them in return. Alec LeSueur's *The Hotel on the Roof of the World: Five Years in Tibet* recounts his years running a hotel in Lhasa; it is delightfully humorous as well as informative about the clashes between Tibet and China. For years, Matteo Pistono smuggled evidence of Chinese atrocities out of Tibet and showed it to Western governments and human rights groups; he combines stories of adventure and spiritual pilgrimage in his fascinating book, *In the Shadow of the Buddha: One Man's Journey of Spiritual Discovery & Political Danger in Tibet*. Marlene Van Niekerk's novel *Agaat* also deals with a unique friendship and oppressive circumstances but in a different part of the world, apartheid-era South Africa.

Stewart, Stanley

Frontiers of Heaven: A Journey to the End of China. Guilford, CT: Lyon's Press, 2004 [1995]. 206 pp. ISBN: 9781592284016

Stewart, a British journalist, journeyed by train and bus from Shanghai to the banks of the Indus, roughly following the old Silk Road and exploring the area beyond the Great Wall, which even the Chinese consider a mysterious land of exiles. Stewart describes the lost cities of Central Asia, the Buddhist monasteries, a Kirghiz wedding on "the roof of the world," and ballroom dancing in the Mountains of Heaven with highly poetic descriptions and a dry wit. His portraits of the individuals he met are particularly fascinating: the Chinese woman with whom he had an affair; the chief judge in Wuwei who carried a cow's head with him; and the sailor who discussed Tang poetry.

Subjects: Great Wall of China; Love Affairs; Rail Travel; Rural Life

Places: China; Pakistan; Tibet

Awards: Thomas Cook Travel Book Award, 1996

Now Try: Stewart has won the Thomas Cook Travel Book Award twice, once for *Frontiers of Heaven* and once for *In the Empire of Genghis Khan: An Amazing Odyssey Through the Lands of the Most Feared Conquerors in History* (annotated in this chapter, in the "Endangered Places" category). Colin Thubron explored some of the same area along the Silk Road as Stewart and wrote about his encounters in *Shadow of the Silk Road,* which is annotated in the "Quests" chapter of this book. Robin Hanbury-Tenison and his wife rode 1,000 miles alongside the Great Wall of China on horseback and, like Stewart, witnessed the changes in China after the Cultural Revolution; their story is told in *Ride Along the Great Wall.*

Tayler, Jeffrey

Angry Wind: Through Muslim Black Africa by Truck, Bus, Boat, and Camel. Boston: Houghton Mifflin, 2005. 252 pp. ISBN: 9780618334674

In 2002, travel writer Tayler crossed the Sahel (the southern region of the Sahara Desert) in order to "hear out the people of the Sahel, to record and transmit their grievances, and to learn their views on the conflict between the West and the Islamic world." He combines historical and political context with interviews and observations to produce a gritty narrative that tackles difficult topics (like female circumcision) and highlights the many paradoxes of the region: Islamic fundamentalism, corruption, an active slave trade, and extreme poverty alongside warm hospitality, patience, and generosity.

Subjects: Deserts; Investigative Stories; Islam; Poverty

Places: Africa; Chad; Mali; Niger; Nigeria; Sahara Desert; Senegal

Now Try: No less than Bill Bryson has called Tayler a rising star among travel writers, and several of his other titles focus on Africa. *Glory in a Camel's Eye: Trekking Through the Moroccan Sahara* tells about a trek that Tayler made across the Moroccan desert with Arab nomads, and *Facing the Congo: A Modern-Day Journey into the Heart of Darkness* recounts the story of his attempt to re-create British explorer Henry Stanley's trip down the Congo River in a canoe. Kevin Kertscher's enjoyable *Africa Solo: A Journey Across the Sahara, Sahel, and Congo* follows a film editor's trip across some of the same countries visited by Tayler in *Angry Wind.* Michael Palin's four-episode series, *Sahara,* is available on DVD and may be of interest to readers who want to see more of the world's largest desert. Fiction set in Africa includes Giles Folen's stunning debut novel about Ugandan dictator Idi Amin's physician, *The Last King of Scotland,* and Nigerian-born Uwem Akpan's collection of stories set in war-torn Africa, *Say You're One of Them.*

Theroux, Paul

The Pillars of Hercules. New York: G.P. Putnam's Sons, 1995. 509 pp. ISBN: 9780399141089

Travel writer Theroux explored the Mediterranean coast by foot, train, and boat, and though his trip was largely without an itinerary, he zigzagged in order to avoid areas of political conflict and therefore spent much of his time visiting the islands of the great sea. In spite of his occasional air of condescension, Theroux is at his best when describing the interesting and curious people he met, both locals and fellow travelers. Theroux is also characteristically testy in this book, but his observations are keen and thoughtful, particularly when he interviews the writers he sought out and obviously admires: Nobel laureate Naguib Mahfouz in Egypt, Emile Habbiby in Israel, and Paul Bowles in Morocco.

Subjects: Authors; Islands; Seas

Places: Africa; Albania; Corsica; Croatia; Egypt; France; Gibraltar; Greece; Israel; Italy; Mallorca; Mediterranean Sea; Morocco; Sardinia; Sicily; Slovenia; Spain; Syria; Tunisia; Turkey

Now Try: Theroux is one of the giants of the travel narrative field, and many of his other titles are annotated in this book: *The Great Railway Bazaar*, his first travel narrative, about a four-month train trip across Europe, the Middle East, and Asia, which the author took in 1975; *The Old Patagonian Express: By Train through the Americas*, about a train trip from Massachusetts to Argentina; and *The Kingdom by the Sea: A Journey Around the Coast of Great Britain*, which recounts his travels around the perimeter of England. Another great travel writer, Eric Newby, also traveled through the countries that border the Mediterranean Sea; his journey is told in his typically hilarious book, *On the Shores of the Mediterranean*. *Mediterranean Winter: The Pleasures of History and Landscape in Tunisia, Sicily, Dalmatia, and Greece* traces the travels of author Robert Kaplan in the mid-1970s through many of the same countries visited by Theroux in *The Pillars of Hercules*. Jan Morris's latest work, *Contact!: A Book of Encounters*, is also a collection of short pieces with an atypically (for her) strong focus on people. The wickedly funny writer Evelyn Waugh recounts his 1929 honeymoon trip to the Mediterranean in the irreverent classic, *Labels: A Mediterranean Journal*. David Abulafia's more recent *The Great Sea: A Human History of the Mediterranean* explains how that sea became so important in the economic and cultural history of the West.

Thubron, Colin

In Siberia. New York: HarperCollins, 1999. 286 pp. ISBN: 9780060195434

Thubron recounts his 15,000-mile solo journey to Siberia, an area as large as Europe and the United States combined and forbidden to Westerners just a few years before his trip. He found barren, uninhabitable tundra and the grim reminders of death camps and massacres, but he also found memorable, resilient people: a peasant who claimed to be the descendent of Rasputin; a Mongol shaman; a scientist pursuing preposterous ideas about magnetic fields; and an archaeologist who believed that civilization began in Siberia. Thubron's keen observations about present-day Siberia are interwoven with historical details about the area, and his precise and meticulous writing captures the contradictions he finds at the core of this vast land.

Subjects: Adventures; Asian History; European History; Prisons; Solo Travelers

Places: Arctic Region; Russia

Awards: ALA Notable Book, 2001; *New York Times* Notable Book, 2000

Now Try: Thubron's earlier book, *Among the Russians*, provides a compelling account of the author's car trip through the Soviet Union in 1980, just as the country was beginning to break apart. Another earlier book by Thubron, *Where Nights Are Longest: Travels by Car Through Western Russia*, describes a 10,000-mile trip through western Russia and features fascinating sketches of the people he met. Douglas Botting describes an earlier trip to Siberia, during the height of the Cold War, in *One Chilly Siberian Morning*. Sharon Hudgins is a food and travel writer, and like Thubron, she focuses on the lives of ordinary people whom she met in Siberia in her vivid book, *The Other Side of Russia: A Slice of Life in Siberia and the Russian Far East*.

Urban Landscapes

Cities are beautiful in ways that are different from the beauty of the more natural destinations of the previous categories of this chapter, and the titles in "Urban Landscapes" evoke that special beauty. In addition to capturing the atmosphere of cities such as Venice in John Berendt's *The City of Falling Angels* or Rio de Janeiro in Ruy Castro's *Rio de Janeiro: Carnival Under Fire*, these titles also celebrate the often colorful and eccentric characters the authors encounter in these cities, both living (the Rat Man of Treviso in John Berendt's *The City of Falling Angels*) and dead (the architect Antonio Gaudi in Robert Hughes's *Barcelona: The Great Enchantress*).

Just as the titles in this category focus on the appeal of cities to some readers, so too will histories and other nonfiction titles set in these cities (Erik Larson's Chicago in *The Devil in the White City: Murder, Magic, and Madness at the Fair That Changed America* or Thad Carhart's Paris in *The Piano Shop on the Left Bank: Discovering a Forgotten Passion in a Paris Atelier*), as well as novels set in specific cities (Donna Leon's Venice-based crime novels, Naguib Mahfouz's Cairo Trilogy, or Lawrence Durrell's Alexandria Quartet).

Berendt, John

The City of Falling Angels. New York: Penguin Press, 2005. 414 pp. ISBN: 9781594200588

Berendt moved to Venice in the days following a mysterious fire that destroyed the historic opera house, La Fenice, and his book follows the reaction of the locals to the fire and his own investigations into its causes. Berendt's investigations became somewhat sidetracked, however, as he became fascinated by the city's colorful characters: a master glassblower, a surrealist artist, an heir to a grand Renaissance palace, the Rat Man of Treviso, contessas, and marchesas. He also tells the stories of various American expatriates who have lived in the city, from Henry James to Ezra Pound, and the book provides an atmospheric and evocative portrait of Venice and its crumbling buildings, twisting passages, and seemingly endless canals.

Subjects: Architecture; Art and Artists; Family Relationships; Investigative Stories; True Crime

Categories: Landscapes and People

Places: Italy; Venice

Now Try: Berendt is best known for his earlier book, *Midnight in the Garden of Good and Evil,* about the murder of a male prostitute at the hands of a respected antique dealer in Savannah, Georgia. One of famed travel writer Jan Morris's best known works is *The World of Venice,* a delightful and very personal guide to the culture and people of the "City of Water." Poet Joseph Brodsky's *Watermark* is another very private look at Venice, although one that is more brooding. A large number of works of fiction are set in Venice, including two marvelous novellas, Daphne du Maurier's chilling *Don't Look Now,* and Thomas Mann's classic story of forbidden love, *Death in Venice.* (The film based on the du Maurier novella was directed by Nicholas Roeg and features one of the most frightening scenes in film history.)

Blount, Roy

Feet on the Street: Rambles around New Orleans. New York: Crown Journeys, 2005. 143 pp. ISBN: 9781400046454

Humorist and writer Blount takes the reader on eight rambles through America's Crescent City, focusing on its architecture, its music, its food, and its people: Truman Capote, Jefferson Davis, Zora Neale Hurston, Jelly Roll Morton, and countless others. Blount's walking tour captures the city from Bourbon Street to the Garden District, from eating live oysters to relishing beignets, from jazz to voodoo, and provides the author's sometimes humorous, but always enthusiastic, impressions of a city that he refers to as "like no other place in America, and yet (or therefore) . . . the cradle of American culture." Written before the destruction of Hurricane Katrina, Blount does speculate on what would happen to the city when the "big one" hits, and his predictions have an eerie prescience.

Subjects: American History; Architecture; Food; Humor; Quick Reads; Walking

Categories: Landscapes and People

Places: New Orleans

Series: *Crown Journeys*

Now Try: After Hurricane Katrina hit, *New Yorker* writer Dan Baum moved to New Orleans to write about the response of its residents to the disaster; he found a number of captivating characters there and writes about them in *Nine Lives: Mystery, Magic, Death, and Life in New Orleans*. When *New York Times* writer Rob Walker relocated to New Orleans with his girlfriend in 2000, he began emailing stories about life there to his friends; these stories are the heart of the captivating *Letters from New Orleans*. Poet Andrei Codrescu provides a collection of sketches of the city's more interesting inhabitants in his poignant love song, *New Orleans, Mon Amour: Twenty Years of Writings from the City*. John Kennedy Toole's Pulitzer Prize winner, *A Confederacy of Dunces*, and Walker Percy's National Book Award winner, *The Moviegoer*, are two superb novels that take place in New Orleans, and Frederick Barthelme's novel *Waveland* is set on the Mississippi coast in the aftermath of Hurricane Katrina and portrays individuals rebuilding their own lives as well as their homes and towns. *Feet on the Street* is part of the *Crown Journeys* series, many of whose titles are annotated in this book. Several of these are amusing in the same way that Blount's book is, especially *The Great Psychedelic Armadillo Picnic: A Walk in Austin* by Kinky Friedman, *Fugitives and Refugees: A Walk in Portland, Oregon* by Chuck Palahniuk, and *Washington Schlepped Here: Walking in the Nation's Capital* by Christopher Buckley.

Boo, Katherine

Behind the Beautiful Forevers: Life, Death, and Hope in a Mumbai Undercity. New York: Random House, 2012. 256 pp. ISBN: 9781400067558

Pulitzer Prize winner and MacArthur grant recipient Katherine Boo spent three years among the individuals living in a slum area in Mumbai and provides a painfully realistic portrayal of their lives, including their hopes and dreams of a better life. Boo's descriptions of enterprising teenagers, scrap-metal thieves, corrupt policemen, and garbage pickers are poignant but unsentimental. Nevertheless, the impact is staggering, and as one reviewer noted, the book will change the reader's view of the world. Boo's book is wonderfully written with a fast pace that reflects the rapid changes taking place in India in general and Mumbai in particular.

Subjects: Globalization; Poverty; Urban Life

Places: India; Mumbai

Now Try: Suketu Mehta's *Maximum City: Bombay Lost and Found*, about the author's return after 21 years to the city in which he grew up, is also annotated in this chapter. Anand Giridharadas was born in the United States of Indian parents and tells of his return to their native country in *India Calling: An Intimate Portrait of a Nation's Remaking*, which focuses on the impact of change on tradition by looking at individuals living in India and their families; the title is annotated in "The Journey" chapter of this book. Arjun Purkayastha captures the furious pace of Mumbai through its crowded train stations in his Kindle book, *Bombay Train: A Stranger's Perspective*. The 2008 British film, *Slumdog Millionaire*, tells the story of a young man from the Mumbai slums; it won the 2009 Academy Award for Best Picture.

Carey, Peter

30 Days in Sydney: A Wildly Distorted Account. New York: Bloomsbury, 2001. 248 pp. ISBN: 9781582341668

Booker Prize winner Carey returned to his home town after nearly two decades abroad and writes a rambling evocation of Australia's largest city. During his month in Sydney, which coincided with the summer Olympics there, Carey interviewed his eccentric friends, surfed and partied a bit too much, and tried to describe the city in terms of the four elements: earth, air, fire, and water. The result is a very personal set of impressions of Sydney, complete with its history (it was founded as a convict colony), its struggles with poor soil and poor weather, its Aborigines, its Harbour Bridge, and its Opera House.

Subjects: Architecture; Indigenous Peoples; Quick Reads

Places: Australia; Sydney

Series: *The Writer and the City*

Now Try: Carey's book is part of Bloomsbury's series, *The Writer and the City,* and fans of literary travel narrative may enjoy other titles in the series, including John Banville's *Prague Pictures,* David Leavitt's *Florence: A Delicate Case,* and Edmund White's *The Flaneur: A Stroll Through the Paradoxes of Paris.* Carey is one of only two writers to win the Booker Prize twice; one of his novels to win that prize is *Oscar and Lucinda,* in which two obsessive gamblers try to transport a glass church from Sydney to a remote coastal town. Although Sydney is only one part of Bill Bryson's excellent book, *In a Sunburned Country* (annotated in the "Travel Humor" chapter of this books), his evocation of that city is first rate; as my editor notes, "no one walks around and describes cities like Bryson does." Clare Naylor's humorous novel, *Dog Handling,* is also set in Sydney and involves a woman who travels there after her fiancé calls off their wedding. Another novel set in Sydney is James Bradley's *The Deep Field,* about a photographer who is sent there to document fossils and who falls in love with a blind paleontologist.

Castro, Ruy

Rio de Janeiro: Carnival Under Fire. New York: Bloomsbury, 2004. 244 pp. ISBN: 9781582341903

Brazilian journalist Castro weaves together the history and daily life of his hometown, including the annual Carnival, the nightlife, the beaches, and the cuisine. The writing is relaxed and almost conversational, full of anecdotes about the city, its architecture, its people, and its music. Castro covers the history of Rio, from the Portuguese explorers who founded it through its long slave trade through its Copacabana and Ipanema days to its regeneration after the capital was moved from Rio to Brasilia in 1960. The less attractive elements of Rio (the drug trade, the favelas, the crime) are covered too, although in less detail.

Subjects: Architecture; Food; Music and Musicians; Quick Reads; South American History

Places: Brazil; Rio de Janiero

Series: *The Writer and the City*

Now Try: Castro emphasizes the importance of music in the history and contemporary life of Rio, and he is also the author of a book on Brazil's best known music, *Bossa Nova: The Story of the Brazilian Music That Seduced the World.* Alma Guillermoprieto's *Samba* may also interest readers who are fascinated by the music of Brazil. Earlier travel narratives on Brazil include *Brazil on the Move* (1963) by noted American writer John Dos Passos and *Brazilian Adventure* (1933) by Peter Fleming, the brother of James Bond's creator, Ian Fleming. Although Edwidge Danticat's *After the Dance: A Walk Through Carnival in Jacmel, Haiti* takes place in a different location, it has a similar feel to Castro's book, and both involve carnival festivities.

Cohn, Nik

The Heart of the World. New York: Knopf, 1992. 371 pp. ISBN: 9780394568690

Cohn, a British journalist, celebrates the squalid and violent world that he finds along Broadway, New York City's Great White Way, from Battery Park to Times Square. He was guided on his journey by a Soviet émigré taxi driver and a transvestite prostitute and, along the way, he encountered a number of eccentric, often doomed characters from both the past and the present. Cohn provides some history of the area as well, from P.T. Barnum's museum of human oddities to the Gilded Age of Stanford White and Evelyn Nisbet. Though his writing may be overly metaphoric and too focused on misfits for some readers, it is a fascinating book.

Subjects: American History

Categories: Landscapes and People

Places: New York City

Awards: Thomas Cook Travel Book Award, 1993

Series: *Vintage Departures*

Now Try: Cohn is best known for his 1975 *New York Magazine* article, "Tribal Rites of the New Saturday Night," which was the source for the film "Saturday Night Fever." He also wrote *Triksta: Life and Death and New Orleans Rap*, a captivating study of rap musicians in New Orleans. Another fascinating look at the less glittering side of New York is Gregory Gibson's *Hubert's Freaks: The Rare-Book Dealer, the Times Square Talker, and the Lost Photos of Diane Arbus*, which recounts the discovery of several never-before-seen prints by legendary photographer Diane Arbus by a down-and-out rare book dealer. Teju Cole's first novel, *Open City*, which has been called "a new landmark in post-September 11 fiction," tells the story of a Nigerian immigrant who wanders around Manhattan, musing on present scenes and past events. Jane Jacobs was an architectural writer living in New York City in 1961 when she published *The Death and Life of Great American Cities*, a highly influential book on urban planning, which argued that planning policies were destroying many inner-city communities. Other more general titles about cities include Joel Kotkin's *The City: A Global History*, which argues that commerce, security and power, and the "sacredness" of urban space lead to successful cities, and Witold Rybczynski's *Makeshift Metropolis: Ideas About Cities,* which focuses on how best to manage the increasingly urban future.

Estrada, Alfredo José

Havana: Autobiography of a City. New York: Palgrave Macmillan, 2007. 275 pp. ISBN: 9781403975096

Estrada, a Havana-born magazine editor, tells the Cuban capital city's story through its landmarks (from the Plaza de Armas, where Havana was founded in 1519, to the Morro Castle that guards the entrance to Havana Bay) and its most famous residents (from the martyr of Cuban independence, José Martí, to Ernest Hemingway). He works hard to be politically neutral and fair minded ("finding a middle ground between political extremes," as the author calls it) and provides a very personal portrait of the city of his birth.

Subjects: Architecture; Latin American History

Places: Cuba; Havana

Now Try: Estrada writes about Havana's historic casino era, and the story of one of these nightclubs (the Tropicana) is told by Rosa Lowinger and Ofelia Fox in *Tropicana Nights: The Life and Times of the Legendary Cuban Nightclub.* T.J. English writes about the 1950s casino era in Havana and claims that the Mob had Cuban dictator Batista "in his pocket" in *Havana Nocturne: How the Mob Owned Cuba and Then Lost It to the Revolution,* and Guillermo Cabrera Infante's dazzling novel, *Three Trapped Tigers,* looks at life in the cabaret society of pre-Castro Cuba. Christopher Baker's *Mi Moto Fidel: Motorcycling Through Castro's Cuba* describes a three-month trip around the island on a motorcycle and celebrates the resilience of the Cuban people. Christopher Hunt followed the path that Castro followed in his 1959 Liberty Caravan through Cuba in *Waiting for Fidel* and writes about the reactions of a wide range of people to Castro's regime. Like Estrada, Yale professor Carlos Eire provides a very personal look at life in Cuba in his memoir, *Waiting for Snow in Havana: Confessions of a Cuban Boy;* Eire writes nostalgically about his life in Cuba before Castro and before he himself was airlifted out of the country to Miami. Pedro Juan Gutiérrez's semi-autobiographical novel, *Dirty Havana Trilogy,* tells the story of an ex-radio journalist who wanders through Havana, surviving on menial jobs and overseeing the decay of the city from his rooftop apartment.

Hughes, Robert

Barcelona: The Great Enchantress. New York: Knopf, 1992. 573 pp. ISBN: 9780394580272 YA

Hughes, a distinguished art critic, writes about the history of the great Catalonian city and its culture in particular. As might be expected from the author of a well-received book on modern art (*The Shock of the New*), Hughes is especially informative about Barcelona's architecture and its most famous architect, Antonio Gaudi. But Hughes is equally knowledgeable of the history of the city and the Catalonian spirit, and he explains the importance of politics to the inhabitants of

Barcelona and their long-standing disagreements with Madrid. The book is long, almost encyclopedic, and contains a great deal of information, but is also witty and clearly written.

Subjects: Architecture; Art and Artists; European History; Humor; Scholarly Writing

Places: Barcelona; Spain

Series: *National Geographic Directions*

Now Try: Hughes is best known for his history of the early days of Australia, *The Fatal Shore: The Epic of Australia's Founding,* and for his recent history of Rome, *Rome: A Cultural, Visual, and Personal History*. Irish writer Colm Toibin's *Homage to Barcelona* is another celebration of the great city and is especially good on the topic of the artists who lived and worked there. George Orwell's classic account of his experiences in the Spanish Civil War, *Homage to Catalonia,* is set in Barcelona and the area surrounding the city. Carlos Ruiz Zafon's intricate, best-selling first novel, *The Shadow of the Wind,* has been described as "a love letter to the city of Barcelona." Manuel Vázquez Montalbán's gripping crime novel, *The Man of My Life,* is set in Barcelona and involves the murder of the son of a rich financier; as one reviewer noted, "Montalbán does for Barcelona what Chandler did for Los Angeles." Two critically well received (but very different films) have been set in Barcelona: Whit Stillman's witty 1994 film, *Barcelona,* which looks at the city through the eyes of two rather shallow Americans; and Mexican director Alejandro González Iñárritu's *Biutiful,* a grim, gritty story that takes place in the Barcelona underworld.

Kotlowitz, Alex

Never a City So Real: A Walk in Chicago. New York: Crown Journeys, 2004. 159 pp. ISBN: 9781400046218

Wall Street Journal writer Kotlowitz tells the story of America's "Second City" through portraits of some of its residents who are trying to make a difference in the lives of others there: union workers, political bosses, social workers, street artists, attorneys, and immigrants. He describes Chicago as "a stew of contradictions" and uses the stories of its people to highlight the political and economic realities of the city and, in turn, the "messy vitalities" of the United States. The book is too short to be comprehensive but instead serves as a snapshot of the city and its lesser known neighborhoods.

Subjects: American History; Essays; Investigative Stories; Quick Reads

Places: Chicago

Series: *Crown Journeys*

Now Try: Kotlowitz is best known for his compelling book about two brothers growing up in a violence-ridden housing project in Chicago, *There Are No Children Here: The Story of Two Boys Growing Up in The Other America*. The contradictions that Kotlowitz finds in Chicago are also reflected in David Grazian's study of the blues clubs there, *Blue Chicago: The Search for Authenticity in Urban*

Blues Clubs. Like Kotlowitz, Studs Terkel explains Chicago through portraits of its people in *Division Street: America*, for which Kotlowitz wrote the introduction. American writer Nelson Algren grew up in Chicago, and his memoir, *Chicago: City on the Make*, has been called "the best book about Chicago" by no less than Studs Terkel. Algren's most famous novel, *The Man with the Golden Arm*, which won the very first National Book Award in 1950, is also set in Chicago and recounts the struggles of Frankie Machine, a backroom card dealer who is addicted to morphine.

Lopate, Phillip

Waterfront: A Walk Around Manhattan. New York: Crown Publishers, 2004. 421 pp. ISBN: 9780609605059

Lopate, a native New Yorker, provides a tour of Manhattan's riverside perimeter, from the Little Red Lighthouse made famous by the 1942 children's book of the same name to Battery Park. He covers many aspects of this part of the city (which he calls "the key to New York's destiny"), including its culture and its history, and includes discussions of writers from Melville to Whitman to Stephen Crane and historical persons from Captain Kidd to Mayor LaGuardia. The sometimes rambling book is full of absorbing information about the piers, wharves, and boardwalks of the borough and is an affectionate look at a lesser appreciated part of the city.

Subjects: American History; Architecture; Essays; Rivers

Places: East River; Hudson River; New York City

Series: *Crown Journeys*

Now Try: An excellent read-alike is Joseph Mitchell's collection of vivid pieces about life on the New York waterfront, *The Bottom of the Harbor*. Another book of interest to readers who enjoyed Lopate's book is Nathan Ward's history, *Dark Harbor: The War for the New York Waterfront*, which recounts the waterfront area and its corruption and crime from the 1930s to the 1950s. *Philadelphia's Lost Waterfront*, by Harry Kyriakodis, is the history of another great city's waterfront area. *Waterfront* is part of the *Crown Journeys* series, several of whose titles are annotated in this book. Titles that are not annotated in this book, but still recommended for readers interested in literary travel narratives, include *Wandering Home: A Long Walk Across America's Most Hopeful Landscape: Vermont's Champlain Valley and New York's Adirondacks* by Bill McKibben; *Hallowed Ground: A Walk at Gettysburg* by James McPherson; *The Great Psychedelic Armadillo Picnic: A Walk in Austin* by Kinky Friedman; *Land's End: A Walk in Provincetown* by Michael Cunningham; *Blues City: A Walk in Oakland* by Ishamel Reed; *City of the Soul: A Walk in Rome* by William Murray; and *Washington Schlepped Here: Walking in the Nation's Capital* by Christopher Buckley.

Mak, Geert

Amsterdam: A Brief Life of a City. Cambridge, MA: Harvard University Press, 2000. 338 pp. ISBN: 9780674003316

Dutch journalist Mak combines history and travel narrative as well as fact and anecdote in this engaging book about "the Venice of the North." Mak follows the city from its 13th-century origins through its heyday as a cultural and financial capital of Europe to its present status as the largest city in and capital of the Netherlands. Mak has a good eye for unusual details, such as the diary of a priest who feared for his life or Rembrandt's drawing of a girl put to death for manslaughter, and writes in an accessible style.

Subjects: Architecture; Art and Artists; European History

Places: Amsterdam; Netherlands

Now Try: Mak is best known for *In Europe: Travels Through the Twentieth Century*, which combines travel narrative with a history of Europe in the 20th century. British travel writer Harry Pearson meanders through one of the Netherlands's neighboring countries, Belgium, in the amusing *A Tall Man in a Low Land: Some Time Among the Belgians*. Fiction readers may also enjoy *Amsterdam: A Traveler's Literary Companion* (edited by Manfred Wolf), which features twenty stories by writers from that city, arranged by geographic sections of Amsterdam. Ian McEwan's dark comedy, *Amsterdam*, won the Booker Prize and is perhaps the quintessential modern novel about the city.

Martin, Judith

No Vulgar Hotel: The Desire and Pursuit of Venice. New York: W.W. Norton & Co., 2007. 330 pp. ISBN: 9780393059328

Judith Martin (a.k.a. Miss Manners) is obsessed with Venice and writes both about "that miracle-from-the-swamp" and her own relationship with it as an admitted "Venetophile." She writes with a gentle wit and provides ample information on Venetian food, painting, and history as well as the city's social life. Being Miss Manners, of course, means that Martin spends a good part of the book advising the reader on how to interact with others and how to behave in general while traveling.

Subjects: European History; Humor; Women Travelers

Places: Italy; Venice

Now Try: Marlena de Blasi's *A Thousand Days in Venice* is perhaps more memoir than travel narrative and tells the story of how the author fell in love with her future husband in Venice. Tiziano Scarpa's brief tribute to "the Queen of the Adriatic," *Venice Is a Fish: A Sensual Guide*, uses parts of the body to symbolize the different areas of Venice. The husband-and-wife team of Louis Begley and Anka Muhlstein have written a wonderful three-part appreciation of Venice, entitled *Venice for Lovers*, which includes a novella by Begley about a young man whose spurned love for a woman is transformed into a love for Venice. Mary McCarthy's colorful *The Stones of Florence and Venice Observed* is a classic portrayal of the history and art of the two Italian cities. While E.M. Forster's *A Room with a View* is set in Florence, it also deals, in a lovely and humorous way, with interactions with other travelers and locals.

Mehta, Suketu

Maximum City: Bombay Lost and Found. New York: Alfred A. Knopf, 2004. 542 pp. ISBN: 9780375403729

Mehta grew up in Bombay (now Mumbai) before his family migrated to New York, and he returned to the city of his youth after a 21-year absence to find "the biggest, fastest, richest city in India." The book is organized around the industries for which Mumbai is known (movies, finance, gangsters, and prostitutes) and captures the complexities of this city of 18 million people, some packed into neighborhoods with a density of one million per square mile. Mehta's writing is spare but full of details, some of them stomach-turning, and while these details may sometimes feel only loosely connected, they provide a fascinating look at a city of both unmatched beauty and unrivaled poverty, intolerance, and violence.

Subjects: Community Life; Culture Clash; Family Relationships; Immigration; Urban Life

Places: India; Mumbai

Awards: Pulitzer Prize for General Nonfiction, Runner-up, 2005; Samuel Johnson Prize, Shortlist, 2005

Now Try: Mehta looks at Mumbai's notorious dance bars in his book, and a more in-depth examination of those places from the point of view of one of the dancers is Sonia Faleiro's moving book, *Beautiful Thing: Inside the Secret World of Bombay's Dance Bars,* which also explores the hypocrisies of middle-class marriage in India and one woman's struggle for personal freedom. In the prologue to *Maximum City,* Mehta acknowledges the influence of V.S. Naipaul, whose trilogy on India (*An Area of Darkness, India: A Wounded Civilization,* and *India: A Million Mutinies Now*) includes visits to Mumbai. Pulitzer Prize winner Katherine Boo provides a painfully realistic portrayal of lives in a slum area in Mumbai in *Behind the Beautiful Forevers: Life, Death, and Hope in a Mumbai Undercity* (annotated in this chapter). William Dalrymple's *City of Djinns: A Year in Delhi* describes the author's stay in India's historical capital; like Mehta, he encountered a wide range of individuals, from whirling dervishes to eunuchs. Two award-winning novels by the Indian-born writer Rohinton Mistry take place in Mumbai: *Such a Long Journey,* about a bank clerk whose family begins to fall apart, and *Family Matters,* about a middle-class Parsi family and its aging patriarch. Gregory David Roberts's massive 2003 novel, *Shantaram,* is also set in Mumbai and tells the story of an Australian bank robber and heroin addict who escapes prison, flees to India, and lives in Mumbai for 10 years; the book is based on events in the author's own life.

Miller, Sam

Delhi: Adventures in a Megacity. New York: St. Martin's Press, 2010 [2009]. 291 pp. ISBN: 9780312612375

Miller provides an enthusiastic walking tour of India's administrative capital, a megalopolis of 18 million people, some of whom live in dismal poverty and some of whom live in luxurious splendor. The author encountered India's many contradictions as he traveled through the city: ancient palaces and brand new metro stations; open-air slaughterhouses and cybercafés; crowded slums and deserted stretches of countryside. He also provides vignettes of historical figures (the Gandhis, the Nehrus, the various rajes) as well as contemporary individuals he meets (a crematorium attendant, police brass band members, cult followers). Miller's appreciation of the city's rich diversity creates a stunning portrait of what the author calls "India's dreamland and its purgatory."

Subjects: Asian History; Walking

Categories: Landscapes and People

Places: Delhi; India

Now Try: William Dalrymple's *City of Djinns: A Year in Delhi* is another writer's celebration of Delhi and one that features encounters with a range of colorful and diverse individuals. Dalrymple's *Nine Lives: In Search of the Sacred in Modern India* may also be of interest; it is annotated in the "Landscapes and People" section of this chapter. Justine Hardy's witty *Scoop-Wallah: Life on a Delhi Daily* follows the author's year in India, working at "The India Express." Madan Vasishta's *Deaf in Delhi* is more memoir than travel narrative and tells the story of an Indian man who became deaf at age 11 and eventually achieved status as a professor in the United States. Delhi lies in the Ganges River Basin, and travel writer Eric Newby's hilarious trip down that sacred river is described in *Slowly Down the Ganges*. Readers interested in a history of India should consider John Keay's *India: A History*, which begins in 3000 BC with the development of agriculture and trade networks, or Barbara D. and Thomas R. Metcalf's shorter work, *A Concise History of Modern India*.

Morris, Jan

Trieste and the Meaning of Nowhere. New York: Simon & Schuster, 2001. 203 pp. ISBN: 9780743201285

Well-known travel writer Morris celebrates this Italian port city, where she was stationed as a soldier at the end of World War II, by telling of its history under the Hapsburgs, its rule by the Nazis, and its role in the Cold War. Describing Trieste as "a blend of the genial and the melancholy" and "a place where regrets, hope and high memories merge," she pays particular attention to the cultural icons who are identified with the city, notably James Joyce, Rainer Marie Rilke, and Sigmund Freud. The book also has elements of memoir; while writing it, Morris announced that it would be her last book, so there is much reflection on her career as a writer and traveler.

Subjects: European History; Memoirs; Quick Reads; Women Travelers

Places: Italy; Trieste

Now Try: Although Morris had announced that *Trieste and the Meaning of Nowhere* would be her last book, she did write others after its publication, including *A Writer's House in Wales*, in which she tells about her house in Wales and reflects on being Welsh; the science fiction novel, *Hav,* which was shortlisted for the 2007 Arthur C. Clarke Award; and *Contact!: A Book of Encounters,* a collection of short pieces with a strong focus on people. Joseph Cary traveled to Trieste to write a book about three writers who lived there in the early 20th century: James Joyce, Italo Svevo, and Umberto Saba; his book, which covers much more than these writers, is entitled *A Ghost in Trieste.* Domnica Radulescu's historical novel *Train to Trieste,* about life under the Ceausescu regime, may appeal to fiction readers.

Quindlen, Anna

Imagined London: A Tour of the World's Greatest Fictional City. Washington, DC: National Geographic, 2004. 162 pp. ISBN: 9780792265610

Journalist, novelist, and book lover Quindlen had read about London in books and finally visited the city in 1995 at the age of 42. *Imagined London* is based on numerous subsequent trips and celebrates not only the fictional city of Sherlock Holmes and Galsworthy's Forsythe Saga but also the very real city where authors such as Henry James, Daniel Defoe, and Evelyn Waugh lived and worked. Quindlen visits Holmes's apartment at 221-B Baker Street, Poet's Corner in Westminster Abbey, the dark back alleys of Dickens's novels, and the Knightsbridge of *Forever Amber*. The book is at once a celebration of the city that Quindlen calls "the capital of literature" and the literature that provided that stature.

Subjects: Authors; Books and Learning; Literary Lives; Quick Reads; Women Travelers

Places: England; London

Series: *National Geographic Directions*

Now Try: No bibliophile's list of books about London would be complete without reference to Helene Hanff's charming books, *84 Charing Cross Road* and *The Duchess of Bloomsbury Street;* the former follows Hanff's 20-year correspondence with a London bookseller, and the latter recounts her 1971 visit to the bookstore in London. Novelist V.S. Pritchett's *London Perceived* is a look at London in the early 1960s and contains a number of references to the great writers who lived in and wrote about the city. Most of the authors that Quindlen discusses in *Imagined London* are from previous centuries; two exceptions are Monica Ali, whose best-known novel, *Brick Lane,* is set in the heart of London's Bangladeshi community, and Zadie Smith, whose first novel, *White Teeth,* follows the lives of two wartime friends in London and was listed as one of *Time* magazine's 100 best English-language novels from 1923 to 2005.

Rodenbeck, Max

Cairo: The City Victorious. New York: Knopf, 1999. 300 pp. ISBN: 9780679446514

Rodenbeck, a western journalist who has spent most of his professional life in Cairo, paints a fascinating portrait of one of the world's oldest cities from the age of the Pharaohs to Mubarak's presidency. He details the changes to the city's layout over the centuries, explains the importance of Islam, considers the ongoing debate between the religious and the secular, and celebrates the spirit of the 15 million inhabitants of the city. Because of the author's personal knowledge of

Cairo, the book reads like an insider's guide to this chaotic metropolis, including visits to hashish dens, bazaars, slums, and small shops.

Subjects: African History; Islam; Urban Life

Places: Africa; Cairo; Egypt

Series: *Vintage Departures*

Now Try: *The Cairo Chronicles,* by Leslie Robin Lewis, describes the year and a half that the author (a young anthropologist) and her husband and children spent in Cairo and also manages to discuss some key ideas in anthropology. In the entertaining book, *Playing Cards in Cairo,* Hugh Miles, a freelance journalist, writes about moving to Cairo and falling in love with an Egyptian doctor whose female friends told him about their lives as Muslim women. Nobel Prize winner Naguib Mahfouz wrote a trilogy of novels about Cairo (*Palace Walk, Palace of Desire,* and *Sugar Street*) that follow the life on an Egyptian family and its patriarch from the 1919 Egyptian Revolution to the end of World War II. Alaa al Aswany's gripping novel, *The Yacoubian Building,* is also set in Cairo and explores the corruption and decadence of Egyptian society during the rule of Mubarak.

Appreciating Nature

What the author of a travel narrative finds and appreciates in a destination may be the plants and animals of that place, and titles in this section evoke the beauty of nature that the author finds at the destination. In some cases, the titles celebrate birds (as in William Fiennes's *The Snow Geese: A Story of Home*); in other cases, animals (as in Tim Flannery's *Chasing Kangaroos: A Continent, a Scientist, and a Search for the World's Most Extraordinary Creature*); and in yet other cases, plants (as in Mark Plotkin's *Tales of a Shaman's Apprentice: An Ethnobotanist Searches for New Medicines in the Amazon Rain Forest*). Regardless, these living things define the author's focus in the titles in this section.

Fans of the travel narratives in this category may also be interested in environmental and nature writing, such as Jonathan Weiner's *The Beak of the Finch: A Story of Evolution in Our Time* or Michael Pollan's *The Botany of Desire: A Plant's-Eye View of the World.* Novels from the point of view of animals (Richard Adams's *Watership Down* or Jack London's *White Fang*) or novels about individuals who work with animals (Dian Fossey's *Gorillas in the Mist* or Graham Billings's *Forbush and the Penguins*) may also be recommended.

Clare, Horatio

A Single Swallow: Following an Epic Journey from South Africa to South Wales. London: Chatto & Windus, 2009. 327 pp. ISBN: 9780701183127

Barn swallows migrate from South Africa to their breeding grounds in Wales and back annually, crossing 6,000 miles, two continents, and

14 countries in the process. Travel writer Horatio Clare followed their migration route on foot as well as by bus, train, and camel, doing his best to keep pace with the birds. Along the way, Clare picked up the local folklore: in South Africa, swallows are "the bird that brings the rain"; in Zambia, they are "the bird that never gets tired"; and in Niger, they are used in witchcraft. She also encountered a number of fascinating people: emerald smugglers, environmentalists, ornithologists, spies, soldiers, and slave laborers, among others. Clare's writing is expressive and somewhat ironic, the travels of the swallows being somewhat less troublesome (no visas, no encounters with police) than those of the author.

Subjects: Birds; Migrations; Swallows

Places: Africa; Algeria; Cameroon; England; France; Morocco; Namibia; Niger; Nigeria; Republic of the Congo; South Africa; Spain; Wales; Zambia

Awards: Dolman Best Travel Book Award, Shortlist, 2010

Now Try: Clare's first book, *Running for the Hills,* was a memoir about the causes of his parents' divorce and the harsh conditions of his childhood; it won a Somerset Maugham Award (given to a writer under the age of 35) in 2007. Alan Tennant's story of following the arctic peregrine falcon on its migratory path is told in *On the Wing: To the Edge of the Earth with the Peregrine Falcon,* which is annotated in this chapter. Another writer who uses birds as a way of looking at the lives of individuals in another culture is Stephen Bodio, whose *Eagle Dreams: Searching for Legends in Wild Mongolia,* also includes ample information on falconry. Michael McCarthy's *Say Goodbye to the Cuckoo* is a quieter and more inwardly focused book about another bird species; McCarthy looks at the reasons for the decline in the migration of birds and the implications that this decline might have for all of us. Fiction readers may also enjoy Nicholas Drayson's sweet, witty novel about a love triangle in Kenya, one that involves bird watching, *A Guide to the Birds of East Africa.*

Fiennes, William

The Snow Geese: A Story of Home. New York: Random House, 2002. 253 pp. ISBN: 9780375507298

Fiennes traveled by rental car, bus, and train from Texas to Baffin Island to follow the snow geese on their spring migration of several thousand miles north to their breeding grounds on the Arctic tundra. He provides detailed descriptions of the people he met and the places he visited, but mostly he muses on the meaning of home, the thrill of being alive and on the move, and our joy in returning home. As with so many books in this section, *The Snow Geese* is about much more than the living thing that is the book's ostensible focus.

Subjects: Birds; Migrations; Snow Geese

Places: Baffin Island; Canada; Texas

Awards: Hawthornden Prize, 2003; Samuel Johnson Prize, Shortlist, 2002

Now Try: Fiennes was recovering from a long illness when he found a copy of Paul Gallico's *The Snow Goose,* which he had read as a child and which inspired his own book. Gallico's short fairy tale is about a wounded goose that brings together a young girl and a deformed lighthouse keeper and may appeal to those who enjoyed *The Snow*

Geese. The strong sense that Fiennes has of home is also reflected in his memoir of growing up in a medieval moated castle in England, *The Music Room: A Memoir*. Readers who are interested in birds and their migratory habits may also enjoy two other books annotated in this section (Peter Matthiessen's *The Birds of Heaven: Travels with Cranes* and Alan Tennant's *On the Wing: To the Edge of the Earth with the Peregrine Falcon*) as well as Brian Harrington's *The Flight of the Red Knot: A Natural History Account of a Small Bird's Annual Migration from the Arctic Circle to the Tip of South America and Back*, about a lesser known bird's migratory habits.

Flannery, Tim

Chasing Kangaroos: A Continent, a Scientist, and a Search for the World's Most Extraordinary Creature. New York: Grove Press, 2007 [2004]. 258 pp. ISBN: 9780802118523 YA

Paleontologist Flannery wandered through the Australian outback on his motorcycle in search of kangaroos, which he calls "the most remarkable animals that every lived, and the truest expression of my country." Like the animal that is the focus of his book, Flannery hops (from subject to subject), discussing everything from the kangaroo's evolution, the Australian environment, the fate of the aborigines, and his own theories of extinction. The book is witty (sometimes a bit bawdy) and fascinating and clearly captures the author's exuberance for the 70-plus species of kangaroo, both those in existence and those that are extinct. The book is part road trip, part natural history, and part wake-up call to the environmental crisis that species like the kangaroo face.

Subjects: Animals; Endangered Species; Environment; Humor; Indigenous Peoples; Kangaroos; Motorcycles; Paleontology; Science

Places: Australia

Now Try: Flannery is best known for his book on global warming, *The Weather Makers*, but his anthology of excerpts from explorers of Australia, *The Explorers: Stories of Discovery and Adventure from the Australian Frontier*, may have more appeal to fans of the travel genre. In *Kangaroo Dreaming: An Australian Wildlife Odyssey*, Edward Kanze tells about a nine-month journey that he and his wife took through Australia in search of kangaroos and some of Australia's other unique animals. Margaret Mittelbach and Michael Crewdson describe a road trip in search of a different marsupial (presumably extinct) in *Carnivorous Nights: On the Trail of the Tasmanian Tiger*. Gwendolyn Gross's novel, *Field Guide* (about a woman who travels to Australia to study fruit bats and ends up searching for her lost professor), may also appeal to readers who enjoyed *Chasing Kangaroos*.

Kincaid, Jamaica

Among Flowers: A Walk in the Himalaya. Washington, DC: National Geographic, 2005. 191 pp. ISBN: 9780792265306

Kincaid's book about her trip with a botanist friend to gather seeds in Nepal is part travel narrative and part gardening book; her Vermont garden, where she intended to plant some of the seeds she gathered, was never far from her thoughts. Kincaid alternated between being ecstatic at the "unreal, magical, extraordinary" beauty of Nepal and being frightened by its rats, its leeches, and its Maoist rebels. Mostly, however, she was exuberant about seeing butterflies, yaks, 30-foot rhododendrons with peeling bark, or Tibetan rhubarb plants. The book does ramble and Kincaid is somewhat self-absorbed, but the descriptions of Nepal and its flora and fauna are wonderful.

Subjects: Animals; Plants; Quick Reads

Categories: The Beauty of the Place

Places: Nepal

Series: *National Geographic Directions*

Now Try: Readers interested in gardening may enjoy Kincaid's *My Garden,* which mixes botanical history, colonial history, and her own gardening experience. Kincaid also wrote the preface to *In the Land of the Blue Poppies: The Collected Plant-Hunting Writings of Frank Kingdon Ward,* a collection of essays about Ward's 22 expeditions to Tibet, China, and Southeast Asia in search of exotic plants. Less exotic but still of interest to those who enjoy gardening as well as travel is Richard Goodman's description of raising a vegetable garden in a small farming town in southern France, the charming *French Dirt: The Story of a Garden in the South of France,* and Joan Marble's *Notes from an Italian Garden,* which recounts her experiences gardening in the central Italian town of Canale.

Mahler, Richard

The Jaguar's Shadow: Searching for a Mythic Cat. New Haven, CT: Yale University Press, 2009. 359 pp. ISBN: 9780300122251

After he read a newspaper account of a jaguar sighting in New Mexico, Mahler, a journalist and tour guide, spent 10 years searching for the elusive big cat, and this book details his travels to Central and South America on that quest. He discusses a wide range of topics related to the jaguar, including their diminishing range and numbers, the history of the species as revealed through its fossil records, the folk tales of the beast as told by native peoples, and attempts to save the species. Mahler tells his tale in a fast-moving style, and the book serves as a reminder of the fragile situation of the jaguar in particular or large predator cats in general.

Subjects: Animals; Endangered Species; Folklore; Indigenous Peoples; Jaguars

Places: Belize; Mexico; Panama

Now Try: Alan Rabinowitz is a field biologist who writes about his scientific and personal experiences in Belize, where he studied jaguars, in *Jaguar: Struggle and Triumph in the Jungles of Belize.* Rabinowitz's *Jaguar: One Man's Struggle To Establish The World's First Jaguar Preserve* documents his attempts to create a sanctuary for jaguars in Belize. Like Mahler, Barry Lopez draws upon science and myth in his book about a different predator (the wolf) and its relationship to humans, *Of Wolves and Men.* Philip Caputo mixes travel narrative and scientific speculation in his examination of another large predator cat in *Ghosts of Tsavo: Stalking the Mystery Lions of East Africa*, and John Henry Patterson's classic *The Man-eaters of Tsavo* treats the same subject. John Vaillant's book, *The Tiger: A True Story of Vengeance and Survival* (a 2011 ALA Notable Book), tells the story of yet another predator cat, in this case, a man-eating Siberian tiger in Russia's Primorye province and the efforts to trap it.

Matthiessen, Peter

The Birds of Heaven: Travels with Cranes. New York: North Point Press, 2001. 349 pp. ISBN: 9780374199449 YA

This book details Matthiessen's travels through more than a dozen countries in search of the fifteen species of migrating crane, eleven of which are on the verge of extinction, as well as the efforts of a small group of dedicated individuals trying to protect them. Matthiessen became a Buddhist priest following a 1973 expedition to the Himalayas, and as might be expected from a Buddhist priest writing about a bird that is considered sacred by many cultures, the quest described in *The Birds of Heaven* is as much spiritual as it is scientific. The author describes the political and social dynamics of the places he visited and reminds the reader of the fragile status of the cranes, who depend on the vanishing wetlands for breeding. His writing conveys the thrill the author feels at every crane sighting and the curiosity and enthusiasm that he still maintains for his subject, and does so in what one reviewer described as "a serendipitous prose as elegant as the stately birds that inspire him."

Subjects: Birds; Cranes; Endangered Species; Environment; Migrations; Spirituality; Wetlands

Categories: Endangered Places

Places: Australia; Bhutan; China; India; Japan; Mongolia; Russia; South Africa; South Korea; Tibet

Awards: *New York Times* Notable Book, 2002

Now Try: Canadian ornithologist Janice M. Hughes also explores the vulnerable state of cranes and the efforts being taken to preserve them in *Cranes: A Natural History of a Bird in Crisis*. Dayton Hyde's *Sandy: The Sandhill Crane Who Joined Our Family* is a more personal story about one man's efforts to save an individual bird. Readers interested in travels in search of rare birds may enjoy Luke Dempsey's gentle and amusing book, *A Supremely Bad Idea: Three Mad Birders and Their Quest to See It All*. Readers looking for books about attempts to save endangered birds should try Bruce Barcott's *The Last Flight of the Scarlet Macaw: One Woman's Fight to Save the World's Most Beautiful Bird*, about an American woman who became the "Jane Goodall of Belize."

Padel, Ruth

Tigers in Red Weather: A Quest for the Last Wild Tigers. New York: Walker & Co., 2006 [2005]. 432 pp. ISBN: 9780802715449

Padel, a poet and great-great-granddaughter of Charles Darwin, describes her two years of travel to more than a dozen countries in search of the elusive wild tiger. She writes about meeting the scientists and conservationists who are trying to protect the remaining 5,000 tigers in the wild from the poaching, trade, and deforestation that threaten their existence. Padel's book addresses the problems of endangered species in general and includes many reflections on her personal life, particularly the end of her long-term relationship. Padel's evocative, poetic voice comes through clearly in this combination of travel narrative, natural history, and memoir that is, unfortunately, less optimistic about the future of its subject than are most of the titles in this category.

Subjects: Animals; Endangered Species; Memoirs; Tigers; Women Travelers

Categories: Discovering One's Self

Places: Bangladesh; Bhutan; Burma; Cambodia; China; India; Indonesia; Laos; Malaysia; Nepal; North Korea; Russia; South Korea; Thailand; Tibet; Vietnam

Awards: Dolman Best Travel Book Award, Shortlist, 2006

Now Try: Tigers have been a favorite subject of travel writers. Travel narrative icon Peter Matthiessen's *Tigers in the Snow* recounts his travels to Russia and Manchuria in search of the Siberian tiger and conveys both anger at the tiger's current predicament and hope embodied in a number of successful conservation efforts. Richard Ives traveled to India, Nepal, and Southeast Asia and writes of his encounters with both friends and enemies of the tiger in *Of Tigers and Men: Entering the Age of Extinction*. Sy Montgomery focuses on the tigers and the people who live in a single swamp area between India and Bangladesh in *Spell of the Tiger: The Man-Eaters of Sundarbans*. John Vaillant's book, *The Tiger: A True Story of Vengeance and Survival* (a 2011 ALA Notable Book), tells the gripping story of a man-eating Siberian tiger in Russia's Primorye province and the efforts to trap it. Peter Matthiessen's *The Snow Leopard* (annotated in this chapter, under "Classics") recounts his 1973 quest for another elusive, almost mythical predator.

Plotkin, Mark

Tales of a Shaman's Apprentice: An Ethnobotanist Searches for New Medicines in the Amazon Rain Forest. New York: Viking, 1993. 318 pp. ISBN: 9780670831371 [Y][A]

Plotkin traveled to the northeast Amazon basin to track the shamans whose extensive knowledge of medicinal plants may help cure some of today's diseases, just as quinine (derived from a tree in the Amazon rain forest) cured malaria. Plotkin is a Harvard ethnobotanist, and the book is a mix of scientific details and anecdotes about the native people the author encountered and obviously had great compassion for. Unfortunately, Plotkin's adventure is overshadowed by the sad recognition that the rain forest and its cornucopia of medicinal plants, as well as the native people whose oral traditions pass on their knowledge of the plants' powers, are rapidly disappearing. Luckily, the author does suggest approaches for preserving the rain forests and their inhabitants.

Subjects: Folklore; Indigenous People; Medicine; Plants; Religion; Rivers

Categories: Endangered Places; Landscapes and People

Places: Amazon River; Brazil; French Guiana; Guyana; Suriname; Venezuela

Now Try: Plotkin's book was the basis for a documentary film, *The Shaman's Apprentice*, which is narrated by Susan Sarandon. Plotkin expands on this work in *Medicine Quest: In Search of Nature's Healing Secrets*, which outlines more uses of indigenous plants and animals in treating diseases. Wade Davis is another Harvard ethnobotanist who journeys to the Amazon in search of the native uses of plants, and he writes about his experiences in *One River*. Mark Honigsbaum's excellent *The Fever Trail: In Search of the Cure for Malaria* (annotated in the "Travel Adventure" chapter) describes the 19th-century search for quinine, reputed to be a cure for malaria, in the Amazon region and the Andes. Sy Montgomery writes about traveling the Amazon in search of a different species (the pink dolphin) in her book, *Journey of the Pink Dolphins: An Amazon Quest*.

Pyle, Robert Michael

Mariposa Road: The First Butterfly Big Year. Boston: Houghton Mifflin Harcourt, 2010. 558 pp. ISBN: 978 0618945399

Pyle crisscrossed the United States (including Alaska and Hawaii) with the goal of seeing 500 of the 800 American species of butterfly in a single year, and his story is as much about the places and people he encountered as it is about the butterflies he chased. Kyle's approach was decidedly low tech (a butterfly net made from a cottonwood limb, 35-year-old binoculars) and his account, while enthusiastic, does not gloss over the difficulties of his journey: the insect bites, the car repairs, the minor injuries, his wife's battle with cancer. Kyle also addresses global warming, fire, pollution, pesticides, human encroachment, and other threats to the butterflies' existence. The resulting book is witty, accessible, and informative.

Subjects: Butterflies; Environment; Global Warming; Humor; Spouses

Places: Alabama; Alaska; Arizona; California; Colorado; Florida; Georgia; Hawaii; Illinois; Kentucky; Louisiana; Maine; Mississippi; Montana; Nevada; New Mexico; Oregon; Tennessee; Texas; Washington; Wisconsin

Now Try: Pyle got much of his inspiration for the butterfly "big year" from Kenn Kaufman, whose entertaining and informative *Kingbird Highway: The Biggest Year in the Life of an Extreme Birder* tells about the "big year" he spent as a 19-year-old attempting to spot as many birds as possible. Lynn E. Barber describes a woman's "big year" in the traditionally male-dominated arena of bird spotting in *Extreme Birder: One Woman's Big Year*. Pyle's earlier book, *Chasing Monarchs: Migrating with the Butterflies of Passage*, covers his attempts to follow individual butterflies on the migratory paths from the northern United States to California and Mexico. Butterfly lovers may also be interested in Fiona Mountain's novel, *Lady of the Butterflies*, which is based on 17th-century English lepidopterist Lady Eleanor Glanville, as well as Kurt Johnson's delightful book about writer Vladimir Nabokov's studies of butterflies, *Nabokov's Blues: The Scientific Odyssey of a Literary Genius*.

Quammen, David

Monster of God: The Man-Eating Predator in the Jungles of History and the Mind. New York: W.W. Norton, 2003. 513pp. ISBN: 9780393051407

Nature writer Quammen traveled to the homes of four "alpha predators" (the lions of the Gir forest in India, the saltwater crocodiles of Northern Australia, the brown bears of the Carpathian Mountains in Romania, and the Siberian tigers of eastern Russia) to explore why we need man-eating animals and what we would lose with their extinction. The book looks at both the animals and the lives of the impoverished human communities that live near or among them and meanders through topics that include history, psychology, philosophy, religion, and ecology (everything from *Beowulf* to *Aliens*). Quammen examines difficult questions without oversimplifying the issues and provides a wealth of detail, background information, colorful anecdotes, and fascinating characters. Not surprisingly, because of this richness of information, *Monster of God* is anything but a quick and easy read.

Subjects: Animals; Bears; Biology; Crocodiles; Environment; Endangered Species; Folklore; Jungles; Lions; Religion; Tigers

Categories: Landscapes and People

Places: Australia; India; Romania; Russia

Awards: ALA Notable Books, 2004; *New York Times* Notable Book, 2003

Now Try: Quammen has written a number of other richly detailed, thought-provoking books about the threatened or real extinction of animal species, including *The Song of the Dodo: Island Biogeography in an Age of Extinction* (annotated in this chapter) and *The Flight of the Iguana: A Sidelong View of Science and Nature*. David Baron explores the complex relationship between humans and another predator, the mountain lion, in *The Beast in the Garden: The True Story of a Predator's Deadly Return to Suburban America.* William Stolzenburg's *Where the Wild Things Were: Life, Death, and Ecological Wreckage in a Land of Vanishing Predators* argues, like *Monster of God*, that predators have an important role in the preservation of the ecological balance. Werner Herzog's documentary film, *Grizzly Man*, may also appeal to readers who are fascinated with the darker side of nature that predators represent.

Quammen, David

The Song of the Dodo: Island Biogeography in an Age of Extinction. New York: Scribner, 1996. 702 pp. ISBN: 9780684800837

Quammen traveled extensively to research this book on island biogeography, which studies how various species are distributed among the world's islands and island-like spaces and which, according to Quammen, yields important insights into the origin and extinction of these species. The details of these travels to Bali (to follow in the footsteps of Alfred Russel Wallace, who co-discovered evolution via natural selection with Darwin), to Guam (to better understand why its birds have been going extinct), and to Madagascar (to learn why it has lost several of its species, including the pygmy hippopotamus) are mixed with a synthesis of a wide range of scientific disciplines to produce a layman's guide to the small island ecosystems that are more prone to creating new species but also more prone to losing them. ("Islands are where species go to die," according to Quammen.) In spite of his focus on extinction and environmental decay, however, *The Song of the Dodo* urges the reader not to abandon hope and is therefore somewhat more optimistic than the author's later work, *Monster of God*.

Subjects: Animals; Endangered Species; Environment; Extinctions; Islands

Categories: Endangered Places

Places: Bali; Brazil; Galapagos; Guam; Hawaii; Komodo; Madagascar; Mauritius; New Guinea; Tasmania

Now Try: Quammen's biography of Charles Darwin, *The Reluctant Mr. Darwin: An Intimate Portrait of Charles Darwin and the Making of His Theory of Evolution*, explores many of the themes discussed in *The Song of the Dodo*, particularly the relationship between Darwin and Alfred Russel Wallace. Like *The Song of the Dodo*, Jared Diamond's *Collapse: How Societies Choose to Fail or Succeed* and Peter Tyson's *The Eighth Continent: Life, Death, and Discovery in the Lost World of Madagascar* (annotated in this chapter) also end on optimistic notes, even though the authors have ample reason to be anything but hopeful. Jonathan Weiner's fascinating book, *The Beak of the Finch: A Story of Evolution in Our Time*, may also be of interest; it follows husband and wife scientists who study the evolution of the beaks of finches on the Galapagos Islands. *The Hungry Tide*, a novel by Amitav Ghosh, explores the conflicts between nature and civilization on an island in the Bay of Bengal. For readers who want to tackle a far more technical work on biogeography, the book to start with is Robert H. MacArthur and Edward O. Wilson's seminal work, *The Theory of Island Biogeography*.

Sacks, Oliver

Oaxaca Journal. Washington, DC: National Geographic, 2002. 159 pp. ISBN: 9780792265214

The noted neurologist writes here about his ten-day trip to southern Mexico in search of ferns. He traveled with other members of the American Fern Society, and their destination was a Mexican state with more species of fern than in all the United States. Although Sacks provides a good bit of information about ferns (that they are older than the dinosaurs, for example), the focus of his journal becomes more than the plants, and while he does convey the excitement one would expect of a lifelong pteridologist, he is also shocked by the poverty he finds in Mexico and thrilled by the history he discovers. In the end, the ferns almost take second stage to the place itself; as Sacks states at the close of the book, "This has turned out to be a visit to a very other culture and place, a visit, in a profound sense, to another time."

Subjects: American History; Ferns; Plants; Poverty; Quick Reads

Places: Mexico

Categories: Landscapes and People

Awards: *New York Times* Notable Book, 2002

Now Try: Sacks is a prolific writer, and any of his many titles would likely please readers who enjoyed *Oaxaca Journal*. Of particular interest to fans of the travel genre is his book, *The Island of the Colorblind*, which chronicles his trip to the Micronesian island of Pingelap to study a community of people with congenital colorblindness and his trip to Guam to investigate a puzzling neurodegenerative disease. Micro-histories, such as Mark Pendergrast's *Uncommon Grounds: The History of Coffee and How It Transformed Our World* and Mark Kurlansky's *Salt: A World History*, may also appeal. Like *Oaxaca Journal*, their authors digress from their ostensible subject material to consider a wider range of topics. For readers more interested in a culinary journey, Susana Trilling's *Seasons of My Heart: A Culinary Journey through Oaxaca, Mexico* is a good option; Trilling and her husband are former New Yorkers living in Oaxaca.

Schooler, Lynn

The Blue Bear: A True Story of Friendship, Tragedy, and Survival in the Alaskan Wilderness. New York: Ecco, 2002. 272 pp. ISBN: 9780066210858 YA

Schooler is an Alaskan guide who was recovering from the brutal death of the woman he loved when he met Japanese photographer Michio Hoshino. The book describes both their travels through remote areas of Alaska on a quest to photograph the elusive "blue" or glacier bear and their growing friendship, which allowed Schooler to deal with the pain of his losses. The book evokes the beauty of the Alaskan landscape and includes a number of reflections on the author's life and the nature of friendship. The search for the glacier bear serves as an allegory, of course, and much of the writing is philosophical, reflective, and even poetic.

Subjects: Animals; Bears; Friendships; Memoirs; Nature

Categories: The Beauty of the Place; Healing Odysseys

Places: Alaska

Now Try: Schooler's *Walking Home: A Traveler in the Alaskan Wilderness, a Journey into the Human Heart* (annotated under "Healing Odysseys") tells of his 2007 solo journey through Alaska and, as does *The Blue Bear*, deals with issues of loss and transition. Schooler also wrote the foreword to *Hoshino's Alaska*, a book of photographs by his late friend. For another book set in Glacier Bay, Alaska, which involves another man's friendship with photographer Michio Hoshino, readers can turn to Kim Heacox's *The Only Kayak: A Journey into the Heart of Alaska*. James Campbell's *The Final Frontiersman: Heimo Korth and His Family, Alone in Alaska's Arctic Wilderness* tells the very personal story of a man who moved to Alaska in the mid-1970s and whose family lives in isolation 130 miles north of the Arctic Circle; the book's treatment of that isolated life and the tragedies faced by the family may appeal to readers who enjoyed *The Blue Bear*. Sam Keith's *One Man's Wilderness: An Alaskan Odyssey* is based on the journals and photographs of Richard Proenneke, who moved to the Alaskan woods in the 1960s. While Jonathan Johnson's moving *Hannah and the Mountain: Notes toward* *a Wilderness Fatherhood* takes place in Idaho, it deals with many of the same themes as does *The Blue Bear*: nature and loss, in Johnson's case, his wife's traumatic miscarriages.

Tennant, Alan

On the Wing: To the Edge of the Earth with the Peregrine Falcon. New York: Alfred A. Knopf, 2004. 304 pp. ISBN: 9780375415517

Tennant logged thousands of miles as he followed the arctic peregrine falcon in a rattletrap Cessna with his pilot, a World War II veteran, from the Texas barrier islands to the Arctic and then back south, through Mexico, Belize, and into the Caribbean. His immediate purpose was to determine the migratory path of these birds and to understand the impact of environmental pesticides on their future survival, but his story is also an exciting adventure, as Tennant and his pilot try to keep their broken-down plane in the air, impersonate state troopers, steal U.S. Army gear, and sneak across international borders. Woven into this action are thoughts about the science of peregrine falcons, pesticides, animal migration, our common origin with birds and other animals, and unless things change, our common uncertain future.

Subjects: Birds; Endangered Species; Environment; Falcons; Migrations

Places: Alaska; Belize; Canada; Mexico; Texas; Wyoming

Awards: New York *Times* Notable Book, 2004

Now Try: Readers who want to know more about peregrine falcons will likely enjoy J. A. Baker's *The Peregrine,* in which the author tracked a pair of peregrines over a single winter in England. Those looking for another title that focuses on the connections between humans and animals should turn to David Abram's *Becoming Animal: An Earthly Cosmology*. The stunningly beautiful Jacques Perrin documentary, *Winged Migration,* can also be recommended to those who are interested in birds in general and in their migratory behavior in particular.

Tyson, Peter

The Eighth Continent: Life, Death, and Discovery in the Lost World of Madagascar. New York: William Morrow, 2000. 374 pp. ISBN: 9780380975778

The world's fourth-largest island is the subject of Tyson's book, which profiles four scientists who were studying the unique island life (80 percent of its plants grow only on Madagascar) before that life disappears. The scientists' work took place in the face of the island's growing human population and concomitant loss of the habitats and diversity of its plants and animals. Tyson, a science journalist, mixes scientific ideas with a history of the island and a personal travelogue and makes the reader feel like a part of the scientific teams as they make their discoveries. He writes with a sense of urgency in the face of an ecological disaster, but also with a sense of guarded optimism.

Subjects: Animals; Endangered Species; Environment; Islands; Plants

Categories: Endangered Places

Places: Madagascar

Now Try: The island of Madagascar is well represented in the travel and natural history literatures. Travel writer Dervla Murphy writes about a trip to Madagascar with her daughter and the gentle, polite people who lived there in *Muddling through in Madagascar*. Mark Eveleigh searches for a mysterious tribe of white pygmies on the island in *Maverick in Madagascar*, and a lemur plantation run by an aristocratic French family is the subject of *Lords and Lemurs: Mad Scientists, Kings With Spears, and the Survival of Diversity in Madagascar* by primatologist Alison Jolly. *The Aye-Aye and I: A Rescue Journey to Save One of the World's Most Intriguing Creatures from Extinction* by the prolific author/naturalist Gerald Durrell describes an expedition to film and capture the rare primate. Finally, more adventurous readers may wish to try William Burroughs's very short apocalyptic novel *Ghost of a Chance*, which tells the story of a pirate captain who set up a utopian colony on 18th-century Madagascar dedicated to protecting the indigenous landscape and lemur population.

Watt, Alison

The Last Island: A Naturalist's Sojourn on Triangle Island. Madeira Park, BC: Harbour Pub., 2002. 192 pp. ISBN: 9781550172966

At 23, Watt made her first trip to Triangle Island, a wildlife sanctuary off the coast of British Columbia, to study puffins and other seabirds. Her mentor at the time was the young biologist Anne Vallée, who died on the island two years after Watt's visit. Written in diary format, *The Last Island* follows Watt when, 16 years later, she returned to Triangle Island to investigate a mysterious decline in the puffin population. With memories of that summer with Vallée constantly with her, Watt mixes native legends, evolutionary theory, scientific knowledge, and an appreciation for nature's delicate balance to recreate the sounds, sights, and textures of the island as well as share her thoughts on friendship and the human spirit.

Subjects: Birds; Diaries; Environment; Friendships; Island; Quick Reads; Scientists; Women Travelers

Places: British Columbia

Awards: Edna Staebler Award, 2003

Now Try: Watt is also a poet, and her first book of poetry, *Circadia*, attempts to capture the lyricism in natural processes such as the weather and the tides. Renée Askins waged a 15-year campaign to restore wolves to Yellowstone National Park, and her inspiring memoir, *Shadow Mountain: A Memoir of Wolves, a Woman, and the Wild*, includes her thoughts about other topics, including her feelings for a friend and a sister who died of cancer. Ann Armbrecht's beautiful memoir *Thin Places: A Pilgrimage Home* is the story of another scientist's inner journey; Armbrecht was an anthropologist living on and off in a small village in Nepal while her marriage in the United States was deteriorating.

Whitty, Julia

Deep Blue Home: An Intimate Ecology of Our Wild Ocean. Boston: Houghton Mifflin Harcourt, 2010. 246 pp. ISBN: 9780618119813

A documentary filmmaker and diver, Whitty writes about traveling the oceans and their shores from the Sea of Cortez to Newfoundland to Antarctica. Her thesis is that the several oceans make up a single "World Ocean" connected by a powerful current that encircles the Earth. She sees that single ocean as both controlling and being controlled by the Earth's climate. The book is a mix of facts, myths, and legends about this "World Ocean" and its ecology. Based on her 30-plus years of observations of whales, birds, dolphins, and other creatures, Whitty warns that our own existence is closely tied to the ecological balance of the ocean and that we ignore its health at our peril.

Subjects: Animals; Environment; Folklore; Mythologies; Oceans; Women Travelers

Categories: Endangered Places

Places: Antarctica; Arctic Region; Galapagos; Mexico; Newfoundland; Sea of Cortez

Now Try: Whitty's books, which include *The Fragile Edge: Diving and Other Adventures in the South Pacific* and a short story collection, *A Tortoise for the Queen of Tonga*, have been described as the "underwater equivalent of an African big-game safari." In his book, *Portrait of the Gulf Stream: In Praise of Currents*, novelist Erik Orsenna traveled to meet scientists and explore many of the themes that Whitty discusses, although his focus is on the Gulf Stream. In spite of the fact that the following titles are more science and less travel narrative, readers interested in the world's oceans and their impact on our future will be well advised to read *The World Is Blue: How Our Fate and the Ocean's Are One*, written by Sylvia Earle, National Geographic's first Explorer in Residence; Susan Casey's *The Wave: In Pursuit of the Rogues, Freaks and Giants of the Ocean* (annotated in the "Quests" chapter); Rachel Carson's classic *The Sea Around Us*; Carl Safina's *Song for the Blue Ocean: Encounters Along the World's Coasts and Beneath the Seas*; Richard Ellis's *The Empty Ocean*; and view the BBC documentary, *The Blue Planet: Seas of Life*.

Endangered Places

The titles in the last section of this chapter, "Endangered Places," focus on what we might call the lost beauty of the destination, on the impending threats to the destination and its ecology. The changes may threaten the environment of the place (for example, the Aral Sea in Tom Bissell's *Chasing the Sea: Lost Among the Ghosts of Empire in Central Asia*) and or they may impact people (as in David Metcalfe's *Out of Steppe: The Lost Peoples of Central Asia*), but there is a strong sense of lost beauty of place in these titles.

Several works of fiction have endangered places as their theme (Edward Abbey's *The Monkey Wrench Gang*, T.C. Boyle's *When the Killing's Done*, or Norman MacLean's *A River Runs through It*), and science fiction is rich with ecologically focused novels (Frank Herbert's *Dune* series or Harry Harrison's *Make Room! Make Room!*). These titles and nonfiction in genres such as environmental or nature writing (Rachel Carson's *Silent Spring* or Aldo Leopold's *A Sand County Almanac: And Sketches Here and There*) may also appeal to readers who have enjoyed the books in the "Endangered Places" category.

Bissell, Tom

Chasing the Sea: Lost Among the Ghosts of Empire in Central Asia. New York: Pantheon Books, 2003. 388 pp. ISBN: 9780375421303

Bissell, who served briefly as a Peace Corps volunteer in Uzbekistan, returned to investigate the rapidly disappearing Aral Sea, half of which lies in that country. The sea was once as large as Lake Michigan but has lost most of its water and will likely disappear by the middle of the 2010s, leaving nothing but desert. Bissell discusses the ecological disaster, its causes, and its impact on the people of Uzbekistan. He and his interpreter Rustam then set out across the country, discussing the history and culture of the region as well as the impact of the Soviets. The book is brutally funny in parts and somewhat depressing toward the end, and it is hard to shake the notion that the Aral Sea may be the first of many ecological disasters to come.

Subjects: Asian History; Conservation; Environment; European History; Friendships; Humor; Seas

Places: Aral Sea; Uzbekistan

Series: *Vintage Departures*

Now Try: For further details about the ecological disaster of the Aral Sea, readers should consult Robert W. Ferguson's *The Devil and the Disappearing Sea: A True Story about the Aral Sea Catastrophe*. A central chapter of Christopher Robbins's travelogue, *Apples Are From Kazakhstan: The Land That Disappeared* (annotated in this section), deals with the shrinking of the Aral Sea. Bissell's book of short stories, *God Lives in St. Petersburg: and Other Stories*, fictionalizes his experiences in Central Asia and captures what one reviewer called "the disorientation and recklessness of life overseas."

Crossette, Barbara

So Close to Heaven: The Vanishing Buddhist Kingdoms of the Himalayas. New York: A.A. Knopf, 1995. 297 pp. ISBN: 9780679418276

Former *New York Times* correspondent Crossette traveled to Bhutan and neighboring areas to explore the religious culture of Tibetan Buddhism, which the author fears is under threat from encroaching modernity. Though Buddhism is the focus of the book, Crossette also considers the politics and societies of the areas she visited. The author interviewed a range of individuals, from the king of Bhutan to ordinary citizens, and provides a sympathetic look at what the author calls "the only laboratory left to us at the end of the 20th century."

Subjects: Buddhism; Religion; Women Travelers

Categories: Landscapes and People

Places: Bhutan; India; Nepal

Series: *Vintage Departures*

Now Try: A number of excellent travel narratives take place in Bhutan. *Beyond the Sky and the Earth: A Journey into Bhutan* is the beautifully written story of author Jamie Zeppa's two years as a teacher in Bhutan. *Buttertea at Sunrise: A Year in the Bhutan Himalaya* by Britta Das tells about the author's time in Bhutan teaching physiotherapy to medical workers there. Katie Hickman's older *Dreams of the Peaceful Dragon: A Journey Through Bhutan* relates her travels in the remote eastern part of the country. Alexandra David-Néel, whose book *My Journey to Lhasa* is annotated in the "Travel Adventure" chapter, was another woman who traveled in the Himalayas; *The Secret Lives of Alexandra David-Neel: A Biography of the Explorer of Tibet and Its Forbidden Practices,* by Barbara and Michael Foster, is a particularly good biography of her. Readers interested in learning more about Buddhism have a number of good titles, including *The Heart of the Buddha's Teaching* by Thich Nhat Hanh, an introduction to the core teachings; *Buddha* by Karen Armstrong, a biography written for the general audience; and Bhante Henepola Gunaratana's *Mindfulness in Plain English,* a very practical guide to meditation.

Ehrlich, Gretel

The Future of Ice: A Journey into Cold. New York: Pantheon Books, 2004. 200 pp. ISBN: 9780375422515

Ehrlich backpacked in the Chilean Andes, spent the winter in a cabin in Wyoming, and sailed on a research ship in Greenland as she explored the impact of global warming on our planet's winter season and considered whether "the end of winter might be the end of life." Her writing is passionate and poetic, filled with beautiful imagery, and captures her personal relationship with the cold. The book is often frightening, as the author considers the implications of the planet's "deseasoning" and tries to alert us to what might be lost if there were no winter.

Subjects: Environment; Global Warming; Quick Reads; Women Travelers

Places: Arctic Region; Chile; Greenland

Now Try: Ehrlich has written a number of books in which she contemplates the impact of places on people. These include *The Solace of Open Spaces,* where she finds peace of mind on a farm in Wyoming, and *In the Empire of Ice: Encounters in a Changing Landscape,* where she describes the people who live on the

Arctic Ocean. Although he is less pointed that Ehrlich, Edwin Way Teale also explores the winter and its impact on our lives in *Wandering Through Winter: A Naturalist's Record of a 20,000-Mile Journey Through the North American Winter* (annotated in the "Classics" section of this chapter). For readers interested in man's impact on the earth's climate, Elizabeth Kolbert's *Field Notes from a Catastrophe: Man, Nature, and Climate Change* may be of interest; it is a more straightforward, less poetic consideration of the issues than Ehrlich. Bill Streever traveled in the Arctic region and speculates on the nature of cold and its importance to the planet in *Cold: Adventures in the World's Frozen Places*. Bill McKibben, whom the Boston *Globe* called "probably the nation's leading environmentalist," and his first book, *The End of Nature*, is regarded as the first book for a general audience that warns of climate change. McKibben's latest book, *Eaarth: Making a Life on a Tough New Planet*, argues that we are already seeing the effects of climate change.

Kaplan, Robert D.

The Ends of the Earth: From Togo to Turkmenistan, from Iran to Cambodia, a Journey to the Frontiers of Anarchy. New York: Vintage, 1997 [1996]. 476 pp. ISBN: 9780679751236

Kaplan travels around the world to explore the question of why some countries cope with the challenges of population growth and resource depletion while others fail so miserably. His discussions with government officials, fellow travelers, and ordinary people present a harrowing report of ecological disaster, civil wars, and flight to the cities. His pessimistic message is that these crises may force states to become more authoritarian or to capitulate to religious fundamentalists; as he notes in Sierra Leone, "The future here could be sadder than the present." *The Ends of the Earth* is a gravely important travel narrative with only glimmers of hope that some cultures and traditions will support stabilizing and regenerative efforts.

Subjects: African History; Asian History; Environment; Politics

Places: Africa; Cambodia; China; Egypt; India; Iran; Pakistan; Sierra Leone; Thailand; Togo; Turkey; Turkmenistan; Uzbekistan

Series: *Vintage Departures*

Now Try: Many of Kaplan's books reach pessimistic conclusions about the areas to which he traveled. These include *Surrender or Starve: Travels in Ethiopia, Sudan, Somalia, and Eritrea*, which examines the ethnic, religious, and class conflicts in those countries, and *Monsoon: The Indian Ocean and the Future of American Power*, which looks at the changes taking place in the countries that border the Indian Ocean. While Paul Collier's *The Bottom Billion: Why the Poorest Countries Are Failing and What Can Be Done About It* is not a travel narrative, it does explore many of the issues that Kaplan explores in *The Ends of the Earth* and presents a slightly more optimistic outlook. Environmental writer Eugene Linden's *The Ragged Edge of the World* is more focused on the impact of commerce and globalism on animal habitats and indigenous people in Vietnam, New Guinea, Borneo, and sub-Saharan Africa.

Kluge, P. F.

The Edge of Paradise: America in Micronesia. New York: Random House, 1991. 244 pp. ISBN: 9780394581781

Kluge was a Peace Corps volunteer in Micronesia in the late 1960s, and when his friend (the second president of Palau) died of an apparent suicide, he returned to hunt for clues about his friend's death and to gain a better understanding of these islands. He starkly depicts the crumbling infrastructure and burdensome debt that hinder the development of these islands and shows the impact of America's presence in an undeveloped part of the world. While Kluge captures the complicated nature of the relationship between the United States without simplistically labeling the villains and the victims, in the end, he suggests that there is no way that "a big place can touch a little one without harming it."

Subjects: Colonialism; Healing Odysseys; Islands

Places: Micronesia; Palau

Now Try: In *Surviving Paradise: One Year on a Disappearing Island,* Peter Rudiak-Gould recounts his year as a teacher on one of the Marshall Islands, a part of Micronesia. Kluge himself has written several novels, including *Biggest Elvis,* which is set in the Philippines near the U.S. naval base of Subic Bay. Oliver Sacks's fascinating book, *The Island of the Colorblind,* is set on two islands in Micronesia: Guam, where Sacks studied a mysterious neurodegenerative disease, and Pingelap, where he found a congenital colorblindness that affected more than 5 percent of the population. Sacks also speculates on a wide range of issues, including the importance of islands and the genesis of disease. Francisco Goldman's political true crime title, *The Art of Political Murder: Who Killed the Bishop,* may also appeal with its story of the murder of Guatemala's leading human rights activist, Bishop Juan Gerardi.

Laurance, William

Stinging Trees and Wait-a-Whiles: Confessions of a Rainforest Biologist. Chicago: University of Chicago Press, 2000. 196 pp. ISBN: 9780226468969

Laurance is a research scientist at the Smithsonian Institute who spent 18 months doing field work in northern Australia in the mid-1980s. The rain forest he found there was beginning to disappear, and the book chronicles what happened to the various species whose habitats were disrupted by loggers and farmers. An accessible and engaging book, *Stinging Trees and Wait-a-Whiles* is sometimes amusing (when describing the eccentricities of field work) and sometimes very serious (when warning about environmental destruction).

Subjects: Animals; Endangered Species; Environment; Landscape; Quick Reads; Scientists

Categories: Appreciating Nature

Places: Australia

Now Try: Tim Flannery's *Throwim Way Leg* describes the author's 15 expeditions to New Guinea, and like *Stinging Trees and Wait-a-Whiles,* captures the more absurd side of field research. By contrast, *A Naturalist and Other Beasts: Tales from a Life in the Field* by George Schaller, of the Wildlife Conservation Society, focuses more on the daily lives of the exotic animals studied by the author. Fiction readers may also enjoy novels about field work, including Ann Patchett's *State of Wonder*, about a scientist who travels to the Amazonian jungle to find the remains of a colleague who died there under mysterious circumstances, and Kira Salak's *White Mary*, about a young female reporter who travels to Papua New Guinea to find a Pulitzer-winning writer who is presumed to be dead but who she thinks may still be alive.

Lewis, Norman

A Goddess in the Stones: Travels in India. New York: H. Holt, 1992 [1991]. 322 pp. ISBN: 9780805019599.

Lewis had an interest in primitive cultures that were threatened by progress, and in 1990, he traveled to India to learn about the nation's tribal people, who had resisted the government's efforts to modernize them but were endangered due to the clearing of their jungle forests. In the eastern state of Orissa, Lewis found villages living by ancient traditions that stood in contrast to the economic miracle of modern India, but in other parts of India, he found more disturbing stories that stood in contrast to the joy and freedom of the tribal people: caste wars in the northwest state of Bihar; people dying in the streets of Calcutta; dowry killings; and infanticides. Lewis writes with a keen eye for detail and a sense of sadness at the impending losses these tribal people will suffer as the modern world continues to encroach.

Subjects: Culture Clash; Hinduism; Indigenous Peoples; Jungles; Modernization

Places: India

Awards: Thomas Cook Travel Book Award, 1992

Now Try: Lewis was once described by no less than Graham Greene as one of the best writers of the 20th century, and his works include other travel narratives about southeast Asia. Shortly after World War II, he visited Burma and wrote about his experience in *Golden Earth: Travels in Burma*. In 1950, his visit to French Indochina led to the bestseller, *A Dragon Apparent: Travels in Cambodia, Laos & Vietnam*, which inspired Graham Greene to write *The Quiet American*. *An Empire of the East: Travels in Indonesia* focuses on his journey to the lesser-known parts of Indonesia, including the Muslim dominated northern tip of Sumatra and the Indonesian half of New Guinea, where an indigenous society was on the verge of collapse.

Metcalfe, Daniel

Out of Steppe: The Lost Peoples of Central Asia. London: Hutchinson, 2009. 241 pp. ISBN: 9780091925529

Metcalfe sought out six ethnic communities in Central Asia that are disappearing as that part of the world modernizes and becomes more homogeneous. One group suffered from the shrinking of the Aral Sea, another represented the last surviving Jews in Central Asia, and another claimed to be the descendants of Genghis Khan's soldiers. Some of his journeys were dangerous, and he disguised himself as a Muslim at one point. Through a mix of historical details, personal stories, and encounters with local characters, Metcalfe both celebrates the area's diversity and laments changes that threaten to eradicate some of these people.

Subjects: Adventures; Asian History; Islam; Minorities

Categories: Landscapes and People

Places: Afghanistan; Kazakhstan; Kyrgyzstan; Pakistan; Tajikistan; Turkmenistan; Uzbekistan

Awards: Dolman Best Travel Book Award, Shortlist, 2010

Now Try: Colin Thubron travels to Kazakhstan as well as the other four Central Asian countries that were once republics of the Soviet Union in *The Lost Heart of Asia*; like *Out of Steppe*, his book does a good job of capturing the lives of the people who live there. Thubron's *Shadow of the Silk Road* (annotated in the "Quests" chapter of this book) is also set in these countries, but the focus is on the historical trading routes that traversed the area. Justin Marozzi traveled through modern Uzbekistan in the footsteps of Tamerlane, the successor to Genghis Khan, in *Tamerlane: Sword of Islam, Conqueror of the World*. The history of the clash between Tsarist Russia and Victorian England for supremacy in Central Asia is recounted in Peter Hopkirk's enjoyable book, *The Great Game: The Struggle for Empire in Central Asia*.

Montaigne, Fen

Fraser's Penguins: A Journey to the Future in Antarctica. New York: Henry Holt and Co., 2010. 288 pp. ISBN: 9780805079425

Montaigne provides a vivid description of the five months he spent with penguin expert Bill Fraser's scientific team in Antarctica. His informative and touching story explains how Antarctica has warmed faster than anywhere on earth in the past 60 years and how that warming has been detrimental to the penguins, which rely on the sea ice for their food and their migratory patterns. Although Montaigne's message is sobering, his depiction of the penguins, the scientists who study them, and the harshly beautiful Antarctic landscape is inspiring.

Subjects: Birds; Endangered Species; Environment; Global Warming; Penguins; Scientists

Categories: Appreciating Nature

Places: Antarctica

Now Try: Dyan de Napoli's *The Great Penguin Rescue: 40,000 Penguins, a Devastating Oil Spill, and the Inspiring Story of the World's Largest Animal Rescue* provides a firsthand account of the rescue of a colony of African penguins after a ship foundered and spilled oil off the South African coast, threatening the lives of nearly 75,000 penguins. The very popular documentary film, *March of the Penguins,* won the 2005 Academy Award for Best Documentary Feature and should appeal to readers who are interested in the emperor penguins of

Antarctica. In *Ghost Country: A Lifetime Spent on the Edge*, Peter Hilary (the son of Sir Edmund Hilary) tells the harrowing story of the author's journey on skis to retrace the 1912 route to the South Pole taken by Robert Scott.

O'Neill, Dan

A Land Gone Lonesome: An Inland Voyage Along the Yukon River. New York: Counterpoint, 2006. 256 pp. ISBN: 9781582433448

"A hundred years ago, thousands of people bustled along this river," O'Neill notes about this journey down the Yukon River in a canoe. "Today, it is a ghost river connecting ghost towns." O'Neill traveled from Dawson City, in Canada's Yukon Territory, to Eagle, Alaska, on the border with Canada, and his trip is as much about the river's boisterous past (the Klondike gold rush, mail delivery by dog sled) as it is about its present, in which the National Park Service is regulating the homesteaders and "river people" out of existence. O'Neill's case against the National Park Service is made against a backdrop of lyrical descriptions of the landscape and portraits of characters who range from the charming to the irascible.

Subjects: Canoeing; Rivers

Places: Alaska; Yukon; Yukon River

Now Try: The homesteaders and "river people" of the Yukon River are also interviewed by John McPhee in his classic book on Alaska, *Coming into the Country* (annotated earlier in this chapter), and it is interesting to read McPhee's book first to note the changes to the area in the thirty years between the two books. In John Hildebrand's *Reading the River: A Voyage Down the Yukon*, the author tells of his return to the Yukon area ten years after he and his wife had attempted to homestead there; his book is also a portrait of the people eking out an existence in this rugged land. For readers who enjoy adventure, John Balzar's *Yukon Alone: The World's Toughest Adventure Race* tells about the 1,000-mile long Yukon Quest, a dog sled race that is farther inland and farther north, and therefore more challenging, than the more famous Iditarod; Balzar's portraits of the mushers and their dogs is compelling.

Raban, Jonathan

Bad Land: An American Romance. New York: Pantheon Books, 1996. 324 pp. ISBN: 9780679442547

The area of eastern Montana that Raban describes in this mix of travelogue and history has already been diminished. The immigrants who settled the area in return for 320 free acres of land saw their hoped-for civilization collapse in little more than a decade in the early part of the 20th century. Raban traveled through abandoned homesteads and barely surviving towns to tell the stories of those who left and those who stayed in this brutal, weather-beaten land. Raban's exquisite writing and point of view as an Englishman living in the states provide insights into this unique time and place in American history and help explain the sense of unrealized dreams that lingers in the western American psyche.

Subjects: Agriculture; American History; American West; Landscapes and People

Places: Montana

Awards: ALA Notable Book, 1998

Series: *Vintage Departures*

Now Try: Steven R. Kinsella's remarkable *900 Miles from Nowhere: Voices from the Homestead Frontier* tells the story of the struggles of the Great Plains homesteaders through their own letters, diaries, and photographs. Carrie Young's *Nothing To Do But Stay* chronicles the pioneering life of the author's Norwegian-born mother in the North Dakota of the early 20th century. *Hell Creek, Montana: America's Key to the Prehistoric Past*, by Lowell Dingus, is ostensibly about dinosaur hunting in Montana but also includes a number of personal reflections on the Montana Freemen and other aspects of the history of the American West. A good young adult novel about homesteading in Montana in the early 20th century is Kirby Larson's heart-warming *Hattie Big Sky*. Readers who are fascinated by Raban's portrayal of a part of the American landscape that has disappeared may also be interested in two photography collections: Brian Vanden Brink's *Ruin: Photographs of a Vanishing America* and Michael Eastman's *Vanishing America*, both of which capture fading bits of Americana, such as mills, grain elevators, movie houses, soda fountains, barbershops, roadside diners, and storefront churches.

Robbins, Christopher

Apples Are From Kazakhstan: The Land That Disappeared. Ashland, OH: Atlas Books, 2008. 296 pp. ISBN: 9780977743384

Robbins's book is, for the most part, a light-hearted but educational look at a country known to few in the West, but chapter 4, "City of the Plain and the Vanishing Sea," deals with the fate of the Aral Sea, the fourth largest lake in the world. The sea has steadily shrunk since the early 1960s, when cotton was introduced into the area, and the fishing communities that once thrived on its shores have disappeared. The chapter serves as a stark cautionary tale.

Subjects: Agriculture; Asian History; Conservation; Environment; Humor; Seas

Places: Aral Sea; Kazakhstan

Awards: Dolman Best Travel Book Award, Shortlist, 2008

Now Try: Tom Bissell's *Chasing the Sea: Lost Among the Ghosts of Empire in Central Asia* (annotated in this section) also discusses the fate of the Aral Sea, although Bissell views the ecological disaster from Uzbekistan. Keith Rosten was a Fulbright Scholar in Kazakhstan during its emergence as an independent nation; he writes about his experiences in the amusing *Once in Kazakhstan: The Snow Leopard Emerges*. Colin Thubron travels to Kazakhstan as well as the other four Central Asian countries that were once republics of the Soviet Union in *The Lost Heart of Asia*; his book is particularly good at capturing the lives of the people who live there.

Stewart, Stanley

In the Empire of Genghis Khan: An Amazing Odyssey Through the Lands of the Most Feared Conquerors in History. Guilford, CT: Lyons Press, 2002 [2000]. 266 pp. ISBN: 9781585747030

Stewart traveled 1,000 miles on horseback across Mongolia, from the ancient capital of Quaraqorum to Dadal, the birthplace of Genghis Khan. Stewart was aided by two guides, who let him sleep in their tents and share their food (mutton and fermented mare's milk). Stewart saw the culture of the nomadic Mongols as dying out, due largely to the brutal introduction of Soviet-style communism; in fact, his disdain for the Russians is clear, and there is a strong streak of sarcasm in his writing. Nevertheless, Stewart evokes the beauty of the country and some of the customs, in particular, a not-to-be-missed description of a nomadic wedding, complete with out-of-control drinking and brawling.

Subjects: Asian History; Nomads

Places: Mongolia

Awards: Thomas Cook Travel Book Award, 2001

Now Try: Tim Severin also rode by horse across Mongolia, but his purpose was more focused: to retrace part of the overland communication system that once linked the great Khan's empire; his experiences are recounted in the vivid book, *In Search of Genghis Khan: An Exhilarating Journey on Horseback across the Steppes of Mongolia.* Stephen Bodio realized a life-long dream when he traveled to Mongolia in search of the eagle hunters he had seen depicted in *National Geographic* as a child; his travel narrative, *Eagle Dreams: Searching for Legends in Wild Mongolia,* also includes ample information on falconry. Erika Warmbrunn's *Where the Pavement Ends* describes the author's spur-of-the-moment bicycle trip through Mongolia, China, and Vietnam and includes details of her month teaching English to children in a Mongolian village; it is annotated in the chapter of this book entitled "Getting There is Half the Fun."

Thomson, Peter

Sacred Sea: A Journey to Lake Baikal. Oxford, England; New York: Oxford University Press, 2007. 320 pp. ISBN: 9780195170511

Thomson, a producer of National Public Radio's *Living on Earth,* spent six months traveling with his brother to Lake Baikal, the oldest, deepest, and largest freshwater lake in the world. In spite of local myths that the lake can clean itself, Thomson discovered that pollutants from local farms and factories had, in fact, introduced contaminants into the food chain, making the fish from the lake unsafe to eat. The compelling, beautifully written book combines travel narrative (the brothers decide not to travel by plane but to take boats and trains instead), personal reflections on Thomson's recent divorce, environmental investigation, and an appreciation of the Russian people.

Subjects: Divorce; Endangered Species; Environment; Healing Odysseys; Lakes

Categories: Landscapes and People

Places: Lake Baikal; Russia

Now Try: In 1990, National Book Award winner Peter Matthiessen traveled to Lake Baikal to investigate threats to the ecological balance of the lake; he describes the lake as well as its flora, fauna, and people in *Baikal: Sacred Sea of Siberia*. Bartle B. Bull's *Around the Sacred Sea: Mongolia and Lake Baikal on Horseback* recounts the travels of three recent Harvard graduates around Lake Baikal and their attempts to document the environmental damage being done to the lake. One of the four trips that Ian Frazier describes in his fascinating travel narrative, *Travels in Siberia* (annotated in this chapter), is a winter trip to the Baikal region.

Tidwell, Mike

Bayou Farewell: The Rich Life and Tragic Death of Louisiana's Cajun Coast. New York: Pantheon Books 2003. 348 pp. ISBN: 9780375420764

Mike Tidwell, a travel and environmental writer, visited the Cajun coast of Louisiana and found that it is disappearing at a rate of 25 acres per day. The impact of humans, through oil and gas drilling or the maintenance of shipping channels, has made these wetlands the most rapidly vanishing landmass on the planet. Finding that few people were discussing the problem, Tidwell uses the book to begin the conversation; he talked to the various groups who inhabit the area (Cajun shrimp harvesters; Vietnamese fishermen; Houma Indians) and detailed their cultures and their lives. Tidwell provides a good scientific background to the situation, makes clear the complexities involved, and also makes the issues both human and real. All the more powerful because it was written before Katrina, *Bayou Farewell* serves as a stark reminder of what we stand to lose unless we address the problems faced by the bayou area.

Subjects: American Indians; Endangered Species; Environment; Wetlands

Categories: Landscapes and People

Places: Louisiana

Series: *Vintage Departures*

Now Try: Tidwell has written a number of books on ecological issues, and *The Ravaging Tide: Strange Weather, Future Katrinas, and the Coming Death of America's Coastal Cities* may be of particular interest to readers interested in preserving the wetlands and other coastal areas. Tidwell's *The Ponds of Kalambayi: An African Sojourn* examines the two years he spent in Zaire as a Peace Corps volunteer and the lessons he learned about the importance of tradition among the villagers he met there. His *Amazon Stranger: A Rainforest Chief Battles Big Oil*, as the title suggests, tells the true story of a primitive people and their leader, an American born to missionary parents.

Trojanow, Ilija

Along the Ganges. London: Armchair Traveller, 2011 [2005]. 135 pp. ISBN: 9781906598914

Hungarian writer Trojanow, who spent five years living in Mumbai, traveled down the Ganges River, from its source in the Himalayas to the Bay of Bengal. In addition to visiting Hindu festivals and reporting on the many clashes between ancient traditions and the modern world, Trojanow expresses concern for the health of the holy river, seeing threats to its existence from dams and the growing population in India, which has doubled in the past 40 years. As Trojanow writes, "The overwhelming majority pollute the river without a thought and believe that a garland and a coconut settle the balance. The holiness of the river relieves them of personal responsibility. Ganga, a goddess after all, should be strong enough to wash away all sins."

Subjects: Environment; Hinduism; Quick Reads; Rivers

Places: Bangladesh; India; Ganges River

Now Try: Eric Newby's classic story of traveling down the Ganges for his 44th birthday is *Slowly Down the Ganges*, which is much more humorous than Trojanow's book. Journalist Julian Crandall Hollick's *Ganga: A Journey Down the Ganges River* is, like Trojanow, more serious and focuses on the ecology and mythology of the river as well as the folk culture of the villages through which the Ganges flows. Trojanow is the author of several travel narratives, including *Mumbai To Mecca: A Pilgrimage to the Holy Sites of Islam*, which describes his pilgrimage to Mecca as well as his own Muslim heritage.

Wheeler, Sara

The Magnetic North: Notes from the Arctic Circle. London: Jonathan Cape, 2009. 354 pp. ISBN: 9780224082211

Wheeler spent two years traveling to all of the countries in the Arctic region, talking to indigenous people, scientists, and explorers and warning of a looming ecological disaster in the melting of the ice caps. Ironically, she found that the melting ice caps may open the area up for even more exploitation, as the retreating ice reveals new oil fields and mineral deposits. Wheeler's book is full of historical facts and details about the lives of those who inhabit these cold lands, but it is also a compelling warning that "The survival of civilisation as we know it hangs on what happens in the Arctic."

Subjects: Environment; Explorers; Global Warming; Indigenous Peoples; Scientists; Women Travelers

Places: Alaska; Arctic Region; Canada; Finland; Greenland; Norway; Russia; Sweden

Now Try: Wheeler's earlier travels at the opposite end of the world, Antarctica, are chronicled in her book, *Terra Incognita: Travels in Antarctica*, which is also annotated in this chapter, under "The Beauty of the Place." *Polar Dream: The First Solo Expedition by a Woman and Her Dog to the Magnetic North Pole* tells the true story of author Helen

Thayer's attempt to become the first woman to ski alone to the North Pole. Bill Streever traveled in the Arctic region and speculates on the nature of cold and its importance to the planet in *Cold: Adventures in the World's Frozen Places*. Fiction readers interested in the Arctic region may enjoy *The Voyage of the Narwhal* by National Book Award winner Andrea Barrett, which follows a voyage to find the lost expedition party of John Franklin.

Consider Starting With . . .

Berendt, John. *The City of Falling Angels*.
Chatwin, Bruce. *In Patagonia*.
Ehrlich, Gretel. *This Cold Heaven: Seven Seasons in Greenland*.
Frazier, Ian. *Travels in Siberia*.
Matthiessen, Peter. *The Birds of Heaven: Travels with Cranes*.
Raban, Jonathan. *Bad Land: An American Romance*.

Fiction Read-Alikes

Anderson, Alison. *Darwin's Wink: A Novel of Nature and Love* follows two naturalists who fall in love while trying to save an endangered bird species on an island off the coast of Mauritius. The novel combines an appreciation of nature with a vivid portrayal of the beauty of the island.

Guterson, David. Guterson's novels and short stories are set in the Pacific Northwest and evoke the beauty of those landscapes. Characters often share a love of the outdoors, as in ***The Other***; work outdoors, as in ***Our Lady of the Forest***; or engage in outdoor activities, as in the collection of stories, ***The Country Ahead of Us, The Country Behind***.

Harrison, Jim. Harrison's works are often set in remote places like Sand Hills in Nebraska, Michigan's Upper Peninsula, and the mountains of Montana. Among his novels that evoke a strong sense of place and an appreciation of nature are ***Wolf: A False Memoir***, about a man searching for wolves in northern Michigan; ***A Good Day to Die***, which involves a road trip to save the Grand Canyon from a proposed dam; and ***True North***, in which the protagonist tries to deal with the damage his family's logging business has done to Michigan's Upper Peninsula.

Henry, Sue. Henry writes two mystery series with a strong sense of place. The first (the *Alaska Mystery* series) is set in Alaska and involves state trooper Alex Jensen and his girlfriend Jessie Arnold. These range from ***Murder on the Iditarod Trail***, in which someone is systematically killing the top competitors in Alaska's best known dogsled race, to 2010's ***Cold as Ice***. Henry also writes the *Maxie and Stretch Mysteries*, about retiree Maxie McNabb and her dachshund, who travel the United States in a Winnebago. The titles in this series take place in Colorado (***The Serpents Trail***), Hawaii (***The Refuge***), and Alaska (***The End of the Road***).

Leon, Donna. Leon is the author of the *Commissario Brunetti* series of crime novels set in Venice and featuring police commissioner Guido Brunetti. Each book explores a specific aspect of Venetian life, beginning with ***Death at La Fenice***, in which a German conductor is found dead during the performance of "La Traviata" at the famous opera house in Venice, and ***Death in a Strange Country***, in which an American soldier's body is found floating in one of the Venetian canals. As of 2011, Leon has published 20 titles in the series.

Mahfouz, Naguib. The late Egyptian writer won the Nobel Prize in Literature in 1988, and his works include the so-called Cairo Trilogy (***Palace Walk***, ***Palace of Desire***, and ***Sugar Street***), all of which focus on the urban landscape of Cairo.

Michener, James. Many of Michener's novels are set in specific countries and have the feel of travel narratives. Among these are ***Mexico***, which focuses on bullfighting but also includes insights into the history and culture of Mexico; ***Caravans: A Novel of Afghanistan***, set in that country just after World War II; ***The Drifters***, which follows six young individuals from different countries as they travel through Spain, Portugal, Morocco, and Mozambique; and ***Poland***, which looks at the lives of three Polish families from the 13th through the 20th centuries.

Notes

1. According to Joyce Saricks, the six elements of appeal are " pacing, characterization, story line, frame and setting, tone and mood, and language and style." *The Readers' Advisory Guide to Genre Fiction* (Chicago: American Library Association, 2009), p. 7.
2. This is consistent with Catherine Ross's observation that "an interest in a particular subject can trump the distinction between fiction and nonfiction. . . . Many readers said that they would become interested in some topic and then read everything they could on it." "Reading Nonfiction for Pleasure: What Motivates Readers?" in *Nonfiction Readers' Advisory*, edited by Robert Burgin (Westport, CT: Libraries Unlimited, 2004), p. 107.
3. Guy Robertson, "Travel Collections: Off the Shelf, On the Road," *Feliciter* 55 (2009): 105.

References

Robertson, Guy. "Travel Collections: Off the Shelf, On the Road." *Feliciter* 55 (2009): 104–6.

Ross, Catherine. "Reading Nonfiction for Pleasure: What Motivates Readers?" In *Nonfiction Readers' Advisory*, edited by Robert Burgin, 105–20. Westport, CT: Libraries Unlimited, 2004.

Saricks, Joyce. *The Readers' Advisory Guide to Genre Fiction*. Chicago: American Library Association, 2009.

Chapter 2

Quests

To be on a quest is nothing more or less than to become an asker of questions.
—Sam Keen, *Fire in the Belly: On Being a Man*

Definition of "Quests"

The definition of travel given in this book's introduction states that travel is an activity that involves a traveler or travelers who go to a destination by some means, *for some purpose*, for some length of time. The titles discussed in this chapter are those that concentrate on the purpose of the travel. As Neal Wyatt notes, "Often writers in this area have many other interests and motivations than a simple trip, and those wider aspects are reflected in their works."[1]

The chapter focuses on five specific purposes. The traveler may go in search of food or history or legends or even a concept or idea, like love, as in Franz Wisner's *How the World Makes Love: And What It Taught a Jilted Groom*. The traveler's purpose may be to repeat the journey of an earlier traveler, as in Richard Bernstein's search for enlightenment while following the path of a seventh-century Buddhist monk in *Ultimate Journey: Retracing the Path of an Ancient Buddhist Monk Who Crossed Asia in Search of Enlightenment*. What links all of the titles in this chapter is the focus on the purpose of the travel, because for some readers, the purpose of the trip will be a key factor in the book's appeal.

My friend Lee was a traveler whose trips had a strong focus on food. Whenever he would return from a trip to London or Paris, he would tell me where and what he had eaten. He kept a journal of his travels, and many of the entries were devoted to the restaurants he had discovered and the meals he had enjoyed. The titles in the "In Search of Food" category would likely appeal to him.

Some of my own trips have had a strong sense of being "In Search of History." For me, the highlight of the trip to China that I took with my wife in 2009 was seeing the terracotta warriors in Xian, reading about them, learning about Qin Shi Huang (the first Emperor of China, who had the warriors made and placed near his tomb to protect him in the afterlife), and shaking hands with one of the farmers who discovered the figures while digging for a well in 1974.

Readers who talk about why they travel or who talk about their travel in terms of the purposes included in this chapter (food, history, legends, concepts, and following in someone's footsteps) or who are interested in one of these areas outside of any connection to travel (foodies and history buffs, for example) may find the titles in this chapter of particular interest.

Appeal of "Quests"

Titles that have been classified as "Quests" tell stories of travel with a purpose, and because the purpose of the individual traveler is key to these stories, the appeal of characterization will be strong. After all, the traveler is in search of food, history, legends, or concepts that are important to her and that reveal an important part of herself to the reader. Bruce Chatwin (*The Songlines*) opens himself to the reader through his obsession with the invisible Aboriginal pathways that created and continually recreate the world. Calvin Trillin bares his gastronomic soul as he tracks down baked oysters, barbecue, and poutine in *The Tummy Trilogy*. Eric Weiner proclaims himself an Eeyore while searching for the concept of happiness in *The Geography of Bliss: One Grump's Search for the Happiest Places in the World*. We get to know these people through their travels and through the purposes behind their travels.

Characterization also becomes crucial in the books categorized as "In the Footsteps of . . . " The character of the traveler remains important, but of equal (if not greater) importance is the character of the earlier traveler in whose steps she is following. Emma Larkin provides insights into the life of one of the 20th century's great writers (*Finding George Orwell in Burma*), and Richard Bernstein helps the reader understand the seventh-century Buddhist monk in whose path of enlightenment he follows (*Ultimate Journey: Retracing the Path of an Ancient Buddhist Monk Who Crossed Asia in Search of Enlightenment*). Tim Butcher tells us about the explorer H. M. Stanley (*Blood River: A Journey to Africa's Broken Heart*), and Tony Horwitz teaches us about Captain Cook by retracing his journeys (*Blue Latitudes: Boldly Going Where Captain Cook Has Gone Before*).

Frame and setting will also be strong appeal factors, as with most of the titles in this book. John Barlow makes the reader taste and smell the northern Spanish province of Galicia while searching for that region's food in *Everything but the Squeal: Eating the Whole Hog in Northern Spain*. The reader feels the winds blowing on St. Helena and feels the isolation and loneliness of that island while searching for the ghost of Napoleon in Julia Blackburn's *The Emperor's Last Island: A Journey to St. Helena*. The reader shivers in the Arctic Region described by Joanna Kavenna while searching for a lost land (*The Ice Museum: In Search of the Lost Land of Thule*) and pulls off leeches alongside Ian Baker while searching for a legendary Himalayan paradise (*The Heart of the World: A Journey to the Last Secret Place*).

The other traditional appeal factors typically play a smaller role in these narratives, and the titles represent a wide variety of pacing, story line, tone and mood, and language and style. Most readers will find something of interest here, whether they are looking for the edgy but enthusiastic tone of Anthony Bourdain (*A Cook's Tour: In Search of the Perfect Meal*) or the intense, personal reflections of the granddaughter of a slave as she visits key sites of the slave trade (Saidiya V. Hartman's *Lose Your Mother: A Journey Along the Atlantic Slave Route*) or a well-written narrative by a highly regarded writer like V. S. Naipaul (*Among the Believers: An Islamic Journey*) or Bruce Chatwin (*The Songlines*).

Readers' advisors working with those who enjoy books in this subgenre have ample opportunity to suggest books from other genres as well. Readers who enjoy travel in search of food, like Anthony Bourdain's *A Cook's Tour: In Search of the Perfect Meal*, may also be drawn to titles in the cooking and food genre that do not necessarily involve travel, even a biography like Jacques Pepin's *The Apprentice: My Life in the Kitchen*. Readers who like travel in search of history, like Rachel Polonsky's recent *Molotov's Magic Lantern: A Journey in Russian History*, may also like history in general, and in the case of Polonsky's book, other titles that deal with Russian cultural history (like James Billington's *The Icon and the Axe: An Interpretive History of Russian Culture* or Suzanne Massie's *Land of the Firebird: The Beauty of Old Russia*) may be suggested. The same is true of the other purposes of travel that are highlighted in this chapter: legends, concepts, and travel in the footsteps of others.

Organization of the Chapter

Like of all the chapters in this book, this chapter begins with "Classics," titles that were published prior to 1990 and that also display universality, multiple levels of meaning, great stories, memorable characters, emotional or though-provoking experiences, and great writing. These titles are likely to be more familiar to both readers and librarians and will help them better understand the nuances of the subgenre and its further categories. The purposes that underlie "Quests" have not changed radically since these earlier titles were published, and so their appeal may be similar to the appeal of more recent titles.

The other categories in the chapter reflect the purposive nature of "Quests" and reflect five different reasons that might motivate such travel. "In Search of Food," as one might guess, includes those titles where the traveler goes in search of food, either a specific kind of food, or the food of a specific country, or food in general. "In Search of History" gathers together titles that describe travel in search of a country's history or the history of some site or even of some object. Titles in the category "In Search of Legends" include those travels in search of legendary (as opposed to historical) places and people. Travelers may also go in search of a concept or an idea, such as happiness or love or ruins, and these are the focus of "In Search of a Concept." Finally, "In the Footsteps of . . ." represents titles in which the traveler follows in the footsteps of an earlier traveler.

Classics

As noted earlier, this book defines classics as travel narratives that were published before 1990. They are intended to represent titles that are more familiar to readers and librarians and that will serve as good entry points into the subgenre of "Quests" and its various categories. Because the purposes that underlie travel have not changed radically over the years, the appeal of these older works may be similar to the appeal of more recent quests. After all, a quest for food by M.F.K. Fisher (*As They Were*) in the 1950s will share many themes and appeal factors with a more recent quest for food by Peter Mayle (*French Lessons: Adventures with Knife, Fork, and Corkscrew*).

The titles listed under "Classics" reflect most of the categories of this subgenre. There are quests in search of food (Calvin Trillin's *Travels with Alice* and *The Tummy Trilogy*), quests in search of history (V. S. Naipaul's *Among the Believers: An Islamic Journey*), quests in search of legends (Bruce Chatwin's *The Songlines*), and quests in the footsteps of others (Caroline Alexander's *One Dry Season: In the Footsteps of Mary Kingsley* and Lesley Downer's *On the Narrow Road: A Journey into Lost Japan*).

Alexander, Caroline

One Dry Season: In the Footsteps of Mary Kingsley. New York: Knopf, 1990 [1989]. 290 pp. 9780394574554

Alexander, a former Rhodes scholar and pentathlete, re-created the 1890s journey taken by the English writer Mary Kingsley into western Africa and found the land and people little changed a century later. Her writing alternates between Kingsley's travels and her own, and the trip is highlighted by the fascinating characters Alexander encountered: a Protestant minister from a cannibal tribe, nuns, truck drivers, a heartbroken European woman whose Gabonese husband had abandoned her. Along the way, Alexander's admiration of the African people deepens.

Subjects: Women Travelers

Categories: In the Footsteps of . . .

Places: Africa; Gabon

Series: *Vintage Departures*

Now Try: Kingsley's *Travels in West Africa* was originally published in 1895 and has never been out of print; it is available now in the *National Geographic Adventure Classics* series. Tanya Shaffer's *Somebody's Heart Is Burning: A Woman Wanderer in Africa* describes the year the author spent in Africa (Kenya, Mali, and Ghana) and, like

Alexander, provides rich descriptions of the people and places Shaffer encounters. Rosemary Mahoney's *Down the Nile: Alone in a Fisherman's Skiff* provides another woman's perspective on Africa, in this case, the Nile River and the individuals who live alongside it. (It is annotated in "A Sense of Place.") In *Mali Blues: Traveling to an African Beat,* Belgian writer Lieve Joris travels to western Africa (Senegal, Mauritania, and Mali) and captures the spirit and music of the individuals there. Bill Bryson visited Kenya to support CARE International, a charity dedicated to the eradication of poverty, and wrote *Bill Bryson's African Diary,* a short but very personal account of his trip.

Chatwin, Bruce

The Songlines. New York: Viking, 1987. 293 pp. ISBN: 9780670806058

This brilliantly written book recounts his journey to the Australian Outback to learn firsthand about the legendary Aboriginal songlines, described by Chatwin as "the labyrinth of invisible pathways which meander all over Australia" and which represent the paths along which the world was created and is constantly being created. Chatwin has his own theories about the songlines, and so the narrative is very much one of ideas, one in which the author develops an appreciation of the nomadic drive in mankind. While Chatwin did travel throughout Australia and met any number of fascinating individuals, the book is controversial in its combination of fiction and nonfiction and in what some reviewers perceived as its simplistic, colonialist views of European and Aboriginal Australians.

Subjects: Anthropology; Culture Clash; Friendships; Spirituality

Categories: In Search of Legends

Places: Australia

Now Try: Chatwin died at age 48, just three years after the publication of *The Songlines,* and readers who enjoy his major travel narratives may be interested in *What Am I Doing Here?,* a collection of his travel stories and essays that was the last of his works to be published during his lifetime; *Anatomy of Restlessness: Selected Writings 1969–1989,* a collection of his unpublished travel tales, short stories, and essays; or *Under the Sun: The Letters of Bruce Chatwin,* a collection of his personal correspondence. Travel writer Tony Horwitz hitchhikes through the Australian Outback in his witty *One for the Road: Hitchhiking Through the Australian Outback,* which is funnier but perhaps less insightful than Chatwin's book. Marlo Morgan's novel, *Mutant Message Down Under,* recounts a four-month journey taken by an American woman through the Australian Outback; like *The Songlines,* it deals with the culture of the Aborigines. Aboriginal writer Alexis Wright won the 2007 Miles Franklin Award for *Carpentaria,* her novel about land rights and the harsh realities of Aboriginal life in Australia; like Chatwin's book, the writing is exquisite, and one reviewer said that "Wright's prose soars between the mythical and the colloquial."

Downer, Lesley

On the Narrow Road: A Journey into Lost Japan. New York: Summit Books, 1989. 280 pp. ISBN: 9780671640477

In 1689, Japanese poet Matsuo Basho traveled through the northern provinces of Japan and later wrote a well-known book about his journey. In 1985, British writer Lesley Downer followed his path in order to discover a more traditional, more provincial Japan than the modern cities we are used to seeing in the media. Downer's integration of Basho's words (particularly his haikus) and her realization that so little has changed in this "lost Japan" make this an enjoyable and enlightening book.

Subjects: Poetry; Women Travelers

Categories: In the Footsteps of . . .

Places: Japan

Now Try: Basho's original journey is recounted in *The Narrow Road to the Deep North and Other Travel Sketches*. Jane Reichhold translated Basho's haiku and published them as a single volume, *Basho: The Complete Haiku*. Sam Hamill's translations of Basho and other masters of haiku are found in *The Sound of Water: Haiku by Basho, Buson, Issa, and Other Poets*. Like Downer and Basho, Alan Booth followed a more rural route (in his case, down the eastern side of Japan) in the classic, *The Road to Sata*, which is annotated in this book's "Getting There Is Half the Fun" chapter. Oliver Statler made the famous 88-temple pilgrimage on the Japanese island of Shikoku in *Japanese Pilgrimage*, a book that captures the complexities of traditional Japanese culture. Leila Philip spent two years as the apprentice to a potter in a remote Japanese village, and she recounts her time there in *Road Through Miyama*.

Fisher, M.F.K.

As They Were. New York: Knopf, 1982 [1955]. 261 pp. ISBN: 9780394524009

This juicy set of essays by prolific food writer Fisher covers some of her travels to French restaurants, Swiss chalets, and Paris train stations as well as her thoughts on crossing the Atlantic on an ocean liner. These are nostalgic pieces that celebrate the joy of cooking and eating and remind us of the importance of food and travel to one's soul. The writing is, for lack of a better word, delicious; W. H. Auden himself said of Fisher, "I do not know of anyone in the United States today who writes better prose."

Subjects: Essays; Food; Women Travelers

Categories: In Search of Food

Places: California; France; Switzerland

Now Try: Among Fisher's other works are two that evoke a strong sense of place: her memoir of life in Aix-en-Provence in the 1940s and Marseille in the 1950s, *Two Towns in Provence: Map of Another Town and a Considerable Town*, and her memoir of three years in

1930s Dijon, *Long Ago In France: The Years In Dijon*. Michael S. Sanders traveled to a tiny, remote French village to study the inner workings of a French restaurant and got absorbed in the life of the village in the evocative *From Here, You Can't See Paris: Seasons of a French Village and Its Restaurant*. Like Fisher, *New Yorker* writer A. J. Liebling understands the importance of good food; he writes about eating and shows off a prodigious appetite in *Between Meals: An Appetite for Paris*. Julia Child arguably writes as well as Fisher and loves French food as much; her book, *My Life in France*, is annotated in "The Expatriate Life" chapter of this book. Fisher celebrated the social aspect of food, and readers who appreciate that theme in her writing may also enjoy two collections of essays written by novelist and *Gourmet* columnist Laurie Colwin, *Home Cooking: A Writer in the Kitchen* and *More Home Cooking: A Writer Returns to the Kitchen*, as well as Judith Moore's mouth watering memoir, *Never Eat Your Heart Out*.

Heyerdahl, Thor

Kon-Tiki: Across the Pacific by Raft. New York: Washington Square Press, 1984 [1950]. 240 pp. ISBN: 9780671726522 Y A

Heyerdahl's expedition across the Pacific, from Peru to Tahiti, was a quest for evidence to support his theory that people from South America could have settled Polynesia. The author and five companions made the 4,300-mile trip on a raft made of 40-foot long logs, and the book follows the project from the building of the raft itself through their 100-plus days at sea, to their crash landing on an island in the South Pacific. The book is written in a simple and direct style, without being overly dramatic, and the reader may have to be reminded that what the author called a "suicidal expedition" was taken in the days before GPS, helicopter rescues, and other technologies.

Subjects: Adventure; Oceans

Categories: In the Footsteps of . . .

Places: Pacific Ocean; Peru; Polynesian Islands; Tahiti

Now Try: Heyerdahl used at least two other expeditions to provide evidence for his theories. *Aku-Aku* recounts a 1955–1956 expedition to Easter Island and other Polynesian islands to research his idea that the great stone statues at Easter Island were carved by people who originally came from Peru. *The Ra Expeditions* chronicles his two attempts to cross the Atlantic Ocean on papyrus boats to show that people from Africa could have sailed to the New World. *Kon-Tiki*, the documentary film about Heyerdahl's expedition, won Best Documentary Feature at the 1951 Academy Awards and remains the only feature film from Norway to win an Academy Award. At the age of 60, William Willis sailed alone across the Pacific Ocean to American Samoa in a primitive raft that he built himself, traveling 2,200 miles farther than Heyerdahl; his remarkable story is told by T. R. Pearson in *Seaworthy: Adrift with William Willis in the Golden Age of Rafting* (annotated in the "Travel Adventure" chapter of this book). P. J. Capelotti recounts the stories of Willis and several others in *Sea Drift: Rafting Adventures in the Wake of Kon-Tiki*, a riveting collection of more than 40 expeditions by individuals inspired by Heyerdahl.

Holmes, Richard

Footsteps: Adventures of a Romantic Biographer. New York: Vintage, 1985. 288 pp. ISBN: 9780670323531

Holmes is a well-known biographer of Shelley and other Romantic figures, and in this book, he follows in the footsteps of four of these writers, trailing Robert Louis Stevenson through the Cévennes Mountains in southern France; Mary Wollstonecraft through revolutionary Paris; Shelley through Italian villages; and French poet Gerard de Nerval through 19th-century Paris. *Footsteps* is an entertaining mix of travel narrative and biography and even autobiography, as Holmes ponders his own life as a biographer and what it means to chronicle the life of another.

Subjects: Authors; Biographies; Poets

Categories: In the Footsteps of . . .

Places: France; Italy; Paris

Series: *Vintage Departures*

Now Try: Robert Louis Stevenson's *Travels with a Donkey in the Cévennes* is considered a pioneer work in travel literature and recounts the author's 12-day solo hike through the mountains in south-central France. A few years after *Footsteps*, Holmes published *Sidetracks: Explorations of a Romantic Biographer*, a collection of essays and other short pieces, some of which include his travels in the footsteps of his subjects, including Zelda and F. Scott Fitzgerald in Paris, Thomas Chatterton in London, and French poet Théophile Gautier in London. Readers who want to know more about the three of the four writers in whose footsteps Holmes followed have plenty of options. Holmes himself wrote a highly regarded biography of Shelley, *Shelley: The Pursuit*, which portrays the poet as a "darker and more earthly" individual than the ethereal character tradition has presented. Frank McLynn's *Robert Louis Stevenson: A Biography* is the definitive biography of the great Scottish writer, but it may be difficult to find, and Philip Callow's *Louis: A Life of Robert Louis Stevenson* is a good alternative. Mary Wollstonecraft, whose 1796 work, *Letters Written During a Short Residence in Sweden, Norway, and Denmark*, is a classic travel narrative, is well served by Janet Todd's biography, *Mary Wollstonecraft: A Revolutionary Life*. There is no good English language biography of the French poet Gerard de Nerval, but his poetry is reasonably accessible, and the Penguin Classic, *De Nerval: Selected Writings*, can be recommended. While it has little to do with travel, Holmes is also the author of one of the most celebrated recent books on the history of science, *The Age of Wonder: The Romantic Generation and the Discovery of the Beauty and Terror of Science*, which won the 2009 Royal Society Prize for Science Books and the 2009 National Book Critics Circle Award for General Nonfiction.

Iyer, Pico

Video Night in Kathmandu: And Other Reports from the Not-So-Far East. New York: Knopf, 1988. 376 pp. ISBN: 9780394550275

Time writer Iyer's quest in *Video Night in Kathmandu* is to "find out how America's pop-cultural imperialism spread through the world's most ancient civilizations." The author spent seven months in 1985 traveling to Asia on four separate visits to track down this phenomenon. He found "Rambo" remakes in Bombay, Bruce Springsteen songs in Manila, burgers in Nepal, and break dancing in Beijing. Iyer brings a unique perspective to his travels; he was born in England to Indian parents who moved to the United States when he was seven. His examination of what he calls "Coca-Colonization" is witty, ironic, and perceptive, and he concludes that the East is changing the West as much as the West is changing the East.

Subjects: Culture Clash; Essays; Humor

Categories: Reflective Journeys

Places: Bali; Burma; China; Hong Kong; India; Japan; Nepal; Philippines; Thailand; Tibet

Series: *Vintage Departures*

Now Try: Iyer is a prolific writer of travel narratives, and several of his titles (*The Global Soul: Jet Lag, Shopping Malls, and the Search for Home*; *Falling Off the Map: Some Lonely Places of the World*; and *The Lady and the Monk: Four Seasons in Kyoto*;) are annotated in this volume. His collection of essays, *Tropical Classical: Essays from Several Directions*, is like *Video Night in Kathmandu* in its focus on the clash of cultures. Like Iyer, Jeff Greenwald can be funny and ironic, and he also addresses issues related to the clash of cultures. In *Shopping for Buddhas,* Greenwald attempts to find the perfect statue of the Buddha in Kathmandu and explores the clash between spirituality and greed. Jean Kwok's novel, *Girl in Translation,* also looks at culture clash in the lives of Asian immigrants to the United States, a mother and her daughter who emigrate from Hong Kong to Brooklyn.

Millman, Lawrence

Last Places: A Journey in the North. Boston: Houghton Mifflin, 1990. 242 pp. ISBN: 9780395436158

Last Places recounts Millman's journey in the mid-1980s along the ancient sea routes of the Vikings from Norway to Newfoundland. Millman traveled solo and visited the lonely places that the Vikings visited in order to better understand them and their heritage and influence. But though the places that he visited were lonely, the journey was filled with encounters with fascinating individuals: speakers of a lost Nordic language in the

Shetlands; a convicted murderer in Reykjavik; an Inuit hermit in Greenland; and a Newfoundlander who warns him about the local version of the Himalayan Yeti. The book is earthy and poetic and laugh-out-loud funny in places.

Subjects: Humor; Solo Travelers

Categories: In the Footsteps of . . .

Places: Faeroe Islands; Greenland; Iceland; Labrador; Newfoundland; Norway; Shetland Islands

Series: *Vintage Departures*

Now Try: Millman likes to travel where few others have been, and *Lost in the Arctic: Explorations on the Edge* is a collection of essays recounting his travels to Arctic lands. *An Evening Among the Headhunters: And Other Reports from Roads Less Taken* is another collection of his essays, these from journeys to far flung places like Tonga, the Bay Islands of the Honduras, and Sark. Gretel Ehrlich's marvelous *This Cold Heaven: Seven Seasons in Greenland* (annotated in this book's chapter on "A Sense Of Place") has much in common with *Last Places,* particularly in its appreciation of the people who inhabit this particular "last place." Jane Smiley's touching novel, *The Greenlanders,* is set in 14th-century Greenland and tells the story of a single family there.

Naipaul, V. S.

Among the Believers: An Islamic Journey. New York: Knopf, 1981. 430 pp. ISBN: 9780394509693

In 1979 and 1980, Naipaul undertook a seven-month quest across the Asian continent to gain a better understanding of the countries in which Islamic fundamentalism was becoming more important. The book was controversial, with some readers finding it prescient and other readers believing that Naipaul was biased against the Muslim world. Regardless, the book is a fascinating look at Islam at a critical juncture in its history, just after the Iranian revolution that replaced the Shah with the Islamic Republic, and Naipaul is a brilliant writer whose portrayals of people and places are precise and insightful.

Subjects: Investigative Stories; Islam; Religion

Categories: In Search of History

Places: Indonesia; Iran; Malaysia; Pakistan

Now Try: In 1998, Naipaul published a sequel to this book, entitled *Beyond Belief: Islamic Excursions Among the Converted Peoples,* in which he again traveled to Indonesia, Iran, Malaysia, and Pakistan and produced a series of revealing vignettes based on the people he encountered. Naipaul is an intriguing individual in his own right, and Patrick French's *The World Is What It Is: The Authorized Biography of V. S. Naipaul* is a fascinating look at his life. Naipaul has published 15 novels to date, and readers wanting to explore his writings might start with *In a Free State* (which won the 1971 Booker Prize and comprises three stories on the theme of the price of freedom) and *A Bend in the River* (which looks at the changes taking place in an unnamed African country after its independence, through the eyes of an Indian Muslim shopkeeper). British author Tim Mackintosh-Smith also travels through Islamic countries as he follows in the footsteps of the great Muslim explorer, Ibn Battutah, in *Travels with a Tangerine: A Journey in the Footnotes of Ibn Battutah.* He provides a fascinating look at both modern day and 14th-century Islam. Ibn Battutah's travels from his native Morocco to Mecca in the 14th century are absorbing and have been abridged by Mackintosh-Smith; this edition is annotated in the chapter of this book entitled "A Sense of Place."

Palin, Michael

Around the World in 80 Days with Michael Palin. London: BBC Books, 1989. 256 pp. ISBN: 9780563208266 YA

Monty Python alumnus Michael Palin followed in the footsteps of Jules Verne's fictional character, Phileas Fogg, and circumnavigated the world on trains, in taxis, by camels, and in balloons (everything but by airplane). Whether he's riding the legendary Orient Express or the more prosaic Amtrak, whether he's policing Venice's canals on a garbage boat or sailing on a dhow across the Persian Gulf and the Indian Ocean, Palin is sharp-eyed and knowledgeable about the countries through which he passed. The book is based on diaries that Palin kept during his journey, which was filmed for BBC television, and the result is witty and colorful, full of Palin's observations about places and people.

Subjects: Circumnavigations; Humor; Illustrated Books

Categories: In the Footsteps of . . .

Places: Africa; Alexandria; Cairo; China; Dubai; Egypt; England; Hong Kong; India; Italy; Japan; Madras; Mumbai; New York City; Saudi Arabia; Shanghai; Singapore; Tokyo; United States; Venice

Now Try: The DVD version of Palin's adventure is easily available and quite exciting, as Palin tried to circle the globe in 80 days in spite of numerous delays. The Jules Verne novel, *Around the World in Eighty Days,* is still a fun read, although some modern readers may feel that Verne is less than sensitive to other people and their cultures. French writer Jean Cocteau also followed the path of Phileas Fogg in 1936 and wrote regular dispatches for a French newspaper; these articles were published together as *Round the World Again in 80 Days* and make fascinating reading, especially in comparison with the original Verne and the later Palin. Palin's book includes a number of photographs, and British comic Stephen Fry's beautifully illustrated *Stephen Fry in America: Fifty States and the Man Who Set Out to See Them All* may also appeal to readers who enjoyed Palin's travel narrative. Anthony Bourdain's *No Reservations: Around the World on an Empty Stomach* is also rich with photographs.

Severin, Tim

The Brendan Voyage. New York: McGraw-Hill, 1978. 292 pp. ISBN: 9780070563353

Severin, an award-winning adventure and travel writer, attempted to sail across the Atlantic in a leather-clad boat to show that St. Brendan the Navigator could have reached North America from Ireland in the sixth century. Although the voyage itself was exciting and dangerous, the most interesting aspect of the book for many readers will be the detailed story of the construction of the boat; Severin admired the skill level of ancient craftsmen as he bought ox hides from a tannery that was centuries old, tracked down harness makers to sew the hides together properly, and found Irish timber for the mast. Written in a straightforward and clear style, *The Brendan Voyage* is an exciting travel narrative as well as an absorbing study of the seafaring technology of a previous time.

Subjects: Adventure;

Categories: In the Footsteps of . . .

Places: Atlantic Ocean; Ireland

Now Try: Severin has re-created several famous journeys: sailing a Bronze Age ship to follow the path of Ulysses in *The Ulysses Voyage: Sea Search for the Odyssey*; building and sailing an eighth-century ship from Oman to China to trace the voyages of Sinbad the Sailor in *The Sinbad Voyage*; riding the trail of the Crusaders from Belgium to Jerusalem in *Crusader: By Horse to Jerusalem*; following the footsteps of Marco Polo on motorcycle in *Tracking Marco Polo*; and building and sailing a bamboo raft across the Pacific in *The China Voyage: Across The Pacific By Bamboo Raft*. *The Voyage of St. Brendan* itself has been translated from the Latin by John O'Meara. Colin Angus (whose *Amazon Extreme: Three Ordinary Guys, One Rubber Raft, and the Most Dangerous River on Earth* and *Lost in Mongolia: Rafting the World's Last Unchallenged River* are annotated in the "Travel Adventure" chapter of this book) and his wife, Julie Angus, describe their self-propelled trip from Scotland to Syria by rowboat and bicycle in *Rowed Trip: A Journey by Oar from Scotland to Syria*. Thor Heyerdahl's works, including *Kon-Tiki* (annotated above) and *Aku-Aku*, are also likely to appeal to readers who enjoyed Severin's book.

Stevens, Stuart

Night Train to Turkistan: Modern Adventures Along China's Ancient Silk Road. New York: Atlantic Monthly Press, 1988. 239 pp. ISBN: 9780871131904

In 1935, travel writer Peter Fleming journeyed to Xinjiang (then known as Chinese Turkestan) to report on the aftermath of the civil war there for *The Times*. Some 50 years later, Stevens and three friends retraced Fleming's steps from Beijing to the remote town of Kashgar. The book recounts their trip in a wildly humorous fashion, particularly their battles with government bureaucrats who seemed determined to prevent them from completing their journey, and their encounters with the woeful Chinese transportation system. In spite of the significant changes in China in recent years, the book is less dated than one might think, because it deals with a remote part of that nation.

Subjects: Humor; Quick Reads; Silk Road

Categories: In the Footsteps of . . .

Places: China; Xinjiang

Now Try: The original trek by Fleming and Ella Maillart took seven months to complete and included travel by train, truck, camel, horse, and foot over 3,500 miles of hostile desert and steep mountains. Fleming's account of the trip can be found in his book, *News from Tartary: A Journey from Peking to Kashmir*, and Maillart's version is recorded in her book, *Forbidden Journey*. Rob Gifford's *Road to China: A Journey into the Future of a Rising Power* (annotated in "The Journey" chapter of this book) also took place on the Old Silk Road, and it is interesting to compare the more capitalist China that Gifford encountered in 2005 with the more ideological China that Stevens encountered in 1985. Peter Hessler's *Country Driving: A Journey Through China from Farm to Factory* is a more contemporary look at the rapid pace of change in China and how it has affected the lives of ordinary citizens.

Trillin, Calvin

Travels with Alice. New York: Ticknor & Fields, 1989. 195 pp. ISBN: 9780899199108

Trillin's witty little book of essays recounts several trips to Europe with his wife Alice and their two daughters and is full of helpful hints on such things as how to judge gelato in Italy and how to fit in at a Paris café. His reflections range from memories of car trips as a child (the son of a grocer) to the elaborate 50th birthday trip he arranged for his wife. Throughout the book, Trillin's love of food and his love for his wife are obvious. One word of warning, though: this is a book to make the reader very hungry.

Subjects: Essays; Food; Humor; Quick Reads; Spouses

Categories: Family Travel; In Search of Food

Places: Barbados; Caribbean; France; Italy; New York City; Spain; United States (Various)

Now Try: Sadly, Alice Trillin died on September 11, 2001, and her husband's tribute to her humor and her "child's sense of wonderment" can be found in the tender and intimate *About Alice*. For readers who enjoy the "foodie" aspect of Trillin's writing, Jeffrey Steingarten's two books, *It Must've Been Something I Ate* and *The Man Who Ate Everything* can be recommended; both contain a high level of appreciation for food and travel. (The latter is annotated in this chapter.) London restaurant critic Jay Rayner's enjoyable *The Man Who Ate the World: In Search of the Perfect Dinner*, in which the author traveled the world, met master chefs, and ate expensive food, may also be of interest.

Trillin, Calvin

The Tummy Trilogy. New York: Farrar, Straus, and Giroux, 1994. 386 pp. ISBN: 9780374524173

This volume contains three of Trillin's classic food-oriented travel narratives, each of which was originally published separately: *America Fried* (1974);

Alice, Let's Eat: Further Adventures of a Happy Eater (1978); and *Third Helpings* (1983). Trillin travels throughout the United States to sing the praises of local food and to decry pretentious restaurants. Whether he's enjoying baked oysters in Wagaman, Louisiana, or fried chicken in Crawford County, Kansas, Trillin (whom Craig Claiborne called "the Walt Whitman of American eats") celebrates the nation's food with a dry wit and an amazing appetite.

Subjects: Essays; Food; Humor; Spouses

Categories: Family Travel; In Search of Food

Places: Japan; Kansas City; Martinique; New York City; United States (Various)

Now Try: Trillin's more recent collection of essays on food and travel, *Feeding a Yen*, is annotated in this chapter. Patricia Volk's *Stuffed: Adventures of a Restaurant Family* is funny and tender, like much of Trillin, and the focus on her restaurant family may appeal to fans of Trillin, whose wife Alice and daughters are often featured in his stories. Titles by "foodies" like M.F.K. Fisher (*The Art of Eating*) or Ruth Reichel (*Tender at the Bone: Growing Up at the Table*) might also be recommended, but they are more memoirs than travel narratives. Jane and Michael Stern's *Roadfood: The Coast-to-Coast Guide to 800 of the Best Barbecue Joints, Lobster Shacks, Ice Cream Parlors, Highway Diners, and Much, Much More* is more travel guide than travel narrative but is indispensible to anyone interested in American food. PBS fans will be familiar with the shows *Sandwiches That You Will Like* and *A Hot Dog Program*, and DVDs for both shows are available; both celebrate American food.

In Search of Food

As noted earlier, narratives in the "Quests" subgenre represent travel that has a motivation besides merely reaching the destination. The purpose of travel may be the traveler's search for and interest in food, and these titles are the focus of this first category. The search may be for a specific kind of food (candy in Steve Almond's *Candyfreak: A Journey through the Chocolate Underbelly of America*) or the food of a specific country (China in Fuchsia Dunlop's *Shark's Fin and Sichuan Pepper: A Sweet-Sour Memoir of Eating in China*) or the food of a specific area of a country (the Spanish province of Galicia in John Barlow's *Everything but the Squeal: Eating the Whole Hog in Northern Spain*) or even the "lost" food of a country or region (Andrew Beahrs's *Twain's Feast: Searching for America's Lost Foods in the Footsteps of Samuel Clemens*). Drinks are included (Kate Hopkins's *99 Drams of Whiskey: The Accidental Hedonist's Quest for the Perfect Shot and the History of the Drink* and Evan McHugh's *Pint-Sized Ireland: In Search of the Perfect Guinness*).

"Foodies" and fans of other food-oriented nonfiction (including folks like my friend Jerry, who just enjoys reading cookbooks) should take particular pleasure in these titles. Because eating is a social activity in many cultures, some of the titles have a strong character appeal. Because food is often a reflection of the culture in which it is eaten, several titles provide insights into the culture of a locality, a good example being Fuchsia Dunlop's *Shark's Fin and Sichuan Pepper: A Sweet-Sour Memoir of Eating in China*, which looks at the economic upheavals taking place in China during her travels there in search of regional cuisines. Several of the titles (John Barlow's *Everything but the Squeal: Eating the Whole Hog in Northern Spain*) are also humorous and will appeal to readers who appreciate a good laugh. Others (like Linda Ellerbee's *Take Big Bites: Adventures Around the World and Across the Table*) are very personal and blend in elements of memoir and self-discovery.

Readers who enjoy titles where the traveler goes in search of food may also be drawn to titles in the cooking and food genres that do not necessarily involve travel, even a biography like Jacques Pepin's *The Apprentice: My Life in the Kitchen* or a history like Deborah Cadbury's *Chocolate Wars: The 150-Year Rivalry Between the World's Greatest Chocolate Makers*. Fiction with strong food themes (Laura Esquivel's *Like Water for Chocolate* or Joanne Harris's *Chocolat*) may also be of interest.

Almond, Steve

Candyfreak: A Journey through the Chocolate Underbelly of America. Chapel Hill, NC: Algonquin Books of Chapel Hill, 2004. 266 pp. ISBN: 9781565124219

The appropriately named Almond is a fiction writer and self-confessed candy freak, and his book is a quest for the delights served up by America's smaller candy makers: Clark Bars in Pittsburgh; Peanut Chews in Philadelphia; Twin Bings in Sioux City; Goo Goo Clusters in Nashville; and Idaho Spuds in Boise. Almond, who claims to have eaten a piece of candy every day of his life, is clearly obsessed and was motivated to write the book by the loss of candies like the chocolate-and-peanut-butter Oompah, the Bit-O-Choc, and his own Madeleine, the Caravelle. *Candyfreak* is a quirky celebration of the individuality of the small companies struggling for survival in a world made more homogeneous by the big three of Mars, Nestle, and Hershey.

Subjects: Business; Candy; Candy Industry; Chocolate; Humor

Places: United States (Various)

Now Try: Almond's essay collection, *(Not That You Asked): Rants, Exploits, and Obsessions*, features his snappy tirades against Sean Hannity, Oprah Winfrey, and other cultural icons, and Almond's book *Rock and Roll Will Save Your Life: A Book by and for the Fanatics Among Us* is part memoir and part paean to rock music; one critic described it as a nonfiction version of Nick Hornby's *High Fidelity*. Almond also contributed an essay to Douglas Bauer's collection of essays on memorable meals, *Death by Pad Thai: And Other Unforgettable Meals*. *Candy and Me*, by Hilary Liftin, is more memoir and less travel, but she does recount her life in terms of the candy that she consumed. Almond discusses the companies that create our chocolate confections, and Deborah Cadbury (yes, that Cadbury family) provides an insider's look at the history of the large chocolate makers in *Chocolate Wars: The 150-Year Rivalry Between the World's Greatest Chocolate Makers*. The competition among candy makers is also captured in the novel *Daalder's Chocolates* by Philibert Schogt, whose protagonist has to close his beloved chocolate shop in the face of competition from one of the giant corporations. Joanne Harris's novel *Chocolat* tells of a woman who sets up a chocolaterie in a small French town, in the process angering the townsfolk both for her decadent treats and for her relationship with a gypsy. The film version, starring Juliette Binoche and Johnny Depp, is scrumptious.

Barlow, John

Everything but the Squeal: Eating the Whole Hog in Northern Spain. New York: Farrar, Straus & Giroux, 2008. 306 pp. ISBN: 9780374150105

Barlow is a novelist and self-professed glutton who lives in the Spanish province of Galicia and who decided to spend a year traveling around the province to eat every part of the pig possible: from cured hams and chorizo to pig bladder pudding. He sought out heirloom hogs that had been rescued from extinction, attended a thousand-year-old ant-throwing festival, and visited Fidel Castro's aunt. The book is more than a treatise on the Galician cuisine, however, and looks at the region's traditions, culture, and inhabitants as well. Barlow is an amiable, funny writer (one reviewer compared him to Bill Bryson), and the book is humorous as well as informative.

Subjects: Animals; Cooking (Pork); Food; Foodies; Humor; Marriage

Places: Spain

Now Try: Peter Kaminsky traveled far and wide (from Kentucky to Burgundy, from Andalucia to Georgia) in his search for the perfect pig in the delightful *Pig Perfect: Encounters with Remarkable Swine and Some Great Ways to Cook Them.* Stéphane Reynaud's *Pork and Sons* is another book that combines travel with an appreciation of the pig; the book also includes 150 recipes. Tasting a slice of *lardo* (pig fat) prepared by Mario Batali was part of what motivated Bill Buford to quit his job at *The New Yorker* and work in restaurant kitchens in order to gain a chef's knowledge of food, as he explains in his memoir, *Heat: An Amateur's Adventures as Kitchen Slave, Line Cook, Pasta-Maker, and Apprentice to a Dante-Quoting Butcher in Tuscany.* Finally, Fergus Henderson's *The Whole Beast: Nose to Tail Eating* may be recommended to readers interested in a cookbook that focuses on eating every part of whatever animal is being served.

Beahrs, Andrew

Twain's Feast: Searching for America's Lost Foods in the Footsteps of Samuel Clemens. New York: Penguin Press, 2010. 323 pp. ISBN: 9781594202599

When Mark Twain traveled with his family in Europe in 1879, he jotted down a list of foods that he had eaten as a young man, foods that he now yearned for, foods like Illinois prairie hens and Nevada lake trout. Beahrs, a novelist and an anthropologist, took this list and searched across the United States to find the dishes in their original regional preparations. His focus is more on the food and less on Twain, and he takes the opportunity to explore a wide range of historical and cultural questions, from the recent industrialization of agriculture to the diet of the slaves to water reclamation in the far West. The book celebrates American regional food and makes a strong argument for being a locavore.

Subjects: American History; Authors ; Cooking; Food

Categories: In the Footsteps of . . .

Places: Arkansas; California; Illinois; Louisiana; Massachusetts; Nevada

Now Try: Twain's list of 80 foods that he had eaten as a young man and that he missed as he toured Europe may be found in *A Tramp Abroad*, which is annotated in the "Travel Humor" chapter of this book. In *America Eats!: On the Road With the WPA—The Fish Fries, Box Supper Socials, and Chitlin Feasts That Define Real American Food*, Pat Willard followed in the footsteps of WPA writers who wrote unpublished accounts of American food fairs and festivals in the 1930s; Willard found that a number of these fairs and foods still exist. Jane Ziegelman's *97 Orchard: An Edible History of Five Immigrant Families in One New York Tenement* does not involve travel but does provide a fascinating portrait of immigrant families in late 19th- and early 20th- century New York (German, Italian, Irish, and Jewish families) through the foods that they ate.

Bourdain, Anthony

A Cook's Tour: In Search of the Perfect Meal. New York: Bloomsbury, 2001. 274 pp. ISBN: 9781582341408

Former chef and Food Network star Bourdain traveled around the world in search of "the perfect meal," by which he means the ideal combination of food, atmosphere, and company. The book is not for those who are squeamish about what and where they eat, as Bourdain's meals included lamb testicles in Morocco, live cobra heart in Vietnam, and reindeer in Russia. It is also not for those who dislike strong language and strong opinions; one reviewer described Bourdain as "Hunter S. Thompson high on paella instead of peyote." Nevertheless, this is the book for foodies who enjoy a good adventure, who understand that eating well is the foundation of living together, and who appreciate the connections between the food, the land, and hard work. Bourdain's enthusiasm is infectious, particularly when he is talking about the things he loves, like the Japanese obsession with quality or the sense of community in small-town Mexico.

Subjects: Cooking; Dark Humor; Essays; Food; Foodies; Quick Reads

Places: Africa; California; Cambodia; France; Japan; Mexico; Morocco; Portugal; Russia; Spain; Vietnam

Awards: *New York Times* Notable Book, 2002

Now Try: Bourdain gained notoriety with *Kitchen Confidential: Adventures in the Culinary Underbelly*, a revealing and somewhat unsettling tour behind the scenes of gourmet restaurants. His later book, *No Reservations: Around the World on an Empty Stomach*, is similar to *A Cook's Tour* but contains many more photographs and is largely a companion book to his Travel Channel show of the same name. Another Travel Channel star, Andrew Zimmern, tells of his travels in search of strange foods (cow vein stew, giant flying ants, raw camel kidneys, and Hunan-style rooster balls) in *The Bizarre Truth: How I Walked Out the Door Mouth First . . . and Came Back Shaking My Head*, another title that the squeamish may wish to skip. While Bourdain and Zimmern focus on interesting foods, Zane Lamprey samples drinks around the world (from Irish whisky to Tanzanian "bee brew") in the aptly titled *Three Sheets: Drinking Made Easy! 6 Continents, 15 Countries, 190 Drinks, and 1 Mean Hangover!*

Ciezadlo, Annia

Day of Honey: A Memoir of Food, Love, and War. New York: Free Press, 2011. 382 pp. ISBN: 9781416583936

Annia Ciezadlo and her husband spent six years serving as correspondents in Baghdad and Beirut, and her mouth-watering memoir of those years focuses on the food and friends that the couple encountered; as Ciezadlo puts it, "I cook to comprehend the place I've landed in." Her passion for food and her examination of the history of Middle Eastern food are mixed with startling scenes of war, narrow escapes, dangerous culture clashes, and struggles to define her identity in these foreign lands. The final chapter of the book contains recipes for many of the dishes she mentions in her narrative. As one reviewer noted, Ciezadlo "reminds us that the best memoirs are kaleidoscopes that blend an author's life and larger truths to make a sparkling whole."

Subjects: Cooking; Culture Clashes; Food; Memoirs; Self-Discovery; Spouses; Women Travelers

Places: Baghdad; Beirut; Iraq; Lebanon

Now Try: Greg and Lucy Malouf explore the cuisines of Lebanon and Syria in their combination cookbook and travel narrative, *Saha: A Chef's Journey Through Lebanon and Syria*; Lucy's narrative of their time in the Middle East is mixed in with Greg's recipes for Bedouin spinach and lentil soup, lamb shawarma, and other delights. Salma Abdelnour was flown out of war-torn Beirut in 1981, when she was nine years old; she returned 30 years later and writes about the rediscovery of home and food there in *Jasmine and Fire: A Bittersweet Year in Beirut*. Cheryl Lu-Lien Tan's *A Tiger in the Kitchen: A Memoir of Food and Family* is another memoir that mixes food with larger issues; after living in the United States for over a dozen years, Tan returns home to Singapore to learn more about her family and its recipes. Deborah Copaken Kogan's memoir of her experiences as a photographer in various war zones, *Shutterbabe: Adventures in Love and War*, may also appeal to readers who enjoyed *Day of Honey*, as may her novel, *Between Here and April*, which explores similar themes.

Cloud, Roy

To Burgundy and Back Again: A Tale of Wine, France, and Brotherhood. Guilford, CT: Lyons Press, 2011. 216 pp. ISBN: 9780762764556

Cloud, who had worked in the wine business for years, traveled to France for the first time in search of wines for his employer. The fact that Cloud did not speak French led him to ask his French-speaking brother to accompany him, and the book focuses as much on the family's history (a strong-willed father who suffered a terrible bicycling accident on his own trip to France, the brother's traumatic divorce, Cloud's own work in the wine business) as it does on the wine regions of Burgundy, the Loire, and the Rhone. There are also charming portraits of French wine producers that Cloud has known and worked with as well as frequent reminders of the ways in which wine connects us to life.

Subjects: Brothers; Family Relationships; Fathers and Sons; Quick Reads; Wine

Places: France

Now Try: Kathryn Borel's father was a wine aficionado who had failed to convey his appreciation of wine to his daughter, but following a tragedy in her life, Borel decided to get to know her father and his passion for wine through a father–daughter French wine trip; their story is told in Borel's *Corked: A Memoir*. Neal I. Rosenthal takes readers on a tour of family-owned vineyards in France and Italy in his book, *Reflections of a Wine Merchant*, which highlights the hard, often unpleasant work of winemaking. In Rex Pickett's amusing novel, *Sideways*, two friends, Miles and Jake, take a road trip through California's wine country to celebrate Jake's last few days of freedom before getting married; the novel is filled with details about wine, wine snobbery, and friendship. *Three Weeks with My Brother*, by Nicholas Sparks and Micah Sparks, tells the story of another trip taken by two brothers, although in a somewhat gentler manner; it is annotated in "The Journey."

Dunlop, Fuchsia

Shark's Fin and Sichuan Pepper: A Sweet-Sour Memoir of Eating in China. New York: W.W. Norton, 2008. 320 pp. ISBN: 9780393066579

Dunlop is a British food writer who has written well-known books on Sichuan and Hunan cuisine. In *Shark's Fin and Sichuan Pepper*, she returned to China to examine the regional cuisines, Chinese attitudes toward food, and the blending of food and politics in the various cooking schools. Dunlop ate and discusses a wide range of food (from mixed vegetables to stir-fried snake) and the chapters include recipes as well as her memories of earlier visits to and culinary training in China. Because the trip on which this book is based took place during the middle of China's economic upheavals, Dunlop is also able to provide insights into the cultural transformations she witnessed.

Subjects: Cooking; Culture Clash; Food; Recipes; Women Travelers

Places: China

Now Try: The cookbooks that made Fuchsia Dunlop famous are *Land of Plenty: A Treasury of Authentic Sichuan Cooking* and *Revolutionary Chinese Cookbook: Recipes from Hunan Province,* both of which include information on the history and geography of two regions. Jen Lin-Liu's evocative memoir and cookbook, *Serve the People: A Stir-Fried Journey Through China,* recounts her years living and working in Shanghai and Beijing, where she attended a culinary school. *Hot, Sour, Salty, Sweet: A Culinary Journey through Southeast Asia,* by Jeffrey Alford and Naomi Duguid, is more cookbook than travel narrative, but the authors do include an impressive knowledge of the countries from which their food comes. *The Last Chinese Chef,* a novel by Nicole Mones, tells the story of a food writer who goes to China to profile a Jewish-Chinese chef and determine the validity of a paternity claim against her late husband. For a slightly different take on Chinese cuisine, one that focuses on the history of Chinese food in America, readers may want to try Jennifer 8. Lee's *The Fortune Cookie Chronicles: Adventures in the World of Chinese Food.*

Ellerbee, Linda

Take Big Bites: Adventures Around the World and Across the Table. New York: Putnam's Sons, 2005. 302 pp. ISBN: 9780399152689

Ellerbee, an Emmy-award-winning journalist, writes about her career assignments around the world and the eating adventures that accompanied those assignments: pho in Vietnam, fried pork rinds in Texas, pâté in France, and caviar aboard Malcolm Forbes's yacht, among others. In addition to her reflections on a life of journalism and eating, Ellerbee shares the intimate details of her battle with breast cancer, her attempts to revive a failing marriage, and her general passion for life. The book is witty and easy to digest, mixes memoir with travel narrative, and ends each chapter with a recipe or two.

Subjects: Cooking; Food; Humor; Recipes; Self-Discovery; Women Travelers

Places: Afghanistan; Alaska; Arizona; Baltimore; Bolivia; California; El Salvador; England; France; Hawaii; Italy; London; New Mexico; New Orleans; New York; Oregon; Paris; Portland; Santorini; Seattle; Texas; Turkey; Vietnam; Wales

Now Try: The *New York Times* reviewed *Take Big Bites* alongside gossip columnist Liz Smith's *Dishing: Great Dish—and Dishes—from America's Most Beloved Gossip Columnist,* which combines anecdotes from Smith's life with descriptions of the food she was eating at the time. The *Times* review also mentioned Nora Ephron's novel, *Heartburn,* in which the author mixes recipes into her story of a woman who realizes that her husband is having an affair. Food writer Ruth Reichl's books may appeal to readers who enjoyed *Take Big Bites,* especially her memoir *Tender at the Bone: Growing Up at the Table,* which focuses on Reichl's relationship with her bipolar mother and her emotionally distant father, and *Garlic and Sapphires: The Secret Life of a Critic in Disguise,* a collection of essays that recount her "adventures" as a food critic for the *New York Times.*

Flinn, Kathleen

The Sharper Your Knife, the Less You Cry: Love, Laughter, and Tears in Paris at the World's Most Famous Cooking School. New York: Viking, 2007. 285 pp. ISBN: 9780670018239

When 30-something Kathleen Flinn's corporate job in London was eliminated, she decided to pursue a lifelong dream and attend the famous French cooking school, Le Cordon Bleu. Her story of surviving the rigors of the elite culinary school (deboning a chicken while leaving its skin intact or chopping live lobsters in half) is interwoven with descriptions of daily life in Paris (buying baguettes and French wine, strolling through the streets) and her developing romance. Flinn includes recipes for dishes as diverse as *Poulet a la Moutarde* (Chicken with Mustard Sauce) and *Chicorees Frisees Classique* (Classic Belgian Endives) and tells her story with a light and amusing style.

Subjects: Coming of Age; Cooking; Education; Food; Humor; Marriage; Memoirs

Places: France; Paris

Now Try: Flinn's second book, *The Kitchen Counter Cooking School: How a Few Simple Lessons Transformed Nine Culinary Novices into Fearless Home Cooks* is not a travel narrative but should have appeal for foodies; Flinn tells of her year-long project to help nine novice cooks hone their cooking skills and, in the process, reports on the state of home cooking in general. Flinn's experiences at Le Cordon Bleu can be compared with those of Julia Child, as recounted in her book, *My Life in France* (annotated in "The Expatriate Life" chapter of this book). Readers interested in celebrity chefs may enjoy Michael Ruhlman's *The Reach of a Chef: Professional Cooks in the Age of Celebrity*, in which the author traveled to Chicago, Las Vegas, and other cities to meet famous chefs and discuss the phenomenon of the celebrity chef.

Fort, Matthew

Eating Up Italy: Voyages on a Vespa. New York: Centro Books, 2006. 296 pp. ISBN: 9781933572024

Fort, a British food writer, combines travel narrative and cookbook in this exploration of Italy through its food, from the relatively commonplace *pasta al forno* to the more adventurous stewed eel and Neapolitan tripe. Mixing descriptions of the Italian cuisine with reflections on the country's history, traditions, and cultures, Fort emphasizes the regional nuances that make each part of the country special and celebrates the people who produce and treasure these diverse foods.

Subjects: Cooking; Food; Recipes

Places: Italy

Now Try: Fort also wrote *Sweet Honey, Bitter Lemons: Travels in Sicily on a Vespa,* which does for the island of Sicily what *Eating Up Italy* does for the mainland. Isabella Dusi takes the reader on a journey through Tuscany to discover the origins of Brunello di Montalcino, a world-famous wine, in *Bel Vino: A Year of Sundrenched Pleasure Among the Vines of Tuscany*. Michael Tucker's *Living in a Foreign Language: A Memoir of Food, Wine, and Love in Italy* is a celebration of the lifestyle, cuisine, and local wine of the central Italian region of Umbria. Fiction readers interested in Italy and food may enjoy Lily Prior's debut novel, *La Cucina: A Novel of Rapture,* in which a heartbroken librarian falls in love with an English chef with whom she shares a love of cooking.

Hopkins, Kate

99 Drams of Whiskey: The Accidental Hedonist's Quest for the Perfect Shot and the History of the Drink. New York: St. Martin's Press, 2009. 308 pp. ISBN: 9780312381080

Hopkins, who writes "The Accidental Hedonist" blog (http://accidentalhedonist.com/), and a friend went in search of the best whiskeys in the world, wandering from distillery to distillery in the United States, Canada, Scotland, and Ireland. The book outlines their quest and includes both a history of the whiskey trade (America's Whiskey Rebellion of 1794, the rivalry between Ireland and Scotland for the best malt, how Prohibition devastated the whiskey industry in the United States) and a discussion of some more technical matters (the art of distilling and the proper ways of drinking whiskey). The book is particularly down-to-earth and lacks the snobbery often associated with books that deal with wine and other drinks.

Subjects: Alcohol; Drinks; Whiskey; Women Travelers

Places: Canada; Ireland; Kentucky; Pittsburgh; Scotland

Now Try: Jason Wilson's *Boozehound: On the Trail of the Rare, the Obscure, and the Overrated in Spirits* documents that author's quest for the best liquors in the world: Mexican tequila, French cognac, Peruvian pisco. Andrew Jefford writes about the seven whiskey distilleries on the Scottish Isle of Islay and provides a history of the island itself in the compelling *Peat Smoke and Spirit*. Max Watman traveled from Colorado to Virginia to document those who produce and sell homegrown alcohol in the enjoyable book, *Chasing the White Dog: An Amateur Outlaw's Adventures in Moonshine*.

Mayle, Peter

French Lessons: Adventures with Knife, Fork, and Corkscrew. New York: Alfred A. Knopf, 2001. 227 pp. ISBN: 9780375405907

Mayle is best known for his books about Provence, but in *French Lessons*, he wanders throughout France in search of food and food festivals: the annual cheese fair at Livarot; the frog's-leg festival in Vitel; the snail fair in Martigny-les-Bains; and the Catholic mass in Richerenches, which gives thanks for a rare and expensive black truffle. As always, Mayle is charming and cultured, and his love of the

French people is obvious. An appetizing mix of dry wit and scrumptious facts, *French Lessons* is a celebration of the tastes and smells of France and especially the French passion for food.

Subjects: Food; Humor; Quick Reads

Places: France

Series: *Vintage Departures*

Now Try: Mayle's books about Provence (*A Year in Provence, Toujours Provence*, and *Encore Provence*) are annotated in this book's chapter on "The Expatriate Life." Georgeanne Brennan's *A Pig in Provence: Good Food and Simple Pleasures in the South of France* is another culinary tour of Provence and its food, including truffles, goat cheese, and garlic. Former Parisian restaurant owner Peta Mathias looks at French cuisine in restaurants, farmhouses, barges, and truck stops in *French Toast: Eating and Laughing Your Way Around France*. Susan Hermann Loomis's *On Rue Tatin: Living and Cooking in a French Town* is more memoir than travel narrative and tells the story of an American who attended a French cooking school and later returned to France to buy and restore a dilapidated convent; the book is filled with recipes and stories about the food of the Normandy region of France. Fiction that focuses on French food includes Muriel Barbery's *Gourmet Rhapsody*, in which a French food critic lies on his death bed and reflects on the flavors of his life, and Nancy Coons's *The Feasting Season*, about an American travel writer who is asked to write a guidebook on French history and who encounters the rich variety of French provincial food as she travels through the country.

McHugh, Evan

Pint-Sized Ireland: In Search of the Perfect Guinness. New York: Thomas Dunne Books/St. Martin's Press, 2007. 280 pp. ISBN: 9780312363666

McHugh, an Australian, and his future wife traveled from the Guinness brewery in Dublin to Westport on Ireland's west coast to Belfast, the capital of Northern Ireland, in search of the perfect pint of the bitter dark liquid called stout. Even though McHugh's first taste of stout was disappointing and even though he decided that stout is an acquired taste, he committed himself to acquiring that taste. The book is filled with wild, hilarious tales of their visits to pubs with locals and other fellow travelers, and in fact, the book is less about stout and more about camaraderie and friendship.

Subjects: Beer; Drinks; Humor

Places: Ireland

Now Try: Pulitzer Prize winner Ken Wells toured the United States to learn more about beer in the enjoyable *Travels with Barley: A Journey Through Beer Culture in America*. Pete McCarthy did a lot of drinking and visiting bars in his delightfully funny exploration of what it means to be Irish, *McCarthy's Bar: A Journey of Discovery in the West of Ireland*, which is annotated in the "Travel Humor" section of this book. David Monagan returned to his roots in Cork,

Ireland, and wrote about the experience (particularly the contrast between the Ireland of the present and that of his memory) in *Jaywalking with the Irish*. One of the best-known recent Irish writers is Frank McCourt, whose memoir *Angela's Ashes* tells of his childhood in Ireland, marked by extreme poverty and alcoholism.

Parker Bowles, Tom

The Year of Eating Dangerously: A Global Adventure in Search of Culinary Extremes. New York: St. Martin's Press, 2007 [2006]. 374 pp. ISBN: 9780312373788

"I wanted to sample everything, however gruesome," writes food journalist Parker Bowles in the introduction to this exploration of some of the world's oddest and most "dangerous" foods. He did eat the truly dangerous (fugu in Japan) but most of his meals were merely disgusting (smelly dog soup in Korea, sea slugs and millipedes in China) or, at best, exciting (the National Fiery Foods and Barbeque Show in Albuquerque). Parker Bowles writes with a self-deprecating humor and lots of references to his British childhood, and the book is an appreciation, not just of the exotic foods of other countries, but also of their cultures and their humanity.

Subjects: Culture Clash; Food; Humor

Places: Albuquerque; China; England; Nashville; Italy; Japan; Korea; Laos; Sicily; Spain; Tokyo

Now Try: Several reviewers compared Parker Bowles to Anthony Bourdain, although without the drugs, profanity, and machismo. Bourdain's *A Cook's Tour: In Search of the Perfect Meal* is annotated in this chapter and includes meals of lamb testicles and live cobra heart. Douglas Bauer collected 20 essays about favorite meals from various writers in *Death by Pad Thai: And Other Unforgettable Meals*, and while they are generally not dangerous, the meals will interest foodies: Amy Bloom on lasagna, Jane Stern on her first post-wedding Thanksgiving, and Steve Almond on lobster pad thai. Moira Hodgson's memoir of meals, *It Seemed Like a Good Idea at the Time: My Adventures in Life and Food*, is another book that will appeal to foodies, although again the foods are less exotic than those discussed by Parker Bowles. Another British writer, Gina Mallet, writes about fast foods, the foods of her childhood, and a host of other food-related topics in the wide-ranging *Last Chance to Eat: The Fate of Taste in a Fast Food World*.

Roahen, Sara

Gumbo Tales: Finding My Place at the New Orleans Table. New York: W.W. Norton, 2008. 293 pp. ISBN: 9780393061673

Roahen, a food writer, presents a culinary tribute to her adopted hometown in this tour of the Crescent City. She bases her thoughts on the French notion of *terroir* (how a region's geography and climate affects its grapes and thereby its wines) and talks about the "emotional *terroir*" of New Orleans, treating readers to a celebration of the major food groups of the city, the history and traditions surrounding these foods, and the people who developed them. The menu of this delicious book includes muffalettas, po'boys, mudbugs, bread pudding, sezeracs, and gumbo as well as the author's observations of New Orleans both before and after Katrina.

Subjects: Food; Women Travelers

Places: New Orleans

Now Try: Like Roahen, Tom Fitzmorris wrote a food column for a New Orleans newspaper; his *Hungry Town: A Culinary History of New Orleans, the City Where Food Is Almost Everything* is another history of New Orleans cuisine, with a particular focus on the aftermath of Katrina. Two of New Orleans's best-known chefs, Emeril Lagasse and Paul Prudhomme, have published cookbooks that may interest readers of *Gumbo Tales*, particularly *Emeril's New New Orleans Cooking* and *Chef Paul Prudhomme's Louisiana Kitchen*. Roy Blount's delightful *Feet on the Street: Rambles Around New Orleans* should appeal to anyone interested in the Big Easy; it is annotated in the chapter entitled "A Sense of Place." In Poppy Z. Brite's novel *Liquor*, the main characters decide to open a restaurant in New Orleans whose entire menu is based on liquor.

Steingarten, Jeffrey

The Man Who Ate Everything: And Other Gastronomic Feats, Disputes, and Pleasurable Pursuits. New York: Alfred A. Knopf, 1997. 514 pp. ISBN: 9780679430889

Steingarten became the food critic at *Vogue* in 1989, and this collection of essays approaches food from so many angles that the *New York Times* called the book "part cookbook, part travelogue, part medical and scientific treatise, part propaganda pamphlet and part self-deprecating self-portrait." His travels include sampling choucroute in Alsace, eating hand-massaged beef in Japan, and searching for the ultimate in ice cream in Sicily. He also tackles such topics as how to bake the perfect sourdough, how to bottle one's own mineral water, and why salt and sugar aren't bad for you. Steingarten can be both funny and argumentative, and the book includes some very good recipes as well.

Subjects: Cooking; Essays; Food; Humor; Recipes

Places: France; Italy; Japan; New York City; Sicily; Venice

Now Try: Steingarten followed up *The Man Who Ate Everything* with an equally hilarious and knowledgeable book, *It Must've Been Something I Ate*, which includes trips to France to witness a pig slaughter and to the Atlantic off North Carolina to fish for bluefin tuna. Steingarten includes some food science in his essays, and readers who are interested in that topic may find Robert Wolke's *What Einstein Told His Chef: Kitchen Science Explained* of interest. Alton Brown, the host of the Food Network's *Good Eats*, focuses on the science behind the food as well, and his trilogy, *Good Eats: The Early Years*, *Good Eats 2: The Middle Years*, and *Good Eats 3: The Later Years* may be of interest. Another male restaurant critic, Frank Bruni, has written *Born Round*, a fascinating memoir that focuses on his battles with his weight and his attempts to learn to love food "just enough."

Trillin, Calvin

Feeding a Yen: Savoring Local Specialties, From Kansas City to Cuzco. New York: Random House, 2003. 197 pp. ISBN: 978–0375508080

This book's 14 mouth-watering essays feature *New Yorker* writer Calvin Trillin as he details his "Register of Frustration and Deprivation," local foods that are practically unavailable outside their native lands. Trillin reminisces about and attempts to track down these homey, ethnic foods sold in small shops in faraway places: *pimientos de Padrón* from Spain, fried fish from the Barbados, *pan bagnats* from France, ceviche from Peru, boudin from Louisiana, posole from New Mexico, fish tacos from San Diego, and barbecue from Kansas City. Members of Trillin's family appear in some of the essays, particularly his late wife Alice and his daughter, who had moved to California and whom Trillin tried to lure back to Manhattan with the promise of "real" bagels. Trillin's dry wit is often self-deprecating but always gentle and good-natured.

Subjects: Essays; Food; Humor; Quick Reads

Categories: Family Travel

Places: Barbados; France; Kansas City; New York City; Nice; Peru; Spain; United States (Various)

Awards: *New York Times* Notable Books, 2003

Now Try: Trillin has written a number of other titles that deal with travel and food, and these might also be appreciated by readers who like *Feeding a Yen*. They include *American Fried: Adventures of a Happy Eater, Alice, Let's Eat: Further Adventures of a Happy Eater, Third Helpings,* and *Travels with Alice,* all of which are annotated in the "Classics" section of this chapter (the first three as *The Tummy Trilogy*). *Vogue* food critic Jeffrey Steingarten's *The Man Who Ate Everything: And Other Gastronomic Feats, Disputes, and Pleasurable Pursuits* is another collection of witty essays featuring strong opinions about what is and isn't good food as well as a wide range of foods, from the perfect piecrust to Alsatian choucroute. Linda Ellerbee's *Take Big Bites: Adventures Around the World and Across the Table* (annotated in this section) is also humorous and full of personal observations that reflect an appreciation of a wide range of foods, particularly ethnic foods. One popular source of local foods is the food trucks that are becoming more popular throughout the United States; Heather Shouse traveled to 18 major cities and interviewed 50 food vendors for her book, *Food Trucks: Dispatches and Recipes from the Best Kitchens on Wheels,* which includes everything from taco carts to ice cream trucks to crepe trailers.

Vanderhoof, Ann

An Embarrassment of Mangoes: A Caribbean Interlude. New York: Broadway, 2003. 305 pp. ISBN: 9780767914024

Vanderhoof writes about the two-year voyage that she and her husband took from Toronto to the Caribbean on a 42-foot sailboat. They dropped anchor in 16 countries and 47 separate islands, enjoying local food and festivities, secluded beaches, and beautiful sunsets. They also faced the challenges of unpredictable weather, the region's poverty, and the tedious chores associated with life on a sailboat, and the book is as much about a voyage of self-discovery as it about discovering "island time." The recipes at the end of each chapter (e.g., lobster curry, mango crisp, Bahamian mac and cheese) will also appeal to foodies.

Subjects: Food; Islands; Sailing; Self-Discovery; Spouses; Women Travelers

Places: Bahamas; Caribbean; Cayman Islands; Dominican Republic; Florida; Georgia; Grenada; New York; North Carolina; Ontario; South Carolina; Toronto; Trinidad and Tobago

Now Try: Readers who liked Vanderhoof's descriptions of Caribbean food may also enjoy Melinda and Robert Blanchard's account of their experience opening a restaurant on the island of Anguilla in *A Trip to the Beach: Living on Island Time in the Caribbean* as well as their cookbook, *At Blanchard's Table: A Trip to the Beach Cookbook.* An earlier book about the Caribbean is Alec Waugh's classic *Love and the Caribbean: Tales, Characters and Scenes of the West Indies*; Waugh was the brother of novelist Evelyn Waugh. In *The Sex Lives of Cannibals, Getting Stoned with Savages,* and *Lost on Planet China* (all annotated in "Travel Humor"), J. Maarten Troost also displays a good sense of humor about accepting different cultures while simultaneously trying to get along with his spouse.

Vanderhoof, Ann

The Spice Necklace: My Adventures in Caribbean Cooking, Eating, and Island Life. Boston: Houghton Mifflin Harcourt, 2010. 459 pp. ISBN: 9780618685370

Vanderhoof, an award-winning food and travel writer, and her husband sailed among the islands of the Caribbean in search of the region's foods: nutmeg and chocolate on the island of Grenada, hot pepper sauce on Trinidad, seaweed on St. Lucia. They also encountered a number of memorable island characters (fishermen, cooks, Rastafarians) who shared recipes and stories about their lives. The book is filled with interesting details about each of the islands they visited, and with humorous stories. Recipes for dishes from stewed goat to mango chow are also included, and the author even suggests alternative ingredients to substitute for items that may be hard to find.

Subjects: Food; Humor; Recipes; Seas; Spouses; Women Travelers

Places: Caribbean; Dominican Republic; Grenada; Guadeloupe; Haiti; Martinique; Saba; St. Kitts; St. Lucia; St. Martin; St. Vincent and the Grenadines; Trinidad and Tobago

Now Try: Melinda and Robert Blanchard chronicle their experience opening a restaurant on the island of Anguilla in *A Trip to the Beach: Living on Island Time in the Caribbean* and follow up with their own cookbook, *At Blanchard's Table: A Trip to the Beach Cookbook.* Herman Wouk's novel *Don't Stop the Carnival* is loosely based on his experiences managing a hotel on one of the U.S. Virgin Islands in the early 1960s.

In Search of History

Another purpose in traveling is to search for history, either the history of a country or countries (Paraguay in John Gimlette's *At the Tomb of the Inflatable Pig: Travels through Paraguay* or the countries that once made up Yugoslavia in Robert D. Kaplan's *Balkan Ghosts: A Journey Through History*) or specific sites within one or more countries (Tony Horwitz's *A Voyage Long and Strange: Rediscovering the New World*) or an event (the Civil War in Tony Horwitz's *Confederates in the Attic: Dispatches from the Unfinished Civil War*) or even an object (the fez in Jeremy Seal's *A Fez of the Heart: Travels Around Turkey In Search Of A Hat*). The traveler may interweave the story that took place many years before with her own experiences, as when Saidiya V. Hartman remembers her grandmother, who was a slave, while visiting Ghana to write about the history of the slave trade in *Lose Your Mother: A Journey Along the Atlantic Slave Route*. The traveler may also draw lessons from her consideration of the individual or event, as when Julia Blackburn reflects on the nature of human relationships in light of Napoleon's exile on St. Helena in *The Emperor's Last Island: A Journey to St. Helena*.

These titles should appeal to readers who are drawn to history as well as to readers of travel narratives. It is worth remembering that Joyce Saricks defines the appeal of frame to include historical setting[2] and that Catherine Ross's research has found that "An interest in a particular subject can trump the distinction between fiction and nonfiction. . . . Many readers said that they would become interested in some topic and then read everything they could on it."[3] The interest in history may also trump the distinction between nonfiction genres such as history and travel.

Consequently, readers who enjoy the titles in this category may also enjoy histories of specific countries (Earl Shorris's *The Life and Times of Mexico*) or even more specific histories, like James Billington's *The Icon and the Axe: An Interpretive History of Russian Culture* or Suzanne Massie's *Land of the Firebird: The Beauty of Old Russia* (both of which deal with Russian cultural history). Such readers may also find historical fiction (Patrick O'Brian's *Aubrey–Maturin* series or James Michener's many country-based novels, like *Mexico, Caravans: A Novel of Afghanistan*, or *Poland*) to be appealing.

Blackburn, Julia

The Emperor's Last Island: A Journey to St. Helena. New York: Pantheon Books, 1991. 277 pp. ISBN: 9780679411505

Blackburn mixes the history of Napoleon's final years on St. Helena with a narrative of her own visit to the island and produces a philosophical reflection on human relationships and, in Napoleon's case, the pain of life in exile from those relationships. Blackburn weaves in other stories as well: the Portuguese nobleman who suffered self-imposed exile on the island for a crime of treason but who also transformed the island into an oasis of extraordinary lushness and beauty; the decline of the island as visitors cut down its trees and exposed the soil to eroding winds; and the island's current state as what the author calls a "training ground for bureaucrats, a ship of fools."

Subjects: 19th Century; Biographies; European History; Quick Reads; Women Travelers

Places: St. Helena

Series: *Vintage Departures*

Now Try: Two of Blackburn's novels have been shortlisted for the Orange Prize: *The Book of Colour,* which begins with a British missionary journeying to an island near Mauritius, and *The Leper's Companions,* about a woman who deals with a loss in her life by joining a group of pilgrims to Jerusalem. Blackburn is also the author of several nonfiction works, including *Daisy Bates in the Desert: A Woman's Life Among the Aborigines,* a biography of an Australian woman who lived in the Australian outback and championed the Aborigines for 43 years. For another book on Napoleon and St. Helena, readers might try Johannes Willms's *Napoleon & St Helena: On the Island of Exile.*

Gimlette, John

At the Tomb of the Inflatable Pig: Travels through Paraguay. New York: Alfred A. Knopf, 2003. 362 pp. ISBN: 9781400041763

Paraguay is a landlocked country in South America and, based on Gimlette's witty history and travelogue, one of the strangest countries in the world. Its national railway has no running trains, for example, and over the years it has served as a haven for Nazis, Mennonites, socialists from Australia, and Islamic extremists. Gimlette has made several visits to the country, beginning when he was 18, and shows an appreciation for the nation while at the same time describing in less than politically correct terms some of the more horrific aspects of Paraguayan history.

Subjects: Humor; South American History

Places: Paraguay

Awards: *New York Times* Notable Book, 2004

Series: *Vintage Departures*

Now Try: Gimlette's latest travel narrative is *Wild Coast: Travels on South America's Untamed Edge,* which focuses on the lesser-known South American countries of Guyana, Suriname, and French Guiana. Robert Carver, whose great-uncle vanished in Paraguay while searching for Inca silver, recounts his journey to that country in *Paradise with Serpents: Travels in the Lost World of Paraguay,* a book that received markedly mixed reviews. Lily Tuck's *The News From Paraguay* is a historical novel told from the point of view of an Irish woman who became the mistress of the son of Paraguay's dictator.

Hartman, Saidiya V.

Lose Your Mother: A Journey Along the Atlantic Slave Route. New York: Farrar, Straus and Giroux, 2007. 270 pp. ISBN: 9780374270827

Hartman, the granddaughter of a slave, makes the history and horror of the Atlantic slave trade more palpable by visiting key sites in Ghana associated with the Middle Passage: holding cells; slave markets; and walled towns built to protect against slave raiders. As the author puts it, "In following the trail of captives from the hinterland to the Atlantic coast, I intend to retrace the process by which lives were destroyed and slaves born." A professor, Hartman writes with a scholarly depth as well as deeply personal reflection and provides an intense but rewarding reconstruction of the lives of those bound for slavery.

Subjects: African Americans; Scholarly Writing; Slavery

Places: Africa; Ghana

Now Try: Readers who want to know more about the Middle Passage may find Stephanie Smallwood's harsh descriptions in *Saltwater Slavery: A Middle Passage from Africa to American Diaspora* to be well researched and informative. Olaudah Equiano's 18th-century memoir, *The Interesting Narrative and Other Writings,* tells how he was kidnapped in Africa at the age of 10, served as a slave to a British naval officer for 10 years, and eventually purchased his freedom. Justin Marozzi traveled through Libya with a colleague and writes about the trip and the history of efforts of British explorers to suppress the African slave trade in *South From Barbary: Along the Slave Routes of the Libyan Sahara.* Barry Unsworth's Booker Prize-winning novel, *Sacred Hunger,* follows the crew of a slave ship from Liverpool to Guinea and through the Middle Passage; the theme of greed is played out against the horrifying details of life aboard a slave ship.

Horwitz, Tony

Confederates in the Attic: Dispatches from the Unfinished Civil War. New York: Pantheon Books, 1998. 406 pp. ISBN: 9780679439783 YA

Horwitz, a Pulitzer Prize-winning war journalist, went in search of the people who keep alive the memory of the War Between the States and the places that are associated with that memory. He talked with those who reenact Civil War battles and those who try to honor their ancestors who fought in the war; he attended a Klan rally and a birthday party given by the Sons of the Confederacy for Stonewall Jackson; he visited Antietam, Gettysburg, and Appomattox. He reflects on his own childhood obsession with the Civil War as well as the ways in which the war is still very much with us all. Although Horwitz clearly has some affinity with the Rebels' cause, he presents a balanced account as well as a good mix of the humorous and the serious, the past and the present.

Subjects: American Civil War; American History; American South; Humor; Investigative Stories; Race Relations

Places: Alabama; Georgia; Kentucky; Mississippi; North Carolina; South Carolina; Tennessee; Virginia

Awards: *New York Times* Notable Book, 1998

Series: *Vintage Departures*

Now Try: Jerry Ellis followed General Sherman's Civil War march through Georgia and gains insight on his native region in *Marching through Georgia: My Walk along Sherman's Route*. *Travels to Hallowed Ground: A Historian's Journey to the American Civil War* by Emory M. Thomas is a short book with interesting insights on the battles that took place at the sites visited by the author. Ken Burns's remarkable documentary series, *The Civil War*, includes many visits to key places in the war. While not a travel narrative, James M. McPherson's book, *For Cause and Comrades: Why Men Fought in the Civil War*, is an excellent examination of the motivations of rank-and-file soldiers for fighting in that war, based largely on their own letters and diaries. Horwitz's dark humor has something in common with Sarah Vowell, whose *Assassination Vacation* (annotated in this chapter) recounts her visits to the sites associated with the first three presidential assassinations, and Hank Stuever, whose *Off Ramp: Adventures and Heartache in the American Elsewhere* looks at offbeat locations, events, and characters in the United States, like a discount funeral home in a strip mall and a group of Texans searching for fragments from the fallen *Columbia* spacecraft.

Horwitz, Tony

A Voyage Long and Strange: Rediscovering the New World. New York: Henry Holt and Co., 2008. 445 pp. ISBN: 9780805076035

Horwitz "roams the annals of early America" in this journey to the sites that mark the history of the United States between Columbus's 1492 "discovery" and Plymouth Rock. Horwitz visited a range of historical places that included Newfoundland, where the Vikings arrived in 1000; the Dominican Republic, which Columbus mistook for the Orient; Daytona Beach, where Ponce de Leon christened Florida; and Roanoke Island, where the ill-fated Lost Colony was attempted. Horwitz interweaves his own travels and portraits of the fascinating people he met with historical accounts and does so with his usual wry sense of humor.

Subjects: 16th Century; American History; Exploration; Explorers; Humor

Places: Dominican Republic; Florida; Massachusetts; Mexico; New Mexico; Newfoundland; North Carolina; Virginia

Awards: ALA Notable Book, 2009; *New York Times* Notable Book, 2008

Now Try: Peter Stark explores American history through "blank spots" on the U.S. map (northern Maine, central Pennsylvania, the Gila desert in New Mexico, and southeast Oregon) in *The Last Empty Places*. John Putnam Demos writes about the experiences of a Puritan minister and his family who were captured by a group of French men and Native Americans and forced to march to Canada in 1704 in *The Unredeemed Captive: A Family Story from Early*

America; the title may appeal to readers who want to read "real" history. Readers interested in more primary sources may enjoy Captain John Smith's *Writings*, which chronicle the first English settlements in North America. Nathaniel Philbrick's novel, *Mayflower: A Story of Courage, Community, and War*, provides a fictional account of the Pilgrim's settlement of New England.

Kaplan, Robert D.

Balkan Ghosts: A Journey Through History. New York: St. Martin's Press, 1993. 307 pp. ISBN: 9780312087012

Kaplan's book serves as both a travel narrative depicting the nations of the Balkan area and a chilling history of the ethnic rivalries in the region, rivalries that would explode in the 1990s into the series of wars in the countries that once made up Yugoslavia. The book is particularly insightful, as it was completed before the first shot of those wars was fired and yet predicts the likely consequences of what the author calls "a confused, often violent ethnic cauldron." Interestingly, the observations on Romania, Bulgaria, and Greece may be the best parts of the book, even if they are less well known than the parts dealing with the former Yugoslavia. Kaplan's book is pessimistic and particularly depressing in its depiction of human depravity

Subjects: European History; Islam; Minorities; Politics; War

Places: Albania; Bulgaria; Croatia; Greece; Macedonia; Romania; Serbia

Awards: ALA Notable Book, 1994

Series: *Vintage Departures*

Now Try: Kaplan repeatedly praises Rebecca West's classic travel narrative on Yugoslavia, *Black Lamb and Grey Falcon*, which discusses the history and culture of the Balkans and was written just before the Nazi invasion of 1941. Sixty years after West's journey, Tony White retraced her footsteps in a collection of essays entitled *Another Fool in the Balkans*; he tries to make sense of the contemporary conflicts by exploring the history and culture of the region. Téa Obreht's riveting novel, *The Tiger's Wife*, is set in a war-torn Balkan country and follows a young doctor on a mercy mission there as she tries to understand why her recently deceased grandfather abandoned his family. *The Tiger's Wife* won the 2011 Orange Prize, making Obreht the youngest winner of the prize in its 16-year history.

Kaplan, Robert D.

Eastward to Tartary: Travels in the Balkans, the Middle East, and the Caucasus. New York: Random House, 2000. 364 pp. ISBN: 9780375502729

In 1998 and 1999, Kaplan traveled slowly (by land and sea but not by air) through what he calls "The New Near East" (the Balkans, Turkey, Syria, Lebanon, Jordan, Israel, the Caucasus, and Central Asia), countries that he sees as the remains of the fallen Soviet and Ottoman empires. The book is something of a follow-up to his *Balkan Ghosts* and shows the same impressive grasp of the area's history and the same astute political analysis. Kaplan also comes to the same pessimistic conclusions as he did in *Balkan Ghosts*, for example, seeing the ethnic and religious rivalries of the area as even more dangerous in our age of increased globalization.

Subjects: Asian History; European History; Islam; Minorities; Politics

Places: Balkans; Central Asia; Israel; Jordan; Lebanon; Syria; Turkey

Awards: *New York Times* Notable Books, 2001

Series: *Vintage Departures*

Now Try: Kaplan traveled through the Horn of Africa and examined ethnic and religious conflicts there in the insightful *Surrender or Starve: Travels in Ethiopia, Sudan, Somalia, and Eritrea*. A good introduction to Kaplan's pessimistic view of the world, one that involves less travel, is *The Coming Anarchy: Shattering the Dreams of the Post Cold War*. Victoria Clark traveled throughout the Balkans as well as Russia, Cyprus, and Turkey to explore the history and current state of the Eastern Orthodox Church in *Why Angels Fall: A Portrait of Orthodox Europe from Byzantium to Kosovo*. Tom Bissell is less pessimistic than Kaplan, but his books cover similar themes and geographical regions as Kaplan. Bissell's book of short stories, *God Lives in St. Petersburg: and Other Stories*, fictionalizes his experiences in Central Asia and captures what one reviewer called "the disorientation and recklessness of life overseas." He recounts his visit to the disappearing Aral Sea in *Chasing the Sea: Lost Among the Ghosts of Empire in Central Asia*, which is annotated in "A Sense of Place."

Polonsky, Rachel

Molotov's Magic Lantern: A Journey in Russian History. London: Faber and Faber, 2010. 388 pp. ISBN: 9780571237807

Polonsky moved to Moscow and settled in an apartment that had been the residence of several members of the Soviet governing elite, including Vyacheslav Molotov, one of Stalin's henchmen. Polonsky used the books in Molotov's library and his old "magic lantern" (image projector) as a way of searching for Russia's Soviet history, visiting the cities of the books' authors, many of whom were executed or sent to the Gulags by Molotov. Part memoir, part travelogue, and part literary history, Polonsky's book is wide ranging, both geographically (the vast landscape of Russia) and intellectually (she discusses the history of collective farming on one page and the poet Anna Akhmatova's honeymoon on the next), and is as rich as the country she seeks to understand.

Subjects: Asian History; Authors; Books and Reading; European History; Memoirs; Women Travelers

Places: Moscow; Russia

Awards: Dolman Best Travel Book Award, 2011

Now Try: Polonsky's book was the victim of a famous negative review on Amazon.com, which turned out to have been secretly written by Orlando Figes, another scholar of Soviet cultural history and the author of *Natasha's Dance: A Cultural History of Russia,* which looks at Russian history through the country's writers, musicians, and artists. Two other cultural histories of Russia, neither of which involves travel to the extent that Polonsky's book does, are Librarian of Congress James Billington wide-ranging 1970 cultural history of Russia, *The Icon and the Axe: An Interpretive History of Russian Culture,* and Suzanne Massie's examination of Russian history from roughly 1000 AD to the revolution of 1917, *Land of the Firebird: The Beauty of Old Russia.* Elif Batuman's hilarious collection of essays, *The Possessed: Adventures with Russian Books and the People Who Read Them,* may also be of interest; it combines memoir and travel narrative and centers on her education in the Russian language and its literature.

Roe, Richard Paul

The Shakespeare Guide to Italy: Retracing the Bard's Unknown Travels. New York: Harper Perennial, 2011. 309 pp. ISBN: 9780062074263

Roe spent over 20 years traveling across Italy in search of the locations of the scenes of Shakespeare's 10 Italian plays, including *Romeo and Juliet, The Merchant of Venice,* and *The Two Gentlemen of Verona.* Roe was attempting to understand how Shakespeare, who apparently never left England, could have set so many of his plays in Italy, and his research on the great playwright, Italian history, and the Italian language will fascinate fans of literature. The level of detail in Roe's work is impressive and includes the likely discovery of Prospero's island from *The Tempest.*

Subjects: 16th Century; 17th Century; Authors; Drama; Shakespeare, William

Places: Italy

Now Try: There are a number of books that mix travel narrative with Shakespearean themes. These include *On the Trail of the Real Macbeth, King of Alba,* in which Cameron Taylor and Alistair Murray travel to Scotland in search of the real Macbeth, and *Shakespeare's Journey Home: a Traveller's Guide through Elizabethan England,* in which Julian Dutton portrays the great writer's annual trip from London to Stratford-on-Avon. The recent film, *Anonymous,* is based on the theory that Edward De Vere, the Earl of Oxford, wrote Shakespeare's plays, a theory that Katherine Chiljan elaborates on in her book, *Shakespeare Suppressed: The Uncensored Truth About Shakespeare and His Works.*

Seal, Jeremy

A Fez of the Heart: Travels Around Turkey In Search Of A Hat. San Diego, CA: Harcourt Brace, 1996. 337 pp. ISBN: 9780156003933

Seal, a British journalist working in Turkey, became fascinated with the fez, introduced in the 1800s by the Ottoman ruler to replace the old-fashioned turban and then banned in 1925 by Kemal Ataturk as a symbol of Turkey's past. As he searched through Turkey to trace the history of the hat, Seal discovered a country still caught between modernization and tradition. His writing is highlighted by memorable descriptions, and because Seal was fluent in the language, he was able to travel beyond the usual tourist sites into the "real" Turkey.

Subjects: Asian History; Culture Clash

Places: Turkey

Now Try: Mary Lee Settle's *Turkish Reflections: A Biography of a Place* also depicts a country where the past and the present are woven together; the book is annotated in "The Journey" chapter of this book. Stephen Kinzer's *Crescent and Star: Turkey Between Two Worlds* is written by the former *New York Times* bureau chief in Istanbul and, while it does not involve travel *per se*, is an excellent introduction to the country. Nobel Prize winner Orhan Pamuk's novel *Snow* involves an exiled poet who returns to Turkey to report on a series of suicides by girls who have been forbidden to wear headscarves. Rose Macaulay's 1956 novel, *The Towers of Trebizond*, is set in Turkey and features a character who wants to emancipate the women of Turkey by encouraging them to wear bathing hats. What Jeremy Seal does with the fez and Turkey, Tom Miller does with the Panama hat and Ecuador in *Panama Hat Trail: A Journey from South America*, which provides a wealth of information about the hat itself as well as the people of Ecuador.

Settle, Mary Lee

Spanish Recognitions: The Roads to the Present. New York: W.W. Norton & Co., 2004. 358 pp. ISBN: 9780393020274

Settle is an award-winning fiction writer who believes that Spain is a country where "history intrudes everywhere." Her endearing travelogue depicts her solo quest at the age of 82 through southern and central Spain for that history, major events like the Moorish invasion in 711 and the expulsion of Moors and Jews in 1492 as well as lesser-known individuals who have contributed to the history of the towns that she visited. Settle shows a deep respect for Spanish culture and customs as well and includes bits of Spanish folklore as she explores ruins and restoration projects.

Subjects: European History; Folklore; Solo Travelers; Women Travelers

Places: Spain

Now Try: Settle died in 2005, a year after the publication of *Spanish Recognitions*. Her memoir, *Learning to Fly: A Writer's Memoir*, which was begun in 2003, follows the path that led her to become a writer. On the subject of Spain, James Michener's, *Iberia: Spanish Travels and Reflections* is the classic travel narrative; it is annotated in this book's chapter on "A Sense of Place." Giles Tremlett focuses on the more recent history of Spain in his insightful

Ghosts of Spain: Travels Through Spain and Its Silent Past, while H. M. van den Brink focuses on the country's tastes and smells in *Spain: Body and Soul*. A lighter travel narrative on Spain can be found in the PBS series, *Spain: A Culinary Road Trip*, which stars Mario Batali, Mark Bittman, and Gwyneth Paltrow and is available on DVD; a companion book, *Spain: A Culinary Road Trip* by Batali and Paltrow, is also available.

Thubron, Colin

Shadow of the Silk Road. New York: Harper Collins Publishers, 2007. 363 pp. ISBN: 9780061231728

Thubron spent eight months traveling the "ghost" of the 7,000-mile Silk Road, the network of ancient trade routes that linked the European world with China for nearly 3,000 years and served as the major path for the exchange of goods and ideas between East and West. His ability to speak both Mandarin and Russian allowed him to speak directly with numerous people on the trip and to describe their attitudes, sentiments, and surprising narrow-mindedness. Thubron's writing is often beautiful, and his insights into China's new economy, the war in Afghanistan, and political upheaval in Iran are engrossing.

Subjects: Asian History; European History; Exploration; Silk Road

Places: Afghanistan; China; Iran; Kazakhstan; Kyrgyzstan; Tajikistan; Turkey; Turkmenistan; Uzbekistan

Now Try: Thubron's earlier travels through China are recounted in *Behind the Wall: A Journey through China* (annotated in the chapter on "A Sense of Place"). Peter Hopkirk writes about several explorers and travelers looking for treasures and buried cities along the former Silk Road in the fascinating *Foreign Devils on the Silk Road*. Rory Stewart's *The Places in Between*, about his risky walk across war-torn Afghanistan, takes place on part of the old Silk Road; the title is annotated in the "Getting There Is Half the Fun" chapter of this book. Michael Chabon's swashbuckling adventure novel, *Gentlemen of the Road: A Tale of Adventure*, takes place on the Silk Road around 950 AD and tells the story of two Jewish bandits in southwest Russia.

Vowell, Sarah

Assassination Vacation. New York: Simon & Schuster, 2005. 258 pp. ISBN: 9780743260039 YA

NPR contributor Vowell mixes travel and history in this delightfully witty examination of the first three presidential assassinations: Lincoln, Garfield, and McKinley. She visited as many sites associated with those events as she could, no matter how tenuous the connection, from Mount Marcy in upstate New York, where Vice-President Teddy Roosevelt learned of McKinley's fate, to the National Museum of Health and Medicine, where fragments of Lincoln's skull are displayed. Vowell explores the social and political environments in which the assassinations took place and draws parallels between the past and the present, seeing similarities between, for example, McKinley's wars in Cuba and the Philippines and the Bush invasion of Iraq.

Subjects: American History; Humor; Presidents; Women Travelers

Places: New York; Vermont; Washington, DC

Now Try: Vowell explores more American history and politics in *The Partly Cloudy Patriot,* a collection of essays based on her travels to Gettysburg, Salem (Massachusetts), Carlsbad Caverns, and other typically American sites. President Lincoln's travel plans play a role in Michael J. Kline's fascinating *The Baltimore Plot: The First Conspiracy to Assassinate Abraham Lincoln.* Readers interested in more information on the McKinley assassination should consider Eric Rauchway's *Murdering McKinley: The Making of Theodore Roosevelt's America,* which focuses on the society and politics of the time of McKinley's death as well as the assassination itself. Kenneth D. Ackerman does much the same for the Garfield assassination in *Dark Horse: The Surprise Election and Political Murder of President James A. Garfield.*

Vowell, Sarah

Unfamiliar Fishes. New York: Riverhead Books, 2011. 238 pp. ISBN: 9781594487873

Vowell traveled to Hawaii to examine the history of the newest state and, in particular, the impact of the New England missionaries who came in the 1820s to Christianize the native people and turn Hawaii into a version of New England. She took her eight-year-old nephew to see tourist landmarks but also to see the places where blood was spilled as the descendants of those New England missionaries slowly took over the islands. In her typical lively manner, Vowell tells the sad story of American annexation, complete with sugar barons, con men, Theodore Roosevelt, and the last Hawaiian queen (Liliuokalani), who wrote the well-known "Aloha 'Oe." Vowell is especially good at connecting the dots of history and manages, as one reviewer put it, to "view history with a visitor's eye."

Subjects: 19th Century; American History; Christianity; Colonialism; Humor; Indigenous Peoples; Women Travelers

Places: Hawaii

Now Try: Vowell's history of the Massachusetts Bay Colony, *The Wordy Shipmates,* has much in common with *Unfamiliar Fishes,* particularly its focus on the religious motivations of those involved in these aspects of American history. Vowell's collections of short essays on a wide range of topics related to American history, *The Partly Cloudy Patriot* and *Take the Cannoli: Stories From the New World,* may also appeal. Julia Flynn Siler's *Lost Kingdom: Hawaii's Last Queen, the Sugar Kings and America's First Imperial Adventure* is a fine history of the American annexation of Hawaii and focuses on the tragic figure of Liliuokalani, the last Hawaiian queen.

Winchester, Simon

The River at the Center of the World: A Journey Up the Yangtze, and Back in Chinese Time. New York: H. Holt, 1996. 410 pp. ISBN: 9780805038880

Winchester uses the Yangtze River as a metaphor for China's history, and as he traveled the length of the world's third longest river, he also traveled "back in time" to gain a sense of the spirit of China and its people. In Shanghai, where the Yangtze ends, Winchester saw the future of China and the people's hope for a future led by the Chinese themselves; in the mountains of Tibet, where the river begins, he found villages largely unchanged for several hundred years. This mixing of travel narrative and history sees Winchester stopping in small towns, like the one that Mao visited during the Long March or the one in which the 1910 revolution that brought Sun Yat Sen to power began, and sharing their histories. *The River at the Center of the World* is a well-researched introduction to Chinese history and culture, disguised as a travel narrative.

Subjects: Asian History; Culture Clash; Rivers; Scholarly Writing

Places: China; Yangtze River; Shanghai; Tibet

Awards: ALA Notable Book, 1998

Now Try: Peter Hessler's *River Town: Two Years on the Yangtze* (annotated in "The Expatriate Life" chapter of this book) is another look at Chinese culture through the lens of a small town on the Yangtze River; it tells the story of Hessler's two years as a teacher in a local college. While not a travel narrative as such, Jung Chang's *Wild Swans: Three Daughters of China* tells the story of modern China through the lives of three generations of Chinese women: the author's grandmother, who escaped slavery in a brothel; her mother, an idealistic Communist; and her own experience as a "barefoot doctor." In his book, Winchester is very critical of the Chinese government's Three Gorges Dam project; in *Before the Deluge: The Vanishing World of the Yangtze's Three Gorges*, river guide Deirdre Chetham uses a handful of towns in the area affected and their citizens to discuss the impact of the project.

In Search of Legends

Just as travelers may search for historical places and individuals, as reflected in the narratives from the previous section, they may also search for legendary places and individuals. These legendary places or individuals, unlike those from the "In Search of History" section, may or may not actually exist.

These legends may represent places, such as the mines of King Solomon that Tahir Shah writes about in his book, *In Search of King Solomon's Mines*, or the waterfall hidden in the Himalayas that is the subject of Ian Baker's quest in *The Heart of the World: A Journey to the Last Secret Place*. They may represent things, such as the Ark of the Covenant in Tudor Parfitt's *Lost Ark of the Covenant: Solving the 2,500 Year Old Mystery of The Fabled Biblical Ark*. They may represent people and their origins, as in Tudor Parfitt's *Journey to the Vanished City: The Search for a Lost Tribe of Israel*. They may even represent legendary beasts, like the African version of the Loch Ness monster that Redmond O'Hanlon searches for in *No Mercy: A Journey to the Heart of the Congo*.

Readers who are fascinated by the legends that are the focus of these travel narratives should find the titles of interest, and though the legends themselves may or may not be fictional, several of the titles set their legends in an historical context that will appeal to readers who enjoy history. Some of the titles have a religious or spiritual focus; for example, Ian Baker's *The Heart of the World: A Journey to the Last Secret Place* is also about the author's spiritual journey. Some of the titles are particularly gripping (Nicholas Clapp's *The Road to Ubar: Finding the Atlantis of the Sands*) and should appeal to readers who enjoy tales told with a degree of suspense. Others, like Christopher Dawes's *Rat Scabies and the Holy Grail: Can a Punk Rock Legend Find What Monty Python Couldn't?*, which includes instructions for building one's own Ark of the Covenant, are funny and should appeal to fans of humor.

Along these lines, readers who are drawn to travel narratives that focus on the search for legendary places and people may find other nonfiction titles dealing with legends (Graham Hancock's *The Sign and the Seal: The Quest for the Lost Ark of the Covenant* or William J. Gibbons's *Mokele-Mbembe: Mystery Beast of the Congo Basin*) to be of interest. Fiction that deals with legends (James Hilton's *Lost Horizon* or Bernard Cornwell's Grail Quest Trilogy) may also appeal to these readers.

Baker, Ian

The Heart of the World: A Journey to the Last Secret Place. New York: Penguin, 2004. 511 pp. ISBN: 9781594200274

Buddhist scholar Baker went in search of a waterfall, hidden deep in the Himalayan Mountains, that serves as the portal to a hidden paradise (or *beyul*), which according to legend, is accessible only to a devout pilgrim who can endure both physical and spiritual challenges. Baker and his team spent years exploring a five-mile area filled with leeches, sheer cliffs, and impassable white water before finally finding the legendary waterfall. Baker provides information on Tibetan Buddhism and his own spiritual journey as well as describing the physical challenges he and his team met and the natural beauty of the land that provided those challenges.

Subjects: Adventure; Buddhism; Exploration; Spirituality

Places: Tibet

Series: *Vintage Departures*

Now Try: In *Frank Kingdon Ward's Riddle of the Tsangpo Gorges*, Baker, Kenneth Cox, and Ken Storm, Jr., write about botanist and explorer Frank Kingdon Ward's expedition into the same area covered in *The Heart of the World*. Michael McRae writes about Kingdon Ward as well as Baker and several others who explored the Tsangpo River Gorge in *The Siege of Shangri-La: The Quest for*

Tibet's Sacred Hidden Paradise. Lost Horizon, James Hilton's classic novel of Shangri-La, the mysterious paradise hidden in the Himalayas, is an obvious fiction counterpart to *The Heart of the World.* Eric Weiner's *The Geography of Bliss: One Grump's Search for the Happiest Places in the World* (annotated in this chapter) includes a visit to Bhutan, which was the model for Hilton's Shangri-La.

Clapp, Nicholas

The Road to Ubar: Finding the Atlantis of the Sands. Boston: Houghton Mifflin, 1998. 342 pp. ISBN: 9780395875964 YA

Clapp, a documentary filmmaker, went in search of the legendary city of Ubar, known in the Koran and "The One Thousand and One Nights" as a wealthy city that Allah caused to disappear into the desert sands because of the sins of its inhabitants. Clapp tells an exciting, absorbing story of discovery as his two expeditions used both modern tools (NASA space photographs) and ancient tools (maps and written accounts) to identify the site of the city. Clapp does an excellent job of keeping the reader in suspense and shows an understanding and appreciation of the peoples of the Arabian Peninsula, with whom he interacted.

Subjects: Adventure; Ancient History; Archaeology; Deserts; Exploration; Middle Eastern History

Places: Arabia; Oman

Awards: ALA Notable Book, 1999

Now Try: Another version of the quest for Ubar is provided by Sir Fiennes Ranulph in the informative *Atlantis of the Sands: The Search for the Lost City of Ubar*; Ranulph had spent 24 years searching for Ubar and eventually worked with Clapp's team to uncover the city. James Rollins's novel *Sandstorm* involves a wealthy British financier who disappears near the site of Ubar and his daughter, who, 20 years later, leads an expedition searching for the city. Jan Morris's *Sultan in Oman* focuses on the same region as the author accompanied the country's ruler on the first crossing of the Omani desert by automobile in 1955.

Clapp, Nicholas

Sheba: Through the Desert in Search of the Legendary Queen. Boston: Houghton Mifflin, 2001. 372 pp. ISBN: 9780395952832 YA

Clapp, sometimes described as "the real Indiana Jones," went in search of the real Queen of Sheba, the only woman in the Bible with political power. To uncover the truth behind the legend, Clapp traveled to Jerusalem, Ethiopia, and Yemen, the latter of which proved to be both the richest and the most dangerous of his destinations. As in *The Road to Ubar,* Clapp mixes ancient information with modern techniques (including satellite images and carbon-14 dating) to uncover the facts behind the legends and myths surrounding the object of his search.

Subjects: Adventure; Ancient History; Archaeology; Bible; Exploration; Middle Eastern History

Places: Africa; Ethiopia; France; Israel; Jerusalem; New York; Yemen

Now Try: Clapp reconstructs the life and death of another (much less famous) individual, gold prospector Chester Pray, in *Who Killed Chester Pray? A Death Valley Mystery,* which meticulously portrays life in the gold rush towns of California in the late 19th and early 20th centuries. Readers who are fascinated by first-person accounts of archaeological discoveries should try Brian M. Fagan's *Eyewitness to Discovery: First-Person Accounts of More Than Fifty of the World's Greatest Archaeological Discoveries.* The Queen of Sheba has been the subject of a number of novels, including India Edghill's *Wisdom's Daughter: A Novel of Solomon and Sheba,* which focuses on the Queen's search for an heir. Tudor Parfitt is often referred to as a "British Indiana Jones," and his books (*Journey to the Vanished City* and *The Lost Ark of the Covenant*) might also be suggested; both titles are annotated in this section.

Dawes, Christopher

Rat Scabies and the Holy Grail: Can a Punk Rock Legend Find What Monty Python Couldn't? New York: Thunder's Mouth Press, 2005. 325 pp. ISBN: 9781560256786

Dawes is a music journalist who discovered that his neighbor, a former punk rock drummer named Rat Scabies, was obsessed with the Holy Grail and a theory that it may be connected with a small town in France. Soon, Scabies had involved Dawes in his quest for the Grail, and they set off across Europe and Great Britain, caught up in tales of the Knights Templar, the Cathars, the Albigensian Crusade, and the Man in the Iron Mask. The book, which includes instructions for building one's own Ark of the Covenant, is (not surprisingly) hilarious and as much a reflection on friendship and the nature of belief as it is on the Grail quest itself.

Subjects: European History; Friendships; Humor; Music and Musicians; Religion

Places: England; France; Italy; Scotland

Now Try: Dawes's book was referred to by one reviewer as "*The Da Vinci Code* gets the punk rock treatment," and anyone interested in the conspiracy theories surrounding the Holy Grail should read that novel by Dan Brown or Henry Lincoln's nonfiction book *Holy Blood, Holy Grail,* which first put forth many of the ideas upon which *The Da Vinci Code* is based. The title essay in Byron Rogers's *The Bank Manager and the Holy Grail: Travels to the Weirder Reaches of Wales* provides anecdotal evidence that the Grail was once deposited in a bank in Aberystwyth, Wales. Like Dawes, Tony Horwitz travels with a close friend in his book, *Blue Latitudes: Boldly Going Where Captain Cook Has Gone Before* (annotated in this chapter). The best-known satire of the Grail legend is probably the film, *Monty Python and the Holy Grail,* and Monty Python member

Terry Jones has written several books with historical themes, including the *Who Murdered Chaucer?: A Medieval Mystery, Terry Jones' Barbarians: An Alternative Roman History,* and *Terry Jones' Medieval Lives.*

Grann, David

The Lost City of Z: A Tale of Deadly Obsession in the Amazon. New York: Doubleday, 2009. 339 pp. ISBN: 9780385513531 YA

In 1925, the British explorer Percy Fawcett went in search of the city of Z, home to an ancient civilization. He and his expedition disappeared, and his fate and that of the city of Z became an obsession for explorers and scientists over the years. David Grann, a writer for *The New Yorker,* became one of the obsessed, and his book recounts both the story of Fawcett and Grann's own sometimes humorous attempt to follow in his footsteps and find the famous lost city. Grann alternates between the two stories, provides vivid details about the Amazon jungle into which he ventured, and presents the mysteries of Fawcett and Z in a compelling, gripping manner.

Subjects: 1920s; Exploration; Explorers; Jungles; Rivers

Categories: In the Footsteps of . . .

Places: Amazon River; Brazil

Awards: ALA Notable Book, 2010; *New York Times* Notable Book, 2009; Samuel Johnson Prize, Shortlist, 2009

Series: *Vintage Departures*

Now Try: Fawcett's son collected his letters, manuscripts, and log books and published them as *Exploration Fawcett: Journey to the Lost City of Z.* Ian Fleming's brother Peter also wrote about Fawcett and a 1932 expedition to locate him in *Brazilian Adventure.* Yossi Ghinsberg and three friends hiked into the Amazon rain forest in Bolivia; they were quickly separated, and Yossi was forced to survive alone for weeks in this most inhospitable of environments. Ghinsberg writes about his experience in *Lost in the Jungle: A Harrowing True Story of Survival,* which is annotated in the "Travel Adventure" chapter of this book. Ann Patchett's novel *State of Wonder* concerns a scientist who travels to the Amazonian jungle to find the remains of a colleague who died there under mysterious circumstances and to find another scientist who is studying the women of an indigenous tribe in order to develop a fertility drug.

Honigsbaum, Mark

Valverde's Gold: In Search of the Last Great Inca Treasure. New York: Farrar, Straus and Giroux, 2004. 348 pp. ISBN: 9780374191702

Honigsbaum, a British journalist and historian, describes his efforts to find a legendary, cursed horde of Inca gold, supposedly hidden in the Andes of Ecuador. The quest involves searches through archives in Spain and England, attempts to decipher confusing maps, and tales of previous treasure hunters who have gone broke, gone mad, or died. Honigsbaum weaves a fascinating mystery, full of dead ends and odd characters, and he eventually trekked through the Andes himself for a firsthand search for the gold.

Subjects: Exploration; Incas; Investigative Stories; 19th Century

Places: Ecuador; England; Spain

Now Try: Peter Lourie's *Sweat of the Sun, Tears of the Moon: A Chronicle of an Incan Treasure* tells of that writer's search for the same gold as Honigsbaum; Lourie decided early on to focus more on the journey and less on the prize, and the book is a portrayal of the South American culture as much as a treasure hunt. In his book, *What Men Call Treasure: The Search for Gold at Victorio Peak,* Robert Boswell goes in search of a treasure that his grandfather was rumored to have discovered and then hidden in caverns in New Mexico. James Rollins's *Excavation* is a fiction page-turner whose plot begins with the discovery of a 500-year-old mummy in the Andes.

Jones, Ann

Looking for Lovedu: Days and Nights in Africa. New York: Alfred A. Knopf, 2001. 268 pp. ISBN: 9780375405549 YA

Feminist writer Jones traveled from one end of Africa to the other in order to find the legendary Lovedu tribe, a matriarchal tribe supposedly ruled by a mystical rain queen and governed by the feminist principles of compromise and understanding. She mixes descriptions of her travel with the history of Africa, observations on the effects of colonialism and tourism on the continent, and reflections on the role of women in the patriarchal societies that dominate Africa.

Subjects: African History; Colonialism; Culture Clash; Women Travelers

Places: Africa; Benin; Cameroon; Central African Republic; Cote d'Ivoire; Democratic Republic of the Congo; Ghana; Kenya; Mauritania; Mali; Morocco; Mozambique; Nigeria; South Africa; Tanzania; Togo; Uganda; Zimbabwe

Series: *Vintage Departures*

Now Try: Tanya Shaffer's *Somebody's Heart Is Burning: A Woman Wanderer in Africa* provides a feminist perspective on her travel to Kenya, Mali, and Ghana following the break-up with her boyfriend. Sarah Erdman's *Nine Hills to Nambonkaha: Two Years in the Heart of an African Village* is more memoir than travel narrative but does an excellent job of portraying the rhythms of daily life in an African village. The Lovedu rain queen may have served as the inspiration for H. Rider Haggard's classic adventure novel, *She: A History of Adventure,* which follows the journey of a Cambridge professor to a lost kingdom in the African interior, one ruled by an all-powerful queen. Tom DeMott's book *Into the Hearts of the Amazons: In Search of a Modern Matriarchy* looks at a matriarchal society on a different continent, the Zapotec women of southern Mexico.

Jubber, Nicholas

The Prester Quest. London: Doubleday, 2005. 516 pp. ISBN: 9780385607025

Prester John was a legendary Christian king during Medieval times, rumored to rule over a Christian nation among the Muslims of Africa or the Middle East. In 1177, Pope Alexander III sent a letter to Prester John via his physician, who promptly disappeared. Over 800 years later, Nicholas Jubber found a copy of the Pope's letter and decided to deliver the letter to the tomb of an Ethiopian king sometimes connected to the fabled king. The resulting book, Jubber's first, is filled with historical anecdotes and insights and lots of enthusiasm. As one reviewer noted, it combines "serious historical research and entertaining escapades with credibility and passion."

Subjects: African History; Christianity; European History; Humor; Prester John

Places: Africa; Ethiopia; Italy; Sudan; Turkey

Awards: Dolman Best Travel Book Award, 2006

Now Try: Science fiction writer Robert Silverberg writes about the legendary Christian ruler in *Realm Of Prester John,* speculating that the myth was fueled by the need for the Christians to have a potential ally in the Crusades against Islam. Umberto Eco's novel, *Baudolino,* tells the story of a peasant boy who is adopted by Emperor Frederic Barbarossa in the 12th century, and who goes in quest of Prester John. Sir John Mandeville was one of those who popularized the story of Prester John; in his 14th-century *Travels* (which are available in a number of editions), he used the legend to encourage Christians to fight to reclaim Jerusalem. Giles Milton's book, *The Riddle and the Knight: In Search of Sir John Mandeville, the World's Greatest Traveler,* is a good introduction to Mandeville.

Kavenna, Joanna

The Ice Museum: In Search of the Lost Land of Thule. New York: Viking, 2006 [2005]. 294 pp. ISBN: 9780670034734

Kavenna went in search of the legendary land of Thule, first described by a 4th-century BC Greek explorer as lying six days north of Scotland. She followed the routes of previous explorers such as Fridtjof Nansen and Richard Burton and visited the Shetland Islands, Iceland, and Greenland, among others. Kavenna explores a number of topics, including the Nazis (who viewed Thule as a lost Aryan homeland), the Cold War (the United States maintains an airbase in Greenland called Thule), and man's impact on the fragile ecosystems of the Arctic. The book contains some beautiful descriptions of the harsh landscape as well as conveying the author's love of these northern lands.

Subjects: Exploration; Explorers; Mythology; Thule; Women Travelers; World History

Places: Arctic Region; Estonia; Greenland; Iceland; Norway; Scotland

Awards: Dolman Best Travel Book Award, Shortlist, 2006

Now Try: Greta Ehrlich's magnificent book about her travels to Greenland, *This Cold Heaven: Seven Seasons in Greenland*, is annotated in the "A Sense of Place" chapter of this book; like Kavenna, she has a love of the countries of the far north. Piers Vitebsky has lived among the Eveny people in Siberia for 20 years, and in *The Reindeer People: Living With Animals and Spirits in Siberia*, he describes their daily lives, culture, and symbiotic relationship with the reindeer. Peter Høeg's novel, *Smilla's Sense of Snow*, is a thriller set in Denmark and an island off the coast of Greenland, but it also explores the relationship of individuals and their societies. Kavenna is also a fascinating novelist; the same skill she has with nonfiction prose is apparent in her two novels, the Orange Award winner *Inglorious* (about a young journalist who quits her job and loses her boyfriend in the months after her mother's death) and *The Birth of Love* (which examines childbirth through the stories of three women from the 19th, 21st, and 22nd centuries).

O'Hanlon, Redmond

No Mercy: A Journey to the Heart of the Congo. New York: Alfred A. Knopf, 1997 [1996]. 461 pp. ISBN: 9780679406556

O'Hanlon went in search of Africa's version of the Loch Ness monster, the legendary *Mokèlé-mbèmbé* of Lake Tele, deep in the forests of the northern Congo. O'Hanlon's description of the dangerous (even foolhardy) journey is both amusing and terrifying, as he and his traveling companions took the long way to the lake, were nearly killed by a village chief, tried to save a baby gorilla, got drunk on the local liquor, and encountered giant eagles and dwarf crocodiles. *No Mercy* is beautifully written, with spellbindingly detailed descriptions of the flora and fauna as well as the quirks of the individuals that O'Hanlon and his colleagues met along the way.

Subjects: Adventure; Animals; Dinosaurs; Humor; Plants

Places: Africa; Republic of the Congo

Series: *Vintage Departures*

Now Try: Cryptozoology is the name given to the study of and search for animals (like the *Mokèlé-mbèmbé*) whose existence has not been proven. Cryptozoologist William J. Gibbons describes several expeditions (including several of his own) to find the *Mokèlé-mbèmbé* in his book *Mokele-Mbembe: Mystery Beast of the Congo Basin*. Loren Coleman and Jerome Clark have written a reference work for those interested in such creatures, *Cryptozoology A To Z: The Encyclopedia of Loch Monsters, Sasquatch, Chupacabras, and Other Authentic Mysteries of Nature*. Helen Winternitz's trip up the Congo River is vividly described in *East Along the Equator: A Journey up the Congo and into Zaire*; she and her boyfriend followed the path of Conrad's *Heart of Darkness* and uncovered monsters of another sort, suggesting that the colonial brutality of the 19th century has merely been replaced by the corruption and exploitation of President Mobutu.

Parfitt, Tudor

Journey to the Vanished City: The Search for a Lost Tribe of Israel. New York: St. Martin's Press, 1993. 278 pp. ISBN: 9780312088293

Parfitt's quest centers on the origins of the Lemba tribe of southern Africa and, specifically, whether they could be one of the lost tribes of Israel. Parfitt began his travels in South Africa, where he witnessed food taboos and circumcision customs that seemed very close to those of the Jewish tradition, and continued through several African nations and into Yemen, where he found local names that corresponded to Lemba clan names. Along the way, Parfitt met fascinating people, from scholars to rain queens, and combined oral tradition, historical evidence, and anthropological observation to also tell the story of modern Africa. An epilogue outlines DNA evidence that appears to link the Lemba with Jewish and Yemeni peoples.

Subjects: African History; Ethnography; Jews and Judaism; Religion

Places: Africa; Malawi; Mozambique; South Africa; Tanzania; Yemen; Zimbabwe

Series: *Vintage Departures*

Now Try: Parfitt also wrote *The Lost Tribes of Israel: The History of a Myth,* in which he travels the world to track down the history of this legendary story. Zvi Ben-Dor Benite's *The Ten Lost Tribes: A World History* is a more scholarly look at the ongoing search for the lost tribes. Hillel Halkin visited the Mizo people of northeast India and attempted to support their claim that they descended from one of the lost tribes of Israel in *Across the Sabbath River: In Search of a Lost Tribe of Israel.* In Tamar Yellin's award-winning novel, *The Genizah at the House of Shepher,* the protagonist learns that her great-grandfather apparently traveled to Babylon in search of the lost tribes of Israel.

Parfitt, Tudor

Lost Ark of the Covenant: Solving the 2,500 Year Old Mystery of The Fabled Biblical Ark. New York: HarperOne, 2008. 380 pp. ISBN: 9780061371035

Parfitt, a British professor in Jewish studies, embarked on a 20-year, often difficult quest to solve the mystery of the Ark of the Covenant, the vessel that is supposed to contain the Ten Commandments. The author attempts to link the Ark with a holy drum of the Lemba tribe that featured in his earlier book, *Journey to the Vanished City: The Search for a Lost Tribe of Israel,* and he tracked ancient documents from Oxford to Jerusalem to Africa and even to New Guinea. The book combines real-life adventure with fascinating historical facts and speculation, and while his conclusions will not convince every reader, they are thought provoking.

Subjects: Adventure; Archaeology; Investigative Writing; Middle East; Religion; World History

Places: Africa; Egypt; England; Ethiopia; Israel; Jerusalem; New Guinea; Zimbabwe

Now Try: Charles Foster took a grueling trek through Middle Eastern deserts to find out more about the Ark of the Covenant in *Tracking the Ark of the Covenant: By Camel,*

Foot, and Ancient Ford in Search of Antiquity's Greatest Treasure. Graham Hancock's *The Sign and the Seal: The Quest for the Lost Ark of the Covenant* presents a different theory on the fate of the Ark and ties its current location to another ethnic group, the Falasha Jews of Ethiopia. Randall Price provides a fairly objective overview of recent research on the Ark of the Covenant in his *Searching for the Ark of the Covenant: Latest Discoveries and Research.* The search for another legendary relic, the Blue Koran, lies behind Tunisian writer Sabiha Al Khemir's gripping novel, *The Blue Manuscript.*

Shah, Tahir

In Search of King Solomon's Mines. New York: Arcade Pub., 2003. 240 pp. ISBN: 9781559706414 Y A

Shah writes about his search for the Biblical land of Ophir, home of the legendary gold mines of King Solomon and the Queen of Sheba. His sources suggested that he start his quest in Ethiopia, and with his guide, Shah searched through the rural Ethiopian countryside, explored both legal and illegal mines, and rode mules to the alleged source of Solomon's gold. Along the way, Shah writes incisively and with humor about the fascinating people he encountered, their history, and their desperate poverty. In fact, in many ways, the book is more about modern Africa and its challenges and less about Shah's search for gold.

Subjects: Adventure; African History; Archaeology; Biblical History; Humor

Places: Africa; Ethiopia; Jerusalem

Now Try: Shah is considered by many to be one of the best modern travel writers. Two of his best titles are *Sorcerer's Apprentice,* which focuses on his apprenticeship to an Indian magician, and *The Caliph's House: A Year in Casablanca,* about his experiences purchasing and renovating a dilapidated palace in the famed Moroccan city. Byron de Prorok's 1942 classic *Dead Men Do Tell Tales* concerns that author's search for King Solomon's mines in Ethiopia. H. Rider Haggard's classic novel, *King Solomon's Mines,* should be read by anyone interested in the legends that surround King Solomon's wealth or anyone just interested in a prototype of the modern adventure novel.

In Search of a Concept

Individuals may also travel in search of a concept or an idea. The best example of this category may be Eric Weiner's *The Geography of Bliss: One Grump's Search for the Happiest Places in the World,* in which the NPR correspondent travels to the Netherlands and eight other countries in search of happiness, consulting the World Database of Happiness and interviewing individuals in the countries he visits in order to explore the concept. In some entries in this category, the narratives have a more intellectual air (Christopher Woodward's *In Ruins: A Journey Through History, Art, and Literature,* in which he reflects on the importance of ruins in European art and literature), while others are more down-to-earth (Franz Wisner's exploration of the concept of love in *How the World Makes Love: And What It Taught a Jilted Groom*).

These titles are likely to have greater appeal for readers who enjoy more abstract, even philosophical writing. In spite of their "heavy" subject matter, however, many of the titles are also very funny (like Pico Iyer's *Falling Off the Map: Some Lonely Places of the World*). Because many of the writers discuss the history of the idea or concept that is the focus of their writing (Nathan and Sharon Hodge, *A Nuclear Family Vacation: Travels in the World of Atomic Weaponry*), readers who enjoy history may also find these titles of interest.

Fans of narratives in this category, with their strong focus on a concept or an idea, may find the focus of micro-histories (Mark Kurlansky's *Salt: A World History* or Mary Roach's *Stiff: The Curious Lives of Human Cadavers*) to be appealing. Because many of the travel narratives in this category are written by journalists, other investigative, exposé, and current affairs titles (Giles Slade's *Made to Break: Technology and Obsolescence in America* or William Langewiesche's *The Atomic Bazaar: The Rise of the Nuclear Poor*) may also be of interest to these readers.

Bennett, Joe

Where Underpants Come from: From Checkout to Cotton Fields—Travels Through the New China and into the New Global Economy. New York: Overlook, 2009. 253 pp. ISBN: 9781590202289

Purchasing a cheap pack of underwear started Bennett wondering about the global economy and specifically who was making money on the transaction. His search for an answer to his question led him to China, where he posed as an underwear buyer to gain access to manufacturer showrooms and factories. Bennett's book is about more than China's meteoric growth in the global economy, though. He also provides a look at the lives of ordinary people there, including the Muslim minority in southern China, and reflects on his own challenges with chaotic traffic, chopsticks, and overcoming his own prejudices.

Subjects: Factory Workers; Humor; Imports; Investigative Stories; Underwear

Places: China; Thailand

Now Try: Economics professor Pietra Rivoli does much the same with t-shirts in her mix of travel narrative and economics, *The Travels of a T-Shirt in the Global Economy: An Economist Examines the Markets, Power, and Politics of World Trade*, in which she interviews cotton farmers in Texas, factory workers in China, and vendors of used clothing in Tanzania. In *Falling off the Edge: Travels Through the Dark Heart of Globalization*, Alex Perry writes about his travels to China, Afghanistan, and Africa to see the effects of globalization first hand and concludes that the prospects for most people are not good. Paul Midler's *Poorly Made in China: An Insider's Account of the China Production Game* takes an insightful, insider's look at business in that country, while fiction readers may enjoy Xialou Guo's novel, *Twenty Fragments of a Ravenous Youth*, which provides a look at contemporary Chinese life through the eyes of a young woman who travels 1,800 miles to seek her fortune in Beijing. William Powers chronicles the efforts of indigenous peoples in Bolivia to defend their rain forests against` the encroachments of the global economy in the informative *Whispering in the Giant's Ear: A Frontline Chronicle from Bolivia's War on Globalization*.

Casey, Susan

The Wave: In Pursuit of the Rogues, Freaks and Giants of the Ocean. New York: Doubleday, 2010. 326 pp. ISBN: 9780767928847

Casey traveled around the world in search of giant ocean waves (some more than 100 feet high) and the sailors, scientists, and extreme surfers who also seek them out. Her story follows the history of the waves, from the stuff of legend to scientific fact, and alternates between the science behind these events and the nearly suicidal attempts of Laird Hamilton and his followers to surf them. The science behind the waves is still relatively new and includes questions about whether global warming will make such waves more likely. In spite of the destructive power of these waves, Casey admires them for their sheer beauty, and her writing conveys the magic of this ferocious natural phenomenon.

Subjects: Adventure; Environment; Investigative Stories; Oceans; Scientists; Surfing

Places: Alaska; Atlantic Ocean; California; England; Hawaii; Iceland; Indian Ocean; Indonesia; Pacific Ocean; South Africa; Tahiti

Awards: *New York Times* Notable Book, 2010

Now Try: Casey is the author of a book about another deadly ocean phenomenon (the great white sharks off the California coast) and the scientists who follow them, *The Devil's Teeth: A True Story of Obsession and Survival Among America's Great White Sharks*. Laird Hamilton, the big wave surfer about whom Casey writes in *The Wave*, has written his own book about the rogue waves and his attempts to conquer them, *Force of Nature: Mind, Body, Soul, And, of Course, Surfing*. In *The Power of the Sea: Tsunamis, Storm Surges, Rogue Waves, and Our Quest to Predict Disasters*, Bruce Parker tells more stories about giant waves and other destructive oceanic forces, including the 2004 Indian Ocean tsunami that left 300,000 people dead.

Clarke, Thurston

Searching for Crusoe: A Journey Among The Last Real Islands. New York: Ballantine Books, 2001. 342 pp. ISBN: 9780345411433

Clarke is a self-described "islomaniac," and his quest is for islands: famous islands (like Mas a Tierra, which inspired *Robinson Crusoe*), holy islands, private islands, and scary islands. He visited Campobello, where Franklin Roosevelt spent his summers as a boy; the island of Patmos, where John was given the vision that became the Book of Revelation; and Phu Quoc, which housed South Vietnam's largest prison camp. He reflects on the importance of islands in our cultures and their personal meaning for him. He talks with local, offbeat characters and decries the fact that most of our islands are being overrun and exploited. *Searching for Crusoe* is a good book for fellow islomaniacs or for readers trying to understand the fascination that some people have with islands.

Subjects: Environment; Islands

Categories: Endangered Places

Places: Cayman Islands; Chile; Greece; Honduras; Indian Ocean; Indonesia; Maldives; Micronesia; New Brunswick; New York; Norway; Pacific Ocean; Republic of Kiribati; Scotland; Vanuatu; Vietnam

Now Try: Dea Birkett's *A Serpent in Paradise* takes the author to Pitcairn Island, where the crew from *Mutiny on the Bounty* founded a colony and where a few dozen descendants of those individuals still live. Melinda and Robert Blanchard chronicle their experience opening a restaurant on the island of Anguilla in *A Trip to the Beach: Living on Island Time in the Caribbean*. Clarke visited the island of Mas a Tierra, where Alexander Selkirk, the model for Robinson Crusoe, was marooned; Defoe's novel, *Robinson Crusoe*, may interest islomaniacs who enjoy *Searching for Crusoe*.

Hansen, Eric

Orchid Fever: A Horticultural Tale of Love, Lust, and Lunacy. New York: Pantheon Books, 2000. 272 pp. ISBN: 9780679451419

The quest in *Orchid Fever* is for the obsession that some individuals have with orchids. Hansen, a travel writer of some note (several of his books are annotated in this volume), focuses on the bizarre world of orchid collectors and the complicated, irrational rules that govern orchid collecting. The author traveled the world of jungles, gardens, orchid shows, and perfume factories (including a trip to Turkey to taste orchid ice cream) to illustrate the many adaptations that the orchids and their growers have developed to survive. Though the book includes a number of facts about orchids and their growth, much of the narrative focuses on the quirky orchid fanciers themselves. A combination of exposé, travelogue, and horticultural history, the book is as much about obsession as it is about the flowers themselves.

Subjects: Horticulture; Investigative Stories; Jungles; Orchids; Plants

Places: Borneo; California; England; France; Germany; Holland; Minnesota; New York; Turkey

Series: *Vintage Departures*

Now Try: The most obvious read-alike is Susan Orlean's *The Orchid Thief*, in which the author travels to Florida to focus on a single individual and his attempts to bend the laws by removing endangered orchids from a state-controlled swamp. (The film *Adaptation* was based on *The Orchid Thief* and may also be of interest to those who enjoy

Orchid Fever.) Readers with a more historical interest in flowers may be interested in Mary Gribbin's *Flower Hunters*, which tells the stories of eleven botanical explorers from the 18th and 19th centuries, and Andrea Wulf's *The Brother Gardeners: Botany, Empire, and the Birth of an Obsession*, which recounts the efforts of 18th-century British botanists to import thousands of previously unknown plant species from the British colonies. Readers who are fascinated by the individuals who collect orchids may enjoy the three Dordogne mysteries of Michelle Wan (*Deadly Slipper*; *The Orchid Shroud*; and *A Twist of Orchids*) and the orchidologist who serves as the sleuth.

Heat-Moon, William Least

Roads to Quoz: An American Mosey. New York: Little, Brown and Co., 2008. 581 pp. ISBN: 9780316110259

Heat-Moon's quirky, wandering book is a series of trips in search of "quoz," described by the author as "anything strange, incongruous or peculiar; at its heart is the unknown, the mysterious." He drove through Maine's North Woods, traveled by boat along the eastern coast of the United States from Baltimore to Florida, rode a bicycle on railroad tracks through the Bitterroot Mountains in Idaho, and followed the less famous Dunbar-Hunter expedition through the lower half of the Louisiana Purchase. The author's well-known love for the back roads comes alive as he describes the people he met along the way, from the artist who turned his cabin into a walk-in kaleidoscope to the caretaker of Jack Kerouac's original scroll manuscript of *On The Road*. *Roads to Quoz* is a long read but one that will be appreciated by readers who enjoy taking the road less traveled.

Subjects: American History; Environment; Geography; Landscapes and People

Places: Arkansas; Baltimore; Colorado; Florida; Georgia; Idaho; Illinois; Indiana; Kansas; Louisiana; Maine; Massachusetts; Maryland; Missouri; Montana; New Hampshire; New Jersey; New Mexico; New York; North Carolina; Ohio; Oklahoma; Pennsylvania; South Carolina; Texas; Utah; Vermont; Virginia; Wyoming

Now Try: In its celebration of the unconventional, *Roads to Quoz* is perhaps most like Heat-Moon's *Blue Highways: A Journey into America*, which is annotated in the "A Sense of Place" chapter of this book. Michael Perry shows an equal appreciation of the diversity and richness in the most seemingly mundane experiences and places in his collection of essays, *Off Main Street: Barnstormers, Prophets & Gatemouth's Gator*, which covers travels from the Vietnam Memorial Wall to Belize. Another collection of articles and essays that reflect the idiosyncrasies of America is *Americana: Dispatches from the New Frontier* by Hampton Sides, whose destinations include a rafting party at the Grand Canyon; the annual motorcycle rally in Sturgis, South Dakota; and Biosphere 2 in Arizona. Bob Greene's first novel, *All Summer Long*, was described by one reviewer as "a sunny, nostalgia-drenched ramble across much of the U.S."; its protagonists wander across the country one summer trying to regain the sense of fun and adventure that summer once embodied for them.

Hodge, Nathan, and Sharon Hodge

A Nuclear Family Vacation: Travels in the World of Atomic Weaponry. New York: Bloomsbury, 2008. 324 pp. ISBN: 9781596913783

The Hodges are a husband-and-wife team of journalists who spent several years touring nuclear weapons sites in the United States, Kazakhstan, Russia, and Iran. Among the sites they visited are Los Alamos, the Nevada Test Site, Congressional bunkers, and a uranium conversion facility in Iran. Along the way, they explore questions about the Cold War and the continued existence of nuclear weapons as well as sites, and they conclude that "much of the infrastructure supporting nuclear weapons continues to exist merely because no one has come up with a compelling reason to shut it down."

Subjects: American History; Atomic Bomb; Cold War; Investigative Stories; Weapons; War

Places: Colorado; Iran; Kazakhstan; Nevada; New Mexico; Pennsylvania; Russia; Tennessee; Washington, DC; West Virginia

Now Try: Tom Vanderbilt writes about a similar road trip among the missile silos, storage bunkers, and test sites of the Cold War in the engaging *Survival City: Adventures among the Ruins of Atomic America*. Trevor Paglen has written two books in which he travels to sites tied to the clandestine operations of the CIA and the U.S. military, like the Area 51 flight test facility in Nevada: *Blank Spots on the Map: The Dark Geography of the Pentagon's Secret World* and the earlier *Torture Taxi: On the Trail of the CIA's Rendition Flights*. Harry Helms's *Top Secret Tourism: Your Travel Guide to Germ Warfare Laboratories, Clandestine Aircraft Bases and Other Places in the United States You're Not Supposed to Know About* is more travel guide than narrative but it covers the same hidden world. Readers interested in nuclear weapons and especially the threats posed by their production by hostile nations such as North Korea and Iran may wish to read William Langewiesche's scary *The Atomic Bazaar: The Rise of the Nuclear Poor*.

Iyer, Pico

Falling Off the Map: Some Lonely Places of the World. New York: Alfred A. Knopf, 1993. 190 pp. ISBN: 9780679422648

Iyer's eight travel essays in *Falling Off the Map* focus on "lonely" places (i.e., countries that are culturally, geographically, or politically isolated). Iyer calls them "shy, defensive, curious places" and is amused by the eccentric and ironic situations that he encountered in each place, from the large hotel for foreign visitors being constructed in North Korea, a country without foreign visitors, to the decision of the Vietnam government to declare 1990 the "Year of Tourism" and then tear down all of its hotels in order to rebuild them. Iyer writes in an impressionistic manner that is full of atmosphere, and while he does point out the comical aspects of the countries he visited, he also clearly loves the people and the places.

Subjects: Essays; Humor; Quick Reads

Places: Argentina; Australia; Bhutan; Cuba; Iceland; North Korea; Paraguay; Vietnam

Series: *Vintage Departures*

Now Try: Iyer's debut novel, *Cuba and the Night*, evokes 1980s Havana in its story of an American photojournalist who falls in love with a beautiful Cuban woman. One of the lonely places that Iyer writes about in *Falling Off the Map* is North Korea, and Barbara Demick's thought-provoking *Nothing to Envy: Ordinary Lives in North Korea* tries to sketch the daily lives of North Koreans through interviews with six defectors from that isolated country. A memoir of life in North Korea that highlights the brutality of its regime is *The Aquariums of Pyongyang: Ten Years in the North Korean Gulag* by Chol-hwan Kang. Like Iyer, Michael Lewis traveled to a number of countries, including Greece, Iceland, and Ireland, and looked at how they dealt with the financial disaster of 2008 in *Boomerang: Travels in the New Third World.*

Iyer, Pico

The Global Soul: Jet Lag, Shopping Malls, and the Search for Home. New York: Knopf, 2000. 303 pp. ISBN: 9780679454335

Iyer's book of essays represents a search for the idea of home as it looks at the impact of globalization on individuals and the prevailing sense of homelessness among frequent travelers. Iyer (an Indian-born, England-educated, California transplant) is one of these "global souls" and sees the world becoming more unicultural, thanks to the influence of global corporations. Iyer finds evidence of this transition in airports such as Dallas-Fort Worth (where the airport is larger than Manhattan), hotels in Hong Kong, the 1996 Summer Olympic games in Atlanta, and schools in Toronto (where over 80 languages are spoken by the students). Some readers may find his conclusions a little stretched, given the evidence, but his writing is crisp and imbued with a deep sense of the spiritual.

Subjects: Consumerism; Essays; Globalization; Home; Investigative Stories; Society

Places: Atlanta; China; Dallas; Hong Kong; Los Angeles; Toronto

Series: *Vintage Departures*

Awards: *New York Times* Notable Book, 2000

Now Try: Isabel Huggan also explores the sense of home and what it feels like to belong to a specific place in *Belonging: Home Away from Home*, which combines memoir and travel narrative and reflections on the craft of writing. Readers who enjoy Iyer's speculations on travel and home may be interested in two more sociological titles. In *The Geography of Nowhere: The Rise and Decline of America's Man-Made Landscape*, James Howard Kunstler considers the changes that the automobile brought to the environments and cultures of the United States; his thoughts include trips to Detroit, Portland (Oregon), and "capitals of unreality" like Atlantic City and Disneyworld. John D. Kasarda and Greg Lindsay suggest in *Aerotropolis: The Way We'll Live Next* that airports will soon be at the center of cities and not on the periphery, thanks to the growing importance of jet travel and global businesses, two factors also explored by Iyer in *The Global Soul*. Readers who enjoy Iyer's thoughts on travel may also enjoy Alain de Botton's extended essay *A Week at the Airport*, a short title that examines how people interact with airports, as well as his *Status Anxiety*, which explores our culture's insatiable search for status.

Kittredge, William

The Nature of Generosity. New York: Knopf, 2000. 276 pp. ISBN: 9780679437529

Montana writer Kittredge combines memoir and travelogue in this philosophical quest for generosity, what the author calls our "ordinary yearning to take physical and emotional care." His travels took him from his childhood on a ranch in Oregon to Alaska, Peru, France, and Venice, and as he reflects on these travels, he also ponders a wide range of topics (from the roots of agriculture to contemporary xenophobia and consumerism) and he considers a wide range of writers (from Walt Whitman and Pablo Neruda to Edmund Wilson and Richard Dawkins). Kittredge admits that his wide-ranging book is "more like a dance than an argument," and though the ideas are sometimes merely touched upon and not explored in depth, the book is still an eloquent argument for the need to recognize both our diversity and our connectedness.

Subjects: Generosity; Memoirs; Philosophy

Places: Alaska; France; Italy; Oregon; Peru; Spain; Venice

Series: *Vintage Departures*

Now Try: *The Nature of Generosity* is something of a sequel to Kittredge's powerful memoir *Hole in the Sky*, which won a PEN West Literary Award and explores the author's coming of age in the American West. Readers interested in the concept of generosity have a number of self-help books to consider, including *The Generosity Factor: Discover the Joy of Giving Your Time, Talent, and Treasure* by Ken Blanchard and S. Truett Cathy and *Enough: Discovering Joy through Simplicity and Generosity* by Adam Hamilton. French writer Jean Giono's fable, *The Man Who Planted Trees*, is the tale of a generous man who brought a deserted valley back to life by planting trees there; the Canadian animated film based on Giono's tale won the 1987 Academy Award for Best Animated Short Film. A darker, more hard-edged story of the generosity of others is told in David Carr's *The Night of the Gun*, which investigates his years as a crack addict and the friends whose generosity helped him recover. Barbara Ehrenreich looks at a different human impulse in *Dancing in the Streets: A History of Collective Joy*, a social history that ranges from Dionysian rituals to rock concerts.

Porter, Bill

Road to Heaven: Encounters with Chinese Hermits. San Francisco: Mercury House, 1993. 220 pp. ISBN: 9781562790417

Porter, who himself spent three years in a monastery in Taiwan, went to China in search of religious hermits, Taoist and Buddhist monks and nuns whose temples and shrines had been destroyed in the Cultural Revolution of the 1960s and 1970s. Porter found these hermits living in huts and caves in the mountains of central China, and his interviews with them provide a fascinating look at these individuals and their search for spiritual wisdom in spite of their government's stance against religion. Porter manages to convey the beauty of the rugged mountainous environment in which these hermits live and to tell their stories with deep respect.

Subjects: Asian History; Buddhism; Quick Reads; Religion; Spirituality; Taoism

Places: China

Now Try: Porter has published several translations of Chinese poetry under the pen name Red Pine, among them *The Heart Sutra, The Clouds Should Know Me by Now,* and *The Diamond Sutra.* He returned to China in 2006 to visit the sites of the first six patriarchs of Zen and wrote *Zen Baggage: A Pilgrimage to China* to tell of his experience. George Crane accompanied former Chinese monk Tsung Tsai to China and Mongolia forty years after Tsai's monastery was destroyed by Red Army troops; their quest is recalled in *Bones of the Master: A Journey to Secret Mongolia.* Readers interested in hermits in general may wish to start with Peter France's book, *Hermits: The Insights of Solitude.* France knows the hermetical life well, having given up a position with the BBC to live alone on a Greek island.

Setterberg, Fred

The Roads Taken: Travels through America's Literary Landscapes. Athens, GA: University of Georgia Press, 1993. 166 pp. ISBN: 9780820315171

Setterberg combines travel narrative and literary history as he recounts his journey to seven places in the United States that are tied to well-known works of literature. He traveled to Willa Cather's hometown in Nebraska and to New Orleans, where Zora Neale Hurston studied voodoo; he searched for moose in the Maine woods of Thoreau and followed Hemingway through the forests of Michigan's upper peninsula. The focus is often on the differences between what Setterberg expected to find, based on the books he had read, and what he actually found, and the author decries what he calls the "blanding" and increasing "sameness" of America.

Subjects: Authors; Literary Lives; Quick Reads

Places: California; Maine; Michigan; Nebraska; Nevada; New Orleans; Texas

Now Try: *How the Heather Looks: A Joyous Journey to the British Sources of Children's Books* was written by Joan Bodger in 1965 but will still appeal to readers who remember Winnie-the-Pooh, Jemima Puddle-Duck, and Toad Hall. *Novel Destinations: Literary Landmarks From Jane Austen's Bath to Ernest Hemingway's Key West* by Shannon McKenna Schmidt and Joni Rendon is closer in spirit to a travel guide than a work of travel narrative, but it does contain reading suggestions as well as information on literary sites in the United States and Europe. Colleen Dunn Bates and Susan La Tempa do much the same for children's literature in *Storybook Travels: From Eloise's New York to Harry Potter's London, Visits to 30 of the Best-Loved Landmarks in Children's Literature*. Anna Quindlen looks at the literary landscape of London, which Quindlen calls "the capital of literature," in her book, *Imagined London: A Tour of the World's Greatest Fictional City* (annotated in "A Sense of Place").

Weiner, Eric

The Geography of Bliss: One Grump's Search for the Happiest Places in the World. New York: Twelve, 2008. 329 pp. ISBN: 9780446580267. YA

Eric Weiner, National Public Radio correspondent and self-proclaimed Eeyore, spent a year seeking out the world's "unheralded happy places" in an attempt to better understand the concept of happiness. His quest began in the Netherlands, with a visit to the Dutch professor who created the World Database of Happiness, and then moved through nine European and Asian countries before returning to the United States. In each country, Weiner explores the notion of happiness by interviewing individuals who live there (experts, random local people, expatriates) and then speculating on how each country's culture contributes to its citizens' notions of happiness and often contrasting these notions with the ideas that most Americans have about being happy. Among other things, Weiner explores why the Swiss are so dull and yet so happy, whether the citizens of Qatar have been able to buy happiness with all their money, and why Moldovans are so unhappy. Weiner focuses more on the people and less on the places that he visits, and his sense of humor, while sometimes dark and edgy, is anything but grumpy.

Subjects: Happiness; Humor; Investigative Stories

Places: Bhutan; England; Iceland; India; Moldova; Netherlands; Qatar; Switzerland; Thailand; United States

Now Try: Another NPR reporter who traveled to Bhutan is Lisa Napoli, who tells her story in the delightful *Radio Shangri-La: What I Learned in Bhutan, the Happiest Kingdom on Earth*. Mary South's mid-life crisis led her to seek happiness by purchasing a 40-foot trawler (without knowing how to pilot it) and eventually take it up the Atlantic coast from Florida to Maine. Her book, *The Cure for Anything Is Salt Water: How I Threw My Life Overboard and Found Happiness at Sea*, will inspire readers who suspect that happiness lies somewhere besides their current jobs; it is annotated in the chapter entitled "Travel Humor." Readers who are interested in the concept of happiness may want to explore Daniel Gilbert's *Stumbling on Happiness*, which argues that our limited imagination gets in the way of our pursuit of happiness; *The How of Happiness*, a self-help book by psychology professor Sonya

Lyubomirsky; Jonathan Haidt's *The Happiness Hypothesis: Finding Modern Truth in Ancient Wisdom*; or even *Against Happiness: In Praise of Melancholy,* in which author Eric Wilson argues that Americans are too interested in being happy.

Weiner, Eric

Man Seeks God: My Flirtations with the Divine. New York: Twelve, 2011. 349 pp. ISBN: 9780446539470

During hospitalization for what turned out to be gas, Weiner (an atheist) was asked by a nurse whether he had found God. Realizing that he hadn't, the former NPR correspondent traveled the world to sample eight different faiths in some detail, beginning with the Sufis, whom Weiner describes as "the drunkards of Islam" and with whose dervishes he tried, rather unsuccessfully, to whirl. In his search for an experience of the divine, Weiner meditated with Tibetan lamas in Nepal, unblocked his *chi* in China, studied the Kabbalah in Israel, and even explored the Raelians (followers of the world's largest UFO-based religion). Throughout it all, he exhibits his usual dilettantish charm, curiosity, and just enough humor.

Subjects: Buddhism; Catholicism; Humor; Islam; Memoirs; Religion; Spirituality; Taoism

Places: California; China; Israel; Las Vegas; Nepal; Turkey

Now Try: Another travel writer who examines various approaches to religion and spirituality is William Dalrymple, whose *Nine Lives: In Search of the Sacred in Modern India* (annotated in the "A Sense of Place" chapter of this book) looks at individuals whose religious paths have been affected by the changes in modern India. Michael Ondaatje, Alexander McCall Smith, Jan Morris, and Paul Theroux are among the contributors to the beautifully photographed book, *100 Journeys for the Spirit,* which includes the personal responses of these and other writers to places like the prehistoric megaliths of Carnac in Brittany and the Shrine of Imam Reza in Mashhad, Iran. Christian George's *Sacred Travels: Recovering the Ancient Practice of Pilgrimage* has a more Christian focus than does Weiner's book, following in the footsteps of spiritual pilgrims as the author travels to Assisi, Ireland, and France to gain a better understanding of his Christian heritage.

Wisner, Franz

How the World Makes Love: And What It Taught a Jilted Groom. New York: St. Martin's Press, 2009. 308 pp. ISBN: 9780312340834

How the World Makes Love is a quest to explore the notion of love by a man who was stood up at the altar. Wisner and his brother visited several foreign countries to talk with people about love, romance, and sex and to learn the most important lessons about love from around the globe. The brothers interviewed everyone with an opinion on the topic, from married couples to serial daters, and tell an often heart-warming story of how people from other countries meet, date, and find love.

Subjects: Family Relationships; Humor; Love Affairs; Male Point of View

Places: Africa; Botswana; Brazil; Egypt; India; Los Angeles; Nicaragua; Prague

Now Try: *How the World Makes Love* is a follow-up to Wisner's earlier *Honeymoon with My Brother,* which is annotated in "The Journey" chapter of this book; that book explains how Wisner was jilted by his bride-to-be. On her solo East Coast journey from Maine to Key West, Lili Wright learned a number of lessons about love, both through her own reflections and through the men whom she encountered; she writes about the trip in *Learning to Float: The Journey of a Woman, a Dog, and Just Enough Men.* Jennifer Cox traveled the world looking for love in *Around the World in 80 Dates,* which is annotated in the "Travel Humor" chapter of this book. Fiction readers who enjoy Wisner's book may also enjoy novels that explore romance from a man's point of view. One possibility is Jonathan Lethem's witty novel, *As She Climbed Across the Table,* about a professor who falls in love with a particle physicist who is too focused on her experiments to return his affection. Another is the delightful Carol Shields novel, *Larry's Party,* which follows a Canadian floral designer through two marriages and divorces and a growing passion for garden mazes.

Woodward, Christopher

In Ruins: A Journey Through History, Art, and Literature. New York: Pantheon Books, 2001. 280 pp. ISBN: 9780375421990

Woodward, the director of the Holburne Museum of Arts in Bath, uses his own travels and those of historical figures like Francis Bacon, Stendhal, and Shelley to reflect on the importance of ruins in European culture. He visited the great ruins in Rome, abandoned palaces, dilapidated Edwardian houses, and crumbling medieval abbeys to provide a wonderful synthesis of the arts, history, and literature and a lively meditation on our own mortality and transience.

Subjects: Art and Artists; European History

Places: England; France; Germany; Greece; Iraq; Ireland; Italy; Turkey

Series: *Vintage Departures*

Now Try: A more modern variety of ruins is explored by Tom Vanderbilt in *Survival City: Adventures among the Ruins of Atomic America,* which is a road trip among ruined missile silos, secret test sites, and other left-overs of the Cold War. British novelist Rose Macaulay wrote *The Pleasure of Ruins* just after World War II and, like Woodward, discusses the aesthetic and moral value of ruins, including her own home, which had been destroyed in the Blitz. In *The Haunts of the Black Masseur,* Charles Sprawson looks at swimmers and swimming in the larger context of literature and culture, much as Woodward does with ruins.

In the Footsteps of . . .

The final category of this subgenre represents travels that involve following in the footsteps of an earlier traveler, many of whom will be well known (the explorer H. M. Stanley, whose travels on the Congo River Tim Butcher retraced in *Blood River: A Journey to Africa's Broken Heart*, or Captain Cook, several of whose voyages were repeated by Tony Horwitz in *Blue Latitudes: Boldly Going Where Captain Cook Has Gone Before*). In some cases, the present-day traveler may compare his own situation to that of the earlier traveler, as when Richard Bernstein reflects on his own search for enlightenment as he follows the path of a seventh-century Buddhist monk in *Ultimate Journey: Retracing the Path of an Ancient Buddhist Monk Who Crossed Asia in Search of Enlightenment*. In others, the present-day traveler may compare the current world with that encountered by the earlier traveler, as when William Dalrymple compares the disappearance of Christianity throughout the Middle East with the crumbling of the Roman Empire that was witnessed by the 6th-century Christian monks in whose footsteps he followed in *From the Holy Mountain: A Journey among the Christians of the Middle East*.

Readers who enjoy these titles in which the traveler follows in the footsteps of an earlier traveler are likely to be interested in the writings of the original traveler (Alexis de Tocqueville's *Democracy in America* or Hsuan Tang's *Journey to the West*) or writings about the original traveler (Richard Alexander Hough's *Captain James Cook: A Biography* or Paul Cartledge's *Alexander the Great*). In some cases, the original traveler may have been a novelist whose fiction is set in exotic locations, such as Robert Louis Stevenson's *Treasure Island* or *South Sea Tales* or George Orwell's *Burmese Days*.

Bell, Gavin

In Search of Tusitala: Travels in the Pacific After Robert Louis Stevenson. London: Picador, 1994. 333 pp. ISBN: 9780330329323

The Samoans referred to Stevenson, who hoped that the South Seas climate would help his tuberculosis and built a mansion there in 1890, as "Tusitala" (Teller of Tales). Bell traveled to Samoa, as well as the Marquesas, Tahiti, Hawaii, and Kiribati, in the footsteps of the great Scottish writer and found traces of the cultures that fascinated him. Bell writes with a fondness both for Stevenson and for the people he met on his own trip and does a wonderful job of evoking the warm breezes and landscape of the South Pacific.

Subjects: Authors; Islands

Places: Hawaii; Kiribati; Marquesas; Micronesia; Pacific Ocean; Polynesia; Samoa; Tahiti

Awards: Thomas Cook Travel Book Award, 1995

Now Try: Other travel writers have followed in Stevenson's footsteps as well. In *The Happy Isles of Oceania: Paddling the Pacific,* Paul Theroux went to Samoa to find out what so attracted Stevenson; his book is annotated in "The Journey" chapter of this book. Scottish writer Christopher Rush worked through his grief over his wife's death by following Stevenson's trail through the Cevennes Mountains of French, a journey of recovery depicted in *To Travel Hopefully: Footsteps in The French Cevennes.* Pamela Stephenson bought a yacht and followed the South Pacific voyage of Robert Louis Stevenson and his wife Fanny; her Pacific journey is told in *Treasure Islands: Sailing the South Seas in the Wake of Fanny and Robert Louis Stevenson.*

Bernstein, Richard

Ultimate Journey: Retracing the Path of an Ancient Buddhist Monk Who Crossed Asia in Search of Enlightenment. New York: A.A. Knopf, 2001. 352 pp. ISBN: 9780375400094

Hsuan Tsang was a seventh-century Chinese Buddhist monk who traveled for 15 years across Asia in search of enlightenment. Bernstein, a *New York Times* correspondent and book critic, followed the monk's journey from western China to India, through harsh deserts and challenging mountain passes. The author's knowledge of the Chinese language and culture (based on his years as a correspondent in Beijing) yielded many insights into the shrines, temples, and other sites he encountered and enabled him to talk with most of the individuals he met on his quest. The lyrical descriptions of places and people combine with Bernstein's reflections on Husan Tsang and on his own loneliness and lack of commitment to relationships to produce a book about enlightenment, both sought after and unexpected.

Subjects: Asian History; Buddhism; Spirituality

Places: China; India; Kazakhstan; Pakistan; Tajikistan

Awards: *New York Times* Notable Book, 2001

Now Try: Hsuan Tsang's own writings about his journey have been translated and published by the University of Chicago in the four-volume *Journey to the West.* Mishi Saran, an Indian woman, also retraced Hsuan Tsang's steps and writes about her journey in a book that combines historical research and reflections on the contemporary world, *Chasing the Monk's Shadow.* Sally Wriggins tells the story of Hsuan Tsang and his travels in the straightforward *The Silk Road Journey With Xuanzang.* One of the four great classics of Chinese literature, *Monkey: A Folk Tale of China,* was originally published in the 16th century and is a fictionalized account of Hsuan Tsang's travels. While Pagan Kennedy's *The First Man-Made Man: The Story of Two Sex Changes, One Love Affair, and a Twentieth-Century Medical Revolution* is primarily about Laura/Michael Dillon's struggles to find his true gender, it is also the story of Dillon's spiritual journey to becoming a Buddhist monk.

Butcher, Tim

Blood River: A Journey to Africa's Broken Heart. New York: Grove Press, 2008 [2007]. 363 pp. ISBN: 9780802118776

Butcher retraced the path of 19th-century explorer H. M. Stanley as he traveled the length of the Congo River from its source at Lake Tanganyika to the Atlantic Ocean by motorbike, canoe, and UN patrol boat. His account of the six-week journey through a country that he sees as "not just undeveloped, but undeveloping" is gripping and filed with stories of atrocity and horror. Butcher, a foreign correspondent for the London *Telegraph*, mixes the Congo's history (Stanley, King Leopold, Lumumba, Mobutu) with his encounters with ordinary Congolese, staff members from the United Nations and humanitarian agencies, and elderly holdovers from the Belgian colonial era to produce an honest, unblinking, grim assessment of an abused, misruled nation.

Subjects: 19th Century; African History; Canoeing; Colonialism; Motorcycles; Rivers

Places: Africa; Congo River; Democratic Republic of Congo

Awards: Dolman Best Travel Book Award, Shortlist, 2008; Samuel Johnson Prize, Shortlist, 2008

Now Try: Jeffrey Tayler's *Facing the Congo: A Modern-Day Journey into the Heart of Darkness* tells the story of that author's attempt to re-create British explorer Henry Stanley's trip down the Congo River in a canoe; Tayler's book is a bit more personal than Butcher's, with as much focus on Tayler's own struggles as on those of the Congo itself. Redmond O'Hanlon's *No Mercy: A Journey Into the Heart of the Congo* is funnier than *Blood River* or *Facing the Congo* and is annotated in "The Journey" chapter of this book. Readers interested in a history of the former Belgian Congo have several good books to select from: Jason Stearns's *Dancing in the Glory of Monsters: The Collapse of the Congo and the Great War of Africa*; Michela Wong's *In the Footsteps of Mr. Kurtz: Living on the Brink of Disaster in Mobutu's Congo*; and Adam Hochschild's brilliant *King Leopold's Ghost: A Story of Greed, Terror, and Heroism in Colonial Africa*. Joseph Conrad's novella, *Heart of Darkness*, is also relevant here; the story of Charles Marlow's search for Kurtz is a classic exploration of the theme of mankind's capacity for evil.

Dalrymple, William

From the Holy Mountain: A Journey among the Christians of the Middle East. New York: Holt, 1998. 483 pp. ISBN: 9780805058734

Dalrymple, the author of several travel narratives, followed the footsteps of two 6th-century Christian monks who had visited caves, monasteries, and hermitages in order to record the wisdom of "the desert fathers." In an ironic parallel, while the earlier monks were witness to the crumbling of the eastern Roman Empire in the face of Muslim conquest, Dalrymple saw his quest as witnessing the disappearance of Christianity from the Middle East, where that religion faces a wide range of challenges: discrimination against Christians in Turkey, warring factions in Lebanon, and holy sites being bulldozed in Israel. The book is sometimes humorous (for example, when discussing the challenges of traveling in the Middle East) but mostly sensitive, both to the people he meets and to the intricacies of the situations in which these modern Christians find themselves.

Subjects: Biblical History; Christianity; Islam; Middle Eastern History; Religion

Places: Africa; Egypt; Greece; Israel; Lebanon; Syria; Turkey

Now Try: John Moscus's *The Spiritual Meadow* served as the inspiration for Dalrymple's quest; it details the travels of St. John Moscus and his younger friend and disciple Sophronius. Sister Benedicta Ward has collected and translated the sayings of over 100 early Christian monastics in *The Sayings of the Desert Fathers: The Alphabetical Collection,* and Laura Swan has examined the lives of the early female ascetics in *The Forgotten Desert Mothers: Sayings, Lives, and Stories of Early Christian Women.* Though it examines a more modern group of religious believers, Dennis Covington's absorbing *Salvation on Sand Mountain: Snake Handling and Redemption in Southern Appalachia* may appeal to readers interested in religious communities.

Horwitz, Tony

Blue Latitudes: Boldly Going Where Captain Cook Has Gone Before. New York: H. Holt, 2002. 480 pp. ISBN: 9780805065411

Horwitz retraced several of Cook's 18th-century voyages, trying to strike a balance between those who see him as a hero who changed the map of the world and those (particularly the indigenous peoples of the lands he opened up) who believe that he did more environmental and cultural harm than good. Horwitz intermingles Cook's voyage story (much of it from Cook's own journals) with his own travels, makes clear the difficulties and hardships of his and Cook's journeys, and even manages to maintain a sense of humor about it all.

Subjects: 18th century; Adventure; Biographies; Exploration; Explorers; Humor; Indigenous Peoples; Sailing

Places: Alaska; Australia; Canada; England; French Polynesia; Hawaii; New Zealand; Tahiti

Awards: *New York Times* Notable Book, 2002

Now Try: Richard Alexander Hough's *Captain James Cook: A Biography* is a good biography of the explorer's life. The abridged *Journals of Captain Cook* are also available from Penguin Classics. Fiction readers may want to try *Mrs. Cook: The Real and Imagined Life of the Captain's Wife* by Marele Day, about the woman who not only survived her famous husband but outlived all of her six children as well. For readers who want more of the adventurous and humorous side of Tony Horwitz, his book about hitchhiking across the Australian Outback, *One for the Road,* can be recommended.

Huler, Scott

No Man's Lands: One Man's Odyssey through The Odyssey. New York: Crown, 2008. 286 pp. ISBN: 9781400082827

After reading Homer's *Odyssey*, NPR contributor Huler decided to trace the twenty-year journey of Odysseus from Troy to Ithaca to better understand the places the great hero visited and the lessons he learned. Huler found the cave of Polyphemus in Sicily and the land of the dead in Italy; he even paddled a rented kayak between Scylla and Charybdis. Huler shares his impressive knowledge of Homer and his take on the themes of the epic: the dangers of ambition and the value of love and family. *No Man's Land* can be rambling and a bit sentimental, but it is pleasantly so and filled with self-deprecating humor and insights into how Homer's great work can apply to our lives.

Subjects: Books and Learning; Family Relationships; Homer; Kayaking; Memoirs; Odysseus; *Odyssey*

Places: Greece; Italy; Mediterranean Sea

Now Try: Huler has written another book with a nautical theme, *Defining the Wind: The Beaufort Scale, and How a 19th-Century Admiral Turned Science into Poetry*, in which he follows in the footsteps of Sir Francis Beaufort and the scale that bears his name. Homer's epic, *The Odyssey*, is an inspiring and enjoyable work, and there are numerous contenders for the best translation; Robert Fitzgerald, Richmond Lattimore, and Robert Fagles have all produced noteworthy translations. Following the Second World War, Ernie Bradford sailed a small yacht in the path of Odysseus and tried to identify the locations of several of the episodes from the epic; he recounts his quest in *Ulysses Found*. The Coen brothers' 2000 film about a chain gang escapee's return home during the Great Depression, *O Brother, Where Art Thou*, has many humorous parallels with Homer's *Odyssey*. Thomas Cahill's introduction to ancient Greek life and thought, *Sailing the Wine-Dark Sea: Why the Greeks Matter*, opens with a discussion of Homer's *Iliad* and the ancient Greek glorification of war.

Jacobs, Michael

Andes. Berkeley, CA: Counterpoint, 2011. 580 pp. ISBN: 9781582437378

Jacobs, who inherited his interest in the Andes from his grandfather, followed in the footsteps of explorer Alexander von Humboldt and Simón Bolívar through the northern and central Andes and in the footsteps of scientist Charles Darwin at the mountain range's southernmost tip. Traveling across seven countries in all, Jacobs encountered assorted characters as well as the historical figures who were important to the region and the ghosts of vanishing indigenous civilizations. Jacobs writes in what one reviewer called "highly condensed and highly idiosyncratic sketches," meandering from topic to topic (from his thoughts on Hugo Chávez to the weather to the cuisine) and alternating between a relaxed persona and one that is awed by the immensity of the landscape through which he passes.

Subjects: Indigenous Peoples; Mountains

Places: Andes Mountains; Argentina; Bolivia; Chile; Colombia; Ecuador; Peru; Venezuela

Now Try: Jacobs's earlier book, *The Factory of Light: Tales from My Andalucian Village,* was shortlisted for the 2004 Thomas Cook Travel Book Award; in that book, he tells about his time in a remote village in the mountains of Andalucía and the town's mysterious "healers." In an interview with *The Browser* (http://thebrowser.com/interviews/michael-jacobs-on-andes), Jacobs recommends five books on the Andes. These include Chris Moss's thorough *Patagonia: A Cultural History,* John Hemming's highly regarded account of the destruction of the Incan empire (*The Conquest of the Incas*), as well as Christopher Isherwood's curmudgeonly classic, *The Condor And The Cows: A South American Travel Diary,* about a six-month tour of Colombia, Ecuador, Peru, Bolivia, and Argentina that Isherwood and his friend took in 1947. Jacobs also recommends Simon Lamb's book about the geological origins of the Andes (*Devil in the Mountain: A Search for the Origin of the Andes*) and Hugh Thomson's travel narrative, *The White Rock: An Exploration of the Inca Heartland* (annotated in "The Journey").

Kriwaczek, Paul

In Search of Zarathustra: The First Prophet and the Ideas that Changed the World. New York: Knopf, 2003 [2002]. 248 pp. ISBN: 9780375415289

Kriwaczek traced the footsteps of Zarathustra, the founder of Zoroastrianism (to the extent that this is possible, given the lack of historical evidence about Zarathustra) and makes the case for the importance of the early prophet to the later monotheistic religions. The author traveled to the prophet's birthplace, Afghanistan, as well as other countries in central Asia to uncover the traces of the religion in both historical settings (the Manicheanist heresy, the Vikings, the Cathars of southern France, Nietzsche) and the present day (the Iranian New Year's celebration of Noruz, a wedding ceremony in Afghanistan). This combination of religious history and travel narrative is a reminder of the common threads that weave through disparate and often conflicting religious traditions.

Subjects: Ancient History; Asian History; Christianity; European History; Islam; Judaism; Religion; Spirituality

Places: Afghanistan; France; Iran; Uzbekistan

Series: *Vintage Departures*

Now Try: Research suggests that the Magi were Zoroastrian priests, and readers interested in another religious history and travel narrative should try Paul William Roberts's *Journey of the Magi: Travels in Search of the Birth of Jesus,* which traces the journey of the Magi through Iran, Iraq, and Syria. The Magi would have followed the ancient "Incense Route," and Barbara Toy made that journey during a dangerous political time in *Traveling the Incense Route: From Arabia to the Levant in the Footsteps of the Magi.* The Persian mystic Mani took elements of Zoroastrianism to form the Manichean religion, and his story is told in a recent novel by the Lebanese author, Amin Maalouf, *The Gardens of Light.*

Larkin, Emma

Finding George Orwell in Burma. New York: Penguin Press, 2005. 294 pp. ISBN: 9781594200526

Larkin, an American journalist who is fluent in Burmese, went to Myanmar (formerly Burma) to trace the footsteps of George Orwell, who went to that country in the 1920s to serve for five years with the British Imperial Police in what was then a colony. She revisited his stops in five areas of the country and, thanks to her fluent Burmese, was able to speak with a number of individuals and gain insight into the current totalitarian state. Larkin writes in a restrained and understated manner and lets the words of the people she meets speak for themselves, without editorializing. As she notes, "All you had to do, it seemed, was scratch the surface of one of the town's smiling residents and you would find bitterness or tears." The book is grim but insightful about the connections between Orwell's themes and the path to tyranny that Myanmar has taken.

Subjects: 1920s; Asian History; Authors; Politics

Places: Myanmar

Now Try: Larkin repeats a joke that is often told in Myanmar, i.e., that Orwell wrote not one novel about the country, but three: *Burmese Days, Animal Farm,* and *1984*. Larkin explains that the first takes place during the British colonial days, and the latter two reflect the current situation. All three would be of interest to readers wanting to learn more about Orwell and Myanmar. Rory Maclean's *Under the Dragon: A Journey through Burma* tells of his return trip to Myanmar and the stories of ordinary people, struggling to survive under the repressive regime. Guy Delisle's *Burma Chronicles* is a graphic (i.e., comic book format) memoir of the author's year in Rangoon, where he depicts daily life under military rule. Daniel Mason's historical novel, *The Piano Tuner,* is set in the jungles of what was then Burma in 1886, telling the story of a shy piano tuner who is sent by the British War Office to repair the rare piano of an army surgeon living in the jungle.

Levy, Bernard Henri

American Vertigo: Traveling America in the Footsteps of Tocqueville. New York: Random House, 2006. 308 pp. ISBN: 9781400064342

Levy, a celebrated French philosopher and journalist, loosely followed the path that another Frenchman, Alexis de Tocqueville, took when he visited the United States in the 19th century. Levy visited places from the Baseball Hall of Fame in Cooperstown (New York) to the Mall of America in Bloomington (Minnesota) and spoke with individuals from John Kerry to Sharon Stone to a waitress in Colorado trying to make ends meet. He speculates on many of Tocqueville's reflections on America ("the tyranny of the majority," for example) and provides his own thoughts about the country, which he admires for its unique brand of democracy. As might be expected of an intellectual like Levy, the writing is sometimes long-winded and philosophical and, as one reviewer put it, "[seething] with provocation and paradox."

Subjects: 19th Century; American History; Philosophy; Politics; Society; Tocqueville, Alexis de

Places: United States (Various)

Now Try: Tocqueville's classic, *Democracy in America,* is readily available and a fascinating travel narrative on its own; the young French aristocrat's observations of 19th-century America and its fledgling democracy are timeless. Levy is known in France for his anti-anti-American stance, and his polemic against the political left, *Left in Dark Times: A Stand Against the New Barbarism,* is a good introduction to his thought. Levy's *War, Evil, and the End of History* is a political travel narrative, in which the author visited five war zones around the world: Angola, Burundi, Colombia, Sri Lanka, and the Sudan. Peter Carey's humorous and insightful novel *Parrot and Olivier in America* is a fictionalized version of Tocqueville's visit to America.

Marozzi, Justin

The Way of Herodotus: Travels with the Man Who Invented History. Cambridge, MA: Da Capo Press, 2008. 348 pp. ISBN: 9780306816215

Historian Marozzi roughly followed the path of Herodotus through Greece, Turkey, Egypt, and Iraq, describing these cultures and places both as Herodotus saw them 2,500 years ago and as they are today. He engaged local individuals (from tour guides to academics), and the book benefits from their wide-ranging perspectives on both past and present. Ironically, although he notes that Herodotus attempted to show all sides of the conflicts about which he wrote, Marozzi himself has a strong anti-American bias, particularly regarding the war in Iraq.

Subjects: Ancient History; Authors

Places: Africa; Egypt; Greece; Iran; Turkey

Now Try: Ryszard Kapuscinski was also inspired by Herodotus, and his memoir of his travels throughout the world as a journalist, *Travels with Herodotus,* is annotated in "The Journey" chapter of this book. Herodotus himself is a very entertaining read, although he apparently believed everything that he was told (he describes gold-digging ants and dog-headed men, for example); his *Histories* are available from Penguin Classics and several other publishers. Marozzi began his travels in Turkey, where Herodotus was born in 480 BC; a delightful book about a year spent by two Americans in a small Turkish village is *Tea & Bee's Milk: Our Year In A Turkish Village.*

Morris-Suzuki, Tessa

To the Diamond Mountains: A Hundred-Year Journey through China and Korea. Lanham, MD: Rowman & Littlefield Publishers, 2010. 201 pp. ISBN: 9781442205031

Australian professor Morris-Suzuki retraces the route taken by Emily Kemp, an artist and explorer who wrote about her travels from northern China to the Diamond Mountains of North Korea a century ago. The mountains have long been revered by poets and religious Koreans, and even though the region has been a site of tension between North and South Korea, Morris-Suzuki was able to travel there and both highlight the changes that have taken place since Kemp visited the region and, as one reviewer stated, put "a human face on the long-suffering people of that pariah state."

Subjects: Mountains; Quick Reads; Women Travelers

Places: China; North Korea; South Korea

Now Try: Not surprisingly, there are few travel narratives with North Korea as the destination. An expatriate narrative of life in North Korea that highlights the brutality of its regime is *The Aquariums of Pyongyang: Ten Years in the North Korean Gulag* by Chol-hwan Kang. Barbara Demick's book, *Nothing to Envy: Ordinary Lives in North Korea,* is not a travel narrative but her attempt to sketch the daily lives of North Koreans through interviews with six defectors from that isolated country, like *To the Diamond Mountains,* attempts to make those who live in North Korea seem more real. The relationships among family members in South Korea are the focus of Kyung-sook Shin's powerful novel, *Please Look After Mom,* in which the family searches for their mother, who has gone missing one afternoon in a Seoul subway station.

Norgay, Jamling Tenzing

Touching My Father's Soul: A Sherpa's Journey to the Top of Everest. San Francisco: HarperSanFrancisco, 2001. 316 pp. ISBN: 9780062516879

Norgay is the son of Tenzing Norgay, the Sherpa guide who climbed to the top of Mt. Everest with Sir Edmund Hillary in 1953. In 1996, Norgay served as the climbing leader for the IMAX film team that just escaped the tragedies made famous by Jon Krakauer's *Into Thin Air. Touching My Father's Soul* is a retelling of that experience as well as a thoughtful memoir of Norgay's own personal development and his efforts to find his identity both in the complex modern world and in the shadow of his father. Norgay interlaces the striking story of his own climb with stories from his father's famous ascent and he provides a fascinating insider's view on the world of the Sherpas.

Subjects: Accidents; Adventure; Climbing and Hiking; Fathers and Sons; Mountains; Self-Discovery; Survival Stories; Weather

Places: Nepal

Now Try: As noted, Norgay was the climbing leader for the 1996 IMAX expedition that aborted its ascent of Everest and avoided the storm that killed eight people; his team had radio contact with the group that died, and participated in rescue attempts. Jon Krakauer's classic *Into Thin Air* is an unforgettable account of that tragic climb; it is annotated in the "Travel

Adventure" chapter of this book. David Breashears, the leader of the IMAX team and the person who made the decision to turn back, tells his version of the story in the compelling *High Exposure: An Enduring Passion for Everest and Unforgiving Places.* Several other survivors of that expedition have written about their experiences, including Beck Weathers, whose *Left for Dead: My Journey Home from Everest* is particularly gripping. Travel writer Jan Morris accompanied the 1953 Hillary-Norgay ascent and first broke the news of the success to the world; she writes about the experience in *Coronation Everest: Eyewitness Dispatches from the Historic Hillary Climb.* Another book in which a climber struggles with the legacy of his father is John Harlin's *The Eiger Obsession: Facing the Mountain That Killed My Father,* in which the author attempts to climb the mountain from which his father fell to his death 40 years earlier.

O'Shea, Stephen

Back to the Front: An Accidental Historian Walks the Trenches of World War I. New York: Walker & Company, 1997 [1996]. 205 pp. ISBN: 9780802713292

In the summer of 1986, journalist and film critic O'Shea walked 450 miles of trenches from the seaside in Belgium to the border of France and Switzerland in order to discover the meaning of the Great War for himself and his generation. O'Shea, whose grandfather fought in World War I, traveled through the battlefields of Somme, Verdun, and Argonne and through lands dotted with cemeteries and monuments. In writing that is poetic, descriptive, and sorrowful, he contemplates the millions of lives needlessly lost through the incompetence of generals and poor battle planning and the deep scar left by the war on Western culture and the Western imagination.

Subjects: European History; Military History; Quick Reads; War; World War I

Places: Belgium; France; Germany; Switzerland

Now Try: Tony Wright's *Turn Right at Istanbul: A Walk on the Gallipoli Peninsula* combines travel narrative and guide with a look at the stories of the young Australians who participated in the disastrous attack on the peninsula in World War I. Nigel Jones, whose uncle was killed near Ypres during World War I, traveled to several battlefields in *The War Walk: A Journey Along the Western Front,* a book that combines his own observations with anecdotes from some of the Great War's last survivors. Another absorbing book about battlefields and the relics of a different war, World War II, is Bill Warnock's *The Dead of Winter: The Battlefield Investigation for Missing GIs Lost During the Bulge.* Robert Graves's *Good-Bye to All That: An Autobiography* is one of the best, if not **the** best, memoirs of World War I. The classic novel about World War I is Erich Maria Remarque's *All Quiet on the Western Front,* which tells the story of a German soldier at the front. A more romantic novel related to "the war to end all wars" is Sebastian Japrisot's engaging novel, *A Very Long Engagement,* which involves a woman who refuses to believe that her fiancé has been killed in the war and searches for him through France in the 1920s. (The film based on the novel, which starred Audrey Tautou, is also called *A Very Long Engagement* and was nominated for a Golden Globe for best foreign language film.)

Raban, Jonathan

Hunting Mister Heartbreak. New York: Edward Burlingame Books, 1991 [1990]. 372 pp. ISBN: 9780060182090

Raban explored the immigrant experience in America by following in the footsteps of several million immigrants and, in particular, the French writer Hector St John de Crevecoeur, the "Mister Heartbreak" of the title and the author of *Letters from an American Farmer* (1782). He sailed from Liverpool, docked in New York, and traveled to Alabama, Seattle, and the Florida Keys. The author's meanderings produce the usual Raban insights, for example, that New Yorkers are either street people or "air people" (rich enough to take elevators to safe places above the streets). The book is also an internal travelogue, with Raban trying out a new personality at every new place that he visits, in essence trying out life as a different sort of American in each region of the country.

Subjects: American History; Immigration

Places: Alabama; England; Florida; Liverpool; New York; Seattle

Awards: Thomas Cook Travel Book Award, 1991

Series: *Vintage Departures*

Now Try: Several of Raban's best books have been written about his travels in America. *Old Glory: A Voyage Down the Mississippi*, about his trip down the great river in an aluminum boat, won the 1981 Thomas Cook Travel Book Award and is annotated in the "A Sense of Place" chapter of this book. *Bad Land: An American Romance*, which was named an ALA Notable Book in 1998, is a journey into the history of eastern Montana. (It is also annotated in the "A Sense of Place" chapter.) *Passage to Juneau: A Sea and Its Meanings* describes a solo voyage he took from Seattle to Alaska via the Inside Passage; it was named an ALA Notable Book in 2000 and is annotated in "The Journey" chapter.

Richardson, Mark

Zen and Now: On the Trail of Robert Pirsig and the Art of Motorcycle Maintenance. New York: Alfred A. Knopf, 2008. 274 pp. ISBN: 9780307269706

Richardson, a journalist, became one of "Pirsig's pilgrims" as he traveled on his motorcycle as closely along Pirsig's original route as possible. The book is about many things: the trip itself and the cities and towns through which he traveled and how they compare now with what they were like when Pirsig visited them 40 years before; Pirsig himself and many of the characters from the book; Richardson's own mid-life crisis; and the impact that *Zen and the Art of Motorcycle Maintenance* has had on his life. Richardson's book is honestly written (he admits to almost committing adultery in South Dakota, he complains that his young sons interfere with his marriage), and while some reviewers did not believe that he understood Pirsig and his great work, Richardson does provide an interesting perspective on that modern classic.

Subjects: Biography; Buddhism; Fathers and Sons; Memoirs; Motorcycles; Philosophy

Places: California; Idaho; Minnesota; Montana; North Dakota; Oregon; San Francisco; South Dakota

Now Try: Pirsig's philosophical classic about a trip with his son from Minnesota to California, *Zen and the Art of Motorcycle Maintenance: An Inquiry into Values*, is annotated in the chapter of this book entitled "The Journey." English professor Ted Bishop rode his motorcycle from the University of Alberta to the University of Texas and speculates about great literature along the way in *Riding with Rilke: Reflections on Motorcycles and Books*. Garri Gallipoli's *The Tao of the Ride: Motorcycles and the Mechanics of the Soul* deftly combines meditations on motorcycling and Eastern spirituality. A more recent popular philosophy book is Matthew Crawford's *Shop Class as Soulcraft: An Inquiry into the Value of Work*, which praises the virtues of working with one's hands.

Rutstein, Harry

The Marco Polo Odyssey: In the Footsteps of a Merchant Who Changed the World. Seattle, WA: B&H, 2008. 271 pp. ISBN: 9780980207606

Rutstein spent 10 years and three separate expeditions retracing Marco Polo's 13,000-mile journey from Venice to China, and his book mixes the old (excerpts from Marco Polo's own writings) with the new (Rutstein's overland travels in a number of different conveyances, from goatskin raft to camel to hitching a ride on a tractor). The stories of Rutstein's travels along the old Silk Road are lively and humorous, and the author includes bits of the history and geography of the places visited along the way.

Subjects: Adventure; Asian History; European History; Exploration; Polo, Marco; Silk Road

Places: Afghanistan; China; Iran; Israel; Italy; Pakistan; Turkey; Venice

Now Try: Marco Polo's own *Travels* is available in many editions, including Everyman's Library and Penguin Classics. Denis Belliveau and Francis O'Donnell spent two years retracing Polo's journey and tell about their experience in the lively book, *In the Footsteps of Marco Polo: A Companion to the Public Television Film.* Tim Severin, whose book *The Brendan Voyage*, is annotated in this chapter, also wrote about following in the footsteps on Marco Polo, but on motorcycle, in *Tracking Marco Polo*. The prize-winning Paul Griffiths novel, *Myself and Marco Polo: A Novel of Changes*, has as its central character Rustichello da Pisa, the cellmate to whom Marco Polo dictated his travels in Genoa, and has that character grow bored and embellish the tales being told to him.

Salak, Kira

Cruelest Journey: Six Hundred Miles To Timbuktu. Washington, DC: National Geographic, 2005. 230 pp. ISBN: 9780792274575

Kira Salak retraced the fatal journey of the great Scottish explorer Mungo Park to become the first person in the world to kayak alone 600 miles on the Niger River of Mali to Timbuktu. The book enumerates the many challenges that she faced (tropical storms, the unbearable and unrelenting heat, hippos, the vagaries of the river itself, men chasing her in wooden canoes) as well as the local people on whom she depended for food and night-time shelter and especially the two slave girls whose freedom she buys at the journey's end. *Cruelest Journey* is not only a page-turning adventure; it is also a story of confronting one's innermost fears.

Subjects: African History; Explorers; Kayaking; Rivers; Slavery; Solo Travelers; Women Travelers

Places: Africa; Mali; Niger River; Timbuktu

Now Try: Salak's first book, *Four Corners: A Journey into the Heart of Papua New Guinea,* tells of her trip deep into Papua New Guinea, including time spent with a tribe that still practiced cannibalism. Salak also wrote a novel, *The White Mary,* about a young female reporter who travels to Papua New Guinea to find a Pulitzer-winning writer who is presumed to be dead but who she thinks may still be alive. Jean-Marie Gibbal has written a very personal description of the land and tribes along the Niger River in his prize-winning *Genii of the River Niger*. Another woman who traveled to Africa, motivated by a plan to help the Zulu tribe's economic development rather than by adventure, was Carol Batrus, whose experiences are told in *When Elephants Fly: One Woman's Journey from Wall Street to Zululand.*

Starr, William W.

Whisky, Kilts, and the Loch Ness Monster: Traveling through Scotland with Boswell and Johnson. Columbia, SC: University of South Carolina Press, 2011. 223 pp. ISBN: 9781570039485

In 2007, journalist and literature enthusiast Starr retraced the 2,800-mile path (in reverse) taken by Samuel Johnson and James Boswell through Scotland in the 18th century. *Whisky, Kilts, and the Loch Ness Monster* mixes his 20th-century observations of the land with the earlier reflections of Johnson and Boswell, making for a fascinating contrast. Starr muses on Scottish history, Scottish fables, and the Scottish people along the way and adds visits to the Outer Hebrides and the Orkney Islands, two places that Johnson and Boswell did not visit. Starr's descriptions of the land are beautiful, his asides are very funny, and the back-and-forth between his observations and those of Johnson and Boswell works surprisingly well.

Subjects: 18th Century; Humor; Quick Reads

Places: Scotland

Now Try: The classic journey of Johnson and Boswell in 1773, which Starr replicates, is recounted in *A Journey to the Western Islands of Scotland and The Journal of a Tour to the Hebrides,* which provides a fascinating look at a culture that was alien to the Enlightenment Europe of the authors. Readers interested in the lives of Boswell and Johnson have their pick of nonfiction (Adam Sisman's riveting book, *Boswell's Presumptuous Task: The Making of the Life of Dr. Johnson*) and fiction (Philip Baruth's *The Brothers Boswell,* a literary thriller set in 1763 London). David Yeadon and his wife spent a year on a small island in the Outer Hebrides, and he recounts that time in *Seasons on Harris: A Year in Scotland's Outer Hebrides,* a slow-paced memoir that mixes personal recollections with stories told by the island's residents. John McPhee's *The Crofter and the Laird* focuses on the residents of another island in the Hebrides and their struggles in the stark, but beautiful surroundings; it is annotated in "The Journey."

Tayler, Jeffrey

River of No Reprieve: Descending Siberia's Waterway of Exile, Death, and Destiny. Boston: Houghton Mifflin, 2006. 230 pp. ISBN: 9780618539093

Tayler steered his custom-made raft 2,400 miles down the 10th longest river in the world, the Lena River, re-creating the Cossack journeys that delineated Russia's eastern borders and annexed Siberia for Ivan the Terrible more than 300 years ago. Traveling from Lake Baikal to the Arctic Ocean, Tayler and his misanthropic guide Vadim journeyed down the unruly, chilling river, through Cossack villages that had not changed for centuries, to the ruins of gulags. *River of No Reprieve* is both a keen portrait of modern-day Siberia and its people, as well as a page-turning adventure in which the author navigates not just a dangerous river but a volatile relationship with his guide as well.

Subjects: Asian History; European History; Rivers

Places: Lake Baikal; Lena River; Russia

Now Try: Six years before *River of No Reprieve,* Tayler published *Siberian Dawn: A Journey Across the New Russia,* in which he traveled over 8,300 miles across Russia, from the port city of Magadan in Siberia to the Polish border, and found poverty, environmental destruction, and a loss of hope among the people. Tayler is also the author of *Murderers in Mausoleums: Riding the Back Roads of Empire Between Moscow and Beijing,* which tells of his later 7,200-mile journey from Moscow to Beijing via the "back roads" (the Caucasus, the Caspian Sea, Kazakhstan, and Inner Mongolia) and the lingering effects of the Soviet era that he found mixed with the hints of capitalism. For a travel narrative that combines fly-fishing in several Russian rivers and social commentary, readers can turn to Fen Montaigne's unique *Reeling In Russia: An American Angler In Russia.*

Thorpe, Nick

8 Men and A Duck: An Improbable Voyage, Reed Boat To Easter Island. New York: The Free Press, 2002. 240 pp. ISBN: 9780743219280

British travel writer Thorpe was a crew member on a reed boat built by adventurer Phil Buck, who intended to sail across the Pacific from Chile to Easter Island in order to test Thor Heyerdahl's theories. The project seemed doomed from the start; reeds absorb water and so the boat was in constant danger of sinking. Thorpe himself had minimal sailing skills, derived mainly from his days as a second-string rower in college, and the voyage faced challenges from sharks to storms to interpersonal conflicts. Thorpe's account is witty, touching, and thrilling, and his eye for detail and talent for asking pointed questions (Where was the life raft?) provide comic relief in the midst of an unbelievably tense situation.

Subjects: Humor; Oceans; Sailing

Places: Chile; Easter Island; Pacific Ocean

Now Try: Heyerdahl's theories are outlined in *Kon-Tiki* (which is annotated in the "Classics" section of this chapter) and *Aku-Aku,* in which the explorer explains his idea that the Easter Island statues were carved by people who originally came from Peru. P. J. Capelotti writes about the 40-plus expeditions that followed Heyerdahl's Kon-Tiki voyage in *Sea Drift: Rafting Adventures in the Wake of Kon-Tiki,* including rafts made of straw, bamboo, and balsa wood. For fiction about Easter Island, readers may turn to Jennifer Vanderbes's debut novel, *Easter Island,* which tells of a woman who followed her anthropologist husband to the island and encountered an inhospitable culture filled with mysteries.

Wood, Michael

In the Footsteps of Alexander the Great: A Journey from Greece to Asia. Berkeley, CA: University of California Press, 1997. 256 pp. ISBN: 9780520213074

Wood, a British journalist, followed the path taken by Alexander the Great and his army from Macedonia to the Indus River in the 4th century BC. The book combines the story of Alexander's conquests with Wood's own travels and attempts to find traces of Alexander's influence in the modern countries of Syria, Iran, and Afghanistan. Wood's writing is enthusiastic and lively and he includes references to ancient Greek texts as well as local legends, many of which see Alexander as anything but great.

Subjects: 4th Century BC; Alexander the Great; Ancient History

Places: Afghanistan; Africa; Egypt; India; Iran; Iraq; Lebanon; Pakistan; Syria; Turkey; Uzbekistan

Now Try: The DVD documentary, *In the Footsteps of Alexander the Great,* serves as a companion to Wood's book and has been well received. Wood has written several "In search of . . ." books, including *In Search of the Trojan War* and *In Search of Myths and Heroes: Exploring Four Epic Legends of the World. Alexander the Great,* by Paul Cartledge, is an accessible biography of the man who conquered most of the known world by the time he was 30. Steven Pressfield's historical novel, *The Virtues of War: A Novel of Alexander the Great,* tells the story of the powerful leader's life from his own point of view.

Young, Gavin

In Search of Conrad. London: Hutchinson, 1991. 303 pp. ISBN: 9780091735241

Young, a British foreign correspondent, was a great admirer of Joseph Conrad and retraced his voyages to southeast Asia, traveling by sea, land, and river and visiting the ports and islands that Conrad had seen, from Singapore to the Straits of Makassar. Young provides rich details about Conrad's world at the end of the 19th century and evokes the atmosphere of the area. An interesting subplot is the fact that Conrad based some of his fictional characters on real people and that Young tried to find marriage and death certificates for these individuals and hunted for their descendants.

Subjects: 19th Century; Authors; Sailing; Seas

Places: Bangkok; Borneo; Celebes Islands; Indonesia; Jakarta; Singapore; Thailand

Awards: Thomas Cook Travel Book Award, 1991

Now Try: Young was well regarded as a travel writer when he died in 2001. In the 1980s, he had the idea of sailing to China and back by whatever ships he could find. His *Slow Boats to China* describes his journey from Europe to China, which required seven months and 23 different boats. The sequel, *Slow Boats Home,* covers the return voyage via the South Seas, Cape Horn, and West Africa. Both reflect the slow pace of such travel and Young's belief in the common humanity of all people. Young also wrote *A Wavering Grace,* a memorial to Vietnam and the Vietnamese family that became the emotional center of his life and whose members he helped to establish new lives in America. Helen Winternitz and her boyfriend followed the path of Conrad's *Heart of Darkness* up the Congo River in *East Along the Equator: A Journey up the Congo and into Zaire.* Conrad's best-known novel, *Lord Jim,* involves a British seaman who abandons a ship in distress and is stripped of his navigation command.

Consider Starting With . . .

Bourdain, Anthony. *A Cook's Tour: In Search of the Perfect Meal.*
Butcher, Tim. *Blood River: A Journey to Africa's Broken Heart.*
Chatwin, Bruce. *The Songlines.*
Grann, David. *The Lost City of Z: A Tale of Deadly Obsession in the Amazon.*
Heyerdahl, Thor. *Kon-Tiki: Across the Pacific by Raft.*
Horwitz, Tony. *Confederates in the Attic: Dispatches from the Unfinished Civil War.*
Kaplan, Robert D. *Balkan Ghosts: A Journey Through History.*
Weiner, Eric. *The Geography of Bliss: One Grump's Search for the Happiest Places in the World.*

Fiction Read-Alikes

Cornwell, Bernard. Among the many fictional treatments of the search for the Holy Grail is Cornwell's Grail Quest trilogy, about Thomas of Hookton's 14th-century travels in search of the holiest of relics. In ***The Archer's Tale,*** Thomas leaves his hometown following a raid that leaves everyone but him dead and joins the English army as an archer to fight in the battles of Brittany and Crécy. After the latter battle, King Edward III learns of the links between Thomas's family and the Grail. In the second novel of the trilogy, ***Vagabond,*** Thomas is sent back to England to find the Grail and becomes involved in the Scottish invasion of 1347. He soon discovers that his cousin, who had murdered Thomas's father, is working with members of the Catholic Inquisition in France to find the Grail as well. In the third novel, ***Heretic,*** Thomas leads a small band of men into southern France, the last place the Grail has been seen, and becomes involved in a bitter local war with others who seek the Grail and in the Black Death. Cornwell's books are marked by strong characters and historical details.

Cussler, Clive. Several of the novels in Cussler's *NUMA Files* series involve searches for historical and legendary objects by Kurt Austin and his colleagues at the National Underwater and Maritime Agency. These include the pre-Columbian artifacts buried in the remains of the *Andrea Doria* in ***Serpent,*** the first novel in the series; a mythical tribal goddess in a Venezuelan rain forest in ***Blue Gold***; and an ancient Phoenician statue and the lost treasures of King Solomon in ***The Navigator***. Cussler's books are fast-paced thrillers with plenty of movement among the various characters and subplots.

Dyer, Geoff. Dyer's 2009 work, ***Jeff in Venice, Death in Varanasi,*** combines two novellas about trips with very different purposes: sensual pleasure and spiritual enlightenment. In the first novella, a cynical British journalist named Jeff travels to Venice to cover a biennial art festival, where he meets and seduces a beautiful American woman. In the second, an unnamed narrator (who may be the same Jeff) comes to India's holy city of Varanasi to write a magazine article and slowly falls under the spell of the Ganges River, shaving his head and wearing a dhoti. Dyer is the author of three other novels (including ***The Search,*** about a man who goes in search of a mysterious woman's husband, and ***Paris Trance,*** about expatriate Brits in Paris) and several works that defy classification into any genre.

Garland, Alex. Garland's celebrated first novel, ***The Beach,*** tells the story of a young English traveler in search of a legendary beach in the Gulf of Thailand that is supposedly inaccessible to tourists. As one reviewer noted, the novel is both "a fast-paced adventure novel" and an exploration of "why we search for these utopias." Another reviewer said that there is "no better book that captures the thrill of travel."

Lanchester, John. Lanchester's debut novel, ***The Debt to Pleasure,*** won the Whitbread Award for Best First Novel and was a *New York Times* Notable Book. The book is something of a parody of foodie memoirs, as the supercilious narrator, Tarquin Winot, reminisces about his childhood, which was spent primarily in France, and about food as he travels from Portsmouth to the south of France. A later novel, ***Fragrant Harbor,*** involves a young Englishman who travels by ship to Hong Kong, where his life intertwines with that of a young Chinese missionary nun whom he meets on the voyage.

Morgan, Marlo. Morgan's novel, ***Mutant Message Down Under***, shares many themes with Bruce Chatwin's *The Songlines*, which is annotated in this chapter. Her account of a trek with Aborigines in the Australian outback, which she claimed to be based on a true experience, was originally self-published and generated quite a bit of controversy when Aboriginal groups felt that she had misrepresented their culture for profit and self-promotion. Her second novel, ***Mutant Message from Forever: A Novel of Aboriginal Wisdom***, tells the story of an Aboriginal woman seeking to reunite herself with her twin brother, who is serving a life sentence in Florida.

Rich, Virginia. Readers who enjoyed titles in the "In Search of Food" category may also enjoy the novels in the *Eugenia Potter Mystery* series, some of which also involve travel. The titles in the series include ***The Cooking School Murders***, which takes place during the protagonist's annual visit to her Iowa home town; ***The Nantucket Diet Murders***, which is set during a midwinter reunion with friends in Nantucket; ***The Blue Corn Murders***, which takes place while Potter is visiting an archaeological camp in Colorado; and ***The Secret Ingredient Murders***, which is set in a vacation home on the Rhode Island coast.

Notes

1. Neal Wyatt, *The Readers' Advisory Guide to Nonfiction* (Chicago: American Library Association, 2007), p. 138.
2. Joyce Saricks, *The Readers' Advisory Guide to Genre Fiction* (Chicago: American Library Association, 2009), p. 7.
3. Catherine Ross, "Reading Nonfiction for Pleasure: What Motivates Readers?" in *Nonfiction Readers' Advisory*, edited by Robert Burgin (Westport, CT: Libraries Unlimited, 2004), p. 107.

References

Ross, Catherine. "Reading Nonfiction for Pleasure: What Motivates Readers?" in *Nonfiction Readers' Advisory*, edited by Robert Burgin, 105–20. Westport, CT: Libraries Unlimited, 2004.

Saricks, Joyce. *The Readers' Advisory Guide to Genre Fiction*. Chicago: American Library Association, 2009.

Wyatt, Neal. *The Readers' Advisory Guide to Nonfiction*. Chicago: American Library Association, 2007.

Chapter 3

The Journey

The only journey is the one within.
—Rainer Maria Rilke

Definition of "The Journey"

The definition of "The Journey," as a subgenre of the travel narrative genre, is captured by the book reviewer for the Vancouver *Sun* in a review of Rick Antonson's *To Timbuktu for a Haircut: A Journey Through West Africa*: "It may seem counterintuitive, but the appeal of travel literature often has less to do with the destination in question than with the character of the traveller." Citing the differences in the Tuscany portrayed by Frances Mayes (*Under the Tuscan Sun*) and Ferenc Máté (*The Hills of Tuscany*), the reviewer notes that "In each book, the milieu serves as a backdrop for the revelation and development of the author's persona. The reader responds not to the locale but to the locale as experienced by the narrator."[1]

The focus of the titles annotated in this chapter is on the traveler or travelers. The traveler may take a trip she hopes will hasten a healing process or distance her from a tragedy, like the death of a spouse or a parent. The traveler may take a trip as a way to gain a deeper understanding of herself. The traveler may gain self-understanding through travel to a new destination or by visiting a country important to her past or to her ancestors or by returning to a place she has visited before. The traveler may share her innermost thoughts and reflections about the trip or the destination, thoughts on issues that transcend the journey itself. The traveler may take a trip with other members of her family, often for the purpose of better understanding herself or the family member or of improving the relationship between them. In all cases, though, the focus of the narrative is on the traveler or travelers and their process of growth or change through travel.

These are titles for readers who appreciate books that share an author's innermost thoughts and reflections. These titles may also benefit readers who have gone through similar challenges (divorce or the death of a family member) or who wish to better understand themselves and believe that they might benefit from reading about others who have undertaken to do the same.

Appeal of "The Journey"

Because the focus of the titles in "The Journey" subgenre is on the individual traveler or travelers, the appeal of characterization is primary. It is hard to write about the personal tragedies of death (Rosé Marie Curteman's *My Renaissance: A Widow's Healing Pilgrimage to Tuscany* or Kerry Egan's *Fumbling: A Journey of Love, Adventure, and Renewal on the Camino de Santiago* or Charles Fergus's *Summer at Little Lava: A Season at the Edge of the World*) and divorce (Peter Jenkins's *A Walk Across America* or Mike Carter's *Uneasy Rider: Travels Through a Mid-Life Crisis*) without engaging in deep and meaningful character development. It is hard to write about the process of discovering one's self (Robert M. Pirsig's *Zen and the Art of Motorcycle Maintenance: An Inquiry into Values* or Lydia Minatoya's *Talking to High Monks in the Snow: An Asian American Odyssey*) without discussing that self in great detail.

Travels to one's previous home (Jamaica Kincaid's *A Small Place* or Bill Bryson's *The Lost Continent: Travels in Small-Town America*) or to the homeland of one's parents (Michael J. Arlen's *Passage to Ararat*) will also call for strong focus on and exploration of the characters involved, either the traveler herself or individuals from the traveler's past. "Reflective Journeys," in which the traveler shares her personal reflections of issues that are larger than the specific journey or its destination (Robert D. Kaplan's *An Empire Wilderness: Travels into America's Future* or W. G. Sebald's *The Rings of Saturn*), are also intensely personal and require self-revelation.

Even the titles of the "Family Travel" category, which tend to be lighter affairs, are strong on character, whether it is a famous novelist coming to better understand his manga-obsessed son (Peter Carey's *Wrong About Japan: A Father's Journey with His Son*), a 50-something woman trying to make friends with her mother (Jane Christmas's *Incontinent on the Continent: My Mother, Her Walker, and Our Grand Tour of Italy*), or two very different brothers learning about one another while traveling around the world (Nicholas and Micah Sparks's *Three Weeks With My Brother*).

The appeal factor of frame and setting will also be strong, as it is with most travel narratives. The Armenian villages of Michael J. Arlen's ancestors (*Passage to Ararat*), the Italy of Barbara Harrison's parents (*Italian Days*), the Antigua where Jamaica Kincaid was born (*A Small Place*), and the Vietnam that Andrew Pham remembers and revisits (*Catfish and Mandala: A Two-Wheeled Voyage through the Landscape and Memory of Vietnam*) are all critical to the stories of these travelers.

Other appeal factors will be important in these Journey narratives, perhaps more so than in many of the other categories. For example, it will likely be important that the pacing of these titles be more relaxed and engrossing than may be the case for other travel narratives. Healing and self-discovery, after all, take time and cannot be rushed, as in Colin Fletcher's six-month journey of self-discovery down the Colorado

River by raft and on foot (*River: One Man's Journey Down the Colorado, Source to Sea*). Journeys to one's home or return trips to places visited previously will lead to slow, unhurried reflections, as will the titles categorized as "Reflective Journeys."

The story lines in these titles tend to be character centered, gentle, thought provoking, and sometimes tragic. Tone and mood may also be important, especially for titles in the "Healing Odysseys" category, which will tend to be darker in tone.

There are, of course, other non-travel genres that may provide books of interest to readers who enjoy the journeys discussed in this chapter. Biographies and memoirs would appear to be rich with such titles. For example, a reader who is drawn to books in which travel helps the traveler overcome adversity, like the death of a spouse, may find John Bayley's *Elegy for Iris* or Joan Didion's *The Year of Magical Thinking* of interest.

Likewise, novels with an emphasis on character as an appeal factor may also appeal to readers who enjoy the titles in this chapter, particularly if those characters are involved in the same kinds of self-discovery and healing as the travelers in the titles in "The Journey."

Organization of the Chapter

This chapter, like all the chapters in this book, begins with "Classics," which represent those titles that were published prior to 1990 and that display universality, multiple levels of meaning, great stories, memorable characters, emotional or though-provoking experiences, and great writing. These titles will probably be more familiar to both readers and librarians and will help them understand the subtleties of the subgenre and its categories. The destinations of the titles in this chapter, as with the chapter on "Quests," may have changed over the years, but the more inward focus of the journeys discussed here will have much in common with other titles in the category, regardless of the time of the travel.

"Healing Odysseys" describe those narratives in which the travel is taken in response to a tragedy or crisis in the traveler's life, with the trip seen as a way to hasten the healing process or perhaps to distance the traveler from the tragedy. These journeys arc distinguished from those in the next category, "Discovering One's Self," where the trip leads the traveler to a deeper understanding of herself without the impetus of life tragedy.

The journeys described in "The Past Is a Foreign Country" are also highly personal but are more concerned with the destination, which is the country in which the traveler was either born or brought up or the country of the traveler's ancestors. Likewise, the focus of "Reflective Journeys" is on the personal reflections of the traveler, with the destination providing the context in which the traveler reflects on issues that transcend the journey. In the narratives of

1 2 3 4 5 6 7

the "Return Trips" category, the traveler returns to a place she has previously visited, but these are not places (unlike those in "The Past Is a Foreign Country") where the traveler has lived for an extended period of time. The final category, "Family Travel," is again focused on the traveler, but in this case, the traveler has undertaken the journey as part of a family, usually as a parent and child.

Classics

Classics, those travel narratives that were published before 1990 and that also display universality, multiple levels of meaning, great stories, memorable characters, emotional or though-provoking experiences, and great writing, represent titles that are more familiar to readers and librarians and that will serve as good entry points into the subgenre of "The Journey" and its various categories. As with the previous subgenre, while the destinations of the titles in this category may have changed a good deal over the years, the more inwardly focused journeys discussed here will still have much in common with other, newer titles in this chapter.

The focus of these titles, as with all of the titles in this chapter, is on the traveler, and the timeless themes include traveling to heal one's self after a tragedy (divorce in the case of Peter Jenkins's *A Walk Across America*), traveling to discover one's self (Robert M. Pirsig's *Zen and the Art of Motorcycle Maintenance: An Inquiry into Values* or Mary Morris's *Nothing to Declare: Memoirs of a Woman Traveling Alone*), returning to one's previous homeland (Jamaica Kincaid's *A Small Place* or Bill Bryson's *The Lost Continent: Travels in Small-Town America*), or returning to the homeland of one's parents (Michael J. Arlen's *Passage to Ararat*).

Arlen, Michael J.

Passage to Ararat. New York: Farrar, Straus & Giroux, 1975. 293 pp. ISBN: 9780374229894

Arlen returned to the Armenian villages of his ancestors in order to learn what his heritage meant and to better understand his father, a well-known author who had apparently disowned that heritage. The book combines elements of memoir and explorations of the relationship between a son and his father with travel narrative, and Arlen also intertwines his personal experiences with the history of a people who have survived multiple attempts to eradicate them. The result is an insightful and touching book.

Subjects: Fathers and Sons; Genocide

Categories: "The Past Is a Foreign Country"

Places: Armenia; Turkey

Awards: National Book Award for Nonfiction, 1976

Now Try: Arlen's earlier book, *Exiles*, is a memoir of his parents and provides some background that will help readers better appreciate *Passage to Ararat*. Philip Marsden investigates the fate of the Armenian people in *The Crossing Place: A Journey Among the Armenians*; he travels to a number of Armenian communities in the Middle East and tries to better understand the culture and the spirit of these people. Michael Bobelian's moving *Children of Armenia: A Forgotten Genocide and the Century-long Struggle for Justice* tells both the story of the 1915 genocide of Armenians by Ottoman Turkey and the subsequent refusal of that country to admit what it had done. Joan London's award-winning novel, *Gilgamesh,* tells the story of an Australian woman and her son, who travel to Soviet Armenia in 1939 to find her son's father.

Bryson, Bill

The Lost Continent: Travels in Small-Town America. New York: Harper & Row, 1989. 314 pp. ISBN: 9780060161583

Bryson was born in the United States but settled in Great Britain in his 20s. In 1987, after 10 years abroad, he returned to the United States and journeyed by car around the country. His two trips (one heading east of his childhood home of Des Moines, Iowa, and one headed west from the same place) covered 38 of the 50 states and focused on the small towns that were the destinations of the family road trips of his youth. He seems largely disappointed by what he found, and though some readers may find his humor to be sharp and incisive, others will find him crabby and unpleasant, even though his tone seems to mellow as the trip progresses.

Subjects: Humor; Small Town Life

Categories: On the Road; Return Trips

Places: United States (Various)

Now Try: Bryson is a prolific travel writer, and several of his titles (including *Notes from a Small Island, In a Sunburned Country,* and *A Walk in the Woods*) are annotated in this book. Bryson returned to the United States in 1995 and wrote another series of pieces about his experiences, entitled *I'm a Stranger Here Myself: Notes on Returning to America After 20 Years Away* and annotated in "The Past Is a Foreign Country" section of this chapter. In 1939, author Henry Miller returned to the United States after ten years in Europe; his mostly negative comments on America and particularly its people can be found in *The Air-Conditioned Nightmare*. Denis Lipman's madcap *A Yank Back to England: The Prodigal Tourist Returns* is the opposite of Bryson's *The Lost Continent*; Lipman is a British citizen who returns to England after 20 years in the United States and travels around that country with his American wife and his British working-class family.

Buruma, Ian

God's Dust: A Modern Asian Journey. New York: Farrar, Straus, Giroux, 1989. 267 pp. ISBN: 9780374164584

Buruma, who has lived in Japan for 10 years, traveled for a year through several Asian countries that were struggling with the question of "How to be modern without losing your cultural sense of self." His non-Asian view of Asia is objective, fresh, and insightful and based on interviews with leaders (Imelda Marcos, for example) as well as ordinary people. Visiting so many countries in such a short amount of time results in a book that is frenetically paced, but the pace parallels the whirlwind pace of change that many of these countries and their people are experiencing.

Subjects: Asian History; Buddhism; Modernization

Categories: Reflective Journeys

Places: Japan; Malaysia; Myanmar; Philippines; Singapore; South Korea; Taiwan; Thailand

Now Try: Buruma's other books are less travel narrative and more political and social observation, but *A Japanese Mirror: Heroes and Villains of Japanese Culture* comes close to being an expatriate narrative, as Buruma lived in Japan for 10 years and was able to gain a great deal of insight into the supposed uniqueness of that culture. British poet and journalist James Fenton spent 14 years in Vietnam, Cambodia, South Korea, and the Philippines in the 1970s and 1980s; he reports on his impressions of developments there in *All the Wrong Places: Adrift in the Politics of the Pacific Rim*. Buruma's observations on Myanmar (then Burma) may be compared with those of Rory Maclean, whose *Under the Dragon: A Journey through Burma* tells of his later visit to Myanmar and the stories of ordinary people, struggling to survive under the repressive regime. The Philippine capital of Manila is the setting for Tess Uriza Holthe's moving novel, *When the Elephants Dance*, about a group of friends and neighbors who huddle together in the basement of a house while the Japanese and Americans battle for control of the city and the islands above.

Crichton, Michael

Travels. New York: Knopf, 1988. 377 pp. ISBN: 9780394562360

Crichton, the author of such best sellers as *Jurassic Park* and *The Andromeda Strain*, writes a combination of memoir and travel narrative here and details a number of his travels in search of enlightenment. Attempting to broaden his Western knowledge base, he focuses particularly on Africa and Asia (tracking animals in Malaysia, climbing Kilimanjaro, and scuba diving with sharks in Tahiti) and becomes more interested in spirituality, experiencing altered states, and developing his psychic powers. These New Age ventures may not appeal to all readers, but Crichton's curiosity and willingness to explore the world's mysteries are engaging.

Subjects: Parapsychology; Spirituality

Categories: Reflective Journeys

Places: Africa; Bangkok; California; Caribbean; England; Ireland; Jamaica; London; Los Angeles; Malaysia; New Guinea; Pakistan; Rwanda; Singapore; Tahiti; Tanzania; Thailand

Now Try: Crichton is a well-known fiction author, and his novel, *Eaters of the Dead*, involves a Muslim ambassador who is kidnapped by Vikings and taken with them on a quest to Scandinavia. His 1980 science fiction novel, *Congo*, tells about an expedition for diamonds and an attempt to find out why the members of a previous expedition were mysteriously murdered. Crichton took time off from his life in Hollywood to travel around the world, an approach advocated by Rolf Potts in his "how to" book, *Vagabonding: An Uncommon Guide to the Art of Long-Term World Travel*. Potts also wrote the highly entertaining *Marco Polo Didn't Go There: Stories and Revelations from One Decade as a Postmodern Travel Writer*, which recounts his travels to places like Libya, Thailand, and India as well as discussing the difference between being a traveler and being a tourist.

Harrison, Barbara Grizzuti

Italian Days. New York: Weidenfeld & Nicolson, 1989. 479 pp. ISBN: 9781555843113

In the mid-1980s, Harrison traveled to Italy to get to know the land of her parents, who had emigrated from there to the United States. She recounts her trip in eight chapters, one devoted to each city or area of Italy that she visited. The journey became more a journey of reconciliation and self-realization as she discovered her remaining relatives in Abruzzi and struggled with the resentments of those who were left behind. The long book (almost 500 pages) is filled with historical anecdotes, personal reflections, and discussions about politics, fashion, and food. Like Italy itself, it is richly chaotic, and some readers may wish that it had been edited into a tighter, less exhausting book.

Subjects: Self-Discovery; Women Travelers

Categories: Discovering One's Self; "The Past Is a Foreign Country"

Places: Florence; Italy; Milan; Rome; Venice

Now Try: In *Italian Neighbors*, Tim Parks writes about the first 10 years he and his wife spent in Verona; like Harrison, Parks captures the crazy vitality of the Italian experience. Dianne Hales traveled to Italy to learn the language and celebrates that language and the culture of Italy in the delightful *La Bella Lingua: My Love Affair with Italian, the World's Most Enchanting Language*. Paul Hofmann, a former *New York Times* bureau chief in Rome, writes about his love for the Eternal City in *The Seasons of Rome: A Journal* and about some of the social problems in Italy (the Mafia, the bureaucracy, the divisions between North and South) in *That Fine Italian Hand*. Other memoirs of Italian family life may also appeal, such as James Beard Award winner Laura Schenone's *The Lost Ravioli Recipes of Hoboken: A Search for Food and Family*.

Jenkins, Peter

A Walk Across America. New York: Morrow, 1979. 288 pp. ISBN: 9780688034276 YA

In 1973, recently divorced and disillusioned by the war in Vietnam, pollution, greed, and a host of social ills, Jenkins decided to walk across the

United States in order to better understand the country. *A Walk Across America* recounts the first leg of his journey, from New York to New Orleans, and contains the stories of the remarkable individuals that Jenkins met along the way: a black family in North Carolina who took him in and treated him as one of their own; a mountain main in West Virginia; and the members of a commune in Tennessee. The journey was also one of self-discovery; as Jenkins notes, "I started out searching for myself and my country and found both."

Subjects: Divorce; Self-Discovery; Walking

Categories: Discovering One's Self; Healing Odysseys

Places: Alabama; California; Georgia; Louisiana; Maryland; Mississippi; New Orleans; New York; North Carolina; Pennsylvania; Tennessee; Virginia; Washington, DC; West Virginia

Now Try: *A Walk Across America* covers the first part of Jenkins's journey across the United States. He and his wife, Barbara Jenkins, whom he met on his trip, write about the second part of the trip (from New Orleans to Oregon) in *The Walk West: A Walk Across America 2*. Jenkins wrote several titles about his journeys through the United States, including *Along the Edge of America*, in which he travels the Gulf Coast from the Florida Keys to Texas, and *Looking for Alaska*, which describes the 18 months that Jenkins and his family spent in Seward, Alaska. Doris Haddock walked from Los Angeles to Washington, DC, at the age of 89 to lobby for campaign finance reform. Her story is told in the inspiring *Granny D: Walking Across America in My 90th Year*, which is annotated in the "Getting There Is Half the Fun" chapter of this book. Jenkins walked across the country with his dog Cooper; another writer who crossed the country with his dog is, of course, John Steinbeck, whose *Travels with Charley: In Search of America* is annotated in the "Getting There Is Half the Fun" chapter of this book. A much earlier walk across the United States is told in Robert Lewis Taylor's Pulitzer Prize-winning novel, *The Travels of Jaimie McPheeters*, which follows a 13-year-old boy and his father as they journey across the country from Kentucky to gold rush California in 1849.

Kincaid, Jamaica

A Small Place. New York: Farrar, Straus, Giroux, 1988. 81pp. ISBN: 9780374266387 YA

In this short but scathing book, Kincaid writes about Antigua, where she was born and lived until age 16. She contrasts the natural beauty of the island with the ugliness of life there for most of the inhabitants as well as the "moral ugliness" of tourism, which she sees as another form of economic imperialism. Kincaid despises the British colonialism of the past, the corrupt government of the present, and the ongoing evils of racism and greed. This is not an easy book to read, in spite of its often poetic writing.

Subjects: Quick Reads; Women Travelers

Categories: "The Past Is a Foreign Country"

Places: Antigua; Caribbean

Now Try: Kincaid is one of several Caribbean women (Edwidge Danticat and Dionne Brand are two others) who write about living in tourist destinations in the powerful anthology, *Stories from Blue Latitudes: Caribbean Women Writers at Home and Abroad.* Ian Thomson's hard-hitting *The Dead Yard: A Story of Modern Jamaica,* which won both the 2010 Dolman Best Travel Book Award and 2010 Ondaatje Prize and is annotated in this chapter, argues that there are two Jamaicas: an idyllic resort and its gang-controlled, drug-ridden, corrupt underbelly. Michelle Cliff's novel, *No Telephone to Heaven,* tells of a young woman who returns to Jamaica (where she was born) and finds a country very different from the tourist destination of advertisements.

Magris, Claudio

Danube: A Sentimental Journey from the Source to the Black Sea. New York: Farrar, Straus and Giroux, 1989. 416 pp. ISBN: 9780374134655

Italian cultural and literary historian Magris used his journey along Europe's Danube River as a way of presenting his thoughts about the history, geography, politics, and literature of the people who live along the winding river. Magris visited centuries-old towns along the river, from its origin in Germany to its end at the Black Sea in Rumania, and his themes are as diverse as the ongoing friction between Greco-Roman and Teutonic civilizations in Europe, the roots of fascism, and Napoleon's link to modern nationalism. Not an easy read, *Danube* is filled with literary and historical references, many of them obscure. (In 2011, the *Guardian* listed *Danube* as one of the 100 greatest nonfiction titles of all time.)

Subjects: European History; Rivers

Places: Austria; Bulgaria; Croatia; Danube River; Germany; Hungary; Moldova; Romania; Serbia; Slovakia; Ukraine

Now Try: *Blue River, Black Sea* by Andres Eames describes that writer's journey along the Danube River by bicycle, by horse, by boat, and on foot and is far lighter in tone than Magris's book, about which Eames says, "The great man exercised his synapses through four hundred pages, displaying immense erudition, leaping between intellectual rooftops and poking his nose down the chimney stacks of downriver nations like a PhD chimney sweep from Mary Poppins." Patrick Leigh Fermor's two books, *A Time of Gifts* and *Between the Woods and the Water* (annotated in the chapter of this book entitled "Getting There Is Half the Fun"), are the classic narratives about the countries along the Danube in the 1930s, as fascism was taking hold. A classic look at one of the world's great rivers can be found in Alan Moorhead's *The White Nile* and *The Blue Nile,* the earlier of which focuses on the individuals who sought the source of the Nile and the latter of which looks at the clash of civilizations and the advances made by the modern, Western world into the lands around the Blue Nile. Both titles are annotated in the "Travel Adventure" chapter of this book.

McPhee, John

The Crofter and the Laird. New York, Farrar, Straus and Giroux 1970. 159 pp. ISBN: 9780374514655

McPhee journeys to the land of his ancestors, the tiny island of Colonsay, 25 miles off the Scottish coast, and provides a rich, almost sacred portrait of the history and personalities of this stark and sparsely populated region of just 138 people. McPhee spends little time discussing himself or his family, opting instead to focus on the lives of the tiny island's families, many of which have lived on the island for 200 to 300 years. The book is brilliantly written, as one would expect of McPhee, and his portrayal of the hard-working inhabitants of Colonsay is beautiful without being sentimental.

Subjects: Quick Reads

Categories: "The Past Is a Foreign Country"

Places: Scotland

Now Try: McPhee has written several books about people who live close to nature, among them the orange farmers in *Oranges* and environmentalist David Brower in *Encounters with the Archdruid*. One reader compared *The Crofter and the Laird* with the poet Donald Hall's book, *Eagle Pond*, about his ancestral home in New Hampshire. Lillian Beckwith has written a series of semi-autobiographical works about her years on a small island in the Scottish Hebrides, much like Colonsay, in the 1960s and 1970s; these include *The Hills Is Lonely*, *The Sea for Breakfast*, and *The Loud Halo*. The portrayal of the idyllic Scottish coast village of Ferness in the Bill Forsyth film, *Local Hero*, may also appeal to readers who enjoyed *The Crofter and the Laird*.

Moorhouse, Geoffrey

The Fearful Void. Philadelphia, Lippincott 1974. 288 pp. ISBN: 9780397010196

Moorhouse set out in the mid-1970s to traverse the Sahara Desert from west to east by foot and by camel, something that no one had done before. Why? Partly to recover from a failing marriage, partly for a "giddy and unique success," and partly to overcome his fear "of annihilation, of being surrounded by what is hostile, of being unwanted, of loss and of being lost." Moorhouse discusses his pre-trip planning (learning to ride a camel, learning Arabic) as well as the frustrations and joys of the aborted journey itself: traveling in the winter to avoid the hottest days of the desert but having to cope with the bitter cold desert nights, dealing with hired help who stole food and spilled water, becoming infested with lice, suffering from dysentery, but seeing Timbuktu and feeling the desert wind in his face.

Subjects: Deserts; Divorce

Categories: Healing Odysseys

Places: Africa; Algeria; Egypt; Libya; Mali; Mauritania; Sahara Desert

Now Try: Moorhouse was not able to finish his daunting journey, but in 1987, Michael Asher and his wife Mariantonietta Peru did become the first people to complete the west-to-east crossing of the Sahara; they recount their ordeal and provide a fascinating view of the cultures of the region in *Two Against the Sahara: On Camelback from Nouakchott to the Nile*. Asher also wrote a grim account of French soldiers killed by desert tribes in an 1880 incident, *Death in the Sahara: The Lords of the Desert and the Timbuktu Railway Expedition Massacre*. Kevin Kertscher hitchhikes through several African countries, including part of the Sahara, in *Africa Solo: A Journey Across the Sahara, Sahel and Congo*. William Langewiesche's *Sahara Unveiled: A Journey Across The Desert* is the classic travel narrative about the Sahara Desert and is annotated in the first chapter of this book, "A Sense of Place." Another title about a traveler attempting to recover from a failed relationship is Kevin Patterson's *The Water in Between: A Journey at Sea*, in which the author takes to sailing to "outrun his broken heart."

Morris, Mary

Nothing to Declare: Memoirs of a Woman Traveling Alone. Boston: Houghton Mifflin, 1988. 250 pp. ISBN: 9780395446379

Morris went to the Mexican town of San Miguel de Allende in search of a place "where life would begin to make sense," and her memoir of the Mexican town and her travels around Central America is a journey of self-understanding. Nevertheless, the book is filled with the local people she met and befriended and with the other expatriates who had come to Mexico to write or paint or search for themselves. While Morris highlights many of the challenges of residing in a foreign land, the lack of familiarity with her surroundings was also the spark that fueled her growing understanding of who she is. *Nothing to Declare* will strike some readers as an inspiring journey of self-discovery, although others may find Morris too self-absorbed.

Subjects: Self-Discovery; Women Travelers

Categories: Discovering One's Self

Places: Bolivia; Guatemala; Honduras; Mexico; San Salvador

Now Try: In 2005, following the death of her father, Morris embarked on a trip down the Mississippi in a houseboat; she tells about the trip and how it helped her reconnect with her past in *The River Queen*. Morris is well known for her psychological novels, and these may appeal to readers who enjoy her travel narratives of self-discovery; *Revenge* involves a woman who believes that her stepmother caused her father's death, and *Acts of God* tells about a woman who returns to her 30th high school reunion and is confronted with the demons of her past. *Go Your Own Way: Women Travel the World Solo* is an anthology of travel essays by women who have, like Morris, traveled alone; its pieces range from one by a traveler lost in the jungles of Borneo to one whose author learns to tango in Buenos Aires. Two other solo women travelers are

Rita Gelman, whose *Tales of a Female Nomad: Living at Large in the World* (annotated in this chapter) recounts her journeys to Mexico and other countries in response to her failing marriage, and Nan Watkins, whose *East Toward Dawn: A Woman's Solo Journey Around the World* tells of her decision at the age of 60 to embark on a solo trip around the world following the dissolution of her 30-year marriage and the death of her 23-year-old son.

Naipaul, V. S.

The Middle Passage: The Caribbean Revisited. New York: A.A. Knopf, 2002 [1962]. 524 pp. ISBN: 9780375407390

In 1960 and 1961, after 10 years in England, Naipaul returned to Trinidad, the island of his birth, and various other areas in and bordering the Caribbean. His purpose was to examine the ways in which the various Caribbean nations have dealt with the legacy of colonialism, and he brought his sharp writer's eye to bear on the history and current situation in the places he visited. *The Middle Passage* exemplifies what many critics see as Naipaul's insensitive depiction of the developing world and its people, and some readers will find Naipaul to be patronizing, disdainful, and even racist. However, others will find his largely pessimistic worldview to be perceptive and justified by the quandary in which the former colonies find themselves.

Subjects: Colonialism

Categories: "The Past Is a Foreign Country"

Places: Brazil; British Guyana; Jamaica; Martinique; Suriname; Trinidad and Tobago

Series: *Picador Travel Classics*

Now Try: Naipaul's semi-autobiographical novel, *Miguel Street,* is set in Trinidad in the 1930s and 1940s and concerns a number of characters with great ambitions that are never realized. Travel writer Paul Theroux writes about his friendship with V.S. Naipaul, who championed Theroux's early work, and the exotic locales in which both men lived and traveled in *Sir Vidia's Shadow: A Friendship across Five Continents.* Anu Lakhan brings the street food of Trinidad to life even without recipes in his celebration of Caribbean food, *Trinidad: Caribbean Street Food;* Peter Laurie does the same for a neighboring island's food in *Barbados: Caribbean Street Food.*

Ondaatje, Michael

Running In the Family. New York: W.W. Norton, 1982. 207 pp. ISBN: 9780393016376

Ondaatje's highly impressionistic book, about returning to his native Sri Lanka in the late 1970s, is part travel narrative, part memoir, and part fiction. Much of the focus is on his family, particularly his heavy-drinking father, who remained in Sri Lanka (then Ceylon) when Ondaatje left to live with his mother in England, and who died in the intervening 25 years, but the author also depicts visits to sites from his turbulent childhood. The book is a fine exploration of one's relationship with one's family and native land, and as one would expect from the author of *The English Patient*, the writing is meticulous and filled with stunning imagery.

Subjects: Family Relationships; Fathers and Sons; Quick Reads

Categories: "The Past Is a Foreign Country"

Places: Sri Lanka

Now Try: Several of Ondaatje's novels have a strong sense of place, in particular *Anil's Ghost*, in which the title character returns to her native Sri Lanka after a long absence and finds the country in the midst of civil war, and *The English Patient*, which is set in North Africa and Italy at the end of World War II. Ondaatje's most recent novel, *The Cat's Table*, tells the story of an 11-year-old boy who journeys from Sri Lanka to London by ship in the early 1950s and the adventures that he and his young fellow voyagers have along the way; the story is told 20 years later from the perspective of the man the boy has grown to be. Mark Stephen Meadows's adventurous *Tea Time with Terrorists: A Motorcycle Journey into the Heart of Sri Lanka's Civil War* describes the author's trip from the capital of Sri Lanka to the home of the Tamil Tigers, who for 30 years had been waging war with the ruling government of the country, in the northern part of the island. Another memoir of fathers and sons is Michael Frayn's *My Father's Fortune: A Life*, a compassionate memoir of his father, a salesman in London who worked his way into the British middle class.

Pirsig, Robert M.

Zen and the Art of Motorcycle Maintenance: An Inquiry into Values. New York: Morrow, 1974. 412 pp. ISBN: 9780688002305 YA

Pirsig's classic works on many levels, one of which is the story of a father's 17-day motorcycle trip with his son from Minnesota to California. It is also a journey into Pirsig's own past and the story of Pirsig's attempts to understand and reconcile himself to that past. The book is punctuated with philosophical discussions, primarily about the notion of "quality," an obsession of Pirsig's, particularly in a world that seems so enthralled by "quantity." Readers who like to tackle the big questions will enjoy the book, and many will find it life changing.

Subjects: Buddhism; Fathers and Sons; Memoirs; Motorcycles; Philosophy; Self-Discovery

Categories: Discovering One's Self; Family Travel

Places: California; Chicago; Idaho; Minnesota; Montana; North Dakota; Oregon; South Dakota

Now Try: Pirsig's novel *Lila: An Inquiry into Morals* was less well received by most readers, although some saw it as a more comprehensive expression of Pirsig's philosophy. Mark Richardson's *Zen and Now: On the Trail of Robert Pirsig and the Art of Motorcycle Maintenance* tells of the author's attempt to follow Pirsig's original route as closely as possible; it is annotated in the "Quests" chapter of this book. Although it does not involve travel, Matthew

B. Crawford's *Shop Class as Soulcraft: An Inquiry Into the Value of Work* is similar to *Zen and the Art of Motorcycle Maintenance* in its philosophical approach to everyday matters and the virtues of working with one's own hands.

Raban, Jonathan

Coasting: A Private Voyage. New York: Simon and Schuster, 1987. 302 pp. ISBN: 9780671454807

When he was 40 years old, Raban made a 2,000-mile solo voyage around Britain in a restored ketch. The book captures his descriptions of the coastline and the places and individuals he encountered on various landings (the Isle of Man features prominently) as well as his reflections on the Falklands War, which was then being waged. *Coasting,* as its subtitle might suggest, is also the most autobiographical of Raban's books, and much of the focus is on his own life, beginning with his childhood as a vicar's son and his ambiguous status as not quite upper middle class. The book is superbly written, with stunning descriptions and poetic passages.

Subjects: Memoirs; Sailing; Seas; Solo Travelers

Categories: Reflective Journeys

Places: England; Scotland; Wales

Series: *Picador Travel Classics; Vintage Departures*

Now Try: Paul Theroux also traveled the perimeter of England, although by train, at the time of the Falklands War; his thoughts on that war and on England can be found in *The Kingdom by the Sea,* which is annotated in "Getting There Is Half the Fun." Almost 30 years after Raban and Theroux, Josie Dew bicycled around the perimeter of her native England; her enjoyable *Slow Coast Home* features her knowledge of local wildlife. Adam Nicolson's account of sailing up the west coasts of Ireland and Scotland and of the remote communities with which he came in contact can be found in *Seamanship: A Voyage Along the Wild Coasts of the British Isles*. Paul Murray's debut novel, *An Evening of Long Goodbyes,* also deals with issues of social class and tells the story of a semi-aristocratic Irish brother and sister who live in a seaside estate near Dublin and suddenly discover that they aren't as rich as they thought.

Theroux, Paul

Sunrise with Seamonsters. Boston: Houghton Mifflin, 1985. 365 pp. ISBN: 9780395382219

Theroux is one of the best-known writers of travel narratives, and this collection of 50 of his earlier essays finds him in a reflective mood, pondering questions as broad as where does Asia begin and as mundane as how to forecast the weather in India. The essays cover the 1960s, 1970s, and early 1980s and include travel to Indonesia, Corsica, Cape Cod, and New York City. Not all of the essays deal with travel (there are pieces on Rudyard Kipling and Ernest Hemingway, for example) but those that do capture Theroux's unique way of seeing and writing about the world.

Subjects: Essays

Categories: Reflective Journeys

Places: Afghanistan; Africa; Cape Cod; Corsica; Indonesia; Ireland; Kenya; Malawi; Myanmar; New York City; Uganda

Now Try: Theroux has published other collections of travel essays, including *Fresh Air Fiend: Travel Writings*, which includes travel to the Yangtze River in China, Uganda, Honduras, and Sicily as well as pieces on fellow travel writers Bruce Chatwin, Graham Greene, and William Least Heat-Moon, and *To the Ends of the Earth*, which consists of episodes from six previously published books by Theroux. *A View of the World: Selected Journalism* by Norman Lewis is another famous travel writer's collection of thoughtful essays, 20 pieces written over a 30-year period and covering travel to Guatemala, Belize, Laos, and Spain, among others. The British essayist A. A. Gill has also written several books of travel essays, including *A. A. Gill Is Away* and *Previous Convictions: Assignments from Here and There*; like Theroux, Gill is sometimes described as caustic.

Twain, Mark

Life on the Mississippi. New York: Oxford University Press, 1996 [1883]. 624 pp. ISBN: 9780195101393

The first part of Twain's classic is a memoir of his life as an apprentice steamboat pilot on the Mississippi before the Civil War and the lessons he learns from his mentor, Horace Bixby, particularly about the art and science of navigating the river. The second part is a travel narrative that recounts Twain's post-war journey down the river from St. Louis to New Orleans and his observations on the changes that are taking place in the country, particularly the growth of the railroads and the large cities. Twain adds a number of tall tales to his narrative, and the book is rich in humor and detail.

Subjects: Humor; Rivers

Categories: Return Trips

Places: Mississippi River; New Orleans; St. Louis

Now Try: Many of Twain's works, both fiction and nonfiction, are travel narratives. These include *The Adventures of Huckleberry Finn*, which involves a journey by Huck and Jim down the Mississippi; *Tom Sawyer Abroad*, in which Tom and Huck ride to Africa in a hot air balloon; *Roughing It*, which tells of his travels in the American West, with stagecoaches and prospecting; *The Innocents Abroad*, which describes a trip to Europe and the Holy Land; and *A Tramp Abroad*, which follows his travels in central and southern Europe. (The latter three are annotated in this book, in the chapter on "Travel Humor.") Readers interested in knowing more about Mark Twain should consult the lively biography by Ron Powers, *Mark Twain: A Life*. Readers interested in the history of the Mississippi River in the first half of the 19th century should consult Lee Sandlin's lively *Wicked River: The Mississippi When It Last Ran Wild*. Robert Lewis Taylor's novel, *Journey to Matecumbe*, follows the travels of a young boy trying to escape the Klan just after the Civil War as he rafts down the Mississippi River and travels on to the Florida Keys.

Healing Odysseys

Life is not always kind, and often, in response to the tragedy or crisis in an individual's life, that person will travel, either to distance herself from the tragedy or to find a place that will hasten the healing process. The life changes that the writers in this section face are varied: spouses divorce (Elizabeth Gilbert, *Eat, Pray, Love: One Woman's Search for Everything Across Italy, India and Indonesia*); husbands die (Rosé Marie Curteman's *My Renaissance: A Widow's Healing Pilgrimage to Tuscany*); fathers die (Kerry Egan's *Fumbling: A Journey of Love, Adventure, and Renewal on the Camino de Santiago*); and mothers are killed by burglars (Charles Fergus's *Summer at Little Lava: A Season at the Edge of the World*). Likewise, the responses of the travelers are varied: Bill Carter (*Fools Rush In: A True Story of War and Redemption*) traveled to the war-torn Balkans to serve as an aid worker following the death of his girlfriend; Mike Carter (*Uneasy Rider: Travels Through a Mid-Life Crisis*) bought a motorcycle and rode around Europe after his wife left him; Rosé Marie Curteman (*My Renaissance: A Widow's Healing Pilgrimage to Tuscany*) studied art and cooking in Italy following the death of her husband; and Colin Thubron journeyed by foot to a sacred Tibetan mountain following his mother's death (*To a Mountain in Tibet*).

These narratives tend to be very personal, so readers who are drawn to the appeal of character should find them of interest. They may also be of interest to readers who are attempting to recover from similar situations. Many of the titles, especially those in which a loved one has died, are filled with grief, and readers should be prepared for the strong emotions these books often contain.

Readers who are drawn to travel narratives that involve a tragedy or crisis in the traveler's life and the subsequent healing process may also be interested in psychology titles about grief and healing (Daphne Ross Kingma's *The Ten Things to Do When Your Life Falls Apart: An Emotional and Spiritual Handbook* or Elizabeth Lesser's *Broken Open: How Difficult Times Can Help Us Grow*), memoirs in which the healing process is a major theme (Joan Didion's *A Year of Magical Thinking* or C. S. Lewis's *Grief Observed*), or novels that deal with a character's healing after a tragedy or crisis (John Banville's *The Sea* or Anne Rivers Siddons's *Off Season*).

Carter, Bill

Fools Rush In: A True Story of War and Redemption. London: Doubleday, 2004. 324 pp. ISBN: 9780385606813

In 1991, filmmaker Bill Carter's girlfriend died in a tragic automobile accident, and he traveled to war-torn Bosnia and Herzegovina as a humanitarian aid worker. There he risked his own life to befriend people trying to live their lives without surrendering to the despair and insanity of war, and his work helped him heal his own wounds. Carter attempts to present the conflict through the eyes of those he tried to help and he does so without taking sides; in fact, he admits that when he first entered Bosnia, he was unsure of the sides and their positions. Carter weaves together his struggle to deal with personal loss with the struggles of the people of Sarajevo.

Subjects: Death; European History; Grief; Memoirs; Minorities; Politics; War

Places: Bosnia and Herzegovina; Sarajevo

Now Try: A number of titles have focused on Sarajevo during the Balkan War. These include *Love Thy Neighbor: A Story of War* by *Washington Post* correspondent Peter Maass, an extremely personal and opinionated look at the war; *Zlata's Diary: A Child's Life in Sarajevo* by Zlata Filipovic, who has been described as a modern-day Anne Frank and who portrays firsthand the horrors of the conflict; and Steven Galloway's novel, *The Cellist of Sarajevo*, about four people trying to survive the war, including the cellist who vows to play for 22 days at the site of a mortar attack that killed 22 people waiting in line to buy bread. Bill Carter directed the award-winning documentary film, *Miss Sarajevo*, based on material that he shot during his stay there, and the short film is a startling complement to *Fools Rush In*. Titles by writer William Vollman, who (like Bill Carter) takes a very personal approach to his nonfiction, may also appeal, particularly *An Afghanistan Picture Show: Or, How I Saved the World* (about his 1982 travels to Pakistan and Soviet-occupied Afghanistan), *Riding Toward Everywhere* (about his life among hoboes, annotated in this book's chapter entitled "Getting There Is Half the Fun"), or his recent Kindle book, *Into the Forbidden Zone: A Trip Through Hell and High Water in Post-Earthquake Japan.*

Carter, Mike

Uneasy Rider: Travels Through a Mid-Life Crisis. London: Ebury Press, 2009. 352 pp. ISBN: 9780091923266

When he was in his early 40s, journalist Mike Carter's wife left him. In response, he bought a BMW motorcycle and took his broken heart on a six-month, 20,000-mile motorcycle trip around Europe. *Uneasy Rider* is the result, and it is both humorous and insightful. Carter encountered a number of colorful characters, re-evaluated his life, and watched his scars begin to heal. Carter is self-deprecating, funny, lyrical, and very likable. There is less focus on the mechanics or romance of motorcycling and more concern with learning about one's self and gaining some level of maturity.

Subjects: Divorce; Humor; Motorcycles; Road Trips; Self-Discovery

Places: Europe (Various)

Now Try: While it takes place in America and not Europe, Robert Pirsig's *Zen and the Art of Motorcycle Maintenance* (annotated in this chapter) is the classic tale of self-discovery on a motorcycle. Jeremy Kroeker's very funny

Motorcycle Therapy: A Canadian Adventure in Central America is about two men who took a motorcycle trip from the Canadian Rockies to Panama in order to flee their failed relationships. Mike Carter also wrote *One Man and His Bike: A 5,000 Mile, Life-Changing Journey Round the Coast of Britain*, about a five-month bicycle trip around the perimeter of Great Britain, motivated not by his personal situation but by his perception that the country's economy and society were in decline. A number of motorcycle travels are annotated in the "Getting There Is Half the Fun" chapter of this book, including Ewan McGregor and Charley Boorman's *Long Way Round: Chasing Shadows Across the World* and *Long Way Down: An Epic Journey by Motorcycle from Scotland to South America*. Richard Russo's fiction may also appeal because of the mid-life crises that many of his male characters are often going through; particularly relevant are *Straight Man*, about an interim English department chair in a Pennsylvania university, and *That Old Cape Magic*, about a creative writing professor and former Hollywood screenwriter who ponders marital and family relationships while traveling to two weddings.

Curteman, Rose Marie

My Renaissance: A Widow's Healing Pilgrimage to Tuscany. Sterling, VA: Capital Books, 2002. 210 pp. ISBN: 9781892123916

Curteman tells two stories here: the story of her husband's long battle with dementia and his death in 1994; and the story of her own journey to Italy, where she recovered from her grief, partly by studying art, the Italian language, and Italian cooking in Florence. She found the beauty of her surroundings and the enthusiasm of the individuals she met to be transforming, in spite of her memories of her husband and her tendency to see him everywhere. Her story of healing and reawakening to life is brief but is told with warmth and a touch of humor.

Subjects: Death; Grief; Quick Reads; Spouses

Places: Italy

Now Try: In *Travels with Rima: A Memoir*, Richard H. Collin writes about his wife's death and his decision to go alone on several trips that he and his wife had planned before her death. After the death of his wife, Scottish writer Christopher Rush worked through his grief by following the trail of Robert Louis Stevenson through the Cevennes mountains of French, a journey of recovery depicted in *To Travel Hopefully: Footsteps In The French Cevennes*. When her best friend was diagnosed with incurable cancer, Wilna Wilkinson undertook the pilgrimage of Santiago de Compostella in northern Spain; the story of her journey and her reflections on the loss of a friend are told in *The Way of Stars and Stones: Thoughts on a Pilgrimage*. Rafael Yglesias's *A Happy Marriage* is a touching novel about marriage and one spouse's grief over the loss of his wife of 30 years.

Egan, Kerry

Fumbling: A Journey of Love, Adventure, and Renewal on the Camino de Santiago. New York: Broadway Books, 2006, [2004]. 230 pp. ISBN: 9780385507660

1 2 3 4 5 6 7

Egan was a student at Harvard Divinity School when her father died and she became paralyzed by grief. In order to heal, she and her fiancé walked the Camino de Santiago, a 400-mile medieval pilgrimage route through northern Spain. Egan describes her "grief to faith journey" by detailing the muddy paths and oppressive heat of the journey, the humble towns where she and her fellow pilgrims stayed, the people she met during the journey, her own feelings of anger and sadness over the loss of her father, and historical and theological issues surrounding the pilgrimage. The book is a vivid, personal account of the recovery of one person's faith; as Egan notes, "Life didn't change, but perspective did."

Subjects: Death; Fathers and Daughters; Grief; Pilgrimages

Places: France; Spain

Now Try: Catholic priest Kevin Codd made the pilgrimage along the Camino de Santiago in order to take stock of his own life; he tells the story of the journey and how it changed his spiritual perspective in *To the Field of Stars: A Pilgrim's Journey to Santiago de Compostela*. Art historian Conrad Rudolph made the same pilgrimage and writes about both his personal experiences and the history of this path in the short but delightful *Pilgrimage to the End of the World: The Road to Santiago de Compostela*. Another Harvard Divinity School graduate, Tom Levinson, recounts his 9,000-mile self-imposed pilgrimage across the United States to talk to people about their individual faiths in the often witty and sometimes poignant *All That's Holy: A Young Guy, an Old Car, and the Search for God in America*. Kate Braestrup's memoir about the death of her husband and her decision to pursue his desire of becoming a minister, *Here If You Need Me: A True Story*, may also appeal.

Fergus, Charles

Summer at Little Lava: A Season at the Edge of the World. New York: North Point Press, 1998. 289 pp. ISBN: 9780374525521

In 1996, Charles Fergus's mother was stabbed to death in her home by a burglar, and the author withdrew with his wife and son to a friend's abandoned, concrete-walled house in an isolated part of Iceland, "itself an outermost house of the Western world," according to Fergus. In this lonely place without roads, heat, electricity, or running water, Fergus was able to deal with his grief and to recover his sense of life's meaning, in spite of a second tragedy that struck his family during his season in Iceland. His healing took place in the middle of Iceland's distinctive geology, wildlife, and history, and in the presence of its dour, self-reliant people, and Fergus vividly evokes both place and people.

Subjects: Death; Family Relationships; Grief

Places: Iceland

Now Try: Fergus was inspired to spend his year of recovery by Henry Beston's book, *The Outermost House: A Year of Life On The Great Beach of Cape Cod,* about a year spent living in a cottage on Cape Cod, and although Beston was not motivated by the death of a relative, his evocations of nature are similar to those of Fergus. In *The Windows of Brimnes: An American in Iceland,* Bill Holmes traveled to a fisherman's cottage in northern Iceland to contemplate the fate of his native America, which he calls "my home, my citizenship, my burden." Terry G. Lacy is an American who has lived in Iceland for over 20 years, and he brings that perspective to *Ring of Seasons: Iceland—Its Culture and History,* which weaves together a number of aspects of Iceland and its people.

Fraser, Laura

An Italian Affair. New York: Pantheon Books 2001. 226 pp. ISBN: 9780375420658

Fraser and her husband had been married for just one year when he left her for his high school sweetheart. She was devastated at first but recovered by taking a trip to Italy and meeting a married French university professor with whom she began an affair that would last for the next two years. The book alternates between Fraser's home in San Francisco and the exotic locations where she and her lover met: Milan; Morocco; London; and the Aeolian Islands. Each rendezvous and its locale is described in sumptuous detail (landscapes, food, drink, sounds), but Fraser manages to avoid idealizing her affair or her journey of recovery.

Subjects: Divorce; Love and Dating; Quick Reads; Women Travelers

Places: Africa; England; Italy; London; Morocco; San Francisco

Now Try: Fraser continues the story that started in *An Italian Affair* with *All Over the Map,* which begins with the end of the affair after her lover announced that he had found someone new; her natural tendency to heal herself through travel was then complicated by an assault in Samoa that left her aware of her vulnerability. When Maria Finn discovered that her husband was having an affair, she recovered by learning to tango, an adventure that eventually took her to Buenos Aires, where she learned that her life was just beginning, in *Hold Me Tight and Tango Me Home.* Writer Suzy Gershman and her husband had always fantasized about living in Paris, and when he died unexpectedly, she moved to Paris alone and began the healing process; her first year is described in *C'est La Vie: An American Woman Begins a New Life in Paris and—Voila!—Becomes Almost French.*

Gilbert, Elizabeth

Eat, Pray, Love: One Woman's Search for Everything Across Italy, India and Indonesia. New York: Viking, 2006. 334 pp. ISBN: 9780670034710

After 30-something writer Gilbert divorced her husband and ended a rebound relationship, she felt depressed and alone. She traveled to Bali (Indonesia) to write an article on yoga vacations, and a medicine man there told her that she would one day return to study with him. She spent the next year traveling around the world in an attempt to recover her sense of self and spent four months in Italy, simply eating and enjoying life, followed by three months in an Indian ashram, pursuing a deeper understanding of her spirituality. Finally, she did return to Bali, where she found a balance between the worldliness of Italy and the spirituality of India. She also found love in the form of a spirited, older Brazilian divorcé. *Eat, Pray, Love* is a book that will likely divide readers: for some, Gilbert's memoir will seem a wise spiritual journey, empowering and filled with rich detail and humor, but for others, she will seem self-absorbed, irritating, and too prone to crying.

Subjects: Coming of Age; Divorce; Food; Friendships; Humor; Love and Dating; Marriage; Prayer; Spirituality; Women Travelers

Places: India; Indonesia; Italy

Awards: *New York Times* Notable Book, 2006

Now Try: Gilbert's *Committed: A Skeptic Makes Peace with Marriage* focuses on her life after *Eat, Pray, Love* and includes a 10-month ramble through Southeast Asia. In *Initiation: A Woman's Spiritual Adventure in the Heart of the Andes,* Elizabeth Jenkins writes about her spiritual experiences in the Andean village of Cuzco, Peru, which were so profound that she returned there to live and study the religious practices of the ancient Incas. Rachel Manija Brown's *All the Fishes Come Home to Roost: An American Misfit in India* may also appeal to fans of *Eat, Pray, Love,* particularly those who are fascinated by Gilbert's time in India; it tells the story of an American woman who came of age on an Indian ashram, where she was the only foreign child. Luca Spaghetti (his real name) was asked to show Gilbert around Rome; his side of the story is recounted in *Un Amico Italiano: Eat, Pray, Love in Rome.*

Hancock, Bill

Riding with the Blue Moth. Champaign, IL: Sports Publishing L.L.C., 2005. 246 pp. ISBN: 9781596701045

Hancock was the coordinator of the NCAA basketball tournament when his son Will died in a 2001 airplane crash that killed nine other members of the Oklahoma State University basketball team and staff. Hancock's response was to bicycle 2,750 miles across the United States in order to deal with his grief, a ride that becomes a metaphor for the author's inner journey. The book mixes touching memories of Hancock's son as well as painful thoughts about the prospect of life without their son for Hancock and his wife with stories of bike riding, the back-road places that Hancock and his wife (who followed him with a tent trailer) passed through, the people they met, and how those people helped them deal with "the blue moth of gloom." For many readers, this will be an inspirational journey lesson on how to endure great loss.

Subjects: Bicycles; Death; Grief; Spouses

Places: United States (Various)

Now Try: Dwight Smith, a former professor in his 60s, lost two sons and his wife in separate incidents and undertook a 13,800-mile solo bicycle journey around the perimeter of the United States; he tells his story of recovery in *One Mile at a Time: Cycling through Loss to Renewal*. Melissa Norton and her husband were not motivated by grief to bicycle across the United States, from Oregon to Maine, but Norton's book, *Just the Two of Us: A Cycling Journey Across America*, does focus on the relationship between the wife and husband as their ride alternates between grueling mountain climbs and nights in upscale inns. Jill Homer's *Be Brave, Be Strong: A Journey Across the Great Divide* begins with the author training for a 2,740-mile bicycle ride from Canada to Mexico along the Continental Divide; however, even before the ride begins, she suffered frostbite during a training ride, and her boyfriend of eight years broke off their relationship. Anne Tyler's novel *The Accidental Tourist* is also about a couple's relationship in the aftermath of the death of their son. Likewise, Wallace Stegner's fine novel, *The Spectator Bird* (which won a National Book Award in 1977), is based on a diary that the protagonist kept during a trip that he and his wife took to Denmark after their only child died.

Jian, Ma

Red Dust: A Path Through China. New York: Pantheon Books 2001. 324 pp. ISBN: 9780375420597

In 1983, the 30 year-old photographer and poet Ma Jian found himself divorced, betrayed by his girlfriend, and facing arrest for "spiritual pollution." Hoping to gain insight into his place in the world, he decided to leave Beijing and spent the next three years traveling south and west with little more than a change of clothes and a copy of *Leaves of Grass*. He wandered through deserts and mountains, down coasts, and into the remotest corners of China. His frank portrait of the country under Deng Xiaoping is vibrant, revealing, and thought provoking.

Subjects: Divorce; Marriage; Memoirs; Walking

Places: Beijing; Burma; China; Tibet

Awards: Thomas Cook Travel Book Award, 2002

Now Try: Ma Jian first became known in the West through his story collection *Stick Out Your Tongue*, which was translated into English in 2006; the stories are set in Tibet and do not idealize traditional Tibetan culture but depict it as harsh and often inhumane. His later novel, *Beijing Coma*, tells the story of the Tiananmen Square protests from the point of view of a protestor who is left in a coma by the violence; the *Financial Times* called it "the great Tienanmen novel." Nobel Prize winner Gao Xingjian's novel, *Soul Mountain*, is the story of a man who journeys through rural China to find a legendary mountain; the novel is partly autobiographical and loosely based on the author's own travels.

Nichols, Peter

Sea Change: Alone Across the Atlantic in a Wooden Boat. New York: Viking, 1997. 238 pp. ISBN: 9780670871797

Following his divorce, Nichols took to the sea in a 27-foot shallow-draft sailboat named *Toad*, attempting to retrace a similar voyage he and his ex-wife had taken some years before. Memories of his failed marriage followed him throughout the trip, particularly when he found and began reading his wife's five-volume diary, the entries of which reminded him of their years together, sailing and arguing through the Virgin Islands and European waters. These memories are mixed with details of the voyage itself, navigating by sextant, adapting to the changing sea and sky, making landfall in the Azores and the Isles of Scilly, and realizing that his boat has a major problem that will put his life in danger. *Sea Change* does an excellent job of conveying Nichols's love of sailing as well as his honesty in dealing with his failed marriage.

Subjects: Adventure; Divorce; Exploration; Humor; Islands; Marriage; Memoirs; Oceans; Sailing; Solitude; Solo Travelers

Places: Atlantic Ocean; Azore Islands; England; Scilly Islands; Texas

Now Try: Nichols also wrote the highly regarded *A Voyage for Madmen*, about nine different individuals who, in 1968 (before satellite weather radar and advanced communication equipment) attempted to become the first person to sail around the world alone without stopping; Nichols does an admirable job of portraying the individuals and their motivations. Toni Murden McClure tells of her own voyage of self-discovery as she tried to become the first woman to row solo across the Atlantic Ocean; her book, *A Pearl in the Storm: How I Found My Heart in the Middle of the Ocean*, also tells about her attempts to "confront [her] demons" and "slay [her] dragons" on the trip. Roz Savage describes her experiences as the only female to enter a demanding rowing race across the Atlantic Ocean in *Rowing the Atlantic: Lessons Learned on the Open Ocean*.

Patterson, Kevin

The Water in Between: A Journey at Sea. New York: Nan A. Talese, 2000 [1999]. 289 pp. ISBN: 9780385498838

Patterson, a former Canadian army doctor, decided to heal his broken heart from a brief but painful love affair by sailing from British Columbia to Tahiti on a 20-year-old, 37-foot sailboat; the fact that Patterson didn't know how to sail and had never been at sea did not deter him in his quest, and he set sail with a copilot who did have sea experience and who was recovering from a broken marriage himself. Patterson's attempt to heal soon became a lesson in patience and self-discipline, as the pair ran into stagnant, overly calm seas and a string of bad luck, including lost anchors and broken generators. Patterson mixes humor and melancholy, solitude and camaraderie in telling his story and mixes in quotations from the writers (Chatwin and Theroux among them) who inspired his odyssey.

Subjects: Doctors; Friendships; Humor; Oceans; Relationships; Sailing

Places: Hawaii; Pacific Islands; Pacific Ocean; Tahiti; Vancouver

Now Try: Tristan Jones lost a leg but, less than a year later, attempted to sail around the world on a 36-foot trimaran; he tells about his attempt in *Outward Leg*, an inspiring and engaging book. Janna Cawrse Esarey and her husband finally married after a decade-long on-again-off-again relationship and set sail on a two-year voyage across the Pacific; the challenges and dangers they faced threatened their marriage as well as their lives, and the story is told in *The Motion of the Ocean: 1 Small Boat, 2 Average Lovers, and a Woman's Search for the Meaning of Wife*. In *Ten Degrees of Reckoning: The True Story of a Family's Love and the Will to Survive* (annotated in the "Travel Adventure" chapter of this book), Hester Rumberg tells the tragic story of her best friend Judith Sleavin, who had set out with her husband and two children in 1993 to sail around the world, a voyage cut short off New Zealand by an accident that killed everyone in the party but Sleavin. The tale of incomparable loss and remarkable survival is gripping. Novels by men that deal with the end of a marriage or a relationship may also appeal; possibilities include Jonathan Tropper's *This is Where I Leave You*, in which a Jewish man has to deal with the death of his father while his own wife is having an affair with his ex-boss, and Martin Page's amusing *The Discreet Pleasures of Rejection*, about a man driven to self-analysis when a woman he has never dated breaks up with him via a message left on his answering machine.

Peart, Neil

Ghost Rider: Travels on the Healing Road. Toronto: ECW Press, 2002. 460 pp. ISBN: 9781550225464

Peart, the drummer for the rock band Rush, lost what was then his only daughter in an automobile accident in 1997 and his common-law wife of 22 years to cancer just 10 months later. He left the band to travel, mourn, and heal on a 55,000-mile motorcycle ride through much of North America, Mexico, and Belize. *Ghost Rider* chronicles his internal and external journeys as he worked through anger and frustration, re-connected with other family members, and took his "little baby soul for a ride," as Peart puts it. Like *Eat, Pray, Love*, readers will likely have sharply divided opinions about *Ghost Rider*: some will see the book as an inspiring tale about a man working through his grief; others will find Peart self-absorbed, arrogant, and dismissive of others.

Subjects: Death; Fathers and Daughters; Grief; Motorcycles; Music and Musicians; Road Trips; Spouses

Places: Belize; Canada; Mexico; United States (Various)

Now Try: Peart is the author of three other travel narratives. *The Masked Rider: Cycling in West Africa* is about a 1988 bicycle tour through Cameroon. *Traveling Music: The Soundtrack of my Life and Times* chronicles another road trip, this time by automobile. *Far and Away: A Prize Every Time* looks at his travels in North and South America and especially his discovery of a town in Brazil with a unique blend of West African and Brazilian music. In *Journeys, Two-Up: On the Road through Grief to Renewal*, Ray Uloth describes his 9,000-mile solo motorcycle journey across the United States and his tour of the Middle East following the death of his wife of 40 years to breast cancer. On February 14, 1884, future U.S. President Theodore Roosevelt's wife and mother both died within hours of one another; devastated, Roosevelt left for the Dakota territories, where he lived as a rancher for two years; he wrote about his experience in the Dakotas in *Hunting Trips of a Ranchman: Sketches of Sport On the Northern Cattle Plains,* although there is no mention of his wife or mother in the book.

Theroux, Paul

The Happy Isles of Oceania: Paddling the Pacific. New York: G.P. Putnam's Sons, 1992. 528 pp. ISBN: 9780399137266

Theroux had recently separated from his wife of 25 years and was awaiting the results of a test for skin cancer when he decided to paddle across the Pacific, from New Zealand to Hawaii, visiting over 50 islands. The trip is filled with Theroux's usual misanthropic observations, but there are also wonderfully written passages and his excellent ear for dialogue. His travels took him hiking through New Zealand's southern mountains, exploring the Australian bush, interviewing the King of Tonga, getting stung by jellyfish, drinking kava, and wondering what drew Robert Louis Stevenson to Samoa and Paul Gauguin to Tahiti. As the trip progresses, Theroux begins to lose some of his hard edge, and by the time he arrives in Hawaii, he seems (at least for Theroux) to have taken on a more positive outlook.

Subjects: Adventure; Cancer; Islands; Kayaking; Oceans; Spouses

Places: Australia; Cook Islands; Easter Island; Fiji; Hawaii; New Zealand; Samoa; Solomon Islands; Trobriand Islands; Tahiti; Tonga; Vanuatu

Now Try: Jonathan Waterman and his wife of one year decided to deal with their disenchantment with life by kayaking down the coastline of Baja California, a story he details in *Kayaking the Vermilion Sea: Eight Hundred Miles Down the Baja.* Ann Linnea turned 43 and felt unfulfilled in her life, so she decided to paddle her kayak with a friend around the 1,200-mile perimeter of Lake Superior in order to prepare herself for the second half of her life; she recounts the odyssey in *Deep Water Passage: A Spiritual Journey at Midlife.* Pamela Stephenson bought a yacht and followed the South Pacific voyage of Robert Louis Stevenson and his wife Fanny; her Pacific journey is told in *Treasure Islands: Sailing the South Seas in the Wake of Fanny and Robert Louis Stevenson.*

Thubron, Colin

To a Mountain in Tibet. New York: Harper, 2011. 227 pp. ISBN: 9780061768262

Following the death of his mother, travel writer Thubron journeyed by foot to Mount Kailas, a sacred place to Buddhists, Hindus, and Jains and the source of four of India's great rivers. Along this short but difficult pilgrimage, Thubron reflects on his grief, his solitude (childless and the last surviving member of his family), and his memories of his family as well as on the political and cultural history of Tibet. Thubron's thoughts of his own family (he discovered and read the love letters exchanged between his parents, "guiltily, fearfully, as if testing water") led him to be particularly sensitive to the family issues of the people he encountered on his journey, and the result is often a moving interchange with these individuals. As with most of Thubron's books, *To a Mountain in Tibet* is thoroughly researched; it is also deeply personal and enchanting.

Subjects: Buddhism; Death; Grief; Hinduism; Jainism; Mothers and Sons; Pilgrimages; Quick Reads; Scholarly Writing

Places: Nepal; Tibet

Awards: *New York Times* Notable Book, 2011

Now Try: Thubron is also the author of several novels, including *The God in the Mountain*, which explores the conflict between the sacred and the worldly when an American mining company attempts to mine a mountain that is the home of a sacred shrine, in an unnamed Mediterranean country. Robert Thurman and Tad Wise also made a spiritual pilgrimage to Mount Kailas, and Thurman's perspective as a leading scholar on Tibetan Buddhism enhances their book about the journey, *Circling the Sacred Mountain: A Spiritual Adventure Through the Himalayas*. Mount Kailas is also the subject of *Tibet's Sacred Mountain: The Extraordinary Pilgrimage to Mount Kailas*, by Russell Johnson and Kerry Moran, a book that features some stunning photographs.

Welborn, Amy

Wish You Were Here: Travels Through Loss and Hope. New York: Image Books, 2012. 245 pp. ISBN: 9780307716385

Welborn is a Catholic writer whose husband Michael died suddenly of a heart attack in 2009. Five months later, still grieving over the loss of her spouse, Welborn traveled to Sicily with her three children, where her visits to ancient ruins and small towns and encounters with what one reviewer called "the beauty of the ordinary and the commonplace" led her to think about her loss, her faith, and the happy memories of her life with Michael, thereby making it possible for her to heal somewhat. *Wish You Were Here* is an extremely vulnerable work filled with a deep sadness, but it is also a testimony to Welborn's faith and love.

Subjects: Catholicism; Death; Family Travel; Grief; Spouses; Women Travelers

Places: Italy; Sicily

Now Try: Rosé Marie Curteman's *My Renaissance: A Widow's Healing Pilgrimage to Tuscany* (annotated in this category) is the story of Curteman's husband's long battle with dementia and his death as well as the story of her subsequent journey to Italy to recover from her grief, partly by studying art, the Italian language, and Italian cooking in Florence. When Jane Hanrahan's husband retired, he and she sold their possessions and set out to travel the world; *A Widow's World* is her story of his death in Ankara and her decision to complete the planned 11-month trip from Turkey to South America. Another testimony to faith and love is C. S. Lewis's *A Grief Observed*, an exploration of the author's bereavement following the death of his wife, Joy Gresham. Joan Didion's *The Year of Magical Thinking* is a remarkable memoir of the writer's life after her husband had died of a heart attack and while their daughter was hospitalized and in a coma; her efforts to make sense of what was happening lack the religious orientation of Welborn's book but may still appeal to readers who were moved by *Wish You Were Here*.

Wisner, Franz

Honeymoon with My Brother: A Memoir. New York: St. Martin's Press, 2005. 274 pp. ISBN: 9780312320904

Franz Wisner's beautiful bride-to-be left him just a few days before their wedding, so Wisner took his younger brother with him to Costa Rica for an already-paid-for honeymoon. That experience inspired the two men to quit their jobs, sell their houses, and spend two years traveling through more than 50 countries, getting to know one another better and (for the elder Franz) getting past the pain of the failed relationship. The book is sometimes funny and sometimes touching, but it is mostly an honest and entertaining story about discovering what love and friendship are all about.

Subjects: Brothers; Friendship

Places: Africa (Various); Asia (Various); Europe (Various); South America (Various)

Now Try: Wisner followed up *Honeymoon with My Brother* with *How the World Makes Love: And What It Taught a Jilted Groom*, which is annotated in the chapter on "Quests" and in which he and his brother travel around the world to learn about love. Nicholas Sparks and his brother Micah Sparks write about their three-week trip around the world in *Three Weeks with My Brother*, which is annotated in this chapter. Rinker Buck writes about the summer of 1966, when he and his brother bought and restored an old Piper Cub airplane and then flew it across the country in *Flight of Passage: A Memoir*. A fictional account of a unique relationship between two brothers is Doug Crandell's amusing and captivating *Hairdos of the Mildly Depressed*, about a Georgia man who cares for his brother, a former playboy who suffered serious brain injury at the hands of a jealous husband. Readers who want slightly happier love stories than the one told by Wisner might consider John Bowe's oral history, *Us: Americans Talk about Love*, or Dave Isay's *All There Is: Love Stories from StoryCorps*.

Discovering One's Self

The most foreign territory will always lie within.
—Sara Wheeler, Terra Incognita: Travels in Antarctica

In many cases, the trip entails less a discovery of some external destination and more a discovery of one's self. This self-discovery may be set in motion by a tragedy in one's life (as in the titles of the previous section) or may be the result of other events in the traveler's life. Journeys of the latter type are the subject of the titles in the present category. Regardless of how these journeys begin, they end with a deeper understanding of self.

The traveler may lose faith in previously held beliefs, as in Daniel Everett's abandonment of both Christianity and Chomskian theories of language in *Don't Sleep, There Are Snakes: Life and Language in the Amazonian Jungle*, or the traveler may find his faith growing stronger, as in Bruce Feiler's *Walking the Bible: A Journey by Land Through the Five Books of Moses*. The traveler may discover her fun side, as in Rachel Friedman's *The Good Girl's Guide to Getting Lost*, or discover an inner resourcefulness that she was unaware of, as in Susan Jane Gilman's *Undress Me in the Temple of Heaven*. The traveler may learn about the nature of his or her own ethnic identity, as in Eddy L. Harris's *Native Stranger: A Black American's Journey into the Heart of Africa* or Lydia Minatoya's *Talking to High Monks in the Snow: An Asian American Odyssey*, or the importance of being alone, as in Ken McAlpine's *Off-Season: Discovering America on Winter's Shore* or Robert Kull's *Solitude: Seeking Wisdom in Extremes: A Year Alone in the Patagonia Wilderness*.

As with the titles in the previous section ("Healing Odysseys"), the titles in this category tend to be very personal, and readers who enjoy the appeal of character should find them of interest. They may also be of interest to readers who find themselves in situations like those of the authors of these books.

Readers who enjoy titles in which the trip leads the traveler to a deeper understanding of herself may also enjoy fiction in which characters engage in self-discovery, as in the novels of Richard Russo (*Straight Man* or *That Old Cape Magic*) or Fannie Flagg's *Fried Green Tomatoes at the Whistle Stop Cafe*. As for nonfiction, both memoirs (Toi Derricotte's *The Black Notebooks: An Interior Journey* or Mary Karr's *Lit: A Memoir*) and self-help titles (Charles Duhigg's *The Power of Habit: Why We Do What We Do in Life and Business* or Don Miguel Ruiz's *The Four Agreements: A Practical Guide to Personal Freedom*) may be of interest.

Everett, Daniel

Don't Sleep, There Are Snakes: Life and Language in the Amazonian Jungle. New York: Pantheon, 2008. 283 pp. ISBN: 9780375425028

Don't Sleep, There Are Snakes is part adventure, part anthropological study, and part crisis of faith. Linguistics professor Everett went to Brazil to live with the Pirahã people in the late 1970s and, as a result, lost two of his cherished beliefs: in the Christianity that he and his wife had hoped to bring to the Pirahã; and in the Chomskian theories of language that he came to test. Everett found that the people were happy enough without the message of salvation and came to embrace that lack of belief himself. He also came to the controversial conclusion that the Pirahã do not share the linguistic characteristics that Chomsky had maintained were universal, that they have no counting system, no pure color terms, and no equivalents to quantifiers like "all" and "some." Unfortunately,

Everett tells his story of discovery in rather drab prose and flat characters; as one reviewer noted, "he lacks the wit and felicitous gift for analogy that enables someone like Pinker to bring structural linguistics to life."

Subjects: Christianity; Indigenous Peoples; Jungles; Linguistics; Marriage; Religion; Scientists; Self-Discovery; Spouses

Places: Brazil

Series: *Vintage Departures*

Now Try: In *Bastard Tongues: A Trailblazing Linguist Finds Clues to Our Common Humanity in the World's Lowliest Languages,* Derek Bickerton describes his research of over 30 years into Creole languages and the exotic locations on four continents where he had conducted this research; his writing is both breezy and witty. Linguistics professor K. David Harrison traveled to Tibet, Siberia, and North America to study the many human languages that are being lost in *When Languages Die: The Extinction of the World's Languages and the Erosion of Human Knowledge;* he uses anecdotes and portraits of the speakers of these dying languages to support his ideas. Paul Colinvaux is an ecologist, not a linguist, but his travels to the Amazon River led him to propose theories about the area's past climate that challenged conventional wisdom; his book is *Amazon Expeditions: My Quest for the Ice-Age Equator*. Steven Pinker's most accessible book on language is *The Language Instinct: How the Mind Creates Language;* one critic called it "a beautiful hymn to the infinite creative potential of language." Barbara Kingsolver's engrossing novel, *The Poisonwood Bible,* may appeal to readers who enjoy Everett's book; in Kingsolver's novel, a missionary family moves from Georgia to the Belgian Congo in 1959. The father's inability to adapt to the culture of the Africa village has disastrous consequences.

Feiler, Bruce

Walking the Bible: A Journey by Land Through the Five Books of Moses. New York: Morrow, 2001. 451 pp. ISBN: 9780380977758

Feiler, a fifth-generation American Jew, undertook this 10,000-mile journey from Turkey's Mount Ararat, where Noah's ark landed after the flood, to Jordan's Mount Nebo, where Moses overlooked the Promised Land, in order to retrace the first five books of the Old Testament. Unsure of his motivations, Feiler compared himself with Abraham, "a traveler, called by some voice not entirely clear that said: Go head to this land, walk along this route, and trust what you will find." As he traveled through the places where Biblical events took place (riding a camel up Mount Sinai, standing where Moses received the Commandments, tasting salt pillars at Sodom and Gomorrah), Feiler became more grounded in his own faith and discovered a sense of the Bible's timeless relevance in his life. *Walking the Bible* is well researched, thought provoking, and filled with vivid descriptions of the land and its people that will increase the reader's understanding of the stage on which these historical and spiritual dramas played out.

Subjects: Bible; Investigative Stories; Jews and Judaism; Middle Eastern History; Religion; Scholarly Writing; Self-Discovery

Places: Africa; Egypt; Israel; Jordan; Turkey

Now Try: Feiler followed up *Walking the Bible* with *Where God Was Born: A Journey by Land to the Roots of Religion*, which begins with the story of Joshua and follows the story of Israel through David, Solomon, and the Diaspora. Feiler is also the author of *Abraham: A Journey to the Heart of Three Faiths*, a biography of the man who unites Judaism, Christianity, and Islam and the story of Feiler's inner journey to understand the connections among these faiths. For readers interested in life in Israel as seen by two individuals who emigrated there and describe their own spiritual journeys, Wendy Orange's *Coming Home to Jerusalem* and David Horowitz's *A Little Too Close to God* can be recommended.

Fletcher, Colin

River: One Man's Journey Down the Colorado, Source to Sea. New York: Alfred A. Knopf, 1997. 400 pp. ISBN: 9780394574219

River mixes memoir and travel narrative as it follows the 67-year-old Fletcher 1,700 miles down the Colorado River by raft and on foot over a six-month period. As he writes about tracing the river from its source in the Wyoming mountains or his raft plunging through the river's perilous rapids, Fletcher recalls the psychological wounds that he suffered in World War II and how those wounds led him to spend his life seeking refuge in nature and long, solitary walks; in fact, he describes his solo trip down the Colorado as "something to pare the fat off my soul . . . to make me grateful, again, for being alive." *River* is Fletcher's last book and is written with a sense of closure; it is as much about making peace with life as it is about traversing the great river.

Subjects: Adventure; Memoirs; Rivers; Self-Discovery; Solitude; Solo Travelers

Places: Arizona; California; Colorado; Colorado River; Mexico; Nevada; Utah

Series: *Vintage Departures*

Now Try: Fletcher's earlier masterpiece on becoming the first person to walk the length of the Grand Canyon is *The Man Who Walked Through Time: The Story of the First Trip Afoot Through the Grand Canyon*. John Wesley Powell led the famous 1869 expedition down the Colorado River that first passed through the Grand Canyon; his classic account of that expedition is *The Exploration of the Colorado River and Its Canyons*. Doug Peacock's *Grizzly Years: In Search of the American Wilderness* does not involve a river but does combine memoir and travel narrative much as Fletcher's *River* does; Peacock served as a medic during the Vietnam War and returned home to shake off his memories of the war by following the grizzly bears that live in the United States. *One Man's Wilderness: An Alaskan Odyssey* by Sam Keith and Richard Proenneke might also appeal; Proenneke went to Alaska to live in solitude and had also suffered some hardships during World War II that made him want to live more healthfully and closer with nature.

Friedman, Rachel

The Good Girl's Guide to Getting Lost: A Memoir of Three Continents, Two Friends, and One Unexpected Adventure. New York: Bantam Books, 2011. 287 pp. ISBN: 9780385343374

"Good girl" Friedman was a well-behaved, parent-pleasing college student who traveled to Ireland during the summer before her senior year in college. She met an uninhibited Australian woman, who awakened Friedman's inner vagabond, and after returning to the United States to finish college, Friedman visited her friend in Australia and then traveled with her through South America. Along the way, she discovered that it's okay to follow one's bliss, to put off one's career, and to set aside old expectations in order to have an adventure of one's own. *The Good Girl's Guide to Getting Lost* is an uplifting and witty reminder that travel changes the traveler.

Subjects: Coming of Age; Friendships; Memoirs; Self-Discovery; Women Travelers

Places: Argentina; Australia; Bolivia; Buenos Aires; Chile; Ireland; Peru

Series: *Vintage Departures*

Now Try: Three other women travelers who quit their corporate jobs to spend a year traveling around the world (Jennifer Baggett, Holly C. Corbett, and Amanda Pressner) write about the lessons they learned in Peru, Kenya, Vietnam, and Australia in *The Lost Girls: Three Friends, Four Continents, One Unconventional Detour Around the World*. Holly Morris also quit her job to travel around the world, but her purpose was more serious, to find women around the world who were working to make significant changes; *Adventure Divas: Searching the Globe for Women Who Are Changing the World* describes her encounters with social activists, artists, and politicians. Judith Fine's *Life is a Trip: The Transformative Magic of Travel* is a collection of essays that reinforce the lesson that Friedman learned about the power of travel to change people. Jane Green's *Swapping Lives* may appeal as well; the book jacket calls this novel about two women (one British, one American) who switch lives a "must-read for every modern woman who's ever considered the road not taken."

Gelman, Rita

Tales of a Female Nomad: Living at Large in the World. New York: Crown Publishers, 2001. 311 pp. ISBN: 9780609606421

Gelman, a 48-year-old children's book author whose marriage was failing, traveled first to Mexico in an attempt to revitalize herself and her marriage. That experience led her to take up a new life of traveling with no set plans, immersing herself in other cultures for extended periods of time, and reconnecting with her true self. Her serendipitous journeys included living among rural villagers in Mexico, sleeping with sea lions on the Galapagos Islands, observing orangutans in the rain forests of Borneo, and finding her spiritual center in Bali. Gelman's book is simply written, as one might expect from a children's writer, and it can border on the self-indulgent, but many readers will see it as an honest depiction of what it's like to give up everything one knows to make one's dreams happen.

Subjects: Friendships; Memoirs; Self-Discovery; Women Travelers; Women Writers

Places: Bali; Canada; Galapagos Islands; Guatemala; Indonesia; Israel; Mexico; New Zealand; Nicaragua; Thailand; United States (Various)

Now Try: Gelman also wrote *Female Nomad and Friends: Tales of Breaking Free and Breaking Bread Around the World,* which follows her travels after *Tales of a Female Nomad* and shares the stories sent to her by readers of her earlier book. Faith Conlon, Ingrid Emerick, and Christina Henry de Tessan edited *Go Your Own Way: Women Travel the World Solo,* a series of essays about independent women travelers, whose tales include being lost in the rain forests of Borneo, learning to tango in Argentina, and following in the footsteps of a 10th-century Viking woman in Iceland. Catherine Watson's book, *Roads Less Traveled: Dispatches from the Ends of the Earth,* describes experiences in Borneo and Bali that are similar to those described by Gelman in *Tales of a Female Nomad.* Alex Miller's novel, *Journey to the Stone Country,* involves an Australian woman whose husband abandons her and who returns to her childhood home in North Queensland; there, she meets an Aboriginal man from her childhood and comes to believe that he holds the key to her future.

Gilman, Susan Jane

Undress Me in the Temple of Heaven. New York: Grand Central Publishing, 2009. 306 pp. ISBN: 9780446578929

In 1986, Gilman and her friend Claire had just graduated from college and decided to journey around the world, starting in China, which had just opened itself to the Western world. Unfortunately, as soon as they arrived, they were in over their heads: hungry, under surveillance, and disoriented. Not surprisingly, they began to unravel, particularly Claire, who began to act strangely, to have hallucinations, and to display signs of paranoia. Encounters with military police and an escape from a rural hospital followed. Gilman tells the story with a mesmerizing, engaging style that turns what began as a typical college student's travel narrative into something more like a compelling thriller that shows just how resourceful someone in difficult circumstances can become.

Subjects: Coming of Age; Culture Clash; Friendships; Self-Discovery; Women Travelers; Women Writers

Places: China

Now Try: Gilman is also the author of *Hypocrite in a Pouffy White Dress,* a memoir about growing up on the Upper West Side of Manhattan in the 1970s, and *Kiss My Tiara: How to Rule the World as a SmartMouth Goddess,* a hilarious how-to book for women. Desi Downey moved from the U.S. Midwest to China when her husband's job was transferred there; much like Gilman and her friend, she found herself thrust into a bewildering new life, which she describes in *Ni Howdy!: An American Woman's (Mal)Adaptation to Life in the People's Republic of China*. Stanford professor of anthropology Hill Gates traveled to China to explore the status of women in that country; her experiences there and her observations are detailed in *Looking for Chengdu: A Woman's Adventures in China*. Rhoda Janzen's memoir, *Mennonite in a Little Black Dress: A Memoir of Going Home*, does not involve travel or China, but its story of a woman whose life was turned upside down after her husband of 15 years left her for a man and after she was injured in an automobile accident may appeal to readers who are drawn to the theme of women dealing with bewildering developments in their lives.

Grange, Kevin

Beneath Blossom Rain: Discovering Bhutan on the Toughest Trek in the World. Lincoln, NE: University of Nebraska Press, 2011. 336 pp. ISBN: 9780803234338

In 2007, Grange hiked Bhutan's Snowman Trek, a 24-day, 216-mile trek through 11 mountain passes (seven of them over 11,000 feet) that is regarded as one of the most difficult hikes in the world. Grange focuses not only on the hazards and trials of the difficult hike (more people have climbed Mount Everest than have completed the Snowman Trek) but also on the history and landscape of Bhutan and on his own internal journey of self-understanding, noting that "There was wisdom to be found by foregoing convenience and embracing difficulty." Grange writes with a light touch of good-natured humor and provides beautiful descriptions of the Himalayas.

Subjects: Adventure; Buddhism; Hiking; Humor; Mountains; Self-Discovery; Spirituality

Places: Bhutan

Now Try: Rick Ridgeway's *Below Another Sky: A Mountain Adventure in Search of a Lost Father* describes another difficult journey with an element of self-discovery; Ridgeway took the daughter of a friend who had died in his arms to Tibet to find the grave site and uses the trip to reflect on his friend and to explore his own spirituality. Nigel Gardener and his son traveled to Bhutan both to trek through its mountains and to re-connect with one another; their story is told in Gardener's book, *In Search of Gross Domestic Happiness: A Father and Son go Trekking in Bhutan*. Science writer Jeremy Bernstein's *In the Himalayas: Journeys through Nepal, Tibet, and Bhutan* is less concerned with inner journeys, but he does mix personal stories with historical and social details about Nepal, Tibet, and Bhutan and he does admit to approaching later trips with a more mature, less naïve perspective. The University of Nebraska Press has published several titles with travel themes, including Patrick Dobson's *Seldom Seen: A Journey into the Great Plains*, about a man who backpacked from Kansas City to Helena, Montana, and wrote about his encounters with small town America, and Daryl Farmer's *Bicycling Beyond the Divide: Two Journeys into the West*, about a 40-year-old man who repeated a 5,000-mile bicycle ride that he had taken 20 years earlier and the changes that have affected both him and the Western United States, through which he rides.

Harris, Eddy L.

Native Stranger: A Black American's Journey into the Heart of Africa. New York: Simon & Schuster, 1992. 315 pp. ISBN: 9780671748975

Harris spent a year traveling through Africa, expecting to find his roots as an African American man. He spent a night in jail in Liberia, visited nomads in Senegal, felt surprisingly happy in South Africa, criticized black officials for their tyranny, hunted gorillas with a British party in Zaire, and ultimately found that, in spite of his race, he was still a stranger and a rich American. As he realized on a river boat in Zaire, "I didn't know where I belonged. It was so strange to be among so many black people and to have so much more in common with the handful of whites." Harris's discovery, told throughout his narrative, that culture, education, and opportunity trump race and skin color is well written, with vivid descriptions and sympathetic observations about the plight of Africa and Africans, and is an honest, hardly romanticized look at Africa.

Subjects: African Americans; African History; Islam; Nomads; Self-Discovery; Society

Places: Africa; Benin; Burkina Faso; Cameroon; Gambia; Guinea-Bissau; Ivory Coast; Liberia; Mali; Mauritania; Morocco; Rwanda; Senegal; South Africa; Togo; Zaire; Zambia; Zimbabwe

Series: *Vintage Departures*

Now Try: Harris is also the author of *Mississippi Solo: A River Quest*, which recounts his canoe trip down the Mississippi; his thoughts on racial issues as he travels from the northern United States south are as thought provoking as his observations on Africa in *Native Stranger*. Keith B. Richburg traveled throughout Africa as a *Washington Post* bureau chief and reflects on the complexities and corruption of that continent in the compelling memoir *Out Of America: A Black Man Confronts Africa*. Readers wishing to better understand Africa may consider the novels of that continent's native writers, like Chinua Achebe's classic *Things Fall Apart* and the more recent *Say You're One of Them* by Uwem Akpan, a collection of five stories set in war-torn Africa and told largely from the perspective of children. *Native Stranger* can be compared with Ekow Eshun's memoir of returning to his native Ghana from England, *Black Gold to the Sun* (annotated in this chapter). Another African American man who writes provocatively on issues of race and community is Nathan McCall, and readers who enjoyed *Native Stranger* may want to consider his nonfiction memoir, *Makes Me Wanna Holler: A Young Black Man in America*, or his novel, *Them*, which explores the dynamics of race in a downtown Atlanta neighborhood.

Kull, Robert

Solitude: Seeking Wisdom in Extremes: A Year Alone in the Patagonia Wilderness. Novato, CA: New World Library, 2008. 355 pp. ISBN: 9781577316329

Years after Kull lost his leg in a motorcycle accident, he traveled to Patagonia to live alone for a year and study the effects of long-term solitude on the body and the mind as well as explore the spiritual questions that had plagued him for his entire life. While his studies were tied to his Ph.D. dissertation and intended to be "purely secular," his journey soon became one of personal growth and enlightenment, which Kull came to see as an ongoing process and not an end state. The book intersperses his journal entries with explorations and observations of the often-intense forces of nature around him. Kull is something of a tortured soul, and while some readers may be put off by what they perceive as narcissism and self-indulgence, others will admire his honesty in showing the bad with the good.

Subjects: Self-Discovery; Solitude; Solo Travelers; Spirituality

Places: Chile

Now Try: Sara Maitland explores solitude, from a 40-day retreat on the Isle of Skye to the silence of the Sinai desert, in *A Book of Silence.* Gregory Couch shares his own physical and spiritual struggles as he climbs various peaks in Patagonia in *Enduring Patagonia.* More philosophical, less travel-oriented books about solitude include Anthony Storr's *Solitude: A Return to the Self,* which includes his analysis of historical figures such as Newton, Kafka, and Beatrix Potter, and Philip Koch's *Solitude: A Philosophical Encounter,* which is based on that writer's understanding of thinkers from Plato and Jesus to Proust and Tillich. Jim Knipfel doesn't write about solitude but he does tackle spirituality in what the book jacket calls an "anti-spirituality spiritual manifesto," *Ruining It For Everybody,* which opens with the line, "Whenever I hear the word 'spiritual,' I reach for my revolver." Knipfel also writes with black humor about going blind and being clinically depressed in *Slackjaw: A Memoir* as well as about his six-month stay in a mental institution in Minneapolis in *Quitting the Nairobi Trio.*

McAlpine, Ken

Off-Season: Discovering America on Winter's Shore. New York: Three Rivers Press, 2004. 290 pp. ISBN: 9781400049738

Freelance writer McAlpine spent a winter driving the east coast of the United States from Key West, Florida, to Lubec, Maine, in search of tales of life in small coastal towns. He talked to fishermen on Tangier Island, Virginia, watched summer homeowners closing up their homes on Ocracoke Island, North Carolina, surfed the nearly frozen ocean in Rhode Island, and spent the night in a ditch in Maine. His vivid descriptions of the people he met along the way are fascinating, but what began as a trip based on McAlpine's interest in the colorful locals who live in these towns soon shifted to a celebration of isolated beaches and deserted inlets as the author discovered that what he was really seeking was the sense of inner peace that came to him sitting alone with the ocean.

Subjects: Oceans; Self-Discovery; Small Town Life; Solitude; Solo Travelers

Places: Connecticut; Florida; Georgia; Massachusetts; Maine; New Jersey; New York; North Carolina; Rhode Island; South Carolina; Virginia

Now Try: McAlpine is also the author of *Islands Apart: A Year on the Edge of Civilization*, in which he travels alone through Channel Islands National Park in California in order to get away from his fast-paced life and just reflect. Gunnar Hansen traveled 2,700 miles along the barrier islands of the United States, from the border with Mexico to North Carolina's Outer Banks, and describes how fragile those islands are in *Islands at the Edge of Time: A Journey To America's Barrier Islands*. Following the 9/11 attack on the World Trade Center, which was across the street from her apartment, Gwendolyn Bounds got away from it all by moving to a small town north of New York City and joining the regulars at a small Irish bar there, a journey she recounts in *Little Chapel on the River: A Pub, a Town and the Search for What Matters Most*.

Minatoya, Lydia

Talking to High Monks in the Snow: An Asian American Odyssey. New York: HarperCollins, 1992. 269 pp. ISBN: 9780060168094

When Minatoya, a second-generation Japanese American, lost her university job in Boston, she traveled to Japan to visit her mother's home village. Through this and subsequent trips (to teach in Okinawa and China and to live in Nepal), she came to terms with her cultural identity and accepted both her Asian heritage and her American spirit. Her struggles with traditional Japanese values and American cultural principles are told in beautiful, lyrical writing and intermingled with stories of growing up in a predominantly Caucasian neighborhood in upstate New York; stories of her mother's family, still divided by a shameful divorce; and stories of her parents' experience in a relocation camp during the war. *Talking to High Monks in the Snow* artfully portrays the passion and intensity of Minatoya's search for a cultural identity.

Subjects: Culture Clash; Divorce; Family Relationships; Friendships; Immigration; Memoirs; Self-Discovery

Places: China; Japan; Nepal

Awards: ALA Notable Book, 1993

Now Try: Minatoya's acclaimed novel, *The Strangeness of Beauty*, further explores the lives of women who are both Japanese and American and who learn to extract the best of both worlds. Garrett Kaoru Hongo's *Volcano: A Memoir of Hawai'i* is a beautiful, lush memoir of growing up in the Hawaiian village of Volcano and living in California in the early 1950s. David Guterson's novel, *Snow Falling on Cedars*, also explores the experiences of Japanese residents in the United States during and after World War II. Bruce Feiler (whose *Walking the Bible* is annotated in this chapter) provides the opposite point of view, that of an American exchange teacher at a Japanese high school near Tokyo, in *Learning to Bow: Inside the Heart of Japan*.

Paterniti, Michael

Driving Mr. Albert: A Trip Across America with Einstein's Brain. New York: Dial Press, 2000. 211 pp. ISBN: 9780385333009

Paterniti's story of driving cross-country to take Einstein's brain to the great physicist's granddaughter works on several levels. It is part history, as Paterniti recounts the story of Dr. Thomas Harvey (who accompanied him on the trip) performing the autopsy on Einstein in 1955 and then removing and keeping the brain as a souvenir at his home. It is part road trio, as the pair visit, among others, writer William Burroughs (a former neighbor of Harvey), the Los Alamos site of the Manhattan Project, and various tourist traps. But the book is also about Paterniti's journey of self-discovery, as he dealt with his feelings for his girlfriend Sara on the trip, thinking about what she meant to him and what their future might be like. *Driving Mr. Albert* is a whimsical and somewhat surreal book that will appeal to readers who enjoy quirky, disjointed tales.

Subjects: Einstein, Albert; Investigative Stories; Physics; Quick Reads; Self-Discovery

Places: California; Kansas; Maine; New Jersey; New Mexico

Awards: *New York Times* Notable Book, 2000

Now Try: In the 1920s and early 1930s, Einstein himself traveled the world and kept diaries in which he recorded his impressions of people and places as well as his thoughts on a wide range of topics; physicist Josef Eisinger provides a summary of these diaries in the delightful *Einstein on the Road*. Ralph Leighton recounts the plans that physicist Richard Feynman made to visit the former country of Tannu-Tuva in the enjoyable *Tuva or Bust! Richard Feynman's Last Journey*; Feynman's personal quirkiness is as good as anything found in *Driving Mr. Albert*. Readers who appreciate the macabre aspect of *Driving Mr. Albert* may find Tilman Spengler's first novel, *Lenin's Brain*, and Ilya Zbarsky's *Lenin's Embalmers* of interest; Spengler's protagonist travels throughout Europe searching for money for his research into locating the brain cells responsible for genius, and Zbarsky's tale of the ultimate fate of Lenin's body is told against the backdrop of Russian history.

Raban, Jonathan

Passage to Juneau: A Sea and Its Meanings. New York: Pantheon Books, 1999. 435 pp. ISBN: 9780679442622

Raban describes his 1,000-mile solo voyage on a 35-foot ketch from his home in Seattle along the Inside Passage between Vancouver Island and the Canadian mainland, into the open water of Queen Charlotte Sound, and back into the "scribble of islands" at Alaska's southern tip. The book is, in Raban's words, a meditation "on the sea, at sea," an engaging, well-informed contemplation of history (including the 18th-century voyage of Captain George Vancouver and his encounters with the seagoing natives who lived along the coast), culture (from Wordsworth to Kwakiutl Indian art), and the difficult passages of his own life (his sadness about his father, who is dying of cancer, and the problems that he sees in his marriage). (In 2011, the *Guardian* listed *Passage to Juneau* as one of the 100 greatest nonfiction titles of all time.)

Subjects: Exploration; Family Relationships; Sailing; Self-Discovery; Solo Travelers

Places: Alaska; British Columbia; Seattle

Awards: ALA Notable Book, 2000

Series: *Vintage Departures*

Now Try: Two of Raban's other travel narrative (*Coasting: A Private Voyage*, about his 2,000-mile solo voyage around Britain, and *Old Glory: A Voyage Down the Mississippi*, about his trip down that great river) also involve travel on the water; both are annotated in this book. Elsie Hulsizer and her husband spent three summers sailing the southeastern Alaskan coast, its fjords and glaciers; she writes about the experience in *Glaciers, Bears and Totems: Sailing in Search of the Real Southeast Alaska*. Jonathan Waterman describes a more northerly journey, a series of solo journeys that he took across the Arctic through Canada's northern islands, in *Arctic Crossing: A Journey Through the Northwest Passage and Inuit Culture*.

Rogers, Susan Fox

Solo: On Her Own Adventure. Seattle, WA: Seal Press, 1996. 270 pp. ISBN: 9781878067746

Rogers provides 23 stories of women traveling alone, describing adventures as varied as simply camping overnight, hiking in the Adirondacks, swimming with dolphins in California, kayaking in Alaska, trekking in Nepal, and spending a year bicycling around New Zealand. Because the women travel alone, their narratives tend to focus on the internal journey as they attempt to push beyond societal norms and discover deeper truths about themselves. *Solo* is an empowering collection of tales about women who have found their inner strength through solo travel.

Subjects: Adventure; Essays; Kayaking; Self-Discovery; Solitude; Solo Travelers; Women Travelers

Places: Alaska; California; Nepal; New York; New Zealand

Now Try: Rogers has also written *Going Alone: Women's Adventures in the Wild*, another collection of inspiring stories about women who find contentment in traveling alone. *Go Your Own Way: Women Travel the World Solo*, edited by Faith Conlon, Ingrid Emerick, and Christina Henry de Tessan, is a series of essays about women traveling the world alone. Anne LaBastille's *Woodswoman: Living Alone in the Adirondack Wilderness* is a classic story of one woman's life alone in the remote Adirondack North Country.

Schooler, Lynn

Walking Home: A Traveler in the Alaskan Wilderness, a Journey into the Human Heart. New York: Bloomsbury, 2010. 262 pp. ISBN: 9781596916739

Schooler (whose book *The Blue Bear: A True Story of Friendship, Tragedy, and Survival in the Alaskan Wilderness* is annotated in the chapter on "A Sense of Place")

dealt with his sense of growing older and his failing marriage by traveling alone by boat across the Gulf of Alaska and then by foot along the coastline. He faced terrible weather, swollen rivers, and hostile grizzly bears as he sought solace and escape in nature. His striking descriptions of nature are mixed with the history of the area, the mythology of the local Tlingit, and his own exploration of the questions that had led him to initiate this journey. The book shares the lessons he learned about life's trials and how these are best endured with the help and community of others and does so in an engrossing, beautifully written manner.

Subjects: Animals; Memoirs; Self-Discovery; Solitude; Solo Travelers; Spouses; Walking

Places: Alaska

Now Try: Erin McKittrick and her husband hiked, skied, and paddled 4,000 miles from Seattle to Alaska's Aleutian Islands; she describes their encounters with rough weather, wild animals, and their own internal anxieties in *A Long Trek Home: 4,000 Miles by Boot, Raft and Ski*. Guy Grieve left a job he hated to live in a remote area of Alaska, far from the nearest human being; he writes of the experience, which included building a log cabin from scratch, in *Call of the Wild: My Escape to Alaska*. Seth Kantner was born in Alaska, and so his book *Shopping for Porcupine: A Life in Arctic Alaska* is more memoir than travel narrative; nevertheless, his tales of hunting caribou and moose and his respect for both the wilderness and the Eskimo traditions provide a strong evocation of place.

Steinbach, Alice

Without Reservations: The Travels of an Independent Woman. New York: Random House, 2000. 278 pp. ISBN: 9780375501883

Pulitzer Prize winner Steinbach took a sabbatical from her job as a *Baltimore Sun* columnist to travel in Europe and rediscover herself. She hoped to seek adventure and independence and to find her core after a lifetime of being defined by her relationships with others: mother, friend, and writer about the lives of other people. She rented a small flat in Paris and later traveled to England, Scotland, and Italy, and eventually discovered that, in spite of her stated desire for independence, what she continually sought out were friendships and human contact. Steinbach, as one might expect, writes with the discerning eye and clean prose of a journalist, and while she reveals her inner thoughts and feelings, she never descends into self-obsession or whining.

Subjects: Friendships; Self-Discovery; Solitude; Women Travelers

Places: England; France; Italy; London; Milan; Oxford; Paris; Rome; Scotland; Venice

Now Try: Steinbach had so much fun on her European trip that she quit her job with the *Baltimore Sun* and decided to travel the world and educate herself, taking cooking classes in Paris and art classes in Kyoto, among others;

she recounts her journeys in *Educating Alice: Adventures of a Curious Woman.* Elisabeth Eaves traveled five continents to find the sense of home she never had as a child; her journeys, which include such exotic locations as Cairo, Papua New Guinea, and Yemen, are described in *Wanderlust: A Love Affair with Five Continents.* Janet Flanner, whose essays from Paris helped inspire Steinbach's trip, served as the Paris correspondent for *The New Yorker* from 1925 through 1975; those influential earlier essays have been published as *Paris Was Yesterday, 1925–1939* and *Paris Journal, 1944–1955.* Marilyn Brant's novel, *A Summer in Europe,* concerns another woman who travels to Europe to rediscover herself; in the case of Brant's heroine, the decision of her boyfriend to postpone their engagement and her aunt's invitation to join her on a summer trip to Europe are the motivations.

Walton, Anthony

Mississippi: An American Journey. New York: Knopf, 1996. 279 pp. ISBN: 9780679446002

At age 30, Walton, an African American poet and writer whose parents left Mississippi to raise a family in a middle-class suburb of Chicago, became aware of the racism he was confronting in New York City and began to question his identity and heritage. "If I was going to have to live out the fate of being black and American," he concluded, "I felt I needed to know what that meant. And that meant Mississippi." Walton's return to his parents' home state to find his roots is chronicled in this book, which covers his travels from the Natchez Trace to the cotton fields of the delta region. Walton writes in an easy, conversational style and weaves stories of his family with those of slaves, Confederate generals, civil rights martyrs, and racist demagogues to produce a moving and insightful portrait of America's racial dilemma as seen in a single state.

Subjects: African Americans; American History; American South; Memoirs; Race Relations; Self-Discovery; Slavery

Places: Chicago; Mississippi; New York City

Series: *Vintage Departures*

Now Try: Another African American man, Eddy Harris, shares his thoughts on racial issues while traveling down the Mississippi River by canoe in *Mississippi Solo: A River Quest.* John Howard Griffin's classic *Black Like Me* is a travel narrative of sorts, in which a white man darkens his skin and pretends to be a black man as he travels through Mississippi and other states of the American South. In 1997, Gary Younge, a black British journalist, retraced the route of the 1960s Freedom Riders through the American South; he shares his unique observations in *No Place Like Home: A Black Briton's Journey through the American South.* Kathryn Stockett's bestseller, *The Help,* depicts race relations and the early civil rights movement in 1960s Mississippi through the lives of well-to-do white families and their African American maids. Another author who writes about race and family relationships is Edward Ball, whose books include *Slaves in the Family* (which won a National Book Award), the story of his search for the descendants of the people enslaved by his family in the antebellum south, and *Peninsula of Lies,* the story of an early white transsexual and her marriage to a young African American mechanic. Paul Hendrickson's *Sons of Mississippi: A Story of Race and Its Legacy* tells of the South and segregation through the stories of several white men who sought to keep James Meredith from attending the University of Mississippi in 1962.

"The Past Is a Foreign Country"

The travelers in the titles in this category all travel to their pasts, either to the countries in which they were born (for example, Edwidge Danticat's *After the Dance: A Walk Through Carnival in Jacmel, Haiti* or Eva Hoffman's *Exit into History: A Journey Through The New Eastern Europe*) or the areas in which they grew up (Frank Conroy's *Time and Tide: A Walk through Nantucket*) or the countries of their ancestors (Louise Erdrich's *Books and Islands in Ojibwe Country: Traveling Through the Land of my Ancestors* or Ted Simon's *The Gypsy in Me: From Germany to Romania in Search of Youth, Truth and Dad*).

In some cases, the journey helps the traveler make peace with her native land, as in Kapka Kassabova's *Street Without a Name: Childhood and Other Misadventures in Bulgaria*; in other cases, as in Ekow Eshun's *Black Gold of the Sun: Searching for Home in Africa and Beyond*, there is no resolution with the past. The stories may be told with a sense of nostalgia and loss, as in Frank Conroy's *Time and Tide: A Walk through Nantucket*, or with a sense of horror at the country's deterioration, as in Peter Godwin's *When a Crocodile Eats the Sun: A Memoir of Africa*, or even with an appreciation for the beauty of the land and its people, as in Teri Maggio's *The Stone Boudoir: Travels Through the Hidden Villages of Sicily*.

Though the elements of healing or self-discovery may not be as strong in these titles as in those of the previous categories in this chapter, these titles are still very personal, given the connections between traveler and destination, and will suit readers who like the appeal of character. Because the destination plays a strong role, though, the appeal of frame is also important in these titles.

Both memoirs and novels in which the main character returns to the country in which she was either born or brought up or the country of the traveler's ancestors may appeal to readers who enjoy the titles in this category. These include memoirs such as Rian Malan's *My Traitor's Heart: A South African Exile Returns to Face His Country, His Tribe, and His Conscience* or Carolyn Jourdan's *Heart in the Right Place*, as well as novels like Jonathan Safran Foer's *Everything Is Illuminated*, in which a young American Jew travels to Ukraine in search of the woman who saved his grandfather's life during World War II.

Brown, Andrew

Fishing in Utopia: Sweden and the Future that Disappeared. London: Granta Books, 2008. 263 pp. ISBN: 9781847080813

Brown spent part of his childhood in Sweden in the 1960s, when the country was known for being affluent and egalitarian. In the 1970s, he returned, married a Swedish woman, and got a job there, working first in a timber mill and then as a journalist. In the 1980s, Brown and his wife divorced, and he left the country. He returned 20 years later and found a very different Sweden, one whose decline he examines while recalling the path of his own life and his love of fishing. Brown's observations can be quite perceptive, especially when he discusses the life of assassinated Swedish Prime Minister Olaf Palme or when he describes the older Swedes he met and their traditional ways of life.

Subjects: Divorce; Memoirs; Politics; Society

Places: Sweden

Awards: Dolman Best Travel Book Award, Shortlist, 2009; Orwell Prize, 2009

Now Try: A particularly delightful book about the traditions and customs of Sweden, many of which are referred to in *Fishing in Utopia*, is Lily Lorenzen's *Of Swedish Ways*. Contemporary Swedish society and its perceived ills are the backdrop of several mystery series, like the police procedurals of Kjell Eriksson, whose main figure, Ann Lindell, takes time off from maternity leave to uncover a killer in *The Princess of Burundi*, the first book in the series. For readers willing to go outside the travel narrative genre, Brown is the author of two well-regarded popular science books. *Darwin Wars: The Scientific Battle for the Soul of Man* examines the two major camps of 20th-century post-Darwinian thought: those like Richard Dawkins and Steven Pinker, who have expanded Darwin's ideas into other areas, including psychology and linguistics; and those like Stephen Jay Gould, who are skeptical about such ideas. *In the Beginning Was the Worm: Finding the Secrets of Life in a Tiny Hermaphrodite* tells the story of three scientists whose research on a simple worm led to the sequencing of the human genome and Nobel Prizes for the three men.

Bryson, Bill

I'm a Stranger Here Myself: Notes on Returning to America After 20 Years Away. New York: Broadway Books, 1999. 288 pp. ISBN: 9780767903813

Humorist Bryson is a native-born American who lived in England for 20 years before returning to the states and writing a collection of articles on American life for London's *Daily Mail* magazine. Bryson contrasts contemporary American culture with contemporary British culture, as well as 1995 American culture with the 1975 culture that Bryson last saw before moving to England. Bryson has a fine eye, and his thoughts about the American tendency to drive from shop to shop even when the shops are within walking distance or the pervasive American fear of being sued or the contrast between the U.S. postal service and its counterpart in England are almost always on target. Bryson is, of course, funny, and there are a number of laugh-out-loud passages, but he also waxes nostalgic for the America he left many years ago.

Subjects: Essays; Humor; Pop Culture

Places: New Hampshire

Now Try: Readers who enjoy Bryson's reminiscences about the America that he left will doubtless enjoy his marvelously funny memoir of growing up in 1950s America, *The Life and Times of the Thunderbolt Kid: A Memoir*. Like Bryson, American Michael

Harling married a British woman and moved to England; his observations on life in his newly adopted country have been captured on his blog (http://postcardsfromacrossthepond.com/) as well as two books: *Postcards from Across The Pond* and *More Postcards from Across the Pond*. E. B. White's *Here Is New York* is "a love letter to the city," written about the city of his youth some years after White had moved to Maine. Readers looking for a foreigner's perspective on the United States may be interested in Beppe Severgnini's *Ciao, America!: An Italian Discovers the U.S.*, in which the Italian newspaper columnist lives in Washington, DC, and comments on everything from Spam to La-Z-Boys.

Conroy, Frank

Time and Tide: A Walk through Nantucket. New York: Crown Publishers, 2004. 141pp. ISBN: 9781400046599

Conroy, who served as the director of the influential Iowa Writers' Workshop from 1987 until his death in 2005, takes a walk through his own memories of Nantucket, which he first visited as a three-year-old boy. His reminiscences include taking a summer job there in 1955 with college friends, playing jazz piano in one of the island's bars, building a house on a small plot of land next to the ocean in the 1960s, and turning an old, failed bar into a thriving club. The book highlights both the changes that have taken place on the island itself as well as the changes that have taken place in the author's life; as Nantucket grew from an isolated island community to a summer home for the very wealthy, Conroy himself grew from a college student to a father through divorce and loneliness to new love with a woman he met on Nantucket. The narrative is told in a series of short essays and is beautifully written, nostalgic, and tinged with sadness and a sense of loss.

Subjects: Divorce; Essays; Quick Reads

Places: Massachusetts; Nantucket

Series: *Crown Journeys*

Now Try: Michael Cunningham's *Land's End: A Walk through Provincetown* is another writer's distinctive look at a small Massachusetts town. Readers who enjoy Conroy's evocation of Nantucket may find novels set on the island appealing. These include Elin Hilderbrand's *Barefoot* and *Nantucket Nights*, Jane Green's *The Beach House*, Nancy Thayer's *Moon Shell Beach*, and Sena Jeter Naslund's *Ahab's Wife, or the Star Gazer*. Conroy himself was a well-regarded writer of both fiction and nonfiction, and readers may also enjoy his memoir *Stop-Time*, which tells of his childhood and early adulthood and which was nominated for the National Book Award in 1967.

Danticat, Edwidge

After the Dance: A Walk Through Carnival in Jacmel, Haiti. New York: Crown Journeys, 2002. 158 pp. ISBN: 9780609609088

Danticat was born in Haiti but emigrated to New York at age 12. In this short, delightful book, she writes about her return to Haiti to attend the annual carnival that her uncle, a Baptist minister, refused to let her attend as a child. During the week prior to the carnival, she walked around the seaside town of Jacmel, pondering the tragic island's history of dictators and invasions and meeting the performers and artists who use the carnival to re-create the legends of the Haitian people. During the carnival itself, she lost herself in the celebration of the crowd and the beauty of the island and its people.

Subjects: Folklore; Memoirs; Quick Reads; Walking

Category: The Beauty of the Place; Landscapes and People

Places: Haiti

Series: *Crown Journeys*

Now Try: Danticat is an award-winning fiction writer, and readers of *After the Dance* may also enjoy her collection of short stories, *Krik? Krak!* and her novel about the 1937 massacre of Haitians in the Dominican Republic, *The Farming of the Bones*, as well as the memoir of her Haitian family, *Brother, I'm Dying*. Zora Neale Hurston's *Tell My Horse: Voodoo and Life in Haiti and Jamaica* is the classic Haitian travelogue, with its firsthand account of voodoo practices in the 1930s. Tracy Kidder's *Mountains Beyond Mountains* is not a travel narrative, but its story of an American physician who has dedicated his life to helping the poor in Haiti is inspiring and deserves to be read by anyone who cares about the people of that nation. A recent history of Haiti is Laurent Dubois's *Haiti: The Aftershocks of History*, which argues that many of Haiti's problems are caused or exacerbated by outsiders, including the United States.

Deb, Siddhartha

The Beautiful and the Damned. New York: Faber and Faber, 2011. 253 pp. ISBN: 9780865478626

Novelist Deb was born and raised in small towns in northeastern India. In 2004, six years after he left home, he returned to his native land to work undercover at a call center in Delhi for *The Guardian*. His experiences there led him to travel across the Indian subcontinent to examine the "new" India of entrepreneurs and the traditional India of farmers and factory workers. Deb tells India's story in five tautly written narratives that focus on rich characters: a management guru who runs a business school for those who can't afford state-run schools, a woman with a graduate degree in botany who defers her dreams in order to work in a fancy restaurant, and a farmer whose village is plagued with suicides. *The Beautiful and the Damned* is a splendid, sensitive overview of India as it deals with globalization.

Subjects: Globalization; Investigative Stories; Rural Life; Society; Urban Life

Places: India

Now Try: Deb's first novel, *The Point of Return*, is semi-autobiographical in nature and is set in a fictional hill-station that closely resembles the northeastern Indian towns in which he grew up. His second novel, *Surface*, is also set in northeast India and concerns a disillusioned Sikh journalist. *The Beautiful and the Damned* has been compared favorably to V. S. Naipaul's books on India, including *An Area of Darkness*, *India: A Wounded Civilization*, and *India: A Million Mutinies Now*, the last of which is annotated in this chapter. Deb's analysis of Indian culture has also been compared with that of Adrian Nicole LeBlanc's *Random Family: Love, Drugs, Trouble, and Coming of Age in the Bronx*, even though LeBlanc's compelling book about two Latino women from the Bronx takes place in a very different place. Geoff Ryman's fascinating near-future science fiction novel, *Air: Or, Have Not Have*, examines the intersection between new technologies and old cultures in a fictional region in western China.

Erdrich, Louise

Books and Islands in Ojibwe Country: Traveling Through the Land of my Ancestors. Washington, DC: National Geographic, 2003. 143 pp. ISBN: 9780792253730

Award-winning writer Erdrich journeyed with her 18-month-old daughter and the girl's father, who is a traditional healer and guide, to the islands of her ancestors in southern Ontario to visit the sacred rock paintings or *atisikan* that her people have worshipped for centuries. Erdrich's intimate and powerful account of the pilgrimage includes many reflections on her love of books and the links between her life as a writer and the tradition of storytelling that has been passed down by the Ojibwe. She contemplates many aspects of Ojibwe language, culture, and traditions and sets these against her own family and contemporary life. *Books and Islands in Ojibwe Country* is a short but well-written evocation of the wisdom of her ancestors.

Subjects: American Indians; Books and Reading; Lakes; Mothers and Daughters; Quick Reads; Self-Discovery

Places: Minnesota; Ontario

Series: *National Geographic Directions*

Now Try: Erdrich is a well-regarded author whose novels include *Love Medicine*, which tells the stories of several families living on an Ojibwe reservation in North Dakota, and *The Beet Queen*, which focuses on the German American community living near that reservation. Another writer, Ariel Dorfman, explores the Atacama Desert of his native Chile in *Desert Memories: Journeys Through the Chilean North*; he uses the trip to explore both the origins of modern Chile and his wife's European ancestors. Readers interested in the Ojibwe tribe should consider Ignatia Broker's *Night Flying Woman: An Ojibway Narrative*, which tells the story of her great-great-grandmother, who witnessed enormous changes and losses for her people.

Eshun, Ekow

Black Gold of the Sun: Searching for Home in Africa and Beyond. New York: Pantheon Books, 2006 [2005]. 229 pp. ISBN: 9780375424182

1 2 3 4 5 6 7

Eshun is an African British writer and artistic director who returned to his native Ghana to help answer the question of where he came from. He was shocked to discover that one of his ancestors was a slave trader, and his trip failed to bring him the resolution that he set out to find. Nevertheless, the trip also led him to realize that his past need not determine the path of his life. Eshun also reflects on his childhood in London, including the difficulties that arose after his father's loss of a job as a result of a military coup in Ghana, and on black figures who also visited Africa in search of their identities, such as W.E.B. Du Bois and Richard Wright. Eshun's journey deals with a number of deep questions about identity and race and is both beautifully written and intellectually stimulating.

Subjects: African History; Colonialism; Memoirs; Quick Reads; Self-Discovery; Slavery

Places: Africa; Ghana; London

Now Try: Sadiya Hartman's *Lose Your Mother: A Journey Along the Atlantic Slave Route* (annotated in the "Quests" chapter of this book) recounts the author's travels on the route taken by captured slaves from Ghana to the Atlantic coast and is as rewarding as it is intense. Eddy Harris's *Native Stranger* (annotated in this chapter) also tells of a black man's journey to Africa to better understand his identity. *A Passage to Africa* by BBC correspondent George Alagiah tells a story that is somewhat the opposite of Eshun's; Alagiah and his parents emigrated from Sri Lanka to Ghana when he was five years old, and the book looks at his experiences growing up as well as the struggles of African nations as they emerged from colonialism.

Giridharadas, Anand

India Calling: An Intimate Portrait of a Nation's Remaking. New York: Times Books/Henry Holt and Co., 2011. 273 pp. ISBN: 9780805091779

Anand Giridharadas was born in the United States of Indian parents and grew up hearing family stories, mixing with Indian expatriates, and visiting his grandparents in India on several occasions. He eventually returned to India, working first for an American management-consulting firm and then as a reporter for the *New York Times/International Herald Tribune*. The jobs allowed him to travel through rural India, where he examined individuals and families living there in order to gain insight on the impact of change on tradition in India. Giridharadas does an especially good job of sharing anecdotes and drawing lessons from them about India's attempts to come to terms with the modern world.

Subjects: Culture Clash; Family Relationships; Investigative Stories; Society

Places: India; Mumbai

Now Try: Several titles have treated the subject of India's struggles between modernity and tradition. These include William Dalrymple's *The Age of Kali: Indian Travels and Encounters*, which is based on his 10 years living and traveling in India and is more pessimistic about the country's chances; he sees India slipping into the age of Kali, "an epoch of strife, corruption, darkness, and disintegration." Edward Luce's *In Spite of the Gods: The Rise of Modern India* also contrasts the great strides that India has made in technology with the poverty and illiteracy with which the country still struggles. Salman Rushdie's novel *Midnight's Children* tells an older story of India, one that takes

1 2 3 4 5 6 7

place during the transition from a British colony to independence and partition in 1947; *Midnight's Children* won the 1981 Booker Prize and was named the best all-time Booker Prize winner in both 1993 and 2008.

Godwin, Peter

When a Crocodile Eats the Sun: A Memoir of Africa. New York: Little, Brown and Co., 2007 [2006]. 344 pp. ISBN: 9780316158947

Godwin returned to his native Zimbabwe when his father suffered a heart attack in 1996, and as he watched his father slowly die, he also watched the deterioration of Zimbabwe under the brutal rule of Robert Mugabe. Godwin's father also revealed a secret (that he was a Polish Jew whose mother and sister had died in the Holocaust) and Godwin draws parallels between being white in Mugabe's Zimbabwe and being Jewish in Nazi Germany. Godwin's deeply personal book is powerful and moving on several levels.

Subjects: African Americans; Authors; Family Relationships; Family Secrets; Fathers and Sons; Jews and Judaism; Multicultural; Race Issues

Places: Africa; Zimbabwe

Awards: ALA Notable Book, 2008

Now Try: Godwin's *Mukiwa: A White Boy in Africa* is his memoir of growing up in Rhodesia during the end of white rule and the transition to black rule; the book won the 1997 Orwell Prize, Britain's most prestigious prize for political writing. Wendy Kahn returned to Zimbabwe, where she had grown up, following the death of her sister there and confronted a past she had tried to ignore; her personal journey is outlined in *Casting with a Fragile Thread: A Story of Sisters and Africa*. Readers interested in Robert Mugabe, the dictatorial ruler of Zimbabwe, might start with Martin Meredith's excellent *Mugabe: Power, Plunder, and the Struggle for Zimbabwe's Future*. Other memoirs about parents and their secrets are *One Drop: My Father's Hidden Life* by Bliss Broyard, whose father was an African American literary critic who passed for a white man, and *The Good Daughter: A Memoir of My Mother's Hidden Life* by Jasmin Darznik, whose Iranian mother had married at 13 and then fled an abusive husband, leaving a daughter behind. Helene Cooper's spectacular memoir, *The House at Sugar Beach: In Search of a Lost African Childhood*, might also appeal; it is set in Liberia and tells how Cooper lived there until a coup drove her, her mother, and her sister to America.

Hoffman, Eva

Exit into History: A Journey Through The New Eastern Europe. New York: Viking, 1993. 410 pp. ISBN: 9780670836499

Hoffman was born in Poland and emigrated to Canada when she was 13. In *Exit into History*, she returned to Poland and traveled to several other countries in Eastern Europe, providing readers with a firsthand account of these nations as they emerged from Soviet rule. The book is filled with interviews with fascinating people: the co-editor of one of Poland's newspapers, who told of hiding in the underground during the Communist years; a Czech woman whose father and husband were prominent activists against the Soviets; and the abandoned children in a Romanian orphanage. The book may strike some readers as uneven in its treatment of the various countries and their people; Hoffman is clearly more comfortable in her native Poland than in Romania and Hungary, for example, and seems less understanding of the latter nations. Nevertheless, her observations are generally sharp, and the individuals she spoke with are captivating.

Subjects: 1990s; Communism; European History; Investigative Stories

Places: Bulgaria; Czech Republic; Hungary; Poland; Romania; Slovakia

Now Try: Hoffman has written an insightful memoir of her life growing up in Canada, *Lost in Translation*. Andrew Nagorski examines many of the same Eastern European nations and individuals as does Hoffman's *Exit into History* in his invigorating *Birth of Freedom: Shaping Lives and Societies in the New Easter Euro*. Another shrewd commentator on the rise of these Eastern European countries in the 1990s is Timothy Garton Ash, whose book *History of the Present: Essays, Sketches, and Dispatches from Europe in the 1990s* is a collection of essays that cover this critical time.

Kapur, Akash

India Becoming: A Portrait of Life in Modern India. New York: Riverhead Books, 2012. 304 pp. ISBN: 9781594488191

Kapur, a journalist who was born in India and educated in the United States, returned to southern India in 2003. At first, he saw the economic growth there as exciting and positive, but he grew to understand that progress also brought problems and disruptions. To better understand these transformations, Kapur portrays the lives of several individuals, including the member of a powerful land-owning family whose importance diminished as the region moved away from an agricultural economy, a well-educated woman who moved to Bangalore to take advantage of better schools for her children and to work as a professional, and a man who was born in extreme poverty as a member of the untouchable class but who became an independent businessman and rose to the middle class. Kapur's book is a fascinating account of the new India and puts a human face on the country's rapid modernization.

Subjects: Culture Clash; Globalization; Modernization; Society

Places: India

Now Try: One reader said that Kapur's book reminded her of Siddhartha Deb's *The Beautiful and the Damned*, but "without the grit"; Deb's overview of Indian and its attempts to deal with globalization is annotated in this chapter. One of the individuals featured in *India Becoming* is a man born into the untouchable class who rose to the middle class; Narendra Jadhav's amazing *Untouchables: My Family's Triumphant Escape from India's Caste System* tells the story of her family's struggles to achieve equality. R.

K. Narayan's collection of short stories about southern India, *Malgudi Days*, is set in the same part of India as Kapur's book and involves many of the same kinds of people that he interviewed.

Kassabova, Kapka

Street Without a Name: Childhood and Other Misadventures in Bulgaria. New York: Skyhorse Publishers, 2009. 337 pp. ISBN: 9781602396456

Kassabova was born in Bulgaria and grew up there during the last 15 years of Communist rule. She and her family moved shortly after the collapse of the Berlin Wall and lived in Britain, New Zealand, and Argentina, among other places, before she decided to return to Bulgaria, following its admission into the European Union. *Street Without a Name* is both a memoir of her dreary childhood in Bulgaria and her return to visit relatives and make a bit of peace with her native country. She found a country massively changed by the events of the late 1980s and attempting to deal with gangsters, poverty, and its own ethnic and historical tensions.

Subjects: 1970s; Coming of Age; Communism; Government; Immigration; Memoirs; Women Travelers

Places: Bulgaria

Awards: Dolman Best Travel Book Award, Shortlist, 2009

Now Try: Cynthia Morrison Phoel, who served in Bulgaria in the Peace Corps, writes about the struggling citizens of the Bulgarian town of Old Mountain in her collection of stories and a novella, *Cold Snap: Bulgaria Stories*. Radka Yakimov's *Dreams and Shadows* is more memoir than travel narrative and tells of her childhood behind the Iron Curtain, her emigration to Canada with her husband's family, and her return to Bulgaria after the fall of Communism. Slavenka Drakulic focuses on the seemingly mundane to reflect the great changes in Eastern Europe in her dazzling look at the post-Communist world, *Cafe Europa: Life After Communism*. Elena Gorkhova's memoir, *A Mountain of Crumbs*, about a strong-willed daughter and an authoritarian mother living in the Soviet Union of the 1960s, may also be recommended.

MacKinnon, J. B.

Dead Man in Paradise: Unraveling a Murder from a Time of Revolution. New York: New Press, 2007 [2005]. 261 pp. ISBN: 9781595581815

In 1965, during the Trujillo dictatorship in the Dominican Republic, journalist MacKinnon's uncle, a Catholic priest, and two policemen were killed under mysterious circumstances. Forty years after the apparent murder, MacKinnon traveled to that Caribbean nation to investigate the killings and to learn more about his uncle and the country in which he was killed. *Dead Man in Paradise* is both a travel narrative and a true-crime thriller, as MacKinnon explores the machismo culture that the former Trujillo followers maintain as well as the nature of Hispaniola, the island that the Dominican Republic shares with Haiti, and the often-violent history of relationships between those two neighbors. MacKinnon tells his haunting story with brilliance, passion, and a staggering eye for detail.

Subjects: American History; Investigative Stories; True Crime

Places: Dominican Republic

Awards: Charles Taylor Prize, 2006

Now Try: In Mark Arax's *In My Father's Name,* the author tries to track down the truth about his father's murder 20 years earlier in Fresno, California. Terri Jentz's *A Strange Piece of Paradise* also mixes travel writing with her quest to finally locate the man who attacked her and a friend while they were camping 15 years earlier. In Mischa Berlinski's first novel, *Fieldwork,* a reporter who moves to Thailand to be with his girlfriend tries to clear the name of an anthropologist wrongfully accused of murder. There are several good books about the Dominican Republic, the setting for *Dead Man in Paradise.* Michele Wucker begins her book about the relationships between the Dominican Republic and Haiti with a cockfight, an image that recurs throughout *Why the Cocks Fight: Dominicans, Haitians, and the Struggle for Hispaniola.* Julia Alvarez's haunting novel, *In the Time of the Butterflies,* takes place during the rise of Trujillo's dictatorship, while the last days of his ruthless regime are told from several viewpoints by Mario Vargas Llosa in his disturbing novel, *The Feast of the Goat.*

Maggio, Teri

The Stone Boudoir: Travels through the Hidden Villages of Sicily. Cambridge, MA: Perseus Pub., 2002. 246 pp. ISBN: 9780738208008

Over 15 years, Maggio traveled to Sicily to explore the land of her grandparents, who shared tales of the Sicilian mountain towns with her when she was a child. Her focus was on these small hill towns, from Polizzi Generosa, where Martin Scorsese's father was born, to Catania, which celebrates the feast of Sant'Agata, who was martyred by having her breasts cut off, to Santa Margherita, the town of her grandparents, which was destroyed in an earthquake in 1968. Maggio is curious, enthusiastic, and fascinated by the details of daily life, from the way Sicilian women hang out their wash to the placement of Sicilian kitchens on the top floor of the house. Her simply written prose brings to life the beautiful landscapes and generous residents of these tiny villages.

Subjects: Memoirs; Small Town Life; Women Travelers

Places: Sicily

Now Try: Maggio's *Mattanza* is a vivid account of the difficult lives of Sicilian fishermen and their epic hunts for bluefin tuna. Mary Taylor Simeti's *On Persephone's Island: A Sicilian Journal* (annotated in this book's chapter on "The Expatriate Life") tells the story of a year in the life of an American woman who married a Sicilian professor and divided her time between Palermo and a working farm. In *A House in Sicily,* Daphne Phelps tells about inheriting a villa in Sicily from her uncle and turning it into an inn.

Moaveni, Azadeh

Lipstick Jihad: A Memoir of Growing Up Iranian in America and American in Iran. New York: PublicAffairs, 2005. 249 pp. ISBN: 9781586481933

Moaveni grew up in California as the child of Iranian exiles, caught between her dreams of an Iran she had never seen and her life as a typical American girl. After she graduated from college, she moved to Iran to become a journalist and "to figure out [her] relationship" with Iran. *Lipstick Jihad* is as much about Moaveni's search for herself (her tense relationship with her mother, her failed romances) as it is about an Iran that seemed at first poised to loosen the grip of its religious leaders with the election of a moderate cleric as president. Nevertheless, the portrait that she does paint of Iran is one not usually seen: the next generation of young people, desperate for change. Moaveni's writing is beautiful, and her candor is impressive.

Subjects: Culture Clash; Journalism; Multicultural Issues; Women Travelers; Women's Studies

Places: Iran

Now Try: Moaveni's second book, *Honeymoon in Tehran: Two Years of Love and Danger in Iran,* tells of her return to Iran for *Time* magazine in 2005 to cover the election of Ahmadinejad, and her subsequent pregnancy and marriage; the book is annotated in "The Expatriate Life" chapter of this book. Like Moaveni, Firoozeh Dumas grew up in America as the child of Iranian parents; her humorous memoir of life in California is told in *Funny in Farsi: A Memoir of Growing Up Iranian in America.* A different kind of return to Iran is told by Terence Ward in *Searching for Hassan: An American Family's Journey Home to Iran;* Ward's family had lived in Iran in the 1960s and returned in 1998 to search for an old Iranian friend who had looked after the family in those earlier days. Marjane Satrapi's graphic memoirs of her life in Iran, *Persepolis: The Story of a Childhood* and *Persepolis 2: The Story of a Return,* are also highly regarded.

Naipaul, V. S.

India: A Million Mutinies Now. New York: Viking, 1991 [1990]. 521 pp. ISBN: 9780670837021

In the early 1960s and again in the mid-1970s, the Nobel Prize winning writer V. S. Naipaul visited India, the land of his parents, and wrote negative, controversial books about what he found there. This book is based on a 1988 trip to India, but here Naipaul is much less pessimistic than he had been in earlier works about the nation, believing that India is now "a country of a million little mutinies," where the yearning for freedom is allowing the people to break free from past traditions about caste. Naipaul interviewed a number of people (a former terrorist, devout Hindus and Muslims, politicians, people of all castes) and most of the book is told in the words of these individuals, largely without judgment on the part of the author.

Subjects: Investigative Stories

Categories: Return Trips

Places: India

Now Try: Naipaul's previous two visits to India resulted in *An Area of Darkness* and *India: A Wounded Civilization*, both of which are far darker and more disillusioned than is *India: A Million Mutinies Now*. Travel writer William Dalrymple's *The Age of Kali: Indian Travels and Encounters* is based on his 10 years living and traveling in India and is more pessimistic about the country's chances, like the earlier works of Naipaul; he sees India slipping into the age of Kali, "an epoch of strife, corruption, darkness, and disintegration." Aravind Adiga's Booker Prize-winning novel, *The White Tiger*, captures a similar sense of the "new India," told through the eyes of a taxi driver.

Palahniuk, Chuck

Fugitives and Refugees: A Walk in Portland, Oregon. New York: Crown Journeys, 2003. 175 pp. ISBN: 9781400047833

Novelist Palahniuk mixes elements of memoir and bizarre travel guide in this tribute to his adopted city. Chapters that discuss the best places to eat or to see ghosts are interspersed with what the author calls "postcards," autobiographical sketches that follow Palahniuk's time in Portland from the early 1980s. There are connections between some of the sites highlighted and Palahniuk's fiction (for example, the 3.5-acre mausoleum that was the setting for his second novel), and the writing is quirky but effective. Some readers may be offended by his chapters on sex clubs and other seedy sides of the city, but others will find a fascinating guide to the offbeat side of the city.

Subjects: Community Life; Humor; Essays; Memoirs; Quick Reads; Urban Life

Places: Portland, Oregon

Series: *Crown Journeys*

Now Try: In addition to his novels, Palahniuk also wrote *Stranger Than Fiction: True Stories*, a collection of essays that includes trips to the regional Olympic trials in Waterloo, Iowa, and a demolition derby in Linn, Washington. Laura O. Foster's *The Portland Stairs Book* is more guidebook than travel narrative, but its focus on the most interesting of Portland's nearly 200 public staircases is as quirky as *Fugitives and Refugees*. Jon Bell's *On Mount Hood: A Biography of Oregon's Perilous Peak* recounts the author's own trip around Oregon's most famous mountain as well as stories about others who have climbed the peak.

Pham, Andrew X.

Catfish and Mandala: A Two-Wheeled Voyage through the Landscape and Memory of Vietnam. New York: Farrar, Straus and Giroux, 1999. 344 pp. ISBN: 9780312267179

Born in Vietnam, Pham and his family came to California as "boat people" in the 1970s. After his sister committed suicide, Pham quit his job and began a bicycle trip through Mexico, the western United States, Japan, and eventually his homeland, Vietnam. The result is a powerfully written, vivid memoir and travel narrative that mixes several themes: his recollections as a refugee; his guilt over his sister's suicide; the stories of the Vietnamese people he meets; the poverty he encounters in his native land; and his feelings of being disconnected from both his revisited homeland and his adopted country. Pham, who was trained as an engineer but quit that profession to become a freelance writer, is a skillful writer, and even readers who are not particularly interested in his themes will likely be impressed by the richness of his prose.

Subjects: Bicycling; Culture Clash; Family Relationships; Immigration; Memoirs; Vietnam War

Places: California; Japan; Mexico; Vietnam

Awards: *New York Times* Notable Book, 1999

Now Try: Pham tells the story of his father's survival through three wars (World War II, the French-Indochina War, and the Vietnam War) in the haunting book, *The Eaves of Heaven: A Life in Three Wars*. Journalist Tom Bissell went with his father, an ex-Marine, as the latter retraced his tour of duty in Vietnam; Bissell mixes travel narrative with his father's memories of the conflict in *The Father of All Things: A Marine, His Son, and the Legacy of Vietnam*. Zoe Schramm-Evans takes a more optimistic view of Vietnam, which she sees as a nation on the brink of massive social and political changes, in her account of her journey from Ho Chi Minh City to Hanoi, *A Phoenix Rising: Impressions of Vietnam*. Nam Le, a Vietnamese-born Australian writer, has published a collection of short stories entitled *The Boat*, in which he explores characters who, as one reviewer put it, are "forced to grapple at the most fundamental level with who they are and what they want or believe"; the stories take place in locations as diverse as the slums of Colombia and the streets of Tehran.

Rogers, Douglas

The Last Resort: A Memoir of Zimbabwe. New York: Harmony Books, 2009. 309 pp. ISBN: 9780307407979

Rogers was born and raised in Zimbabwe and lived with his parents through that country's stressful transition to postcolonial independence. He grew up and left for the United States, but his parents stayed in Zimbabwe and ran a popular game farm and lodge. His parents' thriving business was endangered, however, around 2000, when the country's president, Robert Mugabe, began a program of land redistribution, and Rogers returned to his homeland to find the lodge serving as a refugee camp for displaced whites, a hang-out for illegal diamond dealers, and a marijuana farm. Rogers began to see his parents as somewhat heroic, and *The Last Resort* is a riveting mix of travel narrative, family memoir, and social commentary that is also, in places, wickedly funny.

Subjects: African History; Coming of Age; Family Relationships; Humor

Places: Africa; Zimbabwe

Now Try: Sekai Nzenza-Shand returned to her Zimbabwean home after many years in Australia and examined how AIDS and drought had led to a breakdown in native traditions in *Songs to an African Sunset: A Zimbabwean Story*. There are numerous memoirs about life in the British colony of Rhodesia and its transition to Zimbabwe. Peter Godwin's *Mukiwa: White Boy in Africa* tells the story of his childhood in that country and his return as a journalist covering the changeover to black rule, and his *When a Crocodile Eats the Sun* continues the story by detailing the country's collapse under Mugabe; the latter is annotated in the current section of this book. Alexandra Fuller's *Don't Let's Go to the Dogs Tonight* depicts a white African girl's coming of age during the Rhodesian civil war of the 1970s.

Shadid, Anthony

House of Stone: A Memoir of Home, Family, and a Lost Middle East. Boston: Houghton Mifflin Harcourt, 2012. 311 pp. ISBN: 9780547134666

Shadid, a Pulitzer Prize-winning journalist who died in 2012 while covering the civil war in Syria, returned to his great-grandfather's estate in southern Lebanon in 2011, to rebuild the house after an Israeli rocket had damaged it. *House of Stone* is about Shadid's efforts to restore the old home (complete with the usual dealings with contractors and local workers) as well as his reflections on his family history, the history and future of Lebanon and the Middle East, and the problems the individuals of this region are struggling to solve. Shadid writes movingly and nostalgically of his family while also expressing his frustrations and hope over the current state of affairs in the Middle East.

Subjects: Family Relationships; Memoirs; Middle Eastern History

Places: Lebanon

Now Try: Shadid is also the author of *Legacy Of The Prophet: Despots, Democrats, And The New Politics Of Islam*, which argues that a more democratic Islam is arising from what he sees as the last breaths of a dying Islamic extremism, and the later *Night Draws Near: Iraq's People in the Shadow of America's War*, examines the Hussein dictatorship and the American invasion of Iraq from the point of view of the Iraqi people themselves. Shadid also contributed text to Rania Matar's collection of black-and-white photographs from war-torn Lebanon, *Ordinary Lives*. Another nonfiction book about homes, homelands, and the Middle East is Sandy Tolan's *The Lemon Tree: An Arab, a Jew, and the Heart of the Middle East*.

Simon, Ted

The Gypsy in Me: From Germany to Romania in Search of Youth, Truth and Dad. New York: Random House, 1997. 318 pp. ISBN: 9780679441380

Simon's father, whom he never knew, was a Romania Jew and his mother was German. Following the death of his mother, Simon decided to travel 1,500 miles by foot between the two poles of his ancestry to better understand both his parents and the great changes being wrought in post-Soviet Europe. The book has some gloomy moments, particularly when Simon reflects on the individuals who feel a loss of the security and identity that they had enjoyed under Communism, but the story of finding his father's hometown and original birth record is particularly moving.

Subjects: Communism; European History; Walking

Places: Germany; Poland; Romania; Russia; Ukraine

Now Try: Simon also wrote *Jupiter's Travels: Four Years Around the World on a Triumph,* about his four-year, 78,000-mile journey by motorcycle through 45 countries in the 1970s, and *Dreaming of Jupiter,* in which he retraces that journey at the age of 69. William Blacker's *Along the Enchanted Way: A Story of Love and Life in Romania* recounts the 10 years the author spent in Romania as he watched the old way of life disappear under the wave of modernity; the book was shortlisted for the Dolman Best Travel Book Award in 2010. Romania is also the subject of Caroline Juler's *Searching for Sarmizegetusa: Journeys to the Heart of Rural Romania,* which discusses her travels into the rural areas of this eastern European country. Mikey Walsh's memoir, *Gypsy Boy: My Life in the Secret World of the Romany Gypsies,* describes his youth in a Gypsy community in a forthright, sometimes graphic, manner. The 1993 film, *Latcho Drom,* may also be of interest; it tells the story of a year in the life of the Romany people through their musicians and dancers.

Reflective Journeys

As noted in the introduction to this chapter, the emphasis on the titles of this chapter is the traveler. The current category, "Reflective Journeys," represents titles whose focus is on the reflections of the traveler. Each journey described in these titles provides the context in which the author reflects on issues that are larger than or transcend the specific journey or its destination.

For example, in *An Empire Wilderness: Travels into America's Future,* Robert D. Kaplan used his two trips to the American West, Mexico, and British Columbia as the stimulus for his often-apocalyptic speculations on the future of the United States. In *The Road to Kosovo: A Balkan Diary,* Greg Campbell used his travels to the former Yugoslavia to reflect on the ethnic conflicts and other forces at play in that area's conflicts in the 1990s. The contrast between the past and future of a place is a common theme, as we see in Rob Gifford's *China Road: A Journey into the Future of a Rising Power* or Peter Hessler's *Country Driving: A Journey Through China from Farm to Factory*. Other writers focus their thoughts on the act of travel itself, with Alain de Botton's *The Art of Travel* and Ryszard Kapuscinski's *Travels with Herodotus* being two examples.

The appeal of character is less strong in these titles than in the titles of the previous categories of this chapter, but because several of the writers listed here are highly regarded writers (including Nobel Prize winners Octavio Paz

1 2 3 4 5 6 7

and Jose Saramago and "near Nobel Prize winners" Ryszard Kapuscinski and W.G. Sebald), many of these titles will resonate with readers who are interested in the appeal factor of style or language.

The personal reflections on issues that transcend the journey by the travelers in the titles in this category are similar to both philosophical works and novels with philosophical themes, and these can be recommended to readers who enjoy "Reflective Journeys." Examples of philosophical works include Alain de Botton's *How Proust Can Change Your Life* and *Plato and a Platypus Walk into a Bar: Understanding Philosophy through Jokes* by Thomas Cathcart and Daniel Klein. Novels with philosophical themes run the gamut from Voltaire's *Candide* to Milan Kundera's *The Unbearable Lightness of Being* to David Foster Wallace's *Infinite Jest*.

Campbell, Greg

The Road to Kosovo: A Balkan Diary. Boulder, CO: Westview Press, 1999. 229 pp. ISBN: 9780813335896

Campbell, a freelance journalist, recounts two trips that he made to the former Yugoslavia (one in 1996 to Bosnia and one in 1998 to Kosovo), the campaign of "ethnic cleansing" begun by Milosevic, and the ineffectiveness of the NATO forces in stopping that campaign. Campbell, who stayed with local journalists rather than with the international press corps, offers a gripping insider's view of the Balkan conflict. His descriptions of daily life in the midst of the war are particularly chilling, and his analysis of the forces at play in the conflict (the ethnic conflicts, the underlying dynamics of civil war) is incisive.

Subjects: European History; Islam; Minorities; Quick Reads; War

Places: Bosnia and Herzegovina; Kosovo

Now Try: Another journalist who provides a firsthand look at events in Kosovo is Janine di Giovanni, whose *Madness Visible: A Memoir of War* is a blunt examination of the destruction of the former Yugoslavia following Tito's death. Joe Sacco's *The Fixer: A Story from Sarajevo* is a graphic narrative that tells the story of a "fixer" who leads Western reporters to stories and guides them through the dangerous landscape of postwar Sarajevo and Bosnia. Norwegian journalist Asne Seierstad chronicles the lives of 13 Serbians before, during, and after the fall of Milosevic in *With Their Backs to the World: Portraits from Serbia*. Brian Hall's account of the complicated situation in the Balkans, based on interviews with members of the various religious and ethnic "tribes" in the areas of conflict, *The Impossible Country*, is annotated in the "Sense of Place" chapter of this book.

de Botton, Alain

The Art of Travel. New York: Pantheon, 2002. 255 pp. ISBN: 9780375420825

De Botton discusses a number of aspects of the philosophy of travel in this book of nine essays, presented in five sections: "Departure"; "Motives"; "Landscape"; "Art"; and "Return." De Botton examines a number of themes (from how we imagine places before we actually see them to the effects of deserts and the countryside on us) as well as a number of writers and thinkers: Flaubert's obsession with the Orient and his trip to Egypt, von Humboldt's journey to South America, Wordsworth's travels to England's Lake District, and many others. At his worst, de Botton's observations can be predictable, obvious, and sometimes glib, but at his best, he ties his own travel experiences to those of a wide number of great thinkers.

Subjects: Authors; Essays; Philosophy

Places: Africa; Amsterdam; Barbados; Egypt; England; France; London; Madrid; Netherlands; Spain

Now Try: Readers who enjoy de Botton's philosophical musings on travel may also enjoy his *A Week at the Airport,* a short title that examines how people interact with airports, as well as his other books, which attempt to show the relevance of philosophy to daily life. These include *How Proust Can Change Your Life* and *The Consolations of Philosophy,* which address issues such as friendship, envy, and desire. Phil Cousineau explores the often-disappointing nature of travel for those who journey with a purpose and offers ways to improve the experience in *The Art of Pilgrimage: The Seeker's Guide to Making Travel Sacred.* Television travel guide Rick Steves has written a pensive book on how to travel more consciously, in *Travel as a Political Act.* Readers who enjoyed de Botton's focus on literary figures may also enjoy Paul Fussell's book, *Abroad,* which explores the meaning of travel and its importance to English and American writers, particularly those writing between the two wars. Readers who enjoy de Botton's literary style may also enjoy the travel narratives of Pico Iyer, including *Falling Off the Map: Some Lonely Places of the World* and *The Global Soul: Jet Lag, Shopping Malls, and the Search for Home,* both of which are annotated in the chapter on "Quests." Other offbeat works of philosophy might also appeal, including *Plato and a Platypus Walk into a Bar: Understanding Philosophy through Jokes* by Thomas Cathcart and Daniel Klein.

Gifford, Rob

China Road: A Journey into the Future of a Rising Power. New York: Random House, 2007. 322 pp. ISBN: 9781400064670

Gifford, formerly the China correspondent for NPR, took a six-week, 3,000-mile journey along China's Mother Road from Shanghai into the Gobi Desert, where the paved road meets the ancient Silk Road. The contrast between the booming city of the future and the desolate town at the end of the road pervades this book, and Gifford shows both the prosperity and the poverty, both the individuals who are embracing the future and those who are tied to the past. The author's fluency in Mandarin allowed him to interview a large number of the individuals he met, and he uses these interviews to highlight many of the issues facing what may be the world's next super-power: he met an abortionist who enforces the one child policy, for example, and he visited an AIDS village in Henan

Province. Gifford is even-handed in his approach to these issues, and his writing is entertaining and thought provoking.

Subjects: Asian History; Globalization; Rural Life; Society; Urban Life

Places: China

Now Try: Like Gifford, Peter Hessler's *Oracle Bones* (annotated in the chapter entitled "A Sense of Place") tells of a modern China that is tied to its past. J. D. Brown's *Digging to China: Down And Out In The Middle Kingdom* is an earlier look at China through the eyes of an English teacher at a medical college in northern China in the mid-1980s; it is augmented by insights from two later trips to China, including one just after Tiananmen Square. Alan Paul's wife landed a three-year assignment in Beijing and moved him and their three children to China; he writes about the music and culture he found there and speculates on globalization as well in the uplifting *Big in China: My Unlikely Adventure Raising a Family, Playing the Blues, and Reinventing Myself in Beijing*. Sara Bongiorni's *A Year without "Made in China": One Family's True Life Adventure in the Global Economy* is personal look at just how central China, its factories, and its factory workers are to our lives as consumers in America.

Grescoe, Taras

Sacré Blues: An Unsentimental Journey through Quebec. Toronto: Macfarlane, Walter & Ross, 2000. 315 pp. ISBN: 9781551990484

Grescoe was born in British Columbia but settled in Quebec when he returned to Canada in the mid-1990s. In *Sacré Blues*, he treats the province almost as a foreign destination as he explores the culture, economy, language, and climate of Quebec, as well as the Québécois themselves, with an outsider's perspective. Grescoe's attitude toward Quebec and its inhabitants is somewhat ambivalent: on one hand, he clearly admires the people and seeks out opinions from people on both sides of various controversial issues; on the other, he is quick to condemn those who want self-rule but would never extend that same right to Native Indians. Grescoe can also be irreverently funny, as when he calls Quebec "Canada's smoking section."

Subjects: Culture Clash; Humor

Places: Quebec

Awards: Edna Staebler Award, 2001

Now Try: Grescoe is also the author of *The End of Elsewhere: Travels among the Tourists*, a collection of essays that provides a mix of travel narrative and anthropological observations. For readers interested in a history of French-speaking Canada, Peter N. Moogk's book *La Nouvelle France: The Making of French Canada—A Cultural History* might be a good place to start. In *Sacré Blues*, Grescoe notes the diversity of Quebec; Patricia Burn's *The Shamrock and the Shield: An Oral History of the Irish in Montreal* provides a fascinating oral history of one of the more important ethnic groups in Quebec's largest city, Montreal. A. A. Gill's *The Angry Island*, about Great Britain and the British, is similar to *Sacré Blues* in that Gill is English but doesn't like many things about the country.

Hessler, Peter

Country Driving: A Journey through China from Farm to Factory. New York: Harper, 2010. 438 pp. ISBN: 9780061804090

The subtitle of Hessler's most recent book on China is somewhat misleading. Instead of "a" journey, his book really focuses on several journeys over a seven-year period that began when he acquired his Chinese driver's license in 2001 and began exploring the country. Much of the focus of the book is on driving and particularly on how the Chinese people "take such joy in driving badly," rarely using turn signals or headlights, tailgating and honking, and passing constantly. However, beneath the entertaining surface, the book is about change and how the rapid pace of change in China has affected the lives of ordinary citizens, particularly those he met in the little town north of Beijing where he rented a house. As Hessler points out, "It was all but impossible for people to keep their bearings in a country that changed so fast."

Subjects: Globalization; Investigative Stories; Road Trips; Rural Life; Transportation; Urban Life

Places: China

Awards: *New York Times* Notable Book, 2010

Now Try: Leslie T. Chang explores the massive changes disrupting individual lives in China in *Factory Girls: From Village to City in a Changing China*; like Hessler, she has a talent for seeing larger themes in the lives of everyday people. *Dreaming in Chinese: Mandarin Lessons In Life, Love, And Language* by Deborah Fallows is more memoir than travel narrative, but her portrait of a Chinese culture, based both on the complex Mandarin language and on several other regional languages, is as entertaining as *Country Driving*.

Kaplan, Robert D.

An Empire Wilderness: Travels into America's Future. New York: Random House, 1998. 393 pp. ISBN: 9780679451907

In the 1990s, journalist Kaplan took two trips to the American West, Mexico, and British Columbia in order to talk with a wide range of individuals and uncover the trends that will impact America in the near future. His travels to the fluid borders with Mexico and Canada, to places that highlighted the differences among seemingly similar ethnic groups, and to places where the centralized powers of Washington, DC, seemed irrelevant led him to a gloomy forecast that includes a growing disparity between haves and have-nots, a growing segregation of the population by class and race, and an increase in the importance of the global at the expense of involvement in local communities. Kaplan's insights are keen, provocative, somewhat apocalyptic, and very important.

Subjects: American History; American West; Society

Places: Arizona; Arkansas; British Columbia; California; Colorado; Idaho; Kansas; Mexico; Mississippi; Missouri; Montana; Nebraska; New Mexico; Oklahoma; Oregon; Texas; Utah; Washington; Wyoming

Series: *Vintage Departures*

Now Try: Several of Kaplan's other titles (*The Ends of the Earth, Balkan Ghosts,* and *Eastward to Tartary,* for example) are annotated in this book; all have the same sharp but pessimistic insights as can be found in *An Empire Wilderness.* Timothy Egan explored much of the same geographical area as *An Empire Wilderness* in his collection of 14 essays, *Lasso the Wind: Away to the New West;* Egan focuses particularly on the individuals he encountered during his travels and how they portray what he calls "the basic struggle . . . between the West of possibility and the West of possession." Readers interested in the future of the American West may want to look at Marc Reisner's *Cadillac Desert: The American West and Its Disappearing Water,* which focuses on water, a resource that will become increasingly important and increasingly scarce. Joe Bageant takes an insightful look at another region of the United State (the South) in *Deer Hunting with Jesus: Dispatches from America's Class War.*

Kapuscinski, Ryszard

Travels with Herodotus. New York: A.A. Knopf, 2007. 275 pp. ISBN: 9781400043385

Travels with Herodotus was the last book published by Kapuscinski, a writer often mentioned during his life as a potential Nobel Prize winner, and it is a personal and lively combination of memoir and travel narrative. Kapuscinski's career as a journalist took him first to India with a gift of Herodotus's *Histories* from his boss to accompany him. As he traveled over the years to China, Iran, Africa, and other places, Kapuscinski compared his own journeys and insights with those of Herodotus, whom he came to see as "the first globalist" and "the first to argue that each culture requires acceptance and understanding."

Subjects: Authors; Globalization; Journalism; Memoirs; Politics; War

Places: Africa; China; Greece; India; Iran; Poland

Series: *Vintage International*

Now Try: As noted, Kapuscinski was a highly regarded writer and journalist. His book *Imperium* covers his travels in the disintegrating Soviet Union as well as his personal relationship with that country, and his *Shah of Shahs* looks at the decline and fall of the last Shah of Iran. In spite of the high regard in which he was held, Kapuscinski was also the target of much criticism, particularly for his depiction of Africa and Africans in *The Shadow of the Sun,* his essays on that continent over four decades, which some reviewers felt portrayed people as stereotypes. The Greek writer Herodotus is considered by some to be the world's first travel writer, and his *Histories* are available from Penguin Classics and several other publishers. Justin Marozzi follows in the footsteps of Herodotus in *The Way of Herodotus,* which is annotated in the "Quests" chapter of this book. The themes of acceptance and understanding, both of one's self and of one's fellow travelers, lie at the heart of Damon Galgut's fascinating novel, *In a Strange Room,* which was shortlisted for the 2010 Booker Prize and tells the story of a South African man who wanders through Greece, Africa, and India, forming ties with his fellow travelers.

Mishra, Pankaj

Temptations of the West: How to be Modern in India, Pakistan, Tibet, and Beyond. New York: Farrar, Straus, and Giroux, 2006. 323 pp. ISBN: 9780374173210

Mishra examines the complex and sometimes contradictory relationship between South Asia and the West in eight pieces that are a mixture of travel narrative, journalism, and autobiography. Mishra sees these countries attempting to modernize but crippled by political corruption, poverty, and the long-lived hatred of one tribe for another as he examines a successful Bollywood filmmaker, looks at the "cycle of retribution" between Muslims and Hindus in Kashmir, considers how the atheistic Chinese government sells Tibetan Buddhism to tourists, and scrutinizes Nehru's post-independence politics. By no means an easy read, Mishra's narrative is densely written and thought provoking.

Subjects: Asian History; Buddhism; Culture Clash; Essays; Hinduism; Islam; Memoirs; Sociology

Places: Afghanistan; India; Nepal; Pakistan; Tibet

Awards: *New York Times* Notable Book, 2006

Now Try: Mishra has also written *Butter Chicken in Ludhiana: Travels in Small Town India,* in which he used India's small towns to show that country in transition to modernity, and *An End to Suffering: The Buddha in the World,* about his search in India, Pakistan, and Afghanistan to understand Buddhism's relevance in the modern world. Anand Giridharadas, born in the United States of Indian parents, returned to their native country and examined individuals living there and their families in order to gain insight on the impact of change on tradition in India; he shares those insights in *India Calling: An Intimate Portrait of a Nation's Remaking* (annotated in this chapter, under "The Past Is a Foreign Country"). Pico Iyer also looks at the relationship between the developing world and the spread of culture from the United States in *Video Night in Kathmandu: And Other Reports from the Not-So-Far East.*

Orlean, Susan

My Kind of Place: Travel Stories from a Woman Who's Been Everywhere. New York: Random House, 2004. 282 pp. ISBN: 9780679462934

In 33 wide-ranging essays, Orlean turns her journalist's eye toward a number of offbeat locations and events, including the World Taxidermy Championships in Springfield, Illinois; a fertility blessing ceremony in Bhutan; an African music shop in Paris; a climb up Japan's Mount Fuji; and even her own apartment. Her focus is more on the people and the events than the places, and her ear for dialogue, her intense curiosity about and empathy for the individuals she met, and her thoughts about human nature are particularly strong in these pieces.

Subjects: Essays; Investigative Stories; Women Travelers

Places: Alabama; Australia; Bangkok; Bhutan; Boston; Cuba; France; Havana; Hungary; Illinois; Japan; Miami; Michigan; New York; New York City; New Jersey; Paris; Scotland; Texas; Thailand

Now Try: Orlean is best known for her book *The Orchid Thief,* in which she travels to Florida to interview an orchid "thief" whose attempts to remove endangered orchids from a state-controlled swamp are probably illegal. A collection of her profiles of fascinating individuals, *The Bullfighter Checks Her Makeup: My Encounters with Extraordinary People,* includes stories of the famous (designer Bill Blass and ice skater Tanya Harding) as well as the less famous (the female Spanish matador of the title and a New York taxicab driver who also happens to be an Ashanti king). Another opinionated and outgoing woman writer (although a bit more rough around the edges, especially when it comes to her language) is Hollis Gillespie, whose collection of autobiographical tales, *Bleachy-Haired Honky Bitch: Tales from a Bad Neighborhood,* and essays, *Trailer Trashed: My Dubious Efforts Toward Upward Mobility,* are filled with hilarious and heart-breaking stories. Hank Stuever's *Off Ramp: Adventures and Heartache in the American Elsewhere* also looks at offbeat locations, events, and characters, although most are restricted to these United States, including a wedding in New Mexico and two friends in Texas who share a passion for decorating.

Paz, Octavio

In Light of India. New York: Harcourt Brace, 1997. 209 pp. ISBN: 9780151002221

Nobel Prize winner Paz served as Mexico's ambassador to India from 1962 to 1968 and writes about those experiences and how the people and culture of India affected him in the three essays that make up this very personal book. Paz covers topics as wide-ranging as the caste system, Sanskrit poetry, and the conflicts between Hindus and Muslims, and he writes with a great deal of affection for the Indian people. As might be expected from a writer who won the Nobel Prize for Literature, the writing is accomplished and intellectual.

Subjects: Asian History; Authors; Essays; Hinduism; Islam; Quick Reads

Places: India

Now Try: While Paz is best known as a poet, he occasionally published collections of essays, including *The Double Flame: Love and Eroticism,* which examines the concepts of sex, eroticism, and love in the history of literature; like *In Light of India,* these essays also cover a number of topics, from original sin to artificial intelligence. Another Nobel Prize winner, the Indian economist Amartya Sen, has published a collection of essays about India's intellectual and political history, *The Argumentative Indian: Writings on Indian History, Culture and Identity.* Another highly skilled, poetic Nobel Prize winner is Orhan Pamuk; among his works are the highly personal memoir, *Istanbul: Memories and the City,* and the novel *Snow,* which involves an exiled poet who returns to Turkey to report on a series of suicides by girls who have been forbidden to wear headscarves.

Saramago, Jose

Journey to Portugal: In Pursuit of Portugal's History and Culture. New York: Harcourt, 2000. 452 pp. ISBN: 9780151005871

Saramago, who won the Nobel Prize in Literature in 1998, spent six months traveling across his native country by car from north to south for this book, his only travel narrative. Described by one reviewer as "an ode of love for a country and its rich traditions," the book explores the history and legends of Portugal and its people, describes present-day churches and castles, and both evokes the country's glorious past and regrets that the modern country has not held onto the lessons of that past. While the book is beautifully written, it does assume a certain level of knowledge about Portugal and may be obscure to readers who are not already familiar with that country.

Subjects: Architecture; Art and Artists; Authors; Automobiles; European History

Places: Portugal

Now Try: Saramago did not write another travel narrative, but his last published work, *The Notebook*, is a collection of blog articles from 2008 and 2009 that focus on his political thoughts, many of them having to do with Portugal. There are fewer travel narratives having to do with Portugal than one might expect, but Richard and Barbara Hewitt's delightful *A Cottage in Portugal* does describe that couple's experience buying and renovating a 300-year-old cottage in a remote Portuguese village, and Marianne Gilbert Finnegan's *Dreaming of Portugal: A Memoir* tells about her and her husband's decision to build a house and open an international bookshop in a southern coastal town in Portugal.

Sebald, W. G.

The Rings of Saturn. New York: New Directions, 1998. 296 pp. ISBN: 9780811213783

Sebald, a German writer who was often mentioned as a potential Nobel Prize winner, writes about a walking tour of Suffolk, England, but he uses that walk to think about England's past and to speculate on the country's present state of decline. The range of topics that Sebald considers (from Kafka to Flaubert, from the introduction of the silkworm in Europe to the Irish Civil War) is impressive and, as one reviewer noted, "obliterates time and defies comparison." The writing is dense and brilliant and reflects Sebald's feelings of both the joy and sadness of existence. (In 2011, the *Guardian* listed *The Rings of Saturn* among the 100 greatest nonfiction titles of all time.)

Subjects: Authors; Memoirs; Walking

Places: England

Now Try: Several reviewers have commented on the uniqueness of Sebald's book, although one suggested that it reminded him of *Still Life with a Bridle* by poet and essayist Zbigniew Herbert, which looks at the cultural, artistic, and aesthetic legacy of 17th-century Holland, or Vladimir Nabokov's wonderful autobiography, *Speak, Memory*. Another writer who used his walk to explore intellectual topics is the Norwegian novelist Tomas Espedal's *Tramp: Or the Art of Living a Wild and Poetic Life,* which explores his need (and that of others, including great thinkers from Rousseau to Whitman) to explore the world on foot. Another intellectual, poet Ezra Pound, followed the paths of the troubadours in southern France when he was a young man and considered their impact on western literature; Richard Sieburth edited Pound's notes on these walks in *A Walking Tour in Southern France: Ezra Pound Among the Troubadours* and followed in Pound's footsteps through France himself.

Sesser, Stan

The Lands of Charm and Cruelty: Travels in Southeast Asia. New York: Knopf, 1993. 306 pp. ISBN: 9780679416005

Sesser, a writer for the *New Yorker,* traveled through and presents the darker side of five countries in southeast Asia, chronicling the fear under which even wealthy, educated citizens live in Singapore; the continued devastation caused by unexploded bombs in Laos, left over from the war in the 1960s; Cambodia's apparent view of the genocidal Khmer Rouge as possible saviors of the country; Burma's paranoid, corrupt rulers; and the environmental devastation on Borneo. Sesser contrasts the charm and friendliness of the people in these countries with the oppression and cruelty of their regimes. *The Lands of Charm and Cruelty* is an informative but gloomy book.

Subjects: Asian History; Essays; Politics

Places: Borneo; Burma; Cambodia; Laos; Malaysia; Singapore

Series: *Vintage Departures*

Now Try: British journalist James Fenton provides a similar, although perhaps more cynical, analysis of Cambodia, the Philippines, South Korea, and Vietnam in his book, *All the Wrong Places: Adrift in the Politics of the Pacific Rim.* One of the Asian countries about which Sesser writes is Laos, and Brett Dakin, who spent two years there, provides a compassionate, insightful look at that country in *Another Quiet American: Stories of Life in Laos.* Ross Marlay and Clark Neher take an interesting approach to Asian history in *Patriots and Tyrants* by examining that history through the lives of ten leaders who changed their countries, including Mao Zedong, Mohandas Gandhi, Ho Chi Minh, Pol Pot, and Suharto. For a beautifully written novel set in Cambodia, readers can try Canadian writer Kim Echlin's *The Disappeared,* about a woman who travels to Phnom Penh to find her Cambodian lover, who left her 11 years earlier to return to his native land in search of his family.

Thomson, Ian

The Dead Yard: Tales of Modern Jamaica. London: Faber and Faber, 2009. 370 pp. ISBN: 9780571227617

British journalist Ian Thomson's hard-hitting book argues that there are two Jamaicas (an idyllic resort and its gang-controlled, drug-ridden, corrupt underbelly) and sets out to understand why this is the case. Thompson visited ghettos and plantations to interview a wide number of Jamaicans from all levels of society and found a country tied to its colonial past, one that has "slipped painfully and not entirely from British rule onto a path dictated by the crime and business interests of the United States and its Caribbean neighbors." In spite of his gloomy assessment, Thomson did tease out the hope for a brighter future than many of its citizens hold.

Subjects: Caribbean History; Investigative Stories; Sociology

Places: Caribbean; Jamaica

Awards: Dolman Best Travel Book Award, 2010; Ondaatje Prize, 2010

Now Try: Laurie Gunst's *Born Fi' Dead: A Journey Through The Jamaican Posse Underworld*, about gangs in Jamaica that moved to the United States, is as hard hitting and provocative as Thomson's book. Jamaica's reggae music and the Rastafarian people behind that music are the primary subjects of Robert Roskind's travel narrative, *Rasta Heart: A Journey into One Love*. Although the bulk of Zora Neale Hurston's *Tell My Horse: Voodoo and Life in Haiti and Jamaica* is her firsthand account of voodoo practices in Haiti, her account begins in Jamaica and provides a brief picture of life on that island in the 1930s. Another investigative account of a topic that many people might not realize is still so prevalent is John Bowe's *Nobodies: Modern American Slave Labor and the Dark Side of the New Global Economy*.

Wheeler, Sara

Travels in a Thin Country: A Journey Through Chile. New York: Modern Library, 1999. 304 pp. ISBN: 9780375753657

Wheeler describes her travels through Chile in the early 1990s, as the country was recovering from Pinochet's dictatorial rule. She recounts her 2,600-mile journey from the northern desert to the country's southern tip with a good deal of understated humor. She stayed in haciendas and police stations, met a wide range of local people (from the elite to the eccentric to the down-to-earth), and shares some historical notes about the country.

Subjects: Deserts; Solo Travelers; Women Travelers

Categories: Landscapes and People

Places: Chile

Now Try: Wheeler's narratives about her travels to the Arctic region (*The Magnetic North*) and the Antarctic region (*Terra Incognita*) are also annotated in this book's chapter entitled "A Sense of Place." Writer Ariel Dorfman explores the Atacama Desert of his native Chile in *Desert Memories: Journeys Through the Chilean North*; he uses the trip to explore both the origins of modern Chile and his wife's European ancestors. Another writer, Isabel Allende, discusses Chile in her beautifully written book, *My Invented Country: A Memoir*, which is more memoir than travel narrative. Chile is one of the countries visited by Che Guevara and his friend Alberto Granado, whose nine-month exploration of South America on motorcycle is captured in *The Motorcycle Diaries: Notes on a Latin American Journey* (annotated in "Getting There Is Half the Fun").

1 2 3 4 5 6 7

Winter, Brian

Long after Midnight at the Niño Bien: A Yanqui's Missteps in Argentina. New York: PublicAffairs, 2007. 247 pp. ISBN: 9781586483708

In the 1990s, Winter spent four years as a reporter in Argentina. While he covered the country's dissolution into financial crisis and revolution by day, he learned to tango by night, visiting *milongas* in Buenos Aires, searching for the origins of the dance in salons and brothels, and falling in love with his dance instructor. As Winter learned the dance, he also began to see parallels between the tango and the local character and the country's troubles; through the dance and its rituals, he came to better understand the Argentinean belief that the country is "simultaneously doomed and still the most marvelous place imaginable." Winter writes with humor and intensity about Argentina, its famous dance, and his own search for passion.

Subjects: Dance; Memoirs; Politics; Society

Places: Argentina; Buenos Aires

Now Try: When Maria Finn discovered that her husband was having an affair, she recovered by learning to tango, an adventure that eventually took her to Buenos Aires, where she learned that her life was just beginning, in *Hold Me Tight and Tango Me Home.* Camille Cusumano traveled to Buenos Aires to recover from a failed 15-year relationship and a violent encounter with her ex's new girlfriend; she fell in love with the country and the tango and writes about that love affair in *Tango: An Argentine Love Story.* Readers who are interested in the tango may wish to consult Christine Denniston's *The Meaning of Tango: The Story of the Argentinian Dance,* which explores the history and the essence of the dance. Tomás Eloy Martínez's hallucinatory thriller, *The Tango Singer,* is set in Buenos Aires and involves an American student's quest to find Julio Martel, rumored to be the greatest of all tango singers. The 1997 film, *The Tango Lesson,* about a female filmmaker who meets a tango dancer in Paris, may also appeal to readers who enjoy *Long After Midnight at the Niño Bien.*

Return Trips

In each title in this category, the traveler returns to a place he or she has visited before. Unlike the category "The Past Is a Foreign Country," however, the destination is not a place where the writer has previously lived for more than a year or two.

Instead, the destination may be to a country where the traveler had previously studied (Ana M. Briongos's *Black on Black: Iran Revisited*), previously traveled (Bill Bryson's *Neither Here Nor There: Travels in Europe*), or even previously worked (Cathy N. Davidson's *36 Views of Mount Fuji: On Finding Myself in Japan*). Typically, the theme of comparison between the place once visited and the current place is strong. In some cases, as in Adele Barker's post-tsunami Sri Lanka (*Not Quite Paradise: An American Sojourn in Sri Lanka*), the land has suffered from a natural disaster. In others, as in Myla Goldberg's Prague (*Time's Magpie: A Walk in Prague*) or Mark Taplin's Russia (*Open Lands: Travels Through Russia's Once Forbidden Places*), significant political changes have taken place. In yet others, as in Mary Lee Settle's Turkey (*Turkish

Reflections: A Biography of a Place) or Paul Theroux's Africa (*Dark Star Safari: Overland from Cairo to Cape Town*), the continued growth of Western influence is a cause for concern.

As with the titles in the category entitled "The Past Is a Foreign Country," these titles are very personal, given the connections between traveler and destination, and will appeal to readers who like the appeal of character. However, the strong role played by the destination means that the appeal of frame or setting is also important in these titles.

Novels or stories in which the main character returns to a place she has previously visited may appeal to readers who enjoy the titles in this category. Examples include James Michener's *Return to Paradise* and Alice Adams's short story collection, *Return Trips*.

Barker, Adele

Not Quite Paradise: An American Sojourn in Sri Lanka. Boston: Beacon Press, 2010. 303 pp. ISBN: 9780807000618

In 2001, Adele Barker, a teacher from Arizona, received a Fulbright scholarship to teach and write in Sri Lanka. During that year, she and her son lived in the central highlands of Sri Lanka, discovered the peaceful beauty of the place (in spite of the civil unrest taking place at the time), learned Sinhalese, discovered the local foods and birds, and made numerous friendships in what Barker describes as "not quite paradise." After a tsunami devastated the area in 2004, she returned to Sri Lanka and sought out the friends she had known years before, only to find out that many were lost in the disaster. Her book, which is travel narrative mixed with memoir, is her attempt to describe both the beauty of Sri Lanka and the terrible devastation it suffered.

Subjects: Civil War; Colonialism; Culture Clash; Mothers and Sons; Natural Disasters; Tsunamis; Women Authors; Women Travelers

Places: Sri Lanka

Now Try: Mark Stephen Meadows also explores the island of Sri Lanka in *Tea Time with Terrorists: A Motorcycle Journey into the Heart of Sri Lanka's Civil War* and provides the historical background to the civil war between the Tamil and the Sinhalese. Alison Thompson tells of her trip to Sri Lanka following the tsunami and of her work to help the survivors, work that changed her life, in the inspiring book, *The Third Wave: A Volunteer Story*. Rory Spowers tried to create an organic farm from an abandoned tea estate in Sri Lanka, an experience he chronicles in *A Year in Green Tea and Tuk-Tuks: My Unlikely Adventure Creating an Eco Farm in Sri Lanka*.

Briongos, Ana M.

Black on Black: Iran Revisited. Melbourne, London: Lonely Planet Publications, 2000. 179 pp. ISBN: 9780864427953

The Spanish writer Ana Briongos has made several journeys to Iran since she first visited the country in the 1960s and studied at the University of Tehran in the 1970s, and *Black on Black* tells about her experiences in that country in the 1990s. The focus of the book is the daily lives of her friends and the ways in which they have adapted to the changes brought about by the Islamic revolution of 1979. Her beautifully written descriptions of these individuals combine to provide an elaborate portrait of this most complex country, both during and after the reign of the Shah.

Subjects: Islam; Middle Eastern History; Quick Reads; Women Authors; Women Travelers

Places: Iran

Series: *Lonely Planet Journeys*

Now Try: Poet Roger Housden had long been fascinated with Iran, especially its poetry and music, and he was able to finally visit the country in his 60s; he describes the artists, writers, filmmakers, and religious scholars he met as well as the places he visited in the rich *Saved by Beauty: Adventures of an American Romantic in Iran*, which is annotated in "A Sense of Place." Afshin Molavi traveled extensively in Iran, his homeland, to explore the history and the daily reality of Iran and its peoples in *The Soul of Iran: A Nation's Journey to Freedom*. Hooman Majd's *The Ayatollah Begs to Differ: The Paradox of Modern Iran* is more social commentary than travel narrative, but it should appeal to readers who want to better understand that nation. Marjane Satrapi's graphic memoirs of her life in Iran, *Persepolis: The Story of a Childhood* and *Persepolis 2: The Story of a Return*, may also appeal.

Bryson, Bill

Neither Here nor There: Travels in Europe. New York: Morrow, 1992. 254 pp. ISBN: 9780688103118

In 1972 and 1973, Bryson and his friend Katz backpacked around Europe. In 1990, Bryson retraced that trip, beginning in Norway, where Bryson hoped to see the Northern Lights, and ending in Istanbul, where the author encountered that city's "collective delirium." Compared to Bryson's other travel narratives, *Neither Here nor There* relies more on his personal observations and flashbacks to his earlier trip and less on historical detail and discussions with locals. Still, Bryson writes in his usual make-the-reader-howl-with-laughter style, although his reliance on European stereotypes may strike some readers as a bit xenophobic.

Subjects: Flashbacks; Humor; Quick Reads

Places: Amsterdam; Austria; Belgium; Belgrade; Bosnia and Herzegovina; Brussels; Bulgaria; Cologne; Copenhagen; Croatia; Denmark; Florence; France; Geneva; Germany; Hamburg; Innsbruck; Istanbul; Italy; Liechtenstein; Milan; Naples; Netherlands; Norway; Paris; Rome; Salzburg; Sarajevo; Serbia; Sofia; Stockholm; Sweden; Switzerland; Turkey; Vienna

Now Try: Steve Cooper also trekked through much of western Europe (from southern Italy to El Camino de Santiago in Spain) and writes humorously about his meanderings in *Six Months Walking the Wilds (Of Western Europe): The Long Way to Santiago*. A much earlier journey through Europe is described by Benita Fuchs in *Notes From Across* *the Pond: A Young Woman's European Odyssey in the 1950's*, which tells the story of her seven-year journey through Europe in the 1950s. Backpacking around Europe, as Bryson and Katz did in the 1970s, has always had a certain appeal for the young; Lisa Johnson has collected a number of tales of backpacking in Europe in her book *Rite of Passage: Tales of Backpacking 'Round Europe*. Bryson is, of course, best known as a travel humorist, and several other titles annotated in the "Travel Humor" section of this book might appeal to his fans.

Carey, Alice

I'll Know It When I See It: A Daughter's Search for Home in Ireland. New York: Clarkson Potter, 2002. 291 pp. ISBN: 9780609609842

This book is part memoir of growing up in Queens with Irish immigrant parents (an abusive father and a mother who served as a maid to a Broadway producer) and part story of return to an Ireland that Carey had visited as a child. On their return to Ireland, the author and her husband purchased a ruined Georgian farmhouse and converted the stables into a cottage, a project that stirred up Carey's memories of childhood. She confronts these roots in an honest and sometimes witty manner, struggling to make peace with her poignant past while also overcoming what she terms "the Seven Dwarves of Restoration" and making a new home in the land of her parents.

Subjects: Abuse; Family Relationships; Fathers and Daughters; Memoirs; Mothers and Daughters

Places: Ireland; New York City

Now Try: Joe Queenan's *Closing Time: A Memoir* recounts that writer's Irish Catholic upbringing in Philadelphia and talks of his alcoholic father. Steve Fallon was brought up in an Irish home in Boston, and when he became fascinated with the Gaelic language, he returned to the land of his ancestors to learn the language on Irish soil; his meditation on Irish identity, which includes travels with the ghost of his deceased aunt, is the subject of *Home with Alice: A Journey in Gaelic Ireland*. David Monagan returned to the land of his ancestors in Cork, Ireland, and wrote about the experience (particularly the contrast between the Ireland of the present and that of his memory) in *Jaywalking with the Irish*. Niall Williams and Christine Breen left their publishing jobs in New York City to move to a remote part of Ireland; their story, which is annotated in the chapter on "The Expatriate Life," is told in *O Come Ye Back to Ireland: Our First Year in County Clare*.

Davidson, Cathy N.

36 Views of Mount Fuji: On Finding Myself in Japan. New York: Dutton, 1993. 295 pp. ISBN: 9780525937074

Davidson, an American university professor who first visited Japan in 1980 as part of a faculty-exchange program, tells of several return trips to Japan in this wonderfully rich book. Davidson clearly loved the Japanese culture but was also aware of her status as a *gaijan* (an outsider); she tried to learn the language and the traditions but when offered the chance to live there, decided against it. Her stories about the rituals surrounding a Buddhist funeral and her trip to the "Floating World" where businessmen meet geisha are fascinating, and her observations on the Japanese educational system and the status of Japanese women are insightful. A death in her husband's family also led Davidson to contemplate the pain of suffering loss in a foreign culture and to discuss how different cultures deal with such grief. *36 Views of Mount Fuji* is an intimate look at Japan.

Subjects: Culture Clash; Death and Dying; Memoirs; Self-Discovery; Teaching; Women Travelers

Places: Japan

Now Try: Like Davidson, Bruce Feiler discusses the Japanese educational system, in his case from the point of view of an American exchange teacher at a Japanese high school near Tokyo, in *Learning to Bow: Inside the Heart of Japan*. Alex Kerr moved to Japan as a boy in 1964; his memoir, *Lost Japan*, tells of his life there (particularly his "artistic apprenticeship" in *kabuki* theatre, calligraphy, art collecting, and flower arranging) and how the country has changed. Victoria Abbott Riccardi spent a year in Kyoto, attending a school devoted to Japanese *haute cuisine* and learning about Japanese home cooking from her host family; *Untangling My Chopsticks: A Culinary Sojourn in Kyoto* is her story of being immersed in Japanese cuisine.

Elliot, Jason

An Unexpected Light: Travels in Afghanistan. New York: Picador, 2001. 473 pp. ISBN: 9780312274597

Elliot first visited Afghanistan (the homeland of his ancestors) around 1979, when he accompanied Afghan soldiers fighting against the Soviet invaders. Ten years after that initial encounter and following the victory of the mujahideen, he returned to the war-ravaged country, with his father's contacts in the Afghan Muslim community and with just enough Persian to converse with the people he met. *An Unexpected Light*, his first book, is an incredibly deep portrait of both the Afghan people, who have endured decades of warfare, and the "unexpected light" of Afghan culture that captivated Elliot.

Subjects: Adventure; Investigative Stories; Islam; Politics

Places: Afghanistan

Awards: ALA Notable Book, 2002; *New York Times* Notable Book, 2001; Thomas Cook Travel Book Award, 2000

Now Try: Elliot's second book, *Mirrors of the Unseen, Journeys in Iran*, recounts his four years of travel in Iran and is annotated in an earlier chapter in this book, "A Sense of Place." Jan Goodwin's *Caught in the Crossfire* is the harrowing account of a reporter who disguised herself as a mujahideen and traveled with the Afghan resistance forces for three months. Joel Hafvenstein writes about his three trips to Afghanistan as part of a team trying to discourage farmers there from growing opium poppies; his sobering story is told in *Opium Season: A Year on the Afghan Frontier*. Åsne Seierstad provides another eye-opening look at Afghanistan, reporting on the overthrow of the Taliban from the perspective of everyday citizens in *The Bookseller of Kabul*. Khaled Hosseini's novels, *The Kite Runner* and *A Thousand Splendid Suns*, also provide perspectives on Afghan life, as does *The Swallows of Kabul*, a novel by Yasmina Khadra.

Goldberg, Myla

Time's Magpie: A Walk in Prague. New York: Crown Journeys, 2004. 140 pp. ISBN: 9781400046041

Goldberg lived in Prague in 1993, during Czechoslovakia's split into two nations and Prague's being named the capital of the new Czech Republic. She returned ten years later, after the Velvet Revolution had freed the country from Communism, to portray a fascinating and often bizarre city with a complex past. Like the magpie of the book's title, Goldberg presents "beautiful eclectic bits" of the city's history and its present, from Kafka's grave to the metro's honor system. *Time's Magpie* is a fanciful, quirky, and individualistic guide to a unique city.

Subjects: Communism; European History; Quick Reads; Urban Landscapes

Places: Czech Republic; Prague

Series: *Crown Journeys*

Now Try: Booker Prize winner John Banville also navigates between the city's past and present in *Prague Pictures: A Portrait of the City*, part of Bloomsbury's *The Writer and the City* series. Paul Wilson compiled a collection of 23 stories about Prague in *Prague: A Traveler's Literary Companion*, which includes autobiographical pieces as well as fiction and features writers from Franz Kafka to Ivan Klima. Jan Novak spent a year in the Czech Republic with his wife and children and writes a vivid narrative about daily life in his native country as well as stories of growing up there; the result is the sometimes amusing and sometimes painful *Commies, Crooks, Gypsies, Spooks & Poets: Thirteen Books of Prague in the Year of the Great Lice Epidemic*.

Hansen, Eric

Motoring with Mohammed: Journeys to Yemen and the Red Sea. Boston: Houghton Mifflin, 1991. 240 pp. ISBN: 9780395483473

Hansen returned to Yemen in 1988 to retrieve some travel journals he had buried on a desert island off the Yemeni coast ten years earlier, where he had shipwrecked. As he struggled with the seemingly endless bureaucracy and red tape in his attempt to get approval to return the island, Hansen met a number of colorful individuals, including his guide Mohammed (who carried sheep in his taxi), and came to appreciate Yemen as a country that is both enchanting and exasperating. Hansen chewed the local narcotic (*qat*), visited bathhouses, suffered through the desert heat, and did his best to avoid being taken hostage by one of the Yemeni tribes. His detailed portrait of this Middle Eastern country is entertaining, instructive, and witty.

Subjects: Adventure; Culture Clash; Humor; Islam

Places: Yemen

Series: *Vintage Departures*

Now Try: Kevin Rushby also chewed *qat* in Yemen and became interested enough in the narcotic leaf to return to that country and follow the ancient trade routes of *qat,* which included trips to Yemen, Ethiopia, and Djibouti; his story is told in *Eating the Flowers of Paradise: One Man's Journey Through Ethiopia and Yemen.* Another travel author who sampled the local drug of choice is J. Maarten Troost, whose narrative *Getting Stoned with Savages* (annotated in the "Travel Humor" chapter) tells of his adventures with *kava,* a local intoxicant on the island nations of Fiji and Vanuatu. Jennifer Steil lived in Yemen for a year and served as the clandestine editor of a local newspaper; the lessons she learned about cultural differences, journalism, and her own life are captured in the fascinating book, *The Woman Who Fell from the Sky: An American Journalist in Yemen.* Victoria Clark was born in Yemen and returned several times between 2004 and 2009; her book, *Yemen: Dancing on the Heads of Snakes,* tells of her visits and of the fragile position of this poorest state in the Arab world.

Jenkins, Mark

To Timbuktu: A Journey down the Niger. New York: W. Morrow, 1997. 224 pp. ISBN: 9780688115852

Fifteen years after he and his best friend set out for but failed to reach Timbuktu, the most remote place they could imagine, *Backpacker* writer Mark Jenkins and his friend returned to attempt to reach the fabled city and to become the first to navigate the length of the Niger River, Africa's third longest river. Jenkins and his colleagues first ran the river from its source in Guinea to the ocean, battling killer bees, hippos, and crocodiles, and then Jenkins bought a motorcycle and traveled to Timbuktu, realizing his dream. Along the way, the story is filled with tales of the villages and the people who live along the Niger, as well as explorers who had previously traveled through the same challenging landscape.

Subjects: Adventure; African History; Explorers; Quick Reads; Rivers

Places: Africa; Benin; Guinea; Mali; Niger; Niger River; Nigeria; Timbuktu

Now Try: One of the explorers who inspired Jenkins was Mungo Park, whose classic *Travels in the Interior of Africa* tells of his late 18th-century travels in the dark continent; among other distinctions, Park was the first European to see the Niger River. Two more recent books about Timbuktu are Marq de Villiers's *Timbuktu: The Sahara's Fabled City of Gold,* which combines history and travel narrative, and Frank Kryza's *The Race for Timbuktu: In Search of Africa's City of Gold,* about 19th-century British explorers competing to find the legendary city. Jenkins's trip down the Niger was not particularly prudent or well planned; another such trip down a different river was Tracy Johnston's dangerous rafting expedition in *Shooting the Boh: A Woman's Voyage Down* *the Wildest River in Borneo,* which is annotated in the "Travel Adventures" chapter of this book.

Lamb, Christina

The Sewing Circles of Herat: A Personal Voyage through Afghanistan. New York: HarperCollins, 2002. 338 pp. ISBN: 9780060505264 YA

Lamb, an award-winning British journalist, covered the Afghan-Soviet war in the late 1980s until she was expelled by the Pakistani intelligence agency. After the September 11, 2001, attacks on the United States, she returned to Afghanistan to observe the Afghan people and their beleaguered nation following the fall of the Taliban. Lamb mixes stories from both conflicts, noting that many of the young soldiers she followed in the Afghan-Soviet conflict later became Taliban leaders, and her interactions with numerous Afghan individuals allow her to put a human face on the country's recent history. The sewing circles of her title typify the resourcefulness of these people; under the Taliban, women were allowed to gather together in sewing circles, but these groups were often a cover for book clubs and other gatherings where the women would learn and teach, activities forbidden to them by the Taliban. Lamb's book is a very personal but balanced look at this troubled region.

Subjects: Asian History; Investigative Stories; Islam; Politics; War; Women Travelers

Places: Afghanistan

Now Try: Saira Shah's book, *The Storyteller's Daughter: One Woman's Return to Her Lost Homeland,* mixes memoir and travel narrative and tells of that journalist's journey to Afghanistan to document the brutal reign of the Taliban; the real Afghanistan is contrasted with the stories about the country she heard from her Afghani father while growing up in England. Norwegian journalist Åsne Seierstad lived with a bookseller and his family in Afghanistan's capital and saw the overthrow of the Taliban from the perspective of everyday citizens; her book, *The Bookseller of Kabul,* generated controversy of its own when the bookseller sued the author for defamation. Ann Jones tells the story of post-Taliban Afghanistan with a particular focus on the women of the country in the unsettling *Kabul in Winter: Life Without Peace in Afghanistan.* Readers interested in the portrayal of life in another Islamic country from a woman's perspective may be interested in Azar Nafisi's two books: *Reading Lolita in Tehran* and *Things I've Been Silent About,* both of which provide an insider's look at pre- and post-Shah Iran.

Settle, Mary Lee

Turkish Reflections: A Biography of a Place. New York: Prentice Hall Press, 1991. 233 pp. ISBN: 9780139176753

Novelist Settle lived in Turkey from 1972 to 1974 and then returned in 1989, a visit that she recounts in this book. In addition to her observations of the people she met (invariably hospitable and polite) and the places she visited (the Hagia Sophia, the Blue Mosque, the thermal baths), Settle discusses the history and cultural development of Turkey as a bridge between the East and the West. Although she is clearly disturbed by the growing Western influence in the country (Michael Jackson's music, large luxury hotels), she is still very much in love with Turkey, which she calls "one of the happiest homes I have ever had." Settle's writing is evocative and often dazzling, as might be expected of an author of her stature.

Subjects: Asian History; Memoirs; Women Authors; Women Travelers

Places: Turkey

Now Try: Settle won a 1978 National Book Award for her novel *Blood Tie,* which is set in Turkey and which examines the impact a group of expatriates has on the native Turks who live in a small community on the Aegean Sea. Anastasia M. Ashman and Jennifer Eaton collected 32 stories from expatriate women living in Turkey in *Tales from the Expat Harem: Foreign Women in Modern Turkey*; the women represent seven nations, and their stories range from tales of traveling around the country to tales of everyday life and family traditions. Eric Lawlor portrays a Turkey that is caught between a past represented by its noisy bazaars and a present represented by its attempt to join the European Union in the entertaining *Looking for Osman: One Man's Travels Through the Paradox of Modern Turkey*. The Nobel Prize winner, Orhan Pamuk, has written several novels about modern Turkey, including *The Museum of Innocence,* about the obsessive love of a wealthy businessman for a younger lower-class shop girl, and *The Black Book,* about a lawyer in Istanbul whose wife mysteriously leaves him with no explanation.

Taplin, Mark

Open Lands: Travels Through Russia's Once Forbidden Places. South Royalton, VT: Steerforth Press, 1997. 376 pp. ISBN: 9781883642013

Taplin first visited Russia in 1984 when he was a junior-level diplomat and when most places on the Soviet map were colored red, which meant that travel there was forbidden to foreigners. In 1992, he returned to Russia following the signing of the "Open Lands" agreement with the United States, which allowed him to explore these previously prohibited areas. Much of his journey followed the footsteps of George Kennan, a 19th-century traveler, as he visited former gulags near the Arctic Circle, sacred shrines of Russia Orthodoxy, and black marketeers in Velikiy Ustyug. Taplin has a particularly keen eye for the absurdities of post-Soviet Russian life, and his easy, conversational style produces a highly readable, lively account of the new Russia.

Subjects: Asian History; Communism; European History

Places: Russia

Now Try: During the summer of 1990, journalist Marq de Villiers also visited places in Russia that were typically not open to foreigners; his 2,000-mile boat ride down Russia's most famous river is recounted in *Down the Volga: A Journey Through Mother Russia in a Time of Troubles*. Daniel Kalder's two books, *Lost Cosmonaut: Observations of an Anti-Tourist* and *Strange Telescopes: Following the Apocalypse from Moscow to Siberia,* explore the obscure and bizarre side of Russia and Eastern Europe, from Peter the Great's collection of embalmed babies to exorcisms in the Ukraine. Readers wanting to compare post-Soviet Russia with life under Communism may be interested in Laurens van der Post's classic, *Journey into Russia*, which was written in 1964 and portrays a Russian people whose character seems unchanged in many ways. Ian Frazier's *Travels in Siberia* (annotated in "A Sense of Place") is based on five trips the author made to Siberia over a span of 20 years and includes a focus on the people of the area.

Theroux, Paul

Dark Star Safari: Overland from Cairo to Cape Town. Boston: Houghton Mifflin, 2003. 472 pp. ISBN: 9780618134243

Theroux traveled by train, dugout canoe, "chicken bus," and cattle truck from Egypt to the southern tip of Africa in this return to the continent where, almost 40 years before, he had taught in the Malawi bush country. In spite of Theroux's usual cynicism (particularly about aid workers) and near arrogance, his insights into the impact of decades of Western intervention in Africa are valuable, as are his observations on the changes he saw in Africa since his earlier visits: "Africa is materially more decrepit than it was when I first knew it, hungrier, poorer, less educated, more pessimistic, more corrupt, and you can't tell the politicians from the witch doctors." Theroux writes colorfully and with great skill, an ability that offsets what some readers will see as pessimism and negativity.

Subjects: African History; Canoeing; Rail Travel

Places: Africa; Cairo; Cape Town; Egypt; Ethiopia; Kenya; Malawi; Mozambique; South Africa; Sudan; Tanzania; Uganda

Now Try: Alexandra Fuller returned to Zimbabwe with a white veteran of the Rhodesian War, where he revisited his memories of the bloody conflict; Fuller recounts the experience in *Scribbling the Cat: Travels with an African Soldier*. Julian Smith walked 4,000 miles through eight African countries to follow in the footsteps of 19th-century British explorer Ewart Grogan; Smith tells his own story as well as Grogan's and also describes the many changes to the continent in *Crossing the Heart of Africa: An Odyssey of Love and Adventure*. Binyavanga Wainaina's *One Day I Will Write About This Place: A Memoir* tells the coming-of-age story of a bookish boy growing up in Kenya to become a writer. Like Theroux, Harvard professor Robert Klitgaard found corruption in Africa; his account of trying to get the bankrupt nation of Equatorial Guinea back on its feet is *Tropical Gangsters: One Man's Experience With Development And Decadence In Deepest Africa.*

Theroux, Paul

Ghost Train to the Eastern Star: On the Tracks of the Great Railway Bazaar. Boston: Houghton Mifflin, 2008. 496 pp. ISBN: 9780618418879

Thirty years after the four-month train trip across Europe, the Middle East, and Asia that Theroux described in *The Great Railway Bazaar* (annotated in the chapter entitled "Getting There Is Half the Fun"), Theroux retraced his journey in *Ghost Train to the Eastern Star*, both to discover the changes that had occurred in Europe and Asia since that first trip and to track down the "specter" of his younger self. Theroux provides colorful descriptions of the trains, cities, and countries that are part of his itinerary, adds relevant historical details, and encounters interesting people, including writers such as Pico Iyer and Nobel Prize winner Orhan Pamuk. Some readers may be bothered by Theroux's often bellicose and egotistical attitude, but others will find his strong personality and insightful observations to be nothing short of compelling.

Subjects: Authors; Asian History; European History; Middle Eastern History; Rail Travel; Self-Discovery

Places: Afghanistan; England; France; India; Iran; Italy; Japan; Laos; Myanmar; Pakistan; Russia; Serbia; Sri Lanka; Thailand; Turkey

Now Try: Theroux is best known for his travels by train, and many of these titles (including *The Old Patagonian Express, Riding the Iron Rooster*, and *Dark Star Safari*) are annotated in this book. Fans of Theroux may also enjoy his "novel" *My Other Life*, about a character named Paul Theroux, who has led a life that is very similar to the author's own life. Another travel book that involves repeating an earlier journey is *For Love and a Beetle: A Tale of Two Journeys*, by Ivan Hodge and Petronella McGovern, which tells how Hodge and his wife Beth drove a Volkswagen Beetle in 1961 through Europe and Asia to Calcutta, where they caught a boat to their home in New Zealand, and how they repeated the trip in 1996 in the same automobile, recording (like Theroux) the changes they saw over the 30-plus years.

Thomson, Hugh

The White Rock: An Exploration of the Inca Heartland. Woodstock, NY: Overlook Press, 2003 [2001]. 316 pp. ISBN: 9781585673551

Documentary filmmaker Thomson first led an expedition to the Peruvian Andes in 1982 as a 21-year-old explorer. He returned in 1999 to further explore the Inca ruins there, and *The White Rock* provides details from both journeys. The book also discusses the previous explorations of Hiram Bingham (who discovered Machu Picchu), Gene Savoy (who discovered more than 40 lost Incan cities), and others. Thomson has an abiding respect for the Andes Mountains as well as their treasures and their people, and he is a brilliant storyteller, whose speculations on the lives of the Incas will delight readers interested in that history.

Subjects: Adventure; Explorers; Incas; Mountains; South American History

Places: Peru

Now Try: Thomson also wrote *A Sacred Landscape: The Search for Ancient Peru*, in which he speculates on the function and meaning of many of the archaeological sites in the Andes. The story of explorer Hiram Bingham, who is discussed by Thomson, is told in Christopher Heaney's gripping *Cradle of Gold: The Story of Hiram Bingham, a Real-Life Indiana Jones, and the Search for Machu Picchu*. Gene Savoy, another explorer mentioned in Thomson's book, outlines his own discoveries in *Antisuyo: The Search for the Lost Cities of the Amazon*.

Family Travel

The focus of the titles in this chapter has been on the traveler. Sometimes, travelers take trips as a family, and that family travel is the subject of this category. Family travels involve special dynamics and interpersonal relationships and thereby have an appeal that is different from travel narratives that involve individuals or even groups of unrelated individuals.

With the exception of brothers Nicholas and Micah Sparks (*Three Weeks with My Brother*), the traveling parties in this chapter all involve some variation of parents and children. In most cases, the parent writes about the travel, as in Peter Carey's trip to Japan with his 12-year-old son (*Wrong About Japan: A Father's Journey with His Son*) or Kathryn Harrison's pilgrimage with her daughter on the Camino de Santiago (*The Road to Santiago*), but in some cases, the child is the writer, as in Jane Christmas's trip to Italy with her elderly mother (*Incontinent on the Continent: My Mother, Her Walker, and Our Grand Tour of Italy*). One parent may be involved, as in the titles just mentioned, or both parents may travel, as in Mark Jacobson's *12,000 Miles In The Nick Of Time: A Family Tale*, in which he and his wife travel with their children from Thailand to England. In one case (Mark Leonard's *The Ride of Our Lives: Roadside Lessons of an American Family*), three generations are involved.

The motivations for traveling as a family are many, but the most common reason is to attempt to grow closer or better understand one another, whether it is Peter Carey's attempt to better understand his manga-obsessed son or Jane Christmas's attempt to make peace with her mother.

The focus on family members and interpersonal relationships leads to a strong sense of character, and readers who enjoy titles that deal with such topics should find these titles of particular interest.

Readers who enjoy these narratives about travel undertaken as part of a family may also be interested in psychology and self-help nonfiction that deals with families (Richard Templar's *The Rules of Parenting* or *Raising Kids with Character that Lasts* by Susan and John Yates) as well as memoirs and novels in which families are important. Examples of memoirs with a strong sense of family include Leila Philips's *A Family Place: A Hudson Family Farm, Three Centuries, Five Wars, One Family* and Tom Brokaw's *A Long Way from Home: Growing Up in the American Heartland*, while novels with a similar focus include Harper Lee's *To Kill a Mockingbird* and Jonathan Franzen's *The Corrections*.

Bain, David Haward

The Old Iron Road: An Epic of Rails, Roads, and the Urge to Go West. New York: Viking, 2004. 434 pp. ISBN: 9780670033089

In the summer of 2000, Bain, an expert on the construction of the first transcontinental railroad in the United States, took his wife and two children on a 7,000-mile cross-country journey to follow the path of that railroad. The book is part history and part travel narrative, as Bain typically describes the places he and his family visited (museums, historic sites, abandoned railways, and ghost towns) and then discusses the history of each place. Bain also writes about historical individuals, both famous (Butch Cassidy, Buffalo Bill, and Calamity Jane) and less famous (Edwin E. Perkins, the inventor of Kool-Aid, and Jake Eaton, the "champion gum chewer of the world"). Bain conveys a sense of the conflicts involved in the building of the railroads, both between settlers and Native American Indians and between technology (in this case, the railroads) and nature. He writes with an engaging style that conveys his family's adventures as well as the adventures of those who built the railroad.

Subjects: American History; American Indians; American West; Railroads

Places: California; Colorado; Kansas; Nebraska; Nevada; Utah; Wyoming

Now Try: Rudy G. Hoggard took his family on a train trip across America, from West Virginia to California, in 1996; their 6,000-mile journey through "the backyards of America" is captured in *Family Trackings: Riding the American Rails*. Readers interested in the history of railroads in the American West may want to start with Bain's comprehensive *Empire Express: Building the First Transcontinental Railroad* or Stephen Ambrose's *Nothing Like It In the World: The Men Who Built the Transcontinental Railroad 1863–1869*, although the latter has been less well received than Ambrose's other books. Miriam Toews's quirky *The Flying Troutmans: A Novel* features less history and more extended family road trip when a Canadian woman returns home to find her sister back in a psychiatric ward and her niece and nephew fending for themselves; the unlikely trio travel to the United States to find the children's long-lost father.

Carey, Peter

Wrong About Japan: A Father's Journey with His Son. New York: Knopf, 2005. 158 pp. ISBN: 9781400043118

Novelist Peter Carey's 12-year-old son was obsessed with manga and anime, so Carey took him to Japan to meet Yoshiyuki Tomino, Hayao Miyazaki ("Spirited Away"), and other manga artists and directors of anime films. The cultural gap between Carey and the Japanese individuals he met (his polite host told Carey more than once that he was "wrong about Japan") paralleled the generation gap between the father and his generally uncommunicative son, and both sides learned from one another by the end of the brief trip. Some readers may find the book too brief and its exploration of manga and anime too cursory, but others will enjoy this story of a father who admittedly never quite understands the things that fascinate his son.

Subjects: Anime; Culture Clash; Fathers and Sons; Manga; Quick Reads

Places: Japan

Now Try: Carey is one of only two writers to win the Booker Prize twice; his prize-winning novels are *Oscar and Lucinda* and *The True History of the Kelly Gang*. Mark Tannenbaum and his son Matthew shared a love of baseball and spent a year traveling through the American Midwest and West, attending baseball games, an experience that reaffirmed their love of the game; the delightful book *Between Innings: A Father, a Son and Baseball* recounts their journey. Writer James Dodson took his 10-year-old son, a fan of history and mythology, through Europe in *The Road to Somewhere: A Father, a Son, and a Journey Through Europe*; Dodson was particularly attuned to his son's needs during the trip and to the precious father-son moments. Readers who want to better understand the fascination that many American young people have for Japanese culture can start with *Japanamerica: How Japanese Pop Culture Has Invaded the U.S.*, by Roland Kelts, a lecturer at the University of Tokyo who interviewed a number of people in the anime industry, or Hector Garcia's *A Geek in Japan: Discovering the Land of Manga, Anime, Zen, and the Tea Ceremony*, which is a photograph-heavy travel guide to various aspects of Japanese culture, from *bushido* and *geisha* to *manga* and *anime*.

Christmas, Jane

Incontinent on the Continent: My Mother, Her Walker, and Our Grand Tour of Italy. Vancouver: Greystone Books, 2009. 305 pp. ISBN: 978155365400

On his deathbed, Jane Christmas's father asked her to "make friends with your mother," with whom Christmas had clashed for 50-odd years. A trip to Italy was Christmas's attempt to make peace: "I wanted us to go to Italy to see if I could finally fall in love with her. This trip was my olive branch." Unfortunately, the trip was a disaster, partly because neither mother nor daughter took into consideration the mother's health issues, which ran from diabetes to asthma to incontinence, and partly because they failed to plan properly, going out of season (when restaurants and shops were closed), packing the wrong clothes, and failing to note that Italy isn't very accessible to disabled travelers. Luckily, Christmas writes with a sense of humor, and the book is hilarious as well as an honest portrayal of a mother–daughter relationship that is anything but perfect.

Subjects: Humor; Mothers and Daughters; Women Travelers

Places: Italy

Now Try: Christmas is also the author of *What the Psychic Told the Pilgrim: A Midlife Misadventure on Spain's Camino de Santiago*, which describes her decision to hike the Camino de Santiago de Compostela in northern Spain with fourteen other women in spite of being warned against doing so by a psychic. Sue Monk Kidd and her daughter, Ann Kidd Taylor, had a better experience traveling to Europe than did Jane Christmas and her mother; their journey at critical times in both their lives is told in *Traveling with Pomegranates: A Mother and Daughter Journey to the Sacred Places of Greece, Turkey, and France*. Sue Ellen Haning and her daughter traveled to Italy by backpack and decided to take little cash, no credit cards, and stay with local Italian families; the older Haning writes about their experience in *Two Nuts in Italy*. Another complex, but closer mother–daughter relationship is told in Meg Federico's memoir *Welcome to the Departure Lounge: Adventures in Mothering Mother*, an account of her mother's slow decline that is alternatingly sad and funny. Writer Mary

Gordon's memoir of her mother and the relationship she had with her, *Circling My Mother*, is also candid and powerful.

Cohen, David Elliot

One Year Off: Leaving It All behind for a Round-the-World Journey with Our Children. New York: Simon & Schuster, 1999. 302 pp. ISBN: 9780684836010

Cohen, an author of coffee table books, and his wife decided to get rid of their house, cars, and jobs, and then take their three children on a trip around the world. *One Year Off* tells their story, including the parts that didn't go so smoothly, like losing the kids at the Eiffel Tower or driving through a bad neighborhood in Cape Town at night. But much of the trip did work well, and the family rode camels in the desert, surfed in Australia, explored the Costa Rican jungles, and went white-water rafting in Zimbabwe. The story is told in a series of emails to friends from various stops of their year-long journey, and some readers may find that structure to be a bit limiting. But most will enjoy the good humor and honesty with which the story is told.

Subjects: Circumnavigations; Humor; Family Relationships

Places: Africa; Australia; Bangkok; California; Cambodia; Cape Town; Costa Rica; France; Greece; India; Istanbul; Italy; Johannesburg; Laos; Mumbai; Paris; Phnom Penh; Rome; Sardinia; South Africa; Sydney; Thailand; Turkey; Zimbabwe

Now Try: John Higham quit his job as a rocket scientist and traveled around the world with his wife and two children; their amusing and surprisingly educational story is told in *360 Degrees Longitude: One Family's Journey Around the World*. Russell and Carla Fisher and their two children traveled around the world as well; their book, *WorldTrek: A Family Odyssey*, includes appendices with information for other families considering such a journey. Laura Manske collected 45 essays about traveling with family members in *Family Travel: The Farther You Go, the Closer You Get*; contributors include travel writers Calvin Trillin, Jim Dodson, and Tim Parks as well as comedian Paul Reiser. Benjamin Mee's memoir of uprooting his family to refurbish a zoo and run it as a family business, *We Bought a Zoo: The Amazing True Story of a Young Family, a Broken Down Zoo, and the 200 Wild Animals that Changed Their Lives Forever*, may also appeal to readers who enjoyed *One Year Off*.

Cusk, Rachel

The Last Supper: A Summer in Italy. New York: Farrar, Straus and Giroux, 2009. 239 pp. ISBN: 9780374184032

Cusk, a well-regarded British writer, became disenchanted with what she saw as the "endlessly repeating blankness" of her life, so she set off for Italy for three months with her husband and daughters. They encountered Italian art, Italian food (especially gelato and pasta), the Italian language, and quite a few British expatriates. Cusk's writing is filled with dazzling descriptions and rich similes, some of which may overwhelm at times; for example, when she finishes her *spaghetti alle vongole* at a restaurant and declares, "A pile of empty clam shells remains on my plate like the integuments of a poem whose meaning I have finally teased out." Nevertheless, *The Last Supper* is an intelligent, finely written narrative about the desire to escape to a more exciting, inspiring place.

Subjects: Family Relationships; Women Authors; Women Travelers

Places: Florence; Italy; Rome

Now Try: Cusk's earlier book, *A Life's Work: On Becoming a Mother*, is an honest and unromantic look at motherhood by someone who found the experience less than rewarding. Susan Pohlman and her husband were on the verge of divorce when they decided to spend a year in Italy with their children; *Halfway to Each Other: How a Year in Italy Brought Our Family Home* tells the story of how facing the challenges of living abroad brought the two spouses back together. In 1981, Wallis Wilde-Menozzi and her six-year-old daughter followed her husband of just one year back to his native Italy; *Mother Tongue: An American Life in Italy* describes the difficulties she had adjusting.

Glick, Daniel

Monkey Dancing: A Father, Two Kids, and A Journey To The End Of The Earth. New York: PublicAffairs, 2003. 343 pp. ISBN: 9781586481544

Glick underwent a painful divorce and the death of his older brother to cancer. These heartbreaking experiences and a concern about his children's lack of knowledge of the natural world motivated the long-time environmental reporter to take the kids (a 9-year-old daughter and a 13-year-old son) around the world to see "this planet's amazing animals and environments." As Glick tried to regain balance in his life, he also tried to teach his children about the natural world: diving the Great Barrier Reef, meeting orangutans in Borneo, watching divine monkeys in Bali. For many readers, this book about bonding with one's children and with nature will be nothing short of inspiring.

Subjects: Animals; Circumnavigations; Divorce; Environment; Family Relationships; Fathers and Daughters; Fathers and Sons

Category: Healing Odysseys

Places: Australia; Bali; Borneo; Cambodia; France; Holland; Nepal; Singapore; Switzerland; Thailand; Vietnam

Now Try: Mark Brennand's *Three Blokes in a Dodge: A Clockwise Journey Around the American South West* recounts the trip he and his two sons took following the death of his wife and their mother; he uses her diary entries to explain her role in the family and the depth of her loss. Wendy Knight collected twenty stories of travel involving fathers and daughters in *Far from Home: Father-Daughter Travel Adventures*; Daniel Glick contributed one of the stories, all of which look at how travel impacts these complex relationships.

Harrison, Kathryn

The Road to Santiago. Washington, DC: National Geographic, 2003. 150 pp. ISBN: 9780792237457

Harrison, a novelist, traveled the 400-mile path known as the Camino de Santiago (beginning in France and ending in Santiago, in northwestern Spain) three times, including the trip with her 12-year-old daughter Sarah that opens the book. As her daughter struggled to complete the pilgrimage, Harrison discovered "the grace to quit" and the importance of acceptance. *The Road to Santiago* contrasts the trip she took with her daughter with her previous pilgrimages (one when she was pregnant and another taken solo) and with her memories of her own unloving, emotionally cold mother. The book is extremely well written and also provides compelling portraits of fellow pilgrims along the Camino de Santiago.

Subjects: Mothers and Daughters; Quick Reads; Pilgrimages; Self-Discovery; Women Authors; Women Travelers

Places: France; Spain

Series: *National Geographic Directions*

Now Try: Harrison is best known for her memoir, *The Kiss*, which tells of her father's seduction of her when she was 20. Peter Murtagh, an Irish father, and his 19-year-old daughter Natasha describe their pilgrimage to Santiago de Compostela, the church at the end of the Camino de Santiago, as well as to Ireland's holy mountain in *Buen Camino!: A Father Daughter Journey from Croagh Patrick to Santiago De Compostela*. Actress and new age writer Shirley MacLaine's *The Camino* describes her pilgrimage along the Camino de Santiago, a physically demanding trek that resulted in her losing 10 pounds. Dutch writer Cees Nooteboom's goal was to visit Santiago de Compostela, but she took many detours in her attempt to capture the soul of northern Spain; her meanderings are captured in *Roads to Santiago: Detours and Riddles in the Lands and History of Spain*. Two Australians who traveled the Camino de Santiago, Elizabeth Best and Colin Bowles, have written about their experience in *The Year We Seized the Day: A True Story of Friendship and Renewal on the Camino*; the two barely knew one another, and the challenges of the journey brought them closer together and, at the same time, nearly strained their friendship to the breaking point. Readers thinking about making their own pilgrimage along the Camino de Santiago will do well to consult John Brierly's new guidebook, *A Pilgrim's Guide to the Camino de Santiago*, which includes maps, information on pilgrim hostels, and even spiritual guidelines.

Jacobson, Mark

12,000 Miles in The Nick Of Time: A Family Tale. New York: Atlantic Monthly Press, 2003. 271 pp. ISBN: 9780871138521 YA

In an attempt to show their children the real world and lead them "from pop bondage," Jacobson, a one-time contributing editor to *Rolling Stone*, and his wife took their three children (ages 16, 12, and 9) on a three-month journey from Thailand to England. They saw cremation pyres in India, stood by Moses's burning bush, visited the pyramids and the Angkor Wat, and heard monks chanting in

Nepal. The children alternated between boredom and enchantment, but by the end of the trip, the family seemed more appreciative of the world's variety and of themselves. Extra chapters have been added by the eldest daughter as a kind of counterpoint to her father's narrative, and while some readers may find the narrative a bit tedious and without much insight, others will find it a realistic account of a less-than-perfect family.

Subjects: Family Relationships; Humor

Places: Africa; Cambodia; Egypt; England; France; India; Israel; Jordan; Nepal; Thailand

Now Try: Laurie Pane writes about a seven-year sailing trip around the world with his seven-year-old son and wife-to-be in *Chasing Sunsets: A Practicing Devout Coward's Circumnavigation with His Wife and Son*; the book includes stories by all three members of the family and thereby provides different perspectives on the adventure. Alice Griffin tells of her travels to Norway, Greece, France, and Spain with her two-year-old daughter and husband in *Tales from a Travelling Mum: Navigating Europe with a Babe-in-Arms*, which also offers practical advice for others wishing to travel with small children. Nan Jeffrey's *Bahamas: Out Island Odyssey* is a collection of stories about the travels that she, her husband, and their three children took through the Bahamas; it has some elements of a travel guide as well. Barbara Kingsolver and her family moved to a farm in rural Virginia and decided to eat locally for one year, growing their own vegetables and raising their own poultry, a story told in *Animal, Vegetable, Miracle: A Year of Food Life*; Kingsolver's daughter Camille plays a prominent role in the narrative and is listed as one of the co-authors.

Leonard, Mike

The Ride of Our Lives: Roadside Lessons of an American Family. New York: Ballantine Books, 2006. 230 pp. ISBN: 9780345481498

Mike Leonard, a feature reporter for NBC's *Today Show*, took a road trip in two RVs with his wife, octogenarian parents, three grown children, and one daughter-in-law. The month-long trip from Arizona to the East Coast and finally to Chicago (just in time for the birth of Leonard's grandchild) is filled with visits to places that are part of the family's collective memory, with stories from Leonard's parents, and with various mishaps. Much of the book is quite funny, but there are poignant moments when Leonard reflects on his aging parents and the meaning of life. In the end, Leonard and the other travelers learn that in spite of generation gaps and personality differences, what is most important is family.

Subjects: Family Relationships; Humor; On the Road

Places: Arizona; Chicago; Georgia; Illinois; Louisiana; Maryland; New Jersey; New Mexico; New York; North Carolina; Rhode Island; Texas; Virginia; Washington, DC

Now Try: William McKeen and his 18-year-old son traveled Highway 61 in their Ford Explorer from Thunder Bay, Ontario, to New Orleans; the story of how this road trip brought father and son closer together is told in *Highway 61: A Father-and-Son Journey through the Middle of America*. Mike Leonard's parents were the children of Irish immigrants, and while there is little travel in Frank Gannon's memoir, *Midlife Irish: Discovering My Family and Myself*, his reflections of being the child of Irish immigrants may delight readers who found that aspect of *The Ride of Our Lives* of interest. CBS correspondent Bill Geist's *Way Off the Road: Discovering the Peculiar Charms of Small-Town America* (annotated in "Travel Humor") does not involve his parents, but the offbeat and eccentric comedy as well as the depiction of small-town America is similar to much of Leonard's book.

Peterson, Dale

Storyville, USA. Athens, GA: University of Georgia Press, 1999. 299 pp. ISBN: 9780820321516

Peterson and his two children took a 20,000-mile road trip through the United States, playing a game that they invented and called "Storyville." The game involved finding towns with intriguing names (like Monkeys Eyebrow, Kentucky, or Big Rock Candy Mountain, Utah) and driving to them, then finding local storytellers to explain the origin of the town's name. They began appropriately enough in Start, Louisiana, and finished their travels in, where else, Roads End, Alaska. The result is a delightful book about small-town America, the fascinating individuals who live in small towns, and the never-ending curiosity of children.

Subjects: Fathers and Daughters; Fathers and Sons; Small-Town Life

Category: On the Road

Places: Alabama; Alaska; Arkansas; Arizona; California; Georgia; Illinois; Kentucky; Louisiana; Maine; Maryland; Massachusetts; Minnesota; Mississippi; New York; North Carolina; Ohio; Oklahoma; Oregon; Pennsylvania; South Dakota; Texas; Utah; Washington; West Virginia; Wyoming

Now Try: Robert Sullivan and his family have taken several cross-country trips, and his book *Cross Country: Fifteen Years and 90,000 Miles on the Roads and Interstates of America with Lewis and Clark . . .* details one of those journeys across the United States. Christina Hardyment's pleasant *Heidi's Alp: One Family's Search for Storybook Europe* follows her family as they travel around Europe in search of the real locations of their favorite children's stories. Joe Kurmaskie describes a 4,000-mile bicycle ride across the United States with one son on a bike and a second son in a bike trailer in the very funny book, *Momentum Is Your Friend: The Metal Cowboy and His Pint-Sized Posse Take on America*. Laura Manske is the editor of *Family Travel: The Farther You Go, the Closer You Get*, a collection of 45 essays celebrating traveling as a family and including pieces by notables such as Calvin Trillin, Paul Reiser, and Mary Morris.

Sabar, Ariel

My Father's Paradise: A Son's Search for His Jewish Past in Kurdish Iraq. Chapel Hill, NC: Algonquin Books of Chapel Hill, 2008. 332 pp. ISBN: 9781565124905

Ariel Sabar, a journalist and aspiring rock drummer, admits that he never understood his father, Yona, who was born a Kurdish Jew in Iraq and who became a UCLA professor whose goal was to preserve Aramaic, his native language and the language spoken by Christ. But when the younger Sabar's son was born, he decided to try to close the gap with his father, and the two traveled to Iraq to find Yona's birthplace and Yona's sister, who had been kidnapped as a child. Ariel tells not only the story of his father but also the story of the Kurdish Jews and their need to leave Iraq for Israel. This history and the universal truths associated with it are conveyed in beautiful, vivid language.

Subjects: Fathers and Sons; Jews and Judaism; Languages; Minorities

Places: California; Iraq

Now Try: Dan Jacobson and his son traveled to Lithuania to search for clues about his enigmatic grandfather, Heshel Melamed, the rabbi of the small town in northwest Lithuania; their story is recounted in *Heshel's Kingdom: A Family, a People, a Divided Fate*. Lucette Lagnado's *The Man in the White Sharkskin Suit: A Jewish Family's Exodus from Old Cairo to the New World* is more memoir than travel narrative, but its touching story of the downfall of an Egyptian Jewish family contains themes similar to those of *My Father's Paradise*, such as the striving of one generation to understand another. While on a bicycle trip, Daniel Friedman and his son accidentally discovered the birthplace of his maternal grandmother and the many cousins who lived there; *My Mother's Side: A Journey to Dalmatia* describes this "homecoming" and the lessons about family and community that Friedman learned from his relatives. In Rabih Alameddine's delightfully rich novel, *The Hakawati*, a Los Angeles software engineer returns to Beirut to keep watch over his dying father; while there, the protagonist narrates the story of his family, including his grandfather, who was a *hakawati* or storyteller.

Sparks, Nicholas, and Micah Sparks

Three Weeks with My Brother. New York: Warner Books, 2004. 356 pp. ISBN: 9780446532440

A brochure announcing a three-week trip around the world appealed to writer Nicholas Sparks, and when his wife declined to go with him, he turned to his younger brother Micah. The fun-loving younger brother and the more serious, inwardly focused older brother reflect on the challenges of their childhoods as they recount their journeys to destinations that included Mayan ruins in Guatemala, Machu Picchu in Peru, Ayers Rock in Australia, Angkor Wat in Cambodia, and the Taj Mahal in India. Fans of Sparks will be particularly pleased to learn more about his background.

Subjects: Circumnavigations; Family Relationships; Memoirs

Places: Australia; Cambodia; Easter Island; Ethiopia; Florida; Guatemala; India; Malta; Norway; Peru

Now Try: Brothers Renny and Terry Russell traveled through the American West in the 1950s and 1960s (to places like Yosemite, Point Reyes, and the Grand Canyon) and wrote *On the Loose*, a book that celebrates the beauty of these sites and warns against their destruction. Brothers Lawrence and Lorne Blair traveled for ten years in the Indonesian archipelago, encountering strange animals and even stranger cultures; they chronicle their journey in *Ring of Fire: An Indonesian Odyssey*. Jeff Greenwald's *Snake Lake* is also about the relationship between two brothers: one (the author) who lived in Nepal and was forced to choose between witnessing that country's revolution and returning to the United States to help his brother, who was sinking into depression. Franz Wisner and his brother traveled to several countries to learn about global views of love, romance, and sex in *How the World Makes Love: And What It Taught a Jilted Groom* (annotated in "Quests"); the book is more lighthearted than *Three Weeks With My Brother*. For a pair of novels about sisters who travel together across the United States, readers can try Charles Dickinson's *The Widows' Adventures* (about two elderly sisters, one of whom is blind, who drive from Chicago to Los Angeles) and Pagan Kennedy's *Spinsters* (about two 30-something sisters who drive from Virginia to Arizona following the death of their father in the late 1960s).

Thomas, Elizabeth Marshall

***The Old Way: A Story of the First People.* New York: Farrar, Straus and Giroux, 2006. 343 pp. ISBN: 9780374225520**

In 1950, Thomas (who was then a teenager) joined her father, mother, and brother in an expedition into the Kalahari Desert in southwest Africa to live among the Ju/wasi Bushmen, a tribe of nomadic hunter-gatherers. Thomas reflects on that expedition and on the culture and lives of the Bushmen, calling it a voyage "into the deep past through a time machine" and saying that she felt that she "saw the Old Way, the way of life that shaped us, a way of life that now is gone." She also discusses the tragic fate of these primitive people, who have been forced to coexist with the modern world and who now suffer from poverty, alcoholism, and AIDS.

Subjects: Anthropology; Deserts; Family Relationships; Indigenous Peoples; Modernization; Nomads

Places: Africa; Botswana

Now Try: Thomas wrote an accessible anthropological study of the Ju/wasi, entitled *The Harmless People*; the book was originally written in the 1950s and updated based on field trips taken by Thomas in the 1980s. Her mother, Lorne Marshall, wrote one of the best-known ethnographies of recent times, *The !Kung of Nyae Nyae*. Laurens van der Post tells about his arduous 1957 journey to the same area in *The Lost World of the Kalahari*. The husband and wife team Mark and Cordelia Owens focus on lions, hyenas, and other animals of the Kalahari in their beautifully written book, *Cry of the Kalahari*.

Ureneck, Lou

Backcast: Fatherhood, Fly-fishing, and a River Journey Through the Heart of Alaska. New York: St. Martin's Press, 2007. 286 pp. ISBN: 9780312371517

When Ureneck (the chair of Boston University's journalism department) and his wife divorced, he took his son Adam on a long-promised fishing trip to Alaska, partly to try to reconcile himself to his son, who clearly resented the divorce and felt distant from his father, and partly to try to reach out to his son before he went off to college and possibly out of his father's life. Adam was sullen and critical for much of the trip, and the pair experienced some harrowing moments during their 10-day raft trip down the Kanektok River (for example, when they encountered a massive bear and her cub) as well as the beauty of the Alaskan wilderness. This deeply personal and often painful book explores both that natural wilderness and the equally treacherous workings of human relationships.

Subjects: Adventure; Divorce; Fathers and Sons; Fishing; Rivers

Places: Alaska; Kanektok River

Now Try: William Plummer deals with the death of his estranged father, his own divorce, and his deteriorating relationship with his son Nicky in the memoir, *Wishing My Father Well: A Memoir of Fathers, Sons, and Fly-Fishing*; Plummer used his father's fishing diary and fly-fishing to help him better understand that man. Ron Franscell's *The Sourtoe Cocktail Club: The Yukon Odyssey of a Father and Son in Search of a Mummified Human Toe . . . and Everything Else* recounts the whimsical story of his post-divorce trip to the Yukon with his son. Scott Price's father promised him that if he graduated from college, they would ride their motorcycles together to Alaska; the story of their journey through beautiful scenery and sometimes dangerous back roads is told in *From Maryland to Alaska and Back: A Promise Fulfilled*. Norman Maclean's novella, *A River Runs Through It*, is set in Montana and recalls Maclean's father (a Presbyterian minister), his troubled but talented brother, and the fishing trips that they took.

Consider Starting With . . .

Carey, Peter. *Wrong About Japan: A Father's Journey with His Son.*
Gilman, Susan Jane. *Undress Me in the Temple of Heaven.*
Pham, Andrew X. *Catfish and Mandala: A Two-Wheeled Voyage through the Landscape and Memory of Vietnam.*
Pirsig, Robert M. *Zen and the Art of Motorcycle Maintenance: An Inquiry into Values.*
Raban, Jonathan. *Passage to Juneau: A Sea and Its Meanings.*
Sebald, W. G. *The Rings of Saturn.*
Thubron, Colin. *To a Mountain in Tibet.*

Fiction Read-Alikes

Bowles, Paul. Bowles's best-known novel, ***The Sheltering Sky***, concerns a married couple who travel to North Africa, in part to deal with difficulties in their marriage, but who soon encounter an alien culture they seem incapable of understanding. Bowles explores a number of complex themes related to the uncaring destructiveness of the unfamiliar in this and other novels, including ***Let It Come Down***, about an American man who moves to Morocco to begin a new life but soon descends into a nihilistic world of brothels and drugs, and ***Up Above the World***, about an aging American physician and his much younger wife, who travel to Central America and are trapped by a mysterious young man. Bowles (whose short stories also explore similar themes and are considered literary gems) writes with a clear, direct style that one critic described as "icy, cruel, objective."

Coelho, Paulo. ***The Alchemist*** tells the story of Santiago, a shepherd boy who journeys from Spain to Egypt, where he gains enlightenment and self-understanding through an encounter with a mysterious alchemist. The simple fable has sold over 65 million copies and has been translated into more than 70 languages, supposedly a record for a living author. An earlier novel by Coelho, ***The Pilgrimage***, recounts his experiences on the Camino de Santiago and the lessons he learns about the virtues of simplicity in life. Other novels by Coelho (***Brida***, ***The Zahir: A Novel of Obsession***, and ***The Witch of Portobello***) also feature journeys that lead to spiritual awakenings.

Lee, Chang-rae. In Lee's most recent novel, ***The Surrendered***, June, a Korean War orphan now living in New York and dying of cancer, sells her antique business and sets off for Italy to look for her estranged son. Lee's other novels (***Native Speaker***, ***A Gesture Life***, and ***Aloft***) do not involve travel themes as such, but the first two explore aspects of the immigrant experience.

Maugham, W. Somerset. Maugham's last major novel, ***The Razor's Edge***, has been called one of the greatest travel novels in the English language; its story about a World War I aviator whose quest for the meaning of life takes him to India anticipated the many Westerners who sought wisdom in the East in the 1950s and 1960s. Several of Maugham's other novels, including the autobiographical ***Of Human Bondage*** and ***The Moon and Sixpence***, a fictional version of Paul Gauguin's life, involve travel, and Maugham himself was one of the most significant travel writers of the years between the two world wars.

Mengestu, Dinaw. The Ethiopian-born author's second novel, ***How to Read the Air***, explores the theme of the past as a foreign country and involves Jonas, the son of Ethiopian immigrants, who retraces his parents' honeymoon trip from Peoria to Nashville in order to better understand their lives and his. Mengestu's first novel, ***The Beautiful Things That Heaven Bears***, examines the lives of African immigrants in Washington, DC, and their struggles to reconcile the idealized promises of America with its reality.

Schulze, Ingo. The German writer Ingo Schulze's latest novel, ***Adam and Evelyn***, is a healing odyssey that begins when Evelyn finds her boyfriend Adam, a tailor and dressmaker, sleeping with one of his customers. Evelyn runs off to Hungary with two friends on a long-planned vacation, with Adam in pursuit. The novel includes the strong dialogue that is typical of Schulze as well as elements of romance and suspense (Adam smuggles a woman over the Hungarian border in the trunk of his car). Schulze's earlier collections of short stories (***33 Moments of Happiness: St. Petersburg***

Stories, One More Story, and ***Simple Stories***) include stories with a strong sense of place, including those set in St. Petersburg, Vienna, Estonia, and several small towns in Germany.

Sebald, W. G. Sebald's pensive travel narrative, *The Rings of Saturn* (listed in this chapter) is often categorized as fiction, and several of his other works mix travel narrative with elements of fiction and break down the distinction between fiction and nonfiction. **Vertigo** weaves together the narrator's travels in Italy with those of Stendhal, Casanova, and Kafka before recounting a trip taken by Sebald to his German hometown of "W." ***The Emigrants*** traces the lives of four elderly German/Jewish exiles in England, Austria, and the United States. ***Austerlitz*** tells the story of a man who came to England as part of the *Kindertransport* program that sent German Jewish children to England, and who later goes in search of his past. Sebald's works are typically dense and difficult but rewarding to readers interested in intellectual writing.

Note

1. Cited on the *Africa Travel Magazine* website, http://www.africa-ata.org/antonson.htm.

Chapter 4

Getting There Is Half the Fun

The saying 'Getting there is half the fun' became obsolete with the advent of commercial airlines.
—Henry J. Tillman

Definition of "Getting There Is Half the Fun"

In the introduction to this book, I defined travel as an activity that involves a traveler or travelers who go to a destination *by some means*, for some purpose, for some length of time. The titles discussed in this chapter are those that concentrate on the means of travel.

There are, of course, many conveyances of travel, but this chapter focuses on four that have shown great appeal to readers: travel on foot; travel by train; travel by automobile; and travel by bicycle or motorcycle. For some readers, there is a special attachment to these means of travel and the characteristics of each: the more intimate relationship between the traveler on foot and the lands traveled through or the greater distances covered in less time in an automobile, or the special relationship the motorcycle rider has with her surroundings, as explained by Robert M. Pirsig in *Zen and the Art of Motorcycle Maintenance: An Inquiry into Values*:

> In a car you're always in a compartment, and because you're used to it you don't realize that through that car window everything you see is just more TV. You're a passive observer and it is all moving by you boringly in a frame.
>
> On a cycle the frame is gone. You're completely in contact with it all. You're *in* the scene, not just watching it anymore, and the sense of presence is overwhelming.

I got a sense of the special appeal of trains recently, when my wife and I traveled from our North Carolina home to New York City just before Christmas. Instead of taking the usual flight, we decided to go by train. The train trip took just a couple of hours more than would have been required to drive to the airport, go through security, fly to La Guardia, pick up our luggage, and take a taxi into the city, but the difference between the spacious ride through what Rudy G. Hoggard (*Family Trackings: Riding the American Rails*) called "the backyards of America" and the claustrophobic "cattle car" feeling of most air flights was worth the extra time. I can better understand the romance of rail travel and what Paul Theroux meant when he said, "Ever since childhood, when I lived within earshot of the Boston and Maine, I have seldom heard a train go by and not wished I was on it."

Many of our readers will also be in love with train travel, and the titles in that category of this chapter may appeal to them. When asked about a favorite trip, they may mention one that included rail travel. They may decry the sad state of rail travel in the United States and wonder why we can't be more like Europe. Others will be walkers or motorcyclists or bicyclists or people who long to get in the car and just start driving. Still others will be people who like to read about those means of travel. For all of them, getting there is still half the fun of travel.

Appeal of "Getting There Is Half the Fun"

The titles in this chapter are focused on travel by specific conveyances, so the appeal factor of frame and setting is extremely important. After all, what is important to the reader is that the traveler is not just traveling somewhere but that she is traveling somewhere in a certain way, i.e., on foot, on a train, on the road in a car, or on a bicycle or motorcycle. The method of travel also places the traveler in a specific relationship with the places traveled through, best seen perhaps in the more intimate relationship the traveler on foot has with the land. (Think Jason Goodwin and friends sleeping in haystacks in *On Foot to the Golden Horn: A Walk to Istanbul* or Miles Moreland hiking through the villages and vineyards of France in *Miles Away: A Walk Across France*.)

The appeal of pacing may also parallel the appeal of the specific means of travel. Travel on foot, for instance, tends to be more relaxed and unhurried, as in Alan Booth's walk along the eastern coast of Japan in *The Roads to Sata: A 2,000-Mile Walk Through Japan*. Travel by automobile, on the other hand, may be faster and may cover greater distances, as in Mike Bryan's exploration of the southwestern United States via its interstate highways (*Uneasy Rider: The Interstate Way of Knowledge*).

Character is also important in these narratives, both the character of the traveler herself (the confrontational petulance of Robyn Davidson in *Tracks: A Woman's Solo Trek Across 1,700 Miles of Australian Outback*) or the individuals with whom the traveler travels (Bill Bryson's hilariously misguided friend Katz in *A Walk in the Woods: Rediscovering America on the Appalachian Trail*) or the individuals the traveler encounters (the friendly Iraqis whom Andres Eames encounters in *The 8:55 to Baghdad: From London to Iraq on the Trail of Agatha Christie and the Orient Express*).

Other appeal factors (story line, tone and mood, and language and style) may be present but they are likely to be less important for these titles than they might be for titles in the other travel narrative categories.

Readers who are fascinated by specific types of travel may also be drawn to titles about those conveyances that do not involve travel, and readers' advisors may want to look to other genres, such as biography or history or sports, for suggested titles. Lance Armstrong's *It's Not About the Bike: My Journey Back to Life*, Richard White's *Railroaded: The Transcontinentals and the Making of Modern America*, and Colin Fletcher's *The Complete Walker* come to mind.

Organization of the Chapter

This chapter begins with "Classics," titles published prior to 1990 that display universality, multiple levels of meaning, great stories, memorable characters, emotional or though-provoking experiences, and great writing. These are titles that are likely to be more familiar to readers and librarians, and this familiarity may help readers and librarians better understand the subgenre and its categories. The means of travel have changed over the years, but the conveyances that serve as categories here (foot, rail, car, and bicycle or motorcycle) have changed less than some (such as airplanes). Travel on foot, for example, has always been at a slow pace and along a path that the traveler more or less chooses. By contrast, travel by train has always been faster but along a path chosen by others. Consequently, the appeal of travel by these means may be quite similar from the classic works to the later titles.

The other four categories of this subgenre are all focused on some type of travel. The narratives in "On Foot" focus on travel by walking, a means of travel that is slower and allows the traveler a more intimate connection with the places through which he travels. Those in "On the Rails" involve travel by train, which is slow enough to allow the traveler more time to reflect on the places traveled through and the individuals traveled with, and follows a path prescribed by the tracks, thereby requiring the traveler to take what comes more than in those other forms of travel. Travel by automobile (including travel by truck, by bus, and by hitchhiking), which is faster than travel by foot and more flexible than travel by train, is the focus of "On the Road." Finally, "On Two Wheels" involves traveling by bicycle or motorcycle, a means of travel that is faster than traveling on foot, more flexible than traveling by rail, more intimate than traveling by car, and more physically challenging than traveling by rail or by car.

Classics

As noted earlier, this book defines classics as travel narratives that were published before 1990 and that also display universality, multiple levels of meaning, great stories, memorable characters, emotional or though-provoking experiences, and great writing. Classics are listed in order to highlight titles that are more familiar to readers and librarians and that will serve as good entry points into the subgenre of "Getting There Is Half the Fun" and its various categories.

Though the means by which individuals travel have changed over the years, the conveyances that serve as categories here (foot, rail, car, and bicycle or motorcycle) have changed less than some (such as airplanes) and the appeal and the ambiance of travel by these means may be quite similar from the classic works to the later titles. The slow pace of walking that allows Patrick Leigh Fermor to get a sense of Europe as the Nazis are on the rise in Germany in the 1930s (*A Time of Gifts: On Foot to Constantinople from the Hook of Holland to the Middle Danube*) is similar to the slow pace of Jason Goodwin's walk through Eastern Europe in the 1990s (*On Foot to the Golden Horn: A Walk to Istanbul*), which allows him to get a sense of Europe as the Iron Curtain was falling.

The titles listed under "Classics" here reflect all of the categories of this subgenre: on foot (Alan Booth's *The Roads to Sata: A 2,000-Mile Walk Through Japan* and Robyn Davidson's *Tracks: A Woman's Solo Trek Across 1,700 Miles of Australian Outback*); on the rails (Paul Theroux's *The Great Railway Bazaar* and *The Old Patagonian Express: By Train through the Americas*); on the road (William Least Heat-Moon's *Blue Highways: A Journey into America* and John Steinbeck's *Travels with Charley: In Search of America*); and on two wheels (Che Guevara's *The Motorcycle Diaries: Notes on a Latin American Journey*).

Booth, Alan

The Roads to Sata: A 2,000-Mile Walk Through Japan. Harmondsworth, England: Viking, 1986 [1985]. 281 pp. ISBN: 9780670807765

Alan Booth, who had spent seven years in Japan and who married a Japanese woman, traveled alone by foot from the northernmost point in Japan, Cape Soya, to the southernmost point, the small town of Sata. His trip down the less populated, more rural eastern side of Japan lasted 128 days and covered 2,000 miles. He reports primarily on his encounters with the local people; some treated him as a friend and others treated him rudely, choosing to focus on his status as a foreigner rather than on his fluency in Japanese. Booth's motivation was to better understand the meaning of his time in Japan, but there is little self-reflection in the book, which is instead focused on the rural Japanese people and their traditions.

Subjects: Culture Clash; Solo Travelers; Walking

Categories: On Foot

Places: Japan

Now Try: Booth followed up *The Roads to Sata* with *Looking for the Lost: Journeys Through a Vanishing Japan*, in which he retraces three journeys through Japan, originally taken by a Japanese novelist, the leader of a 19th-century rebellion, and the author of a

12th-century Japanese classic. Will Ferguson's *Hokkaido Highway Blues* (annotated in the "Travel Humor" chapter of this book) was inspired by Booth's book and also involves hitchhiking from one end of Japan to the other. In *The Inland Sea,* Donald Richie explored the Inland Sea of Japan, which serves three of Japan's major islands and which also represents a rural area, less influenced by the West. Maxence Fermine's novel, *Snow,* tells the story of a young Japanese boy at the end of the 19th century who walks across Japan to study haiku with a great artist, and encounters a life-changing vision along the way.

Davidson, Robyn

Tracks: A Woman's Solo Trek Across 1,700 Miles of Australian Outback. New York: Pantheon, 1980. 256 pp. ISBN: 9780394514734 YA

In 1977, Davidson walked from Alice Springs, in the middle of Australia, to Hamelin Pool, on the west coast of the continent, with her dog Diggity and four camels. Her reasons for making the journey are never clear, but her determination and resourcefulness are moving. The descriptions of the Outback are vivid, and her portrayal of the Aborigines is sensitive and supportive. In spite of her occasional offbeat humor, Davidson can be touchy and confrontational at times, but the book itself is a real page-turner and may be, for some readers, a source of inspiration.

Subjects: Adventure; Humor; Solo Travelers; Walking; Women Travelers

Categories: On Foot

Places: Australia

Awards: Thomas Cook Travel Book Award, 1980

Series: *Vintage Departures*

Now Try: Davidson's trip was sponsored by *National Geographic,* which sent Rick Smolan to serve as her photographer. *From Alice to Ocean: Alone Across the Outback* is a collection of Smolan's photographs alongside excerpts from *Tracks,* a presentation that highlights the difficulties of her journey as well as the harsh beauty of the Outback. Davidson also wrote *Desert Places,* about the arid Thar country of northwest India and the nomads who live there. Cynthia Clampitt's *Waltzing Australia* is a combination memoir and travel narrative by a woman who quit her corporate career and moved to and fell in love with Australia. *Voss,* a novel about a German exile who set off to explore the unmapped Australian Outback in the 1840s and the lover he left behind, is generally considered the greatest work of the Australian novelist Patrick White, who won the 1973 Nobel Prize in Literature.

Fermor, Patrick Leigh

Between the Woods and the Water. New York: Viking, 1986. 248 pp. ISBN: 9780670811496

This book is a sequel to Fermor's earlier title, *A Time of Gifts* (annotated further on), in which Fermor walks from the Netherlands to what was then Czechoslovakia. *Between the Woods and the Water* follows him from Czechoslovakia into Hungary and to the Iron Gate, which separated the kingdom of Yugoslavia (now Serbia) from Romania. Fermor was just a teenager at the time of his journey, and yet he wandered unguided through Hungary and Transylvania, attending parties with former aristocrats, pondering the history of the Hapsburgs and the gothic architecture of Romania, relaxing with gypsies, and talking with rich landowners. As one reviewer noted, *Between the Woods and the Water,* even more than *A Time of Gifts,* "is a portrait of an enviable mind, a mind that is simultaneously open to experience and wise, or at least subtle and clear-thinking, but refined by a liberal education."

Subjects: European History; Walking

Categories: On Foot

Places: Budapest; Czech Republic; Hungary; Romania; Serbia

Awards: Thomas Cook Travel Book Award, 1986/87

Now Try: Fermor planned a third volume to cover his journey to its completion in Constantinople, but it was never finished. However, a "near-finished" version was uncovered in 2011, and Fermor's publisher, John Murray, announced plans to publish the final volume in 2013. Fermor also wrote *A Time to Keep Silence,* which tells of his visits to some of Europe's monasteries and his thoughts on the meaning of silence and solitude. Fermor's first award-winning book was *The Traveller's Tree: A Journey Through the Caribbean Islands,* which tells about his journey to the islands of the Caribbean, including Guadeloupe, Martinique, Barbados, Trinidad, and Haiti. That book won the 1950 Heinemann Foundation Prize for Literature.

Fermor, Patrick Leigh

A Time of Gifts: On Foot to Constantinople from the Hook of Holland to the Middle Danube. New York: Harper & Row, 1997. 291 pp. ISBN: 9780060112240

In 1933, the 18-year-old Fermor decided to walk from the Netherlands to Constantinople. The time at which Fermor traveled was a fascinating one (before Communism had taken hold in Eastern Europe, when monarchies still ruled the Balkans and just after Hitler had come to power) and, because he is writing 40 years after the trip, Fermor is able to reflect on the contrasts between what he saw as he walked through these countries and what eventually transpired. This contrast between past and present is paralleled by the contrast between the older, more sophisticated Fermor and the impressions the younger, more enthusiastic Fermor recorded in a dairy during his journey, passages of which are quoted in the book. The poetic descriptions of the countryside and the people he encountered are nothing short of beautiful and stand in stark contrast to the destruction that Europe would face in the years following his trek. (In 2011, the *Guardian* listed *A Time of Gifts* among its 100 greatest nonfiction titles of all time.)

Subjects: European History; Walking

Categories: On Foot

Places: Austria; Czech Republic; Germany; Netherlands; Prague; Slovakia; Vienna

Now Try: Nicholas Bouvier's *The Way of the World* is another classic story of a young man wandering through a number of countries (Greece, Turkey, Iran, Afghanistan, India, and Pakistan) at a critical time for those nations, the early 1950s. Fermor wrote several other travel narratives, including *Mani: Travels in the Southern Peloponnese,* about his trip to the isolated Mani peninsula in Greece, and *Roumeli: Travels in Northern Greece,* about his travels through the rugged countryside of northern Greece and Macedonia.

Guevara, Ernesto (Che)

The Motorcycle Diaries: Notes on a Latin American Journey. Melbourne ; New York: Ocean Press, 2003 [1968]. 175 pp. ISBN: 9781876175702 YA

In 1952, when the future revolutionary Che Guevara was a 23-year-old medical student, he and his older friend Alberto Granado spent nine months exploring South America, beginning in Buenos Aires. They traveled primarily by motorcycle (a single-cylinder 1939 bike dubbed "The Mighty One") but also went by steamship, raft, horse, bus, and automobile (by hitchhiking). As Guevara witnessed the exploitation and mistreatment of mine workers, communists, and lepers, and as he contrasted their current degraded state to that of their once great Incan ancestors, his political consciousness was awakened and he became committed to bringing about social change. The journal is intelligently written and reflects the feelings and thoughts of a young man beginning to embrace his life's work as a revolutionary.

Subjects: 1950s; Communism; Motorcycles; Politics; Poverty; Quick Reads; Road Trips

Categories: On Two Wheels

Places: Argentina; Buenos Aires; Chile; Colombia; Ecuador; Miami; Panama; Peru; Venezuela

Now Try: The film based on the book, *The Motorcycle Diaries,* was well received and stars Gael Garcia Bernal as the young Guevara. Two other diaries of Guevara have been published as *Che: The Diaries of Ernesto Che Guevara*; one covers the guerilla movement led by Castro in Cuba in 1959, and the second covers his travels in Bolivia in the 1960s, where he was eventually captured and killed. Guevara's companion, Alberto Granado, published his version of the journey in *Traveling with Che Guevara: The Making of a Revolutionary,* and highlights the poverty and corruption that Guevara also saw. New York writer Patrick Symmes followed the route taken by Guevara and Granado in 1952 in order to better understand what they saw and how it changed Guevara; his travel narrative and his rather balanced observations on Latin America's fate after Guevara appear in *Chasing Che: A Motorcycle Journey in Search of the Guevara Legend.*

Hansen, Eric

Stranger in the Forest: On Foot across Borneo. Boston: Houghton Mifflin, 1988. 286 pp. ISBN: 9780395440933

Stranger in the Forest describes Hansen's seven-month 1982 walk across the third largest island in the world, Borneo, and back again. Hansen was the first Westerner to walk across the island and did so largely thanks to the help of the Penan, a local indigenous people, because his own preparations were practically worthless: the dialect of Malay that he learned was not the one used in the interior of the island, his maps were inaccurate and outdated, and he could not carry enough food for the crossing. The journey was filled with adventure (he went through the thick rain forest for four weeks without seeing the sun, his diet included bee larvae and boa constrictors, small cuts developed into festering wounds, and many of the natives believed him to be an evil spirit come to kill them for their blood) but in the end, the book is a tribute to the author's resilience, humor, and good luck (as well as to the natives' generosity).

Subjects: Adventure; Humor

Categories: On Foot

Places: Borneo

Series: *Vintage Departures*

Now Try: Several titles about journeys to Borneo are annotated in this book. These include two in the chapter on "Travel Adventure" (*All Elevations Unknown: An Adventure in the Heart of Borneo* by Sam Lightner, Jr., and *Shooting the Boh: A Woman's Voyage down the Wildest River in Borneo* by Tracy Johnston) and one in the chapter on "Travel Humor" (*Into the Heart of Borneo* by Redmon O'Hanlon). Tom Schmidt's *Bumbling Through Borneo* tells the humorous story of an American architect who journeys into the heart of the island. A novel set in Borneo is C. S. Godshalk's *Kalimantaan,* which involves a 19th-century British subject who set out as an explorer but became the ruler of a private raj on the north coast of Borneo.

Heat-Moon, William Least

Blue Highways: A Journey into America. Boston: Little, Brown, 1982. 421 pp. ISBN: 9780316140638

In 1978, Heat-Moon lost both his wife and his job and, as a result, decided to embark on a 13,000-mile journey through the backroads of 38 of the 50 American states, referred to as "blue highways" because they were colored blue on his maps. His respect for the many individuals he meets along the way and his willingness to listen to their stories ("He has a genius for finding people who have not even found themselves," as one critic put it) as well as his reflections on small-town and rural America, American Indian culture and history, and his own personal issues weave together to create a wonderfully profound appreciation of the nation's small-town charm, which Heat-Moon sees as being rapidly lost. The book is wickedly funny in places and represents a truly classic road trip.

Subjects: Humor; Road Trips

Categories: Healing Odysseys; On the Road

Places: Alabama; Arizona; California; Georgia; Idaho; Illinois; Indiana; Kentucky; Louisiana; Maine; Maryland; Michigan; Minnesota; Mississippi; Montana; Nevada; New Hampshire; New Jersey; New Mexico; New York; North Carolina; North Dakota; Oregon; Rhode Island; South Carolina; Tennessee; Texas; Vermont; Washington; West Virginia; Wisconsin

Now Try: Heat-Moon's other travel narratives are annotated in other parts of this book: *River-Horse: The Logbook of a Boat Across America,* in this chapter; *Roads to Quoz: An American Mosey,* in the chapter on "Quests"; and *PrairyErth (A Deep Map): An Epic History of the Tallgrass Prairie Country,* in the chapter on "A Sense of Place." *Blue Highways* begins when Heat-Moon loses his job as a college professor; Douglas G. Brinkley is a college professor who combines history and life lessons in *The Majic Bus: An American Odyssey,* which chronicles a six-week experimental class aboard a sleeper bus that visits 30 states. Bill Bryson also visited back-roads America in his book, *The Lost Continent: Travels in Small-Town America* (annotated in the chapter entitled "The Journey"), but he is less appreciative of that landscape than is Heat-Moon. Elizabeth Berg's novel, *The Pull of the Moon,* recounts the story of a 50-year-old woman who takes to the backroads in response to her midlife crisis; her letters to her husband and her diary entries describe the people she meets and the decisions she makes about her life.

Seth, Vikram

From Heaven Lake: Travels Through Sinkiang and Tibet. London: Chatto & Windus, 1983. 178 pp. ISBN: 9780701127008

Seth was a student at Nanjing University in China in the early 1980s when he decided to hitchhike to his home in India for the summer. The trip was demanding, from its path through forbidden Tibet to the hours spent in the truck cab with a chain-smoking, eccentric driver. Seth, who would later become a novelist, provides marvelous descriptions of the stark beauty of the countries through which he traveled, sad observations of the aftermath of China's cultural revolution in the smashed temples and destroyed works of art, wonderful portraits of the generous people with whom he interacted, and incredible details of the cultures, like the

1 2 3 4 5 6 7

mosque in Sinkiang where the Islamic scriptures were carved into the walls in both Arabic and Chinese.

Subjects: Memoirs; Quick Reads

Categories: On the Road

Places: China; India; Nepal; Tibet

Awards: Thomas Cook Travel Book Award, 1983

Now Try: John Dwyer traveled through much of the same territory that Seth did and describes his trip, which included drinking snake blood in southwest China and being smuggled into Tibet, in *High Road To Tibet: Travels in China, Tibet, Nepal and India*. Renowned travel writer Robert Byron recounts an even earlier journey through Tibet and India in the 1930s in his classic book, *First Russia, Then Tibet: Travels through a Changing World*; like Seth, Byron describes the many changes being felt by the countries through which he traveled. Seth compares the autocratic communist government of China with the fledging democracy of India, and this theme also lies at the heart of Aravind Adiga's Booker Prize winning novel, *The White Tiger*. Yiyun Li's grim novel, *The Vagrants*, also explores the aftermath of the Cultural Revolution in China, through the execution of a former Red Guard leader in a provincial town in the late 1970s.

Steinbeck, John

Travels with Charley: In Search of America. New York: Penguin Books, 2002 [1962]. 214 pp. ISBN: 9780142000700 YA

Travels with Charley recounts Steinbeck's 1960 road trip through America with his poodle Charley, a trip that Steinbeck took to get back in touch with the country: "I've lost the flavor and taste and sound of it. I'm going to learn about my own country." Steinbeck drove his camper (named Rosinante, after Don Quixote's horse) from New York to California and back to the American south, where he was shocked by the racism he encountered. Through it all, Steinbeck speculated on a variety of topics (the vast size of the country, the loss of regional speech, the love of people for their dogs) and met a number of fascinating people. Steinbeck's skill as a writer is evident throughout the book, which provides an absorbing portrait of the country and its people just before the Vietnam War.

Subjects: Animals; Campers; Dogs; Quick Reads; Road Trips

Categories: On the Road

Places: California; Connecticut; Illinois; Indiana; Louisiana; Maine; Michigan; Minnesota; Montana; New York; North Dakota; Ohio; Oregon; Texas; Washington; Wisconsin; Wyoming

Now Try: Steinbeck won the Nobel Prize for Literature in 1962, and his most famous novel, *The Grapes of Wrath*, involves the travels of the Joad family from their farm in

Oklahoma to California. In 1947, Steinbeck made the first of several trips to the Soviet Union and thereby became one of the first Westerners to visit many parts of that country since the communist revolution. He wrote about those experiences in *A Russian Journal*. Bill Barich was inspired by *Travels with Charley* to drive across the United States and report on the America revealed in its small towns in *Long Way Home: On the Trail of Steinbeck's America*. Bruce Fogle was also inspired by Steinbeck's book and traveled around the United States and Canada in a motor home with his golden retriever, a story told in *Travels with Macy*. Lars Eighner's *Travels with Lizbeth* is the first-person account of a homeless man who hitchhikes from Texas to California with his dog and, like *Travels with Charley*, includes some pointed observations about the country.

Theroux, Paul

The Great Railway Bazaar. Boston: Houghton Mifflin, 1975. 342 pp. ISBN: 9780395207086

This is Theroux's first (and, some critics would argue, his finest) travel narrative, describing a four-month train trip across Europe, the Middle East, and Asia, which the author took in 1975. The book features some of the world's best-known railway lines, including the Orient Express, the Tehran Express, India's Grand Trunk Express, and the Trans-Siberian Railway. Theroux's main subjects are the trains themselves and the passengers he encountered, and he shares his usual strong opinions of people and places. Theroux is a writer that some readers love for his keen observations and brilliant writing, but others find him misanthropic and tedious.

Subjects: Asian History; European History; Middle Eastern History; Rail Travel

Category: On the Rails

Places: Afghanistan; England; France; India; Iran; Italy; Japan; Laos; Myanmar; Pakistan; Russia; Serbia; Sri Lanka; Thailand; Turkey

Series: *Picador Travel Classics*

Now Try: Thirty years after the trip described in *The Great Railway Bazaar*, Theroux retraced his journey in *Ghost Train to the Eastern Star: On the Tracks of the Great Railway Bazaar* (annotated in "The Journey"). One of the trains that Theroux rides in his book, the Orient Express, is well known for being the setting of one of Agatha Christie's finest mysteries, *Murder on the Orient Express*, as well as Graham Greene's novel of betrayal, *Stamboul Train*. Theroux is also a fine novelist, and while his novel about a family that leaves the United States to settle in the jungles of Central America, *The Mosquito Coast*, does not involve trains, it is his best-known work of fiction. The film version of the novel, which was directed by Peter Weir and starred Harrison Ford, is equally powerful.

Theroux, Paul

The Kingdom by the Sea: A Journey around the Coast of Great Britain. Boston: Houghton Mifflin, 1983. 353 pp. ISBN: 9780395346457

In the summer of 1982, during the Falklands War, Theroux traveled around the coastline of Great Britain and Northern Ireland, mainly by train, and found a number of British citizens willing to talk about themselves and their country. Typical of Theroux, he did his best to avoid tourist destinations, and so much of his time was spent in decaying seaside resorts like Hartlepool and Margate. The book is a compelling and perceptive portrayal of England in the 1980s, arguably at its dreariest and at the height of the unemployment and poverty that many of its citizens had to endure.

Subjects: Rail Travel; Small Town Life

Categories: On the Rails

Places: England; Northern Ireland; Scotland; Wales

Now Try: Bill Bryson's *Notes from a Small Island* (annotated in the chapter on "Travel Humor") is that author's farewell tour of his adopted country; Bryson traveled only by public transportation and offers observations as scathing in places as any of Theroux's. In *Eleven Minutes Late: A Train Journey to the Soul of Britain* (annotated in this chapter), Matthew Engel travels the railroads of Great Britain and explores their history. Ian Marchant does much the same in *Parallel Lines: Or, Journeys on the Railway of Dreams*, although his focus is more nostalgic for the better days of the railway system. Trains are the scene for a number of Agatha Christie's mysteries, including *4:50 From Paddington: A Miss Marple Mystery*, which involves a murder on one train seen by a witness on a train running parallel to it.

Theroux, Paul

The Old Patagonian Express: By Train through the Americas. Boston: Houghton Mifflin, 1979. 404 pp. ISBN: 9780395277881

In 1978, Theroux decided to travel from his childhood home in Massachusetts to the small town of Esquel, Argentina, entirely by rail. Theroux provides detailed descriptions of the trains he rode, the places he passed through, and especially the people he met (a woman in Veracruz looking for a long-lost love, a bogus priest in Colombia, the author Jorge Luis Borges in Argentina). He also provides his thoughts on a wide range of topics: the differences between the American and Mexican sides of the Rio Grande, the poverty of the indigenous Indians in Mexico, the violence of a soccer match he watched in El Salvador. Theroux, as usual, is perceptive, but he is also curmudgeonly, and many readers are turned off by his sarcasm and critical remarks about his fellow travelers.

Subjects: Rail Travel

Categories: On the Rails

Places: Argentina; Colombia; Costa Rica; Ecuador; El Salvador; Guatemala; Mexico; Panama; Peru; United States

Now Try: Patagonia has been the subject of several travel narratives, most notably Bruce Chatwin's highly-regarded *In Patagonia* (annotated in the chapter on "A Sense of Place"), which is based on that writer's six-month trip to Theroux's ultimate destination, and Anne Whitehead's *Bluestocking in Patagonia: Mary Gilmore's Quest for Love and Utopia at the World's End*, the true story of an aspiring writer who travels with her husband to found a Socialist utopia in Paraguay. Gregory Crouch's *Enduring Patagonia* is an adventure travel narrative about the author's three expeditions to climb a series of peaks on the border of Chile and Argentina. Robert Kull built a cabin in Patagonia to study the impact of isolation on a human being (himself) and relates the experience in *Solitude: Seeking Wisdom in Extremes: A Year Alone in the Patagonia Wilderness*. Bolivian author Juan de Recacoechea's captivating novel, *Andean Express*, involves a 1952 murder on the overnight train from Bolivia to Chile.

Theroux, Paul

Riding the Iron Rooster: By Train Through China. New York: Putnam's, 1988. 480 pp. ISBN: 9780399133091

Theroux explored China and Tibet by train in the late 1980s, a decade after the Cultural Revolution and the death of Mao, and reports here on what he found. He visited both major cities like Beijing and Guangzhou and remote villages along little-used rail lines, and he tried to avoid the usual tourist destinations. His survey of the two countries is intimate and includes fascinating portraits of the people he met and spoke with, particularly about the changes they had experienced. As usual, Theroux is grouchy, even cynical, but his writing is keen and finely detailed.

Subjects: Rail Travel

Categories: On the Rails

Places: Beijing; China; Guangzhou; Tibet

Awards: Thomas Cook Travel Book Award, 1989

Now Try: Theroux is a prolific writer of travel narratives, and several of his titles are annotated in this book. In addition to a number that involve travel by train, Theroux's books also include *The Pillars of Hercules* (annotated in "A Sense of Place"), in which he explores the Mediterranean coast by foot, train, and boat; *The Kingdom by the Sea: A Journey Around the Coast of Great Britain* (annotated above), in which he travels around the coastline of England; and *The Happy Isles of Oceania: Paddling the Pacific* (annotated in "The Journey"), in which he explores 51 islands in the South Pacific, traveling by collapsible kayak. In *Sky Train: Tibetan Women on the Edge of History*, activist Canyon Sam visits Tibet by train to describe four women whose lives were fundamentally changed by the Chinese occupation of their country. Readers who are interested in train travel may enjoy Carlos A. Schwantes's beautifully illustrated memoir of a life riding trains, *Just One Restless Rider: Reflections on Trains and Travel*.

On Foot

The titles is this category all feature travel by walking, a means of travel that is slower than the other methods of transportation and allows the traveler a more intimate connection with the places through which he travels. The slower pace of walking may also enable the traveler to have richer exchanges with traveling partners (Jason Goodwin and his two friends in *On Foot to the Golden Horn: A Walk to Istanbul*) or strangers encountered on the trip (Nicholas Crane's *Clear Waters Rising: A Mountain Walk Across Europe*) or both (as in the case of Bill Bryson's *A Walk in the Woods: Rediscovering America on the Appalachian Trail*, in which he not only interacts with his friend Katz but with other hikers on the trail).

Travel on foot is a more active pursuit for the traveler and allows her more control over the path than does rail travel or travel on the road. Consequently, these walks may have a purpose, as in Nathan Gray's attempt to become the first person to walk the length of the Great Wall of China (*First Pass Under Heaven: One Man's 4000-Kilometre Trek Along the Great Wall of China*) or Doris Haddock's trek across the United States to lobby for campaign reform (*Granny D: Walking Across America in My 90th Year*). On the other hand, they may involve no specific itinerary and may be more like Tim Cahill's rambles through Yellowstone in *Lost In My Own Backyard: A Walk in Yellowstone National Park.*

Many of the titles in this category feature aspects of other travel subgenres and categories (humor in Bill Bryson's *A Walk in the Woods: Rediscovering America on the Appalachian Trail*, religious themes in Christopher Somerville's *The Golden Step: A Walk Through the Heart of Crete*, or political themes in Raja Shehadeh's *Palestinian Walks: Notes on a Vanishing Landscape*), and readers with an interest in those types of titles may find these of interest.

Fans of travel narratives that involve walking will likely find books on walking in general (*The Complete Walker IV* by Colin Fletcher and Chip Rawlins or Rebecca Solnit's *Wanderlust: A History of Walking*) to be of interest, as well as biographies or memoirs of famous walkers (John Muir's *A Thousand-Mile Walk to the Gulf* or Colin Fletcher's *The Man Who Walked Through Time: The Story of the First Trip Afoot Through the Grand Canyon*). Fiction that involves long walks, like Charles Frazier's *Cold Mountain* or Marly Youmans's *Catherwood*, may also appeal.

Bryson, Bill

A Walk in the Woods: Rediscovering America on the Appalachian Trail. New York: Broadway, 1998. 276 pp. ISBN: 9780767902526 YA

Bryson, a native of the U.S. Midwest who had been living in England for 20 years, returned to the states and decided to reconnect to the landscape by hiking the 2,100-mile Appalachian Trail. Unfortunately, Bryson was somewhat ill prepared for the trip, lacking any real backpacking experience, and he made matters worse by traveling with his overweight, junk food obsessed friend Steven Katz.

The result is a hilarious narrative, filled with witty observations about himself, about Katz, about the people they met, and about the situation. However, it is also an educational narrative, as Bryson is full of information about the trail and the sites they saw on it.

Subjects: Climbing and Hiking; Friendships; Humor; Mountains; Quick Reads; Walking

Places: Appalachian Trail

Now Try: Bryson has written a number of travel narratives, including *Notes from a Small Island, I'm a Stranger Here Myself: Notes on Returning to America After 20 Years Away, The Lost Continent: Travels in Small-Town America,* and *In a Sunburned Country,* all of which are annotated in this book. Readers who find themselves laughing out loud at Bryson's often self-deprecating wit may want to venture outside travel and try his wonderful memoir of growing up in 1950s America, *The Life and Times of the Thunderbolt Kid: A Memoir*. The Appalachian Trail is well represented in the travel literature, although few of the titles share Bryson's humorous style. Good titles include David Miller's *AWOL on the Appalachian Trail,* Kelly Winters's *Walking Home: A Woman's Pilgrimage on the Appalachian Trail,* Adrienne Hall's *A Journey North: One Woman's Story of Hiking the Appalachian Trail,* Leslie Mass's *In Beauty May She Walk: Hiking the Appalachian Trail at 60,* and Bill Irwin's *Blind Courage*. Irwin's book is particularly inspiring, as the author hiked the trail in spite of being blind. Bryson's wry humor is similar to that of Redmond O'Hanlon, whose *In Trouble Again: A Journey Between the Orinoco and the Amazon* and *Into the Heart of Borneo* are annotated in the "Travel Humor" chapter.

Cahill, Tim

Lost In My Own Backyard: A Walk in Yellowstone National Park. New York: Crown Journeys 2004. 138 pp. ISBN: 9781400046225.

Cahill lived 50 miles from the world's first national park but admits that he knew very little about it: "I live fifty miles from the park, but proximity does not guarantee competence. I've spent entire afternoons not knowing exactly where I was, which is to say, I was lost in my own backyard." The book describes Cahill's wanderings in the park, particularly those that were away from the paved roads to which most tourists stick. He encountered animals (bears of various persuasions, wolves, and coyotes) and a variety of natural phenomena (fumaroles, geysers, glaciers, mudpots, petrified forests, and waterfalls). As always, Cahill mixes a wealth of information with his unmatched sense of humor.

Subjects: Animals; Environment; Hiking; Humor; Quick Reads; Walking

Places: Montana; Yellowstone National Park; Wyoming

Series: *Crown Journeys*

Now Try: A more sobering account of visits to the 20-million-acre park is *Death in Yellowstone: Accidents and Foolhardiness in the First National* by Lee

Whittlesey, which describes the deaths of more than 250 people, most of which occurred because of human mistakes and negligence. Gary Ferguson lived for a year in Hawks Rest, the most remote corner of Yellowstone, and tells about what he sees as a fragile ecosystem under threat in *Hawks Rest: A Season in the Remote Heart of Yellowstone.* Ferguson is also the author of *Walking Down the Wild: A Journey Through the Yellowstone Rockies,* which tells of his 500-mile hike through the park's mountains and reiterates his sense that the Yellowstone ecosystem needs to be protected. Diane Smith's epistolary novel, *Letters from Yellowstone,* follows a 19th-century female botanist's summer with a group of male scientists who are surprised when she turns out to be a woman; the novel explores the early history of the park as well as the struggles of a woman to gain the respect of her male colleagues.

Crane, Nicholas

Clear Waters Rising: A Mountain Walk Across Europe. London: Viking, 1996. 374 pp. ISBN: 9780670868391

Newly married and just turning 40, British geographer Crane decided to journey on foot through some of the remotest parts of Europe, travelling along the chain of mountains that runs from Cape Finisterre on the coast of Galicia in northwest Spain to Istanbul. The 17-month, 6,200-mile journey took him through the Pyrenees, France's Massif Central, the Alps, the Carpathians, and finally the Balkans. At first, Crane seemed to avoid other people, but as the trek continued, he softened and his interactions with and observations of those he met are particularly interesting. Crane is funny in places, always optimistic and resilient, and an excellent writer.

Subjects: Climbing and Hiking; Humor; Mountains; Walking

Places: Austria; Bulgaria; France; Italy; Poland; Romania; Slovakia; Spain; Switzerland; Turkey; Ukraine

Awards: Thomas Cook Travel Book Award, 1997

Now Try: Crane is a delightful writer, and readers who enjoy *Clear Waters Rising* may be interested in his other books. In *Great British Journeys,* he retraces the journeys of eight earlier travelers, including Gerald of Wales, who explored that country in seven weeks in 1188, and H. V. Morton, who crossed England by automobile in the 1920s. In *Two Degrees West,* he follows the longitude line of the title, which runs through the center of England, and provides a look at England in the 1990s. One of the writers who inspired Crane's journey in *Clear Waters Rising* was Robert Louis Stevenson, whose *Travels with a Donkey in the Cévennes* recounts the author's 12-day solo hike through the mountains in south-central France.

Goodwin, Jason

On Foot to the Golden Horn: A Walk to Istanbul. New York: Henry Holt, 1995. 278 pp. ISBN: 9780805040821

Goodwin and two friends walked through Eastern Europe from Gdansk, on Poland's Baltic coast, to the Golden Horn in Istanbul. Their journey was adventurous enough (sleeping in haystacks, drinking with Gypsies, dealing with hostile customs officials) but it also took place during an extremely important time, as the Iron Curtain was falling and a new Europe was going through its birth pangs. The story of this spectacular walk is told in crisp, vivid detail and with a touch of self-deprecating humor.

Subjects: Communism; European History; Friendships; Humor; Walking

Places: Bulgaria; Czech Republic; Hungary; Istanbul; Poland; Romania; Slovakia; Turkey

Now Try: Goodwin followed up *On Foot to the Golden Horn* with *Lords of the Horizons: A History of the Ottoman Empire,* a quirky history that some readers have found charming and others have found incomprehensible. Readers who want to know more about Goodwin's destination, Istanbul, may appreciate the sad, highly personal memoir by Nobel Prize winner Orhan Pamuk, *Istanbul: Memories and the City*. John Freely's *Istanbul: The Imperial City* is more history than travel narrative, but the fact that Freely taught in Istanbul makes it a more personal history. *The Dervish House,* a novel by British science fiction writer Ian McDonald, takes place in Istanbul in the near future and weaves together the stories of six people whose lives intersect in surprising ways, with the city itself playing an important role. Dave Eggers's debut novel, *You Shall Know Our Velocity,* also concerns two friends who travel around the world, but these friends are giving away a large sum of money that one of them has come into.

Gray, Nathan

First Pass Under Heaven: One Man's 4000-Kilometre Trek Along the Great Wall of China. Auckland, NZ: Penguin Books, 2004. 267 pp. ISBN: 9780143020677

In 2000, Gray attempted to become the first person to walk the entire length (about 2,500 miles) of the Great Wall of China. His journey included several companions (a Buddhist monk, a Jewish photojournalist, a Catholic recording artist, and a Mormon golfer) in an attempt to mark the millennium with a show of cultural, racial, and religious harmony but soon encountered challenges from the weather (blizzards), harassment by the Chinese police, and the journey itself (thirst and starvation). In addition to telling the inspiring story of his trek, Gray also provides a good bit of information about the history of the Wall and enlightening insights into China's political climate.

Subjects: Great Wall of China; Hiking; Politics; Walking

Places: China

Now Try: Photographer William Lindesay's *The Great Wall Revisited: From the Jade Gate to Old Dragon's Head* is lavishly illustrated and uses the photographs to show the differences between the Great Wall today and the one depicted in earlier drawings and photographs. Lindesay also ran over 1,500 miles along the Great Wall, a two-year obsession that he describes in *Alone on the Great Wall*. Robin Hanbury-Tenison and his wife rode 1000 miles alongside the Great Wall on horseback and witnessed the changes in China after the Cultural Revolution; their story is told in *Ride Along the Great Wall*. Readers who enjoy *First Pass Under Heaven* may also enjoy the many "stunt memoirs" that have become popular in recent years. These include Richard Preston's *The Wild Trees: A Story of Passion and Daring*, about California's coastal redwood trees and the recreational climbers who scale them, and A. J. Jacobs's *My Life as an Experiment: One Man's Humble Quest to Improve Himself by Living as a Woman, Becoming George Washington, Telling No Lies, and Other Radical Tests*, in which the author performs a series of life "experiments," such as outsourcing his daily tasks to a team in India and speaking nothing but the truth for a month.

Haddock, Doris, and Dennis Burke

Granny D: Walking Across America in My 90th Year. New York: Villard Books, 2001. 285 pp. ISBN: 9780375505393 YA

Beginning in January 1999, Doris Haddock (aka "Granny D") walked across the United States, from Los Angeles to Washington, DC, to lobby for campaign finance reform. Along the way, she spoke with people about her cause, encouraged them to write to their legislators, gave speeches, and marched in parades. Fourteen months and 3,200 miles after she started, Granny D arrived at the steps of the Capitol, accompanied by over 2,000 supporters and the national and international media. Haddock endured deserts, Rocky Mountains, Southern humidity, and Northeast blizzards to fulfill her purpose, and she tells her story with a good sense of humor and a sprinkling of wisdom.

Subjects: Elderly; Politics; Walking; Women Travelers

Places: Arizona; Arkansas; California; Kentucky; Maryland; New Mexico; Pennsylvania; Tennessee; Texas; Washington, DC; West Virginia

Now Try: Haddock continued her political work until she died at the age of 100; she and Dennis Burke wrote *Granny D: You're Never Too Old to Raise a Little Hell* as a follow-up to her book about walking across the United States. Audrey McCollum traveled to Papua New Guinea, where she met Pirip Kuru, a tribal woman who had founded a women's rights organization there; the story of their friendship and attempts to improve the lot of rural women is told in *Two Women, Two Worlds*. Scott Hunt traveled around the world to meet a number of individuals who are fighting for peace and justice, including the Dalai Lama, Jane Goodall, and Aung San Suu Kyi; their words and his reflections are found in his book, *The Future of Peace: On the Front Lines with the World's Great Peacemakers*. Fans of the 90-something Granny D may also enjoy Elizabeth and Sarah Delany's memoir, *Having Our Say: The Delany Sisters' First 100 Years*.

Morland, Miles

Miles Away: A Walk across France. New York: Random House, 1992. 238 pp. ISBN: 9780679425274

In 1989, Morland, a 45-year-old banker, gave up his high-pressure job and backpacked 350 miles across France (from the Mediterranean to the Atlantic) with Guislaine, whom he had divorced after 13 years of marriage and then remarried. *Miles Away* recounts their preparations for the trip, the blistering trek itself through farmyards, dusty villages, and vineyards, the history of the French countryside through which they pass, and the sheer joy that they felt in being together. Morland, who describes himself as a "middle-aged wreck," tells the story with charm and humor.

Subjects: Divorce; Humor; Marriage; Quick Reads; Walking

Places: France

Now Try: *Washington Post* writer L. Peat O'Neil hiked from the Atlantic to the Mediterranean through the Pyrenees Mountains between Spain and France and wrote about the experience in *Pyrenees Pilgrimage: Walking Across France*; the book also shares recipes, wines, and practical tips for others who wish to make the same journey. Robin Neillands also walked 700 miles from the English Channel to the Mediterranean through French backroads and villages; his reflections on the local people, the history of the areas he passed through, and the wonderful cuisine are captured in *Walking Through France: From the Channel to the Camargue*. When poet Ezra Pound was a young man, he followed the paths of the troubadours in southern France; Richard Sieburth edited Pound's notes on these walks in *A Walking Tour in Southern France: Ezra Pound Among the Troubadours* and followed in Pound's footsteps through France himself. Hiking in the Dordogne region of France forms the backdrop of Michelle Wan's debut novel, *Deadly Slipper*, in which woman goes to France to look for clues about her twin sister's disappearance there 20 years earlier; the novel is filled with wonderful descriptions of the region and details of the local cuisine.

Sandham, Fran

Traversa: A Solo Walk Across Africa, From the Skeleton Coast to the Indian Ocean. London, New York: Duckworth Overlook, 2007. 274 pp. ISBN: 9780715637029

Fran Sandham, a former *Rough Guides* editor who was working at a London bookshop when the idea struck him, writes about his solo trek on foot across Africa, from the Skeleton Coast in Namibia, which borders the Atlantic Ocean, to Bagamoyo in Tanzania, which borders the Indian Ocean. Sandham tells of his encounters with dangers as varied as animals (lions, snakes, cockroaches the size of mice), malaria, bandits, and land mines as well as stories of those who went before him, such as Livingstone and Stanley. Sandham wavered between determination and self-doubt throughout the trip, and he is a likeable and self-deprecating storyteller.

Subjects: African History; Humor; Solo Travelers; Walking

Places: Africa; Malawi; Namibia; Tanzania; Zambia

Now Try: Julian Smith followed in the footsteps of 19th-century British explorer Ewart Grogan by walking 4,000 miles through eight African countries; Smith tells his own story as well as Grogan's and the story of Africa's changes as a continent in *Crossing the Heart of Africa: An Odyssey of Love and Adventure*. Rick Ridgeway walked 300 miles from Mount Kilimanjaro to the Indian Ocean and told his story in *The Shadow of Kilimanjaro*, which includes reflections on Kenya's colonial history and its struggles as a developing nation. Paula Constant and her husband walked from Trafalgar Square in London to the edge of the Sahara Desert in Morocco, a yearlong, 3,100-mile journey that she recounts in *Slow Journey South: Walking to Africa*. The Travel Channel series *Africatrek* recounts the journey of a newly married couple's trek on foot across the African continent, and is available on DVD.

Shehadeh, Raja

Palestinian Walks: Notes on a Vanishing Landscape. New York: Scribner, 2008. 200 pp. ISBN: 9781416569664

Shehadeh is a Palestinian human rights lawyer and writer who has lived on the West Bank since 1948. For decades, he has found comfort in walking, and the book uses six of his walks to tell the story of the struggles, disappointments, and hopes of the Palestinian people. Shehadeh describes a beautiful landscape of hills, rivers, sacred springs, and famous landmarks like the Shuqba Caves, Wadi Qelt, and the Dead Sea, but he also describes the disappearance of his treasured freedom to walk through the countryside as the area has become the site of standoffs between Palestinians and Israeli settlers. *Palestinian Walks* is an intensely personal account of life in one of the world's most troubled regions.

Subjects: Islam; Jews and Judaism; Middle Eastern History; Quick Reads; Walking; War

Places: Palestinian Territories

Awards: Orwell Prize, 2008

Now Try: Shehadeh is also the author of *When the Birds Stopped Singing: Life in Ramallah Under Siege*, which describes his experiences during the Israeli invasion of his West Bank city in 2002, and the autobiographical *Strangers in the House: Coming of Age in Occupied Palestine*. Like Shehadeh, American Pamela J. Olson lived in Ramallah; she tells about her two years there as an editor for the Palestine *Monitor* in her book, *Fast Times in Palestine*. Greg Myre and Jennifer Griffin reported from Jerusalem for the *New York Times* and Fox News respectively and also raised a family there; they write about how the Israeli–Palestinian conflict has transformed into a new kind of war, one with fewer clear, decisive military victories, in *This Burning Land: Lessons from the Front Lines of the Transformed Israeli-Palestinian Conflict*. Sandy Tolan's *The Lemon Tree: An Arab, a Jew, and the Heart of the Middle East* looks at the Arab–Israeli conflict through the lives of a Palestinian refugee, a Jewish settler, and the home that the latter lives in and that the former's father built and fled during the 1948 formation of Israel. Suad Amiry's *Sharon and My Mother-in-Law: Ramallah Diaries*, about the challenges of daily life in the West Bank town of Ramallah, may also appeal.

Somerville, Christopher

The Golden Step: A Walk through the Heart of Crete. London: Haus Publishing, 2007. 318 pp. ISBN: 9781904950974

Somerville, who wrote the "Walk of the Month" column for London's *Daily Telegraph* for 15 years, hiked 300 miles from the eastern coast of Crete to its western coast with only a map (and a rather unreliable map at that), a walking stick, a compass, and very little Greek. Along the way, he enjoyed the hospitality of the locals, crossed mountains and gorges, and lived without a mobile phone or other technological conveniences. There is a religious theme to the book, as Somerville began his journey on Easter and ended it on Whitsun (Pentecost) at the Monastery of the Golden Step, whose golden steps can only be seen by the pure, according to legend. There is also a good bit of reflection on the history and people of Crete, with whom Somerville is clearly enamored.

Subjects: Hiking; Islands; Religion; Walking

Categories: Landscapes and People

Places: Crete

Series: *Armchair Traveller Series*

Now Try: Crete has been the subject of several good travel narratives, and Barry Unsworth's *Crete* is annotated in the "A Sense of Place" chapter of this book. Others include Jeffrey Collman's *Walks with Crete's Spring Flowers*, which recounts the author's botanical walks in Crete over the past ten years; Dilys Powell's 1973 classic, *Villa Ariadne*, which is both an autobiography and a portrait of the island; and Anthony Cox's *Still Life in Crete*, in which the author and his wife retire to a corner of western Crete and write about their experiences. Part of Haruki Murakami's novel, *Sputnik Sweetheart*, is set on an unnamed Greek island, much like Crete; a college student falls in love with a classmate who later disappears from the Greek island, where she has accompanied a businesswoman with whom she has apparently fallen in love.

Stevenson, Andrew

Summer Light: A Walk across Norway. Melbourne, Oakland: Lonely Planet Publications, 2002. 235 pp. ISBN: 9781864503470

Stevenson lived in Norway for five years and walked and cycled from Oslo to Bergen with his new love Annabel to introduce her to the country's splendid fjords and mountains. The pair stayed on cliff-top farms, climbed the country's highest mountains, and took a side trip to Spitzbergen, north of the Arctic Circle. Stevenson's vivid, affectionate account of their trip includes portraits of the people they met along the path (particularly rural Norwegians) and their way of life, speculations on the Norwegian light and its effect on the people there, and occasional mishaps, like getting stuck in a snowdrift or two.

Subjects: Arctic Regions; Bicycling; Mountains; Quick Reads; Walking

Places: Norway

Series: *Lonely Planet Journeys*

Now Try: Joanna Kavenna's *The Ice Museum: In Search of the Lost Land of Thule* (annotated in the "Quests" chapter of this book) includes some exceptional sections on Norway. Ian Mitchell recounts his trip into the Norwegian fjords on a 30-foot yacht and speculates on Norway's place in the modern world in *Isles of the North: A Voyage to the Lands of the Norse.* Eric Dregni and his pregnant wife spent a year in Norway, thanks to Eric's Fulbright Fellowship; he writes about that year and the birth of their son there in the engaging *In Cod We Trust: Living the Norwegian Dream.* Another meandering story about a man and his new love is Michael Perry's memoir, *Truck: A Love Story,* in which the part-time medical technician sets out to fix an old pickup truck and falls in love with a local woman.

Stewart, Rory

The Places in Between. Orlando, FL: Harcourt, Inc., 2006 [2004]. 299 pp. ISBN: 9780156031561

The Places in Between, Stewart's first book, recounts his January 2002 walk across Afghanistan territory still loosely held by the Taliban. Stewart had been warned against making this journey; as one member of the Afghan Security Service told him, "It is mid-winter. There are three meters of snow on the high passes, there are wolves, and this is a war. You will die, I can guarantee." Luckily for Stewart, he survived, thanks to his knowledge of Persian and Muslim customs and thanks to the kindness of the many strangers whom he met. Stewart's focus, in fact, is on these strangers (some kind, some terribly cruel, some supporters of the Taliban, some drug dealers, and some simple farmers) and less on himself. Superbly written with an understated humor and a conversational style, the book provides many insights into this nation of conflict.

Subjects: Adventure; Asian History; Humor; Islam; Walking

Places: Afghanistan

Awards: Ondaatje Prize, 2005; *New York Times* Notable Book, 2006

Now Try: Stewart's next book, *The Prince of the Marshes: And Other Occupational Hazards of a Year in Iraq,* describes a year spent serving as a provincial governor in Iraq; it is annotated in this book, in the chapter entitled "The Expatriate Life." Post-Taliban Afghanistan is also the subject of *Come Back to Afghanistan: A California Teenager's Story* by Said Hyder Akbar and Susan Burton, which tells of Akbar's visits to his father, who had become the governor of an Afghan province; Akbar finds himself in several dangerous situations but, like Stewart, tells his story with both humor and insight. Ted Rall spent time in Afghanistan during the U.S. bombing and mixes columns he wrote for the *Village Voice* with a graphic novel that captures his observations of that time in *To Afghanistan and Back: A Graphic Travelogue.*

Watkins, Paul

The Fellowship of Ghosts: A Journey through the Mountains of Norway. Washington, DC: National Geographic, 2004. 233 pp. ISBN: 9780792267997

Watkins walked alone through Norway's three inland mountain ranges: the alpine Rondane; the severe Dovrefjell; and the icy, jagged Jotunheimen ("Home of the Giants" in Norse folklore). He based his journey on guidebooks written long ago by long-dead writers, hence the "fellowship of ghosts" that accompanied him. His writing is sometimes overdone as he describes a beautiful but harsh land, with blue fields of snow and valleys bordered by incredibly high cliffs, but his attempts to examine the effect that this bleak wilderness has on his senses and on the identity of the Norwegian people is often stirring.

Subjects: Hiking; Mountains; Self-Discovery; Solitude; Solo Travelers; Walking

Places: Norway

Now Try: Watkins is a well-regarded writer whose novel *Thunder God,* about a fisherman's son who is believed to hold one of the greatest secrets of the Norse religion, involves travel to Constantinople, the Balkan area, and Wales. In *Notes for the Aurora Society,* Jim O'Donnell walked 1,500 miles through Finland, another Scandinavian country, to learn about that country's history and to explore the connection between the Finns and their land. The Norwegian novelist Tomas Espedal's *Tramp: Or the Art of Living a Wild and Poetic Life* explores his need (and that of others, including great thinkers from Rousseau to Whitman) to explore the world on foot. Patti Jones Morgan followed her husband to Norway, where he worked on a North Sea oil project; she writes about her struggles with solitude, with cultural differences, and with the Norwegian language in *Island Soul: A Memoir of Norway.*

Wren, Christopher S.

Walking to Vermont: From Times Square into the Green Mountains—A Homeward Adventure. New York: Simon & Schuster, 2004. 273 pp. ISBN: 9780743251525

On his last day of work, foreign correspondent Wren walked out of the Manhattan office of the *New York Times* and set off on foot for the retirement home that he and his wife had bought in Vermont, over 400 miles away. Wren encountered a number of problems (an overweight backpack, blisters, weather, and his fear of bears), but dealing with these issues and the daily routine helped him forget about the problems of the world, which he had covered in his work, and appreciate the beauty of nature. He also encountered a number of colorful characters and learned that every hiker had a story to share. Most of all, though, Wren discovered his new self and conveys the joy of that discovery.

Subjects: Climbing and Hiking; Memoirs; Retirement; Self-Discovery; Walking

Places: New York City; Vermont

Now Try: Much of Wren's walk took place on the Appalachian Trail; in *AWOL on the Appalachian Trail,* David Miller tells how his life was changed as he pursued his dream of hiking the complete length of that trail. Jennifer Pharr Davis hiked the Appalachian Trail shortly after she graduated from college and hoped that the experience would help her decide what to do with her life; she recounts the challenges she met and the lessons she learned in *Becoming Odyssa: Epic Adventures on the Appalachian Trail*. Wren's destination was Vermont, which is where Bill McKibben began the walk he describes in *Wandering Home: A Long Walk Across America's Most Hopeful Landscape: Vermont's Champlain Valley and New York's Adirondacks,* an eloquent, rapturous celebration of the Adirondack area. Fans of walking in general may enjoy Geoff Nicholson's *The Lost Art of Walking: The History, Science, and Literature of Pedestrianism,* which is part history, part memoir, and part social commentary.

On the Rails

Travel by rail has a unique appeal. It is slower than air travel and allows the traveler more time to reflect on the places traveled through and the individuals traveled with. It often involves travel through the "hidden" side of the land (the back lots, the small towns, the countryside) and thereby provides the traveler with a different perspective on the places traveled through. Unlike traveling on foot, on bicycle or motorcycle, or by car, travel by rail follows a path prescribed by the tracks, and the traveler takes what comes more than in those other forms of travel.

Because of these aspects of rail travel, readers of these books will find fascinating character sketches (for example, Tom Allen's *Rolling Home: A Cross-Canada Railroad Memoir* or Terry Pindell's *Making Tracks: An American Rail Odyssey*) and intimate portraits of the countries through which the authors have traveled (Miles Brendin's *Blood on the Tracks: A Rail Journey from Angola to Mozambique* or Terry Pindell's *Yesterday's Train: A Rail Odyssey Through Mexican History*).

There is also often a sense of sadness in these titles (as in Tom Allen's *Rolling Home: A Cross-Canada Railroad Memoir*), for in some countries (the United States and Canada, in particular), the railroads have fallen on hard times.

Readers who find these narratives that involve travel by train to be of interest may also enjoy books about railroad history (Stephen E. Ambrose's *Nothing Like it in the World: The Men Who Built the Transcontinental Railroad, 1863–1869* or David Haward Bains's *Empire Express: Building the First Transcontinental Railroad*) or fiction set on trains (Leo Tolstoy's *Anna Karenina* or Howard Bahr's *Pelican Road*). Interestingly, a large number of mysteries are set on trains, and these (like Agatha Christie's *Murder on the Orient Express* or Patricia Highsmith's *Strangers on a Train*) may also be recommended.

Allen, Tom

Rolling Home: A Cross-Canada Railroad Memoir. Toronto, New York: Penguin/Viking, 2001. 298 pp. ISBN: 9780670884735

Allen, the host of CBC Radio's "Music & Company," crossed Canada by train with his family. Traveling from Halifax to British Columbia and then north to Hudson's Bay, they rode two-car dayliners that were held together with duct tape, and luxury cruisers packed with wealthy tourists. They met passengers from honeymooners to abandoned spouses and railway employees that included engineers, cooks, and porters, and the portraits of these individuals are occasionally touching. The narrative is partly a celebration of the importance of the Canadian railway system, which provides a vital link for many remote communities to the rest of the world, and its rich history, and partly a lament for a system that has seen its funding drastically reduced.

Subjects: Rail Travel; Small Town Life

Places: Alberta; British Columbia; Canada; Halifax; Manitoba; New Brunswick; Nova Scotia; Ontario; Quebec; Saskatchewan; Toronto; Vancouver; Winnipeg

Awards: Edna Staebler Award, 2002

Now Try: When Terry Pindell learned that the Canadian government had proposed large cutbacks to its passenger train services, he decided to explore that country's railway system for a year; he documents his travels and the history of the Canadian railway system in *Last Train to Toronto: A Canadian Rail Odyssey*. Pindell also traveled on Amtrak's 31 passenger train lines in the United States and wrote an account of those trips in *Making Tracks: An American Rail Odyssey*, which is annotated in this chapter. Greg McDonnell's *Passing Trains: The Changing Face of Canadian Railroading* focuses on the aspects of Canadian railways that are fading away and includes over 200 color photographs. *Destination Murder*, one of Donald Bain's Jessica Fletcher (*Murder, She Wrote*) mysteries, is set on a train trip through British Columbia.

Bredin, Miles

Blood on the Tracks: A Rail Journey from Angola to Mozambique. London: Picador, 1994. 257 pp. ISBN: 9780330330336

Bredin followed the route of the colonial railways through southern Africa and encountered three civil wars in the five countries that he visited, a reflection of the grim state of affairs in southern Africa. His travels from the Atlantic coast of Angola, where the former bustling center of the African slave trade lies in decay, to the Indian Ocean took place on a railway system that carried everything from diamonds and copper to refugees and food to mercenaries and weapons. Parts of this book about a journey through some of Africa's poorest countries are written with a dry humor, while other parts are terrifying.

Subjects: African History; Colonialism; Humor; Rail Travel; War

Places: Africa; Angola; Democratic Republic of the Congo; Mozambique; Zambia; Zimbabwe

Now Try: Another African railway trip is described by Denis Boyles in *Maneater's Motel and Other Stops on the Railway to Nowhere: An East African Traveler's Nightbook;* like Bredin, Boyles is alternately funny and grim in his descriptions of Africa. Rick Ridgeway walked 300 miles from Mount Kilimanjaro to the Indian Ocean and told his story in *The Shadow of Kilimanjaro,* which includes reflections on Kenya's colonial history and its struggles as a developing nation. While George Alagiah's *A Passage to Africa* does not involve rail travel, the BBC correspondent's story of emigrating with his parents to Ghana when he was five years old does mix outrage at the continent's past and hope for its future. Readers who enjoyed *Blood on the Tracks* may also enjoy general history books on colonialism and Africa, such as Adam Hochschild's horrifying *King Leopold's Ghost: A Story of Greed, Terror, and Heroism in Colonial Africa.*

Diski, Jenny

Stranger on a Train: Daydreaming and Smoking around America with Interruptions. New York: Picador USA, 2002. 280 pp. ISBN: 9780312283520

Stranger on a Train is based on two railway trips, the first across the southern United States and the second, a year later, around the perimeter of the country from New York to Portland, Oregon, and back. Diski, a British novelist, combines confessional memoir and cultural commentary with her somewhat halfhearted travel narrative (her editor wanted her to "put in more landscape and scenery") to produce a book that is fascinating and often humorous in its examination of America and Americans and of Diski herself, her smoking habit and other obsessions, her moral judgments of other people, and the occasional insights from her life.

Subjects: Humor; Memoirs; Rail Travel; Smoking; Solitude; Women Travelers

Places: Alabama; Arizona; California; Colorado; Delaware; Florida; Georgia; Idaho; Illinois; Indiana; Louisiana; Maryland; Minnesota; Mississippi; Montana; New Jersey; New Mexico; New York; North Carolina; North Dakota; Ohio; Oregon; Pennsylvania; South Carolina; Texas; Utah; Virginia; Washington; Washington, DC; Wisconsin

Awards: Thomas Cook Travel Book Award, 2003

Now Try: The emptiness of the American landscape that Diski depicts in *Stranger on a Train* is similar to the snowy emptiness she depicts in an earlier memoir and travel narrative, *Skating to Antarctica,* which weaves beautiful descriptions of her trip to that frozen continent with disturbing stories from her childhood. Diski's self-revelatory style is also apparent in her book, *On Trying to Keep Still,* which mixes descriptions of her year-long journey to New Zealand and digressions on topics as various as aging and trying to keep warm. In *Stranger on a Train,* Diski refers to Evelyn Waugh's novel, *A Handful of Dust,* which involves a journey to South America and whose sardonic tone is similar to Diski's. Diski's confessional style is similar to that of Janice Deaner in the novel, *The Body Spoken,* about a woman who confides to a stranger on a train that she has been living as a man for the past five years.

Eames, Andres

The 8:55 to Baghdad: From London to Iraq on the Trail of Agatha Christie and the Orient Express. Woodstock, NY: Overlook Press, 2006. 403 pp. ISBN: 9781585678020

Eames, a British travel writer, retraced a solo journey taken by Agatha Christie in 1928, after she and her first husband had ended their marriage. Eames rode in elegant cars that were salvaged from the original Orient Express and stayed in the same hotels as the great mystery writer. The resulting book combines travel narrative, literary biography, and history, as Eames recounts not just the story of Christie's trip but also the story of the Orient Express itself. The timing of Eames's trip (just prior to the Second Gulf War) was perhaps not the best, but he managed to meet friendly people, even in Iraq, where an explosion almost ended his trip prematurely.

Subjects: Authors; Rail Travel

Categories: In the Footsteps of . . .

Places: Baghdad; Belgrade; Bulgaria; Croatia; Damascus; Iraq; Istanbul; Serbia; Sofia; Syria; Turkey; Zagreb

Now Try: In addition to the obvious read-alike, Agatha Christie's *Murder on the Orient Express*, fiction readers may also enjoy Graham Greene's *Stamboul Train*, which tells a story of love and betrayal among a group of persons traveling from Belgium to Istanbul on the famous train. Eames is also the author of *Blue River, Black Sea*, which describes his journey along the Danube River by bicycle, by horse, by boat, and on foot. While Alexander Frater's *Beyond the Blue Horizon* involves travel by air instead of by train, it may be of interest to readers who enjoyed *The 8:55 to Baghdad* because of Frater's mix of past and present as he travels around the world using only routes that the pre-World War II Imperial Airways would have flown. Agatha Christie's *An Autobiography*, a new edition of which was released in 2011, is the great writer's story of her life and how she became a mystery writer.

Engel, Matthew

Eleven Minutes Late: A Train Journey to the Soul of Britain. London: Macmillan, 2009. 323 pp. ISBN: 9780230708983

Engel, who considers the railway system to be "the ultimate expression of Britishness," explored the system and its history by traveling as much of the network of trains as possible, talking to passengers and railway employees, and uncovering the most charming and bizarre train in Britain, the most beautiful branch line, and the rudest employee. In spite of its many humorous passages and witty observations, the book is a sad paean of sorts for a once-proud system that has suffered from both nationalization and privatization, although as Engel concludes, "It is not the politicians, in the final analysis, who are responsible for the mess. It is us, because we let them do it."

Subjects: Economics; Humor; Politics; Rail Travel

Places: England

Awards: Dolman Best Travel Book Award, Shortlist, 2010

Now Try: Ian Marchant's *Parallel Lines* is a more personal account of Britain's railways, in which the author makes a distinction between "the railway of reality" and "the railway of romance." *On the Slow Train: Twelve Great British Railway Journeys* by Michael Williams is more travel guide than travel narrative but it captures the same nostalgia for the former greatness of the British railway system that Engel reflects in *Eleven Minutes Late*. A more straightforward historical account of the British railway system is Christian Wolmar's *Fire & Steam: A New History of the Railways in Britain*, while a more salacious tale is Kate Colquhon's *Murder in the First-Class Carriage: The First Victorian Railway Killing*. For fiction, readers can turn to the *Robert Colbeck* mysteries of Edward Marston, all of which involve British trains. The first of the series, *The Railway Detective*, takes place in 1851, when a mail train from London to Birmingham is derailed and its gold and mail are stolen.

Goldstein, Robert M.

The Gentleman from Finland: Adventures on the Trans-Siberian Express. Seattle, WA: Rivendell Pub., 2005. 230 pp. ISBN: 9780976328803

Goldstein's narrative about his 1987 journey across the fading Soviet Union describes more ordeal than travel. He began by spending two days aboard what he believed to be the Trans-Siberian Express, only to discover that he was on the wrong train. His ticket mistakenly identified him as a Finn when he was really a Mexican-American-Russian-Jew. He spoke little Russian and carried an outdated phrase book. He encountered an old woman who stole his only pair of shoes, smugglers who stashed contraband under his bunk, and a beautiful Russian woman who rescued him from disaster in one city but who may have been a KGB agent. *The Gentleman from Finland* is both humorously self-deprecating and poignant, as Goldstein became obsessed by the knowledge that his ancestors had migrated from Russia and by his desire to learn more about them.

Subjects: Humor; Quick Reads; Rail Travel

Places: Russia

Now Try: Goldstein also wrote the very funny *Riding With Reindeer: A Bicycle Odyssey Through Finland, Lapland, and Arctic Norway*, which describes his nearly disastrous ride across Finland while mixing in the history and culture of this Scandinavian country. William Bleasdale's *Trans-Siberian Railway Journey: Russia, Morocco, Thailand and Malaysia* is based on the author's day-to-day notes made during his rail journeys and includes many of his beautiful color photographs. Canadian writer Bill Murray also rode on the Trans-Siberian Express and writes about that experience along with 14 other stories of travel to Bhutan, Borneo, Burma, and a number of other countries in the enjoyable *Common Sense and Whiskey: Travel Adventures Far from Home*. With its oddball characters and its portrait of post-Soviet Russia, Stuart M. Kamisky's *Murder on the Trans-Siberian Express: A Porfiry Petrovich Rostnikov Novel* is a fictional homage to the world's longest railway.

Kisor, Henry

Zephyr: Tracking a Dream across America. New York: Times Books/Random House, 1994. 338 pp. ISBN: 9780812919844

Kisor, the book editor and literary columnist at the *Chicago Sun-Times*, rode Amtrak's California Zephyr from Chicago to Oakland, commenting on its history (the train wrecks, the robberies, the pioneers, and the fortune hunters) and the breathtaking beauty of the scenery along its route. He watched the crew (engineers, cooks, and stewards) prepare for the trip and talked with a wide range of passengers that included Reno-bound retirees, book lovers, gourmands, and train buffs. The resulting book will appeal to anyone who gets a thrill out of riding a train.

Subjects: American History; American West; Rail Travel

Places: Chicago; Denver; Oakland; Reno; Salt Lake City

Now Try: James McCommons wrote *Waiting on a Train: The Embattled Future of Passenger Rail Service: A Year Spent Riding Across America*, about a year that he spent riding trains, including the California Zephyr, through several regions of the United States; he both bemoans the current state of the country's railway system and speculates on its future. Patrick Poivre d'Arvor's *First Class: Legendary Train Journeys Around the World* celebrates eleven famous railroad lines, including the California Zephyr. Railroad fans and foodies may both be drawn to James D. Porterfield's *Dining By Rail: The History and Recipes of America's Golden Age of Railroad Cuisine*, which attempts to "preserve a record of one of the ways we used to eat." In the novel *Loco Motive*, Mary Daheim's mystery-solving librarian and innkeeper, Judith Flynn, takes Amtrak's Empire Builder from Seattle to Boston and, on the way, encounters the murder of a famous daredevil.

Pindell, Terry

Making Tracks: An American Rail Odyssey. New York: Henry Holt and Company, 1991. 399 pp. ISBN: 9780805017403

In 1988, Pindell rode 30,000 miles on all of Amtrak's 31 passenger train lines, a trip that included all but three of the 48 contiguous states. *Making Tracks* mixes travel narrative and railroad history as Pindell relates his adventures crisscrossing the nation on the Montrealer, the Crescent, and the

Meridian, among others, and documents the frustrations of the current American rail system as well as its past glory. Less deliberate and journalistic than Kisor's *Zephyr* (annotated above), Pindell is particularly good at describing the people he happens to encounter on the trains: the sports fans, the Vietnam veterans, the business failures, foreign exiles and foreign students, and even an actor who rides the train in order to study people.

Subjects: American History; Rail Travel

Places: United States (Various)

Now Try: *Booked on the Morning Train: A Journey Through America* by George F. Scheer III, describes a more personal train journey than does *Making Tracks,* and its author also finds more vigor and life in the train system than does Pindell. Rudy G. Hoggard recounts the 1996 railroad trip that he and his family made from West Virginia to California, in order to see his oldest son, who was in the Air Force; *Family Trackings: Riding the American Rails* tells their story of riding through the "backyards of America." Richard Troxell traveled over 10,000 miles on the trains in Texas and writes down their history of train wrecks, railroad towns, and train robbers in *Texas Trains*. David Baldacci is best known for his faced-paced thrillers, but his romantic holiday novel, *The Christmas Train,* about a man who meets his former lover on a train, is set on two Amtrak lines, the Capitol Limited from Washington, DC, to Chicago and the Southwest Chief from Chicago to Los Angeles. Readers who would prefer the usual Baldacci can try *Divine Justice,* the beginning of which takes place on a train from Washington, DC, bound for New Orleans.

Pindell, Terry

Yesterday's Train: A Rail Odyssey through Mexican History. New York: Henry Holt and Company, 1997. 377 pp. ISBN: 9780805037913

Pindell, who has traveled by train across the United States (*Making Tracks: An American Rail Odyssey*) and Canada (*Last Train to Toronto: A Canadian Rail Odyssey*), here reports on his railway travels through Mexico, which he found to be "a nation besieged by its history." As usual, Pindell mixes descriptions of the landscapes he saw (deserts, mountains, coasts, and farming country) with historical accounts of these places (the meeting of Cortez and Moctezuma in Mexico City, the fate of the Tarahumara Indians in Copper Canyon). He also reflects on the character of the Mexican people, based on his visits to individual homes and to areas most tourists never see, and while recognizing the many differences between Mexico and the United States, *Yesterday's Train* is generally sympathetic with the Mexican people and their culture.

Subjects: American History; Rail Travel

Places: Mexico

Now Try: Paul Theroux's classic *The Old Patagonian Express* (annotated in this chapter) includes rides on two Mexican trains: the Aztec Eagle from San Antonio, Texas, to Mexico City and on El Jarocho from Mexico City to Veracruz. While it does not involve train travel, Daniel Hernandez's *Down and Delirious in Mexico City: The Aztec Metropolis in the Twenty-First Century* does provide a fascinating look at the Mexican people and the western hemisphere's largest city. Readers interested in a good history of Mexico in general should consider Earl Shorris's hefty (800 pages) *The Life and Times of Mexico*. For a fiction read-alike that takes place in mid-1960s Mexico, readers can try Dorothy Gilman's debut Emily Pollifax novel, *The Unexpected Mrs. Pollifax,* in which the elderly widow becomes a CIA agent and goes to Mexico City to pick up some important microfilms.

Vollmann, William T.

Riding Toward Everywhere. New York: Ecco, 2008. 206 pp. ISBN: 9780061256752 YA

Vollmann, a National Book Award winner for his fiction, tells the story of a different kind of train travel: the illegal kind. In spite of the fact that he was almost 50 years old, had a wife and young child, had suffered a series of strokes and a broken pelvis, and had won a number of literary prizes, Vollmann broke into rail yards and hopped freight trains, apparently for the pure joy and freedom of it. *Riding Toward Everywhere* describes a number of these rides and the hoboes, tramps, and prostitutes with whom he crossed paths. In spite of his obvious talents as a writer, Vollmann's prose here is rough and jarring, and the book is somewhat aimless, more rumination than narrative. Nevertheless, the description of this underside of American life is fascinating, and Vollmann writes with an intense passion.

Subjects: American West; Hoboes; Quick Reads; Rail Travel

Places: California; Idaho; Utah; Wyoming

Now Try: Ted Conover also describes life among the hoboes in his first book, *Rolling Nowhere: Riding the Rails with America's Hoboes* (which is annotated in "The Expatriate Life" chapter of this book). For practical information on hopping trains, interested readers can be directed to Duffy Littlejohn's *Hopping Freight Trains in America* or Josh Mack's *The Hobo Handbook: A Field Guide to Living by Your Own Rules*. Vollmann won a National Book Award for his historical novel, *Europe Central,* which takes place in the 20th-century central Europe of individuals such as composer Dmitri Shostakovich, artist Käthe Kollwitz, film director Roman Karmen, and poet Anna Akhmatova. Vollmann has also published *The Atlas,* a semi-autobiographical work drawn from his travels around the world. Vollmann is not for everyone, but people who like him really like him; another writer who elicits that kind of reaction is Jack Kerouac, whose work is discussed in the "Fiction Read-Alikes" at the end of this chapter.

On the Road

Travel by automobile is faster than travel by foot, thus allowing the traveler to cover greater distances, as in Tim Cahill's attempt with endurance driver Gary Sowerby to drive the 15,000-mile long Pan-American Highway between

Argentina and Alaska (*Road Fever: A High-Speed Travelogue*) or Jeroen van Bergeijk's hilarious road trip from Holland to Africa (*My Mercedes is Not [Crossed-out] for Sale: From Amsterdam to Ougadougou—An Auto-Misadventure Across the Sahara*).

Travel by automobile is more flexible than travel by train, and the traveler can more easily set her own itinerary rather than being governed by where the tracks go. Some travelers seek out the back roads and small towns (Brad Herzog's *Turn Left at the Trojan Horse: A Would-Be Hero's American Odyssey*) while others (Mike Bryan's *Uneasy Rider: The Interstate Way of Knowledge*) are fascinated by the interstate highways, and still others (*Horatio's Drive: America's First Road Trip* by Dayton Duncan and Ken Burns) drive even where there are no roads.

Most of the travelers in this category go by automobile, but travel by truck (Manchán Magan's *Truck Fever: A Journey Through Africa*), bus (David McKie's *Great British Bus Journeys: Travels Through Unfamous Places*), and hitchhiking (Tom Parry's *Thumbs Up Australia: Hitching the Outback*) are also included.

Titles in other genres may also appeal to readers who enjoy travel narratives that involve automobiles and other vehicles. These might include histories of automobiles (Douglas Brinkley's *Wheels for the World: Henry Ford, His Company, and a Century of Progress, 1903–2003* or Paul J. Ingrassia's *Crash Course: The American Automobile Industry's Road from Glory to Disaster*), more sociological works (Tom Vanderbilt's *Traffic: Why We Drive the Way We Do*), and fiction where automobiles or road trips play an important role (Jack Kerouac's *On the Road* or Roland Merullo's *Breakfast with Buddha*).

Bergeijk, Jeroen van

My Mercedes is Not [Crossed-out] for Sale: From Amsterdam to Ougadougou—An Auto-Misadventure Across the Sahara. New York: Broadway Books, 2008. 210 pp. ISBN: 9780767928694

Dutch journalist van Bergeijk had an idea: he could make some quick money by buying a dilapidated 1988 Mercedes with 220,000 kilometers on its odometer in Amsterdam and reselling it in a Third World country. His hilarious book mixes travel narrative with cultural commentary with thoughts on automobiles, including a visit to the Mercedes plant in Bremen, as it recounts the three-month trip from Holland through Morocco and several other African countries, across the Sahara Desert, to Burkina Faso. Van Bergeijk details the many obstacles that he encountered: mine fields, corrupt officials, ever more corrupt guides, bandits, the lack of food and water, and the contrasting abundance of sandstorms. Luckily, the author's patience and high-spirited optimism carried him through the trip, and he relates the story with plenty of good humor.

Subjects: Automobiles; Culture Clash; Deserts; Humor; Quick Reads; Road Trips

Places: Africa; Amsterdam; Burkina Faso; Germany; Ghana; Ivory Coast; Mauritania; Morocco; Netherlands; Sahara Desert; Senegal; Western Sahara

Now Try: Peter Chilson explored the roads and vehicles of the West African nation of Niger in *Riding the Demon: On the Road in West Africa,* in which he focuses on the local bush taxis to explain the history and psyche of the people in this remote land. While Neil Peart's *The Masked Rider: Cycling in West Africa* depicts his travels on a motorcycle, he and van Bergeijk explored many of the same countries in Africa. Carl Hoffman reminds us that travel in many parts of the world is dangerous; his book *The Lunatic Express: Discovering the World . . . via Its Most Dangerous Buses, Boats, Trains, and Planes* describes the author's quest to travel the world's most dangerous modes of transportation: trains in Africa and India; buses in South America; ferries in Indonesia; airlines in Cuba; and trucks in Afghanistan.

Bryan, Mike

Uneasy Rider: The Interstate Way of Knowledge. New York: Alfred A. Knopf, 1997. 349 pp. ISBN: 9780679416715

Mike Bryan uses his travels in the southwestern United States to refute the idea that the "real" America is to be found only on the back roads. Instead, Bryan argues, the interstate highways of the nation are full of eccentric individuals and quirky attractions. His sample size may be limited to Texas and three other states, but he provides plenty of evidence to support his argument: a snake farm where tourists can purchase mice with which to feed the snakes; the world's only "No Smoking" ranch; motel operators; state troopers; and traveling salesmen. His argument that life along the interstates is anything but dull and sterile is interwoven with thoughts on America's pioneer spirit and the history of road building.

Subjects: American History; American West; Highways; Small Town Life

Places: Arizona; California; New Mexico; Texas

Series: *Vintage Departures*

Now Try: William Least Heat-Moon makes the opposite argument to Bryan in *Blue Highways: A Journey into America,* in which he argues that the "real" America is found on the small back roads that are marked in blue on road maps; the book is annotated in the "A Sense of Place" chapter of this book. Claude Clayton Smith's *Lapping America: A Man, A Corvette, and the Interstate* is another celebration of the interstate system in the United States; it recounts Smith's circumnavigation of the contiguous 48 states via the interstate highways and supports Bryan's argument that the interstates get a "bum rap." Larry McMurtry provides a very personal and cranky look at America's interstate highways in *Roads: Driving America's Great Highways*. For a fictional road trip set in New Mexico, readers may enjoy Cathryn Alpert's hilarious first novel, *Rocket City,* in which a woman is driving across the New Mexico desert to marry her high school sweetheart when she meets a hitchhiking dwarf.

Cahill, Tim

Road Fever: A High-Speed Travelogue. New York: Random House, 1991. 278 pp. ISBN: 9780394576565

Cahill served as the co-driver for endurance driver Gary Sowerby in an attempt to break the Guinness Book of World Records time for driving the 15,000-mile long Pan-American Highway between Ushuiaia, Argentina, and Prudhoe Bay, Alaska. Cahill describes the 23-and-a-half day trip with his usual cleverness and sense of humor, even when discussing the lack of chemistry between him and the moody Sowerby or his "soap box" issues like global warming, the destruction of the rain forests, and the United States involvement in foreign governments. While the trip itself left little time for sightseeing, the first half of the book (in which Cahill and Sowerby contacted officials in the countries they intended to pass through and discussed their customs laws) does examine the cultures of those countries.

Subjects: Highways; Humor

Places: Alaska; Alberta; Argentina; British Columbia; Canada; Chile; Colombia; Colorado; Costa Rica; Ecuador; El Salvador; Guatemala; Honduras; Mexico; Montana; New Mexico; Nicaragua; Panama; Peru; Yukon

Series: *Vintage Departures*

Now Try: Cahill specializes in bizarre journeys, and several of his books (*Lost In My Own Backyard: A Walk in Yellowstone National Park, A Wolverine Is Eating My Leg, Jaguars Ripped My Flesh, Hold the Enlightenment,* and *Pass the Butterworms: Remote Journeys Oddly Rendered*) are annotated in this book. Joseph Yogerst explored the southern half of the Pan American Highway (from northern Mexico to southern Argentina) and wrote about his experiences in *Long Road South: The Pan American Highway*; the book was published by the National Geographic Society and consequently includes many beautiful photographs. Ed Culberson became obsessed with riding his motorcycle through an 80-mile, jungle-filled gap in the Pan American Highway; his exploits are described in *Obsessions Die Hard: Motorcycling the Pan American Highway's Jungle Gap.*

Condon, Sean

Sean and David's Long Drive. Melbourne, Oakland: Lonely Planet Publications, 1996. 289 pp. ISBN: 9780864423719

Condon grew bored working as a copywriter in an advertising agency in Australia and decided to conquer that boredom by driving seven weeks around central and eastern Australia with his friend David O'Brien. Their 8,700-mile road trip (all of which was driven by O'Brien) is recounted in diary form in *Sean and David's Long Drive,* which documents the continent's odder sights as well as the drinking, smoking, and chatting in which Condon and O'Brien indulged along the way. One reviewer described Condon as "a Gen-X cross between Bill Bryson and Dave Barry," and Condon's humor is definitely sarcastic with a compassionate edge.

Subjects: Friendships; Highways; Humor; Pop Culture 1

Places: Australia

Series: *Lonely Planet Journeys*

Now Try: A couple of years later, Sean and David traveled across the United States, and their amusing, if somewhat loopy, journey through that country is described in Sean Condon's *Drive Thru America.* Condon also wrote the very funny *My Dam Life,* about the three years he and his wife spent in Amsterdam, 2
where his wife was transferred just before the magazine for which she worked folded, and where the couple decided to nevertheless make a go of it. Condon has been compared with Bill Bryson, and Bryson's *In a Sunburned Country* (annotated in the "Travel Humor" chapter of this book) is an extremely funny, entertaining account of his visit to Condon's native Australia. A road trip through the Australian Outback that leaves the independent main char- 3
acter and her estranged father stranded lies at the heart of Australian writer Nikki Gemmell's evocative novel, *Alice Springs.*

Duncan, Dayton, and Ken Burns

Horatio's Drive: America's First Road Trip. New York: Alfred A. Knopf, 2003. 173 pp. ISBN: 9780375415364 YA 4

In 1903, a Vermont doctor named Horatio Nelson Jackson made a $50 bet that he could drive an automobile from San Francisco to New York in 90 days. The wager sounds reasonable enough until you realize that there were only 150 miles of paved roads in the country at that time, that the auto had just one gear, that its top speed was 30 mph, and that no one had attempted such a feat before. *Horatio's Drive* tells the story of Jackson 5
and his traveling companions (mechanic Sewall Crocker and a bulldog named Bud) as they tried to overcome bad roads, no roads, bad maps, bad directions, and corporate-sponsored rivals and tried to become road trip pioneers. The Duncan and Burns volume is a companion piece to a PBS documentary and includes a number of vintage photographs and letters.

Subjects: American History; Automobiles; Doctors; Illustrated Books; Quick 6
Reads; Road Trips

Places: Albany; Buffalo; California; Cheyenne; Chicago; Cleveland; Idaho; Illinois; Indiana; Iowa; Nebraska; New York; New York City; Ohio; Omaha; Oregon; Pennsylvania; Sacramento; San Francisco; Wyoming

Now Try: As noted, the book served as a companion to the PBS documentary, *Horatio's Drive,* and readers who enjoyed the book will likely enjoy the 7
film as well. In contrast to the dearth of roads that Horatio Jackson encountered, the United States now has plenty of roads, and Larry McMurtry writes about the longest of these in *Roads: Driving America's Great Highways,* a very

personal look at America's interstate highways. Readers interested in the early days of the automobile in the United States would do well to begin with *Pioneers, Engineers, And Scoundrels: The Dawn Of The Automobile In America,* a well-researched history by Beverly R. Kimes. John McPhee's *Uncommon Carriers,* about people who transport all sorts of goods (particularly on the roads) may also be of interest, particularly as part of his narrative involves his own cross-country trip alongside the owner and driver of a chemical tanker carrying hazardous materials.

Herzog, Brad

Turn Left at the Trojan Horse: A Would-Be Hero's American Odyssey. New York: Citadel, 2010. 307 pp. ISBN: 9780806532028

Herzog's introspective cross-country RV road trip began in Seattle, Washington, and ended at his high school reunion in Ithaca, New York. Along the way, Herzog considered his own life's journey as well as a wide range of topics, including death, immortality, leadership, friendship, self-awareness, and especially heroism. As he pondered these weighty topics, he considered both classical examples (Athena, Zeus, Hercules, and Theseus) as well as their more recent counterparts (Daniel Boone, Meriwether Lewis, Chuck Yeager, Calamity Jane, firefighters, police officers, and ranchers). He also stopped at any place whose name referred back to the ancient Greeks: the Cyclopes Café in Seattle; Troy, Oregon; Iliad, Montana; Siren, Wisconsin; and Pandora, Ohio. *Turn Left at the Trojan Horse* is a curious and generally uplifting journey through an America where heroes still live.

Subjects: Heroism; Humor; Self-Discovery; Small Town Life

Categories: Discovering One's Self

Places: California; Montana; New York; Ohio; Oregon; Washington; Wisconsin

Now Try: Herzog is also the author of *States of Mind* and *Small World: A Microcosmic Journey*. The former is subtitled "A Search for Faith, Hope, Inspiration, Harmony, Unity, Friendship, Love, Pride, Wisdom, Honor, Comfort, Joy, Bliss, Freedom, Justice, Glory, Triumph, and Truth or Consequences in America" and tells how he and his wife drove across the United States, searching for those virtues among the residents of small-town America. Like Herzog, Kirk Robinson found a deep connection with the past in his travels; *Hiking Through History: Hannibal, Highlanders, and Joan of Arc* tells how he hiked through Spain, France, and Italy, following in the footsteps of Hannibal and Joan of Arc.

Maclean, Rory

Stalin's Nose: Travels Around the Bloc. Boston: Little, Brown and Co., 1992. 233 p. ISBN: 9780316542395

Just two weeks after the fall of the Berlin Wall, Maclean accompanied his German aunt and her pet pig across Eastern Europe in a battered, rather unreliable East German automobile. The trip is funny and surreal (one of the destinations is Budapest, where the aunt hoped to replace her lost false teeth), and Stalin's nose does make an appearance: it came from a bronze statue that was pulled down during a 1956 uprising in Hungary. The book is also informative, given the changes in Eastern Europe that Maclean witnessed, and it represents the first of several travel narratives by the British writer.

Subjects: Communism; European History; Humor

Places: Berlin; Budapest; Czech Republic; Germany; Hungary; Moscow; Poland; Prague; Romania; Russia

Now Try: Maclean has written eight travel narratives, and several of these have won awards or been shortlisted for major prizes. *Under the Dragon: A Journey through Burma* tells of his return to Burma 10 years after he had first visited that country and portrays both the beauty of the place and the repression of its regime. *Magic Bus: On the Hippie Trail From Istanbul to India* recounts his attempt to retrace the "hippie trail" of the 1960s and 1970s through Turkey, Iran, Afghanistan, and Pakistan. Like *Stalin's Nose,* both books focus on countries and people undergoing great changes. Slavenka Drakulic also discusses the great changes in Eastern Europe by focusing on the seemingly mundane in her look at the post-Communist world, *Cafe Europa: Life After Communism.* The historical account of the preservation of Lenin's body for viewing in Red Square, *Lenin's Embalmers,* by Ilya Zbarsky and Samuel Hutchinson, may also be of interest. In Travis Nichols's epistolary novel, *Off We Go Into the Wild Blue Yonder,* the narrator takes his grandfather and girlfriend on a road trip to the Polish village where the grandfather had been shot down during World War II and helped to survive by a Polish woman whom they hope to find.

Magan, Manchán

Truck Fever: A Journey through Africa. London: Brandon Books, 2008. 277 pp. ISBN: 9780863223891

In the early 1990s, Magan, who later became a documentary filmmaker, traveled for six months from London to Nairobi in a refurbished Army truck with 18 strangers, including schoolgirls, nurses on vacation, a man who claimed to be a former torturer in the British Army, and a locksmith who claimed to be a UFO abductee. The trip was filled with adventures and mishaps (coming face-to-face with gorillas and pygmies, risking disease when drinking water from polluted streams, traveling with a guide who tended to abandon them when things got difficult, and being robbed of money, passports, and food) but in spite of it all, Magan saw the journey as one of self-discovery, full of experiences that helped him develop as a person. The author also provides anecdotes and observations about the nature of Africa and the trials of living and travelling in developing countries.

Subjects: Colonialism; Humor; Poverty; Self-Discovery

Categories: Discovering One's Self

1 2 3 4 5 6 7

Places: Africa; Benin; Burkina Faso; Cameroon; Central African Republic; Democratic Republic of the Congo; England; Kenya; London; Morocco; Nairobi; Niger; Nigeria

Now Try: Magan is the author of two other travel narratives, although neither reports on a journey quite as harrowing as the one in *Truck Fever*. *Angels & Rabies: A Journey through the Americas* recounts a backpacking trip he took through parts of South America and North America. *Manchán ' s Travels: A Journey through India* follows Magan and his brother through India as they searched for sites and individuals to include in a documentary film they had been commissioned to make. Ayun Halliday writes with a more shocking sense of humor than does Magan, but many of the situations she got herself into in *No Touch Monkey!: And Other Travel Lessons Learned Too Late* were as bizarre as those faced by Magan in *Truck Fever*.

McKie, David

Great British Bus Journeys: Travels through Unfamous Places. London: Atlantic Books, 2006. 359 pp. ISBN: 9781843541325

McKie took the public bus system to explore many of Britain's smaller, unknown towns, what the author calls "not very special places that do not often get written about." His journey (which started in Leeds, where he was born, and ended in London) included visits to quaint towns with grand names (like Frinton-on-Sea, Claxford St Andrew, Tumby Woodside, Yaddlethorpe, and Bradwell-juxta-Mare) and reflects McKie's passion for the secret history and variety of Great Britain, as told in its small towns. The book is filled with vivid descriptions, witty observations, obscure details, and the occasional cup of tea with fellow travelers.

Subjects: Buses; European History; Small Town Life

Places: England; Scotland; Wales

Awards: Dolman Best Travel Book Award, Shortlist, 2007

Now Try: Bill Bryson traveled around his adopted England by public transportation and hiking, focusing on small towns as well as some larger cities, in *Notes from a Small Island* (annotated in the "Travel Humor" chapter of this book). Stuart Maconie went in search of Middle England in *Adventures on the High Teas: In Search of Middle England*, in which the author visited a number of towns in England (Meriden, Chipping Norton, Bath, and Oxford, among others) in search of a place, a culture, or a way of life. Travis Elborough's *The Bus We Loved: London's Affair with the Routemaster* is a nostalgic history of the red double-decker buses that were, according to the author, the last buses to be proper buses. The road trip through the English countryside to the Shetland Islands in Jonathan Coe's witty novel, *The Terrible Privacy of Maxwell Sim*, is taken by car, not bus, but the protagonist's wandering route is similar to that taken by McKie.

Parry, Tom

Thumbs Up Australia: Hitching the Outback. London, Boston: Nicholas Breasley Publ., 2006. 281 pp. ISBN: 9781857883909

Parry decided to hitchhike nearly 8,000 miles across Australia's Outback with his reluctant, pouty French girlfriend, loosely following the paths of the first people to cross the continent. As might be expected, the two met some strange, eccentric characters on those dusty back roads (hippies, Aboriginal elders, former miners) and ran across some quirky places: remote waterholes, cattle farms, Aboriginal communities, and hippie communes. *Thumbs Up Australia* is down-to-earth and hilarious and captures the spirit of the people and the land that Parry encountered.

Subjects: Humor; Indigenous Peoples

Places: Australia

Awards: Dolman Best Travel Book Award, Shortlist, 2007

Now Try: Travel writer Tony Horwitz also hitchhiked through the Australian Outback in his witty *One for the Road: Hitchhiking Through the Australian Outback*; like Parry, Horwitz wanted to see the "real" Australia, but he did spend a bit more time in pubs than did Parry and his girlfriend. Joe Bennett lived ten years in New Zealand before he decided to get to know the country better by hitchhiking around it; he tells the story of his journey in *A Land of Two Halves: An Accidental Tour of New Zealand*. For readers who are fascinated by hitchhiking, the collection of stories edited by Tom Sykes and Simon Sykes, *The Hitchers of Oz: An Anthology of Hitchhiking Stories and Observations from Australasia and Beyond*, will be of interest; among the authors of the collected pieces are writers J. P. Donleavy and Alan Dean Foster, actor Sam Neil, and rapper Chuck D.

Rogers, Jim

Adventure Capitalist: The Ultimate Investor's Road Trip. New York: Random House, 2003. 357 pp. ISBN: 9780375509124

Rogers, a Columbia University finance professor and the founder of a global investment partnership, mixes investment advice and travel narrative in this story of his turn-of-the-millennium road trip around the world with his fiancée in a custom-built yellow Mercedes convertible. The idea was to travel through over 100 countries and thereby get a better sense of the global marketplace; as Rogers puts it, "I know that one can learn more about a country from speaking to the madam of a brothel or a black marketeer than from meeting a foreign minister." The trip, which covered a record 152,000 miles and 116 countries, reinforced Rogers's belief in the ingenuity and resourcefulness of individuals and his disdain for governments.

Subjects: Automobiles; Circumnavigations; Economics; Finance; Globalization

Places: Africa; Angola; China; Colombia; East Timor; Iceland; Myanmar; Russia; Saudi Arabia; Sudan

Now Try: Rogers is the author of the earlier *Investment Biker* (annotated in this chapter under "On Two Wheels"), in which he traveled around the world by motorcycle in order to better understand investing in foreign markets. Rogers also wrote *A Bull in China: Investing Profitably in the World's Greatest Market,* which is perhaps more an investment guide than a travel narrative, but his visits to China's largest winemaker and other companies in the country itself may appeal to travel readers. Michael Lewis's *Boomerang: Travels in the New Third World* also mixes travel narrative with finance, as Lewis traveled to some of the countries hit hardest by the financial disaster of 2008, including Greece, Iceland, and Ireland. Readers with an interest in non-traditional economies and the patience for a bit more scholarly read might also consider Sudhir Venkatesh's *Off the Books: The Underground Economy of the Urban Poor.*

Rushin, Steve

Road Swing: One Fan's Journey into the Soul of American Sports. New York: Doubleday, 1998. 245 pp. ISBN: 9780385482295

Rushin, a writer for *Sports Illustrated,* recounts a long road trip he made just before turning 30 to various sites made famous by American sports: the boyhood home of Larry Bird in French Lick, Indiana; the cornfield near Dyersville, Iowa, where *Field of Dreams* was filmed; and as many sports halls of fame as he could identify. While it may feel a bit rushed to some readers, *Road Swing* is generally well written; Rushin has a knack for capturing the way "real" people speak and a great sense of humor, even about something as obviously serious for him as sports.

Subjects: Baseball; Basketball; Football; Golf; Humor; Quick Reads; Soccer; Sports

Places: United States (Various)

Now Try: There are a number of travel narratives with sports themes. Brad Null and Dave Kaval, for example, visited all 30 major league baseball parks in less than 40 days and provide detailed information about each park in *The Summer That Saved Baseball: A 38-Day Journey to Thirty Major League Ballparks.* Tim Parks followed fans of an Italian soccer team for a year and documents the experience in *A Season with Verona* (annotated in "The Expatriate Life" chapter of this book). In *The Sportsman: Unexpected Lessons from an Around-the-World Sports Odyssey,* professional football player Dhani Jones tells about his travels around the world filming an off-season television show called *Dhani Tackles the Globe.* Jim Yardley's amusing *Brave Dragons: A Chinese Basketball Team, an American Coach, and Two Cultures Clashing* tells the true story of the Shanxi Brave Warriors, the worst team in China's professional basketball league, the American coach they hired to turn the team around, and the culture clashes that resulted. Charles Rosen's funny and touching novel, *The House of Moses All-Stars,* tells the story of a Jewish basketball team's road trip across the United States during the Great Depression.

Sullivan, Robert

Cross Country: Fifteen Years and 90,000 Miles on the Roads and Interstates of America . . . New York: Bloomsbury Pub., 2006. 389 pp. ISBN: 9781582345277

The full subtitle of this book pretty much summarizes the book—*Fifteen Years and 90,000 Miles on the Roads and Interstates of America with Lewis and Clark, a Lot of Bad Motels, a Moving Van, Emily Post, Jack Kerouac, My Wife, My Mother-in-Law, Two Kids, and Enough Coffee to Kill an Elephant*. Sullivan, a contributing editor for *Vogue*, claims to have driven over 90,000 miles across the United States over the years and recounts here one particular trip, a five-day crossing with his wife and two kids in a rented Impala. The trip was filled with stops and side treks (the Columbia River Gorge, where Sullivan talks about the Lewis and Clark expedition; Jack Kerouac's gas station in Longmont, Colorado), and the book mixes a charming travel narrative with a long contemplation of the American road trip.

Subjects: Automobiles; Family Relationships; Highways; Humor

Places: Colorado; Minnesota; Montana; New York; Oregon; Pennsylvania; Wisconsin

Now Try: Sullivan's other books have been about subjects other than travel, but the subjects are fascinating and may interest readers who find his digressions in *Cross Country* to be engrossing. *The Meadowlands: Wilderness Adventures on the Edge of a City* is a natural history of the New Jersey swamps. *Rats: Observations on the History and Habitat of the City's Most Unwanted Inhabitants* is a history of rodents in New York City. *A Whale Hunt: How a Native-American Village Did What No One Thought It Could* is an account of a Washington state American Indian tribe's revival of their whaling tradition. For readers more interested in a pure history of the American interstate system, Tom Lewis's *Divided Highways: Building the Interstate Highways, Transforming American Life* can be recommended.

On Two Wheels

Traveling by bicycle or motorcycle is faster than traveling on foot, more flexible than traveling by rail, more intimate than traveling by car, and more physically challenging than traveling by rail or by car. These aspects of two-wheel travel are part of the appeal of the titles in this category. (It should, of course, be noted that there are important differences between motorcycle travel and bicycle travel. Motorcycling is much faster than bicycling, and the latter allows the traveller to see more detail in the landscape, much like walking or hiking. While books on motorcycling and bicycling have been joined together in this category, the astute readers' advisor will be aware of these distinctions and thereby be better able to match titles with readers.)

The travelers in these titles cover a great deal of territory. Dan Austin and his colleagues rode 4,800 miles across the United States (*True Fans: A Basketball Odyssey*). Ewan McGregor and Charley Boorman rode their motorcycles 20,000 miles from London to New York City via Europe, Asia, and Canada (*Long Way Round: Chasing Shadows Across the World*) and then from the northern tip of Scotland to the southernmost tip of South Africa (*Long Way Down: An Epic Journey by Motorcycle from Scotland to South America*).

Because a bicyclist or motorcyclist is more in control of her itinerary, the travel may be more purpose-driven, as in Jim Malusa's goal of riding his bicycle to the lowest points on six of the Earth's seven continents (*Into Thick Air: Biking to the Bellybutton of Six Continents*) or Tim Moore's attempt to ride the Tour de France in the weeks prior to that 2,256-mile race (*French Revolutions: Cycling the Tour de France*).

Travel by bicycle or motorcycle also puts the traveler more closely in touch with her surroundings and often leads to interesting speculations on the destination, as in David Byrne's fascinating *Bicycle Diaries* or Dervla Murphy's observations on the devastation of AIDS in Africa in *The Ukimwi Road*. Likewise, travel by bicycle or motorcycle puts the rider closer to individuals along the way, and the travelers on these conveyances often interact with interesting people, as in the impoverished but friendly people that Lynette Chiang met in Cuba (*The Handsomest Man in Cuba: An Escapade*).

Finally, the physical challenges encountered by bicycle and motorcycle riders also play a large role in these titles. These include the inclement weather and potential rapists encountered by Karen Larsen on her motorcycle trip from New Jersey to Alaska (*Breaking the Limit: One Woman's Motorcycle Journey through North America*) and the Pyrenees mountains through which Polly Evans rode (*It's Not About the Tapas: A Spanish Adventure on Two Wheels*).

Titles about bicycling or motorcycling as a sport (Lance Armstrong's *It's Not About the Bike: My Journey Back to Life* or Mat Oxley's *Stealing Speed: The Biggest Spy Scandal in Motorsport History*), titles about the history of bicycles or motorcycles (David Herlihy's *Bicycle: The History* or Paul Garson's *Born to Be Wild: A History of the American Biker and Bikes, 1947–2002*), and fiction where bicycles or motorcycles play an important role (Ron McLarty's *The Memory of Running* or Greg Moody's *Cycling Murder Mystery* series) may also appeal to fans of the titles in this category.

Austin, Dan

True Fans: A Basketball Odyssey. Guilford, CT: Lyons Press, 2005. 214 pp. ISBN: 9781592287796

Austin, his brother, and a friend rode their bicycles 4,800 miles across the United States "to see America . . . to get to know the people and to see if they were as heroic as we'd always believed." Their odyssey stretched from Venice Beach, California, to Springfield, Massachusetts, and involved dozens of basketball games in small-town parks and school yards as well as having those who helped the three travelers (the preacher who let them sleep in his church, the miner who offered them money he could scarcely afford, and many others) sign their basketball, which was then donated to the NBA Hall of Fame. *True Fans* is both about pursuing one's dreams and about the "true fans" who helped make the trio's dream come true.

Subjects: Basketball; Bicycles; Quick Reads; Small Town Life

Places: Baltimore; Boston; California; Colorado; Connecticut; Illinois; Indiana; Iowa; Las Vegas; Maryland; Massachusetts; Nebraska; Nevada; New York; New York City; Pennsylvania; Philadelphia; Utah; Washington, DC; West Virginia

Now Try: Austin's film documentary about the trip, also called *True Fans,* won the People's Choice Award at the Banff Film Festival and may be of interest to those who enjoyed the book. Alex Chambers traveled to all 13 home arenas of the teams in the women's professional basketball league and wrote about his passion for the game in *13 Teams: One Man's Journey with the WNBA*. Although *Across America by Bicycle: Alice and Bobbi's Summer on Wheels* by Alice Honeywell and Bobbi Montgomery doesn't involve sports, it does involve a cross-country bicycle ride, in this case by two retirement-age women who traveled from Oregon to Maine; like the trio in *True Fans,* Honeywell and Montgomery met and were helped along by many fascinating people. A cross-country bicycle trip and a helpful man who claims to be a professional basketball player are part of the plot of James McManus's quirky novel, *Going to the Sun,* in which a 30-year-old woman bicycles from Chicago to Alaska, where she had helped her boyfriend commit suicide seven years earlier.

Byrne, David

Bicycle Diaries. New York: Viking, 2009. 297 pp. ISBN: 9780670021147

Talking Heads leader David Byrne reports on his bicycle riding through several of the world's major cities. His reflections on what he saw as he pedaled fill the book and cover such disparate topics as music, fashion, architecture, the visual arts, globalization, and politics. (As might be expected, his observations on music are particularly insightful.) His thoughts are presented in short pieces, and so the book has a random, almost haphazard, feel, but the book also contains a strong ecological message, that the sustainability of our cities depends on the adoption of alternative means of transportation, like the bicycle.

Subjects: Bicycles; Cities; Transportation; Urban Planning

Places: Argentina; Australia; Berlin; Buenos Aires; England; Germany; Istanbul; London; Manila; New York City; Philippines; San Francisco; Sydney; Turkey

Now Try: Another musician, Neil Peart (the drummer of the band Rush), writes about his travels through West Africa in *The Masked Rider: Cycling in West Africa.* Peart differs from Byrne in that he rides a motorcycle, but the books are similar in that they both feature the writers' personal reflections on a wide range of topics. The political and ecological issues related to bicycling are discussed by Jeff Mapes in *Pedaling Revolution: How Cyclists Are Changing American Cities,* a book that explores bicycling in cities such as Amsterdam, San Francisco, and New York.

Chiang, Lynette

The Handsomest Man in Cuba: An Escapade. Guilford, CT: Globe Pequot, 2007. 257 pp. ISBN: 9780762743902

Thirty-something Chiang quit her IT job in Australia, left her boyfriend, and set out to discover the world. *The Handsomest Man in Cuba* recounts her journey through that island on a fold-up bicycle, a tent, a sleeping bag, a small stove, and $2,000 in cash. Cycling through Cuba's varied terrain alone for three months, she stayed with local people and in campsites and did her best to make friends and get to know the locals. Her easygoing, sometimes hilarious, book portrays Cuba as a complex country, filled with warm and friendly but incredibly poor people.

Subjects: Bicycling; Communism; Humor; Islands; Poverty; Small Town Life; Solo Travelers; Women Travelers

Places: Cuba

Now Try: Irish writer Dervla Murphy's *Full Tilt: Ireland to India with a Bicycle* is the classic solo journey by a woman on a bicycle; she shares with Chiang a strong sense of rapport with the local people she encountered on her trip. Interestingly, Murphy also visited Cuba, and she reports on her journey there in *The Island That Dared: Journeys in Cuba*; however, she did not travel by bicycle or solo (she took along her daughter and three granddaughters). American Isadora Tattlin (a pseudonym) followed her European businessman husband to Cuba when he was stationed in Havana in the 1990s and wrote *Cuba Diaries: An American Housewife in Havana,* which portrays the country during this period of relative liberalization. Fiction readers interested in Cuba may enjoy two novels by Oscar Hijuelos: *Beautiful Maria of My Soul,* told from the point of view of the heroine of his most famous book (*The Mambo Kings Play Songs of Love*); and *A Simple Habana Melody,* about a Cuban musician who returns to the island after being mistakenly imprisoned by the Nazis during World War II.

Evans, Polly

It's Not About the Tapas: A Spanish Adventure on Two Wheels. London, New York: Bantam, 2003. 301 pp. ISBN: 9780553815566

Evans had grown tired of her job as the senior editor of Hong Kong's biggest entertainment weekly and so she gave it all up to travel around Spain by bicycle. Her adventure turned out to be more than she had bargained for (the physically challenging Pyrenees, being nearly derailed by goats and pigs, and overly enthusiastic suitors) but she enjoyed every bit of it. Her comical narrative includes a good bit of history of the regions through which she traveled (including oddities like the king who collected pickled heads and the queen who toured the country with her husband's rotting corpse) and some mouth-watering food.

Subjects: Bicycling; Food; Humor; Solo Travelers; Women Travelers

Places: Spain

Now Try: Evans is the author of several amusing travel narratives. *Fried Eggs with Chopsticks: One Woman's Hilarious Adventure into a Country and a Culture Not Her Own* (annotated in the "Travel Humor" chapter of this book) recounts her solo trip across China by plane, train, bus, boat, and even mule. *On a Hoof and a Prayer: Exploring Argentina at a Gallop* tells about her journey to Argentina to fulfill her childhood dream of learning to ride a horse. At 43, Nancy Brook left the corporate world and the frustrating world of post-divorce dating to bicycle 700 miles through France and recover her sense of self; she chronicles her journey in *Cycling, Wine and Men: A Midlife Tour de France*. Other memoirs in which women pursue their dreams and interests might also appeal to these readers; two possibilities are Elizabeth Bard's *Lunch in Paris: A Love Story with Recipes* (annotated in "The Expatriate Life") or Judith Matloff's *Home Girl: Building a Dream House on a Lawless Block*, about a foreign correspondent who decides to return to her native New York City and purchase a brownstone in Harlem.

Larsen, Karen

Breaking the Limit: One Woman's Motorcycle Journey through North America. New York: Hyperion, 2004. 358 pp. ISBN: 9780786868704

Larsen, who was between finishing her Masters degree and starting a new job, decided to ride her motorcycle from Princeton, New Jersey, to the tip of the Arctic Circle in Alaska and back, partly just to do it and partly to meet her biological father for the first time and her biological mother's family, including half-brothers and sisters whom she had never met. With little more than her bike and the barest of essentials, Larsen challenged her endurance as well as some of her long-held beliefs, examining such questions as why people take risks and what a family is. Larsen does a particularly good job of describing the challenges she faced (violent thunderstorms, nearly frozen fingers, the constant dirt and filth of the road, potential rapists, and a break-up with her boyfriend) and the emotional ups and downs she experienced.

Subjects: Family Relationships; Motorcycles; Women Travelers

Places: Alaska; Canada (Various); Colorado; Michigan; Nevada; New Jersey; New York

Now Try: Carla King explored the small towns on the U.S. borders with Mexico and Canada in her tale of a four-month, 10,000-mile journey, *American Borders: A Solo Circumnavigation of the United States on a Russian Sidecar Motorcycle*; like Larsen, she is particularly good at describing the many challenges she faced. Lois Pryce rode her motorcycle 20,000 miles from Alaska to Argentina and recounts the trial-filled journey with charm and humor in *Lois on the Loose: One Woman, One Motorcycle, 20,000 Miles across the Americas*. Dorothy Friedman describes how she and her youngest son bonded on a motorcycle trip from Los Angeles to South Dakota and on to Canada in *Trail of the Dove: How a Mother and Her Grown Son Learned to Love Each Other on a Cross-Country Motorcycle Journey*. The tone of Erika Lopez's hilarious novel, *Flaming Iguanas: An Illustrated All-Girl Road Novel Thing*, is the opposite of Larsen's serious narrative, but both involve women riding motorcycle cross country to reunite with their fathers.

Malusa, Jim

Into Thick Air: Biking to the Bellybutton of Six Continents. San Francisco: Sierra Club Books, 2008. 321 pp. ISBN: 9781578051410

Writer and botanist Malusa rode his bicycle to the lowest points on six of the seven continents (Antarctica, whose lowest point is buried in snow and ice, was excluded). His trips (to Argentina's Laguna del Carbón; Lake Eyre, Australia; Death Valley, California; Lake Assal, Djibouti; the Dead Sea, on the border of Israel and Jordan; and the Caspian Sea in Russia) are recounted with both a scientist's eye for detail and a sense of humor; his descriptions of these faraway lands and their people are sometimes laugh-out-loud funny. Malusa also focuses on the larger question of why people travel in the first place.

Subjects: Adventure; Bicycling; Friendships; Humor; Sports

Places: Argentina; Australia; Death Valley, California; Djibouti; Israel; Jordan; Russia

Now Try: Dominic Gill is another bicyclist who set off on a journey with a curious agenda: he not only intended to pedal from Prudhoe Bay, Alaska, to the southernmost city in South America; he rode a tandem bicycle and invited strangers to ride along with him. Gill's story is told in *Take a Seat: One Man, One Tandem and Twenty Thousand Miles of Possibilities*. Mark Beaumont pedaled around the world in a world record 81 days in 2008 and writes about his adventure in *The Man Who Cycled the World*. Barbara Savage's sometimes inspiring *Miles from Nowhere: A Round the World Bicycle Adventure* tells about another around-the-world bicycle trip, this one taken by Barbara and her husband, shortly before her death in a bicycle accident. *Travels with Willie: Adventure Cyclist* is a collection of Willie Weir's columns for *Adventure Cyclist* magazine and covers bicycle trips to a number of countries, including Colombia, Cuba, Thailand, and Turkey.

McGregor, Ewan, and Charley Boorman

Long Way Down: An Epic Journey by Motorcycle from Scotland to South America. New York: Atria Books, 2008 [2007]. 341 pp. ISBN: 9781416577454

Yes, that Ewan McGregor. The famous actor (*Trainspotting, Star Wars, Moulin Rouge*) and his actor friend rode their motorcycles from John O'Groats at the northern tip of Scotland to Cape Agulhas at the southernmost tip of South Africa, in 2007. The account of their three-month journey includes original diary entries and captures their joy at being on the road and discovering different cultures, although several reviewers felt that it lacked the innocent delight of their previous book, *Long Way Round* (annotated below).

Subjects: Humor; Men's Friendships; Motorcycles

Places: Africa; Botswana; Egypt; England; Ethiopia; France; Italy; Kenya; Libya; Malawi; Namibia; Rwanda; Scotland; South Africa; Sudan; Tanzania; Tunisia; Uganda; Zambia

Now Try: *Long Way Down* was made into a 10-part television series, which has been released on DVD; fans of the book may enjoy the series as well. Boorman is the author of three other travel narratives, all involving motorcycles. *Race to Dakar* describes Boorman's participation in the Dakar Rally from Lisbon to Dakar, often described as the most challenging race on the planet. *By Any Means: The Brand New Adventure from Wicklow to Wollongong* recounts his trip from England to Sydney, Australia, which Boorman took "by any means" except airplane; his modes of transportation included train, horse, boat, kayak, elephant, and of course, motorcycle. He uses the same "by any means" approach in *Right to the Edge: Sydney to Tokyo By Any Means,* in which he describes his trip from Australia to Japan by motorcycle, quad bike, hovercraft, canoe, and paraglider. Readers looking for what one reviewer called an "antidote to the *Long Way Down*" might enjoy classic motorcycle journalist Steve Wilson's *Short Way Up: A Classic Ride Through Southern Africa—5,000 Solo Miles on a 1950s Ariel,* which describes his 6,000-mile trip through Africa, partly for fun and partly to raise money for a school in Zambia.

McGregor, Ewan, and Charley Boorman

Long Way Round: Chasing Shadows Across the World. New York: Atria Books, 2004. 312 pp. ISBN: 9780743499330

What began as a daydream turned into a 20,000-mile, four-month motorcycle ride from London to New York City the long way, via Europe, Asia, and Canada. In addition to the descriptions of the countries through which they rode and the people with whom they interacted, the themes of friendship and the bonds among all people are also explored throughout the book. McGregor and Boorman gained a particular appreciation for how small the world is and how interconnected we all are. The two also talk a good bit about their bikes; fans of motorcycles will enjoy these passages, but other readers may not.

Subjects: Adventure; Humor; Men's Friendships; Motorcycles

Places: Belgium; Canada; Czech Republic; England; France; Germany; Kazakhstan; Mongolia; Russia; Slovakia; Ukraine; United States

Now Try: As with *Long Way Down, Long Way Round* was made into a television series, and the seven episodes have been released on DVD. Emilio Scotto was given an atlas when he was eight years old, and he dreamed of traveling to every country in the world; *The Longest Ride: My Ten-Year 500,000 Mile Motorcycle Journey* describes how he fulfilled that dream, rode through Mexico during an earthquake, met Muhammad Ali, was attacked by cannibals in Sierra Leone, and was blessed by the pope. Another round-the-world motorcycle trip is described by Ted Simon in *Jupiter's Travels: Four Years around the World on a Triumph,* which describes his four-year, 78,000-mile journey by motorcycle through 45 countries in the 1970s. Yet another is Dan Walsh's *Endless Horizon: A Very Messy Motorcycle Journey around the World,* which is alternately cynical, hopeful, and very funny.

Moore, Tim

French Revolutions: Cycling the Tour de France. New York: St. Martin's Press, 2002 [2001]. 277 pp. ISBN: 9780312290450

Moore tackled the 2,256-mile route of the Tour de France, the world's most watched sporting event, in the weeks prior to the race itself.

Unfortunately, he was not a world-class athlete (he was in his late 30s and hadn't ridden a bicycle since adolescence) and he didn't care much for the local French people along the way. Moore tried to recreate the ride as experienced by the professionals: he had his legs depilated, he tried to urinate while cycling, and he even cheated, by skipping some parts of the route. The result is one of the funniest sports books ever, but one that also includes enough history of the Tour de France to interest the most avid biker.

Subjects: Bicycling; Humor; Sports

Places: France

Now Try: Moore has written a number of other humorous travel narratives, one of which involves bicycling: in *Frost On My Moustache: The Arctic Exploits of a Lord and a Loafer*, he rode a bicycle across Iceland as he attempted to follow in the footsteps of 19th-century explorer Lord Dufferin. While his book *Do Not Pass Go* does not involve bicycling, it is based on an amusing premise: Moore visited every place in London that is named on the board of the 1930s British version of Monopoly, places like Old Kent Road and Mayfair. Moore's very funny *Travels with My Donkey: One Man and His Ass on a Pilgrimage to Santiago* is annotated in the "Travel Humor" chapter of this book. Tim Krabbe's engrossing novel, *The Rider*, is the first person account of a competitive cyclist in the 85-mile Tour de Mont Aigoual, one of the most challenging legs of the Tour de France. Another novel about the Tour de France is Dave Shields's *The Race: A Novel of Grit, Tactics, and the Tour de France*, which explores a young American's opportunity to compete in that race and the intense pressure that results.

Murphy, Dervla

The Ukimwi Road. London: John Murray, 1993. 276 pp. ISBN: 9780719552502

Ukimwi is Swahili for AIDS, and the 60-something travel writer Dervla Murphy rode her bicycle 3,000 miles through the epicenter of Africa's AIDS crisis, observing the devastating impact of the disease, droughts, and economic collapse on the local people. Murphy sharply criticizes the well-meaning Westerners who tried to help but who didn't understand the societies they were working with and who tried to impose their own values. Murphy's straightforward and sometimes heartbreaking book recounts the hopeless economic and political situation of these countries but also offers a small ray of hope in the stories of women who were beginning to work together to find solutions to a seemingly insoluble problem.

Subjects: AIDS; Bicycling; Poverty; Women Travelers

Places: Africa; Kenya; Malawi; Tanzania; Uganda; Zambia; Zimbabwe

Now Try: Murphy is the author of nearly three dozen travel narratives, most of which involve solo travel on a bicycle. Her best-known work may be her first, *Full Tilt: Ireland to India with a Bicycle*, which describes her journey from Ireland to India, through some very inhospitable terrain that ranged from snow and ice in the mountains to scorching desert. Her first trip to Africa is recounted in her book, *In Ethiopia with a Mule*, which reflects her sense of humor in spite of being robbed three times and suffering both exhaustion and illness. Actress Angelina Jolie has seen the victims of violence and disease in her role as a Goodwill Ambassador for the United Nations High Commissioner for Refugees; she writes about some of those experiences in *Angelina Jolie: Notes from My Travels*. Another inspiring account of a woman working quietly to better the world is Melissa Faye Greene's *There Is No Me Without You: One Woman's Odyssey to Rescue Africa's Children*.

Richman, Jana

Riding in the Shadows of Saints: A Woman's Story of Motorcycling the Mormon Trail. New York: Crown Publishers, 2005. 299 pp. ISBN: 9781400045426

Richman, who was raised a Mormon but who left the faith, decided to make the same journey that seven of her eight Mormon great-grandmothers had made in the mid-19th century, from Illinois to Salt Lake City, Utah. Unlike her ancestors, though, Richman made the journey alone and by motorcycle. However, like her ancestors, she is also searching for a kind of peace and faith, and much of the book is about the author's spiritual reflections, unresolved family issues, and attempts to understand her mother in particular. Richman works in visits to Mormon graveyards, discussions with missionaries, and stories of her female ancestors and tells her story in an intimate, appealing manner.

Subjects: 19th Century; Family Relationships; Mormonism; Mothers and Daughters; Motorcycles; Solo Travelers; Women Travelers

Places: Illinois; Iowa; Nebraska; Utah; Wyoming

Now Try: John J. Newkirk's *The Old Man and the Harley: A Last Ride Through Our Fathers' America*, about the author's retracing of his father's earlier cross-country motorcycle ride during the Great Depression has the same focus on history that Richman's book has. Karen Larsen's *Breaking the Limit* (annotated in this chapter) may also appeal; it tells about another woman traveling on a motorcycle and the family issues that she needed to resolve. Readers who are interested in the Mormon faith and its history may be fascinated by *I Walked to Zion: True Stories of Young Pioneers on the Mormon Trail*, a collection of excerpts from journals and personal histories written by children and young adults who walked the Mormon trail in the 19th century. A much stranger account of a woman traveling in search of actual religious relics is Anneli Rufus's *Magnificent Corpses: Searching through Europe for St. Peter's Head, St. Claire's Heart, St. Stephen's Hand, and Other Saintly Relics*. Fiction readers interested in the Church of the Latter Day Saints may enjoy the nine-part *Work and the Glory* series of historical novels by Gerald N. Lund, which begins with *Pillar of Light* and includes *So Great a Cause* and *All Is Well*, both of which follow the Mormon faithful on their trail from Illinois to Utah.

Rogers, Jim

Investment Biker: On the Road with Jim Rogers. New York: Random House, 1994. 402 pp. ISBN: 9780679422556

Finance professor Rogers rode around the world on his motorcycle to gain a better understanding of how to invest in foreign markets. His trips through 52 countries with his girlfriend Tabitha took almost two years and were punctuated by such adventures as eating locusts in Zaire, learning how to trade currency on the black market, and being helped by an Irish biker gang. Mixed in with the travel narrative is investment advice: why Zimbabwe is doomed to fail, why Chile succeeded, and why the U.S. economy may have seen its best days. Rogers also writes a lot about the people he "bumped into" during the trip and what he learned from them.

Subjects: Circumnavigations; Economics; Finance; Globalization; Motorcycles

Places: Africa (Various); Argentina; Austria; Beijing; Botswana; Buenos Aires; Chile; China; Europe (Various); Ireland; Istanbul; Japan; Kazakhstan; New York; Russia; South Africa; South America (Various); Turkey; Zambia; Zimbabwe

Now Try: Rogers followed up the success of *Investment Biker* with *Adventure Capitalist* (annotated in this chapter), in which he writes about traveling through over 100 countries in a custom-built Mercedes convertible; that book is also filled with investment advice. Another travel narrative with an economics slant is Pietra Rivoli's *The Travels of a T-Shirt in the Global Economy: An Economist Examines the Markets, Power, and Politics of World Trade*, in which the author visited cotton farmers in Texas, factory workers in China, and used-clothing vendors in Tanzania to gain a better understanding of the global economy. Another writer who shares Rogers's faith in globalization and free markets is Thomas Friedman, whose works on those topics include *The Lexus and the Olive Tree: Understanding Globalization* and *The World Is Flat: A Brief History of the Twenty-First Century*.

Smith, Roff Martin

Cold Beer and Crocodiles: A Bicycle Journey into Australia. Washington, DC: Adventure Press, National Geographic Society, 2000. 284 pp. ISBN: 9780792279525

Smith, a native New Englander who had lived in Australia for 15 years, decided that he knew little about his adopted country; so he abruptly quit his job and set out to bicycle 10,000 miles through cities, mountains, deserts, and of course, the Outback. Smith struggled through much of the nine-month trip (riding through rugged terrain, battling winds and dust and flies, fighting up steep mountain grades and across burning deserts, staying at remote sheep and cattle stations, conserving water) but in the end, he found a new home and learned from the people he encountered what being an Australian is about.

Subjects: Bicycling; Deserts; Mountains; Solo Travelers

Places: Australia

Now Try: Tony Horwitz was working in an office in Sydney when he got the urge to see more of Australia; his story of hitchhiking through the Australian Outback is told in *One for the Road: Hitchhiking Through the Australian Outback*. Quentin van Marle rode his bicycle 4,000 miles from the north of Australia to the south of the continent and tells his story in *Boomerang Road: A Pedalling Pom's Australian Odyssey*. Another Down Under bicycling narrative is Josie Dew's *Long Cloud Ride: A Cycling Adventure Across*

New Zealand, which recounts the author's 6,200-mile ride through Australia's neighbor during the wettest, stormiest year on record.

Warmbrunn, Erika

Where the Pavement Ends: One Woman's Bicycle Trip Through Mongolia, China & Vietnam. Seattle, WA: Mountaineer Books, 2001. 249 pp. ISBN: 9780898866841

With little forethought or training, Warmbrunn rode her bicycle 5,000 miles through Mongolia, China, and Vietnam. She describes both the challenges of her journey (eating sheep's head in Mongolia, dealing with bureaucrats in China, being accosted by two young men) and the beauty of the people she met and their customs. Warmbrunn, who spent a month teaching English to children in a Mongolian village, also has an excellent eye for detail, which allows her to contrast the countries: the frigid weather and childlike adults of Mongolia, the tropical beaches and war-weary children of Vietnam. Her sensitivity and openness to the people of these three countries allows her to appreciate their lifestyles and to write about the experience with humor and insight.

Subjects: Bicycling; Teaching; Women Travelers

Places: China; Mongolia; Vietnam

Now Try: Journalist Louisa Waugh writes about the year she spent in a remote western village in Mongolia in *Hearing Birds Fly: A Nomadic Year in Mongolia;* her portrayal of the villagers and their culture is reminiscent of Warmbrunn. Jill Lawless visited Mongolia in the late 1990s and writes about a country awakening from years of isolation in *Wild East: Travels in the New Mongolia.* When Mongolia opened itself to the West, Jasper Becker was one of the first westerners to visit the country; his reflections on what he saw and especially the lasting effects of Russian and Chinese rule over the area are found in *Mongolia: Travels in the Untamed Land.* Translated fiction set in Mongolia is scarce, but readers can try Christopher Howard's *Tea of Ulaanbaatar,* a rambling novel about a Peace Corps worker stationed in the country's capitol in the late 1990s, or Galsan Tschinag's moving young adult novel, *The Blue Sky,* about a Tuvan boy in the Mongolian mountains in the 1950s.

Consider Starting With . . .

Bryson, Bill. *A Walk in the Woods: Rediscovering America on the Appalachian Trail.*

Chiang, Lynette. *The Handsomest Man in Cuba: An Escapade.*

Diski, Jenny. *Stranger on a Train: Daydreaming and Smoking around America with Interruptions.*

Heat-Moon, William Least. *Blue Highways: A Journey into America.*

Maclean, Rory. *Stalin's Nose: Travels Around the Bloc.*
Stewart, Rory. *The Places in Between.*
Theroux, Paul. *The Great Railway Bazaar.*

Fiction Read-Alikes

Christie, Agatha. Christie's best-known mystery, ***Murder on the Orient Express,*** is set on the famous long-distance passenger train, which carries detective Hercule Poirot from Constantinople to Paris. She also wrote ***The Mystery of the Blue Train,*** which again involves Poirot, this time on a train bound for the French Riviera, on which an American heiress is murdered and her famous ruby goes missing. Another Poirot mystery, ***Death on the Nile,*** takes place on a boat traveling down the Nile River. By setting these mysteries on trains and boats, Christie made it easier for the suspects to be detained while Poirot's "little grey cells" did their work.

Greene, Graham. Greene set one of his early thrillers, ***Stamboul Train,*** on the Orient Express as it runs between Ostend (Belgium) and Istanbul; the novel weaves together the lives of several characters who happen to be traveling together. A better-known novel of Greene's, ***Travels With My Aunt,*** is also set in part on the Orient Express and follows the travels of a conventional, retired banker and his eccentric, adventurous Aunt Augusta across Europe and to South America. Greene also wrote ***Journey Without Maps,*** a highly-regarded travel narrative about a four-week walk through Liberia in 1935, as well as several novels that have a strong sense of place: ***The Power and the Glory*** (Mexico); ***The Heart of the Matter*** (British West Africa); ***The Quiet American*** (Vietnam); ***Our Man in Havana*** (Cuba); and ***The Comedians*** (Haiti).

Highsmith, Patricia. The chance encounters with strangers that is a feature of rail travel figures prominently in Highsmith's classic thriller, ***Strangers on a Train,*** in which one of the strangers (Bruno) offers to kill the other's (Guy's) wife in exchange for Guy killing Bruno's father. Another of Highsmith's classics, ***The Talented Mr. Ripley,*** involves travel, when young Tom Ripley is asked by a shipping magnate to go to Italy and persuade his son Dickie to return to the United States.

Kerouac, Jack. As one reviewer noted, "Few books capture the headlong momentum and pure joy of the road like" Kerouac's classic autobiographical novel, ***On the Road***. That book, which the Modern Library ranked as one of the 100 best English-language novels of the 20th century, is based on several road trips Kerouac and his friends made in the United States in the late 1940s and early 1950s. Kerouac's ***The Dharma Bums*** also involves travel and contrasts the narrator's life outdoors, bicycling and hiking through the West, with his life in the city.

MacLean, Alistair. MacLean's only historical novel, ***Breakheart Pass,*** is set on a train traveling through the Nevada territory in the winter of 1873. As the train goes higher into the mountains, more people disappear or are killed, slowly revealing that almost no one on the train is truthful. MacLean also wrote two thrillers that rely on and evoke the harsh environment of the Arctic area: ***Bear Island*** and ***Ice Station Zebra***.

McLarty, Ron. In 2004, thanks to praise from Stephen King, McLarty was able to find a publisher for his novel, ***The Memory of Running***, which involves an overweight Vietnam veteran who bicycles across the United States in order to reclaim the body of his dead sister in Los Angeles. McLarty mixes humor with heartbreak as his hero rediscovers his life along the way.

Moody, Greg. Fans of bicycling may enjoy Moody's five books in the *Cycling Murder Mystery* series. In the first of the series, ***Two Wheels***, a world champion cyclist dies in an explosion and Will Ross, his replacement on the cycling team, begins to suspect that the death was anything but accidental. In ***Perfect Circles***, Ross and the team ride in the Tour de France. In ***Derailleur***, Ross is joined by cyclist and love interest Cheryl Crane; the two ride through the Colorado mountains in ***Deadroll***. In ***Dead Air***, Ross is pursued by both a killer driven by revenge and a manipulative television reporter.

Robbins, Tom. The ultimate novel about hitchhiking is undoubtedly Robbins's ***Even Cowgirls Get the Blues***, with its protagonist, Sissy Hankshaw, and her enormously large thumbs. As with many of Robbins's novels, this one covers a wide range of topics (from free love and drug use to animal rights and religion) and includes a number of offbeat, memorable characters.

Whiteside, Diane. Whiteside writes Western romances and is best known for her *Texas Vampires Paranormal Romance* series. In addition to relying on a strong sense of place in her stories, typically set in small towns in the Old West, Whiteside has written at least one novel that is set on a cross-country train, ***The Northern Devil***, in which her protagonist is trapped on a private train with a man intent on stealing her inheritance. Another of her romances, ***The River Devil***, takes place on a different kind of conveyance, a riverboat on the Mississippi and Missouri rivers.

Chapter 5

The Expatriate Life

The true heart of a place does not come in a week's vacation.
To know it well . . . one must "wait its occasions."
—Ellen Meloy, *The Anthropology of Turquoise: Meditations on Landscape, Art, and Spirit*

Definition of "The Expatriate Life"

To return to the definition given in the introduction to this book, travel is an activity that involves a traveler or travelers who go to a destination by some means, for some purpose, *for some length of time*. The titles discussed in this chapter are those that are defined largely by the length of time spent by the traveler in her destination. They represent stays of at least one or two years or, in some cases, a lifetime; they also include narratives in which the traveler lives with a "foreign" group of people for a longer time.

The traditional distinction between an expatriate (someone who lives in a foreign country out of choice) and an exile (someone who is forced to live in a foreign country) is also consistent with this book's definition of a travel narrative as a book in which one or more travelers take a *voluntary* trip. Although there are some excellent books by exiles (Ariel Dorfman's *Heading South, Looking North: A Bilingual Journey*, for example), the titles in this chapter are written by expatriates, individuals who voluntarily spent longer periods of time in foreign lands, what Stoddard Martin called "voluntary exiles."[1]

For many readers, the idea of traveling to another country and living there for an extended period of time holds a certain appeal or romance. They long for a more intimate knowledge of a place and its people than the traveler typically gains in the few days or weeks most trips encompass. They want a deeper, richer experience than the one provided by shorter trips or "If It's Tuesday, This Must Be Belgium" tours. As one of the participants in a 2009 open chat about expatriate literature said, "If travel writing is a chance to travel vicariously, expat lit is a chance to live abroad vicariously."[2] As another participant noted, "Traveling doesn't give you enough time to 'see'. You have to live it."[3]

Living in a foreign country or with a foreign people for a lengthy period of time also engenders a variety of challenges. Some of these are challenges that may not be faced by shorter-term travelers at all, and some are challenges that may not be faced by shorter-term travelers to quite the same degree. A short-term traveler who has difficulty with the language of the destination country, for example, can get by or find an interpreter, but an expatriate must learn the language in order to function in her new country. A traveler will likely stay in a hotel, but an expatriate will need a home, complete with a kitchen and plumbing that will have to be kept in working order. Larger issues, such as assimilation and identity, may also affect the expatriate but not the short-term traveler.

The motivations of the expatriates in the titles in this chapter are varied, and so is their appeal to readers. Some expatriates grew tired of their lives and decided to chuck it all for a new life in a new country. Some moved to their foreign homes with spouses and stayed after their marriages dissolved. Some fell in love in a foreign country, married, and made that country home. Some had dreamed of living abroad all of their lives and were finally able to realize those dreams. Some spent time abroad as students or as teachers or as writers on fellowship or as Peace Corps volunteers. Those who decided to live with a foreign group of people did so out of a desire to better understand these people.

Most of our readers won't actually live abroad, but many of them may wish that they could. My friend Paul, for example, is a Francophile who has good friends near Crécy in northern France. He visits them almost annually, for two or three weeks at a time, and I'm convinced that given half a chance, he'd move to France and become an expatriate. If I ever hear that he won the lottery, I'll start looking for him there.

A lot of our readers are like Paul, and the titles in this chapter on expatriate narratives should help satisfy their longings for life in another country.

Appeal of "The Expatriate Life"

Two of the traditional appeal factors are extremely important to the titles in this chapter on "The Expatriate Life": frame and setting and characterization. The importance of frame and setting is especially apparent in the titles of the first two subgenres, "A Year or Two in . . ." and "Living Abroad." In the former, the sense of newness and discovery of a place play an important role, while in the latter, it is the growing depth of understanding of the place that will attract readers. Think about the Provence of Peter Mayle (*A Year in Provence* or *Encore Provence: New Adventures in the South of France* or *Toujours Provence*) or the Tuscany of Frances Mayes (*Under the Tuscan Sun: At Home in Italy* or *Bella Tuscany: The Sweet Life in Italy* or *Every Day in Tuscany: Seasons of Italian Life*) or the China of Peter Hessler (*River Town: Two Years on the Yangtze*) and you get a good sense of the importance of frame and setting to these titles.

Characterization is also a critical appeal factor for these titles, which are invariably filled with wonderful, sometimes quirky characters: Peter Mayle's neighbors, Massot, Faustin, and Menicucci in the Provence books; the local Italians whom Frances

Mayes meets in her Tuscany trilogy; the servant Farah in Isak Dinesen's *Out of Africa*; Sachiko, the Japanese woman with whom Pico Iyer falls in love (*The Lady and the Monk: Four Seasons in Kyoto*); the 14th Dalai Lama in Heinrich Harrer's *Seven Years in Tibet*; or Gertrude Stein and F. Scott Fitzgerald in Ernest Hemingway's *A Moveable Feast*.

Characters are also important in the section entitled "Living with Others," which focuses on groups of individuals, like the Gypsies of Fernanda Eberstadt's *Little Money Street: In Search of Gypsies and Their Music in the South of France* or Isabel Fonseca's *Bury Me Standing: The Gypsies and Their Journey*, the Indian eunuchs of Zia Jaffrey's *The Invisibles: A Tale of the Eunuchs of India*, and the soccer hooligans of Bill Buford's *Among the Thugs*.

The other traditional appeal factors of story line, pacing, tone and mood, and language and style will be less important but may play important roles in specific titles.

Readers who are drawn to the titles in this chapter may also be drawn to titles from genres outside travel narratives, and the readers' advisor should be prepared to help the reader cross those boundaries. Biographies, memoirs, and histories, in particular, seem rich with possibilities. A memoir such as Stein's *The Autobiography of Alice B. Toklas* or a biography like Jeffrey Meyers's *Hemingway: A Biography* or a history like William Wiser's *The Crazy Years: Paris in the Twenties* might all be reasonable read-alikes for Ernest Hemingway's *A Moveable Feast*, for example, not to mention novels and short stories by any of the lost generation writers who lived in Paris in the 1920s.

Likewise, readers interested in expatriate narratives, with its greater sense of living the foreign experience, may also find titles from Immersion Journalism to be of interest. Titles like *Word Freak: Heartbreak, Triumph, Genius, and Obsession in the World of Competitive Scrabble Players* by Stefan Fatsis, *Newjack: Guarding Sing Sing* by Ted Conover, and *Animal, Vegetable, Miracle: A Year of Food Life* by Barbara Kingsolver all share with expatriate narratives the sense of living in another culture.

Interestingly, several of these expatriate narratives involve buying and fixing up old houses (Peter Mayle's *A Year in Provence*, Frances Mayes's *Under the Tuscan Sun: At Home in Italy*, Lawrence Durrell's *Bitter Lemons of Cyprus*) and may appeal to do-it-yourself types or individuals who enjoy HGTV. Details like these may be the key to building a good relationship with these readers.

Organization of the Chapter

The first category in this chapter is "Classics," which represent titles published prior to 1990 that also display universality, multiple levels of meaning, great stories, memorable characters, emotional or though-provoking experiences, and great writing. These are titles that are likely to be more familiar to readers and librarians, and this familiarity may help readers and librarians better understand the subgenre and its categories, especially given the fact that the appeal of living a longer time abroad or living among others has not changed a great deal over the years.

Two of the other categories are distinguished by the length of time involved in the expatriate experience. "A Year or Two in . . ." consists of narratives in which the traveler spends a year or two in the destination, thus combining a sense of wonder at the newness of the land and its people with the time to develop a deeper understanding of the place and the individuals who live there. By contrast, the titles in the "Living Abroad" category are those in which the traveler spends more than a year or two in another country, thus allowing the sense of wonder at the newness of the land and its people to begin to wear off and the understanding of the place and the individuals who live to grow.

The fourth category of this subgenre, "Living with Others," is somewhat different and involves the traveler living not so much in a foreign country as with a group of individuals whose world is foreign to the traveler. The groups with which these individuals identify (Gypsies, indigenous Mexican tribes, soccer fans) represent ties that are as strong as those defined by the borders of many nations.

Classics

As noted earlier, this book defines classics as travel narratives that were published before 1990 and that also display universality, multiple levels of meaning, great stories, memorable characters, emotional or though-provoking experiences, and great writing. These titles are intended to be more familiar to readers and librarians and to thereby serve as good entry points into the subgenre of "The Expatriate Life" and its categories. Because the appeal of spending a longer time abroad or of living among other people has not changed radically over the years, the appeal of these older works (like Isak Dinesen's *Out of Africa*) may not differ greatly for many readers from the appeal of newer counterparts, like Sarah Erdman's *Nine Hills to Nambonkaha: Two Years in the Heart of an African Village* or Kuki Gallman's *I Dreamed of Africa*.

The titles listed under "Classics" reflect the categories of this subgenre and include short stays, like the year that music critic Mark Hudson spent in a Gambian village in *Our Grandmothers' Drums: A Portrait of Rural African Life and Culture*, as well as longer stays, like Isak Dinesen's 17-year life in Kenya in the marvelous *Out of Africa*. There are even short stays that turn into longer stays, like Peter Mayle's *A Year in Provence*, which turned into several years and several books. Finally, there are stories of living with others, like Ted Conover's year spent riding the rails with hoboes in *Rolling Nowhere: Riding the Rails with America's Hoboes* and Robert D. Kaplan's time among the mujahideen in *Soldiers of God: With Islamic Warriors in Afghanistan and Pakistan*.

Several countries are also represented, including the China of Mark Salzman (*Iron and Silk*), the Cyprus of Lawrence Durrell (*Bitter Lemons of Cyprus* and *Prospero's Cell: A Guide To The Landscape And Manners of The Island Of Corfu*), the France of Ernest

Hemingway (*A Moveable Feast*) or Peter Mayle (*A Year in Provence*), the Kenya of Isak Dinesen's *Out of Africa*, and the Tibet of Heinrich Harrer (*Seven Years in Tibet*).

Conover, Ted

Rolling Nowhere: Riding the Rails with America's Hoboes. New York: Viking Press, 1984. 274 pp. ISBN: 9780670603190 YA

Investigative journalist Conover spent a year riding the rails, becoming a tramp himself, in order to learn more about hoboes. Much of the narrative focuses on the members of this underclass whom Conover met and his experiences with them, but there is also a good bit of focus on Conover's thoughts about what he had undertaken, his fears about the project, and how he felt his behavior and attitude were changed. In spite of the violence, scarcity, addiction, and isolation of the hobo life, Conover clearly felt sympathy for these individuals, especially when he realized that they did not have the luxury of returning home when the project was finished

Subjects: Investigative Stories; Rail Travel

Categories: Living with Others; On the Rails

Places: Arizona; California; Colorado; Idaho; Missouri; Montana; Nebraska; Nevada; North Dakota; Oregon; Utah; Washington; Wyoming

Series: *Vintage Departures*

Now Try: Conover followed *Rolling Nowhere* with *Coyotes*, about a year he spent with migrant Mexican workers, crossing the U.S.–Mexican border four times and traveling with the workers through California, Arizona, Idaho, and Florida; Conover claims that "Mexican farm workers were the new American hoboes." Wayne Iverson combines the lessons he learned in more than 12 years of hopping trains as well as those learned in seven years as a practicing monk in *Hobo Sapien: Freight Train Hopping Tao and Zen*. Eddy Joe Cotton spent six years on the road and recounts his story in *Hobo: A Young Man's Thoughts on Trains and Tramping in America*; he also provides a history of hoboes in the United States and some practical advice for those who also want to hit the road. William T. Vollmann also encountered hoboes when he hopped freight trains, an experience he writes about in *Riding Toward Everywhere* (annotated in the chapter entitled "Getting There Is Half the Fun"). Conroy is best known as an "immersion journalist," and other writers in that genre (like Barbara Ehrenreich, whose *Nickel and Dimed: On (Not) Getting By in America* examined the lives of America's working poor) may appeal to readers who enjoy *Rolling Nowhere*.

Dinesen, Isak

Out of Africa. New York: Modern Library, 1983 [1938]. 389 pp. ISBN: 9780394604985

"I had a farm in Africa at the foot of the Ngong Hills," opens this classic expatriate memoir. For 17 years, Baroness Karen Blixen, a Danish aristocrat who would later write under the pen name of Isak Dinesen, owned and operated a coffee plantation in Kenya, near Nairobi. Blixen and her husband, a Swedish baron, came to Kenya from Denmark, and when they separated in 1921, she stayed and managed the farm by herself. The book, which is written in a brilliant and wistful style, recounts the visits that her lover (big-game hunter Denys Finch-Hatton) paid, the Africans who lived on the farm, the eventual failure of the farm, and the decision to sell it and return to Denmark.

Subjects: 1910s; 1920s; Colonialism; Farms; Memoirs; Women Travelers

Categories: Living Abroad

Places: Africa; Kenya

Now Try: Dinesen's *Letters From Africa, 1914–1931* provides more insight into the writer's mind and her daily life on the farm in Kenya. Judith Thurman won a 1983 National Book Award for her biography of the great writer, *Isak Dinesen: The Life of a Storyteller*. The four stories gathered in Dinesen's *Shadows of the Grass* also capture her love of the African people and the land itself. Elspeth Huxley was the child of white pioneer settlers in Kenya; her memoir, *The Flame Trees of Thika: Memories of an African Childhood,* tells the story of her childhood on a coffee farm during the same years that Dinesen ran her farm. Moritz Thomsen joined the Peace Corps in his 60s, was posted to Ecuador, and returned some years later to live permanently and run a farm with his best friend; he recounts his experience in *The Farm on the River of Emeralds*. Alexandra Fuller's *Don't Let's Go to the Dogs Tonight,* which depicts a white African girl's coming of age during the Rhodesian civil war of the 1970s, may also appeal to Dinesen fans.

Durrell, Lawrence

Bitter Lemons of Cyprus. London: Faber & Faber, 2000 [1957]. 276 pp. ISBN: 9780571201556

British author Lawrence Durrell spent 1953–1956 on the island of Cyprus, which was a British colony at the time. *Bitter Lemons of Cyprus* recounts those years, from the author's adventures buying and maintaining a house and his experiences as an English teacher at a local school to the political turmoil and violence that overcame Cyprus and led to the departure of Durrell and other British nationals. Durrell captures the dreamlike beauty of the island and the remote village of Bellapaix, where he lived, and the idiosyncrasies of the villagers, both Greek and Turkish. Durrell tells this heart-breaking story in delicate, crafted prose.

Subjects: 1950s; Authors; Colonialism; Islands; Memoirs; Small Town Life; Teaching

Categories: Living Abroad

Places: Cyprus

Now Try: Durrell was a well-regarded travel writer, and many of his short pieces as well as excerpts from his longer writings have been collected in *The Lawrence Durrell Travel Reader,* which includes several essays on the Mediterranean islands of Cyprus, Corfu, Rhodes, and Sicily. Travel writer Colin Thubron visited Cyprus in 1974, just before Turkey invaded the island, and writes about his 600-mile walk around the island in *Journey into Cyprus*. For a better understanding of the issues separating the Greeks and the Turks on Cyprus, readers can consult Yiannis Papadakis's *Echoes from the Dead Zone: Across the Cyprus Divide*; Papadakis, a Greek, set out to understand both communities and the concerns that have divided them. Durrell's fiction, particularly *The Alexandria Quartet*, about the lives of British expatriates living in Alexandria before and during World War II, may also appeal.

Durrell, Lawrence

Prospero's Cell: A Guide To The Landscape And Manners of The Island Of Corfu. London: Faber and Faber, 1975 [1945]. 168 pp. ISBN: 9780 571048410

Durrell and his first wife lived on the Greek island of Corfu from 1937 to 1941, and *Prospero's Cell* is the story of their life there, with its swimming, fishing, sailing, good food, and wine. The book, which is brilliantly written in journal form, is part memoir, part history, and part travel narrative. The sunny Greek island is contrasted with the grey, industrialized England that Durrell and his wife had left, and the lively new friends they met also brighten the story, at least until their charming idyll was abruptly ended with the outbreak of World War II, when Durrell and his wife left for Alexandria, Egypt.

Subjects: 1930s; Authors; Islands; Memoirs; Quick Reads; Spouses

Category: Living Abroad

Places: Corfu; Greece

Now Try: *Prospero's Cell* was Durrell's first travel narrative, and he would go on to write others about the Greek islands, including *Reflections on a Marine Venus*, about the island of Rhodes just after World War II, and *The Greek Islands*, which describes several of the Greek islands, their histories, and their mythological importance. Lawrence Durrell's younger brother Gerald wrote his memoir of life as a child on Corfu from 1935 to 1939 in his Corfu Trilogy (*My Family and Other Animals*; *Birds, Beasts, and Relatives*; and *The Garden of the Gods*), but his version of events does not always agree with that of his older brother, suggesting that at least part of *Prospero's Cell* may be fictionalized. In 2002, Eleni N. Gage decided to rebuild her ancestral home in a village near the border of Greece and Albania; the story of her attempt to fulfill this dream, in spite of battles with the local bureaucracy, is told in the earnest *North of Ithaka: A Granddaughter Returns to Greece and Discovers Her Roots*.

Harrer, Heinrich

Seven Years In Tibet. New York: Jeremy P. Tarcher/Putnam, 1997 [1953]. 329 pp. ISBN: 9780874778885

Harrer, an Austrian mountaineer, and his friend escaped from a British internment camp in India during the Second World War and traveled to

Lhasa, the capital of Tibet. The two spent seven years in Lhasa, and Harrer describes the experience, the culture and people of Tibet (at that time, a mysterious, isolated country), and his friendship with the 14th Dalai Lama. China's invasion of Tibet in 1950 led to Harrer's departure from that country, but his book captures a culture that no longer exists.

Subjects: 1940s; Buddhism; Memoirs; Mountains; World War II

Category: Living Abroad

Places: India; Lhasa; Tibet

Now Try: Harrer later wrote *Return to Tibet: Tibet After the Chinese Occupation*, about what he observed on his 1982 return to Tibet as part of one of the first groups allowed in by the Chinese; he contrasts the happy, vivid country and people he had seen in the 1940s with the drab, dismal Tibet that was the end product of Chinese occupation. *Seven Years in Tibet* was originally the sequel to *The White Spider*, Harrer's account of the first successful climb of the Eiger, a Swiss mountain in the Bernese Alps, in 1938. Harrer became friends with the current Dalai Lama during his original visit to the country, and readers interested in that spiritual leader's life may want to read *My Land and My People: The Original Autobiography of His Holiness the Dalai Lama of Tibet*.

Hemingway, Ernest

A Moveable Feast. New York: Scribner, 2009 [1964]. 240 pp. ISBN: 9781416591313

"If you are lucky enough to have lived in Paris as a young man, then wherever you go for the rest of your life, it stays with you, for Paris is a moveable feast." Hemingway's memoir of his life in Paris in the 1920s with his first wife is filled with portraits of other expatriates, including F. Scott Fitzgerald, Ezra Pound, and Gertrude Stein, as well as European writers like Ford Madox Ford, Hilaire Belloc, and James Joyce. Many of the cafes, bars, hotels, and apartments mentioned by Hemingway can be found in modern Paris.

Subjects: 1920s; Authors; Memoirs; Quick Reads

Categories: Living Abroad

Places: France; Paris

Now Try: Noel R. Fitch's *Walks In Hemingway's Paris: A Guide To Paris For The Literary Traveler* is more travel guide than travel narrative, but fans of *A Moveable Feast* will enjoy its visits to the areas frequented by Hemingway and his colleagues. David Lebovitz's *The Sweet Life in Paris: Delicious Adventures in the World's Most Glorious—and Perplexing—City* describes the pastry chef author's experiences as an expatriate in Paris in more recent times; the book includes 50 recipes. Diane Johnson's *Into a Paris Quartier: Reine Margot's Chapel and Other Haunts of St.-Germain* is a long essay that celebrates the 6th arrondissement of Paris, which was one of Hemingway's hangouts. A recent biography that looks at Hemingway's life after Paris is Paul Hendrickson's rich *Hemingway's Boat: Everything He Loved in Life, and Lost, 1934–1961*, which focuses particularly on the writer's love of the sea, fishing, and his boat. Hemingway lived in Paris during the 1920s with his first wife, Hadley, and she is the subject of Paula McLain's novel about their life together during that fast-living time, *The Paris Wife*.

Hudson, Mark

Our Grandmothers' Drums: A Portrait of Rural African Life and Culture. London: Secker & Warburg, 1989. 321 pp. ISBN: 9780436209598

Music critic Hudson spent a year living in a village in Gambia, observing the daily life and participating in the rituals of the people there. Hudson was eventually, and surprisingly, invited to join one of the women's societies and he found them to be more independent and empowered than he expected, in spite of their lives of hard work, circumcision, and arranged marriages. Hudson is frank and honest in recounting his personal and emotional involvement in the life of this small African village.

Subjects: Culture Clash; Small Town Life

Categories: Living with Others; A Year or Two in . . .

Places: Africa; Gambia

Awards: Thomas Cook Travel Book Award, 1990

Now Try: Hudson also wrote *The Music in My Head*, a novel about a collector of African music who traveled to Africa in search of the continent's greatest musician; the novel highlights the complex relationship between Europeans and Africans. Susana Herrera's *Mango Elephants in the Sun: How Life in an African Village Let Me Be in My Skin* tells about the author's experience as a Peace Corps volunteer in northern Cameroon and how her life in the village allowed her to forget her painful childhood. Anthropologist Katherine A. Dettwyler gives a very personal account of her work with malnourished children in Mali in *Dancing Skeletons: Life and Death in West Africa*; the book explores the author's own thoughts, biases, joys, and sorrows as well as the ethnographic details of the subject.

Kaplan, Robert D.

Soldiers of God: With Islamic Warriors in Afghanistan and Pakistan. Boston: Houghton Mifflin, 1990. 258 pp. ISBN: 9780395521328

Kaplan, an American journalist and author of several travel narratives (*Balkan Ghosts, Eastward to Tartary, The Ends of the Earth*), went to Afghanistan in the 1980s to write about the guerilla war against the Soviet Union. He traveled with the mujahideen and writes about a conflict he felt was not being adequately reported; hc portrays the fighters as peasants reacting to the invasion of their land, not as religious fanatics. Among the mujahideen he met was the 30-year-old Hamid Karzai, who would later become the president of Afghanistan. Kaplan gives the reader a good feel for the history of the country and its conflict with the Soviet Union, as well as a close look at the people he met, the land, the food, and the culture.

Subjects: Asian History; Islam; Politics; War

Categories: Living with Others

Places: Afghanistan

Series: *Vintage Departures*

Now Try: Kaplan traveled to what he sees as the frontiers of the American empire (Afghanistan, Colombia, Fallujah, Mongolia, the Philippines, Yemen) and praised the efforts of the American soldiers stationed in those parts of the world in *Imperial Grunts: On the Ground with the American Military, from Mongolia to the Philippines to Iraq and Beyond*. For a different perspective on the Soviet conflict in Afghanistan, readers may try *The Hidden War: A Russian Journalist's Account of the Soviet War in Afghanistan* by Artyom Borovik, described by one reviewer as "alternately fascinating and horrific." Ali Ahmad Jalali compiled over 100 interviews with mujahideen veterans and published *Afghan Guerrilla Warfare: In the Words of the Mujahideen Fighters*, a fascinating look at the conflict from the Afghan side. In *Cables from Kabul: The Inside Story of the West's Afghanistan Campaign*, former British ambassador to Afghanistan Sherard Cowper-Coles offers a high-level account of how Britain was drawn into the Afghan War and why that war was a military fiasco. Another journalist known for his close rapport with soldiers was Ernie Pyle, who reported during World War II; his stories have been collected in the volumes *Brave Men* and *Here Is Your War: Story of G.I. Joe*.

Mayle, Peter

A Year in Provence. New York: Vintage Books, 1991 [1990]. 207 pp. ISBN: 9780679731146 YA

When Mayle and his wife purchased a 200-year-old farmhouse and moved to southern France with their two dogs, he intended to spend his time writing a novel. Instead, he created a travel narrative genre: buy an old house in an interesting part of the world, move there, and write about the challenges with a good bit of humor. Mayle and his wife encountered everything from the local ways of measuring time, lazy builders, unruly workers, unexpectedly bad weather, tax-dodging lawyers, and underground truffle hunters. The book is written with a wonderful, dry wit, and Mayle's characterizations of the local people (from his grumpy, fox-hunting neighbor Massot to the perpetual pessimist Faustin to the clarinet-playing plumber Menicucci) will delight many readers.

Subjects: Community Life; Food; Gentle Reads; Homes; Humor; Memoirs; Quick Reads; Seasons; Spouses

Categories: Living Abroad

Places: France

Series: *Vintage Departures*

Now Try: Mayle followed up *A Year in Provence* with two other books based on his life there, *Toujours Provence* and *Encore Provence* (both annotated in this chapter). *A Year in Provence* was turned into a successful television mini-series, and fans of the book may enjoy the DVD of that series. A more serious and more intellectual look at expatriate life in Provence is provided by Nicholas Woodsworth in *Seeking Provence: Old Myths, New Paths*; the author ruminates on everything from Cezanne to Nietzsche. Although Lawrence Durrell is most often associated with the islands of the Mediterranean, he did live for more than 30 years in the Provence region of France; his memories of that place are captured in *Caesar's Vast Ghost: Aspects of Provence.* Betsy Draine and Michael Hinden bought a small stone house in southwest France in 1985 and recount the experience in their charming book, *A Castle in the Backyard: The Dream of a House in France.* Mark Greenside's hysterically funny *I'll Never Be French (No Matter What I Do): Living in a Small Village in Brittany* looks at an American's life in yet another French province, this one at the westernmost edge of France.

Orwell, George

Down and Out in Paris and London. New York: Harcourt Brace Jovanovich, 1961 [1933]. 213 pp. ISBN: 9780156262248

In 1927, Orwell was living in London and contributing stories to various journals when he decided to investigate the lives of downtrodden individuals living in poverty. He first moved to Paris, where he washed dishes at an upscale hotel, and then to London, where he lived in a world of tramps and street people. While parts of the book are apparently fictitious, it is largely factual and a stark portrayal of life among the bitterly poor: the dirt, the noise, the begging, the vagrancy. The book is not for the squeamish, particularly Orwell's detailed descriptions of filthy kitchens, bug-infested beds, and other unpleasant aspects of a life of extreme poverty.

Subjects: 1920s; Investigative Stories; Memoirs; Poverty

Categories: Living with Others

Places: England; France; London; Paris

Now Try: Another classic work that documents living conditions among the poor in a major city is Jacob Riis's *How the Other Half Lives: Studies Among the Tenements of New York,* which was written in 1890. Writer/photographer Nick Danziger spent most of 1994 living among the homeless and unemployed in England, Scotland, Wales, and Northern Ireland; his chilling documentary of the lives of these marginalized individuals is *Danziger's Britain: A Journey to the Edge.* Matthew O'Brien's *My Week at the Blue Angel: And Other Stories from the Storm Drains, Strip Clubs, and Trailer Parks of Las Vegas* looks at the lives of those living in poverty in Las Vegas, "a side of Sin City that remains an afterthought," as one reviewer put it. Ted Conover describes life among a specific group of homeless in America (hoboes) in his book, *Rolling Nowhere: Riding the Rails with America's Hoboes* (annotated in this chapter). More modern investigations of poverty might also be suggested, such as Gabriel Thompson's *Working in the Shadows* or David Shipler's *The Working Poor.*

Paul, Elliot

The Last Time I Saw Paris. London: Sickle Moon Books, 2001 [1942]. 322 pp. ISBN: 9781900209137

Elliot Paul had published three novels when he moved to the Latin Quarter of Paris, where he stayed until the outbreak of World War II. His portrayal of the demise of the great city during the period between the two world wars is engaging and filled with witty portrayals of the hoteliers, government clerks, prostitutes, taxidermists, grocers, and goldfish salesmen who live on the same street as the author. The book has strong political overtones (many of the characters are described in terms of their politics, for instance) and is a moving depiction of the soul and spirit of the French people.

Subjects: 1920s; 1930s; Authors; European History; Memoirs; World War II

Categories: Living Abroad

Places: France; Paris

Now Try: Paul returned to Paris and his beloved Rue de la Huchette in 1949, writing about the neighborhood and many of his pre-war friends in *Springtime in Paris*. Alex Karmel's *A Corner in the Marais: Memoir of a Paris Neighborhood* is a more recent depiction of life in one of Paris's more famous districts; Karmel also provides a good bit of architectural and historical information about his adopted neighborhood. John Baxter mixes his story of moving to Paris from Australia and falling in love with tales of the erotic side of Parisian history, including stories about celebrities from Salvador Dali to Josephine Baker, in *We'll Always Have Paris: Sex and Love in the City of Light*. Baxter most recently published *The Most Beautiful Walk in the World: A Pedestrian in Paris*, which recounts his yearlong experience as a "literary walking tour" guide in Paris. Elaine Dundy's 1958 novel, *The Dud Avocado*, recounts the hilarious misadventures of the young American Sally Jay Gorce as she tries to experience life to its fullest in 1950s Paris. Dundy's second novel, *The Old Man and Me*, was written in 1964 and follows Gorce to London, where she is older but no wiser.

Salzman, Mark

Iron and Silk. New York: Random House, 1986. 211 pp. ISBN: 9780394551562 YA

In the early 1980s, Salzman spent two years in Changsha, the capital of China's Hunan province, teaching English and studying martial arts. *Iron and Silk* describes his experience in 30 short episodes, all written with compassion and self-deprecating humor. Salzman was clearly respectful of the sometimes peculiar Chinese customs he encountered, and he is not afraid to describe his many blunders as an outsider. He also learned not just the techniques of martial arts or calligraphy, but the underlying meaning of these practices as well. *Iron and Silk* is a brief but appreciative look at the China of the early 1980s.

Subjects: Culture Clash; Martial Arts; Memoirs; Quick Reads; Teaching

Categories: Living Abroad

Places: China

Series: *Vintage Departures*

Now Try: Salzman's first novel, *The Laughing Sutra*, is also set in China and is a fable about an orphan boy who was raised by a Buddhist monk and who granted the monk's dying wish by going on a quest from China to San Francisco to find the missing scripture known as the Laughing Sutra. American Matthew Polly also traveled to China to study martial arts and writes about that experience in *American Shaolin: Flying Kicks, Buddhist Monks, and the Legend of Iron Crotch: An Odyssey in the New China*; his narrative involves his growth as a practitioner of kung fu as well as his growing understand of Chinese culture. Pamela Logan's *Among Warriors: A Pilgrim in Tibet* recounts the story of Logan, a longtime karate student, and her attempt to travel alone to a remote area of Tibet in order to meet and learn from the famed Khampa warriors.

Simeti, Mary Taylor

On Persephone's Island: A Sicilian Journal. New York: Knopf, 1986. 329 pp. ISBN: 9780394549880

Simeti traveled to Sicily in 1962 to do volunteer work but then fell in love with and married a Sicilian professor and remained in Sicily. *On Persephone's Island* tells the story of one year in her life, 1983, and alternates between her life running her husband's family farm and Palermo, where her husband taught and her children attended school. Simeti's wonderfully written book captures the beauty of the countryside, the rhythm of the farm work, the customs of the Sicilian people, and the history and mythology of the island. It also captures her loneliness and isolation as an outsider, and her portrait of Sicily does not gloss over the island's imperfections: political corruption and the influence of the Mafia.

Subjects: Farming; Islands; Spouses

Categories: Living Abroad

Places: Italy; Sicily

Series: *Vintage Departures*

Now Try: Simeti and pastry cook Maria Grammatico co-wrote *Bitter Almonds: Recollections and Recipes from a Sicilian Girlhood*, about Grammatico's childhood in an orphanage in Sicily in the late 1950s, where she learned to make her pastries. Teri Maggio brings to life the beautiful landscapes and big-hearted residents of the tiny Sicilian mountain villages where her grandparents lived in *The Stone Boudoir* (annotated in "The Journey" chapter of this book). Peter Robb spent over 14 years in Sicily, Naples, and other parts of southern Italy; he writes about the region and especially the power of organized crime in this part of the country in *Midnight in Sicily: On Art, Food, History, Travel and la Cosa Nostra.*

Turnbull, Colin M.

The Forest People. New York: Simon & Schuster, 1968 [1961]. 295 pp. ISBN: 9780671640996

Turnbull, a British American anthropologist, spent three years living with the Mbuti pygmies in the Congo region of Africa. Turnbull was not just an observer of these hunter-gatherers but also shared in their daily lives and learned their customs firsthand. He writes in an informal, accessible, and exuberant style about the hunting parties, the ceremonies around girls coming of age, the circumcision rites, their intense love for their forest world, and their relationships with the surrounding villagers.

Subjects: Anthropology; Indigenous People

Categories: Living with Others

Places: Africa; Democratic Republic of Congo

Now Try: Turnbull's other classic work is *The Mountain People*, about his two-year stay with the Ik people of Uganda; as with the Mbuti of *The Forest People*, Turnbull became closely involved in the day-to-day lives of the Ik. Turnbull's biography, *In the Arms of Africa*, by Roy Richard Grinker, may also be of interest to readers of his books. Other works of anthropology that transcend that genre by portraying the subject peoples in a more intimate manner include Marjorie Shostak's *Nisa: The Life and Words of a !Kung Woman* and Elizabeth Marshall Thomas's *The Harmless People*, both about the rituals and lifestyles of the !Kung tribe of Africa's Kalahari Desert.

Williams, Niall, and Christine Breen

O Come Ye Back to Ireland: Our First Year in County Clare. New York: Soho Press, 1987. 233 pp. ISBN: 9780939149070

Williams and Breen abandoned their publishing careers in New York City to move to a small family farm in County Clare, Ireland. Their plans to write and paint soon gave way to simple survival: their home turned out to be dirt-floored and drafty, they lacked sufficient peat to keep it warm, their crop was threatened by blight, and they desperately missed their luxuries like orange juice and a fat Sunday paper. In spite of the challenges, they stuck it out and learned the skills needed to meet these challenges, including how to deal with the nearly incessant rain. Their adjustments to the new life are told in an honest and delightful manner.

Subjects: Farming; Small Town Life

Categories: Living Abroad

Places: Ireland

Now Try: Williams and Breen have written several books about the couple's life in County Clare. The first of these, *When Summer's in the Meadow*, recounts their disappointment on learning that they can't have children and their subsequent decision to adopt a child. *Pipes Are Calling: Our Jaunts through Ireland* follows the family as they explore the backroads of western Ireland. Their latest book about life in Ireland, *The Luck of the Irish: Our Life in County Clare*, is less romantic than the previous titles and finds the couple with two children, part-time jobs, and concerned about the decline of Irish farming. When Jack and Barbara Maloney's children grew up and moved out, the couple moved from the American Midwest to Scotland; *The Wee Mad Road: A Midlife Escape to the Scottish Highlands* tells about their first two years there and how they had to adjust to life in the small Scottish village in which they settled.

A Year or Two in . . .

The length of time that an individual lives in another country is an important factor in the way in which the traveler's story is told. Shorter stays typically feature a sense of wonder at the newness of the land and its people, which may wear off with longer stays. But the fact that the traveler spends a year or two in the destination also means that she has time to develop a deeper understanding of the place and the individuals who live there than would be the case for the shorter visits described in most of the titles in the previous chapters.

The titles in this category represent a wide range of countries: from Patricia Storace's Greece (*Dinner With Persephone: Travels in Greece*) to Karin Muller's Japan (*Japanland: A Year in Search of Wa*). Some of the destinations are as safe and serene as Paul Collins's small Welsh town of Hay-on-Wye (*Sixpence House: Lost in a Town of Books*); others are as dangerous as Azadeh Moaveni's Iran (*Honeymoon in Tehran: Two Years of Love and Danger in Iran*) or Rory Stewart's post-invasion Iraq (*The Prince of the Marshes: And Other Occupational Hazards of a Year in Iraq*).

The titles also represent a wide range of themes, including religion (William Dalrymple's *City of Djinns: A Year of Delhi* or Robert J. Hutchinson's *When in Rome: A Journal of Life in Vatican City*), AIDS (Sarah Erdman's *Nine Hills to Nambonkaha: Two Years in the Heart of an African Village*), self-discovery (David Mura's *Turning Japanese: Memoirs Of A Sansei*), and even love (Pico Iyer's ethereal *The Lady and the Monk: Four Seasons in Kyoto*).

Readers who enjoy these titles, in which the traveler spends a year or two in the destination, may also enjoy histories of the countries involved, memoirs written by individuals native to these countries, or fiction that takes place in these countries. For example, fans of Karin Muller's *Japanland: A Year in Search of Wa* may be interested in James McClain's *Japan: A Modern History* or Sayo Masuda's *Autobiography of a Geisha* or the novels of Haruki Murakami.

Ahmed, Qanta

In the Land of Invisible Women: A Female Doctor's Journey in the Saudi Kingdom. Naperville, IL: Sourcebooks, Inc., 2008. 454 pp. ISBN: 9781402210877

Ahmed is a British-born Muslim female doctor who was denied a visa to remain in the United States and who then spent two years working as a physician in Saudi Arabia. She recounts a number of incidents that highlight the clash between traditional values and modern reality: women who lay naked on the operating table but were required by custom to have their faces concealed, being able to operate medical equipment but forbidden by law to drive a car. Her perspective is fascinating but complicated; she is both a devout Muslim who went on a pilgrimage to Mecca and a feminist who is critical of the oppression of women in the country.

Subjects: Culture Clash; Doctors; Islam; Medicine; Memoirs; Women Travelers

Places: Saudi Arabia

Now Try: Patrick Notestine's *Paramedic to the Prince: An American Paramedic's Account of Life Inside the Mysterious World of the Kingdom of Saudi Arabia* provides another glimpse inside Saudi Arabia from a medical worker's viewpoint, although Notestine is male and much of his book involves working with Saudi royalty; nevertheless, like Ahmed, he provides a fascinating look inside a world that remains hidden to most readers. Jean Sasson's *Princess: A True Story of Life Behind the Veil in Saudi Arabia* is the story of a Saudi princess whom the author met while living in Saudi Arabia, and highlights the terrible conditions that even privileged women in that country endure. Another woman who writes about her experience in a Muslim country is Audra Grace Shelby, whose *Behind the Veils of Yemen* tells of her time as a missionary in Yemen.

Collins, Paul

Sixpence House: Lost in a Town of Books. New York: Bloomsbury, 2003. 246 pp. ISBN: 9781582342849

Collins, his wife, and son moved from San Francisco to the small Welsh town of Hay-on-Wye with the idea of settling down in this town of 1,500 people and 40 antiquarian bookstores. *Sixpence House* tells the story of their time there, Collins's work in one of the bookstores, their attempts to purchase a reasonably affordable house that wasn't falling down, and Collins's work on his first book. Collins tells his story with a good bit of droll wit and with numerous digressions into obscure trivia. In large part, *Sixpence House* is the story of one man's love of books; bibliophiles, in particular, will love the book.

Subjects: Authors; Books and Reading; Humor; Small Town Life

Places: Wales

Now Try: Collins worked on his first book, *Banvard's Folly*, while in Hay-on-Wye; that book offers thirteen biographical sketches of individuals who were once famous but are now unknown, including the American painter John Banvard, who completed a 15,000-square-foot painting of the Mississippi River. The Canadian crime reporter Jeremy Mercer traveled to Paris after naming an underworld source in a book and receiving threats; he tells about his work as an unpaid employee at the famous bookstore, Shakespeare & Company, and the eccentric characters who frequented the store in the amusing *Time Was Soft There: A Paris Sojourn at Shakespeare & Co.* Bibliophiles should also enjoy Helene Hanff's marvelous classics, *84 Charing Cross Road* and *The Duchess of Bloomsbury Street*, the latter of which recounts her 1971 journey from the United States to the bookstore in London.

Dalrymple, William

City of Djinns: A Year of Delhi. New York: HarperCollins Publishers, 1993. 351 pp. ISBN:9780002157254

Historian and writer William Dalrymple spent a year in the historical capital of India (which he called a city with "a bottomless seam of stories") and writes about his encounters with individuals from a wide range of religious backgrounds, including Sufi dervishes, attendees at a Hindu feast, and Muslims observing Ramadan. Dalrymple provides an entertaining overview of both the history of the city, as seen in its ancient ruins and the epic stories from the Mahabharata, and the experience of living in the contemporary city. He also explores the more violent side of the city's history, from the 1857 mutiny against British rule to the Partition massacres in 1947 to the riots that followed the assassination of Indira Gandhi in 1984.

Subjects: Asian History; Buddhism; Christianity; Hinduism; Islam; Judaism; Memoirs; Religion; Spirituality

Places: Delhi; India

Awards: Thomas Cook Travel Book Award, 1994

Now Try: *City of Djinns* was Dalrymple's second book, following *In Xanadu*, which traced the path taken by Marco Polo from Jerusalem's Church of the Holy Sepulchre to Xanadu, the summer seat of Kubla Khan, in Inner Mongolia. Dalrymple's *Nine Lives: In Search of the Sacred in Modern India* (annotated in the "A Sense of Place" chapter of this book) looks at individuals whose religious paths have been affected by the changes in modern India. Sarah Macdonald's *Holy Cow: An Indian Adventure* (annotated in this chapter) includes that author's reflections on Delhi, where her boyfriend was stationed for two years. Sam Miller's *Delhi: Adventures in a Megacity* (annotated in "A Sense of Place") also examines the many contradictions of India's administrative capital.

Doerr, Anthony

Four Seasons in Rome: On Twins, Insomnia, and the Biggest Funeral in the History of the World. New York: Scribner, 2007. 210 pp. ISBN: 9781416540014

Novelist and short story writer Anthony Doerr received the prestigious Rome Prize from the American Academy of Arts and Letters, which included a yearlong fellowship in Rome. *Four Seasons in Rome* describes that year, during which Doerr was distracted from work on his novel, both by the museums, food, people, and events of Rome (the death of Pope John Paul II, for example) and by the writer's family, which included twin sons who were just six months old at the beginning of the year. Doerr's writing is keen and wonderfully descriptive, capturing the uniqueness of the Eternal City and its seasons.

Subjects: Authors; Family Relationships; Fathers and Sons; Memoirs

Categories: Urban Landscapes

Places: Italy; Rome

Now Try: Eleanor Clark's *Rome and a Villa* describes another American who traveled to Rome on a fellowship to write a novel, one who was also lured away from completing the novel by the charms of Rome; her book depicts everyday life in Rome in the late 1940s and early 1950s and is filled with information on Roman art and architecture. *Satyr Square: A Year, a Life in Rome* by Leonard Barkan tells the story of a Princeton professor's yearlong sabbatical in Rome; a professor of comparative literature, Barkan fills his narrative with references to literature, art, music, food, and wine. H. V. Morton's *A Traveler in Rome* is the classic travel narrative of Rome in the 1950s; many of his observations about Italian culture are as fresh and pertinent today as when they were written. A recent cultural history of Rome that has received good reviews is Robert Hughes's *Rome: A Cultural, Visual, and Personal History*; Hughes is the former art critic for *Time* magazine and presents the cultural past, spectacle, and power of the great city.

Erdman, Sarah

***Nine Hills to Nambonkaha: Two Years in the Heart of an African Village.* New York: Henry Holt, 2003. 322 pp. ISBN: 9780805073812**

Erdman was a Peace Corps volunteer in a small village in the poor, dusty, predominantly Muslim northern Ivory Coast at the end of the 1990s. She found herself caught between the need to bring progress to the people of the village and the need to respect their traditions, caught between the needs for better childhood nutrition and better AIDS awareness and the people's belief in sorcery and magic. ("How do you promote behavior change so that people have more control over the state of their bodies but stop at the threshold where important traditions get destroyed?" she wondered.) She delivered babies, staged plays about AIDS, held a healthy baby contest but still mourned a little when electricity came to the village a week before she left. Erdman's chronicle of her time in Nambonkaha is beautifully written and filled with a wondrous respect for the people with whom she lived.

Subjects: AIDS; Medicine; Memoirs; Peace Corps; Poverty; Village Life

Places: Africa; Ivory Coast

Now Try: Kris Holloway was also a Peace Corps volunteer in an African village (this one in Mali) and her memoir of her time there and her friendship with the village's overworked midwife is *Monique and the Mango Rains: Two Years with a Midwife in Mali.* Mike Tidwell's *The Ponds of Kalambayi: An African Sojourn* examines the two years he spent in Zaire as a Peace Corps volunteer and is similar to Erdman's book in focusing on the lessons he learned about the importance of tradition among the villagers he met there. *From the Center of the Earth: Stories Out of the Peace Corps* is Geraldine Kennedy's collection of 13 true stories written by Peace Corps volunteers about their experiences in various countries; all display a strong sense of unexpected insight gained from the cultures in which they worked.

Hessler, Peter

River Town: Two Years on the Yangtze. New York: HarperCollins Publishers, 2001. 402 pp. ISBN: 9780060195441

Only three years after China allowed the Peace Corps into the country, Hessler spent two years as a Peace Corps volunteer in a Sichuan province town on China's Yangtze River, teaching English literature at a local college. Drawing from the journals he kept during this period, Hessler describes his experience as one of only two foreigners in the city in the past 50 years, tells of his struggles learning the language and culture, and describes everyday life with references to the history of China. The characters he met (the dutiful students, the local noodle shop owner with big dreams, the optimistic and patriotic party member) are described with a rich depth, as is the congested, polluted city itself. A poignant sense of transience pervades the book, too, as we are reminded that the very existence of the town is threatened by the Three Gorges Dam, which was being built while Hessler lived there.

Subjects: Books and Learning; Community Life; Culture Clash; Education, Humor; Peace Corps; Rivers; Teaching

Places: China; Yangtze River

Awards: ALA Notable Book, 2002; *New York Times* Notable Book, 2001

Now Try: *River Town*, Hessler's first book, was followed by *Oracle Bones* and *Country Driving*, both of which provide a closer look at individuals trying to cope with the major changes taking place in China today; both are annotated elsewhere in this book. A review of Michael Levy's recent memoir, *Kosher Chinese: Living, Teaching, and Eating with China's Other Billion*, compared that book to *River Town*; Levy's book recounts the story of his Peace Corps mission to teach English in Guiyang, China, deep in the heart of China. Deborah Fallows and her husband (*Atlantic* correspondent James Fallows) moved to China, and she writes about the challenges of the language and the culture in *Dreaming in Chinese: Mandarin Lessons in Life, Love, and Language*. China is currently experiencing history's largest migration as 130 million citizens have moved from their rural homes to urban centers in search of jobs; in *Factory Girls: From Village to City in a Changing China* Leslie T. Chang explores this phenomenon by following two teenage girls as they moved to and worked in one of the new factory cities.

Hutchinson, Robert J.

When in Rome: A Journal of Life in Vatican City. New York: Doubleday, 1998. 388 pp. ISBN: 9780385486477

Hutchinson (a frequent writer on Catholicism) and his family moved to Rome so that he could explore what he calls "the spiritual and political center" of the Catholic church. The result of these explorations is a sometimes irreverent but always informative book about the history of the Vatican and its present. (Typical of Hutchinson's style is his detailed description of the magnificent treasures of St. Peter's followed by the remark, "Who dusts all of this stuff?") He looks into the sex lives of various popes, discusses how Vatican archaeologists found and then lost the bones of St. Peter, talks to the pope's personal tailor, and visits a museum constructed entirely from human bones, all of which makes the papacy and its long struggle for sanctity and power more accessible.

Subjects: Catholicism; European History; Papacy; Religion

Places: Italy; Rome; Vatican City

Now Try: Although Irish novelist Colm Toibin was no longer a practicing Catholic, he traveled throughout Europe to explore how the Catholic church impacts the lives of its followers in *The Sign of the Cross: Travels in Catholic Europe*. Paul Hofmann spent 30 years in Rome and served as the bureau chief of the *New York Times* there; he writes about the Eternal City and its quirky characters in *The Seasons of Rome: A Journal*. In *As the Romans Do: An American Family's Italian Odyssey*, Alan Epstein celebrates the food and the people of Rome based on his expatriate life there since 1995. Anneli Rufus's spectacularly strange travelogue *Magnificent Corpses: Searching through Europe for St. Peter's Head, St. Claire's Heart, St. Stephen's Hand, and Other Saintly Relics* might also appeal to readers who enjoy *When in Rome*; Rufus visited over two dozen of Europe's most famous relics, from St. Anthony's severed tongue to St. Catherine's head.

Iyer, Pico

The Lady and the Monk: Four Seasons in Kyoto. New York: Knopf, 1991. 337 pp. ISBN: 9780679403081

Iyer went to Kyoto to live in a monastery and learn about Zen Buddhism from the inside. During his year there, he learned about Zen, about Japanese culture, and about Kyoto, one of the world's loveliest cities. He also fell in love. *The Lady and the Monk* explores both religion and romance, as Iyer struggles with the rigor and discipline of Zen and falls in love with Sachiko, a young, married Japanese woman with two children who is trying to free herself from the constrained role that women have traditionally played in Japan. Iyer paints a loving and delicate portrait of Sachiko and the lessons she taught him about the Japanese world.

Subjects: Buddhism; Culture Clash; Love Affairs

Places: Japan; Kyoto

Series: *Vintage Departures*

Now Try: James Sullivan's *Over the Moat: Love among the Ruins of Imperial Vietnam* recounts his journey to Vietnam, where he fell in love with a shop worker in Hue; like Iyer, Sullivan explores both the complexities of the foreign culture and those associated with falling in love. Deborah Boliver Boehm traveled to Japan in the 1960s to "get away from Zen" but ended up living next door to a Zen monastery and falling in love with one of the monks; her story is told with sensuality and humor in *A Zen Romance: One Woman's Adventures in a Monastery*. The theme of Western men falling in love with Japanese women and learning about the Japanese culture through the relationship is central to both James Michener's novel about Japan after World War II, *Sayonara*, and James Clavell's novel about feudal Japan, *Shogun*. Alan Brown's humorous novel, *Audrey Hepburn's Neck*, flips the perspective and tells the story of a 23-year-old Japanese cartoonist who is obsessed with slim American women; set in contemporary Tokyo, the book deals with the erotics of cultural differences, prejudices of various sorts, and the many ways in which globalization has affected the lives of young Japanese men and women.

Lucas, John

92 Acharnon Street: A Year in Athens. London: Eland, 2007. 219 pp. ISBN: 9780955010538

In 1984, Lucas traveled to Greece to teach English literature for a year at the University of Athens. Though he shows no illusions about the problems facing Greece (the inept bureaucracy delayed his first payment until Christmas), he did fall in love with the tavernas, the crazy traffic, the proximity to the beautiful blue waters of the Aegean, and the conviviality of its people. Lucas writes about Greece's recent history (its mistreatment by the Allies after World War II, its painful civil war, and the cruelties of the junta that ruled the country from 1967 to 1974), but his focus is on the contemporary daily life of this gritty city.

Subjects: European History

Categories: Urban Landscapes

Places: Athens; Greece

Awards: Dolman Best Travel Book Award, 2008

Now Try: Sofka Zinovieff's *Eurydice Street: A Place in Athens* describes her move to Athens with her Greek-born husband and two young daughters and her attempts to adjust to life there. In *Oedipus on a Pale Horse: Journey through Greece in Search of a Personal Mythology,* David Sheppard mixes a travel narrative about his 10 weeks in Greece with memories of painful incidents in his own life (including the disappearance of his daughter) and details from Greek mythology as he tries to make sense of his life and build his "personal mythology." Jill Dudley's *Ye Gods!: Travels in Greece* is a lighter look at one couple's travels through Greece, complete with tales about the ancient Greek myths and the influence of the Greek Orthodox Church.

Macdonald, Sarah

Holy Cow: An Indian Adventure. New York: Broadway Books, 2003 [2002]. 291 pp. ISBN: 9780767915748

Macdonald spent two years in India when her boyfriend, a television correspondent, was stationed in New Delhi. Her visit began unceremoniously when she developed a bad case of pneumonia and was hospitalized. When she recovered, she decided to explore India as much as she could and so she wandered through the "spiritual smorgasbord" of India: learning the language, making friends, meditating, seeking out an Ayurvedic "miracle healer," bathing in the Ganges, studying Buddhism in Dharamsala, visiting an ashram, and singing with Sufis. Her portrait of

India captures the richness of its cultures and customs as well as the overcrowding, the grime, and the pollution. Macdonald is witty and sometimes even outrageous, but she clearly grew to love the country and develop an appreciation for its complexities.

Subjects: Buddhism; Christianity; Hinduism; Humor; Islam; Judaism; Memoirs; Religion; Spirituality; Women Travelers

Places: Delhi; India

Now Try: William Dalrymple's *City of Djinns: A Year in Delhi* (annotated in this category) describes the author's stay in India's historical capital; like Macdonald, he encountered individuals from a wide range of religious backgrounds, including Sufi dervishes, attendees at a Hindu feast, and Muslims observing Ramadan. Lucy Edge searched for enlightenment at various yoga schools and ashrams in India; she tells her story with the same kind of humor as Macdonald in *Yoga School Dropout: A Hilarious, Hapless and Desperate Quest for Mystic Indians and Tantric Bliss*. Katherine Russell Rich traveled to India as a freelance writer and fell in love with the country and the Hindi language; her book, *Dreaming in Hindi*, tells of her immersion in the language and in the culture of India itself.

Mayes, Frances

A Year in the World: Journeys of a Passionate Traveller. New York: Broadway, 2006. 420 pp. ISBN: 9780767910057

Mayes is best known for her books about Tuscany (annotated in this chapter's section on "Living Abroad"), but *A Year in the World* tells about visits she and her husband made to a dozen other beautiful places, including Portugal, several locations on the Mediterranean, England, and Scotland, where they attempted to live like the locals, renting houses, shopping in the neighborhood markets, and wandering the streets. Mayes evokes the splendor of each place and writes particularly well about the local cuisines: lemon gelato in Italy; tapas in Seville; blood oranges in Andalucia. She also addresses the art, architecture, and history of her destinations, although not in any great detail.

Subjects: Food; Seas; Spouses; Women Travelers

Places: Africa; Capri; Crete; England; France; Greece; Italy; Mediterranean Sea; Morocco; Portugal; Scotland; Spain; Turkey

Now Try: Most travel narratives focus on a single destination, but occasionally multiple destinations are the subject of a book. Jennifer Baggett, Holly C. Corbett, and Amanda Pressner quit their corporate jobs in Manhattan to spend a year traveling around the world, including Peru, Kenya, Vietnam, and Australia; they describe the experience in *The Lost Girls: Three Friends, Four Continents, One Unconventional Detour Around the World*. In *Incognito Street: How Travel Made Me a Writer*, Barbara Sjoholm describes a three-year ramble through Europe (including stops in Spain, England, France, and Norway) and how that long journey helped her find her voice as a writer. Elizabeth Gilbert's visit to three countries (*Eat, Pray, Love: One Woman's Search for Everything Across Italy, India and Indonesia*) is annotated in this book's chapter, "The Journey."

Moaveni, Azadeh

Honeymoon in Tehran: Two Years of Love and Danger in Iran. New York: Random House, 2009. 340 pp. ISBN: 9781400066452

Moaveni's book about returning to Tehran in 2005 to cover the election of Mahmoud Ahmadinejad for *Time* magazine is more personal than her earlier *Lipstick Jihad* (annotated in "The Journey" chapter) and recounts how she fell in love with an Iranian man, moved in with him, became pregnant, then got married, and moved to London. Moaveni interweaves the story of her personal life with the social and political issues of life in Iran and with the relationship between her and Mr. X, the "political handler" assigned by the Iranian Ministry of Intelligence to follow her and learn what she's writing and who her sources are. Moaveni provides a fascinating look at several aspects of life in Iran, from dating behaviors to class distinctions, from dress requirements for women to Internet access and satellite television.

Subjects: Culture Clash; Journalism; Love Affairs; Marriage; Multicultural Issues; Pregnancy; Women Travelers

Places: Iran; Tehran

Now Try: Christiane Bird spent three years as a child in Iran with her family and returned in 1998 to explore whether the dream-like land of her memory had really become the harsh world being portrayed by the Western media; her sensitive narrative of the contradictions she found in Iran is *Neither East Nor West: One Woman's Journey through the Islamic Republic of Iran*. Readers interested in another woman's portrayal of Iran should find Azar Nafisi's two books, *Reading Lolita in Tehran* and *Things I've Been Silent About*, fascinating. Both are more memoir than travel narrative, particularly the latter, but both provide an insider's look at pre- and post-Shah Iran. Roxana Saberi was an Iranian American journalist in Iran in 2009 when she was arrested and convicted on espionage charges before being released on appeal; her story of this harrowing experience is told in *Between Two Worlds: My Life and Captivity in Iran*.

Muller, Karin

Japanland: A Year in Search of Wa. Emmaus, PA: Insert Trefoil Rodale, 2005. 307 pp. ISBN: 9781594862236

Muller, a Swiss American documentary filmmaker, went to Japan in search of the inner peace (or *wa*) she felt was missing from her life. Her host family and numerous Japanese friends helped her experience the wide variety of Japanese culture: the corporate and dating cultures of the cities; communities of sumo wrestlers, kabuki performers, and geisha; a Yamabushi ascetic mountain cult; and the 900-mile Shikoku

Pilgrimage. While Muller writes with a light, engaging style, she is also honest about the complexities of being a Westerner in Japan; she openly discusses the deterioration of her relationship with her host family, for example. Whether Muller found *wa* is an open question, but her telling of the journey will fascinate many readers.

Subjects: Culture Clash; Humor; Memoirs; Women Travelers

Places: Japan

Now Try: Muller is also the author of *Hitchhiking Vietnam: A Woman's Solo Journey in an Elusive Land,* in which she recounts her 6,400-mile trek across Vietnam, from the Mekong Delta to the Chinese border, and *Along the Inca Road: A Woman's Journey into an Ancient Empire,* which follows her six-month trip through Ecuador, Peru, Brazil, and Chile. Kate Williamson takes a more visual approach to her yearlong stay in Kyoto in *A Year in Japan,* which includes watercolor illustrations that portray various aspects of the life and culture of Japan. Rebecca Otowa has lived in Japan since 1978, having married into a traditional Japanese family; her experiences, and especially her thoughts of what she gave up to become a part of this very different society, are outlined in *At Home in Japan: A Foreign Woman's Journey of Discovery*.

Mura, David

Turning Japanese: Memoirs of A Sansei. New York: Atlantic Monthly Press, 1991. 376 pp. ISBN: 9780871134318

In the mid-1980s, Mura, a third-generation Japanese American poet, spent a year in Japan with his wife as part of a creative artist exchange. The book chronicles his search for identity and his attempt to make sense of his upbringing as an Asian American in a Jewish neighborhood in Chicago. Mura's attempts to discover Japanese culture (he studied the Japanese dance form known as *butoh* and the Japanese *Noh* theatre, he met Japanese radicals and writers, he struggled to learn Japanese) paralleled his attempts to discover himself. The book is written with the beautiful rhythm one might expect of a poet and is anything but a light read as Mura delves into thought-provoking discussions about race, relationships, politics, and history.

Subjects: Culture Clash; Family Relationships; Memoirs; Self-Discovery

Places: Japan

Now Try: Mura's *Where the Body Meets Memory: An Odyssey of Race, Sexuality and Identity* is a memoir of his experience coming of age as a Japanese American in the United States; it is not a travel narrative but it does explore many of the issues that Mura discusses in *Turning Japanese*. Lydia Minatoya, a second-generation Japanese American, tells of coming to terms with her cultural identity through visits to Japan, China, and Nepal in *Talking to High Monks in the Snow* (annotated in "The Journey" chapter of this book). Rahna Reiko Rizzuto, the daughter of a Japanese American mother, returned to Hiroshima to gain a better understanding of her heritage; *Hiroshima in the Morning* describes her trip, her interviews with survivors of the World War II bombing, and how her quest was changed by the events of September 11, 2001.

Stewart, Rory

The Prince of the Marshes: And Other Occupational Hazards of a Year in Iraq. Orlando, FL: Harcourt, Inc., 2006. 396 pp. ISBN: 9780151012350

Six months after the U.S.-led invasion of Iraq, British diplomat and travel writer Stewart was appointed the coalition deputy governor of Maysan, a province of 850,000 people in the southern marshlands. Stewart provides an insider's view of the rebuilding efforts in Iraq as he worked with the Iraqis to deal with the usual challenges (patching roads and buildings, dealing with a flood) as well as the unusual (mediating a tribal war, regulating religious flagellants, an attack on coalition offices). *The Prince of the Marshes* is rich in detail, somewhat remorseful, and sometimes disturbing but it is also a balanced portrayal of post-war Iraq by a writer who seems not to have preconceived notions of who's right.

Subjects: Culture Clash; Islam; Middle Eastern History; Politics; War

Places: Iraq

Now Try: Stewart is best known for his first book, *The Places in Between*, about his 2002 walk across Afghanistan territory that was still held by the Taliban; the title is annotated in the "Getting There Is Half the Fun" chapter of this book. Canadian journalist Hadani Ditmars traveled to Iraq just after the invasion and reported on life in the streets in the poignant *Dancing in the No-Fly Zone: A Woman's Journey Through Iraq*. For readers interested in yet another glimpse at post-war Iraq, Rajiv Chandrasekaran's *Imperial Life in the Emerald City: Inside Iraq's Green Zone* provides a fascinating look at the occupational administration, headquartered in the Green Zone around Saddam Hussein's former palace.

Storace, Patricia

Dinner With Persephone: Travels in Greece. New York: Pantheon Books, 1996. 398 pp. ISBN: 9780679421344

American poet Storace spent a year in Athens ("at the intersection of a prostitute and a saint") and describes Greece and the people she found there, living between a proud past and a complex, sometimes doubt-ridden present. She is as interested in describing contemporary Greece as she is in recounting stories of its past, and her writing leaps from one thing to another, from an object encountered to a historical parallel or a mythic reference or a more recent anecdote, from a pop song or a soap opera to an ancient church ritual or the story of Dionysus bringing the gift of wine to Naxos. Storace's thoughtful reflections provide a rich and refreshing portrait of modern Greece.

Subjects: European History; Memoirs; Women Travelers

Places: Athens; Greece

Awards: *New York Times* Notable Book, 1996

Series: *Vintage Departures*

Now Try: Sofka Zinovieff moves to Athens with her Greek-born husband and two young daughters in *Eurydice Street: A Place in Athens*, which describes her attempts to adjust to life there. In the 1930s, the great writer Henry Miller spent a year with British author Lawrence Durrell on the island of Corfu; this visit and how it healed the writer's soul are described by Miller in *The Colossus of Maroussi*. Another writer, Emma Tennant, describes the years she spent visiting her parents' home in Corfu in *A House in Corfu: A Family's Sojourn in Greece*. Fiction readers who are interested in Greece may enjoy the Louis DeBernieres novel, *Corelli's Mandolin*, which takes place on the Greek island of Cephallonia and explores the impact of Nazi occupation on the inhabitants, or Panos Karnezis's *Little Infamies*, a collection of short stories about individuals in a nameless Greek village, including a priest, a prostitute, a doctor, the mayor, a centaur, and a parrot that recites Homer.

Living Abroad

As noted in the introduction to the previous category, when the traveler spends more than a year or two in another country, the sense of wonder at the newness of the land and its people often begins to wear off and the understanding of the place and the individuals who live there may deepen.

Many of the travelers write enthusiastically about life in their new homes (like Julia Child in *My Life in France*), while others (like Elizabeth Bard in *Lunch in Paris: A Love Story with Recipes*) are very clear about the challenges that living in a foreign country present. Still others (like Kuki Gallman in *I Dreamed of Africa* or Rosamond Carr in *Land of a Thousand Hills: My Life in Rwanda*) convey a deep love for their adopted countries in spite of the terrible events they have witnessed.

The motivations of these long-term expatriates are also varied. Some, like Annie Hawes (*Extra Virgin: A Young Woman Discovers the Italian Riviera, Where Every Month Is Enchanted*) or Tony Cohan (*On Mexican Time: A New Life in San Miguel*), became dissatisfied with life in their native countries. Others, like Kuki Gallman (*I Dreamed of Africa*), had always dreamed of living abroad. Still others, like *The New Yorker*'s Adam Gopnik (*Paris to the Moon*), just happened to be stationed abroad.

Two of the best-known travel writers of recent decades (Frances Mayes and Peter Mayle) are featured in this section, but there are also lesser-known travelers (like Annie Hawes and Tim Mackintosh-Smith) who deserve a wider audience.

Readers who enjoy these titles, in which the traveler spends more than a year or two in another country, may also enjoy histories of the countries involved, memoirs written by individuals native to these countries, or fiction that takes place in these countries. For example, readers who like Adam Gopnik's *Paris to the Moon* may also enjoy Graham Robb's *Parisians: An Adventure History in Paris* or Simone de Beauvoir's memoir, *The Prime of Her Life*, or Diane Johnson's novel, *Le Divorce*.

Bard, Elizabeth

Lunch in Paris: A Love Story with Recipes. New York: Little, Brown and Co., 2001. 324 pp. ISBN: 9780316042796

Bard, an American journalist working in London, went to Paris for a weekend, had lunch with a handsome Parisian, and never came home. The book is a charming but honest expatriate memoir that describes how Bard fell in love with her husband and her adopted city, especially its food. The author doesn't downplay the challenges of creating a life in a foreign country or the difficulties of being an American in Paris as she learns how to buy fresh figs, how to gut a fish, and how to soothe homesickness with chocolate soufflé. The book includes some very tasty recipes.

Subjects: Culture Clash; Food; Love Affairs; Recipes; Women Travelers

Places: France; Paris

Now Try: Bard writes a blog entitled "Lunch in Paris" (http://www.elizabethbard.com/), and those who enjoy her book may wish to keep up with her further adventures through that blog. Kristin Espinasse is another blogger (http://french-word-a-day.com/) who moves from America to France to marry and start a family; her book, *Words in a French Life: Lessons in Love and Language from the South of France,* is less about food and more about the French language. Espinasse is also the author of *Blossoming in Provence,* which is filled with short anecdotes about her life in France. Kim Sunee's *Trail of Crumbs: Hunger, Love, and the Search for Home* details her story of adoption from South Korea to New Orleans and eventual move to France, where she too discovers the importance of food and cooking in creating a sense of home. Sarah Turnbull's *Almost French: Love and a New Life in Paris,* which tells the story of another journalist who went to Paris to stay with a man, is annotated elsewhere in this chapter. Gail Jones's third novel, *Dreams of Speaking,* involves a female Australian academic who travels to Paris to conduct research and forms a friendship with an older Japanese man, who is a survivor of Nagasaki and an expert on Alexander Graham Bell; their deepening friendship is explored in a lyrical, poetic style.

Carr, Rosamond Halsey, and Ann Howard

Land of a Thousand Hills: My Life in Rwanda. New York: Viking, 1999. 248 pp. ISBN: 9780670887804

In the late 1940s, Carr left her job as a fashion illustrator in New York City and accompanied her hunter-explorer husband to what was then the Belgian Congo; when they divorced, she stayed in neighboring Rwanda and managed a flower plantation. *Land of a Thousand Hills* tells of Carr's 50 years there, during which time she witnessed the decline and fall of colonialism, observed wars of independence, visited her friend Dian Fossey and her mountain gorillas, was evacuated during the gruesome 1994 genocide, and returned to turn her plantation into a shelter for some 100 orphaned children. In spite of the terrible events she witnessed, Carr's writing is filled with vivid descriptions and conveys both a love for her adopted country and a deep appreciation for its people.

Subjects: African History; Colonialism; Divorce; Farms; Genocide; Memoirs; Politics; War

Places: Africa; Rwanda

Now Try: Anyone wanting to make sense of the Rwandan genocide should read Philip Gourevitch's moving book, *We Wish to Inform You That Tomorrow We Will be Killed With Our Families: Stories from Rwanda* or Jean Hatzfeld's oral history *Life Laid Bare: The Survivors in Rwanda Speak.* Stephen Kinzer's *A Thousand Hills: Rwanda's Rebirth and the Man Who Dreamed It* focuses on Rwanda's president, Paul Kagame, and his attempts to rebuild the country and reconcile its peoples. Another woman who made an African country her home, Lisa St. Aubin de Terán, writes of her experience in the inspiring *Mozambique Mysteries;* like Carr, she set up aid organizations: a school and a nonprofit organization to promote sustainable development in Southern Africa.

Child, Julia, and Alex Prudhomme

My Life in France. New York: Alfred A. Knopf, 2006. 317 pp. ISBN: 9781400043460 YA

This charming expatriate memoir tells the story of Child's years in France (1948–1954), where her husband Paul was assigned to head the exhibits office of the U.S. Information Service. She arrives in Paris unable to cook or speak French but soon enrolls at Le Cordon Bleu cooking school and sets about writing a French cookbook with two friends. The book deals primarily with her culinary adventures but also paints a portrait of France in the years following the war. The book was finished after Child's death by her great-nephew and is written in the zesty, enthusiastic style that Child made famous on her television shows.

Subjects: Cooking; Food; Women's Contributions

Places: France; Paris

Now Try: Noel Riley Fitch's *Appetite for Life: The Biography of Julia Child* provides a rich picture of her life. Londoner Kathleen Flinn pursued her dream of attending Le Cordon Bleu and writes about the experience in *The Sharper Your Knife, the Less You Cry: Love, Laughter, and Tears in Paris at the World's Most Famous Cooking School.* While it does not involve the expatriate life or travel, Julie Powell's *Julie and Julia* will likely appeal to fans of *My Life in France.* Powell's attempt to cook all 500-plus recipes in Child's *Mastering the Art of French Cooking* is endearing and witty, and the film (*Julie and Julia*) is equally delightful.

Cohan, Tony

On Mexican Time: A New Life in San Miguel. New York: Broadway Books, 2000. 289 pp. ISBN: 9780767903189

In the late 1980s, Cohan and his wife became dissatisfied with life in Los Angeles (the price of real estate, the robberies and killings in their neighborhood) and decided to move to San Miguel de Allende in central Mexico, eventually purchasing and renovating a nearly ruined 250-year-old hacienda there. *On Mexican Time* describes Cohan's love affair with his Mexican home, the beauty of its medieval

Moorish architecture, its fresh flowers, its native fruits, its brightly colored native clothing, and its colorful characters: "the guy who killed the same man twice," Jack Kerouac's sidekick Neil Cassidy (who died in San Miguel de Allende), and other expatriates. Much of the book is also focused on Cohan's own transformation from a fast-paced city dweller to a more relaxed, more connected individual.

Subjects: Community Life; Homes

Places: Mexico

Now Try: Like Cohan, Susan McKinney de Ortega was trying to escape the crime often associated with big city life, although in her case the crime was more personal: rape and the shame that followed it. She tells of her "escape" to Mexico and being pursued by a much younger Mexican man in *Flirting in Spanish: What Mexico Taught Me About Love, Living, and Forgiveness.* Hugh Thomson first fell in love with Latin America at the age of 18, following an adventure in Mexico; in *Tequila Oil: Getting Lost in Mexico* (which was shortlisted for the 2010 Dolman Best Travel Book Award) he explores a more dangerous side of the country than is usually depicted in travel narratives. Maria Finn Dominguez has collected over 30 essays by travelers to Mexico in *Mexico in Mind,* including D. H. Lawrence, poet Muriel Rukeyser, William Burroughs, and Ray Bradbury. Other narratives about the importance of "home" include Jane Brox's *Here and Nowhere Else: Late Seasons of a Farm and Its Family* and Adam Gopnik's *Through the Children's Gate: A Home in New York.*

Gallman, Kuki

I Dreamed of Africa. New York: Viking, 1991. 314 pp. ISBN: 9780670836123

As a child in Italy, Gallman was fascinated with Africa. At 25, she and her husband bought a ranch in Kenya and spent many blissful days tracking elephants, hunting buffalos, building a house, and vacationing on the Kenyan coast. But tragedy struck as her husband was killed in an automobile accident and her son died from a snakebite, and Gallman was left alone. To deal with her grief, she turned the ranch into a living memorial for her husband and son and dedicated it to the preservation of local plants and wildlife. Even though its writing style is sometimes overblown and overly romantic, *I Dreamed of Africa* is both beautiful in its evocation of the African landscape and moving in its tale of personal tragedy.

Subjects: Death and Dying; Family Relationships; Farms; Memoirs

Places: Africa; Kenya

Now Try: Gallman followed *I Dreamed of Africa* with *African Nights: True Stories from the Author of I Dreamed of Africa,* a collection of short stories of her life in Kenya that attempt to capture both her joys and struggles after the tragedies described in the previous book. Melinda Atwood moved to Kenya following the death of her mother and a legal battle over her will; her rejuvenation in

Africa and her curiosity about Africa's mysteries are the focus of *Jambo, Mama: Memories of Africa*. Elspeth Huxley's *The Flame Trees of Thika: Memories of an African Childhood* tells the story of her childhood on a coffee farm in Kenya in the 1910s and early 1920s. Any story of a European woman settling in Kenya will invite comparisons with Isak Dinesen's *Out of Africa* and Beryl Markham's *West With the Night* (annotated in this chapter and in the "Travel Adventure" chapter respectively).

Gopnik, Adam

Paris to the Moon. New York: Random House, 2000. 338 pp. ISBN: 9780679444923

From 1995 to 2000, Gopnik lived in Paris and wrote a series of articles on Paris life for *New Yorker* magazine. *Paris to the Moon* collects these essays as well as some previously unpublished pieces; they provide reflections both on Paris (the cafes, French cooking, the Luxembourg Gardens, strikes, the Tuileries, the Musée d'Orsay) and on parenthood; the Gopniks went to Paris with an infant son and gave birth to a daughter while they were there. Gopnik was clearly in love with Paris but also comments on its warts: the bureaucracy, the pompous attitudes, the brooding over France's decline as a world power. His intelligence and charm make this what one reviewer called "the finest book on France of recent years."

Subjects: Essays; Family Relationships; Memoirs

Places: France; Paris

Awards: *New York Times* Notable Book, 2000

Now Try: Gopnik's family returned to New York City in 2000, and Gopnik wrote *Through the Children's Gate* about their relocation to the city and its transformation as "a children's city." Gopnik also edited *Americans in Paris: A Literary Anthology*, a collection of stories, letters, and memoirs by Americans who came to the City of Light as statesmen, students, and tourists; these include Jefferson, Franklin, Emerson, Twain, Stein, Fitzgerald, and others. Another writer for the *New Yorker*, Edmund White, shares his thoughts on Paris in *The Flaneur: A Stroll Through the Paradoxes of Paris*, the first book in Bloomsbury's series, *The Writer and the City*. Like Gopnik, Thad Carhart captures both the magic and the frustrations of Paris in his story of buying a piano there and taking up the instrument again in his wonderfully written expatriate memoir, *The Piano Shop on the Left Bank: Discovering a Forgotten Passion in a Paris Atelier*. Eric Hazan's *The Invention of Paris: A History in Footsteps* is more of a travel guide, with a focus on the sites of importance in the city's political, literary, and artistic history.

Hawes, Annie

Extra Virgin: A Young Woman Discovers the Italian Riviera, Where Every Month Is Enchanted. New York: HarperCollins Publishers, 2001. 337 pp. ISBN: 9780060198503

In 1983, Annie Hawes and her sister Lucy were fed up with life in cold, foggy London, and so they moved to the sunny olive groves of the small town of Diano San Pietro in Italy's Liguria region. Their planned brief stay turned into years as they became captivated by the charming, eccentric characters of the town and became integrated into that tight-knit community. Food plays a large role in the book, from the region's rosemary skewered sausages to lessons in spotting wild asparagus or telling good mushrooms from bad. Hawes writes with an easy-going humor, a dose of humility, and a real love for the region.

Subjects: Community Life; Food; Humor; Women Travelers

Places: Italy

Now Try: To date, Hawes has written three other books about her travels. *Ripe for the Picking* continues her story of daily life in Liguria; she portrays the local people as interesting rather than extraordinarily curious or amusing, and she is more likely to blame herself for not understanding the local customs than question the customs themselves. *Journey to the South: A Calabrian Homecoming* recounts her sometimes comic and chaotic visit to the Calabrian home of her friend Ciccio's extended family. *A Handful of Honey: Away to the Palm Groves of Morocco and Algeria* finds Hawes leaving Italy for a trip to northern Africa in search of a small oasis town in the Sahara Desert.

Mackintosh-Smith, Tim

Yemen: The Unknown Arabia. London: John Murray, 1997. 280 pp. ISBN: 9780719556227

Mackintosh-Smith has been fascinated with Yemen since he was a teenager and has lived there since 1982. His book combines travel narrative, memoir, and history to describe Yemen as the most fascinating but least known country in the Arab world, a country where men regularly chew narcotic *qat* leaves, where shepherdesses tend their flocks in gold sequined dresses, where the Queen of Sheba once ruled, whose capital was once the seat of the Arab world's only Communist regime. *Yemen* is filled with enthralling details and tantalizing digressions about a largely unexplored land.

Subjects: Islam; Memoirs; Middle Eastern History

Places: Yemen

Awards: *New York Times* Notable Book, 2000; Thomas Cook Travel Book Award, 1998

Now Try: Victoria Clark was born in Yemen and returned there in 2004 and 2009; her portrayal of a dangerously unstable country and its history can be found in *Yemen: Dancing on the Heads of Snakes*. Eric Hansen's return trip to Yemen is filled with colorful individuals and exasperating battles with the local bureaucracy; it is described in *Motoring with Mohammed: Journeys to Yemen and the Red Sea* (annotated in "The Journey" chapter of this book). Though much has changed in the country, Freya Stark's classic account of her 1937–38 expedition to Yemen may still be of interest; *A Winter in Arabia: A Journey Through Yemen* helped establish her reputation as a travel writer.

Mayes, Frances

Bella Tuscany: The Sweet Life in Italy. New York: Broadway, 1999. 286 pp. ISBN: 9780767902830

The middle book of Mayes's trilogy of expatriate memoirs about her life in Italy, *Bella Tuscany* describes how a sabbatical from her teaching position in San Francisco allowed the author to spend her first spring at Bramasole, her house in the Tuscan village of Cortona. Mayes describes her attempts to revive the villa's gardens, her deepening friendships with local Italians, and the joys and frustrations of the ongoing restoration of her property. As with her other books, Mayes writes with passion and mixes her descriptions of daily events with thoughts on food (recipes included), wine, and the Italian language.

Subjects: Community Life; Food; Homes; Memoirs; Recipes; Women Authors

Places: Italy

Now Try: Fans of Mayes will doubtless enjoy the four Italian books of Marlena de Blasi, which begin with *A Thousand Days in Venice,* the story of how she fell in love with and married a Venetian banker; the book is strong on romance and food. De Blasi followed that book with *A Thousand Days in Tuscany: A Bittersweet Adventure,* in which the couple purchased an old farmhouse in "a place that still remembers real life." *The Lady in the Palazzo: At Home in Umbria* followed, as de Blasi and her husband bought, renovated, and moved into the ballroom of a rundown medieval palazzo. The tetralogy is topped off by *That Summer in Sicily: A Love Story,* which recounts the couple's visit to an old castle in the Sicilian mountains and the incredible story of the woman who ruled over the castle. Like the Mayes trilogy, de Blasi's books all contain ample references to the food, wine, and colorful local people of Italy, and all are vividly and affectionately written.

Mayes, Frances

Every Day in Tuscany: Seasons of Italian Life. New York: Broadway, 2010. 306 pp. ISBN: 9780767929820

Mayes's love affair with Italy continues in the last installment in her trilogy as she brings the reader up to date with changes that have taken place since *Bella Tuscany.* Having completed the renovations on her villa, Mayes is able to reflect more on the delights of her experience in Tuscany: her engagement with the people of the nearby hill town, the art of Cortona's noted Renaissance painter Luca Signorelli, the joys of eating food grown in her own garden, and of course, more recipes. In *Every Day in Tuscany,* Mayes seems more relaxed than in her previous books and continues to convey the richness and complexity of her life in Tuscany.

Subjects: Art and Artists; Community Life; Food; Recipes; Women Authors

Places: Italy

Now Try: Food plays a major role in Mayes's three books, and readers may want more titles that mix travel narrative with Italian food. Along those lines, the trilogy of books by the Hungarian-Canadian author Ferenc Máté may be recommended. In *The Hills of*

Tuscany: A New Life in an Old Land, he recounts the search that he and his wife undertook in the late 1980s to find their dream house in Tuscany and how they settled on a renovated stone farmhouse in the central Italy countryside. In *A Vineyard in Tuscany: A Wine Lover's Dream,* Máté tells how he and his wife renovated the villa and turned it into an award-winning winery. Finally, *The Wisdom of Tuscany: Simplicity, Security, and the Good Life* (like Mayes's third book) finds Máté and his wife settling into their new life and singing the praises of the land and the people of Tuscany.

Mayes, Frances

Under the Tuscan Sun: At Home in Italy. New York: Broadway, 1997 [1996]. 280 pp. ISBN: 9780767900386

The first of Mayes's books about Tuscany, *Under the Tuscan Sun* tells how Mayes, who was teaching writing at San Francisco State University, and her husband came to purchase a dilapidated farmhouse in Tuscany and restore it over a two-year period. Fans of Mayes and her trilogy will enjoy her stories of renovating the villa, working in the garden, exploring nearby towns, and interacting with the local people, all told in a rich, sensual style: fruits and vegetables are lush, rains are pelting, vineyards are surrounded by a violet-blue haze. But readers who like a straightforward narrative may not find her rather rambling, stream-of-consciousness approach to their liking.

Subjects: Community Life; Food; Gentle Reads; Homes; Memoirs; Women Authors

Places: Italy

Awards: *New York Times* Notable Book, 1997

Now Try: Television actors Michael Tucker and Jill Eikenberry purchased a 350-year-old stone cottage in Umbria; Tucker describes their love of Italian food, their struggles with the Italian language, and their friendships with local people in the often humorous *Living in a Foreign Language: A Memoir of Food, Wine, and Love in Italy.* Fans of Mayes's book and trilogy may enjoy the 2003 film, *Under the Tuscan Sun,* which was loosely based on the book of the same name; Diane Lane did a particularly good job portraying the author. Readers who don't quite "get" Mayes might enjoy James Hamilton-Patterson's hilarious novel, *Cooking with Fernet Branca,* which is a satire of the foreigners-fall-in-love-in-an-old-Italian-house genre.

Mayle, Peter

Encore Provence: New Adventures in the South of France. New York: Knopf, 1999. 226 pp. ISBN: 9780679441243

This is the third of Mayle's three books about his life in southern France, written after four years in Long Island, away from his beloved Provence. *Encore Provence* consists of 14 essays on a variety of topics (from the flirtatious habits of French butchers to Mayle's recipe for the perfect French village, from the perfume business to his beginner's guide to Marseille) and reveals new insights on themes that will be familiar to Mayle's readers. Mayle seems even more focused on food than usual (most of the essays include at least one meal) and, in one essay, defends Provence against the attacks of a *New York Times* food critic who wrote that the old Provence of good, fresh food no longer exists.

Subjects: Community Life; Essays; Food; Humor; Memoirs; Quick Reads

Places: France

Series: *Vintage Departures*

Now Try: M.F.K. Fisher's classic *Two Towns in Provence: Map of Another Town and a Considerable Town* tells of her life in Aix-en-Provence in the 1940s and Marseille in the 1950s; her portrait of an earlier Marseille can be compared with Mayle's description in one of the essays of *Encore Provence*. The gritty and humorous *Cherries from Chauvet's Orchard: A Memoir of Provence* by Ruth Phillips, the wife of an English painter, tells of the couple's decision to move to Provence and fix up both an old house and their own relationship. British actress Carol Drinkwater's *The Olive Farm: A Memoir of Life, Love, and Olive Oil in the South of France* also recounts the purchase and renovation of a villa in Provence (this one with an olive vineyard) and is the first of a series of books that include *The Olive Season, The Olive Harvest, The Olive Route, The Olive Tree*, and *Return to the Olive Farm*. Joanne Harris's novel, *Blackberry Wine,* tells the story of a once-famous writer who purchases a cottage in a remote French village and is inspired by the house and memories of his childhood summers to write again.

Mayle, Peter

Toujours Provence. New York: Alfred A. Knopf, 1991. 241 pp. ISBN: 9780679402534

Mayle's sequel to *A Year in Provence* is a slower book than its predecessor, and the initial sense of wonder first experienced by Mayle when he moved to Provence has diminished a bit, but *Toujours Provence* continues to provide the warm humor and delicious portrayals of life, people, and food in southern France that Mayle began in his previous book. Mayle again examines the quirks of the Provençal life (purchasing over-the-counter medications at the apothecary, the farmer's market in the center of Avignon) and recounts his own adventures: the celebrity that followed the publication of his first book, slipping a suitcase of expensive truffles past British customs, and searching for gold Napoleons in his backyard.

Subjects: Community Life; Food; Humor; Memoirs; Quick Reads

Places: France

Series: *Vintage Departures*

Now Try: There are a number of good books written by expatriates living in Provence. Vicki Archer's *My French Life* tells how she and her husband bought and restored a 17th-century house in Saint-Rémy-de-Provence; it includes a number of beautiful photographs. Yvone Lenard's collection of essays about her life in southern France, *The Magic of Provence: Pleasures of Southern France,* begins when she and her husband purchased a run-down house in the mountainous Luberon region; her focus, though, is less on the house and more on the individuals they met. Georgeanne Brennan's story of her transformation from a novice cheese maker to an award-winning cookbook author, *A Pig in Provence: Good Food and Simple Pleasures in the South of France,* focuses on her time in Provence, where she learned to make fresh goat cheese and came to appreciate the ability of food to bring people together.

Rodi, Robert

Seven Seasons in Siena: My Quixotic Quest for Acceptance Among Tuscany's Proudest People. New York: Ballantine Books, 2011. 260 pp. ISBN: 9780345521057

Chicago writer Robert Rodi fell in love with Siena, a Tuscan town centered on the pomp and circumstance that surround the twice-yearly Palio horse race for which the town is known. In *Seven Seasons in Siena,* Rodi contrasts the Italian appetite for life that he found in Siena with what he calls "the dismaying anemia of modern American culture" and tells how he struggled to fit into this world as a gay American writer. His stories of sometimes successful, sometimes calamitous attempts to immerse himself in life in Siena are told with humor and brio.

Subjects: Community Life; Horses; Humor; GLBTQ

Places: Italy; Siena

Now Try: Dario Castagno and Rodi wrote *Too Much Tuscan Sun: Confessions of a Chianti Tour Guide* and *A Day in Tuscany: More Confessions of a Chianti Tour Guide,* about the former's experiences as a guide of customized tours through Italy's Chianti region; Castagno also belongs to the Caterpillar contrada in Siena, which won the 2003 Palio. Phil Doran and his wife bought a 300-year-old house in a Tuscan village and moved there from Los Angeles, a story told in the amusing memoir, *The Reluctant Tuscan: How I Discovered My Inner Italian.* Anne Fortier's first novel, *Juliet,* is set in Siena, where the protagonist (Julie) travels when she inherits a key to a safety deposit box there and is told that it may lead her to a family treasure. Readers interested in the author's struggles as a gay man in another country may also enjoy the GLBTQ travel collections by Raphael Kadushin, *Wonderlands: Good Gay Travel Writing* and *Big Trips: More Good Gay Travel Writing.*

Stewart, Chris

Driving Over Lemons: An Optimist in Andalucía. New York: Pantheon Books, 1999. 248 pp. ISBN: 9780375410284

The one-time drummer for the rock group Genesis, Chris Stewart, bought a small hill farm (complete with almond trees, olives, and lemon groves) in the Andalucia region of Spain, just south of Granada, a farm on the wrong side of the river and with no access road, water supply, or electricity. His amusing and insightful recounting of the experience is filled with wonderful characters (particularly his resourceful peasant neighbor Domingo) and delightful memories, like watching his daughter Chloë grow and thrive there. Stewart does a fine job of conveying the rich beauty of the land, its smell, the elements against which he and his wife struggled, and the incredible people who helped them.

Subjects: Community Life; Farms; Friendships; Gentle Reads; Homes; Humor; Rural Life

Places: Spain

Series: *Vintage Departures*

Now Try: Stewart has written two sequels about his work farming in Spain, *A Parrot In The Pepper Tree* and *The Almond Blossom Appreciation Society*, and fans of *Driving Over Lemons* will no doubt enjoy these as well. The former focuses on a parrot that joined the household, as well as Stewart's earlier life, playing drums for Genesis, shearing sheep in Sweden, and learning flamenco guitar during an earlier visit to Spain. The third book in the trilogy includes Stewart's daughter teaching him about teenage social life in Spain and Stewart's work at an immigrants' advice center in Granada. For another look at an expatriate working a farm in southern Europe, readers may enjoy Scottish writer Peter Kerr's story of the challenges and successes of raising oranges on the Spanish island of Majorca, *Grammar Lessons: Translating a Life in Spain*.

Turnbull, Sarah

Almost French: Love and a New Life in Paris. New York: Gotham, 2003 [2002]. 304 pp. ISBN: 9781592400386

Turnbull, a 20-something Australian, met a dashing Parisian man at a dinner party in Bucharest and agreed to stay with him in Paris for a week. One week became two, and after a four-month excursion around Europe, Sarah returned to Paris to live permanently. Adapting to Paris turned out to be harder than expected, though, and *Almost French* chronicles Turnbull's first two years, during which she tried to assimilate and deal with the more perplexing aspects of life in the City of Lights. Her outsider's perspective on French fashion, food, and politics is most interesting.

Subjects: Culture Clash; Food; Love Affairs; Politics

Places: France; Paris

Now Try: Catherine Sanderson's *Petite Anglaise* recounts the adventures of a young British woman who lives in Paris and writes a blog of the same name as the book; her life with a lover and their daughter became somewhat unglued when one of her blog's readers pursued her and tempted her to leave the life that she had built for herself. Rachel Spencer, another 20-something, journeyed to Paris to seek work as an *au pair* for the wealthy; her attempts to serve as nanny to three rowdy children while learning the language and discovering herself is told with wit and humor in *Au Paris*. Writer Suzy Gershman and her husband had always fantasized about living in Paris, and when he died unexpectedly, she moved to Paris alone and began the healing process; her first year is described in *C'est La Vie: An American Woman Begins a New Life in Paris and—Voila!—Becomes Almost French*. Elaine Sciolino, the Paris bureau chief of the *New York Times*, explains the role that seduction (in the broadest sense of the word) plays in French life in *La Seduction: How the French Play the Game of Life*.

Living with Others

Included in this subgenre, "The Expatriate Life," is a category of titles in which the traveler lives not so much in a foreign country as with a group of individuals whose world is entirely foreign to the traveler. After all, countries are an artifact of politicians and geographers, and in many cases, the groups with which individuals identify (the Gypsies of Fernanda Eberstadt's *Little Money Street: In Search of Gypsies and Their Music in the South of France* or the indigenous Mexican tribe of Jeff Biggers's *In the Sierra Madre* or even the soccer hooligans of Bill Buford's *Among the Thugs*) represent stronger ties than those defined by the borders of a nation.

Many of the groups portrayed here are outsiders in their societies, like the Gypsies among whom Isabel Fonseca lived (*Bury Me Standing: The Gypsies and Their Journey*) or the Indian eunuchs of Zia Jaffrey's fascinating book, *The Invisibles: A Tale of the Eunuchs of India*. Others represent groups associated with work, like the West African salt miners of Michael Benanav's *Men of Salt: Crossing the Sahara on the Caravan of White Gold* or the circus performers of Bruce S. Feiler's *Under the Big Top: A Season with the Circus*. Still others are tied together by sports, like the soccer fans that Tim Parks followed in *A Season with Verona*.

The titles represented here typically have a heavy focus on people and should therefore appeal to readers interested in a strong sense of character.

Readers interested in narratives in which the author lives with a group of individuals whose world is foreign to her may also enjoy titles from Immersion Journalism such as *Newjack: Guarding Sing Sing* by Ted Conover or *Animal, Vegetable, Miracle: A Year of Food Life* by Barbara Kingsolver. They may also be interested in other titles about the particular groups highlighted in the titles in this category, like Gypsies or soccer fans, and both nonfiction titles (David Crowe's *A History of the Gypsies of Eastern Europe and Russia* or Chuck Culpepper's *Bloody Confused!: A Clueless American Sportswriter Seeks Solace in English Soccer*) and fiction titles (Joanne Harris's *Chocolat* or Roddy Doyle's *The Van*) may be suggested.

Benanav, Michael

Men of Salt: Crossing the Sahara on the Caravan of White Gold. Guilford, CT: Lyons Press, 2006. 220 pp. ISBN: 9781592287727 YA

Benanav lived for 40 days with West African salt miners who were traveling 500 miles across the Sahara Desert to bring back slabs of solid salt to sell in the local markets. Benanav and his guide Waid spent much of the trip out just trying to connect with the miners, but the trip back (being sleepless and miserable, facing the dangers of sandstorms and dwindling supplies, surviving by burning camel dung for fire) was an ordeal worth writing about. Benanav writes about his adventure in an engaging manner, with ample details, both about the trip itself and the history of the salt caravans.

Subjects: Adventure; Caravans; Deserts; Nomads; Quick Reads; Salt

Places: Africa; Mali; Sahara Desert

Now Try: Benanav traveled among the nomadic Tuareg people of the Sahara, who are the subject of Jeremy Keenan's fascinating *Sahara Man: Travelling with the Tuareg*, about his life in the camps of the indigo-clad nomads in the 1960s and his return in 1999 to see how they had fared, given the changes that had come to that part of Africa. Frank Kryza's *The Race for Timbuktu: In Search of Africa's City of Gold* tells the story of 19th-century British explorers competing to find the legendary city, whose primary objects of commerce were salt, gold, and slaves. For readers who want to know more about salt, Mark Kurlansky's *Salt: A World History* is a popular micro-history with a worldwide focus, while Paul Lovejoy's *Salt of the Desert Sun: A History of Salt Production and Trade in the Central Sudan* is a more scholarly history of salt production and trade in Africa.

Biggers, Jeff

In the Sierra Madre. Urbana, IL: University of Illinois Press, 2006. 184 pp. ISBN: 9780252031014

Award-winning journalist Jeff Biggers spent a year among the Raramuri people of the Sierra Madre Mountains in northwest Mexico, chopping wood, planting corn, attending corn beer celebrations, and serving as a jack-of-all-trades. The book includes engaging portraits of historical figures (the French poet Artaud, the young George Patton, Geronimo, Pancho Villa) as well as those who lived around him: the elderly couple with whom he stayed, the musician who played a stringed instrument named after him. Biggers creates a captivating and absorbing history of an area that is at the same time famous ("The Treasure of the Sierra Madre") and unknown.

Subjects: Indigenous Peoples; Mountains; Quick Reads

Places: Mexico

Now Try: Richard Grant's *God's Middle Finger: Into the Lawless Heart of the Sierra Madre* follows the author through his arduous journey through these mountains, where he was chased by cocaine-snorting, half-drunk Mexican gang members trying to kill him. Readers interested in the Raramuri people among whom Biggers lived may enjoy the more scholarly, beautifully illustrated *Tarahumara: Where Night Is the Day of the Moon*, by Bernard L. Fontana and John P. Schaefer, which provides more information on these people and their history. *The Treasure of the Sierra Madre*, John Huston's classic film about two Americans who convince an old prospector to help them mine for gold in the Sierra Madre Mountains, was selected in 1990 for preservation in the United States

National Film Registry by the Library of Congress as a "culturally, historically, or aesthetically significant" film.

Buford, Bill

Among the Thugs. New York: Norton, 1992 [1991]. 317 pp. ISBN: 9780393033816

American writer and *Granta* editor Bill Buford attempted to understand the British phenomenon of soccer hooliganism by living among violent British football supporters for eight years, attending soccer matches, befriending fans of various teams (especially Manchester United), witnessing a number of riots (notably in Turin and at the 1990 World Cup in Sardinia), and being beaten twice by police. He also attended meetings of the far right, whites-only National Front, one of which turned violent. Buford's account of his experiences is compelling and his insights into the behavior of these thugs are thought provoking.

Subjects: Crime; Investigative Stories; Soccer; Sports; Violence

Places: England; Italy

Series: *Vintage Departures*

Now Try: Martin King and Martin Knight's *Hoolifan: 30 Years Of Hurt* tells the story of soccer hooligan King's life as a member of the Chelsea Headhunters and attempts, like *Among the Thugs*, to explain the social context of hooliganism. Franklin Foerr's *How Soccer Explains the World: An Unlikely Theory of Globalization* uses the game as it is played in different countries to better understand how international forces affect politics and life around the globe. Another writer who infiltrated gangs is Sudhir Venkatesh, whose *Gang Leader for a Day: A Rogue Sociologist Takes to the Streets* explains how he lived among the gangs of young people in Chicago's projects and how a symbiotic relationship between those gangs and their community has developed. Although a much gentler take on the subject, Nick Hornby's popular memoir *Fever Pitch* is also about extreme soccer fandom.

Eberstadt, Fernanda

Little Money Street: In Search of Gypsies and Their Music in the South of France. New York: Knopf, 2006. 242 pp. ISBN: 9780375411168

Novelist Eberstadt moved with her husband and children to Perpignan, a town in the south of France that happened to have one of the largest Gypsy settlements in Western Europe. *Little Money Street* tells how she tried for 18 months to make contact with members of a Gypsy band and was finally invited into their closed circle, where she gathered insights on the strange and puzzling world of the Gypsies: the jobless, mostly illiterate men and their homebound wives, who are bullied, betrayed, and often beaten. Her portrayal of the social life, customs, and music of this misunderstood and secretive group is richly detailed, sensitive, and fascinating.

Subjects: Community Life; Gypsies; Music and Musicians; Racism

Places: France

Series: *Vintage Departures*

Now Try: Eberstadt's most recent novel, *Rat,* concerns a young girl growing up with a single mother in a rough neighborhood in southern France, who runs away with her adopted Algerian brother to London to find her father; the grittiness of the life described by Eberstadt in her novel is similar to that of the Gypsies described in *Little Money Street.* Garth Cartwright journeyed through the Balkans in search of Gypsy musicians and interviewed and photographed many of them for his book, *Princes Amongst Men: Journeys with Gypsy Musicians.* Susan Salguero's *The Gachi, My Gypsy Flamenco Quest* is a compelling portrait of the flamenco music of the Gypsies of Spain and shows both the romance and pain of their way of life. The 1993 film, *Latcho Drom,* is a beautiful film that tells the story of a year in the life of the Romany people through their musicians and dancers.

Feiler, Bruce S.

Under the Big Top: A Season with the Circus. New York: Scribner, 1995. 288 pp. ISBN: 9780684197586

Feiler spent eight months as a clown with the Clyde Beatty-Coles Brothers circus in the southern and northeastern United States, touring with performers from more than a dozen countries, learning the hierarchy and code of conduct of the circus, working a demanding schedule, and finding life in the circus to be a microcosm of life in the United States. Feiler mixes circus history with his own experiences and shows a great deal of respect for his fellow circus performers, portraying them as human beings who enjoy humorous moments, suffer pain, and persevere.

Subjects: Circuses

Places: Alabama; Connecticut; Florida; Georgia; Maryland; Massachusetts; New Hampshire; New Jersey; New York; North Carolina; Pennsylvania; South Carolina; Virginia; Washington, DC

Series: *Armchair Traveller Series*

Now Try: Feiler is the author of two other travel narratives. *Walking the Bible: A Journey by Land Through the Five Books of Moses* tells of a 10,000-mile journey he took to retrace the first five books of the Old Testament; it is annotated in "The Journey" chapter of this book. *Learning to Bow: Inside the Heart of Japan* relates his experience as an American exchange teacher at a Japanese high school near Tokyo. Nell Stroud joined a series of circuses at age 18 and traveled in England and Germany as well as the United States; her experiences are detailed in *Josser: The Secret Life of a Circus Girl.* Cathy Day's *The Circus In Winter* is a collection of 11 short stories that portray the day-to-day lives of circus performers in Indiana during the late 19th and early 20th centuries. Erin Morgenstern's popular novel *The Night Circus* also shares the circus as a setting. The documentary series *Circus,* shown on many PBS stations and portraying a "season in the life" of the Big Apple Circus, might also appeal to these readers.

Fonseca, Isabel

Bury Me Standing: The Gypsies and Their Journey. New York: Knopf, 1995. 322 pp. ISBN: 9780679406785

Following the revolutions of 1989, Fonseca lived and traveled with Gypsies in several Eastern European countries, entering their world and listening to their stories. She provides vivid portraits of individuals living on the edge of society (poets, itinerants, Gypsy kings, child prostitutes) as well as an understanding of the language, culture, and taboos of this large and landless minority. Fonseca also traces Gypsy history, from their exodus out of India and their enslavement in medieval Romania to their massacre by the Nazis and forced assimilation by Communist regimes. *Bury Me Standing,* which takes its title from a Gypsy proverb ("Bury me standing. I've been on my knees all my life.") that reflects the sad plight of these people, is both beautifully written and well researched.

Subjects: Community Life; European History; Gypsies; Racism; Scholarly Writing

Places: Albania; Bulgaria; Czech Republic; Poland; Romania; Slovakia

Series: *Vintage Departures*

Now Try: Jan Yoors's *The Gypsies* is the classic account of the author's life with a wandering band of Gypsies that he joined when he ran away from his affluent home at the age of 12; he tells the story of their constant struggle to survive as free nomads. Yoors also published his photographs of the Gypsies with excerpts from his previous book as *The Heroic Present: Life Among the Gypsies.* Anne Sutherland's *Gypsies: The Hidden Americans* is a somewhat dry, scholarly study but its subject (the 500,000 Rom who represent the largest group of Gypsies in the United States) is interesting. Kate Furnivall's historical novel, *The Red Scarf,* is set in a 1930s Siberian labor camp and features gypsy characters who are central to the story.

Grant, Richard

American Nomads: Travels with Lost Conquistadors, Mountain Men, Cowboys, Indians, Hoboes, Truckers, and Bullriders. New York: Grove Press, 2003. 311 pp. ISBN: 9780802117632

English writer Richard Grant wandered through the United States (mostly in the Southwest) for 15 years, celebrating his wanderlust and that of the individuals with whom he lived: rodeo cowboys, truck drivers, Native Americans, hoboes, tie-dyed concert followers, flea market traders, and retirees who live year round in their pricey RVs. Grant also traces the history of wandering in the New World, with stories of Apache riders and Comanches, frontiersmen, buckskinners, cowboys, and Spanish explorers. Grants writes in a rich, comic style and uses the lives of these

American nomads to show how one can stray from the mainstream in pursuit of the American dream of freedom.

Subjects: American History; American Indians; American West; Hoboes; Humor

Places: Arizona; California; Colorado; Kansas; Montana; Nebraska; Nevada; New Mexico; Oklahoma; South Dakota; Texas; Utah; Wyoming

Awards: Thomas Cook Travel Book Award, 2004

Now Try: Grant is also the author of *God's Middle Finger: Into the Lawless Heart of the Sierra Madre,* which follows the author through the Sierra Madre Mountains, where he narrowly escaped death at the hands of cocaine-snorting, half-drunk Mexican gang members. He also wrote *Crazy River: Exploration and Folly in East Africa,* in which he set out to make the first descent of an uncharted river in Tanzania. All of his books reflect his recklessness, wit, and curiosity. In *American Nomads,* Grant traveled with a number of retirees in their RVs, and readers who find that life attractive may enjoy Ken Halloran's amusing *Travel Tales . . . : An Old Retiree, His RV, His Dog, and His Woman (Not Necessarily in Order of Preference) Hit the Road,* about his experiences traveling the United States in his RV.

Jaffrey, Zia

The Invisibles: A Tale of the Eunuchs of India. New York: Pantheon Books, 1996. 293 pp. ISBN: 9780679415770

While attending a friend's wedding in India, freelance writer Jaffrey encountered members of the *hijra* caste of men who dress as women, are often castrated, and live together. Jaffrey employed both her status as an outsider and her Indian family's connections to examine this phenomenon more closely, interviewing many *hijras* herself and writing about this sometimes taboo topic with great sensitivity and respect for the *hijras*. Her tantalizing journey through India to find out more about these "eunuchs" explores their lives, rituals, and history.

Subjects: Eunuchs; Gender Issues; Investigative Stories; GLBTQ; Women Travelers

Places: India

Series: *Vintage Departures*

Now Try: Anthropologist Serena Nanda's cultural study, *Neither Man Nor Woman: The Hijras of India,* is a more scholarly treatment of the *hijra* caste of India. Gayatri Reddy's *With Respect to Sex: Negotiating Hijra Identity in South India* is yet another scholarly ethnography of the group. For a close look at another group of men who take on female roles, readers may consult *Ladyboys: The Secret World of Thailand's Third Gender,* which includes intimate portraits of nine transgendered individuals.

Parks, Tim

A Season with Verona: Travels Around Italy in Search of Illusion, National Character, and . . . Goals! New York: Arcade Pub., 2002. 447 pp. ISBN: 978155 9706285

Writer Tim Parks, who had lived with his family in Verona for 20 years, decided in early 2000 to travel to every soccer match that his favorite team, Hellas Verona, had scheduled. His purpose was to better understand "how people relate to football . . . how they dream this dream at once so intense and so utterly unimportant." The book's 34 chapters correspond to the team's 34 matches, and each chapter includes an account of the match as well as Parks's thoughts about topics as diverse as nationhood, crowd psychology, authority, and influence. The fans with whom Parks traveled were an unpleasant and rowdy lot (racists and vandals, in some cases), and Parks wonders why this is the case, mixing cultural analysis with an appreciation of the emotional highs and lows of sports.

Subjects: Racism; Soccer; Sports

Places: Italy

Now Try: Parks has written two books on expatriate life in Italy. In *Italian Neighbors: Or, A Lapsed Anglo-Saxon in Verona,* he tells about the first ten years that he spent in Verona, capturing a passionate but amiable world of his adopted home village, Montecchio. The sequel, *Italian Education,* focuses on the experience of raising a son and a daughter there and includes a number of observations about child rearing in Italy. Novelist Nick Hornby's first book, *Fever Pitch,* is one of the most highly regarded memoirs on soccer and consists of a number of short essays about the Arsenal team's ups and downs between 1968 and 1992 and how their playing related to developments in Hornby's own life. Two other books about the power of soccer are Franklin Foer's *How Soccer Explains the World: An Unlikely Theory of Globalization,* which looks at the role of soccer role in various cultures to examine the reach of globalization, and Paul Cuadros's inspiring *A Home on the Field: How One Championship Soccer Team Inspires Hope for the Revival of Small Town America,* about a small town in North Carolina and its struggles with immigration, racism, and poverty.

Consider Starting With . . .

Child, Julia, and Alex Prud'homme. *My Life in France.*
Fonseca, Isabel. *Bury Me Standing: The Gypsies and Their Journey.*
Hessler, Peter. *River Town: Two Years on the Yangtze.*
Iyer, Pico. *The Lady and the Monk: Four Seasons in Kyoto.*
Mayle, Peter. *A Year in Provence.*
Salzman, Mark. *Iron and Silk.*
Stewart, Chris. *Driving Over Lemons: An Optimist in Andalucía.*

Fiction Read-Alikes

Durrell, Lawrence. The writer's famed Alexandria Quartet involves the intertwined lives of several British expatriates living in Alexandria before and during World War II. In the first novel, ***Justine***, the narrator Darley attempts to recover from his tragic affair with Justine Hosnani, a beautiful, rich, mysterious woman married to a wealthy Egyptian. The second novel, ***Balthazar***, is named for Darley's friend, a doctor and mystic, who re-interprets Darley's version of the story from a more intellectual point of view. The third novel, ***Mountolive***, is a straightforward, third-person narrative of events, and the final volume, ***Clea***, shows Darley as he heals and becomes capable of loving Clea Montis, an elusive and emotionally veiled painter.

Freudenberger, Nell. The stories in the 30-something American author's debut short story collection, ***Lucky Girls***, are set in India and Southeast Asia and are told from the perspective of young female expatriates who find themselves in exotic locations, trying to live by new and unfamiliar rules. The two novels that followed (***The Dissident*** and ***The Newlyweds***) both concern expatriates of a different sort, Asians who move to the United States. Freudenberger writes beautifully and depicts realistically complex characters, which one critic described as "yearning for something they can't quite understand, but which they know is out there somewhere."

Hemingway, Ernest. In addition to the memoir of his life in Paris in the 1920s, ***A Moveable Feast*** (annotated in this chapter), Hemingway wrote ***The Sun Also Rises***, which tells the story of a group of American and British expatriates on a sojourn from Paris to Paloma, where they watch the annual running of the bulls and the bullfights. The novel captures the spirit of the expatriates who came of age during World War I and were termed "the lost generation" by Gertrude Stein.

James, Henry. James, an expatriate himself, wrote several works that involve American expatriates in Europe and feature the theme of American innocence. The two best known of these are the novella ***Daisy Miller***, which portrays the courtship of a beautiful but naïve American girl by Frederick Winterbourne (an American who has lived most of his life in Europe), and ***The Portrait of a Lady***, which tells the story of Isabel Archer, a young American woman who inherits a large amount of money and then becomes the victim of the schemes of two American expatriates.

Johnson, Diane. Like James, Johnson writes about the clash of American and European cultures. Her work is, of course, lighter and funnier and more contemporary than James and includes ***Le Divorce, Le Mariage***, and ***L'Affaire***, all of which look at the cultural disconnections of Americans in France. Her most recent novel, ***Lulu in Marrakech***, examines the cultural clashes of Islam and the West.

Lowry, Malcolm. Lowry's expatriate novel, ***Under the Volcano***, tells the story of an alcoholic British ex-consul in a small Mexican town and his disintegration and death on Mexico's Day of the Dead. Lowry's novel has been compared with Dante's *Inferno* and Joyce's *Ulysses* and was recently ranked by the Modern Library as number 11 on its list of the 100 best English-language novels of the 20th century.

Rush, Norman. Rush won the 1991 National Book Award for his novel, ***Mating***, which is set in the expatriate community in Botswana in the 1980s and involves an American anthropologist who falls in love with a charismatic American man who runs an experimental, women-only village in the Kalahari. His latest novel, ***Mortals***, is also set in Botswana and examines the lives of three Americans there. His earlier collection of stories, ***Whites,*** was nominated for the Pulitzer Prize and portrays American and European expatriates dealing with the poverty and drought of Botswana; it is lighter and more accessible than the novels. All feature a strong sense of place and convincing characters.

Sklepowich, Edward. Urbino Macintyre is an American expatriate writer living in Venice and the protagonist in a series of mysteries by Sklepowich, appropriately called the *Urbino Macintyre Mystery Series*. There are now nine titles in the series, beginning with ***Death in a Serene City,*** which links the murder of a Venetian laundress with the theft of the thousand-year-old body of Santa Teodora, and ends with ***The Veils of Venice,*** which focuses on the stabbing death of a contessa. The titles in the series all evoke the splendor and atmosphere of Venice.

Notes

1. Stoddard Martin, *The Great Expatriate Writers* (New York: St. Martin's Press, 1992), p. 1.
2. thandelike, "05–25–09 Expatriate Literature, Open Chat," May 25, 2009. http://litchat.net/past-litchats/05–25–09-expatriate-literature-open-chat/.
3. mdbenoit, "05–25–09 Expatriate Literature, Open Chat," May 25, 2009. http://litchat.net/past-litchats/05–25–09-expatriate-literature-open-chat/.

Reference

Martin, Stoddard. *The Great Expatriate Writers*. New York: St. Martin's Press, 1992.

Chapter 6

Travel Humor

The human race is far too stupid to be deterred from tourism by a mere several million years of bad experiences.
—Dave Barry, *Dave Barry's Only Travel Guide You'll Ever Need*

Definition of "Travel Humor"

The last two chapters of this book are devoted to two special subgenres of travel narrative: "Travel Humor" and "Travel Adventure." These subgenres do not derive from the definition of travel, given in the book's introduction, as an activity that involves a traveler or travelers who go to a destination by some means, for some purpose, for some length of time. Instead, "Travel Humor" and "Travel Adventure" are two subgenres that overlap both stylistically and thematically with other genres, "Humor" and "Adventure."

"Travel Humor" can be considered a subgenre of the travel narrative where the purpose of the narrative is to make the reader laugh. Alternatively, it can be considered a subgenre of the Humor genre where the humor is presented in the context of a travel situation, typically to a place that is foreign to the traveler. "Travel Humor" is represented by Mark Twain poking fun at his fellow passengers on a trip to the Holy Land in *The Innocents Abroad,* as opposed to Twain poking fun at religious beliefs in general in *Letters from the Earth.* "Travel Humor" is Bill Bryson finding plenty to laugh about in Australia in his book, *In a Sunburned Country,* as opposed to Bryson finding plenty to laugh about in his life growing up in Des Moines in *The Life and Times of the Thunderbolt Kid.*

Interestingly, "Humor" is, by far, the most frequently used subject heading in this book. It applies to over half again as many titles as do either of the next most frequently used subject headings ("Quick Reads" and "Women Travelers") and applies to titles in almost all of the chapters in this book; only the chapter on "Travel Adventure" is exempt. There is significant humor in books that focus on travel destinations (Robert Byron trying to coax his automobile through unfriendly terrain *The Road to Oxiana*), on books that focus on the purpose of the trip (Monty Python alumnus Michael Palin's traveling in the footsteps of Phileas Fogg, *Around the World in 80 Days with Michael Palin*), on books that focus on the means of travel (Bill Bryson joking with his friend Steven Katz as they hike the Appalachian Trail in *A Walk in the Woods: Rediscovering America on the Appalachian Trail*), and on books about the expatriate experience (Peter Mayle's amusing neighbors in *A Year in Provence*). There is even humor to be found in the intense situations portrayed in healing journeys (Mike Carter's self-deprecating humor in *Uneasy Rider: Travels through a Mid-Life Crisis* or the mix of humor and melancholy in Kevin Patterson's *The Water in Between: A Journey at Sea*).

Why so many travel narratives should involve humor is a fascinating question, and without delving too deeply into theories about the philosophy of humor, suffice it to say that travel puts people into situations that are often funny because they are awkward or uncomfortable or, well, foreign. In the hands of some writers, these situations would be portrayed as irksome and annoying. In the hands of a humorist, these situations are portrayed as amusing and comical.

Some readers like humor in their travel reading. Of the authors highlighted in this book, Bill Bryson may be their favorite. Or Mark Twain. Or Eric Newby. Or Pete McCarthy. These readers like to think that they can see the humorous side of things when they travel. They laugh when they can't figure out how the *Federbett* on a German bed works (does one crawl in it or sleep under it) or when they realize that they've butchered the French language yet again or when they've injured themselves with chopsticks one more time.

One of my friends laughed a lot when he took the wrong bus once in Jerusalem and ended up in the desert, surrounded by several people, none of whom spoke English or French or German or any language in which he might have barely made himself understood. He had to laugh, in fact, to keep from crying. Luckily, my friend had plenty of experience laughing at the travel narratives of many of the writers in this chapter, including Mark Twain, whose book, *The Innocents Abroad*, includes his own hilarious and insightful thoughts about a trip to Jerusalem.

Appeal of "Travel Humor"

For "Travel Humor," tone or mood is the most important of the traditional elements of appeal. As Joyce Saricks notes, "How do we identify the tone of books? Generally, as we read, we recognize clues and can see how the author creates his or her tone: with *humor* or tension"[1] (emphasis mine).

As the name implies, the tone of "Travel Humor" is, in a word, humorous. These are books that will cause the reader to laugh, to guffaw, to chortle, and to chuckle. Their humor may range from the witty to the satirical to the self-effacing to the mischievous. The humor may be as understated as Eric Newby's "short walk" up a 20,000-foot, previously unclimbed glacial peak (*A Short Walk in the Hindu Kush*) or as outrageous as Redmon O'Hanlon's attempt to "party with" the world's most violent indigenous tribe (*In Trouble Again: A Journey Between the Orinoco and the Amazon*). The traveler may poke fun at others, as Bill Bryson frequently does, or at himself, as Tim Cahill does so well. Even the titles of the books may be funny: *A Wolverine Is Eating My Leg; Karma Cola; Around the World in 80 Dates;* and *Greasy Rider.*

Because of the wide range of humor reflected in these titles, the readers' advisor will need to understand the many types of humor and to appreciate the fact that certain kinds of humor will appeal to one reader and, at the same time, offend another. Pete McCarthy's humor ("God works in mysterious ways, especially after a few drinks"), for example, will upset some readers as sacrilegious, and many readers will be annoyed with Bill Bryson's humor at the expense of his fellow travelers. (One can read the reviews of Bryson's books on Amazon.com or Goodreads.com to gain an appreciation of how one reader will be offended by something that greatly amuses another reader.)

Beyond the appeal of tone or mood, character, story line, and frame or setting may also be somewhat important to readers of these titles. Character, for example, may be important and may function as the basis for much of the humor in these titles. The author may poke fun at himself (Griff Rhys Jones's *To the Baltic with Bob: An Epic Misadventure*) or at the individuals whom she meets (the many men that Jennifer Cox dated in *Around the World in 80 Dates*) or both (Tim Moore's *Travels with My Donkey: One Man and His Ass on a Pilgrimage to Santiago*).

Story line serves an important role in certain "Travel Humor" narratives. The titles of the "Wit and Wisdom" category, for instance, are thought provoking and teach as well as amuse; their pearls of wisdom are cleverly inserted between the jokes. One learns a lot about Alfred Wallace, who co-discovered natural selection with Darwin, while laughing at Redmon O'Hanlon's amusing account of a journey to Borneo (*Into the Heart of Borneo*), just as one gains a better understanding of African history and tourism in general while also enjoying Rick Antonson's droll observations during his trip to Timbuktu (*To Timbuktu for a Haircut: A Journey through West Africa*). Likewise, many of the titles in the category entitled "Crazy Ideas" feature action-oriented story lines that center on outrageous premises. Tony Hawks makes a bet that he can hitchhike around the perimeter of Ireland in one calendar month with a small refrigerator (*Round Ireland with a Fridge*), and the story takes off from there.

Frame or setting is also important in many of these titles. After all, the category is "*Travel* Humor," and so the destinations will often be part of the humor. Eric Newby's *A Short Walk in the Hindu Kush*, for example, would be far less funny if he and his friend had taken an impulsive trip to a less forbidding place than the mountains of Afghanistan.

Other appeal factors, like pacing and language or style, are also important in humor in general and travel humor in particular, such as the wonderful writing of Truman Capote's *The Muses Are Heard: An Account*.

When working with readers who enjoy "Travel Humor," librarians should also remember that the "Humor" genre in general may also contain titles of interest to these readers. Readers' advisors should be ready to suggest titles like *The Year of Living Biblically* by A. J. Jacobs or Stephen Fry's biography, *Moab is My Washpot*, or even humorous fiction titles, like Joseph Heller's *Catch-22* or John Kennedy Toole's *A Confederacy of Dunces* or Kingsley Amis's *Lucky Jim* or anything by P. G. Wodehouse.

Organization of the Chapter

This chapter on "Travel Humor" begins with "Classics," defined in this book as titles that were published prior to 1990 and that display universality, multiple levels of meaning, great stories, memorable characters, emotional or though-provoking experiences, and great writing, thereby making them more likely to be more familiar to readers and librarians. The familiarity of these titles may help readers and librarians better understand the nuances of this subgenre and its various categories. While the destinations of these trips may have changed a great deal over the years represented by these titles, the humor is still fresh.

Beyond that, there are just two categories in this chapter. Some humorous titles also teach, and these are captured in "Wit and Wisdom," which represents titles in which the humor is mixed in with a good bit of knowledge about the destination or the individuals the traveler meets. By contrast, the titles in "Crazy Ideas" are just funny in their premises and motivations. The reader is not required to learn anything; the reader is simply required to laugh.

Classics

Any reader who holds the misguided belief that older writings on "Travel Humor," such as the pre-1990 classics in this section, don't retain their hilarity needs only to sit down with Mark Twain's 1869 work, *The Innocents Abroad*. That book alone should be enough to dissuade the reader of such an ill-advised notion. The books in this first category of the chapter on "Travel Humor" have not been pulled out because they are somehow less funny or even quaintly old-fashioned in their humor; instead, they have been listed together here because they are likely to be more familiar to readers and librarians and should therefore serve as good entry points into the subgenre and categories of "Travel Humor."

Both categories in this subgenre are well represented by the classics. One gains a great deal of both wit and wisdom from Mark Twain's travel narratives (*The Innocents Abroad* or *A Tramp Abroad*, in particular), and one learns a lot about the "packaging" of Eastern spirituality to the West while laughing out loud with Gita Mehta's *Karma Cola: Marketing the Mystic East*. Eric Newby's decision to take *A Short Walk in the Hindu Kush* with little or no preparation is as crazy an idea as any traveler has ever had, perhaps matched only by Redmon O'Hanlon's stated purpose of traveling to the Amazon to "party with" the world's most violent tribe, the Yanomami (*In Trouble Again: A Journey Between the Orinoco and the Amazon*).

Cahill, Tim

Jaguars Ripped My Flesh. New York: Bantam Books, 1987. 306 pp. ISBN: 9780553342765

Cahill, one of the founding editors of *Outside* magazine, has a knack for finding the humorous in seemingly life-threatening situations. Whether he's diving with sharks, caving in Kentucky, filming poison sea snakes in the Philippines, or skydiving in California, Cahill maintains his sense of humor and then moves on unflappably to the next challenge. In these 30-some essays, Cahill comes across as both articulate and humble: "Personally, I've found that it doesn't pay to take these accomplishments too seriously. I spend a lot of time laughing at myself."

Subjects: Adventure; Essays; Humor

Categories: Crazy Ideas

Places: Africa; Alaska; Australia; Guyana; Kentucky; Mexico; Montana; North Dakota; Peru; Philippines; Rwanda; Utah; Venezuela; Washington; Wyoming

Series: *Vintage Departures*

Now Try: Fans of Cahill will likely enjoy the compilation that Keath Fraser edited, *Bad Trips*, which asked various writers to tell about their worst journeys: Wilfred Thesiger tells of a camel ride across the Arabian desert, Anita Desai complains about the cold in Norway, and Umberto Eco writes about staying in a tacky hotel in Southern California. Doug Lansky does much the same in *There's No Toilet Paper on the Road Less Traveled: The Best of Travel Humor and Misadventure*, which includes pieces by Dave Barry on the difficulties of ordering a beer in Japan and Richard Sterling on trying to eat deep-fried potato bugs in Myanmar. *Braving Home: Dispatches from the Underwater Town, the Lava-Side Inn, and Other Extreme Locales* by Jake Halpern has a similar feel, although his topic is somewhat different; he reports on places where people really should not live and the people who do live there, like the bed and breakfast at the foot of an active volcano in Hawaii or the 14-story indoor city of Whittier, Alaska.

Cahill, Tim

A Wolverine Is Eating My Leg. New York: Vintage, 1989. 302 pp. ISBN: 9780679720263

As Cahill says in one of the 18 essays in this book, "Risk is a part of therapy. You can put your life on the line in order to save your soul." And take risks he did, as these essays find Cahill white water rafting in the Himalayas, coming within 10 feet of gorillas, going avalanche skiing, searching for Bigfoot, and descending 40-story-high precipices in caves. Even the less adventurous essays still have the feeling of someone pushing the edge of the envelope: he wanders through the ruins of Jonestown, which is strewn with corpses; he ice fishes; he scuba dives. Through it all, he maintains a wicked sense of humor and is not averse to poking fun at himself, even when there is a sense of impending disaster.

Subjects: Adventure; Essays; Humor; Investigative Stories

Categories: Crazy Ideas

Places: Africa; California; Georgia; Guyana; India; Marquesas; Montana; New Hampshire; Oregon; Philippines; Rwanda; Santa Cruz Islands; Venezuela; Wisconsin

Series: *Vintage Departures*

Now Try: Cahill edited *Not So Funny When It Happened: The Best of Travel Humor and Misadventure,* a collection of amusing travel tales by 36 writers, including Dave Barry, Bill Bryson, J. P. Donleavy, Anne Lamott, Mark Salzman, and David Sedaris. Roger Rapoport and Marguerita Castanera edited a similar collection, *I Should Have Stayed Home: The Worst Trips of the Great Writers,* which includes (among others) Paul Theroux's account of Christmas in Central Africa and Eric Hansen's tale of a night with the homeless in Grand Central Station. Rosemary Caperton, Anne Mathews, and Lucie Ocenas edited a similar collection of misadventures, all involving women travelers, *The Unsavvy Traveler: Women's Comic Tales of Catastrophe.* Readers who enjoy Cahill will likely appreciate adventure narratives that involve whitewater rafting, avalanche skiing, and other activities about which Cahill writes. Although not humorous, Todd Balf's *The Last River: The Tragic Race for Shangri-la* tells the story of a whitewater trip on Tibet's fabled Tsangpo River based on the accounts of those who undertook the run. William A. Kerig's book about avalanche skier Trevor Peterson and his tragic death in the snow is *The Edge of Never: A Skier's Story of Life, Death, and Dreams in the World's Most Dangerous Mountains.*

Capote, Truman

The Muses Are Heard: An Account. New York: Random House, 1956. 182 pp. ISBN: None

Capote's account of The Everyman's Opera trip to the Soviet Union in the 1950s to stage *Porgy and Bess* is mischievously witty and details every challenge and mishap that the company encountered: small, overheated rooms in St. Petersburg; programs that weren't ready for opening night; tawdry stores and working-class bars; meals of yogurt and raspberry soda instead of the hoped-for caviar. *The Muses Are Heard* is filled with satirical details but does manage to highlight the few positive events, as when the cultural ministry sets up a Christmas tree in the hotel lobby.

Subjects: 1950s; Cold War; Communism; Culture Clash; Drama; Humor; Quick Reads

Categories: Wit and Wisdom

Places: Russia

Now Try: Capote's most famous work of creative nonfiction, *In Cold Blood,* is neither humorous nor a travel narrative, but its evocation of the American heartland represents a strong sense of place. In 1947, John Steinbeck made the first of several trips to the Soviet Union as one of the first Westerners to visit many parts of that country since the communist revolution; he wrote about his experiences in *A Russian Journal.*

Another well-regarded writer associated with St. Petersburg in particular is the Nobel Prize winner Joseph Brodsky. Two of his essays on his native city ("A Guide to a Renamed City" and "In a Room and a Half") are available in *Less Than One: Selected Essays*.

Mehta, Gita

Karma Cola: Marketing the Mystic East. New York: Simon and Schuster, 1979. 201 pp. ISBN: 9780671250836

In the late 1960s, thousands upon thousands of Westerners (the Beatles, drugged-out hippies, rich kids from Hollywood) went to India in search of spiritual enlightenment. Mehta, an Indian writer who had also lived in England and the United States, skewers both the Western "pilgrims" and the gurus who were happy to turn the ancient traditions of their religion into a commodity and exploit their disciples all the way to the bank. Mehta's humor is sharp but also angry and sad, as she mourns the way in which her country's traditions were packaged and sold to the naïve.

Subjects: 1960s; Buddhism; Hinduism; Humor; Quick Reads; Religion; Spirituality

Categories: Wit and Wisdom

Places: India

Now Try: Mehta is also the author of *Snakes and Ladders: Glimpses of Modern India,* which captures the many contradictions of India as well as any recent book. Cleo Odzer's autobiographical *Goa Freaks: My Hippie Years in India* provides a less judgmental account of some of the Westerners who came to India in search of spiritual awakening and, in the case of her friends, drugs. Philip Goldberg's *American Veda: From Emerson and the Beatles to Yoga and Meditation: How Indian Spirituality Changed the West* is not a travel narrative but it does serve as a reminder that Westerners were seeking spiritual enlightenment in India long before the 1960s, and it traces the impact of the Vedic tradition on individuals as diverse as Ralph Waldo Emerson, John Coltrane, and J. D. Salinger. The Indian writer Manil Suri mixes Hindu mythology with comedy in his story of Vishnu, the handyman in a Mumbai apartment building, who reflects on his life and the lives of the individuals living in the building; the novel, *The Death of Vishnu,* paints a cynical portrait of modern India.

Newby, Eric

A Short Walk In the Hindu Kush. Hawthorn, Victoria, Australia: Lonely Planet, 1998 [1958]. 255 pp. ISBN: 9780864426048

Newby may not have been the first travel writer to recount a disastrous trip to an inhospitable place by a traveler who was totally unprepared, but *A Short Walk In the Hindu Kush* may be the best of this sub-subgenre.

Newby describes the impulsive, ill-advised trip he and his friend Hugh took in 1956 to a remote corner in Afghanistan that had not been visited by a European in some 50 years. Newby's humor focuses on his own lack of preparation for the trip, the quirks of the individuals he encountered, and the jams in which he and Hugh invariably found themselves. Typical of Newby's understated humor is the very title of the book: the "short walk" included a nearly successful attempt to scale Mir Samir, a 20,000-foot high, previously unclimbed glacial peak.

Subjects: Friendships; Humor; Mountains

Categories: Crazy Ideas

Places: Afghanistan

Series: *Picador Travel Classics*

Now Try: Eric Newby is a brilliant, unbelievably funny travel writer. The collection, *A Merry Dance around the World: The Best of Eric Newby,* is a good introduction to his work; it includes such misadventures as rowing 1,200 miles down the Ganges River, cycling around Ireland during five months of unceasing rain, and cleaning out a pigsty during a gale near Cape Horn. *Departures and Travels* is another collection of Newby's travels and recounts several trips taken by him and his wife; destinations include Yemen, China, Russia, Scotland, Syria, and Siena. Some reviewers consider Peter Fleming's *Brazilian Adventure* (about an expedition to locate a missing explorer in 1920s Brazil) to be the earliest of the black-comedy "bad trips."

O'Hanlon, Redmond

Into the Heart of Borneo. New York: Vintage, 1985. 191 pp. ISBN: 9780394544816

O'Hanlon had a clear sense of the dangers that awaited him on his 1983 journey to a part of Borneo that had remained untouched since the 1920s (his own list included vipers, cholera, crocodiles, ticks, tuberculosis, malaria, rabies, and 1,700 types of parasitic worms) but he went anyway, along with his friend and poet James Fenton and three native guides. This was the aging, overweight British naturalist's first travel narrative and one of his best, not only funny beyond belief but also observant and filled with facts about everything from Darwin's co-discoverer of natural selection, Alfred Wallace, to glorious descriptions of the fauna and flora of the rain forest, especially the nearly extinct Sumatran Rhinoceros that motivated O'Hanlon's journey.

Subjects: Animals; Exploration; Friendships; Humor; Islands; Plants; Quick Reads

Categories: Crazy Ideas; Wit and Wisdom

Places: Borneo

Series: *Picador Travel Classics; Vintage Departures*

Now Try: Brian Row McNamee's *With Pythons & Head-Hunters in Borneo* recounts that writer's journey in the footsteps of O'Hanlon's 1983 expedition; he describes his trek in great detail and throws in ample facts about the history of the island as well. Like O'Hanlon's account, Andro Linklater's amateur anthropological study of the headhunters on Borneo, *Wild People: Travels with Borneo's Head-Hunters,* is alternately funny and revolting; his discussion of the bloodsucking leeches on the island is definitely not for the squeamish. John Wassner understood the dangers of traveling through the lands controlled by Borneo's headhunters, but like O'Hanlon, he made the journey anyway; his description of life in the jungle, which he found quite agreeable, is *Espresso with the Headhunters*.

O'Hanlon, Redmond

In Trouble Again: A Journey between the Orinoco and the Amazon. New York: Atlantic Monthly Press, 1989 [1988]. 272 pp. ISBN: 9780871132499

"Imagine a PBS documentary hosted by the Monty Python troupe," said one reviewer of O'Hanlon's classic about his ill-advised, four-month trip into the bug-infested rain forest along the Amazon River in Venezuela. The lunacy of O'Hanlon's trip was clear from the start: his stated purpose was to meet and "party with" the Yanomami tribe, generally regarded as one of the most violent people on the planet. O'Hanlon is insanely funny, and his fearlessness, trusting nature, and stubbornness carry him from one crazy situation to the next.

Subjects: Animals; Humor; Indigenous People; Rivers

Categories: Crazy Ideas

Places: Amazon River; Venezuela

Series: *Vintage Departures*

Now Try: Greg Emmanuel's *Extreme Encounters: How It Feels to Be Drowned in Quicksand, Shredded by Piranhas, Swept Up in a Tornado, and Dozens of Other Unpleasant Experiences* has an element of black humor about it, even though the purpose of the book is to describe some of life's most dangerous situations; included in the book is a chapter on the dangers of the Amazon River, which focuses mainly on the piranha and snakes that lurk there. Travel writer Eric Newby's hilarious trip down another river is described in *Slowly Down the Ganges*; Newby's humor is more droll and understated than O'Hanlon's. Wade Davis's *One River: Explorations and Discoveries in the Amazon Rain Forest* shares none of the humor of O'Hanlon's book but does share location; it discusses both the plants of the Amazon region and the dangerous expeditions taken by Davis's mentor, Harvard biologist Richard Evans Schultes, in the area beginning in the 1930s. O'Hanlon fans may also appreciate the writing of the creator of Gonzo journalism, Hunter S. Thompson, particularly *Hell's Angels: The Strange and Terrible Saga of the Outlaw Motorcycle Gangs, Fear and Loathing in Las Vegas*, and *The Rum Diary*.

O'Rourke, P. J.

Holidays in Hell: In Which Our Intrepid Reporter Travels to the World's Worst Places and Asks, "What's Funny About . . ." New York: Atlantic Monthly Press, 1988. 257 pp. ISBN: 9780871132406

Political satirist O'Rouke is a self-described "Trouble Tourist—going to see insurrections, stupidities, political crises, civil disturbances and other human folly because . . . because it's fun." He took his gonzo sarcasm to a number of trouble spots for this collection (storming the barricades of student protesters with riot police in Seoul, interviewing Communist insurrectionists in the Philippines, going undercover dressed as an Arab in the Gaza Strip, commenting on the various ways that the guards at security checkpoints in Beirut mispronounce "passport") and produced the perfect book for anyone with a cynical, irreverent view of the world's troubled spots.

Subjects: 1980s; Essays; Humor; Journalism; Politics; War

Categories: Crazy Ideas

Places: Australia; Beirut; El Salvador; Europe (Various); Florida; Israel; Jerusalem; Lebanon; Massachusetts; Mexico; Nicaragua; Panama; Philippines; Poland; Seoul; South Africa; South Carolina; South Korea; Warsaw

Series: *Vintage Departures*

Now Try: O'Rourke has written a number of political satires that include travel, including *Give War a Chance: Eyewitness Accounts of Mankind's Struggle Against Tyranny, Injustice, and Alcohol-Free Beer,* which includes his dispatches from the 1991 Gulf War, and *All the Trouble in the World: The Lighter Side of Overpopulation, Famine, Ecological Disaster, Ethnic Hatred, Plague, and Poverty,* which includes his visit to the Czech Republic to show that a socialist government can't solve its ecological problems any better than a free market government can. Fans of O'Rourke may also enjoy Chuck Thompson's writing; his acidic *Smile When You're Lying: Confessions of a Rogue Travel Writer* attempts to demolish the fantasies of readers of travel magazines by showing the underbelly of travel, including his own "hate list" of least favorite destinations: New Zealand, Colorado, Austin, and the entire Caribbean.

Stevens, Stuart

Malaria Dreams: An African Adventure. New York: Atlantic Monthly Press, 1989. 236 pp. ISBN: 9780871132789

Stevens and a former model traveled to the Central African Republic to retrieve a friend's Land Rover, but he was robbed within ten minutes of entering the country and soon discovered that the Land Rover was nowhere to be found. His solution was to buy a "new" Land Rover and drive it back to Algeria to meet up with his wife. Stevens's quest was filled with the problems that confront travelers in Africa (bureaucracy, bribery, scarcity) and his life was saved more than once through sheer dumb luck and the presence of a beautiful female companion. Wonderfully written, Stevens captures the shrewdness, creativity, humor, and appreciation of the illogical that held him together through his "African adventure."

Subjects: Automobiles; Culture Clash; Humor

Categories: Crazy Ideas

Places: Africa; Algeria; Cameroon; Central African Republic; Chad; Mali; Niger

Now Try: Stevens's highly regarded first book, *Night Train to Turkistan* (annotated in the "Quests" chapter of this book), recounts how Stevens and three friends retraced the 1935 journey of travel writer Peter Fleming to Xinjiang (then known as Chinese Turkestan); like *Malaria Dreams*, it is wildly humorous. *French Lessons in Africa: Travels With My Briefcase in French Africa* by Peter Biddlecombe is another humorous account of travel in Africa; his tales of ten years of travel through Francophone West Africa include everything from white magic in Benin to locusts in Mali and Italian ice cream parlors in the middle of the Sahara. Brandon Wilson's *Dead Men Don't Leave Tips: Adventures X Africa* recounts his honeymoon on a seven-month, 10,000-mile safari across 17 African nations; the author captures the challenges of traveling in countries where the rules change daily with a great deal of wit.

Twain, Mark

Following the Equator: A Journey Around the World. Washington, DC: National Geographic Society, 2005 [1899]. 440 pp. ISBN: 9780792238768

Mark Twain made a good bit of money from his writing and speaking, but he lost even more money on investments, including a typesetting machine that was made obsolete in the 1890s by the Linotype. In order to pay off his creditors, he undertook a tour of the British Empire in 1895 with his wife and daughter and published an account of the trip in 1897 as *Following the Equator*. The book weaves humorous tales (some of them fictional, like the story of Cecil Rhodes making his fortune by finding a newspaper in the belly of a shark) with Twain's criticism of racism and imperialism (for example, his comparison of Australia's treatment of Aboriginal peoples with the American slave system).

Subjects: 19th Century; Circumnavigations; Humor

Categories: Wit and Wisdom

Places: Atlantic Ocean; Australia; Calcutta; England; Fiji; Hawaii; Honolulu; India; Indian Ocean; Mauritius; Mumbai; New Zealand; Pacific Ocean; Sri Lanka; South Africa; Vancouver

Now Try: Robert Cooper's *Around the World With Mark Twain* followed the path taken by Twain in *Following the Equator* and is filled with information about Twain during that trip, the condition of his cold here, the hotel he stayed in there, the officials he ate lunch with at another place. Betty Wetzel also followed Twain's itinerary in her book, *After You, Mark Twain: A Modern Journey Around the Equator*. The 2000 PBS video, *On the Trail of Mark Twain* with Peter Ustinov, is a good companion piece to Twain's book; among other places, Ustinov visits a leper colony in Hawaii and a monastery in Tibet. Several readers have compared Michael Malone's humor in his laugh-out-loud novel, *Handling Sin*, to Twain's; Malone's book involves a man who travels from North Carolina to New Orleans to find his father, who has escaped from the hospital with a young female mental patient and who has left his son a list of bizarre items to gather and bring with him.

Twain, Mark

The Innocents Abroad. New York: Literary Classics of the U.S., 1984. 1027 pp. ISBN: 9780940450257 (Paired with *Roughing It.*)

In 1867, shortly after his first success as a writer, "The Celebrated Jumping Frog of Calaveras County," Twain toured Europe and the Middle East and wrote a collection of travel letters, which he later collected as the book *The Innocents Abroad.* Published in 1869, it was the first of Twain's travel books. Its humor ranges from lighthearted to bitter and biting as Twain pokes fun at fellow passengers, the citizens of the countries he visited, his own expectations and reactions, the Bible (the scene in which his fellow passenger throws rocks at a turtle to make it sing because the Bible refers to "the song of the turtle" is priceless), and the overly romantic travel literature of the day. (In 2011, the *Guardian* listed *The Innocents Abroad* as one of the 100 greatest nonfiction titles of all time.)

Subjects: 19th Century; Humor; Middle Eastern History; Religion

Categories: Wit and Wisdom

Places: Africa; Athens; Atlantic Ocean; Damascus; Egypt; Florence; France; Gibraltar; Greece; Israel; Istanbul; Italy; Jerusalem; Lebanon; Paris; Rome; Russia; Syria; Turkey; Venice

Now Try: Twain is America's premier humorist, and readers who enjoy his travel narratives may also enjoy his humorous essays in general. A good starting point would be Twain's *Letters from Earth,* which include "The Damned Human Race," in which Twain proves that the snake is a higher form of life than the English earl, and "Fenimore Cooper's Literary Offenses," a hysterical send-up of that author's writings. Another great American humorist, James Thurber, lends his name to the Thurber Prize for American Humor, which was won in 2001 by David Sedaris for *Me Talk Pretty One Day*. The book is not a travel narrative *per se,* but the second half describes the author's expatriate life in Normandy with his partner Hugh and in particular his attempts to learn the French language. (Twain would have approved. Consider this line from *The Innocents Abroad*: "Occasionally, merely for the pleasure of being cruel, we put unoffending Frenchmen on the rack with questions framed in the incomprehensible jargon of their native language, and while they writhed, we impaled them, we peppered them, we scarified them, with their own vile verbs and participles.")

Twain, Mark

Roughing It. New York: Literary Classics of the U.S., 1984. 1027 pp. ISBN: 9780940450257 (Paired with *The Innocents Abroad.*) YA

Roughing It was the second of Twain's travel books, published in 1872, and served as a prequel to *The Innocents Abroad.* It covered the author's six years in Nevada, San Francisco, and Hawaii (then called the Sandwich Islands) and served as a portrait of the western frontier for many of its readers. Among other things, Twain wrote about visiting Salt Lake City and meeting Brigham Young, gold and silver prospecting, real-estate speculation, and traveling to Hawaii. Loosely structured around Twain's attempts to strike it rich, *Roughing It* provides a good deal of insight into the old West while being entertaining and funny.

Subjects: 19th Century; American West; Humor

Categories: Wit and Wisdom

Places: United States

Now Try: Another American humorist who is associated with the American West and who traveled extensively, both in the United States and abroad, is Will Rogers. Although he never wrote a travel narrative *per se,* some of his witty observations based on his travels can be found in books like *Never Met a Man I Didn't Like*. Ben Yagoda's *Will Rogers: A Biography* is a good introduction to the life of the cowboy humorist and provides some insight into his life as a world traveler. Patrick de Witt's strangely funny Western, *The Sisters Brothers: A Novel,* displays a quirkier sense of humor than either Twain or Rogers; its story involves a journey from Oregon to San Francisco and then to the Sierra foothills by two brothers hired to track down and kill a prospector.

Twain, Mark

A Tramp Abroad. New York: Oxford University Press, 1996 [1880]. 631 pp. ISBN: 9780195101379

A Tramp Abroad is the third of Twain's travel books; it was published in 1880 and served as a sequel to *Innocents Abroad*. In the book, Twain and his friend Harris traveled through central and southern Europe. The trip was intended to be on foot, but the pair soon took trains, carriages, and barges; in fact, Twain claimed that the longest walk of the trip was the 47 miles he spent wandering around his dark hotel room while trying to find his bed. The humor of the book focuses primarily on debunking the myths of European glory and on the situations that Twain and Harris encounter, as well as their reactions to those situations. The book contains several appendices, including the inspired piece, "The Awful German Language."

Subjects: 19th Century; Friendships; Humor; European History

Categories: Wit and Wisdom

Places: France; Germany; Italy; Switzerland

Now Try: Any number of humorous titles involve Americans traveling to or living in Europe and the misadventures that result. Harriet Welty Rochefort, who married a French man and lived in Paris, takes on the French in *French Toast: An American in Paris Celebrates the Maddening Mysteries of the French.*

David Conte tells of living in Germany in his collection of charmingly funny essays, *The Frankfurt Files: Tales of an American in Germany*. *The Venice Experiment: A Year of Trial and Error Living Abroad* by Barry Frangipane and Ben Robbins recounts the year that Barry and his wife spent in Venice; they found plenty to laugh at in their encounters with the Italian bureaucracy and even in the high tides that threatened their ground-floor apartment.

Wit and Wisdom

Beyond the classics, the first category of "Travel Humor" in this book is "Wit and Wisdom," which represents those titles in which the humor is mixed in with a good bit of knowledge about the destination or the individuals the traveler meets. The reader learns quite a lot about Australia, its rich history, and its incredible flora and fauna while chuckling over the many amusing passages in Bill Bryson's *In a Sunburned Country*, and the reader gains a better understanding of oceanic drift, the global economy, and the consumer culture while laughing through Donovan Hohn's *Moby-Duck: The True Story of 28,800 Bath Toys Lost at Sea . . .*

These titles feature many kinds of humor, including the wry wit of Rick Anderson (*To Timbuktu for a Haircut: A Journey through West Africa*), the self-deprecating humor of Tim Cahill (*Hold the Enlightenment*), the gentle humor of Polly Evans (*Fried Eggs with Chopsticks*), the offbeat and eccentric comedy of Bill Geist (*Way Off the Road: Discovering the Peculiar Charms of Small-Town America*), and the edgier wisecracks of Joe Queenan (*Queenan Country: A Reluctant Anglophile's Pilgrimage to the Mother Country*). But more importantly, all will appeal to readers who want to learn something while they are laughing.

Readers who enjoy these humorous titles that also teach may enjoy a number of other humorous titles that do not involve travel, including nonfiction like David Sedaris's *Me Talk Pretty One Day* or Tina Fey's *Bossypants* and fiction like P.G. Wodehouse's many novels (*Right Ho, Jeeves* and *The Code of the Woosters* for starters) or Kingsley Amis's *Lucky Jim*.

Antonson, Rick

To Timbuktu for a Haircut: A Journey through West Africa. Toronto: Dundurn Group, 2008. 256 pp. ISBN: 9781550028058

Antonson, the president of Tourism Vancouver, responded to his midlife crisis by deciding to spend a month without work, without his Blackberry, and without family obligations. He then decided to realize his childhood dream of traveling overland to Africa and specifically to the legendary city of Timbuktu. One reviewer described this book as "a little bit of Bill Bryson, a little bit of Michael Palin, and quite a lot of Bob Hope on the road to Timbuktu," and the book is filled with Antonson's wry humor. The author recounts his travels by train, by four-wheel drive vehicle, by boat, by camel, and by foot, and along the way he provides the reader with a history of Timbuktu (a city that, at its peak, rivaled

London and Venice as a trading center), his thoughts on tourism as an act of learning, and plenty of droll observations.

Subjects: African History; Humor

Places: Africa; Mali

Now Try: Another amusing travel narrative set in Africa is Brandon Wilson's *Dead Men Don't Leave Tips: Adventures X Africa,* in which he describes his honeymoon on a seven-month, 10,000-mile safari across 17 African nations, where the rules seem to change daily. Phil Gray describes his trek up Africa's Mount Kilimanjaro with equal parts humor and physical exertion in *Kilimanjaro via the Marangu Route: "Tourist Route" My Ass.* Antonson argues that travel is a means of education and a way to break down the barriers between people; television travel guide Rick Steves makes similar arguments in his thoughtful book, *Travel as a Political Act.*

Bryson, Bill

In a Sunburned Country. New York: Broadway Books, 2000. 307 pp. ; ISBN: 9780767903851

Bryson's travels through "the only island that is also a continent, and the only continent that is also a country" is both funny enough to make readers laugh until they cry and extremely informative. In fact, it's often both, as when Bryson explains that Australia is the most dangerous place on the planet: "If you are not stung or pronged to death in some unexpected manner, you may be fatally chomped by sharks or crocodiles, or carried helplessly out to sea by irresistible currents, or left to stagger to an unhappy death in the baking outback." From its beautiful beaches to its arid deserts, from its cities to its famed Outback, from its kangaroos to its 12-foot earthworms, Bryson depicts the richness of Australia through humorous anecdotes and entertaining accounts.

Subjects: Australian History; Humor

Places: Australia

Now Try: Paul Carter recounts his attempt to circumnavigate Australia in a bio-diesel motorcycle in the maniacally funny *Is That Thing Diesel?* (Carter also wrote *Don't Tell Mom I Work on the Rigs: She Thinks I'm a Piano Player in a Whorehouse,* which is not a travel narrative and has nothing to do with Australia but is too good a title to pass up.) Readers interested in Australia (but not necessarily travel humor) should consider the series of books on Australian cities by leading Australian authors, which the University of New South Wales Press has put together. So far, titles include *Sydney,* by novelist Delia Falconer; *In Search of Hobart,* by freelance writer Peter Timms; and *Brisbane,* by journalist Matthew Condon. Bryson's comprehensive look at Australia is paralleled by Matthew Condon's novel, *The Trout Opera,* which spans 100 years of Australian history and tells the story of a man who plays a part in a failed school play in 1906 and is later selected to be featured at the opening ceremony of the 2000 Olympics in Sydney.

Bryson, Bill

Notes from a Small Island. New York: Morrow, 1996. 324 pp. ISBN: 9780688147259

When Bryson decided in 1994 to move back to his native United States after 20 years in England, he wanted to take one last tour around Great Britain (mostly by public transportation) to bid it farewell. The resulting book moves between the hilarious and the endearing, as Bryson sends up various aspects of British life and history (the Tories, George Orwell, George III, William Wordsworth) while clearly admiring the fortitude of a people who withstood the Blitz: the "British are so easy to please. It is the most extraordinary thing. They actually like their pleasures small." As always, Bryson is very funny and very informative.

Subjects: Architecture; European History; Flashbacks; Humor; Living Abroad

Places: England; Scotland; Wales

Now Try: Denis Lipman is the opposite of Bill Bryson, a native Englishman who lived in Washington, DC, and made an annual trip back to England to visit his aging parents. Then he married an American, and she decided to add sightseeing to his annual pilgrimage home. The result, which Lipman describes in his bittersweet book, *A Yank Back to England: The Prodigal Tourist Returns*, is that he re-discovered his native land. Stuart Maconie is from Wigan, in what is known as "Northern England." After living "down south" in London and the midlands, he returned to his native North to reconnect, an amusing journey that he relates in *Pies and Prejudice: In Search of the North*. Kate Fox's delightfully witty book, *Watching the English: The Hidden Rules of English Behaviour*, is not a travel narrative as such but its insights into British behavior should be enjoyable to travel buffs, especially those who love the British Isles.

Cahill, Tim

Hold the Enlightenment. New York: Villard, 2002. 297 pp. ISBN: 9780375507663

Cahill refers to these 30 humorous essays as "a representative sampling of my life," and they are told in his usual self-deprecating manner. The title essay finds him in Jamaica, trying to learn yoga, and as is typical for Cahill, much of the humor derives from his feeling totally out of place. His other essays cover topics much more adventurous: searching for the endangered Caspian tiger in Iraq, diving into shark-infested waters off South Africa, hunting platypus in Australia, visiting salt mines in Mali during a sand storm. Luckily for the reader, Cahill never fails to find the amusing, even in the most extreme situations.

Subjects: Adventure; Essays; Humor

Places: Africa; Argentina; Australia; Bali; British Columbia; Colombia; Ecuador; Idaho; Iraq; Jamaica; Mali; Montana; Nevada; Republic of the Congo; Rwanda; South Africa; Tanzania; Washington

Series: *Vintage Departures*

Now Try: Jennifer J. Leo collected 35 humorous travel essays in *What Color Is Your Jockstrap?: Funny Men and Women Write from the Road*, including one by Tim Cahill about his boyhood memories of snapping turtles and how they led to a fear of freshwater lakes. Leo also edited *The Thong Also Rises: Further Misadventures from Funny Women on the Road*, which includes essays by women travelers, including one on going to the bathroom with a pig in Thailand and another on attending a nude wedding ceremony in Jamaica. Tim Cahill wrote the introduction to *Hyenas Laughed at Me and Now I Know Why: The Best of Travel Humor and Misadventure*, a collection of essays edited by Sean O'Reilly, Larry Habegger, and James O'Reilly; essay writers include Calvin Trillin, Dave Barry, and Anne Lamott.

Cahill, Tim

Pass the Butterworms: Remote Journeys Oddly Rendered. New York: Villard, 1997. 283 pp. ISBN: 9780679456254 Y A

Cahill shares 24 more stories from his adventures around the world, most of which appeared in *Outside* magazine and most of which are also very funny. He visited recent cannibals in New Guinea, kayaked among the Queen Charlotte Islands off British Columbia, and attended the world spear fishing championship in Peru. In addition to the pieces that feature his typically self-effacing, sometimes corny humor, there are one or two more serious essays, including one in which Cahill accompanies a friend whose son was murdered to the river in Peru where the murder occurred; Cahill tells the story with great skill and even greater sympathy for the father.

Subjects: Adventure; Essays; Humor

Places: Alaska; Arctic Region; Bonaire; British Columbia; Caribbean; Honduras; Indonesia; Mongolia; Montana; New Guinea; Pacific Ocean; Peru; Wyoming

Series: *Vintage Departures*

Now Try: Cahill is also the author of *Pecked to Death by Ducks*, yet another collection of amusing essays about topics as varied as firewalking, diving with sharks, and caving. One of the essays from *Pass the Butterworms* is included in *Testosterone Planet: True Stories from a Man's World*, edited by Sean O'Reilly, Larry Habegger, and James O'Reilly; this collection of 29 humorous essays about men and their adventures includes pieces by Jon Krakauer, Bill Bryson, Sebastian Junger, and others. Another humorous travel writer is Jeff Greenwald, whose *The Size of the World* is annotated in this chapter; a collection of 30 of his earlier essays is *Scratching the Surface: Impressions of Planet Earth from Hollywood to Shiraz*. Other humor authors who have been described, like Cahill, as self-effacing, may be of interest as well. These include Dave Barry (*I'll Mature When I'm Dead: Dave Barry's Amazing Tales of Adulthood* and *Dave Barry's Only Travel Guide You'll Ever Need*), A. J. Jacobs (*The Year of Living Biblically* and *Drop Dead Healthy: One Man's Humble Quest for Bodily Perfection*), and Gerald Durrell (*My Family and Other Animals* and *A Zoo in My Luggage*).

Evans, Polly

Fried Eggs with Chopsticks: One Woman's Hilarious Adventure into a Country and a Culture Not Her Own. New York: Delta Trade Paperbacks, 2006. 300 pp. ISBN: 9780385339933

When Evans read that the Chinese had built enough roads to circle the Earth 16 times, she decided to go see the progress for herself. What she found was a nation still in the middle of that progress, with squawking chickens, pot holes, and bear-infested jungles still a part of life. Evans's solo trip across China by airplane, train, bus, boat, and mule took in Shanghai, Xian, and even the border with Tibet. In spite of the challenges of the trip (little knowledge of the language, loneliness, and a bad cold), Evans clearly enjoyed the trip and writes about it with a gentle sense of humor and a sprinkling of trivia, like the fact that Sinbad the Sailor was based on a Chinese eunuch nicknamed San Bao.

Subjects: Culture Clash; Humor; Memoirs; Multicultural Issues; Solo Travelers; Women Travelers; Women Writers

Places: China; Mongolia

Now Try: Evans has written a number of travel narratives, including *It's Not About the Tapas* (annotated in the "Getting There Is Half the Fun" chapter), and they all feature a tender, sometimes kooky sense of humor. In *Kiwis Might Fly*, Evans traveled by motorcycle around New Zealand, in spite of the fact that she had little biking experience. *On a Hoof and a Prayer: Exploring Argentina at a Gallop* recounts her trip to Argentina to fulfill a childhood dream of learning to ride a horse. In *Mad Dogs and an Englishwoman: Travels with Sled Dogs in Canada's Frozen North*, Evans worked with a dog sled team that ran the famous Yukon Quest race between Fairbanks, Alaska, and Whitehorse, Canada. Humorist Nora Ephron (*I Feel Bad About My Neck: And Other Thoughts On Being a Woman* and *Wallflower at the Orgy*) may also appeal to readers who enjoyed *Fried Eggs with Chopsticks.*

Ferguson, Will

Beauty Tips from Moose Jaw: Travels in Search of Canada. Edinburgh: Canongate, 2005. 342 pp. ISBN: 9781841956312

Ferguson mixes tales from the road and trivia in this hilarious account of his travels in his native Canada. He spent three years going from one end of the country to the other, from Cape Spear on the Nova Scotia coast to Victoria, British Columbia, in the west, from large cities like Montreal and Toronto to smaller sites like Fort Vermilion, Alberta, and L'Anse aux Meadows in Newfoundland. Ferguson sometimes traveled alone and sometimes traveled with his family, but he always traveled with his sense of humor, his love of Canada's rich diversity, and his appreciation of interesting tidbits of history.

Subjects: Canadian History; Essays; Humor; Small Town Life

Places: Alberta; British Columbia; Canada; Manitoba; Newfoundland; Nova Scotia; Ontario; Quebec; Saskatchewan

Now Try: Ferguson's first book was *Why I Hate Canadians,* which skewered various aspects of life in Canada, including politics, culture, and attitudes toward the United States. Will Ferguson and his brother Ian then wrote *How to Be a Canadian,* an hysterical guide to such things as "Canadian Cuisine—and How to Avoid It," "Regional Harmony (Who to Hate and Why)," and "How to Make Love Like a Canadian." John Stackhouse's *Timbit Nation: A Hitchhiker's View of Canada,* like *Beauty Tips from Moose Jaw,* paints a portrait of Canada from its various roadside attractions, historic sites, and seemingly unremarkable towns. Fans of Canadian humor may enjoy DVDs of past episodes of *The Red Green Show,* which parodies various topics, including home improvement, fishing, and outdoor shows.

Geist, Bill

Way Off the Road: Discovering the Peculiar Charms of Small-Town America. New York: Broadway, 2007. 240 pp. ISBN: 9780767922722

Emmy Award-winning CBS correspondent Bill Geist traveled across the United States to gather amusing stories of the country's eccentric sites and offbeat characters. Whether he's meeting a Kansas cook who specializes in roadkill or visiting the cow chip capital of the world (Beaver, Oklahoma), Geist's humor is good natured and focuses on small towns like Nederland, Colorado (which features the Frozen Dead Guy Festival) or Huntsville, Texas (home of the Church of the Holy BBQ).

Subjects: Essays; Humor; Quick Reads; Road Trips; Small Town Life

Places: Alabama; Arizona; California; Colorado; Florida; Illinois; Indiana; Iowa; Kansas; Minnesota; Mississippi; Nebraska; Nevada; North Carolina; Oklahoma; Tennessee; Texas; Wisconsin

Now Try: Geist specializes in short essays about odd characters and quirky places in the United States; another collection of such stories is his *Monster Trucks & Hair In A Can: Who Says America Doesn't Make Anything Anymore?* Another writer who focuses on bizarre small towns, particularly in the Western United States, is Bill Graves, whose *On the Back Roads: Discovering Small Towns of America* features the town farthest from a railroad, the largest producer of soda ash, and other odd superlatives. Bill Bryson also visited small towns along America's back roads in his book, *The Lost Continent: Travels in Small-Town America* (annotated in the chapter entitled "The Journey"), but he has less appreciation for the charm of their quirks than does Geist. Fans of Geist may also enjoy other good-natured books on small-town life in America, such as Bob Greene's wistful *Once Upon a Town: The Miracle of the North Platte Canteen,* about a small town in Nebraska that Greene calls, "The best America there ever was. Or at least, whatever might be left of it."

Hohn, Donovan

Moby-Duck: The True Story of 28,800 Bath Toys Lost at Sea and of the Beachcombers, Oceanographers, Environmentalists, and Fools, Including the Author, Who Went in Search of Them. New York: Viking, 2011. 402 pp. ISBN: 9780670022199

Just as Melville's *Moby Dick* is about more than a white whale, so is Donovan Hohn's *Moby-Duck* about more than bath toys. When Hohn first heard the story of 28,800 rubber ducks lost at sea when a container fell from a ship sailing from China to Seattle, his curiosity got the better of him and he began a search for the ducks, trying to determine where they came from and where they eventually washed up. His quest led him to the shores of Alaska and then to an area of the Pacific Ocean known as "the Great Garbage Patch" and eventually to the Chinese factory where the toys were produced. While the story of the rubber ducks turned out to be somewhat inaccurate in its details, it did provide Hohn with the opportunity to gain and share knowledge in a wide range of areas: the science of oceanic drift, environmental issues, the global economy, and our consumer culture. Hohn's dilatory style and combination of humor and scientific knowledge is a little bit Bill Bryson and a little bit John McPhee.

Subjects: Environmental Writing; Humor; Investigative Stories

Places: Alaska; China; Hawaii; Pacific Ocean; Polar Regions

Awards: *New York Times* Notable Book, 2011

Now Try: Curtis Ebbesmeyer, an oceanographer who traces the ocean's currents through athletic shoes and bathtub toys that have spilled from freighters, has written *Flotsametrics and the Floating World: How One Man's Obsession with Runaway Sneakers and Rubber Ducks Revolutionized Ocean Science* with Eric Scigliano, providing an accessible guide to theories of ocean currents called gyres; like *Moby-Duck*, it is both entertaining and informative. Skye Moody's *Washed Up: The Curious Journeys of Flotsam and Jetsam* also looks at items that wash up on our beaches and how they affect the food chains of marine animals. The toys that were lost at sea in Hohn's book were made of plastic, not rubber, and readers may enjoy Susan Freinkel's micro-history, *Plastic: A Toxic Love Story*, which analyzes our relationships with plastic through eight common items, including the comb, the credit card, and the soda bottle.

Horwitz, Tony

Baghdad Without a Map, and Other Misadventures in Arabia. New York: Dutton, 1991. 276 pp. ISBN: 9780525249603

Horwitz followed his journalist wife, Geraldine Brooks (*Nine Parts of Desire: The Hidden World of Islamic Women*), to Cairo in the late 1980s and spent two years visiting 15 countries, trying to pick up assignments as a freelance journalist himself. He shopped for the local narcotic qat in Yemen, met anti-American protesters in Iran, ate camel's meat in the desert, watched really bad belly dancers in Egypt, and shook hands with lepers in Sudan. His book is wildly funny but serious and empathetic at the same time. While describing both the danger ("Most trips . . . began with a choice between the world's ten most likely to be hijacked airlines") and the hilarious situations into which he fell, Horwitz manages to put a human face on the region as he portrays a people pulled by the traditional forces of religion and the modern forces of globalization.

Subjects: Culture Clash; Islam; Middle Eastern History

Places: Africa; Baghdad; Beirut; Cairo; Egypt; Iran; Iraq; Israel; Lebanon; Libya; South Sudan; Sudan; Tehran; Yemen

Now Try: Horwitz is a shrewd and witty writer, and several of his titles (*A Voyage Long and Strange*, *Confederates in the Attic*, and *Blue Latitudes*) are annotated in this book. Pamela J. Olson tells of her two years in Ramallah, Palestine, where she was an editor for the Palestine *Monitor*, in her book, *Fast Times in Palestine*; like *Baghdad Without a Map*, Olson's book is funny and perceptive. Hugh Pope's *Dining with al-Qaeda: Three Decades Exploring the Many Worlds of the Middle East* is less humorous than either Horwitz or Olson but is equally insightful and based on his 30 years of living and traveling in the Middle East. Fans of Horwitz may find similar humor in the books of Jon Stewart and the other writers of *The Daily Show*, including *Earth: A Visitor's Guide to the Human Race* and *America: A Citizen's Guide to Democracy Inaction*.

Leo, Jennifer L., ed.

Sand In My Bra And Other Misadventures: Funny Women Write From The Road. San Francisco: Travelers' Tales, 2003. 194 pp. ISBN: 9781885211927

Leo has pulled together 28 short, funny stories about misadventures suffered by women travelers as diverse as Anne Lamott, Ellen Degeneres, and Sarah Vowell. Their stories include Nancy Bartlett's well-intentioned but disastrous attempt to wear a *chador* to a Kuwait shopping mall, Joann Jornak's experience of being chased by a herd of African elephants, Annalisa Valentine's story of getting bitten by a goddess-possessed healer in Kathmandu, and Jennifer Leo's own experience nightclubbing with a prude in Bangkok's infamous Patpong sex district.

Subjects: Essays; Humor; Quick Reads; Women Travelers

Places: Africa; Australia; Bangkok; Canada; China; Europe (Various); France; Greece; Hong Kong; Indonesia; Italy; Kenya; Kuwait; Mexico; Nepal; Tahiti; Thailand; United Arab Emirates; United States (Various); Zambia

Now Try: Leo followed up *Sand in My Bra . . .* with several other collections. *More Sand in My Bra: Funny Women Write from the Road, Again!* contains 29 more tales of mishaps and bad trips, including Tamar Shepard's experience on Vietnam's so-called "booze cruise" and Suzanne Schlosberg's visit to a sex camp. *The Thong Also Rises: Further Misadventures from Funny Women on the Road* includes 32 more essays by women travelers, including Jennifer Cox's "Hot Date with a Yogi" and Elizabeth Asdorian's "The Naked and the Wed," about a nude wedding ceremony in Jamaica. Humorous memoirs by other forthright women may also appeal to readers who enjoyed *Sand in My Bra and Other Misadventures*; these include Meghan Daum's *Life would Be Perfect If I Lived In that House* or Jen Lancaster's many memoirs, of which the first was *Bitter Is the New Black: Confessions of a Condescending, Egomaniacal, Self-Centered Smartass, Or, Why You Should Never Carry A Prada Bag to the Unemployment Office.*

Moore, Tim

Travels with My Donkey: One Man and His Ass on a Pilgrimage to Santiago. New York: St. Martin's Press, 2004. 328pp. ISBN: 9780312320829.

There are a number of travel narratives about the spiritual pilgrimage to the Spanish cathedral of Santiago de Compostela (Kerry Egan's *Fumbling* and Kathryn Harrison's *The Road to Santiago* are both annotated in this book), but none is as funny as Moore's book, which he dedicated to his donkey, Shinto. Moore ridicules his fellow pilgrims and himself as he recounts his struggles with the 500-mile trek, the elements, and his stubborn companion. The usual challenges of locating food and lodging along the way were made even more complicated by the fact that he needed to accommodate the donkey. Wedged between his portraits of other travelers and his stories of coaxing Shinto across bridges are sections on the history of the pilgrimage.

Subjects: Animals; Humor; Pilgrimages

Places: France; Spain

Now Try: Moore's *French Revolutions: Cycling the Tour de France,* about his attempt to follow the 2,256-mile route of the Tour de France, even though he hadn't ridden a bicycle since adolescence, is annotated in the "Getting There Is Half the Fun" chapter of this book. Interestingly, *Travels with My Donkey* is not the only comic travel narrative about the Santiago de Compostela pilgrimage. German comedian Hape Kerkeling also tackled the grueling path, in spite of being overweight and badly out of shape; his self-deprecating humor is mixed with a good bit of sincerity and self-discovery in *I'm Off Then: Losing and Finding Myself on the Camino de Santiago.* Kevin O'Hara traveled the 1,800-mile coastline of Ireland with a donkey in *Last of the Donkey Pilgrims* in order to fulfill a promise made to his homesick Irish mother; the resulting book is humorous, whimsical, and touching. Readers may also enjoy the writings of humorists who center their comedy on religious issues, like Lewis Black's *Nothing's Sacred* and *Me of Little Faith* or Christopher Moore's *Lamb: The Gospel According to Biff, Christ's Childhood Pal.*

Queenan, Joe

Queenan Country: A Reluctant Anglophile's Pilgrimage to the Mother Country. New York: Henry Holt, 2004. 240 pp. ISBN: 9780805069808

In 2002, Queenan (an American-born writer with a British wife) traveled solo around Great Britain to capture "the feelings, both positive and negative, that I have developed toward my wife's native land." The result is what the writer himself called "an affectionate jeremiad," filled with wisecracks and observations about the British character. Queenan has his definite likes (British literature, late-night train rides, a nice cup of tea) and dislikes (Andrew Lloyd Webber, Chelsea football supporters, John Lennon) and he is not shy about sharing them. His humor is edgy and merciless but he mixes his comments with historical bits (visits to Hadrian's Wall or the Durham Cathedral) that are quite informative.

Subjects: Culture Clash; Humor; Society; Solo Travelers

Places: England

Now Try: Queenan has written several books, and readers who enjoy the sharp humor of *Queenan Country* may also enjoy *My Goodness: A Cynic's Short-Lived Search for Sainthood,* which describes his attempt to atone for his former sins and become a "Very Good Person." Another American, J. R. Daeschner, writes about England and, in particular, its curious rituals in *True Brits: A Tour of Great Britain in All its Bog-Snorkelling, Shin-Kicking, and Cheese-Rolling Glory;* among the events described are the Cooper's Hill Cheese Roll, the shin-kicking contests from the Cotswold Olimpicks, and the Abbots Bromley Horn Dance, designed to promote fertility. In the early part of the 20th century, the Canadian Stephen Leacock was the best-known humorist in the English-speaking world. His books, which can be difficult to locate, include *My Discovery of England,* which was written in the 1920s. Another humorous book that looks at the British character is A. A. Gill's witty tirade, *The Angry Island: Hunting the English.*

Troost, J. Marteen

Getting Stoned With Savages: A Trip through the Islands of Fiji and Vanuatu. New York: Broadway, 2006. 239 pp. ISBN: 9780767921992

As in *The Sex Lives of Cannibals* (annotated below), Troost and his wife moved to another pair of South Pacific island nations (Fiji and Vanuatu, in this case) and while she worked for a nonprofit, Troost explored the cultures of the islands. Again, Troost found that the islands weren't exactly paradise and presented a range of challenges, including volcanic tremors, cyclones, shark-infested waters, aggressive prostitutes, and the local intoxicant, *kava*. Troost integrates the history of the area into his amusing narrative and also considers heavier topics, such as his responsibilities as a new father after his son was born on Fiji.

Subjects: Culture Clash; Drugs; Humor; Islands; Society; Spouses

Places: Fiji; Melanesia; Vanuatu

Now Try: In *Solomon Time: An Unlikely Quest in the South Pacific,* Will Randall tells of his decision to leave teaching, go to the Solomon Islands, and set up a project to improve the lives of the islanders; his story is told with a sweet humor and charm. Michael Moran explores the relatively unknown Melanesian islands of the Coral, Solomon, and Bismarck Seas in *Beyond the Coral Sea: Travels in the Old Empires of the South-West Pacific;* he writes with a dry sense of humor, particularly about historical figures like anthropologist Bronislaw Malinowski. Dave Hart's *Solomon Boy: An Island Journal,* about his stay in a rural village in the Solomon Islands, is not primarily travel humor, but some of the incidents described by the author (eating bat meat and the legs of the rhinoceros beetle) are amusing. Fans of Troost may also enjoy humorist Chuck Klosterman, particularly *Sex, Drugs, and Cocoa Puffs: A Low Culture Manifesto,* which covers topics as diverse as the television show, *Saved by the Bell,* and the Celtics–Lakers rivalry, and the equally scattershot *Eating the Dinosaur.*

Troost, J. Maarten

Lost on Planet China: The Strange and True Story of One Man's Attempt to Understand the World's Most Mystifying Nation . . . New York: Broadway Books, 2008. 382 pp. ISBN: 9780767922005

Troost thought about moving with his family of four to China (a country that he terms "the new wild west") and set out on something of a reconnaissance trip across that country, from the cities of Shanghai and Beijing to the less urban Gobi Desert and Tibetan border. Troost recounts his adventures (dodging drivers in Shanghai, eating yak in Tibet, and seeing Chairman Mao's tomb) and does his best to convince the reader that China remains a largely unknown and often overwhelming world unto itself. Troost writes with his characteristic blunt humor mixed with informative side tracks.

Subjects: Culture Clash; Humor; Society; Spouses

Places: Beijing; China; Shanghai

Now Try: One reviewer said of Jason Barbacovi's *Me and Chairman Mao,* "If David Sedaris lived in China, this is the book he would write." Barbacovi takes a sarcastic, irreverent look at various aspects of life in China based on his six-month tour of the country. Dean Barrett searched China for a utopia that had been described by a 4th-century Chinese poet; his experiences are detailed in the very funny *Don Quixote in China: The Search for Peach Blossom Spring*. James Fallows and his wife moved to China in 2006, where he observed the country's emergence as a powerful player in the world economy; his book, *Postcards from Tomorrow Square: Reports from China,* is not humorous but is extremely perceptive.

Troost, J. Marteen

The Sex Lives of Cannibals: Adrift in the Equatorial Pacific. New York: Broadway, 2004. 272 pp. ISBN: 9780767915304

The first of Troost's travel narratives, *The Sex Lives of Cannibals* recounts the two years he and his wife spent on Kiribati, a tiny island nation in the South Pacific. Troost describes the colorful characters and bizarre situations he encountered on what he first thought would be an island paradise but soon realized lacked any real food except fish, suffered from extreme heat and toxic water, and was governed by what he termed "coconut Stalinism." Mixed in with the sharp humor are Troost's occasional rants against foreign aid workers who ignore local culture and the real needs of the islanders, as well as Americans who are ignorant of their own history, in this case, the many lives lost in the World War II Battle of Tarawa.

Subjects: Culture Clash; Humor; Islands; Society

Places: Kiribati; Micronesia

Now Try: Larry McMurtry's *Paradise* describes that writer's trip to Tahiti and the Marquesas in the early 2000s; McMurtry, like Troost, was out of his element (traveling with "island junkies" with whom he had little in common, running out of reading material) but writes about the experience with a gentle sense of humor and reflections on his parents. In *Surviving Paradise: One Year on a Disappearing Island*, Peter Rudiak-Gould recounts his year as a teacher on one of the Marshall Islands, a part of Micronesia. *Micronesian Blues: The Adventures of an American Cop in Paradise* by Bryan Vila and Cynthia Morris tells of Vila's six years training law enforcement personnel in Micronesia; his expectations of working and living in paradise were, like Troost's, quickly dashed. Arthur Grimble's classic memoir, *A Pattern of Islands*, was originally published in 1952 but has recently been re-published; it tells about Grimble's time in the Gilbert and Ellice Islands (now Kiribati and Tuvalu) in the 1920s, including an episode when he was used as bait for a giant octopus.

Waite, Terry

Travels with A Primate: Around the World with an Archbishop. London: HarperCollins, 2000. 240 pp. ISBN: 9780007106325

In the early 1980s, prior to his four-year captivity in Lebanon, Waite served as an assistant to the Archbishop of Canterbury. *Travels with a Primate* is a humorous account of their travels around the world. Waite describes many of the funnier moments (the Archbishop was nearly suffocated in a homemade "Popemobile" in rural Canada and was gripped a bit too tightly by a koala bear during a photo shot in Australia) and does so with understatement and obvious affection for the Archbishop.

Subjects: Christianity; Humor; Religion

Places: Africa (Various); Alaska; Australia; China; England; New York City; Scotland

Now Try: Jerry Ellis's *Walking to Canterbury: A Modern Journey Through Chaucer's Medieval England* provides a fascinating look at the author's walk from London to Canterbury along the pilgrims' path and his description of the history of that pilgrimage. Robert Hutchinson's *When in Rome*, about his visits to the Vatican, is an irreverent and informative look at "the spiritual and political center" of another branch of the Christian church; it is annotated in the "Expatriate Life" chapter of this book. Waite's autobiographical *Taken on Trust* (which was "written" in his head while he was a hostage in Lebanon) and *Footfalls in Memory* (reflections on the books that he read while in captivity) are not travel narratives nor humor, but they provide a fascinating look at Waite and what he endured.

Crazy Ideas

Some accounts of travel are funny from the get go, and these make up the category called "Crazy Ideas." After all, how could Tony Hawks's plan to hitchhike around the perimeter of Ireland in a month with a refrigerator by his side (*Round Ireland with a Fridge*) be anything but hilarious? How could Pete McCarthy's meanderings around Ireland (*McCarthy's Bar: A Journey of Discovery in the West of Ireland*) fail to amuse when he starts with a travel rule that states, "Never Pass a Bar That Has Your Name On It"?

As with the titles in the previous category, the reader will find many kinds of humor in these narratives, and readers' advisors may need to make some fine distinctions between readers who will enjoy the grumpy humor of Griff Rhys Jones, who sails to St. Petersburg with two other inept sailors (*To the Baltic with Bob: An Epic Misadventure*), those who will enjoy instead the offbeat humor of Eric Nuzum as he travels through the world of vampires (*The Dead Travel Fast: Stalking Vampires from Nosferatu to Count Chocula*), and those who will be better served by the gentle humor of Brad Newsham as he searches for someone to invite to the United States, all expenses paid (*Take Me With You: A Round-The-World Journey to Invite a Stranger Home*).

Readers who are drawn to the "Crazy Ideas" titles may also enjoy other humorous titles that do not involve travel, particularly "stunt memoirs" like Danny Wallace's *Yes Man* or Noelle Hancock's *My Year with Eleanor* and fiction like Michael Chabon's *Wonder Boys* or Douglas Adams's *Hitchhiker's Guide to the Galaxy.*

Cox, Jennifer

Around the World in 80 Dates. New York: Downtown, 2005. 374 pp. ISBN: 9781416513155

After her boyfriend broke up with her, Cox, the head of public relations for Lonely Planet, decided to date her way around the planet, visiting 18 countries in six months in search of Mr. Right. She met "Skate Date" in Paris, "High Roller" in Las Vegas, "Love Professor" in Sweden, "Dead Date" in Italy, and "Penguin Ranger" in Australia, among others, and her dates ranged from the reasonably good to the hilarious to the awkward to the downright scary. Along with observations about the countries she visited, Cox also discusses international dating habits and offers her opinions on which nation's men are the best dates: Americans, because they don't jump so quickly from date to marriage. Her tale is told with a fresh sense of humor and includes Cox's reflections on what it means to find a soul mate.

Subjects: Circumnavigations; Humor; Love and Dating; Women Travelers

Places: Amsterdam; Athens; Australia; Bangkok; Barcelona; Beijing; Berlin; China; Copenhagen; Denmark; England; France; Germany; Greece; Italy; Japan; Las Vegas;

Lisbon; London; Los Angeles; Malaysia; Netherlands; New Zealand; Paris; Portugal; San Francisco; Seattle; Spain; Stockholm; Sweden; Thailand; Tokyo; United States

Now Try: Like Cox, a break-up with her boyfriend led Karen Wheeler to travel; unlike Cox, she settled down in one country (France) and describes her new life, complete with a new romance or two, in the charming and funny *Tout Sweet: Hanging Up My High Heels for a New Life in France*. Elisabeth Eaves's *Wanderlust: A Love Affair with Five Continents*, which describes her travels across five continents, also looks at her search for romance and her growing understanding that she does better with long-distance relationships than with traditional ones. Maria Dahvana Headley spent two years trying to find the right mate in New York City before she decided that she was too picky and resolved to say "Yes" to anyone who asked her out; her year of dating everyone from her apartment building's maintenance man to a homeless man (*The Year of Yes*) isn't travel, but it is a humorous look at dating.

Deck, Jeff, and Benjamin D. Herson

The Great Typo Hunt: Two Friends Changing the World, One Correction at a Time. New York: Crown, 2010. 269 pp. ISBN: 9780307591074

Deck, an associate editor in Washington, DC, and Herson, a book seller, traveled across the United States and parts of Canada, correcting spelling and grammatical mistakes in road signs, restaurant menus, and other signage: things like the misspelled "Oak Lawn Cemetary" sign or the misplaced apostrophe in "The Johnson's" house sign. During their ten-week tour, the pair found 437 typos and corrected 236 of them, speculating along the way about the decline in education and the importance of literacy. They also landed in federal court after they corrected a 1932 hand-painted sign at the Grand Canyon that the prosecutor described as "a priceless historic artifact," and of course the court documents in *United States of America v. Jeff Deck and Benjamin Herson* were filled with typos. In spite of their legal run-in, the pair maintained a sense of humor throughout their quest for proper punctuation.

Subjects: Friendships; Grammar; Humor; Road Trips

Places: Alabama; Arizona; California; British Columbia; Canada; Georgia; Idaho; Illinois; Indiana; Kentucky; Louisiana; Maryland; Massachusetts; Minnesota; New Hampshire; New Mexico; New York; North Carolina; Ohio; South Carolina; South Dakota; Texas; Wisconsin

Now Try: Fans of proper punctuation will also enjoy Bethany Keeley's *The Book of "Unnecessary" Quotation Marks: A Celebration of Creative Punctuation*, which includes photos of the offending signs and Keeley's witty retorts. Lynne Truss's popular humor title *Eats, Shoots, and Leaves: The Zero Tolerance Approach to Punctuation* might also appeal. Jen Yates's *Cake Wrecks: When Professional Cakes Go Hilariously Wrong* is similar, although the focus is on cakes instead of signs; as one might imagine, cake mistakes aren't limited to punctuation.

Two other travel narratives with a focus on language are Dianne Hales's *La Bella Lingua: My Love Affair with Italian, the World's Most Enchanting Language,* which describes her journey to Italy to learn the language and celebrates that language, and Katherine Russell Rich's *Dreaming in Hindi,* which tells of her immersion in the language and the culture of India. Readers who are interested in these aspects of language may also be fascinated by Simon Loxley's history of fonts, *Type: The Secret History of Letters,* as well as the 2007 documentary film, *Helvetica.*

Ferguson, Will

Hokkaido Highway Blues: Hitchhiking Japan. New York: Soho Press, 1998. 433 pp. ISBN: 9781569471333

Ferguson, the author of such works of travel humor as *Beauty Tips from Moose Jaw* (annotated in this chapter), was teaching English in Japan when he decided to hitchhike the country (from Cape Sata in the south to Cape Soya in the north) in order to see Japan "not as a spectator, but as a participant." His 2,000-mile trip began in the tropics and ended in a snowstorm, and his observations range from the poetic to the amusing and even profane. Among the targets of his humor are the food, the Japanese fascination with pornography, and their butchering of the English language.

Subjects: Culture Clash; Humor; Walking

Places: Japan

Now Try: Ferguson followed the path taken by Alan Booth in the classic work, *The Roads to Sata* (annotated in "Getting There Is Half the Fun"), although Ferguson walked from south to north, the opposite direction of Booth; Ferguson also took himself much less seriously than did Booth. During his journey, the Canadian-born Ferguson was often mistaken for an American, something that may not have irritated him, given his first book, *Why I Hate Canadians,* a hilarious examination of the foibles of Canada's citizens. Ferguson is also the author of *Beyond Belfast: A 560-Mile Walk Across Northern Ireland on Sore Feet,* which describes his walk around the perimeter of Northern Island and which won the Stephen Leacock Memorial Medal for Humour in 2010.

Greenwald, Jeff

The Size of the World: Once Around Without Leaving the Ground. Old Saybrook, CT: Globe Pequot Press, 1995. 420 pp. ISBN: 9781564406231

Greenwald had traveled extensively by the time he approached his 40th birthday, but most of that travel had been by airplane, and Greenwald was concerned that airplanes had taken away from the joy of traveling. So he set out to circle the globe without leaving its surface. What began as a simple enough premise soon turned into a remarkable and often hilarious nine-month journey that included scaling an active volcano in Guatemala, riding a raft across the Persian Gulf, saving a baby snow leopard in Tibet, and spending his 40th birthday stuck in the middle of the Sahara. As one reviewer put it, "Phileas Fogg meets Woody Allen."

Subjects: Adventure; Circumnavigations; Deserts; Humor; Mountains

Places: Africa; Guatemala; Morocco; Nepal; Tibet

Now Try: Greenwald is the author of several humorous travel narratives. The first, *Mister Raja's Neighborhood: Letters from Nepal,* recounts his trip to Kathmandu to write a novel only to find writer's block in another country. The second, *Shopping for Buddhas,* provides more tales of his trips to Nepal and also offers more serious insights into Nepalese culture. His latest book, *Snake Lake,* is also about Nepal but is more serious, as Greenwald was torn between witnessing that country's revolution and returning to the United States to help his brother, who was sinking into depression.

Hawks, Tony

Playing the Moldovans at Tennis. New York: Thomas Dunne Books, 2001 [2000]. 248 pp. ISBN: 9780312280109

This is another funny book about another insane bet by Tony Hawks, which began when Hawks and a friend were watching England shut out Moldova in soccer. Hawks, a former junior tennis champion, wagered that he could track down the starting 11 Moldovan players and beat them all at tennis or else strip naked and sing the Moldovan national anthem in public. Needless to say, Hawks traveled to Moldova, with side trips to Northern Ireland and Israel (where one player had been traded), and ran up against bureaucracy, diplomacy, and the language barrier in his attempt to make good on the bet. At its best, *Playing the Moldovans at Tennis* can make a reader laugh out loud and gasp for air.

Subjects: Humor; Sports

Places: Israel; Moldova; Northern Ireland

Awards: Samuel Johnson Prize, Shortlist, 2000

Now Try: Elijah Wald has a standing bet that he can hitch across the United States faster than a bus can travel; his book *Riding with Strangers: A Hitchhiker's Journey* provides ample evidence that he could win that bet. Tony Hawks is also a singer, one of whose songs was a top-20 hit in Albania; his absurdly funny *One Hit Wonderland* recounts his travels to Nashville, Africa, and Albania to find the right sound. Moldova is not a country featured in many travel narratives, but Stephen Henighan's *Lost Province* does recount his experiences as an English man in Moldova and especially his interactions with his host family.

Hawks, Tony

Round Ireland with a Fridge. New York: Thomas Dunne Books, 2000 [1998]. 247pp. ISBN: 9780312242367

TV comedian Hawks made a drunken bet that he could hitchhike around the perimeter of Ireland in one calendar month with a small refrigerator. One of the results is this hilarious book, which recounts his travels, the local people he met along the way, and the national radio show that began covering his trip and made him a celebrity. An easy, entertaining read, *Round Ireland with a Fridge* is as much a tribute to the good-natured people of Ireland as it is an uproarious book based on a goofy idea.

Subjects: Community Life; Quick Reads; Walking

Places: Ireland

Now Try: Hawks is apparently an impulsive individual, and this trait led him to buy a house in the Pyrenees, where he planned to master the piano. The story of this adventure is told in sidesplitting fashion in *A Piano in the Pyrenees: The Ups and Downs of an Englishman in the French Mountains*. Dave Gorman's whimsical *Are You Dave Gorman?* is the result of another drunken bet; in this case, Gorman and his friend Danny Wallace travel 24,000 miles to meet all of the Dave Gormans in the world. In *Shakespeare My Butt!: From Marsupial Elvis to No Place . . . on the Trail of the Pointless Quest,* John Donoghue decides to visit some of the more bizarrely named places in England; while a drunken bet is not involved, the premise is still humorous. Titles like *Round Ireland with a Fridge* have been dubbed "stunt memoirs"; another of these is Danny Wallace's *Yes Man,* in which the author decides to say "Yes" to anything that anyone asks of him.

McCarthy, Pete

McCarthy's Bar: A Journey of Discovery in the West of Ireland. New York: St. Martin's Press, 2000 (2001). 320 pages. ISBN: 9780312272104

McCarthy's meanderings around Ireland hinged on a number of travel rules, including "Never Pass a Bar That Has Your Name On It," "Never Eat in a Restaurant with Laminated Menus," and "Never Bang on About How Wonderful Some Unspoiled Place is, Because Next Time You Go There, You Won't be Able to Get In." McCarthy was born and raised in England, but his mother was Irish, and much of the motivation for his journey was his sense that he belonged more to Ireland than to the country of his birth. His humor in wicked and often sacrilegious ("God works in mysterious ways, especially after a few drinks"), but his love of Ireland and its people is undeniable.

Subjects: Humor; Memoirs; Road Trips

Categories: In Search of an Idea; "The Past Is a Foreign Country"

Places: Ireland

Now Try: Readers who want more Ireland have an embarrassment of riches from which to choose: everything from history (Thomas Cahill's excellent *How the Irish Saved Civilization*) to memoirs (Frank McCourt's unforgettable *Angela's Ashes*) to fiction (James Joyce's coming-of-age story, *A Portrait of the Artist as a Young Man*). In his book, McCarthy mentions the films *Ryan's Daughter* and *The Quiet Man,* both of which were filmed in parts of Ireland that he visited; these and other films about Ireland (*Waking Ned Devine* and *The Secret of Roan Inish* are just two of many) may also be of interest to readers who can't get enough of the Emerald Isle.

McCarthy, Pete

The Road to McCarthy: Around The World In Search of Ireland. London, New York: Fourth Estate, 2004. 368 pp. ISBN: 9780007162123

McCarthy traveled the world in search of what it means to be a McCarthy and, by extension, what it means to be Irish. With his wonderful ear for conversation and his eye for the odd and peculiar, McCarthy wandered to destinations as diverse as Dublin; Tasmania; New York City; Butte, Montana (according to the census, "the most predominantly Irish city in the US"); McCarthy, Alaska; and Morocco, where he found the head of the McCarthy clan. McCarthy is particular funny when he highlights the differences between America and England ("Why do American showers knock you over, while ours have all the oomph of a dolly's watering can?") and even waxes philosophical on occasion ("In a world that lives increasingly in the moment, it's important to remember where we've come from, or we may wake up one morning unable to remember who we are.").

Subjects: Family Relationships; Humor

Places: Africa; Alaska; Australia; Caribbean; Ireland; Montana; Morocco; New York City

Now Try: Another amusing Irish pilgrimage is described by Australian Evan McHugh, whose *Pint-Sized Ireland: In Search of the Perfect Guinness* tells of his search for the best pint of Guinness on the island. David Monagan returned to his roots in Cork, Ireland, and wrote about the experience (particularly the contrast between the Ireland of the present and that of his memory) in *Jaywalking with the Irish*. Monagan then explored his adopted country and its recent fall from financial grace in the more matter-of-fact but still delightful *Ireland Unhinged: Encounters with a Wildly Changing Country*.

Melville, Greg

Greasy Rider: Two Dudes, One Fry-Oil-Powered Car, and a Cross-Country Search for a Greener Future. Chapel Hill, NC: Algonquin Books, 2008. 257 pp. ISBN: 9781565125957

The subtitle says it all. Journalist Melville and his college friend Iggy drove from Vermont to California in a 1985 Mercedes retooled to run on vegetable oil that the two begged from restaurants along the way. Why? To prove that it's possible to drive coast to coast without paying a cent for fossil fuel. The description of the trip itself and the often strained interactions between the two men is funny enough, but even more entertaining are the side trips the pair took (to Al Gore's Tennessee mansion, to Google's solar-powered headquarters, to a wind turbine farm, to a supposedly green Wal-Mart) and the reflections on the future of alternative fuels that these provoke. The book is both funny and thought provoking.

Subjects: Alternative Fuels; Automobiles; Friendships; Road Trips

Places: California; Colorado; Illinois; Indiana; Iowa; Minnesota; Nebraska; Nevada; New York; Ohio; Pennsylvania; South Dakota; Utah; Vermont; Wisconsin; Wyoming

Now Try: Melville and Iggy roughly follow the route taken by Horatio Nelson Jackson, who drove across the United States in 1903, a trip described by Dayton Duncan and Ken Burns in *Horatio's Drive: America's First Road Trip*, which is annotated in the "Getting There Is Half the Fun" chapter of this book. While Doug Fine's *Farewell, My Subaru: An Epic Adventure in Local Living*, is not a travel narrative, it is a wonderfully funny story about a man who replaces his Subaru with a truck powered by vegetable oil after he moves to a ranch in New Mexico and tries to become as green as possible. In Ben Bova's novel *The Green Trap*, the brother of a murdered microbiologist travels from California to Cambridge, Massachusetts, to solve his brother's murder and publicize his discovery of a cheap, safe way to produce hydrogen fuel.

Newsham, Brad

Take Me With You: A Round-The-World Journey to Invite a Stranger Home. San Francisco: Travelers' Tales, 2000. 350 pp. ISBN: 9781885211514

In 1974, when Brad Newsham was 22 years old and traveling in Afghanistan, he wrote a promise in his diary: "Someday, when I am rich, I am going to invite someone from my travels to visit me in America." A dozen years later, Newsham had become a Yellow Cab driver, far from rich, but still committed to his promise. So he took a three-month trip around the world to ask someone who had never left his native country to come to the United States, all expenses paid. Newsham's gentle sense of humor not only underlies the telling of the story, it also allowed him to easily make friends and find out about their dreams and wishes. *Take Me With You* is a beautiful book that reminds us of our shared humanity.

Subjects: Friendships; Humor

Places: Africa; California; Egypt; India; Kenya; Philippines; South Africa; Tanzania; Zambia; Zimbabwe

Now Try: Newsham also wrote *All the Right Places: Traveling Light Through Japan, China, and Russia*, about his travels through those countries following his failed marriage; it is written with the same gentle humor as *Take Me With You*. Tanya Shaffer describes her volunteer efforts to do good in West Africa and the deep personal relationships that she was able to establish in *Somebody's Heart Is Burning: A Woman Wanderer in Africa*. Will Randall also sought to do good by saving a slum school in the Indian city of Poona, an experience described in his poignant and funny book, *Indian Summer: A Good Man in Asia*. Peter Lovenheim's thought-provoking *In the Neighborhood: The Search for Community on an American Street, One Sleepover at a Time* tells about one man's quest to become more informed about and involved with his neighbors and community.

Nuzum, Eric

The Dead Travel Fast: Stalking Vampires from Nosferatu to Count Chocula. New York: Thomas Dunne Books/St. Martin's Press, 2007. 242 pp. ISBN: 9780312371111 YA

Nuzum went on a hilarious quest for vampires, trying to figure out in particular why they have become so popular in our culture. His travels took him to Transylvania on a tour hosted by the actor who played Eddie Munster, to Las Vegas's only topless vampire review, to Goth clubs, and to haunted houses. He slept in a coffin and even drank his own blood, all in an attempt to better understand the vampire phenomenon. From Bram Stoker to Buffy the Vampire Slayer, Nuzum examines this offbeat world with an even more offbeat sense of humor.

Subjects: Humor; Vampires

Places: California; England; Oregon; Romania; San Francisco

Now Try: Paul Bibeau also traveled to Romania to get a better understanding of the history behind the vampire myth in his hilarious combination of travel narrative and cultural investigation, *Sundays with Vlad: From Pennsylvania to Transylvania, One Man's Quest to Live in the World of the Undead.* In *It Started with Dracula: The Count, My Mother, and Me,* author Jane Congdon visited Bucharest, the Carpathian Mountains, and the Black Sea, following in the footsteps of Dracula; she also revisited and healed the scars of her childhood with an alcoholic mother. Nina Auerbach's *Our Vampires, Ourselves* is a thoughtful examination of vampires in our literature and culture, from Byron to Anne Rice; Auerbach sees vampires as a reflection of each era's social and political values.

Pollack, John

Cork Boat: A True Story of the Unlikeliest Boat Ever Built. New York: Pantheon Books, 2004. 291 pp. ISBN: 9780375422577 YA

Washington speechwriter Pollack fulfilled a childhood dream by building a boat entirely of wine corks and floating it down the Douro River in Portugal. His story, which is told with charm and a disarming sense of humor, recounts the many obstacles he overcame: convincing bartenders, Navy stewards, and White House staffers to collect corks for him, gathering over 15,000 rubber bands to hold the corks together, finding a brilliant but disorganized partner, and managing over 100 volunteers as they assembled the boat from over 165,000 corks. Pollack also discusses the history of corks and rubber bands, the importance of pursuing one's childhood dreams, and the maiden voyage of his unique boat in Portugal, where he became a national celebrity. As one reviewer put it, "Pollack's absurd quest seems not merely charming but heroic."

Subjects: Boating; Government; Rivers

Places: Portugal; Washington, DC

Now Try: Pollack was realizing a childhood dream with his boat; poet Gwyneth Lewis was following the advice of a tarot card reader when she decided, with her husband, to set sail for Brazil, a less than smooth journey that is recounted in *Two in a Boat: The True Story of a Marital Rite of Passage*. Douglas Whynott's *A Unit of Water, A Unit of Time: Joel White's Last Boat* may appeal to readers who enjoyed the boat building and human interest aspects of *Cork Boat*; it tells the inspiring story of Maine boat builder Joel White (son of E. B. White), who pursued his dream of designing and building wooden boats, even while he was dying of lung cancer.

Rhys Jones, Griff

To the Baltic with Bob: An Epic Misadventure. London: Michael Joseph, 2003. 403 pp. ISBN: 9780718146252

Comedian Griff Rhys Jones pursued his obsession with the nautical by purchasing an old 45-foot yacht and sailing with two friends to St. Petersburg. The book is funny in a grumpy but self-deprecating way and focuses on the many disagreements between the friends: Griff is a stickler for keeping the boat neat and tidy, all three men seem to be suffering midlife crises, and all are inept as sailors. There are also amusing observations about the people they met in the various towns in which they docked, particularly the contrast between the practical and modest Scandinavians and the more pompous British and Russians.

Subjects: Humor; Men's Friendships; Sailing

Places: Denmark; England; Finland; Latvia; Netherlands; Russia

Now Try: Rhys Jones has also written an engaging tour of Britain's rivers, *Rivers: One Man and His Dog Paddle into the Heart of Britain*, and a rather amusing autobiography, *Semi-Detached*, in which he describes his suburban childhood and loving parents in great detail. Farley Mowat's *The Boat Who Wouldn't Float* is another humorous tale of sailing; his plan to purchase a boat and sail the seas was grounded when the boat he purchased leaked like a sieve. Gregory Jaynes dealt with his midlife crisis by booking passage on a cargo ship bound for the South Pacific; the story of his potentially gloomy journey aboard an icebreaker with inedible food and a surly Russian crew that could speak little English is told with a delightful sense of humor in *Come Hell or High Water: A Really Sullen Memoir*. For a collection of amusing short tales of yachting, readers may enjoy *Chasing the Horizon: "The Life and Times of a Modern Sea Gypsy"* by the curiously named Cap'n Fatty Goodlander. Few novels are funnier than Jerome K. Jerome's *Three Men in a Boat*, the hilarious account of a boating holiday on the Thames; in 2009, it was ranked by *Esquire* as # 2 on that magazine's list of the 50 funniest books ever.

South, Mary

The Cure for Anything Is Salt Water: How I Threw My Life Overboard and Found Happiness at Sea. New York: HarperCollins, 2007. 211 pp. ISBN: 9780060747022

Mary South, a successful 40-something book editor, decided to deal with her midlife crisis by quitting her well-paying job, purchasing a 40-foot trawler (without knowing how to pilot it), taking a nine-week course in seamanship, and sailing it up the Atlantic coast from Florida to Maine. Her trip up the coast, accompanied by another student from her seamanship class and a novice, is interspersed with flashbacks that explain how she quit her job and got where she was. South also shares her thoughts on previous relationships, sexual identity, and family issues as well as the therapy that her voyage provided. The book is a witty and engaging testimonial to the power of pursuing one's dreams.

Subjects: Family Relationships; Humor; Memoirs; Sailing; Self-Discovery

Places: Atlantic Ocean; Florida; Georgia; Maine; New York; North Carolina; South Carolina; Virginia

Now Try: Gwendolyn Bounds gave up her *Wall Street Journal* position after the September 11 attacks and got away from it all by moving to a small town north of New York City and joining the regulars at a small Irish bar there, a journey she recounts in *Little Chapel on the River: A Pub, a Town and the Search for What Matters Most*. Linda Greenlaw, who was the captain on the sister ship of the *Andrea Gail* (of *The Perfect Storm* fame), gave up swordfishing and returned to her parents' home off the coast of Maine; she tells about her new life, fishing for lobster, in *The Lobster Chronicles: Life On a Very Small Island*.

Stewart, Chris

Three Ways to Capsize a Boat: An Optimist Afloat. New York: Broadway, 2010. 178 pp. ISBN: 9780307592378

Stewart, the original drummer for the rock band Genesis, also spent one summer as the skipper of a yacht in the Greek Islands. A friend offered him the job, and he accepted, in spite of the fact that he had never sailed before and didn't really know where to start. The hilarious adventures that ensued included finding the yacht in disrepair, getting seasick, setting the yacht on fire, and capsizing it. In spite of these problems, Stewart followed his experience in the Greek Islands by sailing across the Atlantic Ocean in a re-creation of Leif Eriksson's original route to Vinland. There is a good bit of nautical terminology in *Three Ways to Capsize a Boat*, but the book is otherwise hilarious, entertaining, and quite well written.

Subjects: Humor; Islands; Oceans; Quick Reads; Sailing; Seas

Places: Atlantic Ocean; Greece; Mediterranean Sea

Now Try: Stewart is also the author of three very funny titles about his life on a Spanish farm (*Driving Over Lemons*, *A Parrot in the Pepper Tree*, and *The Almond Blossom Appreciation Society*) the first of which is annotated in the chapter titled "The Expatriate Life." Damian Horner and his wife Siobhan Horner left their London lives and explored the canals of France on a small boat with their two children; they tell their story in the very funny book, *For Better For Worse:*

One Family, One Boat, and One Brand New Life. Hal Roth and his wife sailed a small boat along the Turkish coast and among the Greek Islands, following the path taken by Odysseus, in *We Followed Odysseus;* the book tells both the story of their voyage and that of the hero of *The Odyssey.*

Stiller, Eric

Keep Australia on Your Left: A True Story of an Attempt to Circumnavigate Australia by Kayak. New York: Forge, 2000. 411 pp. ISBN: 9780312874582

Stiller was a kayak salesman in New York who joined an Australian male model in an attempt to paddle around the 10,000-mile perimeter of Australia in a kayak. Stiller describes the many challenges of the journey, from the natural (12-foot waves, heavy rains, crocodiles, and sharks) to the psychological (sheer tedium, exhaustion, and his partner's disregard for preparation and planning). *Keep Australia on Your Left* is a book that divided reviewers: some loved the book for its honest portrayal of the challenges Stiller and his partner encountered, and some hated it for what many described as its whiny tone.

Subjects: Humor; Friendships; Kayaking; Oceans

Places: Australia

Now Try: Two books by Chris Duff also describe attempts to circumnavigate large islands. *On Celtic Tides: One Man's Journey Around Ireland by Sea Kayak* describes Duff's 1,200-mile journey around the Emerald Isle, and *Southern Exposure: A Solo Sea Kayaking Journey Around New Zealand's South Island* tells of his 1,700-mile journey around the larger but less populous South Island of New Zealand. Joe Glickman tells the story of Freya Hoffmeister, a 46-year-old woman who circumnavigated Australia alone in a sea kayak, in *Fearless: One Woman, One Kayak, One Continent.* A more reflective kayak narrative is Victoria Jason's *Kabloona in the Yellow Kayak: One Woman's Journey Through the North West Passage,* which recounts the 4,660-mile journey taken by a grandmother of two who was recovering from a stroke.

Consider Starting With . . .

Bryson, Bill. *In a Sunburned Country.*
Evans, Polly. *Fried Eggs with Chopsticks: One Woman's Hilarious Adventure into a Country and a Culture Not Her Own.*
Hawks, Tony. *Round Ireland with a Fridge.*
McCarthy, Pete. *McCarthy's Bar: A Journey of Discovery in the West of Ireland.*
Newby, Eric. *A Short Walk in the Hindu Kush.*
Twain, Mark. *The Innocents Abroad.*

Fiction Read-Alikes

Dennis, Patrick. Dennis gave the world one of its great fictional characters, his deceased father's eccentric sister, Mame. His 1955 novel, ***Auntie Mame: An Irreverent***

Escapade, introduces her when the 10-year-old narrator (Patrick) is sent to live with her following the death of his parents. In the sequel, ***Around the World With Auntie Mame***, Patrick graduates from prep school and is taken by Mame on a pre-college trip around the world, one that includes adventures in Paris, London, Venice, Russia, and the high seas. Both novels have aged well and are still delightfully hilarious.

Jerome, Jerome K. There are few travel novels (in fact, few novels of any genre) funnier than Jerome's ***Three Men in a Boat*** and its sequel, ***Three Men on the Bummel***. The former is a hilarious account of a boating holiday on the Thames; although published in 1889, the novel's humor is still fresh. In 2009, it was ranked by *Esquire* as # 2 on that magazine's list of the 50 funniest books ever. The sequel involves the same three characters on a cycling tour of Germany.

Kirshenbaum, Binnie. The American novelist and short story writer is known for writing that mixes dark humor with tinges of sadness. Her latest novel, ***The Scenic Route***, is the story of a divorced and recently unemployed woman who travels by car through Europe with a married man, with whom she shares amusing stories about her family. Another Kirshenbaum novel, ***Hester Among the Ruins***, involves a New York woman who travels to Munich to research the life of a German historian, with whom she falls in love.

Millet, Lydia. Millet is a 40-something American writer with a dark sense of humor. Her most recent two novels form the first legs of a trilogy and involve travel themes. In the first, ***How the Dead Dream***, T., a young real estate developer, is forced by a series of calamities to a tropical island, where he journeys up a jungle river to visit an animal preserve. In the second, ***Ghost Lights***, Hal, the mild-mannered bureaucrat husband of one of T.'s workers, volunteers to fly to Belize in search of T., and the novel follows the ways in which the trip changes him. There's a bit of Conrad's *Heart of Darkness* hanging over both novels, especially the latter.

Portis, Charles. Portis, once referred to as "the least-known great writer in America," has written at three hilarious novels about travel, all of which feature his very dry sense of humor and a simple, straightforward style. His first novel, ***Norwood***, tells the story of ex-Marine Norwood Pratt and the bizarre characters he meets on a wild trip through the South to New York City and back to his hometown of Ralph, Texas, via stolen cars, hopped trains, and buses. His best-known work, **True Grit**, features the strong-willed 14-year-old girl Mattie Ross and the deputy marshal she hires to help track down the man who murdered her father. Finally, what may be his funniest novel, ***Dog of the South***, involves Ray Midge, a man who sets off after his wife, who has run off to Mexico with her ex-husband and Ray's credit cards and car.

Waugh, Evelyn. Waugh's ***A Handful of Dust*** is one of the funniest books in the English language and ends with its protagonist, Tony Last, refusing to grant his wife a divorce and instead traveling to Brazil on an expedition. Tony becomes stranded in the jungle following the death of his expedition companion and eventually stumbles upon an isolated tribal village, where he is nursed back to health and then held captive by an Englishman, who forces Tony to remain in the village and read Dickens to him. Waugh was also a travel writer, and his journeys through Ethiopia and the British African colonies serve as the backdrop for a work of nonfiction (*Remote People*) as well as for ***Black Mischief***, a comic novel about the emperor of a fictional African nation and his attempts to modernize the country.

Note

1. See Saricks's long and informative discussion of tone and mood, "At Leisure with Joyce Saricks: Tone and Mood," *Booklist*, April 1, 2010. http://www.booklistonline.com/ProductInfo.aspx?pid=4102541&AspxAutoDetectCookieSupport=1.

Reference

Saricks, Joyce. "At Leisure with Joyce Saricks: Tone and Mood." *Booklist*, April 1, 2010. http://www.booklistonline.com/ProductInfo.aspx?pid=4102541&AspxAutoDetectCookieSupport=1.

Chapter 7

Travel Adventure

Adventure is a path. Real adventure—self-determined, self-motivated, often risky—forces you to have firsthand encounters with the world. The world the way it is, not the way you imagine it. Your body will collide with the earth and you will bear witness. In this way you will be compelled to grapple with the limitless kindness and bottomless cruelty of humankind—and perhaps realize that you yourself are capable of both. This will change you. Nothing will ever again be black-and-white.
—Mark Jenkins, *A Man's Life: Dispatches from Dangerous Places*

Definition of "Travel Adventure"

Adventure, a genre that Neal Wyatt calls "the X Games of the reading world,"[1] stands on its own as one of the major divisions of nonfiction; it is, after all, the first chapter in Sarah Statz Cords's *The Real Story: A Guide to Nonfiction Reading Interests*. However, there are in the world of nonfiction, as in the real world of nations, disputed boundaries, areas like Kashmir or Arunachal Pradesh, where classification is less than clear and distinct, where there is no one simple category to which a title should be assigned. One of these less-than-perfect borders is the one that separates Travel and Adventure.

Imagine a Venn diagram with two big circles, one labeled "Travel" and the other labeled "Adventure." The titles in this chapter are those in the intersection or overlap between those two circles. The rest of the Travel circle contains the titles in the other chapters of this book, and the rest of the Adventure circle contains the titles in the other subgenres of Adventure, which, according to Sarah Statz Cords, include Sports Adventures, Cons and Card Games, War Stories, and Espionage and Intrigue.[2] The other two subgenres outlined by Cords (Survival and Disaster Stories and Historical and Exploration Adventure) overlap with the Travel genre, for the most part.

The titles in this chapter on "Travel Adventure" are those that recount travel to destinations to engage in what most individuals would consider dangerous activities or travel that resulted in unexpected adventure. As might be expected, there are stories of mountain climbing, river rafting, and circumnavigations. There are several attempts to be the first to do something: the first person to fly solo across the Atlantic from east to west, the first person to sail around the world alone, or the first group to raft the Amazon River from its source to the sea. The adventure may be restricted to a single destination or may involve years of general, but risky, travel.

For the titles in the "Travel Adventure" subgenre, travel (and in particular the destination of the travel and thereby the site of the adventure) plays an important role in the narrative. The frozen beauty of Antarctica also threatens the traveler with a cold, icy death by hypothermia. The breathtaking majesty of a river flowing through deep gorges also threatens to capsize the rafter. Mountains may be "the stairways to God's heart" but they also threaten the climber with death or injury.

For these titles, though, adventure (in the sense of putting one's safety and even one's life at risk) also plays an key role, whether intended, as in a rafting trip down a previously untraversed river or the attempt to climb the world's highest peak, or accidental, as the result of a sinking ship that leaves the sailor stranded on a small raft in the Atlantic Ocean or the result of being kidnapped and held captive by guerillas. For the reader, the sense of danger is the attraction, whether the danger was expected or not.

Readers of travel adventures are generally an easy lot to identify. They often engage in adventurous activities themselves (they climb mountains, they go whitewater rafting) or they enjoy reading about people who do those things. They like fast-paced stories, and anything less white-knuckled than Sebastian Junger's *A Perfect Storm* or Jon Krakauer's *Into Thin Air* may strike them as boring. Luckily, there are plenty of exciting titles in this chapter to keep their adrenaline flowing.

Appeal of "Travel Adventure"

As with travel humor, tone or mood is the most important of the traditional elements of appeal for "Travel Adventure." As Joyce Saricks notes, "How do we identify the tone of books? Generally, as we read, we recognize clues and can see how the author creates his or her tone: with humor or *tension* . . ."[3] (emphasis mine).

With "Travel Adventure," the tone is one of tension or suspense. Invariably, these titles keep the reader on the edge of her seat, wondering how Steven Callahan can keep himself alive on a five-and-a-half-foot inflatable raft for two-and-a-half months (*Adrift: Seventy-six Days Lost at Sea*) or wondering which of Valerian Albanov's crew members will survive their 18-month trek across the frozen Arctic ice (*In the Land of White Death: An Epic Story of Survival in the Siberian Arctic*). These are the riveting page turners that many readers yearn for.

Story line and pacing are also important. There must, after all, be an adventure, and that adventure must be told in a action-oriented, compelling manner, like Candice Miller's suspenseful tale of Theodore Roosevelt's attempt to find the headwaters of the Rio da Duvida and trace it north to the Amazon River (*The River of Doubt: Theodore Roosevelt's Darkest Journey*). No one ever wrote a laid-back adventure narrative.

Characterization is also important. As Sarah Statz Cords notes, "its stories of exploration, sports triumph, survival, and intrigue do leave the door open for a secondary appeal to burst through—primarily in the form of the hero."[4] We meet a number of fascinating heroes in these books: explorers like Hiram Bingham, who "discovered" Macchu Picchu (*Lost City of the Incas: The Story of Machu Picchu and its Builders*); solo travelers like Joshua Slocum, who became the first person to sail around the world alone (*Sailing Alone Around The World: The First Solo Voyage Around the World*); adventurous women like Isabella L. Bird (*A Lady's Life in the Rocky Mountains*) and Lucy Jane Bledsoe (*The Ice Cave: A Woman's Adventures from the Mojave to the Antarctic*); and mountain climbers like Heidi Howkins (*K2: One Woman's Quest for the Summit*).

Obviously, frame and setting will be important to some readers as well. Certain readers will find fascination in wild rivers, like the previously untraversed Yenisei River in Mongolia and Russia (Colin Angus's *Lost in Mongolia: Rafting the World's Last Unchallenged River*), or mountains, like Mount Everest (described so vividly in John Krakauer's *Into Thin Air: A Personal Account of the Mount Everest Disaster*), or even specific places, like the Polar region of Fergus Fleming's *Ninety Degrees North: The Quest for the North Pole.*

Readers who enjoy "Travel Adventure" may, of course, also enjoy adventure that does not involve or focus on travel. Readers' advisors working with these individuals should be ready to recommend titles of a more general adventure nature, like Robert Lindsey's *The Falcon and the Snowman: A True Story of Friendship and Espionage* or Frank Abagnale's *Catch Me If You Can: The Amazing True Story of the Youngest and Most Daring Con Man in the History of Fun and Profit!*

Organization of the Chapter

This chapter begins, as have the others, with "Classics," titles that were published prior to 1990 and that also display universality, multiple levels of meaning, great stories, memorable characters, emotional or though-provoking experiences, and great writing. These titles are likely to be more familiar to both readers and librarians and will help them better understand the nuances of the "Travel Adventure" subgenre and its categories. The date of publication may be less relevant here than with other subgenres; a good adventure is always a good adventure, after all, and in fact, older adventures, made before GPS and helicopter rescues, may be even more compelling than their newer counterparts.

The first distinction in the non-classic titles is between adventures that went as planned ("Thrill Seekers") and those where something went terribly wrong ("Unexpected Adventures"). To understand the difference (which is sometimes subtle) compare, for example, the circumnavigations of Jesse Martin (*Lionheart: A Journey Of The Human Spirit*) and Jessica Watson (*True Spirit: The True Story of a 16-Year-Old Australian Who Sailed Solo, Nonstop, and Unassisted Around the World*) with the disastrous voyages described by Hester Rumberg (*Ten Degrees of Reckoning: The True Story of a Family's Love and the*

Will to Survive), John and Jean Silverwood (*Black Wave: A Family's Adventure at Sea and the Disaster That Saved Them*), and Michael J. Touglas (*Overboard!: A True Blue-Water Odyssey of Disaster and Survival*). While the former two titles are not short on accounts of danger and thrills, their authors expected that level of adventure when they set sail. By contrast, the individuals in the latter three titles did not anticipate the tragic accidents, sheer terror, and deaths that they experienced. There is a very subtle difference between the appeal of the planned adventure and the adventure that is thrust upon one, and this distinction in categories attempts to reflect that difference.

The fourth and final subgenre is entitled "They Were Heroes" and includes titles written *about* the adventurer or adventurers by someone not directly involved in the adventure, where the adventure took place before 1990 but the account was published after the classic cut-off date above. These titles display a greater sense of objectivity and context than might a first-person account. The trade-off is, of course, their lack of immediacy and insight that a first-person narrative might offer, although in most cases, the titles do make use of primary sources such as diaries and memoirs.

Classics

As with the other chapters, classics are those "Travel Adventure" titles that were published before 1990 and that also display universality, multiple levels of meaning, great stories, memorable characters, emotional or though-provoking experiences, and great writing. These titles are likely to be more familiar to readers and librarians and may serve as good entry points into the subgenre. Indeed, part of the appeal of these titles is the fact that their adventures took place before their destinations were mapped and before the advent of GPS, helicopter rescues, and other technologies that make such expeditions seem less dangerous.

Some of the adventures and adventurers will be well known to most readers: Hiram Bingham's "discovery" of Machu Picchu (told in his *Lost City of the Incas: The Story of Machu Picchu and its Builders*) and Robert Scott's doomed expedition to the South Pole (recounted by Apsley Cherry-Garrard in *The Worst Journey in the World*). Others may be less familiar: for example, Isabella Bird (*A Lady's Life in the Rocky Mountains*), Alexandra David-Néel (*My Journey to Lhasa: The Classic Story of the Only Western Woman Who Succeeded in Entering the Forbidden City*), and Fitzroy MacLean (*Eastern Approaches*).

Bingham, Hiram

Lost City of the Incas: The Story of Machu Picchu and Its Builders. London: Weidenfeld & Nicolson, 2002 [1948]. 274 pp. ISBN: 9780297607595

In 1911, a local Peruvian farmer led Bingham (at the time a lecturer at Yale) to the Incan site of Macchu Picchu, which was then unknown to the outside world. Bingham's book, a bestseller when it was published, recounts the story of his "discovery" as well as the last days of the Incan empire and provides an overview of subsequent archaeological work in the area and Bingham's own theories about the Incans. Bingham writes with an enthusiasm and immediacy that heightens the sense of adventure surrounding his explorations.

Subjects: Adventure; Archaeology; Exploration; Explorers; Incas; Mountains; South American History

Categories: Thrill Seekers

Places: Peru

Now Try: *Turn Right at Machu Picchu: Rediscovering the Lost City One Step at a Time*, by Mark Adams, tells of the author's attempt to rediscover Macchu Picchu in much the same way as Bingham, by hiking and exploring the Vilcabamba region of Peru and ending up at the famed Incan site; it was named an ALA Notable Book for 2012. Carol Cumes and Romulo Lizarraga Valencia focus more on Andean spirituality and folklore in *Journey to Machu Picchu: Spiritual Wisdom from the Andes*. As noted in the "Quests" chapter, Hugh Thomson's *The White Rock* discusses Bingham's explorations and discovery of Macchu Picchu. Christopher Heaney's riveting *Cradle of Gold: The Story of Hiram Bingham, a Real-Life Indiana Jones, and the Search for Machu Picchu* is a good biography of the explorer. For fiction readers, A. B. Daniel's historical trilogy about the Incas ends with the novel, *The Light of Machu Picchu*, which centers on the love of an Inca princess and a Spanish conquistador.

Bird, Isabella L.

A Lady's Life in the Rocky Mountains. Norman, OK: University of Oklahoma Press, 1960. 254 pp. ISBN: 9780806113289

Bird was a middle-class woman in Victorian England who broke with tradition and explored the world. She was a sickly child, and in 1854, her doctor suggested that she travel in order to improve her health. She explored Australia, Hawaii (then known as the Sandwich Islands), and because she had heard that its air was especially good for the sick, Colorado. *A Lady's Life in the Rocky Mountains* contains her letters to her sister Henrietta, written during Bird's six-month journey through the Colorado Rockies in 1873. She described in vivid detail climbing the 14,000-foot-high Long's Peak as well as the people she met (most of whom she disliked but one with whom she had a romantic attachment) and the natural wonders she saw.

Subjects: 19th Century; Adventures; American West; Letters; Solo Travelers; Women Travelers

Categories: Thrill Seekers

Places: Colorado

Now Try: Bird wrote several travel narratives, including *The Hawaiian Archipelago: Six Months Amongst Palm Groves, Coral Reefs, and Volcanoes of the Sandwich Islands*, her account of traveling to Hawaii in 1863 and her dangerous climb up Mauna Loa, and *The Golden Chersonese: A 19th-Century Englishwoman's*

Travels in Singapore and the Malay Peninsula, which describes her travels in Malaysia and Singapore in the 1880s. Janet Robertson writes about other women who explored the Colorado Rockies following the Pikes Peak gold rush of the 1850s (including Julia Archibald Holmes, the first woman on record to climb a Colorado mountain, and Coral Bowman, who started an American school of technical climbing) in her compelling book, *The Magnificent Mountain Women: Adventures in the Colorado Rockies.* Elinore Pruitt Stewart's *Letters of a Woman Homesteader* recounts a young widowed mother's experience working on a Wyoming ranch in the early 1900s. Mary Austin's classic about the American Southwest, *The Land of Little Rain,* which was originally published in 1903, may also appeal to readers who enjoy Isabella Bird, although much of Austin's focus is on the environment and not the individuals she encountered.

Callahan, Steven

Adrift: Seventy-six Days Lost at Sea. Boston: Houghton Mifflin, 1986. 234 pp. ISBN: 9780395382066

In February 1982, at the start of a transatlantic yacht race, Callahan's sloop sank, and he found himself clinging to a five-and-a-half foot inflatable raft with just three pounds of food and eight pints of water. *Adrift* recounts his attempts to stay alive for two-and-a-half months, living off the fish he caught, drinking water he distilled, fighting off sharks, repairing his damaged raft, and struggling with his own sanity. The book is written in a compelling and absorbing style, with plenty of details, both about Callahan's attempts to survive and about his thoughts and fears during the experience.

Subjects: Accidents; Adventure; Oceans; Sailing; Solo Travelers; Survival Stories

Categories: Unexpected Adventures

Places: Atlantic Ocean

Now Try: Callahan admits to having read Maurice and Maralyn Bailey's *Staying Alive: 117 Days Adrift,* about that couple's 1973 survival on a raft following the sinking of their yacht in the Pacific Ocean, and Dougal Robertson's *Survive the Savage Sea,* about the Robertson family's 37-day ordeal on a raft and a dinghy after their yacht was sunk by killer whales in the Pacific. Michael J. Tougias's *Overboard!: A True Blue-Water Odyssey of Disaster and Survival* (annotated in this chapter) recounts the adventures of three crew members who survived the sinking of their sailboat in the stormy Atlantic in 2005. Yann Martel's fantasy adventure novel *Life of Pi* tells the story of an Indian boy who survives over 200 days, stranded on a small boat in the Pacific Ocean with a Bengal tiger; the novel won the Booker Prize in 2002.

Cherry-Garrard, Apsley

The Worst Journey in the World. New York: Carroll & Graf, 1997 [1922]. 607 pp. ISBN: 9780786704378

Cherry-Garrard was one of three survivors of the ill-fated 1910–1913 British expedition to the South Pole, led by Robert Scott, and his account of that journey is a highly regarded memoir that focuses on the difficulties encountered by the explorers, the causes of the expedition's failure, and the meaning of life. Cherry-Garrard tells the story in gripping, horrific terms and yet with the wide-eyed wonder and innocence of the young man that he was at the journey's beginning. The high regard in which Cherry-Garrard's book is held is reflected in the fact that when *National Geographic Adventure* listed "The 100 Best Adventure Books of All Time," *The Worst Journey in the World* was listed first.

Subjects: Adventure; Exploration; Explorers; Memoirs; Survival Stories

Categories: Unexpected Adventures

Places: Antarctica

Series: *Picador Travel Classics*

Now Try: Robert Scott's own journals, published by the Oxford University Press as *Journals: Scott's Last Expedition*, provide a vivid look at the expedition from the leader's point of view, including both the beauty of the stark environment of Antarctica and the growing desperation of the team members. Roland Huntford's *The Last Place on Earth* is a fascinating account of the race between Scott and his successful rival, Norwegian explorer Roald Amundsen, and contrasts Amundsen's better preparation and planning against the more romantic notions of Scott. Amundsen's own account of the expedition is captured in *The South Pole: An Account of the Norwegian Antarctic Expedition in the "Fram" 1910–1912*, in which the explorer details the frostbite, snow blindness, and other challenges his team encountered. An excellent biography of Cherry-Garrard is Sara Wheeler's *Cherry: A Life of Apsley Cherry-Garrard*.

Dana, Richard Henry, Jr.

Two Years Before The Mast: A Personal Narrative. New York: Library of America, 2005 [1840]. 926 pp. ISBN: 9781931082839 YA

In 1834, 19-year-old Harvard student Richard Dana went to sea, hoping to improve his health. He served as a common sailor on the *Pilgrim*, a brig bound for California at a time when it was still owned by Mexico, and wrote about the adventures he found at sea: storms, whales, scurvy and other hardships, and a mad captain. The book is fascinating for its portrayal of seafaring life in the 19th century, as well as its portrayal of California before the Gold Rush. The style is straightforward enough but filled with nautical terminology that will send many readers scurrying to the dictionary.

Subjects: 19th Century; Oceans; Seas

Categories: Thrill Seekers

Places: Atlantic Ocean; California; Massachusetts; Pacific Ocean

Now Try: Another book about 19th-century sailing life is Charles Tyng's *Before the Wind: The Memoir of an American Sea Captain, 1808–1833*, which tells how Tyng rose from cabin boy to become a ship's captain and a wealthy merchant. A look at modern-day sailors is provided by John McPhee in *Looking for a Ship*, which describes that author's trip from Charleston, South Carolina, through the Panama Canal and down the Pacific coast of South America. A more recent book that describes the lawlessness and anarchy of the oceans and recounts piracy, legal disputes, and the conflict between the need for shipping companies to make a profit and the need to preserve the environment is William Langewiesche's *The Outlaw Sea: A World of Freedom, Chaos, and Crime*. *Two Years Before the Mast* is a natural doorway to fiction about seafarers of the 19th century, including C. S. Forester's *Hornblower* series (beginning with *Mr. Midshipman Hornblower*) and Patrick O'Brian's *Aubrey-Maturin* series (beginning with *Master and Commander*).

David-Néel, Alexandra

My Journey to Lhasa: The Classic Story of the Only Western Woman Who Succeeded in Entering the Forbidden City. Boston: Beacon Press, 1986 [1927]. 310 pp. ISBN: 9780807059005

David-Néel was a fiercely independent Belgian French explorer whose best-known journey was to Lhasa in 1924, where she traveled disguised as a male pilgrim. Her book describes the four-month, treacherous journey in the dead of winter (sleeping on rocks and snow, going hungry and thirsty, traveling by starlight) and tells how she became the first European woman to set foot in the "forbidden" city of Lhasa. David-Néel's knowledge of Sanskrit and Buddhism and her fluency in the Tibetan language make her account all the more informative.

Subjects: Adventure; Buddhism; Memoirs; Solo Travelers; Women Travelers

Categories: Thrill Seekers

Places: Lhasa; Tibet

Now Try: David-Néel wrote several books about Tibet and its religion, including *Magic and Mystery in Tibet*, an intriguing description of some of the country's more unusual religious practices, including psychic heat and telepathy, and *The Secret Oral Teachings in Tibetan Buddhist Sects*, a straightforward explanation of Mahayana Buddhism. Two good biographies of David-Néel are also available: *The Secret Lives of Alexandra David-Neel: A Biography of the Explorer of Tibet and Its Forbidden Practices*, by Barbara and Michael Foster, and Ruth Middleton's *Alexandra David-Neel: Portrait of an Adventurer*. Other titles by or about pioneering women may also be of interest; these include Georgina Howell's biography of "the female Lawrence of Arabia," *Gertrude Bell: Queen of the Desert, Shaper of Nations*, and Beryl Markham's autobiography *West with the Night* (annotated below). Another, more recent option is Norah Vincent's fascinating *Self-Made Man: One Woman's Journey into Manhood and Back*, which tells the story of a woman who disguised herself as a man in order to observe the world of men from the inside.

Kane, Joe

Running the Amazon. New York: Knopf, 1989. 277 pp. ISBN: 9780394553313

In 1985, Kane joined a multinational team of ten men and one woman hoping to become the first group to travel the entire length of the Amazon River, 4,200 miles from its source in the Peruvian Andes to the Atlantic Ocean. Kane provides a thrilling firsthand account of the expedition, especially its many challenges, which included finding the river's source, navigating unmapped gorges and areas occupied by the Shining Path rebels, dealing with corrupt border guards and drug smugglers, and the defection of team members. Traveling by raft, by kayak, and on foot, the original team eventually shrank to four, and Kane tells their story with a very readable, understated style.

Subjects: Adventure; Canoeing; Exploration; Kayaking; Rivers

Categories: Thrill Seekers

Places: Amazon River; Brazil; Colombia; Ecuador; Peru

Series: *Vintage Departures*

Now Try: Kane is also the author of *Savages*, about the Huaorani Indians of Ecuador and their struggles with international oil companies who were exploiting the Amazon with poor environmental practices. Redmon O'Hanlon's misadventures among the uncharted parts of the Venezuelan Amazon are recounted in the hilarious *In Trouble Again: A Journey Between Orinoco and the Amazon*, which is annotated in the "Travel Humor" chapter of this book. Wade Davis's *One River: Explorations and Discoveries in the Amazon Rain Forest* is both about the plants of the region and the dangerous expeditions taken by Davis's mentor, Harvard biologist Richard Evans Schultes, in the Amazon region, beginning in the 1930s.

Lansing, Alfred

Endurance: Shackleton's Incredible Voyage. New York: Carroll & Graf, 1999 [1959]. 282 pp. ISBN: 9780786706211

In 1914, Ernest Shackleton (who had served as third officer on Scott's first expedition to Antarctica) undertook to cross the continent from sea to sea, via the South Pole. However, his ship, the *Endurance*, was soon trapped and then crushed by the ice, leaving Shackleton and his 28-man crew stranded. Lansing's inspiring and captivating book was based on diaries of the crew and interviews with the survivors; it recounts how the men drifted on the ice for over a year before they were able to launch lifeboats to Elephant Island, from which Shackleton and a crew of five sailed to South Georgia Island, where they arranged to have the rest of the crew rescued.

Subjects: Adventure; Exploration; Explorers; Memoirs; Survival Stories

Categories: They Were Heroes; Unexpected Adventures

Places: Antarctica

Now Try: Shackleton's own version of the expedition, from its inception to the final evacuations of his crew, is told in *South: The Endurance Expedition*. Frank Arthur Worsley, the captain of the *Endurance*, provides an even more powerful and concise version of the events, with ample praise for Shackleton, in *Endurance: An Epic of Polar Adventure*. Caroline Alexander's *The Endurance: Shackleton's Legendary Antarctic Expedition* includes the photographs of Frank Hurley, the expedition's photographer, which re-create the stark beauty of the

Antarctic region as well as the destruction of the ship and the daily struggles of the crew to stay alive. Two films about the voyage (*Shackleton: The Greatest Survival Story of All Time*, a biopic starring Kenneth Branagh, and *"The Endurance": Shackleton's Legendary Antarctic Expedition*, a documentary narrated by Liam Neeson) are also available.

MacLean, Fitzroy

Eastern Approaches. Alexandria, VA: Time/Life Books, 1980 [1962]. 562 pp. ISBN: 9780809435654

Maclean, who is generally considered to be one of the inspirations for Ian Fleming's character James Bond, found himself bored with life as a junior diplomat in the British embassy in Paris. He requested a posting in Moscow, received it, and in 1937, traveled to the Soviet Union. *Eastern Approaches* recounts his adventures as a diplomat in Moscow, his travels throughout the Soviet Union and especially the usually forbidden area of Central Asia, his work with the British Army and the Special Air Service in North Africa during World War II, and his years with Tito and his troops, which were fighting to liberate Yugoslavia from Nazi control. The book is written with the dry wit and shrewd observations that one might expect of the man on whom James Bond was modeled.

Subjects: 1930s; 1940s; Adventure; Espionage; European History; Memoirs; World War II

Categories: Thrill Seekers

Places: Afghanistan; Africa; Armenia; Azerbaijan; Bosnia and Herzegovina; China; Croatia; Egypt; England; Georgia; India; Iran; Iraq; Italy; Kazakhstan; Kyrgyzstan; Libya; Montenegro; Morocco; Moscow; Pakistan; Russia; Serbia; Tajikistan; Turkmenistan, Uzbekistan

Now Try: In the late 1980s, MacLean wrote *Portrait of the Soviet Union*, which captures his perceptions of Russia and especially what were then the republics of Uzbekistan, Kazakhstan and Georgia. Another writer who traveled through Central Asia in the 1930s was Peter Fleming, the brother of James Bond's creator Ian Fleming; his book *News from Tartary: A Journey from Peking to Kashmir* describes his 3,500-mile journey from Beijing to Kashmir and especially the political situation in what was then Chinese Turkestan. Many of MacLean's adventures took place in Central Asia, where the British Empire and the Russian Empire had fought for supremacy since Victorian Days; the "Great Game," as that rivalry is often called, is the subject of Peter Hopkins's superb history, *The Great Game: The Struggle for Empire in Central Asia*. As noted above, MacLean was one of the inspirations for the James Bond character, and Ian Fleming's novels, particularly *From Russia, With Love* may appeal to readers of *Eastern Approaches*.

Markham, Beryl

West with the Night. San Francisco: North Point Press, 1983 [1942]. 293 pp. ISBN: 9780865471184 YA

No less a writer than Ernest Hemingway said of Markham's book, "she has written so well, and marvelously well, that I was completely ashamed of myself as a writer." Whether Markham actually wrote the book herself or not is a matter of some controversy; but regardless, this story of her life in Kenya and her days as a bush pilot there is spellbinding and will take the reader back to a world of trailblazing pilots. Markham, who became the first person to fly solo across the Atlantic from east to west, was a remarkable individual, and her story is told with more soul-searching and self-awareness than Isak Dinesen's *Out of Africa,* another classic about a British woman living in Kenya.

Subjects: 1920s; 1930s; Adventure; Aviation; Coming of Age; Women Authors; Women Travelers; Women's Contributions

Category: Thrill Seekers

Places: Africa; Kenya

Now Try: In the 1940s, Markham also wrote eight stories for magazines such as *Ladies' Home Journal* and *Collier's;* Mary S. Lovell has collected these stories about Markham's life in Kenya in *Splendid Outcast: Beryl Markham's African Stories.* Lovell is also the author of *Straight on Till Morning: A Biography of Beryl Markham,* a well-researched and engrossing book. Lovell believes that Markham did write *West with the Night,* a claim disputed by Errol Trzebinski's biography, *The Lives of Beryl Markham,* which argues that Markham's third husband was the real author of the book. The best known of the pioneering women in aviation is, of course, Amelia Earhart, and good biographies include Candace Fleming's *Amelia Lost: The Life and Disappearance of Amelia Earhart* and Ric Gillespie's *Finding Amelia: The True Story of the Earhart Disappearance.*

Moorehead, Alan

The Blue Nile. New York: Harper & Row, 1972. Rev ed. 336 pp. ISBN: 9780060130114

Moorehead, a war correspondent, wrote *The Blue Nile* shortly after *The White Nile* (annotated below), and while the earlier book focused on the individuals who sought the source of the Nile, *The Blue Nile* is more concerned with the clash of civilizations (Napoleonic France in Egypt, Victorian England in what was then Abyssinia) and the advances made by the modern, Western world into the previously isolated lands around the Blue Nile. Moorehead's understanding of the ebbs and flows of the civilizations along the Nile is striking and he evokes both the moods of the Nile and the lands through which it flows.

Subjects: 19th Century; Adventure; Exploration; Rivers; World History

Categories: They Were Heroes

Places: Africa; Egypt; Ethiopia; Nile River; Sudan

Now Try: Moorehead is also the author of *Gallipoli,* a classic work about the disastrous Allied campaign against the Turks, which resulted in the tragic loss of Australian and New Zealand troops, and *Cooper's Creek: Tragedy and Adventure in the Australian Outback,* which describes an 1860 expedition through the Outback to find a route from Melbourne to the northern coast of Australia. In 2004, geologist Pasquale Scaturro and his partner, filmmaker Gordon Brown, became the first individuals to navigate the Blue Nile; Scaturro and Richard Bangs describe the expedition in *Mystery of the Nile: The Epic Story of the First Descent of the World's Deadliest River* (annotated in this chapter).

Moorehead, Alan

The White Nile. New York: Harper & Row, 1971. 368 pp. ISBN: 9780060130497

As noted above, *The White Nile* focuses on the individuals who sought to discover the source of the Nile and to colonize the countries in the Nile Region in the second half of the 19th century, including Richard Francis Burton, Charles George Gordon, Dr. David Livingstone, and Henry Morton Stanley. Moorehead's account of these larger-than-life characters and their stories of heroism is informative and often riveting.

Subjects: 19th Century; Adventure; Colonialism; Exploration; Geography; Rivers; World History

Categories: They Were Heroes

Places: Africa; Nile River; Rwanda; South Sudan; Sudan; Tanzania; Uganda

Now Try: Martin Dugard's *Into Africa: The Epic Adventures of Stanley and Livingstone* is an excellent examination of the two explorers, beginning in 1866 with Livingstone's search for the source of the Nile. Tim Jeal's *Explorers of the Nile: The Triumph and Tragedy of a Great Victorian Adventure* is a more recent treatment of many of the individuals described by Moorehead in *The White Nile.* Edward Rice's *Captain Sir Richard Francis Burton: A Biography* is a good introduction to the life of the great British explorer, who also sought the source of the Nile among the Great Lakes of Africa. A straightforward historical novel about Burton and the British explorer John Speke is William Harrison's *Burton and Speke,* which highlights the differences between the two personalities and the friction these differences caused.

Nansen, Fridtjof

Farthest North: The Voyage and Exploration of the Fram, 1893–1896. New York: Modern Library, 1999 [1897]. 508 pp. ISBN: 9780375754722

Nansen was a Norwegian explorer who won international recognition for his attempt to reach the North Pole in his ship *Fram* between 1893 and 1896. Though he did not reach the pole, his team did reach the farthest northern point ever recorded, and when Nansen returned, he immediately wrote this account of the voyage. The book was an instant success and reflects the determined spirit and eye for detail that allowed Nansen to push farther north than anyone had previously done, in spite of snowdrifts, ice floes, polar bears, scurvy, hunger, and in Nansen's case, being left for dead.

Subjects: Adventure; Exploration; Explorers; Memoirs; Survival Stories

Categories: Thrill Seekers

Places: Arctic Region

Now Try: Roland Huntford (who also wrote *The Last Place on Earth*, about the race to the South Pole between Scott and Amundsen) is the author of *Nansen*, a fascinating biography of the Norwegian explorer. In 2005, explorer Tom Avery replicated the journey taken by Robert Peary and his team, using the same equipment that Peary had used, in order to prove that the U.S. explorer could have done what he claimed; the experiences of Avery and his team are captured in the thrilling book, *To the End of the Earth: Our Epic Journey to the North Pole and the Legend of Peary and Henson*. The rivalry between Peary and explorer Fredrick Cook and each man's claim to have reached the North Pole first are outlined in Bruce Henderson's *True North: Peary, Cook, and the Race to the Pole*. *Polar Dream: The First Solo Expedition by a Woman and Her Dog to the Magnetic North Pole* tells the story of author Helen Thayer's attempt to become the first woman to ski alone to the North Pole.

Slocum, Joshua

Sailing Alone around the World: The First Solo Voyage around the World. New York: Penguin Books, 1999 [1900]. 273 pp. ISBN: 9780140437362

Between 1895 and 1898, Slocum, an experienced sailor, became the first person to sail around the world alone. His three-year journey on a 37-foot sloop is detailed in *Sailing Alone around the World*, which relates his experiences in a very modest, diffident manner, in spite of the many perils he faced: gales, loneliness, fatigue, pirates, and an attack by Yahgan Indians of the coast of Tierra del Fuego. Slocum put in at several ports and describes the individuals he met at these places. There is a good bit of sailing jargon throughout the book, but there are also very accessible reflections on loneliness, particular that felt by a single individual encountering the vast, watery spaces of our planet.

Subjects: 19th Century; Adventure; Circumnavigations; Oceans; Sailing; Solo Travelers

Categories: Thrill Seekers

Places: Ascension Island; Australia; Azores; Brazil; Canary Islands; Cape Verde Islands; Chile; Devil's Island; Fiji; Gibraltar; Grenada; Marquesas Islands; Massachusetts; Mauritius; Nova Scotia; Polynesia; Samoa; South Africa; St. Helena; Trinidad; Uruguay; Wales

Now Try: Geoffrey Wolff has written a well-researched biography of Slocum, *The Hard Way Around: The Passages of Joshua Slocum*. Bernard Moitessier describes his participation in the first *Sunday Times* Golden Globe Race, a non-stop, solo, around-the-world yacht race in 1968 and 1969 in *The Long Way*; while Moitessier pulled out of the race after seven months, he continued to sail alone for three more months, and his book highlights the fatigue and loneliness that he felt. The Golden Globe Race pitted nine sailors against one another and the elements; the story of the race and the one man who crossed the finish line is told in Peter Nichols's enjoyable book, *A Voyage for Madmen*.

Tomlinson, H. M.

The Sea and the Jungle. Barre, MA: Imprint Society, 1971 [1912]. 221 pp. ISBN: 9780876360118

Henry Major Tomlinson was working as a newspaper journalist in 1909 when the opportunity arose to take a trip to South America aboard the tramp steamer *Capella,* which was delivering cargo deep into the jungles of Brazil. At the time of his journey, the upper area of the Madeira River was wild, unmapped, and inaccessible, and the book details his wild winter crossing of the Atlantic Ocean and his time at the construction site of the Madeira-Mamore railway. The book is written with a combination of modesty, humor, and sense of adventure.

Subjects: 1900s; 1910s; Adventure; Jungles; Oceans; Quick Reads; Rivers

Categories: Thrill Seekers

Places: Amazon River; Atlantic Ocean; Brazil

Now Try: The Amazon River is the site of many adventure stories, including Scott Wallace's *The Unconquered: In Search of the Amazon's Last Uncontacted Tribes,* which follows a 2002 attempt to gather information about an uncontacted tribe known for their skill at the use of curare-poisoned arrows. Phillipe Descola spent three years among the Jivaro Indians of the upper Amazon and writes about the experience in *The Spears of Twilight: Life and Death in the Amazon Jungle.* After his loss as a third-party candidate in the presidential election of 1912, Theodore Roosevelt attempted the first descent of an unmapped tributary of the Amazon River, an adventure that almost led to his death; that story is told by Candice Millard in the gripping book, *The River of Doubt: Theodore Roosevelt's Darkest Journey,* which is annotated in this chapter.

Thrill Seekers

This chapter makes a distinction between adventures that went as planned and those that resulted from something going terribly wrong. The former titles are included under "Thrill Seekers" and should appeal to readers who enjoy reading about thrilling adventures and expeditions as well as the planning that went into these trips. These trips were intended to be adventures, and the participants get their money's worth.

Travel narratives in the "Thrill Seekers" category include trips down rivers (the Amazon in Colin Angus and Ian Mulgrew's *Amazon Extreme: Three Ordinary Guys, One Rubber Raft, and the Most Dangerous River on Earth* or the Tsangpo River of Peter Heller's *Hell or High Water: Surviving Tibet's Tsangpo River*) as well as mountain climbs (the world's second highest mountain in Heidi Howkins's *K2: One Woman's Quest for the Summit* or the highest mountain in Borneo in Sam Lightner, Jr.'s *All Elevations Unknown: An Adventure in the Heart of Borneo*). Lucy Jane Bledsoe journeys through deserts and through the frozen Antarctic landscape in *The Ice Cave: A Woman's Adventures from the Mojave to the Antarctic,* while others go to other extremes and, like James M. Tabor in *Blind Descent: The Quest to Discover the Deepest Place on Earth,* explore the deepest caves on the earth. Still others attempt to sail around the world alone as teenagers: Jesse Martin in *Lionheart: A Journey Of The Human Spirit* or Jessica Watson in *True Spirit: The True Story of a 16-Year-Old Australian Who Sailed Solo, Nonstop, and Unassisted around the World.*

Books about the activities that are central to the titles in this category, like mountain climbing (Ronald C. Eng's *Mountaineering: The Freedom of the Hills* or Craig Luebben's *Rock Climbing: Mastering Basic Skills*) and whitewater rafting (Jeff Bennett's *The Complete Whitewater Rafter*) may also be of interest to fans of the titles in "Thrill Seekers." Fiction centered on the types of adventure (Anita Shreve's *A Change in Altitude* or Alice Walker's *Now Is the Time to Open Your Heart*) may also be recommended.

Angus, Colin

Lost in Mongolia: Rafting the World's Last Unchallenged River. New York: Broadway Books, 2003. 270 pp. ISBN: 9780767912808

Angus followed up his rafting trip down the Amazon (see the next entry, *Amazon Extreme*) by taking a team rafting down the previously untraversed Yenisei River in Mongolia and Russia. There are both amazing moments (at one point, Angus is separated for 12 days from the rest of the crew with little gear in the middle of a river in Mongolia) and splendid characters (the Irkutsk mafioso Vladimir, or Remy and Olya, a pair of born-again Christians who meet in the middle of Siberia), and the 3,400-mile trip from the river's remote source in Central Asia to its mouth in the Arctic Ocean is described with both humor and spectacular detail.

Subjects: Adventure; Exploration; Quick Reads; Rivers; Rafting

Places: Mongolia; Russia

Now Try: Eugene Buchanan's story of four Americans and ten Latvians who rafted down the Bashkaus River in Russia, *Brothers on the Bashkaus: A Siberian Paddling Adventure*, has many of the same elements as *Lost in Mongolia*: rafting down a wild river; plans that go awry; clashes of cultures; and colorful characters. Richard Bangs and Christian Kallen describe their 4,000-mile rafting adventure down China's Yangtze River in 1987 in *Riding the Dragon's Back: The Race to Raft the Upper Yangtze*; they also discuss earlier explorers in the region and previous attempts to navigate the river in its entirety. Bangs is also the author of *The Lost River: A Memoir of Life, Death, and Transformation on Wild Water*, about an attempt to run the Tekeze River in Ethiopia several years after Bangs's best friend had died on an expedition down the same river.

Angus, Colin, and Ian Mulgrew

Amazon Extreme: Three Ordinary Guys, One Rubber Raft, and the Most Dangerous River on Earth. New York: Broadway, 2002 [2001]. 240 pp. ISBN: 9780767910507

"I didn't expect to die of thirst—certainly not at twenty-seven," opens this adrenaline-filled narrative. Angus joined Australian Ben Kozel and South African Scott Borthwick in an attempt to become one of the first teams to raft the Amazon River from its source to the sea. The trio followed the route taken by Joe Kane's 1985 historic first-ever descent of the Amazon River from source to sea, and the book captures the determination that carried them through the five-month trip. Their misadventures, blunders, and near-death experiences are told with a sense of humor and an understated style that is both engrossing and entertaining.

Subjects: Adventure; Exploration; Rafting; Quick Reads; Rivers

Places: Amazon River

Now Try: As noted, Angus and Mulgrew's adventure was inspired by Joe Kane's *Running the Amazon,* which is annotated in the "Classics" section of this chapter. Angus is also the author of two other travel adventures: *Beyond the Horizon: The First Human-Powered Expedition to Circle the Globe,* about his attempt to become the first person to sail around the world in a self-propelled vehicle (he succeeded, but there is much debate about whether his route constituted a true circumnavigation) and *Rowed Trip: A Journey by Oar from Scotland to Syria,* which Angus and his wife Julie co-authored, about the couple's journey from Scotland to Syria by rowboat and bicycle.

Bangs, Richard, and Pasquale Scaturro

Mystery of the Nile: The Epic Story of the First Descent of the World's Deadliest River. New York City: G.P. Putnam's Sons, 2005. 294 pp. ISBN: 9780399152627

In 2004, geologist Pasquale Scaturro and his partner, filmmaker Gordon Brown, became the first individuals to navigate the Blue Nile, a 114-day journey described here in breathtaking detail by Scaturro and Bangs. The book combines the story of their 3,260-mile trip (complete with dangerous rapids, man-eating crocodiles, exposure to malaria, extreme weather, petty local officials, and armed guerilla fighters) with the history of previous attempts to descend the great river and some discussion of the history and politics of the surrounding region.

Subjects: Adventure; Exploration; Kayaking; Rivers

Places: Africa; Egypt; Ethiopia; Nile River; Sudan

Now Try: In 1999, Virginia Morrell was on the crew that became the first to descend the Nile in a single, unbroken journey; she writes about the experience in *Blue Nile: Ethiopia's River of Magic and Mystery.* Richard Snailham describes an earlier expedition into the northern gorge of the Blue Nile, one that resulted in the drowning death of one of the crew members, in *The Blue Nile Revealed: The Story of the Great Abbai Expedition, 1968.* Scaturro and Brown were partly motivated to run the Nile by the hope of making a film about the great river; that film, *Mystery of the Nile,* is available on DVD and captures both the expedition and the scenery.

Bledsoe, Lucy Jane

The Ice Cave: A Woman's Adventures from the Mojave to the Antarctic. Madison, WI: Terrace Books/University of Wisconsin Press, 2006. 172 pp. ISBN: 9780299218447

In *The Ice Cave,* Bledsoe, an award-winning novelist and LGBT writer who has served as the writer-in-residence in Antarctica, provides 11 essays that focus on her relationships with the wilderness and the balance of confidence and uncertainty that lies at the heart of adventure. The essays find her biking across mountains, encountering wolves in Alaska, searching for mountain lions, and backpacking alone into the wilderness. The essays vividly portray nature and explore with a soul-searching honesty a wide variety of topics that include human conflict and solitude.

Subjects: Adventure; Animals; Deserts; Essays; GLBTQ; Mountains; Quick Reads; Solitude; Solo Travelers; Women Travelers

Places: Alaska; Antarctica; California; Caribbean; Colorado; Wyoming

Now Try: Bledsoe has written two books about her time in Antarctica. *How to Survive in Antarctica* is part travel narrative and part collection of survival tips and is aimed at young adult readers. *The Big Bang Symphony: A Novel of Antarctica* is a fictional account of scientists, artists, and other women stationed in Antarctica and the interactions among them. Bledsoe's collection of 20 stories of lesbian travelers, *Lesbian Travels: A Literary Companion*, was a finalist for the 1998 Lambda Literary Award in Nonfiction. Gillian Kendall's *Something to Declare: Good Lesbian Travel Writing* is another collection of travel essays by lesbian writers, including Lesléa Newman's story of the awakening of her sexuality and artistic talent while working on a kibbutz in Israel. Another fascinating story of a woman surviving a different kind of challenge in Antarctica is Jerri Nielsen's memoir of treating her own cancer while on a research trip there, *Ice Bound: A Doctor's Incredible Battle For Survival at the South Pole* (by Nielsen and Mary Anne Vollers).

Heller, Peter

Hell or High Water: Surviving Tibet's Tsangpo River. Emmaus, PA: Rodale, 2004. 278 pp. ISBN: 9781579548728

Heller, a seasoned kayaker, was commissioned by *Outside* magazine in 2002 to accompany a team of world-class kayakers who were attempting to shoot Tibet's fabled Tsangpo River, the deepest dry-land rift in the world, three times deeper and eight times steeper than the Colorado River's Grand Canyon, and sometimes called "the Mount Everest of rivers." The result is an exciting and sometimes frightening account of their descent, mixed with a portrait of Tibet and its political situation. Heller does an excellent job of portraying the individuals in the expedition, from the team leader, who directed a good bit of animosity toward Heller, to the porters, who stole the team's supplies and threatened mutiny.

Subjects: Adventure; Kayaking; Rivers

Places: China; Tibet; Tsangpo River

Now Try: Dustin Knapp's documentary film of the Tsangpo River descent, "*Into the Tsangpo Gorge*" is available in DVD and complements Heller's book with its breathtaking scenery. Todd Balf's book about an earlier attempt to run the Tsangpo in 1998 is *The Last River: The Tragic Race for Shangri-la*; although Balf tells the story based on the accounts of others, he is able to convey the excitement of the attempt as well as one who was there. Wick Walker did take part in that ill-fated expedition, and his firsthand account is *Courting the Diamond Sow: A Whitewater Expedition on Tibet's Forbidden River*.

Howkins, Heidi

K2: One Woman's Quest for the Summit. Washington, DC: National Geographic, 2001. 270 pp. ISBN: 9780792279969

The world's second highest mountain, K2, is often referred to as "the savage mountain," because of the difficulty of its ascent; it ranks second among the world's 14 tallest mountains in terms of fatalities and has steeper slopes and worse weather than Everest. Howkins had long dreamed of climbing K2 and was granted permission to do so in 1997. She tells her story as a series of tales told to a hitchhiker whom she picked up just south of the Canadian border, and that story is inspiring, riveting, and filled with details of such quotidian matters as how she went to the bathroom, how she got water, and what she ate. Howkins is particularly good at refraining from romanticizing her efforts, remarking that "I once heard someone define Himalayan climbing as the 'art of suffering.' I understand the suffering part, but I'm not sure I fully grasp the artistic challenge."

Subjects: Adventure; Climbing and Hiking; Mountains; Women Travelers

Places: China; Pakistan

Now Try: There are a number of good books about K2 and the various attempts to climb it. Ed Viesturs and David Roberts recount several climbs from the late 1930s through the disastrous 2008 season, in which 11 climbers died within 36 hours, in the thrilling book, *K2: Life and Death on the World's Most Dangerous Mountain*. Graham Bowley focuses on that 2008 disaster and the icefall that killed almost a dozen climbers in his chilling *No Way Down: Life and Death on K2*. Nepal's Annapurna is even more deadly than K2, and Arlene Blum writes about the 1978 expedition of 13 women up that peak, making them the first Americans and the first women to scale Annapurna, in *Annapurna: A Woman's Place*. Lynn Hill's *Climbing Free: My Life in the Vertical World* is more oriented to the sport of rock climbing, but her courage and strength should appeal to fans of Howkins's book.

Lightner, Jr., Sam

All Elevations Unknown: An Adventure in the Heart of Borneo. New York: Broadway, 2001. 239 pp. ISBN: 9780767907569.

Lightner, a rock climber of some repute, was part of the first team to climb one of Borneo's highest mountains, Bukit Batu Lawi. His story of the expedition is interspersed with the story of Tom Harrisson, a British soldier sent to recruit and arm the natives in the area (many of them headhunters) against the Japanese occupiers during World War II. This mix of present-day adventure, World War II history, and the present-day culture of the people of Borneo is wonderfully entertaining.

Subjects: 1940s; Adventure; Climbing and Hiking; Mountains; Quick Reads; World War II

Places: Borneo; Malaysia

Now Try: Tom Harrisson told his own story in the hard-to-find *World Within: A Borneo Story*; his mention of the mountain inspired Lightner and his colleagues to find and climb the peak. Judith M. Heimann tells another story of Borneo and World War II in *The Airmen and the Headhunters: A True Story of Lost Soldiers, Heroic Tribesmen and the Unlikeliest Rescue of World War II*; her book is based on interviews with several of the Dayak tribespeople directly involved. A fascinating look at Borneo from the environmentalist point of view is Linda Spalding's *A Dark Place in the Jungle: Following Leakey's Last Angel into Borneo*, which recounts the efforts of Birute Galdikas (like Jane Goodall and Dian Fossey, trained by Louis Leakey) to study and preserve the orangutans of Borneo. For a novel set in Borneo, readers may enjoy C. S. Godshalk's *Kalimantaan*, about an English adventurer who establishes himself as the rajah of an independent state in the 1840s.

Martin, Jesse

Lionheart: A Journey Of The Human Spirit. St. Leonards, NSW, Australia: Allen & Unwin, 2000. 253 pp. ISBN: 9781865083476 Y A

Martin tells the true story of how he became, at 18, the youngest person to sail around the world alone, nonstop, and unassisted. The book details the two years of planning that made the 328-day trip in a 37-foot yacht possible, as well as the challenges the teenager faced, including storms and waves, his near collision with a freighter, various mechanical and electrical failures, the threat of pirates, and the isolation of being thousands of miles from any other human being. Martin's story of how he achieved his dream is inspirational and should particularly appeal to teens.

Subjects: Circumnavigations; Oceans; Sailing; Solitude; Solo Travelers

Places: Atlantic Ocean; Australia; Indian Ocean; Pacific Ocean

Now Try: Martin's journey is also depicted in the film, *Lionheart—The Jesse Martin Story*, which was released in 2001. Martin followed up *Lionheart* with *Kijana: The Real Story*, which describes the less successful voyage that he and four friends took from Australia to Indonesia. In May 2010, Jessica Watson completed her 210-day trip around the world in a 33-foot boat, breaking Martin's record to become the youngest person to complete the journey; her book, *True Spirit: The True Story of a 16-Year-Old Australian Who Sailed Solo, Nonstop, and Unassisted Around the World*, is annotated below. Robin Lee Graham's 1972 book *Dove* tells of his sailing trip as a teenager around the world, solo but with stops, on a 24-foot sloop; like *Lionheart*, his story is inspiring.

McCauley, Lucy (ed.)

Women in the Wild: True Stories of Adventure and Connection. San Francisco, CA: Travelers' Tales, 1998. 292 pp. ISBN: 9781885211217

McCauley has collected 33 stories from women adventurers and travelers about the bond between women and places of solitude, danger, and wilderness. Some of the stories are traditional, sports-oriented adventures: Tracy Johnston recounts rafting down the Boh River in Borneo; Margo Chisolm reports on ascending to a basecamp on Mount Everest; and McCauley herself tells about climbing an active volcano in Guatemala. Other essays focus on wildlife: Jane Goodall writes about living with chimpanzees in the Congo jungle; Lynne Cox tells of rescuing an injured pelican on the Pacific; and Joanna Greenfield remembers surviving a hyena attack in Israel. The stories are short but all are inspiring and well written.

Subjects: Adventure; Essays; Women Travelers

Places: Africa (Various); Bolivia; Borneo; Ecuador; Guatemala; Hawaii; Hong Kong; Iceland; India; Ireland; Israel; Italy; Kenya; Mexico; Nepal; New Zealand; Peru; Republic of the Congo; Sicily; Spain; United States (Various); Vietnam

Now Try: McCauley has edited several other books of essays about women travelers, including *A Woman's Path: Women's Best Spiritual Travel Writing* (with Amy Greimann Carlson and Jennifer L. Leo) and *The Best Women's Travel Writing 2009: True Stories from Around the World* (with Faith Adiele). Susan Fox Rogers edited *Going Alone: Women's Adventures in the Wild,* a collection of 20 essays by women traveling solo, hiking in Nepal, hiking in Alaska and Antarctica, and sailing on the open ocean. Rachel Da Silva's collection of stories about women involved in mountain climbs, *Leading Out: Mountaineering Stories of Adventurous Women,* is more narrowly focused, but many of the 27 stories are equally inspiring.

Murphy, Dallas

Rounding the Horn: Being the Story of Williwaws and Windjammers, Drake, Darwin, Murdered Missionaries and Naked Natives—a Deck's-eye View of Cape Horn. New York: Basic Books, 2004. 358 pp. ISBN: 9780465047598

Murphy sailed to the remote Cape Horn, at the southernmost tip of South America, in 2000 on a 53-foot sloop. *Rounding the Horn* describes that trip, as well as several more famous trips taken to the cape, including those of Ferdinand Magellan, Sir Francis Drake, and Captain Robert Fitzroy (with Charles Darwin on board). These tales of previous voyages, Murphy's enthusiasm for his own journey, his interactions with the few native Yaghan people who remain there, and his knowledge as a sailor drive the narrative. The result is an engrossing story that captures the challenges and dangers that Murphy faced in reaching this bleak, distant corner of the world.

Subjects: Adventure; Cannibalism; Indigenous Peoples; Oceans; Sailing

Places: Argentina; Chile

Now Try: John Kretschmer sailed east to west around Cape Horn in a 32-foot sailboat, an extremely dangerous voyage that he describes in *Cape Horn to Starboard*. Father and son David and Daniel Hays built their own 25-foot sloop and sailed it around Cape Hope, an adventure that they recount in *My Old Man and the Sea: A Father and Son Sail Around Cape Horn*. Laurence Bergreen followed the path of Magellan's trip around the world, including his passage through Cape Horn, in the well-told *Over the Edge of the World: Magellan's Terrifying Circumnavigation of the Globe*.

O'Hanlon, Redmond

Trawler: A Journey Through the North Atlantic. New York: Knopf, 2005. 339 pp. ISBN: 9781400042753

Travel writer O'Hanlon joined the crew of a fishing boat that was forced by its owner's economic situation to set sail in the North Atlantic during a near hurricane, while other boats were returning to port. O'Hanlon, who began the trip terribly seasick as the ship lurched through the rough seas, eventually found his sea legs and helped the crew of five fill the hull with deep sea fish. The book is both about the crew, whose occupation is one of the most dangerous in England and who typically go days without sleep and work hard just to avoid slipping off the deck and into the sea, and about his own experience as a fish out of water. As with many of O'Hanlon's trouble-filled journeys, the book is told in a manic, rambling style.

Subjects: Adventure; Fishing; Hurricanes; Oceans

Places: Atlantic Ocean; Scotland

Series: *Vintage Departures*

Now Try: Sebastian Junger's gripping narrative, *The Perfect Storm: A True Story of Men Against the Sea,* tells the story of a single fishing boat and its encounter with one of the worst storms of the century; like *Trawler,* it provides a stark portrayal of the dangerous lives of the fishermen. Douglas A. Campbell writes about four clam boats that were lost in the North Atlantic in 1999 in the absorbing book, *The Sea's Bitter Harvest: Thirteen Deadly Days on the North Atlantic.* The reality television series, *Deadliest Catch,* portrays life aboard fishing vessels in the Bering Sea and may also appeal to readers who enjoy *Trawler;* DVDs of several seasons of the series are available. Two excellent books can be recommended to readers who are interested in fish: Mark Kurlansky's *Cod: A Biography of the Fish that Changed the World* and Paul Greenberg's *Four Fish: The Future of the Last Wild Food,* which examines salmon, tuna, bass, and cod.

Tabor, James M.

Blind Descent: The Quest to Discover the Deepest Place on Earth. New York: Random House, 2010. 286 pp. ISBN: 9781400067671

Tabor, a former contributing editor for *Outside* magazine, recounts the dangerous search for the deepest cave on the earth by following two teams, one led by the obsessive American Bill Stone and the other led by the Russian Alexander Klimchouk. Stone's team explored southern Mexico's Cheve cave, while Klimchouk's team entered Krubera, a freezing 7,000-foot deep supercave in the Republic of Georgia. Tabor focuses on the dangers inherent in such extreme caving, including deadly falls, killer microbes, sudden burial, asphyxiation, claustrophobia, anxiety, and hallucinations far underneath the ground in a lightless world. The resulting book is a pulse-pounding page turner.

Subjects: Adventure; Caves; Exploration

Places: Mexico; Republic of Georgia

Now Try: Tabor's *Forever on the Mountain: The Truth Behind One of Mountaineering's Most Controversial and Mysterious Disasters* is equally exciting and describes the tragic fate of a seven-man mountain climbing team that was stranded on Alaska's Mount McKinley in 1967 during a brutal storm. William Stone and Barbara am Ende set a record for the deepest cave dive in the Western hemisphere in 1994; they tell their story with Monte Paulsen in the gripping *Beyond the Deep: The Deadly Descent into the World's Most Treacherous Cave*. Sheck Exley's *Caverns Measureless to Man* is that caver's memoir and outlines many of his accomplishments over a 30-year career.

Watson, Jessica

True Spirit: The True Story of a 16-Year-Old Australian Who Sailed Solo, Nonstop, and Unassisted Around the World. New York: Atria, 2010. 356 pp. ISBN: 9781451616316 YA

In May 2010, 16-year-old Jessica Watson completed a 210-day trip around the world in a 33-foot boat to become the youngest person to complete the circumnavigation unassisted and nonstop. *True Spirit* is the story of that voyage, told as a combination of blog entries and Watson's commentary. The book covers events prior to the voyage (her inspirations, her planning, her parents' attempts to come to terms with her decision) as well as the details of the circumnavigation itself: what she ate, what she read, the problems she encountered and how she solved them. For many readers, the story of this teenager's adventure will be pure inspiration.

Subjects: Circumnavigations; Oceans; Sailing; Solitude; Solo Travelers; Women Travelers

Places: Atlantic Ocean; Australia; Indian Ocean; Pacific Ocean

Now Try: Watson was inspired by the earlier circumnavigation of Jesse Martin, whose *Lionheart* is annotated in this chapter. Tania Aebi's *Maiden Voyage* tells how in 1987 she became the youngest person to sail around the world; her book is particularly strong on self-discovery and reflection. The story of the first person to sail around the world nonstop and single-handed is recounted in Robin Knox-Johnston's gripping *A World of My Own: The First Ever Non-stop Solo Round the World Voyage*.

Unexpected Adventures

By contrast with the planned adventures of the previous section, the adventures described in the titles in "Unexpected Adventures" were not planned, at least not to the extent that they were experienced. John Krakauer and the climbers up Mount Everest expected some level of adventure but not the level of tragedy described in *Into Thin Air: A Personal Account of the Mount Everest Disaster*. Valerian Albanov (*In the Land of White Death: An Epic Story of Survival in the Siberian Arctic*) and his crew may have set out on a dangerous voyage, but they did not expect to be trapped in ice and to spend

18 months traveling across the ice in an attempt to be saved. Aron Ralston (*Between a Rock and a Hard Place*) was on a simple weekend hike when he became trapped. Tom Hart Dyke and Paul Winder (*The Cloud Garden: A True Story of Adventure, Survival, and Extreme Horticulture*) were searching for rare orchids when they were kidnapped by guerillas and held captive for months. Glen Heggstad (*Two Wheels Through Terror: Diary of a South American Motorcycle Odyssey*) was traveling innocently enough through Colombia on his motorcycle when terrorists captured him.

These titles should appeal to readers who enjoy the pace and excitement of an adventure story but who also appreciate the precarious nature of life and the strength of the human spirit in the face of a world turned upside down.

Fiction centered on similar unexpected adventures (Jo Bannister's *Death in High Places* or Stephanie Rowe's *Ice*) may also be of interest to readers who enjoy the titles in this category, as may memoirs of individuals who overcame other obstacles in their lives (poverty and racism in the case of Claude Brown's *Manchild in the Promised Land* or rape in the case of Trisha Meili's *I Am the Central Park Jogger: A Story of Hope and Possibility*), thus repeating the theme of the resilience of the human spirit.

Albanov, Valerian

In the Land of White Death: An Epic Story of Survival in the Siberian Arctic. New York: Modern Library, 2000. 205 pp. ISBN: 9780679641001

Albanov was one of only two survivors of the 1912 Brusilov expedition; his book recounts that tragic attempt to traverse the Northeast Passage. Albanov served as the navigator for the Saint Anna, which found itself frozen in ice, due largely to the incompetence of its captain. After spending a year and a half on board, waiting for the ice to thaw and suffering from inadequate provisions, Albanov and 13 crewmen left the ship and attempted to reach Franz Josef Land, 235 miles away. Eighteen months later, in spite of an inaccurate map, blizzards, disintegrating ice floes, attacks by polar bears, starvation, sickness, snowblindness, and mutiny, Albanov and one of his crew reached their destination and were rescued. Albanov's account of the trek is gripping and well written, what one reviewer called "as lean and taut as a good thriller."

Subjects: Adventure; Exploration; Explorers; Polar Regions; Quick Reads; Survival Stories

Places: Arctic Regions; Russia

Now Try: The story of British explorer John Franklin's famous expedition in search of the Northwest Passage is told by Owen Beattie and John Geiger in *Frozen in Time: The Fate of the Franklin Expedition*, a chilling book about the disappearance of the expedition and subsequent attempts to find the members. Scott Cookman also examines the Franklin expedition in *Ice Blink: The Tragic Fate of Sir John Franklin's Lost Polar Expedition*; he attributes much of the tragedy to Franklin's reliance on untested technologies, including the steam engine and canned provisions. Andrea Barrett's *Voyage of the Narwhal* is a fictionalized account of a mission to find the last traces of the Franklin expedition. Jennifer Niven's account of the doomed 1913 Canadian Arctic Expedition, *The Ice Master*, describes what one reviewer called, "the worst-planned arctic exploration in history"; only 11 of the 25 crew members survived after their ship was crushed and sunk.

Ghinsberg, Yossi

Lost in the Jungle: A Harrowing True Story of Survival. New York: Skyhorse Pub., 2009. 314 pp. ISBN: 9781602393707

Yossi Ghinsberg and three friends hiked into the Amazon rain forest in Bolivia, expecting a manageable adventure in which they would find uncharted villages and forgotten tribes. After a pleasant enough start, however, things began to go wrong, and following a number of disagreements among themselves, the team split into two groups of two people each. A rafting accident then separated Yossi from his partner Kevin, and Yossi was forced to survive alone for weeks in this most inhospitable of environments, without a knife or a map or even minimal survival training. Ghinsberg's story is gripping and celebrates the individual's will to survive in the most extreme situations.

Subjects: Adventure; Friendship; Jungles; Survival Stories

Places: Bolivia

Now Try: Self-described jungle addict Simon Chapman traveled to the Bolivian jungles in search of the Mono Rey or "King Monkey," a giant ape that had been described by Colonel Percy Fawcett on his ill-fated expedition of 1925; in *The Monster of the Madidi: Searching for the Giant Ape of the Bolivian Jungle*, Chapman tells the story of his trek with humor and vivid descriptions of life in the jungle. Travel writer Hassoldt Davis and his new wife, filmmaker Ruth Staudinger, took their honeymoon journeying down an unexplored river in the jungles of French Guiana; Davis describes their trip in *The Jungle and the Damned*. A classic adventure tale of the South American jungles is Tobias Schneebaum's *Keep the River on Your Right*, which describes his 1955 journey to the Peruvian Amazon in search of a tribe of cannibals and his life among those indigenous people.

Hart Dyke, Tom, and Paul Winder

The Cloud Garden: A True Story of Adventure, Survival, and Extreme Horticulture. Guilford, CT: Lyons Press, 2004 [2003]. 323 pp. ISBN: 9781592284306

The Darién Gap is a 99-mile long stretch of jungle on the border between Colombia and Panama. It is so dense and impassable that it is the only stretch of land to interrupt the 16,000-mile Pan American Highway. In addition, it is so dangerous that even the Lonely Planet guidebook for the area simply warns, "Don't even think about it." In spite of these risks, botanist Hart Dyke and banker Winder traveled there in 2000, hoping to find rare orchids. Instead, they were kidnapped by FARC guerillas and held captive for nine months, during which they were threatened with death. *The Cloud Garden* recounts their ordeal and is told with a blend of riveting suspense and humor.

Subjects: Adventure; Friendships; Horticulture; Jungles; Kidnapping

Places: Colombia; Panama

Now Try: In 1989, the 18-year-old Andrew Egan explored the Darién Gap; his account of the adventure, *Crossing the Darien Gap: A Daring Journey Through a Forbidding and Enchanting and Roadless Jungle That Is the Only Link by Land Between North America and South America,* was written over 20 years later and is filled with encounters with strange people and stranger animals. The Darién Gap represents the narrowest part of the isthmus between Central and South America and was thought in the 19th century to be the best place for a canal; Todd Balf writes about the 1854 U.S. expedition that sought to find a path across the Gap in a fascinating history, *The Darkest Jungle: The True Story of the Darien Expedition and America's Ill-Fated Race to Connect the Seas.* Martin Mitchinson followed the path that Balboa took across the area in 1513; he recounts that journey in Balboa's footsteps in *The Darien Gap: Travels in the Rainforest of Panama.* Another journalistic account of being kidnapped can be found in Garry Leech's *Beyond Bogotá: Diary of a Drug War Journalist in Colombia.*

Heggstad, Glen

Two Wheels through Terror: Diary of a South American Motorcycle Odyssey. Center Conway, NH: Whitehorse Press, 2004. 275 pp. ISBN: 9781884313493

Adventure motorcyclist and former Hell's Angel Heggstad was on a 25,000-mile motorcycle journey from southern California to the tip of South America when Colombian terrorists captured him and forced him to march through the jungle carrying heavy equipment. Heggstad's mental and physical training as a martial arts instructor allowed him to endure five weeks of captivity and eventually secure his freedom, after which he had another motorcycle sent to him and completed his original trip.

Subjects: Adventure; Kidnapping; Motorcycles

Places: Colombia

Now Try: Mark Stephen Meadows's *Tea Time with Terrorists: A Motorcycle Journey into the Heart of Sri Lanka's Civil War* describes another motorcycle trip and another group of terrorists, the Tamil Tigers, who for 30 years had been waging war with the ruling government of Sri Lanka. In 2001, missionaries Martin and Gracia Burnham were captured and held hostage by a Muslim extremist group in the Philippines; Gracia Burnham's powerful book, *In the Presence of My Enemies,* tells the story of their year-long captivity and the rescue that resulted in her husband's death. The internal conflicts of Colombia are depicted in Silvana Paternostro's memoir about returning to that country after 30 years in the United States, *My Colombian War: A Journey Through the Country I Left Behind.*

Johnston, Tracy

Shooting the Boh: A Woman's Voyage down the Wildest River in Borneo. New York: Vintage Books, 1992. 256 pp. ISBN: 9780679740100

Journalist Johnston's expedition down the Boh started off well but then went awry: she lost her duffle bag filled with river gear on the flight to Borneo; the company planning the expedition was irresponsible; that part of the river had never been traveled; the participants didn't realize how dangerous the trip was until they were already on the river; and Johnston herself began having menopausal hot flashes. In spite of the many challenges (bees that feast on human sweat, foot fungus, raging rapids, and perhaps an evil river spirit), Johnston remained surprisingly upbeat, with a real sense of humor in spite of it all.

Subjects: Adventure; Jungles; Rafting; Rivers

Places: Borneo

Series: *Vintage Departures*

Now Try: Johnston's book is excerpted in Lucy McCauley's collection of stories about women adventurers, *Women in the Wild: True Stories of Adventure and Connection,* which is annotated in this chapter. Unlike Johnston, Patricia C. McCairen rafted alone; she tells of her 25-day solo journey down the Colorado River in *Canyon Solitude: A Woman's Solo River Journey Through the Grand Canyon,* which is as much about her internal journey and celebration of solitude as it is about rafting down the Colorado. Ann Linnea's *Deep Water Passage: A Spiritual Journey at Midlife* tells about her 65-day solo kayak journey around Lake Superior, another very spiritual quest.

Krakauer, Jon

Into Thin Air: A Personal Account of the Mount Everest Disaster. New York: Villard, 1997. 293 pp. ISBN: 9780679457527 YA

On assignment from *Outside* magazine, Krakauer, an experienced climber, accompanied a 1996 team on a guided ascent of Mount Everest. That ascent ended in disaster; after reaching the summit, four of Krakauer's teammates died during the descent in the middle of a blizzard. Krakauer's very personal account became well known for its criticisms of several aspects of the ascent: for the growing use of commercial guides, who took otherwise unqualified individuals on the climb, thus leading to dangerous situations; for the competition between two guide companies that may have led one team not to turn back at a pre-designated point; and for his own presence as a journalist, which may have added pressure on the teams to complete the ascent. Simply put, *Into Thin Air* is an unforgettable page-turner.

Subjects: Accidents; Adventure; Climbing and Hiking; Death and Dying; Friendships; Investigative Stories; Mountains; Sports; Survival Stories; Weather

Places: Nepal

Awards: ALA Notable Book, 1998

Now Try: Krakauer was very critical of the Russian climber and guide, Anatoli Boukreev, who descended the summit prior to his clients, apparently to prepare for potential rescue efforts; Boukreev rebuts Krakauer's allegations that he made a number of poor decisions in his own book, *The Climb: Tragic Ambitions on Everest* (co-authored with G. Weston DeWalt). Two other expedition members, Beck Weathers and Lene Gammelgaard, also wrote about their experiences of the disastrous climb. Weathers, who was abandoned as dead and who spent 18 hours in sub-zero temperatures on the mountain before staggering back to camp, describes his harrowing experience in *Left for Dead: My Journey from Everest*. Gammelgaard's book, *Climbing High: A Woman's Account of Surviving the Everest Tragedy*, tells how her triumph as the first Scandinavian woman to scale Everest turned to tragedy in the ensuing disaster, but her book is very even-handed and does not dwell on finding blame for what happened. Yet another climber who was on Everest during the tragedy described by Krakauer, Ed Viesturs, has written a memoir of his experiences as one of the few people to climb all 14 8,000-meter peaks, *No Shortcuts to the Top: Climbing the World's 14 Highest Peaks*.

Morrison, Dan

The Black Nile: One Man's Amazing Journey Through Peace and War on the World's Longest River. New York: Viking, 2010. 307 pp. ISBN: 9780670021987

When peace "broke out" in Sudan, foreign correspondent Morrison (along with a childhood friend who had never been outside the United States) decided to canoe the White Nile from Uganda to Cairo. What began as a buddy story, however, quickly turned into what one reviewer called "a gritty chronicle of the troubles facing a modern Africa." Morrison encountered warring tribes, a hidden oil war, secret dams, militia gunfire, and abandonment, when halfway through the trip, his friend returned to the United States with their canoe. Morrison managed to maintain his sense of humor while he made his way north by any means possible, and explains the historical events and tribal tensions that trouble the area, particularly the Sudan region, today.

Subjects: Adventure; African History; Canoeing; Friendships; Rivers

Places: Africa; Cairo; Egypt; Nile River; South Sudan; Sudan; Uganda

Now Try: Much of Morrison's book takes place in pre-division Sudan, and while Mark Bixler's *The Lost Boys of Sudan: An American Story of the Refugee Experience* is not a travel narrative *per se*, it does highlight the troubles caused by the Sudanese civil war and the impact on the people of Sudan. British travel writer Stanley Stewart's *Old Serpent Nile: A Journey to the Source* is less well known than his other books and represents a diary of his travels through Egypt, Sudan, and Uganda to find the source of the Nile. Christopher Ondaatje's *Journey to the Source of the Nile: An Extraordinary Quest to Solve the Riddle of the World's Longest River* mixes his own travels along the river with 19th-century explorations and includes his stunning photographs.

Ralston, Aron

Between a Rock and a Hard Place. New York: Atria, 2005. 354 pp. ISBN: 9780743492812
YA

What started off as a simple weekend hike turned into one of the most incredible survival stories ever told when a boulder came loose and pinned Aron Ralston's right hand and wrist against a canyon wall. After six days with little water, food, or warm clothing and with the knowledge that he had told no one where he was going, Ralston eliminated his escape options one by one and finally did the unthinkable, amputating his own arm with a dull, dirty knife in order to survive and then rappelling one-armed down a hill and hiking six miles before being found. Ralston tells the story in stark detail but without being gruesome or shocking; in fact, the story is told with a certain amount of humor.

Subjects: Accidents; Adventure; Mountains; Solo Travelers; Survival Stories

Places: Utah

Now Try: The film based on Ralston's book, *127 Hours,* stars James Franco and is readily available on DVD; it was nominated for six Academy Awards. In 1999, Jerri Nielsen was serving as a physician in Antarctica, when she discovered a lump on her breast; *Ice Bound: A Doctor's Incredible Battle For Survival at the South Pole,* by Nielsen and Mary Anne Vollers, tells how she was forced to perform a biopsy and treat herself with chemotherapy until she could be rescued. Piers Paul Read's 1974 classic *Alive: The Story of the Andes Survivors* tells the story of the Uruguayan rugby players whose airplane crashed in the Andes and who survived by resorting to cannibalism. Nando Parrado and Vince Rause have written another account of that event, *Miracle in the Andes: 72 Days on the Mountain and My Long Trek Home,* which supplements Read's account with deeper, more personal reflections on the event.

Rumberg, Hester

Ten Degrees of Reckoning: The True Story of a Family's Love and the Will to Survive. Aukland, New Zealand: Penguin, 2009. 272 pp. ISBN: 9780143011354

Rumberg tells the tragic story of her best friend Judith Sleavin, who had set out with her husband and two children in 1993 to sail around the world on a 47-foot boat. Three years into the voyage, their family adventure was cut short off New Zealand when a freighter, cruising without lights or radar, plowed into their sailboat and killed everyone in the party but Judith. Rumberg depicts both the events leading up to the accident and the accident itself, but the focus of the book is on Sleavin's survival, her strength and determination, and her memories of her family.

Subjects: Accidents; Adventure; Death and Dying; Family Relationships; Oceans; Sailing; Survival Stories

Places: New Zealand; Pacific Ocean

Now Try: Nick Schuyler and Jere Longman tell about another tragedy at sea in *Not Without Hope,* in which three of the four friends who went on a fishing trip off the

Florida coast died when their boat's anchor was stuck and capsized the boat
in the face of a huge storm. Another woman's tale of survival (although one
that involved hiking instead of sailing) is Amy Racina's courageous *Angels* 1
in the Wilderness: The True Story of One Woman's Survival Against All Odds, in
which she tells about hiking in the California Sierras, falling 60 feet and breaking both legs, surviving the pain and fear for four days and nights, and finally
being rescued. Any reader interested in tragedies at sea should start with
Sebastian Junger's gripping narrative, *The Perfect Storm: A True Story of Men*
Against the Sea, which tells the story of a single fishing boat and its encounter
with one of the worst storms of the century. Another memoir of tragedy and 2
its aftermath is Terri Jentz's *A Strange Piece of Paradise,* which mixes travel writing with the author's quest to finally locate the man who attacked her and a
friend while they were camping 15 years earlier.

Silverwood, John, and Jean Silverwood

3

Black Wave: A Family's Adventure at Sea and the Disaster That Saved Them. New York: Random House, 2008. 226 pp. ISBN: 9781400066551

Businessman John Silverwood and his wife, both experienced sailors, decided to set aside their lives and take their four children, ages 3 to 14, on
the seas aboard their 55-foot catamaran. For two years, things went well
as they visited remote islands and watched dolphins and migrating tor- 4
toises. Then, near the end of their voyage, they hit a coral reef in the South
Pacific and had to fight to survive. Their fascinating story is told in two
parts: Jean's soul-baring narrative of the shipwreck and its effects on the
family members; and John's description of the 1855 wreck of the *Julia Ann*
on the same reef and the parallels with his family's experience. Both narratives are engrossing, although readers interested in a more subjective
view of events may prefer Jean's telling of the story. 5

Subjects: Accidents; Adventure; Family Relationships; Oceans; Quick Reads; Sailing; Survival Stories

Places: Pacific Ocean; Tahiti

Now Try: Another family's tale of tragedy at sea is told by Richard Logan and
Teri Duperrault Fassbender in *Alone: Orphaned on the Ocean,* about Fassbender's survival of what appears to have been the murder of her family by the man 6
hired to sail the yacht that they had chartered; the book is as much a true crime
mystery as it is a tale of survival. Tony Bullimore's *Saved: The Extraordinary Tale*
of Survival and Rescue in the Southern Ocean tells the amazing story of his survival on a yacht that capsized 1,500 miles off the coast of Australia; Bullimore
mixes events from his own life with the hour-by-hour account of his rescue.
Readers interested in families and sea tragedies may find Bernie Chowdhury's
The Last Dive: A Father and Son's Fatal Descent into the Ocean's Depths of inter- 7
est; Chowdhury tells the story of Chris and Chrissy Rouse, who died while
attempting to explore a sunken German U-boat off New York. Judith Guest's
Ordinary People may also appeal to readers of *Black Wave;* the novel deals with
a family trying to cope with the aftermath of their son's sailing death.

Simpson, Joe

Touching the Void: The True Story of One Man's Miraculous Survival. New York: Perennial, 2004 [1988]. 218 pp. ISBN: 9780060730550 YA

Joe Simpson and his climbing partner, Simon Yates, had just made the first-ever ascent of the west face of the 21,000-foot Siula Grande peak in the Andes when disaster struck and Simpson fell off an ice cliff, breaking his leg. Yates tried to lower his friend to safety but was eventually forced to cut the rope tying them together or face being pulled to his own death. Certain that his friend was dead, Yates returned to base camp, consumed with grief and guilt over abandoning him. Simpson, however, did survive the fall and eventually crawled back to their tents just a few hours before Yates had planned to leave. The two friends' harrowing experience is told in a tight, yet detailed manner that emphasizes bravery, endurance, and friendship.

Subjects: Accidents; Adventure; Friendships; Mountains; Quick Reads; Survival Stories

Places: Peru

Now Try: The documentary film, *Touching the Void,* was named the Best British Film at the 2003 BAFTA Awards and is available on DVD. Simpson also wrote *This Game of Ghosts,* about his childhood, past climbing experiences, and the period following *Touching the Void.* Another survival story that focuses on the theme of friendship is *The Ledge: An Adventure Story of Friendship and Survival on Mount Rainier* by Jim Davidson and Kevin Vaughan, who climbed Mt. Rainier only to meet with an accident that left them trapped in an 80-foot crevasse. James Tabor's *Forever on the Mountain: The Truth Behind One of Mountaineering's Most Controversial and Mysterious Disasters* describes another mountain climbing tragedy, this one involving a seven-man team that was stranded on Alaska's Mount McKinley in 1967 during a brutal storm. The hero of James Salter's novel, *Solo Faces,* goes to southern France to climb mountains in the Alps and becomes involved in the daring one-man rescue of a team of climbers during a storm; unfortunately, the rescue brings him a level of fame that he did not want.

Tougias, Michael J.

Overboard!: A True Blue-Water Odyssey of Disaster and Survival. New York: Scribner, 2010. 212 pp. ISBN: 9781439145746

Four days into their voyage, an enormous storm struck the crew of a 45-foot sailboat in the Atlantic Ocean off Connecticut, washing the captain and first mate overboard and leaving the remaining three novice crew members to fend for themselves as the storm and the ocean slowly tore their boat apart. Their thrilling story and the equally electrifying tale of the Coast Guard's rescue are told in a vivid and suspenseful manner that fully captures the misery, sea sickness, and sheer terror experienced by the survivors.

Subjects: Accidents; Adventure; Oceans; Quick Reads; Sailing; Weather

Places: Atlantic Ocean

Now Try: Tougias is also the author of *Fatal Forecast: An Incredible True Tale of Disaster and Survival at Sea,* about the struggles of eight lobster fishermen to survive a gigantic storm off the coast of Cape Cod, and *The Finest Hours: The True Story of the U.S. Coast Guard's Most Daring Sea Rescue,* about the valiant efforts of the Coast Guard to rescue the men aboard two oil tankers that split in two during a storm off New England in February 1952. Kalee Thompson's *Deadliest Sea: The Untold Story Behind the Greatest Rescue in Coast Guard History* recounts the story of another Coast Guard rescue, involving a sinking fishing trawler in the Bering Sea off Alaska in March 2008.

They Were Heroes

The final subgenre in this chapter, "They Were Heroes," has a more complicated definition than do most of the other subgenres. First, these are titles that were written *about* the adventurer or adventurers by someone not directly involved in the adventure. Second, these are titles about adventures that took place before the 1990 cut-off date for "Classics." Finally, these are titles that were published after that cut-off date.

Consequently, these narratives benefit from a greater sense of objectivity and a better sense of context than would the first-person descriptions of the adventures. For example, Candice Millard's *The River of Doubt: Theodore Roosevelt's Darkest Journey* will be more objective than Roosevelt's own firsthand account of his trip, *Through the Brazilian Wilderness,* which was published in 1914, and will be better able to set the trip in the context of Roosevelt's political career. On the other hand, such titles may lack the immediacy and insight of first-person accounts, although several make liberal use of diaries, memoirs, and interviews.

Only two of the titles (Candice Millard's *The River of Doubt: Theodore Roosevelt's Darkest Journey* and T. R. Pearson's *Seaworthy: Adrift with William Willis in the Golden Age of Rafting*) take place entirely in the 20th century, so the appeal of adventure in an era before modern inventions will interest some readers.

These titles also include a wide range of settings, from the mountains of Fergus Fleming's *Killing Dragons: The Conquest of the Alps* to the deserts of Dean King's *Skeletons on the Zahara: A True Story of Survival* to the polar region of Fergus Flemings' *Ninety Degrees North: The Quest for the North Pole.*

Readers who enjoy these titles may also wish to try a wide variety of other historical exploration titles or True Adventure nonfiction with an historical bent. Robert Kurson's book about two deep-sea divers who found a U-boat shipwrecked off the New Jersey shore, *Shadow Divers: The True Adventure of Two Americans Who Risked Everything to Solve the Last Mysteries of World War II,* and Ben Mcintyre's biography of a Pennsylvania Quaker who traveled to Afghanistan in the 19th century, *The Man Who Would Be King: The First American in Afghanistan,* are two possibilities. Readers for whom the titles in this category have appeal may also enjoy reading the primary sources (the diaries and memoirs) upon which these accounts have been based. Examples include Ernest Shackleton's own version of the *Endurance* expedition, *South: The Endurance Expedition*, or the version provided by Frank Arthur Worsley, the captain of the *Endurance*, *Endurance: An Epic of Polar Adventure*.

Fleming, Fergus

Killing Dragons: The Conquest of the Alps. New York: Atlantic Monthly Press, 2000. 398 pp. ISBN: 9780871137784

Fergus portrays the first explorers of the Swiss Alps, particularly Mount Blanc and the Matterhorn, beginning in the early 1700s. His engrossing look of these individuals is filled with quirky details about their eccentricities and witty observations, and follows the changes in our relationship with those mountains, from superstition and awe (until the mid-1700s, Mont Blanc was known as Mont Maudit, "the Accursed Mountain," and the common belief was that dragons lived among the mountains) to scientific exploration to nationalistic competition to the current obsession with adventure and risk. *Killing Dragons* is an enjoyable and informative history of the exploration of the Swiss Alps.

Subjects: 18th Century; 19th Century; Exploration; Explorers; Mountains

Places: Alps; Switzerland

Awards: *New York Times* Notable Book, 2001

Now Try: One of the early heroes of Alps expeditions was the Englishman Edward Whymper, the first man to reach the summit of the Matterhorn; his own story of climbing the Alps has been edited by Anthony Brandt and published as *Scrambles Amongst the Alps*. Another English mountaineer, Albert Mummery, is mentioned only briefly by Fleming, but he was the first man to attempt to reach the top of one of the 14 Himalayan peaks that are over 8,000 meters in height; his story of his expeditions in the Alps is *My Climbs in the Alps and Caucasus*. Twentieth-century French climber Gaston Rébuffat's classic, *Starlight and Storm: The Conquest of the Great North Faces of the Alps*, has recently been re-released as part of the *Modern Library's Exploration* series; as one reviewer noted, "you could get a nosebleed just reading this book."

Fleming, Fergus

Ninety Degrees North: The Quest for the North Pole. New York: Grove Press, 2001. 470 pp. ISBN: 9780802117250

Fleming describes the major expeditions that tried to reach the North Pole between 1845 and 1969, using various means, including skis, hot-air balloons, dirigibles, ships, and the explorers' own two feet. These include the better-known expeditions of Franklin, Nansen, and Peary as well as plenty of lesser-known attempts, many of which failed miserably. Fleming's fascinating book combines journal entries and other details of the expeditions to portray the often-eccentric individuals who were obsessed with reaching the North Pole.

Subjects: 19th Century; Exploration; Explorers; Polar Regions

Places: Arctic Region

Awards: *New York Times* Notable Book, 2002

Now Try: Fleming also wrote *Barrow's Boys: A Stirring Story of Daring, Fortitude, and Outright Lunacy,* which serves as something of a prequel to *Ninety Degrees North,* albeit with a larger scope; it portrays the teams of naval officers that John Barrow, England's Second Secretary to the Admiralty, sent on various explorations in the 19th century, opening up Africa to the world and discovering Antarctica along the way. One of them, who accompanied John Franklin on three Arctic expeditions, was George Back. Unlike Franklin, Back lived to tell about his journeys; Peter Steele has written a well-researched biography of Back, entitled *The Man Who Mapped the Arctic: The Intrepid Life of George Back, Franklin's Lieutenant.* Alec Wilkinson's book, *The Ice Balloon: S. A. Andree and the Heroic Age of Arctic Exploration,* tells the story of the Swedish explorer who attempted to fly to the North Pole in a hydrogen balloon in 1897, what one military officer at the time called "the most original and remarkable attempt ever made in Arctic exploration." A more academic history of the British obsession with polar exploration is Francis Spufford's moving book, *I May Be Some Time: Ice and the English Imagination.*

Fleming, Fergus

The Sword and the Cross: Two Men and an Empire of Sand. New York: Grove Press, 2003. 349 pp. ISBN: 9780802117526

Fleming examines France's attempts to colonize northern Africa in the 19th and 20th centuries, following its conquest of Algeria in 1830, and gives particular attention to two men: Charles de Foucauld, a playboy who became an ascetic, and Henri Laperrine, a stern career soldier who founded the Camel Corps. Laperrine, with Foucauld as his guide, traveled across the Sahara in the first decade of the 20th century, and Fleming presents the story as both a forgotten chapter in the history of Europe's colonization of Africa and as a tale of friendship between two fascinating and very different men.

Subjects: 19th Century; 1900s; African History; Colonization; Deserts; Friendship

Places: Africa; Algeria; Sahara Desert

Now Try: Another history of the French exploration and conquest of the Sahara is Douglas Porch's *The Conquest of the Sahara,* which is less focused on the individuals who are at the heart of Fleming's book. There are a number of good biographies of Charles de Foucauld, who was beatified in 2005; these include Jean-Jacques Antier's *Charles de Foucauld* and Ali Merad's *Christian Hermit in an Islamic World: A Muslim's View of Charles de Foucauld.* Foucauld lived and worked among the Tuareg, a nomadic people in the Sahara, and Jeremy Keenan's fascinating *Sahara Man: Travelling with the Tuareg,* about his life in the camps of these people in the 1960s, may be of interest to readers of *The Sword and the Cross.* William Langewiesche's *Sahara Unveiled: A Journey across the Desert* remains the classic travel narrative about the Sahara Desert and is annotated in the first chapter of this book, "A Sense of Place."

Herlihy, David V.

The Lost Cyclist: The Epic Tale of an American Adventurer and His Mysterious Disappearance. Boston, MA: Houghton Mifflin Harcourt, 2010. 326 pp. ISBN: 9780547195575

Herlihy recounts the story of Frank Lenz, an American cyclist who disappeared in Turkey in 1894 while attempting to cycle around the world. Herlihy sets the story within the context of the 1880s, when bicycling first gained popularity and a number of cyclists were using it as a tool of exploration; he also presents Lenz as a champion of the smaller "safety bicycle" that was the precursor to the modern road bicycle. The story of Lenz's difficulties in China, his disappearance in Turkey, the tension between the Turks and Armenians, the bicyclist sent by an American magazine to investigate the disappearance, and the resolution of the mystery is extremely well researched and a fascinating look at the early days of cycling.

Subjects: 19th Century; Bicycling; Circumnavigations; Scholarly Writing

Places: Athens; China; Greece; Pittsburgh; Turkey; Vancouver

Now Try: Herlihy is also the author of *Bicycle: The History*, a well-illustrated story of the vehicle's development from the 1700s, when it was seen as an alternative to the horse-drawn carriage. Readers who are fascinated by the disappearances of travelers have a number of works to try. These include Geoffrey Wolff's *The Hard Way Around: The Passages of Joshua Slocum*, which includes an account of Slocum's 1909 disappearance after he set sail to South America on the same ship that he had used to become the first person to sail around the world single-handedly (see Slocum's *Sailing Alone around The World*, which is annotated in this chapter). American writer Ambrose Bierce traveled to Mexico in 1913, where he joined Pancho Villa's army as an observer and then disappeared; Ray Morris, Jr., provides a good biography of the writer, *Ambrose Bierce: Alone in Bad Company*. Perhaps the most famous disappearance, however, is that of Amelia Earhart, whose 1937 attempt to fly around the world failed when she and her navigator mysteriously disappeared; Candace Fleming's *Amelia Lost: The Life and Disappearance of Amelia Earhart* is one of many books that deal with the famous flyer.

Hodgson, Barbara

No Place for A Lady: Tales Of Adventurous Women Travelers. Berkeley, CA: Ten Speed Press, 2002. 216 pp. ISBN: 9781580084413

Hodgson depicts a number of women who set out on adventures from the 17th through the 19th centuries and, in doing so, not only endured challenges from exotic diseases and inhospitable weather to plagues of scorpions and other life-threatening situations but also sacrificed respectability. These include well-known authors like Mary Shelley and Mme. de Stael, travel writers like Isabella Bird (the author of *A Lady's Life in the Rocky Mountains*, annotated in this chapter), and less well-known adventurers, like Lady Ann Fanshawe, who disguised herself as a cabin boy to confront a band of Spanish pirates. Hodgson's book is well illustrated and includes portraits, historical maps, and drawings.

Subjects: 17th Century; 18th Century; 19th Century; Women Travelers

Places: Africa (Various); Central America (Various); China; Egypt; Europe (Various); India; Iran; Japan; Middle East (Various); North America (Various); Pacific Islands (Various); Russia; Saudi Arabia; South America (Various); Tibet

Now Try: Hodgson is also the author of *Dreaming of East: Western Women and the Exotic Allure of the Orient*, which depicts women from the 18th, 19th, and 20th centuries who traveled to the eastern Ottoman Empire in order to find greater freedom. Alexandra Lapierre provides portraits of 31 women adventurers (including Fanny Vandegrift, who traveled extensively with her husband, Robert Louis Stevenson, and Nellie Bly, who traveled around the world in 71 days) in *Women Travelers: A Century of Trailblazing Adventures 1850–1950*. Another collection of portraits of women adventurers from the last two centuries is Sharon M. Hannon's *Women Explorers: Women Who Dare*.

Honigsbaum, Mark

The Fever Trail: In Search of the Cure for Malaria. New York: Farrar, Straus & Giroux, 2002 [2001]. 397 pp. ISBN: 9780374154691

Malaria, which was little understood until the middle of the 17th century, had afflicted mankind for much of its history, and Honigsbaum describes the search by largely English explorers for quinine, reputed to be a cure for the disease. Quinine was derived from the bark of the rare red cinchona tree, and Honigsbaum portrays explorers such as Richard Spruce, a botanist who spent 15 years searching the Amazon and Andes for the bark, in spite of his own poor health; Charles Ledger, a trader of cinchona bark, whose explorations of Bolivia and Chile left him economically devastated; and Sir Clements Markham, known as the "father" of polar exploration, who successfully transported the plant from Peru. *The Fever Trail* is Honigsbaum's first book, and he does an especially good job of clearly presenting the science behind the story, telling the story in a compelling manner, and reminding the reader that malaria continues to be a devastating disease for much of the world.

Subjects: Adventure; Exploration; Health Issues; Investigative Stories; Medicine

Places: South America (Various)

Now Try: *Quinine: Malaria and the Quest for a Cure That Changed the World* by Flammetta Rocco is another history of quinine, which includes descriptions of the author's own travels as well as her experience growing up in Africa and being infected with malaria herself. Malaria still infects 500 million people every year and kills about 1 million of them, and journalist Sonia Shah provides a history of the disease and our efforts to contain it in *The Fever: How Malaria Has Ruled Humankind for 500,000 Years*; she shows how our hopes for a cure continue to be dashed. For the reader who wants to shorter history of the disease, Randall M. Packard's *The Making of a Tropical Disease: A Short History of Malaria* is a good alternative to Shah.

King, Dean

Skeletons on the Zahara: A True Story of Survival. Boston, MA: Little, Brown 2004. 351 pp. ISBN: 9780316835145

In 1815, Captain James Riley and the crew of the *Commerce* were shipwrecked off the coast of Africa. Within hours of being washed ashore, they had confronted hostile native tribesmen, lost one crewmember to those tribesmen, and confined themselves to a rickety longboat as they tried, without success, to escape. Riley and his crew were eventually captured by desert nomads, sold into slavery, and dragged along through the heart of the Sahara Desert as slaves. Along the way, the Americans encountered murder, starvation, plagues of locusts, sandstorms, dehydration, and hostile tribes that roamed the desert. In the middle of these challenges, Riley hatched a daring scheme to save his men. *National Geographic* sponsored King on an expedition to retrace Riley's terrible journey, and King made extensive use of Riley's memoir.

Subjects: 19th Century; Desert; Islam; Survival Stories; Slavery

Places: Africa; Mali; Morocco; Sahara Desert; Western Sahara

Now Try: Riley's own account of his ordeal, *Sufferings in Africa: The Incredible True Story of a Shipwreck, Enslavement, and Survival on the Sahara,* was first published in 1817 and was highly regarded in the 19th century; Abraham Lincoln listed it alongside the Bible and *Pilgrim's Progress* as one of the books that most influenced his thinking. Readers who are fascinated by Riley's story may also be drawn to tales of long walks to freedom even if those long walks are through extreme cold instead of the extreme heat faced by Riley and his men. One example is Josef M. Bauer's *As Far as My Feet Will Carry Me: The Extraordinary True Story of One Man's Escape from a Siberian Labor Camp and His 3-Year Trek to Freedom,* about German paratrooper Clemens Forell's escape from a Soviet gulag and his 8,000-mile trek across the frozen landscape to freedom in Persia. Another example is David Howarth's *We Die Alone: A WWII Epic of Escape and Endurance,* which recounts the escape of Jan Baalsurd, a Norwegian commando, from the Nazis during World War II and his journey across the Norwegian tundra.

Millard, Candice

The River of Doubt: Theodore Roosevelt's Darkest Journey. New York: Doubleday, 2005. 416 pp. ISBN: 9780385507967

Following his defeat as a third-party candidate in the 1912 Presidential election, Roosevelt traveled to South America to attempt to find the headwaters of the Rio da Duvida ("the River of Doubt," later renamed Roosevelt River in his honor) and trace it north to the Amazon River. During the trip down the river, Roosevelt suffered a minor leg wound followed by a tropical fever that resembled malaria; soon, he was unable to walk, suffering from chest pains, fighting a fever of 103°F, and delirious. At one point, realizing that his condition was a threat to the survival of the others, Roosevelt insisted that he be left behind. Millard's account of this expedition is compelling and suspenseful and does an excellent job of setting the story within the context of Roosevelt's political life as well as the history of South American exploration.

Subjects: 1910s; American History; Exploration; Explorers; Presidents; Rivers; Survival Stories

Places: Amazon River; Brazil

Awards: *New York Times* Notable Book, 2005

Now Try: Roosevelt's own account of his adventure is *Through the Brazilian Wilderness,* which was published in 1914; it is essentially his diary of the trip and reflects his enthusiasm for exploration and adventure. Candice Millard followed up *The River of Doubt* with *Destiny of the Republic: A Tale of Madness, Medicine and the Murder of a President,* about the assassination of an earlier U.S. President, James A. Garfield; her ability to place the event within a larger context is similar to what she does with Roosevelt's adventure. Theodore Roosevelt has been well-served by several excellent biographies, including two that won National Book Awards: Edmund Morris's *The Rise of Theodore Roosevelt* and David G. McCullough's *Mornings on Horseback: The Story of an Extraordinary Family, a Vanished Way of Life and the Unique Child Who Became Theodore Roosevelt.*

Pearson, T. R.

Seaworthy: Adrift with William Willis in the Golden Age of Rafting. New York: Crown Publishers, 2006. 280 pp. ISBN: 9780307335944

William Willis became a sailor at 15. At 45, he single-handedly freed his landlady's brother from Devil's Island. At 60, he sailed alone across the Pacific to American Samoa in a primitive raft he built, going 2,200 miles farther than Thor Heyerdahl had done. At 70, he took a second raft across 11,000 miles of ocean from South America to Australia. At 75, on his third attempt at a solo crossing of the Atlantic Ocean in a small rowboat, he died and was lost at sea. Pearson's summary of Willis's life is fascinating and told with just enough humor.

Subjects: Biography; Oceans; Sailing; Solo Travelers

Places: Atlantic Ocean; French Guiana; Pacific Ocean

Now Try: Willis was not the only individual inspired by Thor Heyerdahl to raft across the Pacific and the Atlantic, and P. J. Capelotti recounts the stories of Willis and several others in *Sea Drift: Rafting Adventures in the Wake of Kon-Tiki,* a riveting collection of more than 40 expeditions. David Pearlman was another adventurer who was inspired by Heyerdahl; Alec Wilkinson's *The Happiest Man in the World: An Account of the Life of Poppa Neutrino* tells how Pearlman changed his name and became the only person to sail across the Atlantic on a raft made from garbage.

Roberts, Jason

A Sense of the World: How a Blind Man Became History's Greatest Traveler. New York: HarperCollins Publishers, 2006. 382 pp. ISBN: 9780007161065 YA

James Holman was a British adventurer in the 18th and 19th centuries who became known as "the Blind Traveler." A tropical illness contracted in his early 20s left him blind and suffering from debilitating pain and limited mobility. In spite of his limitations and at a time when blind individuals were thought to be helpless, he used "human echolocation" to explore the world, traveling a quarter of a million miles (including an 1822 trip around the world from west to east) and publishing several best sellers before falling into obscurity. Roberts provides a meticulously researched and inspiring account of Holman's life.

Subjects: 18th Century; 19th Century; Biography; Blindness; Circumnavigations; Scholarly Writing

Places: Australia; Austria; Belgium; China; France; Germany; Italy; Netherlands; Russia; Switzerland

Now Try: Holman's own writings are available from public-domain electronic sources like Google books or Project Gutenberg. The three best known are *The Narrative of a Journey through France, etc.* (published in 1822), *Travels through Russia, Siberia, etc.* (1825), and *A Voyage Round the World* (four volumes, 1827–1832). Erik Weihenmayer, left blind at age 13 by a degenerative eye disorder, overcame this devastating disability to climb Mount McKinley, Kilimanjaro, Yosemite's El Capitan, and Aconcagua's Polish Glacier; his inspiring and incredible story is told in *Touch the Top of the World: A Blind Man's Journey to Climb Farther than the Eye Can See: My Story*. Another powerful story of overcoming disability in a different sense is Dick Hoyt's *Devoted: The Story of a Father's Love for His Son*, about the author's many marathon and triathlon runs, pushing his wheelchair-bound son as Team Hoyt. Robert Kurson's *Crashing Through: A Story of Risk, Adventure, and the Man Who Dared to See*, may also be of interest; Kurson tells the story of Mike May, who was blinded at age three, became a downhill skier, joined the CIA, and then regained partial vision at the age of 46.

Slung, Michele

Living with Cannibals and Other Women's Adventures. Washington, DC: National Geographic Society, 2000. 243 pp. ISBN: 9780792276869

Slung selected 16 stories of women travelers dating from 1797 forward, from National Geographic's extensive collection of first-person narratives by women explorers, and provides these inspiring, sometimes humorous, sometimes tragic stories in *Living with Cannibals and Other Women's Adventures*. Some of the women portrayed are well known (like Dian Fossey and Amelia Earhart) while others deserve to be better known (like oceanographer Sylvia Earle and mountain climber Catherine Destivelle). Slung pairs past adventurers with their contemporary counterparts, such as astronaut Shannon Lucid with aviator Amelia Earhart. The stories are inspiring, particularly those of the earlier women, who battled not just the elements and the physical challenges but also more stringent cultural expectations.

Subjects: Biography; Quick Reads; Women Travelers

Places: Africa; Arctic Region; Borneo; France; India; Indonesia; Italy; Malaysia; Rwanda; Switzerland

Now Try: Marybeth Bond's *A Woman's World: True Life Stories of World Travel* collects over 50 stories of women travelers and adventurers, including Lexie Hallahan's "Surfing is Better than Sex" and Ruth Bond's "Granny Shoots the Rapids." Twelve years later, Bond published a second collection of stories, *A Woman's World Again: True Stories of World Travel*, which includes 33 tales of adventure and travel in locales as varied as Ireland, Turkey, and Niger. *Wild Writing Women: Stories of World Travel* is another collection of stories by women adventurers; the stories include traveling on a motorcycle in China and playing on the edge of a volcano in Hawaii.

Soskice, Janet

The Sisters of Sinai: How Two Lady Adventurers Discovered the Hidden Gospels. New York: Alfred A. Knopf, 2009. 316 pp. ISBN: 9781400041336

In 1892, Scottish identical twin sisters Agnes and Margaret Smith discovered the earliest Syriac version of the Gospels known thus far. Soskice's account of their discovery and their other contributions to Biblical scholarship focuses on the daring nature of their physical journey to the Middle East at a time when few Westerners traveled in the region. *The Sisters of Sinai* also highlights their spiritual journey, as the sisters overcame their lack of formal training and the derision of male scholars to become well-regarded scholars. Soskice tells the story of the twin sisters in a fascinating, can't-put-it-down style.

Subjects: 19th Century; Bible; Biography; Middle Eastern History; Women Travelers

Places: Africa; Egypt; England

Now Try: In 1870, Agnes Smith published *Eastern Pilgrims: The Travels of Three Ladies*, about her and her sister's earlier travels to Egypt and what was then Palestine. In 1898, she published *In the Shadow of Sinai: A Story of Travel and Research from 1895 to 1897*, about their later travels. Both are available from the public-domain electronic source, archive.org. The Smith sisters also brought back from Egypt fragments of the Cairo Geniza, a collection of Jewish manuscript fragments dating as far back as 870 AD; the story of those manuscripts is told by Adina Hoffman and Peter Cole in the beautifully written *Sacred Trash: The Lost and Found World of the Cairo Geniza*.

Consider Starting With . . .

Cherry-Garrard, Apsley. *The Worst Journey in the World.*
King, Dean. *Skeletons on the Zahara: A True Story of Survival.*
Krakauer, Jon. *Into Thin Air: A Personal Account of the Mount Everest Disaster.*
Millard, Candice. *The River of Doubt: Theodore Roosevelt's Darkest Journey.*
Ralston, Aron. *Between a Rock and a Hard Place.*

Watson, Jessica. *True Spirit: The True Story of a 16-Year-Old Australian Who Sailed Solo, Nonstop, and Unassisted Around the World.*

Fiction Read-Alikes

Bennett, Robert P. Bennett has written two titles in the *Blind Traveler* series: ***Blind Traveler Down a Dark River*** and ***Blind Traveler's Blues***. Both involve a blind man using a GPS unit to navigate the world and should appeal especially to readers who enjoyed Jason Roberts's *A Sense of the World: How a Blind Man Became History's Greatest Traveler* (annotated in this chapter).

Defoe, Daniel. ***Robinson Crusoe*** is arguably the best-known survival tale in English literature. In addition to his 27-year stay on the Island of Despair, Crusoe endures an earlier two-year stint in slavery and a later trek across the Pyrenees to Lisbon to reclaim the profits from his Brazilian estate. Defoe wrote a sequel, ***The Farther Adventures of Robinson Crusoe***, which is less well known and includes Crusoe's return to the island on which he was stranded as well as Madagascar, Southeast Asia, China, and Siberia.

Dickey, James. Dickey's ***Deliverance*** tells the story of four middle-aged men who take a weekend canoe trip down a river in the Georgia backwoods, a trip that soon turns into a harrowing, unexpected adventure when they are accosted by two hillbillies. Dickey was also a highly regarded poet, having won a National Book Award in 1965 for his collection of poems, *Buckdancer's Choice*. He also wrote an adventure novel, ***To the White Sea***, about an American tail gunner who parachutes into Tokyo during the final months of World War II and attempts to stay alive by heading north, out of the city and across Japan, and ***Alnilam***, a novel about a blind father who journeys to an Air Corps training base where his son has been reportedly killed in an accident.

Keneally, Thomas. The Booker Prize-winning Australian novelist wrote two novels based on polar explorations. In ***The Survivor***, a professor who believes that he had abandoned his friend and the leader of an ill-fated Antarctic expedition 40 years ago is shaken by the news that the man's body has been discovered in the ice. ***Victim of the Aurora*** is about another doomed expedition to the South Pole, this one loosely based on Ernest Shackleton's first expedition of 1909, and involves a murder investigation into the death of the expedition's press representative. Keneally is, of course, best known for his novels about historical events, including *Schindler's Ark, The Chant of Jimmy Blacksmith, Gossip from the Forest*, and *Confederates*.

Long, Jeff. American writer Long is an experienced mountain climber; he won the 1993 Boardman Tasker Prize for Mountain Literature with his novel, ***The Ascent***, which tells the story of ten men and two women who scale the more dangerous "dark" side of Mt. Everest. In addition to its depiction of the physical and psychological challenges of such a climb, the novel also plays off the diverse motivations and backgrounds of the team members and the conflicts between the Chinese and Tibetans. Several of Long's other novels also involve mountain climbing, including ***Angels of Light***, about a group of fanatical rock climbers living year-round in Yosemite National

Park, and ***The Wall,*** which deals with two friends who try to scale Yosemite's 3,600-foot-high El Cap, only to discover the body of someone who apparently fell off the cliff and a cave man who attacks the climbers and steals the body.

Mulvihill, William. Mulvihill is best known for his desert survival novel, ***The Sands of Kalahari,*** which recounts an unexpected adventure involving seven people who hire a private airplane to fly them to South Africa after their original airplane is unable to fly. The new airplane crashes in the African desert, and the six survivors set off in the hot sun across an arid landscape in search of civilization. The book was made into a 1965 movie of the same name.

Wheeler, Richard S. Wheeler, who won the 2001 Owen Wister Award for lifelong contributions to the field of Western literature, wrote ***Snowbound,*** a novel based on an incident in the life of the American explorer, John Frémont, whose team was trapped in the snow of the Colorado mountains in the winter of 1848 and 1849. Faced with starvation and freezing to death, Frémont had to risk everything for the group's survival. Wheeler is the author of over 70 books, including two (*Fool's Coach* and *Masterson*) that have won the annual Spur Award for Best Western Novel.

Notes

1. Neal Wyatt, *The Readers' Advisory Guide to Nonfiction* (Chicago: American Library Association, 2007), p. 151.
2. Sarah Statz Cords, *The Real Story: A Guide to Nonfiction Reading Interests* (Westport, CT: Libraries Unlimited, 2006), pp. 3–29.
3. Saricks's discussion of tone and mood is "At Leisure with Joyce Saricks: Tone and Mood," *Booklist*, April 1, 2010. http://www.booklistonline.com/ProductInfo.aspx?pid=4102541&AspxAutoDetectCookieSupport=1.
4. Cords, *The Real Story*, p. 5.

References

Cords, Sarah Statz. *The Real Story: A Guide to Nonfiction Reading Interests*. Westport, CT: Libraries Unlimited, 2006.

Saricks, Joyce. "At Leisure with Joyce Saricks: Tone and Mood," *Booklist*, April 1, 2010. http://www.booklistonline.com/ProductInfo.aspx?pid=4102541&AspxAutoDetectCookieSupport=1.

Wyatt, Neal. *The Readers' Advisory Guide to Nonfiction*. Chicago: American Library Association, 2007.

Appendix A

Travel Narrative Book Awards

This appendix lists the major awards that are given to books in the travel narrative genre on a regular basis or that have periodically been given to travel narrative titles.

American Library Association Notable Book

The Notable Books Council of the American Library Association has selected 25 notable fiction, nonfiction, and poetry books for adult readers annually since 1944. The council has been a committee of the Reference and User Services Association (formerly the Reference and Adult Services Division) since 1972. For further information, see http://www.ala.org/rusa/awards/notablebooks.

American Library Association Notable Books that are annotated in this book include:

2011, Ian Frazier, *Travels in Siberia*
2010, David Grann, *The Lost City of Z: A Tale of Deadly Obsession in the Amazon*
2009, Tony Horwitz, *A Voyage Long and Strange: Rediscovering the New World*
2008, Peter Godwin, *When a Crocodile Eats the Sun: A Memoir of Africa*
2007, Peter Hessler, *Oracle Bones: A Journey between China's Past and Present*
2004, David Quammen, *Monster of God: The Man-Eating Predator in the Jungles of History and the Mind*
2002, Jason Elliot, *An Unexpected Light: Travels in Afghanistan*
2002, Peter Hessler, *River Town: Two Years on the Yangtze*
2001, Colin Thubron, *In Siberia*
2000, Jonathan Raban, *Passage to Juneau: A Sea and Its Meanings*
1999, Nicholas Class, *The Road to Ubar: Finding the Atlantis of the Sands*
1998, Jon Krakauer, *Into Thin Air: A Personal Account of the Mount Everest Disaster*
1998, Jonathan Raban, *Bad Land: An American Romance*
1998, Simon Winchester, *The River at the Center of the World: A Journey Up the Yangtze, and Back in Chinese Time*
1994, Robert D. Kaplan, *Balkan Ghosts: A Journey Through History*
1993, Lydia Minatoya, *Talking to High Monks in the Snow: An Asian American Odyssey*
1993, Richard Shelton, *Going Back to Bisbee*

Charles Taylor Prize

The $25,000 Charles Taylor Prize is awarded "to the author whose book best combines a superb command of the English language, an elegance of style, and a subtlety of thought and perception." The prize was first awarded in 2000, 2002, and 2004; since then, it has been given annually. Further information is available at http://www.thecharlestaylorprize.ca/index.asp.

Titles annotated in this book that have received the Charles Taylor Prize include:

2006, J. B. MacKinnon, *Dead Man in Paradise: Unraveling a Murder from a Time of Revolution*

Dolman Best Travel Book Award

The Dolman Best Travel Book Award is the only major travel book award in Britain that is open to all writers. It was first given in 2006, just two years after the Thomas Cook Travel Book Award was abandoned by its sponsor. The annual prize of £1,000 to £2,500 is organized by the Author's Club in Great Britain and is both sponsored by and named for club member William Dolman. The winner is announced in July of each year. For further information, see http://dolmanprize.wordpress.com/about/.

Past winners, all of which are annotated in this book, have been:

2011, Rachel Polonsky, *Molotov's Magic Lantern: A Journey in Russian History*
2010, Ian Thomson, *The Dead Yard: Tales of Modern Jamaica*
2009, Alice Albinia, *Empires of the Indus: The Story of a River*
2008, John Lucas, *92 Acharnon Street: A Year in Athens*
2007, Claire Scobie, *Last Seen in Lhasa: The Story of an Extraordinary Friendship in Modern Tibet*
2006, Nicholas Jubber, *The Prester Quest*

Edna Staebler Award

The Edna Staebler Award for Creative Non-Fiction is a $10,000 award given annually to a Canadian writer of a first or second published nonfiction book. The award was established by writer and literary journalist Edna Staebler and was first awarded in 1991. Additional information about the prize can be found at http://www.wlu.ca/homepage.php?grp_id=2529.

Titles annotated in this book that have received the Edna Staebler Award include:

2003, Alison Watt, *The Last Island: A Naturalist's Sojourn on Triangle Island*
2002, Tom Allen, *Rolling Home: A Cross-Canada Railroad Memoir*
2001, Taras Grescoe, *Sacré Blues: An Unsentimental Journey Through Quebec*

Hawthornden Prize

The Hawthornden Prize, one of the oldest British literary prizes, was founded in 1919 by Alice Warrender and is awarded annually to an English writer for the best work of "imaginative literature." The award was first given in 1919, and there have been numerous years without a recipient. For further information, see the Wikipedia entry at http://en.wikipedia.org/wiki/Hawthornden_Prize.

Titles annotated in this book that have received the Hawthornden Prize include:

2002, William Fiennes, *The Snow Geese: A Story of Home*
1977, Bruce Chatwin, *In Patagonia*

National Book Award for Nonfiction

The National Book Award for Nonfiction is one of four National Book Awards, given annually by the National Book Foundation. The $10,000 awards recognize outstanding literary works by U.S. citizens. Since 1950, there has been a General Nonfiction category, and from 1964 to1983, there were multiple nonfiction categories. Further information about the awards can be found at the National Book Foundation Website (http://www.nationalbook.org/index.html), and a list of winners in all categories from 1950 through 2009 is at http://www.nationalbook.org/nbawinners_category.html.

Titles annotated in this book that have won the National Book Award for Nonfiction include:

1986, Barry Lopez, *Arctic Dreams: Imagination and Desire in a Northern Landscape*
1976, Michael J. Arlen, *Passage to Ararat*
1979, Peter Matthiessen, *The Snow Leopard*

New York Times Notable Books

Every December since 2004, the New York *Times* has selected 50 fiction and 50 nonfiction titles to appear in a list of "100 Notable Books of the Year." From 1997 through 2003, a longer list of "Notable Books of the Year" appeared.

Titles annotated in this book that have been included on the *New York Times* annual list of notable books include:

2011, Donovan Hohn, *Moby-Duck: The True Story of 28,800 Bath Toys Lost at Sea and of the Beachcombers, Oceanographers, Environmentalists, and Fools, Including the Author, Who Went in Search of Them*
2011, Colin Thubron, *To a Mountain in Tibet*
2010, Susan Casey, *The Wave: In Pursuit of the Rogues, Freaks and Giants of the Ocean*
2010, Ian Frazier, *Travels in Siberia*
2010, Peter Hessler, *Country Driving: A Journey Through China from Farm to Factory*
2009, David Grann, *The Lost City of Z: A Tale of Deadly Obsession in the Amazon*
2008, Tony Horwitz, *A Voyage Long and Strange: Rediscovering the New World*
2008, Robert Mcfarlane, *The Wild Places*
2007, Rosemary Mahoney, *Down the Nile: Alone in a Fisherman's Skiff*
2006, Elizabeth Gilbert, *Eat, Pray, Love: One Woman's Search for Everything Across Italy, India and Indonesia*

2006, Peter Hessler, *Oracle Bones: A Journey between China's Past and Present*
2006, Pankaj Mishra, *Temptations of the West: How to be Modern in India, Pakistan, Tibet, and Beyond*
2006, Rory Stewart, *The Places in Between*
2005, Candice Millard, *The River of Doubt: Theodore Roosevelt's Darkest Journey*
2004, John Gimlette, *At the Tomb of the Inflatable Pig: Travels through Paraguay*
2004, Alan Tennant, *On the Wing: To the Edge of the Earth with the Peregrine Falcon*
2003, David Quammen, *Monster of God: The Man-Eating Predator in the Jungles of History and the Mind*
2003, Calvin Trillin, *Feeding a Yen: Savoring Local Specialties, From Kansas City to Cuzco*
2002, Anthony Bourdain, *A Cook's Tour: In Search of the Perfect Meal*
2002, Fergus Fleming, *Ninety Degrees North: The Quest for the North Pole*
2002, Edward Gargan, *The River's Tale: A Year on the Mekong*
2002, Tony Horwitz, *Blue Latitudes: Boldly Going Where Captain Cook Has Gone Before*
2002, Peter Matthiessen, *The Birds of Heaven: Travels with Cranes*
2002, Oliver Sachs, *Oaxaca Journal*
2001, Richard Bernstein, *Ultimate Journey: Retracing the Path of an Ancient Buddhist Monk Who Crossed Asia in Search of Enlightenment*
2001, Gretel Ehrlich, *This Cold Heaven: Seven Seasons in Greenland*
2001, Jason Elliot, *An Unexpected Light: Travels in Afghanistan*
2001, Fergus Fleming, *Killing Dragons: The Conquest of the Alps*
2001, Peter Hessler, *River Town: Two Years on the Yangtze*
2001, Robert D. Kaplan, *Eastward to Tartary: Travels in the Balkans, the Middle East, and the Caucasus*
2000, Adam Gopnik, *Paris to the Moon*
2000, Pico Iyer, *The Global Soul: Jet Lag, Shopping Malls, and the Search for Home*
2000, Tim Mackintosh-Smith, *Yemen: The Unknown Arabia*
2000, Michael Paterniti, *Driving Mr. Albert: A Trip Across America with Einstein's Brain*
2000, Colin Thubron, *In Siberia*
1999, William Least Heat-Moon, *River-Horse: The Logbook of a Boat Across America*
1999, Andrew X. Pham, *Catfish and Mandala: A Two-Wheeled Voyage through the Landscape and Memory of Vietnam*
1998, Tony Horwitz, *Confederates in the Attic: Dispatches from the Unfinished Civil War*
1997, Frances Mayes, *Under the Tuscan Sun: At Home in Italy*
1996, Patricia Storace, *Dinner With Persephone: Travels in Greece*

Ondaatje Prize

The Ondaatje Prize is an annual £10,000 award that has been given since 2004 to a work of fiction, nonfiction, or poetry that evokes the "spirit of a place" and that is written by a citizen or resident of the British Commonwealth or the Republic of Ireland.

The prize is awarded by the Royal Society of Literature, and more information is available at the society's website at http://www.rslit.org/content/ondaatje.

Titles annotated in this book that have won the Ondaatje Prize are:

2010, Ian Thomson, *The Dead Yard: Tales of Modern Jamaica*
2005, Rory Stewart, *The Places in Between*

Orwell Prize

The Orwell Prize has been awarded annually since 1994 to the book that comes closest to George Orwell's ambition to "make political writing into an art." The prize was founded in 1993 by Orwell biographer Bernard Crick, who used money from the royalties of the hardback edition of his biography of Orwell. Its sponsors include Orwell's adopted son Richard Blair, Reuters, *The Political Quarterly*, Blackwell Publishing, Media Standards Trust, and A. M. Heath & Company. Further information can be found at http://theorwellprize.co.uk/.

Orwell Prize winners that are annotated in this book are:

2009, Andrew Brown, *Fishing in Utopia: Sweden and the Future that Disappeared*
2008, Raja Shehadeh, *Palestinian Walks: Notes on a Vanishing Landscape*

Pulitzer Prize for General Nonfiction

The Pulitzer Prize for General Nonfiction has been awarded since 1962 for a distinguished book of nonfiction by an American author that is not eligible for consideration in another Pulitzer category. For more information, including a list of past winners and finalists, see http://www.pulitzer.org/bycat/General-Nonfiction.

Titles annotated in this book that have received the Pulitzer Prize for General Nonfiction include:

1966, Edwin Way Teale, *Wandering Through Winter: A Naturalist's Record of a 20,000-Mile Journey Through the North American Winter*

Thomas Cook Travel Book Award

The Thomas Cook Travel Book Award was begun by the Thomas Cook Company in 1980 to encourage and reward the art of literary travel writing. The company ended its support for the award and awarded the last prize in 2004. The award has been superseded by the Dolman Best Travel Book Award.

Winners of the award, all of which are annotated in this book, were:

2004, Richard Grant, *Ghost Riders: Travels with American Nomads* (published in the United States as *American Nomads: Travels with Lost Conquistadors, Mountain Men, Cowboys, Indians, Hoboes, Truckers, and Bullriders)*
2003, Jenny Diski, *Stranger on a Train: Daydreaming and Smoking around America With Interruptions*

2002, Ma Jian, *Red Dust: A Path Through China*
2001, Stanley Stewart, *In the Empire of Genghis Khan: An Amazing Odyssey Through the Lands of the Most Feared Conquerors in History*
2000, Jason Elliot, *An Unexpected Light: Travels in Afghanistan*
1999, Philip Marsden, *The Spirit-Wrestlers: A Russian Journey*
1998, Tim Mackintosh-Smith, *Yemen: Travels in Dictionary Land Nomads* (published in the United States as *Yemen: The Unknown Arabia*)
1997, Nicholas Crane, *Clear Waters Rising: A Mountain Walk Across Europe*
1996, Stanley Stewart, *Frontiers of Heaven: A Journey to the End of China*
1995, Gavin Bell, *In Search of Tusitala: Travels in the Pacific After Robert Louis Stevenson*
1994, William Dalrymple, *City of Djinns*
1993, Nick Cohn, *The Heart of the World*
1992, Norman Lewis, *A Goddess in the Stones: Travels in India*
1991, co-winners: Jonathan Raban, *Hunting Mister Heartbreak: A Discovery of America*; Gavin Young, *In Search of Conrad*
1990, Mark Hudson, *Our Grandmothers' Drums*
1989, Paul Theroux, *Riding the Iron Rooster*
1988, Colin Thubron, *Behind the Wall: A Journey Through China*
1986/87, Patrick Leigh Fermor, *Between the Woods and the Water*
1985, Patrick Marnham, *So Far From God: Journey to Central America*
1984, Geoffrey Moorhouse, *To The Frontier*
1983, Vikram Seth, *From Heaven Lake: Travels Through Sinkiang and Tibet*
1982, Tim Severin, *The Sinbad Voyage*
1981, Jonathan Raban, *Old Glory: An American Voyage*
1980, Robyn Davidson, *Tracks*

Author-Title Index

Place Index

Subject Index

Feeding a Yen: Savoring Local Specialties, From Kansas City to Cuzco, 106

About the Author

ROBERT BURGIN, PhD, is a consultant to libraries and a former professor at North Carolina Central University's School of Library and Information Sciences. He edited Libraries Unlimited's *Nonfiction Readers' Advisory* and coedited *The Readers' Advisor's Companion*. He also served as the first editor of Libraries Unlimited's *Real Stories* series. Burgin earned his doctorate in library science from the University of North Carolina at Chapel Hill.